Lecture Notes in Computer Science   15404

Founding Editors

Gerhard Goos
Juris Hartmanis

Editorial Board Members

Elisa Bertino, USA
Wen Gao, China

Bernhard Steffen, Germany
Moti Yung, USA

Services Science

Subline of Lecture Notes in Computer Science

Subline Editors-in-Chief

Athman Bouguettaya, *RMIT University, Melbourne, Australia*
Michael P. Papazoglou, *University of Tilburg, The Netherlands*

Subline Editorial Board

Boualem Bentallah, Australia
Murthy Devarakonda, USA
Carlo Ghezzi, Italy
Chi-Hung Chi, Tasmania
Hani Jamjoom, USA
Ingolf Krueger, USA

Paul Maglio, USA
Klaus Pohl, Germany
Stefan Tai, Germany
Yuzuru Tanaka, Japan
Christopher Ward, USA

More information about this series at https://link.springer.com/bookseries/558

Walid Gaaloul · Michael Sheng ·
Qi Yu · Sami Yangui
Editors

Service-Oriented Computing

22nd International Conference, ICSOC 2024
Tunis, Tunisia, December 3–6, 2024
Proceedings, Part I

Editors
Walid Gaaloul
Telecom SudParis
Évry, France

Qi Yu
Rochester Institute of Technology
Rochester, NY, USA

Michael Sheng
Macquarie University
Sydney, NSW, Australia

Sami Yangui
LAAS-CNRS
Toulouse, France

ISSN 0302-9743　　　　　　　ISSN 1611-3349　(electronic)
Lecture Notes in Computer Science
ISBN 978-981-96-0804-1　　　ISBN 978-981-96-0805-8　(eBook)
https://doi.org/10.1007/978-981-96-0805-8

© The Editor(s) (if applicable) and The Author(s), under exclusive license
to Springer Nature Singapore Pte Ltd. 2025

This work is subject to copyright. All rights are solely and exclusively licensed by the Publisher, whether the whole or part of the material is concerned, specifically the rights of translation, reprinting, reuse of illustrations, recitation, broadcasting, reproduction on microfilms or in any other physical way, and transmission or information storage and retrieval, electronic adaptation, computer software, or by similar or dissimilar methodology now known or hereafter developed.
The use of general descriptive names, registered names, trademarks, service marks, etc. in this publication does not imply, even in the absence of a specific statement, that such names are exempt from the relevant protective laws and regulations and therefore free for general use.
The publisher, the authors and the editors are safe to assume that the advice and information in this book are believed to be true and accurate at the date of publication. Neither the publisher nor the authors or the editors give a warranty, expressed or implied, with respect to the material contained herein or for any errors or omissions that may have been made. The publisher remains neutral with regard to jurisdictional claims in published maps and institutional affiliations.

This Springer imprint is published by the registered company Springer Nature Singapore Pte Ltd.
The registered company address is: 152 Beach Road, #21-01/04 Gateway East, Singapore 189721, Singapore

If disposing of this product, please recycle the paper.

Preface

We are delighted to welcome you to the proceedings of the 22nd International Conference on Service-Oriented Computing (ICSOC 2024), held in the beautiful city of Tunis, Tunisia, from December 3 to December 6, 2024. ICSOC is the premier international forum that brings together academics, industry researchers, developers, and practitioners to share and discuss groundbreaking work in the field of Service-Oriented Computing (SOC). The conference provides a high-quality platform for advancing our knowledge on various aspects of SOC, including business-process management, distributed systems, cloud/edge/fog computing, security and privacy, Internet of Things (IoT), and emerging technologies like quantum computing, blockchain, artificial intelligence, machine learning, big data analytics, and green IT solutions. This year's edition continued the tradition of fostering cross-community scientific excellence, gathering experts from diverse fields such as cyber-physical systems, software engineering, and smart services. ICSOC has a rich history of successful editions in cities around the world, including Rome (Italy), Seville (Spain), Dubai (UAE), Toulouse (France), Hangzhou (China), Málaga (Spain), Banff (Canada), Goa (India), Paris (France), Berlin (Germany), Shanghai (China), Paphos (Cyprus), San Francisco (USA), Stockholm (Sweden), Sydney (Australia), Vienna (Austria), Chicago (USA), Amsterdam (The Netherlands), New York (USA), and Trento (Italy), among others. We are excited to build upon this legacy as we explore the future of service-oriented technologies and their role in shaping the evolving digital landscape.

This year's call for papers generated substantial and increasing interest from the community. The conference continued with the two-round submission and double-blind review process established over the past three editions. In addition to the traditional track on Service-Oriented Technology Basics and Trends, the conference featured three specialized tracks: (1) AI for Services and as-a-Service, (2) Novel Service Frameworks for Cloud Continuum and Smart Environments, and (3) Emerging Technologies. Each track was overseen by a dedicated chair, ensuring a high standard of review.

The conference attracted 255 valid paper submissions co-authored by researchers, practitioners, and academics from 44 countries across all continents. 60 submissions were desk-rejected. Afterward, each submission underwent a thorough review process, with at least three reviewers evaluating the papers in a double-blind manner, followed by discussions moderated by a Senior Program Committee (PC) member. The Program Committee consisted of 167 experts in service-oriented computing and related fields, including 139 PC members and 28 Senior PC members, representing countries from across all continents.

In the first round, 41 papers were submitted. Of these, 2 were recommended for "minor revision and resubmission", and 14 required "major revision and resubmission". In the second round, 214 research papers were submitted, including 11 resubmissions from the first round. For papers resubmitted from the first round, the authors' responses to the reviewers and the quality of their revisions were thoroughly evaluated. The outcomes were as follows: 2 papers recommended for "minor revision and resubmission" were accepted as full papers. Of the 9 papers requiring "major revision and resubmission", 2 were accepted as full papers, and 4 were accepted as short papers. Among the newly submitted papers in the second round, 33 were accepted as full papers, with 15 more selected as short papers. The industry track received 7 submissions, and 3 were accepted as full papers. The acceptance rate for full papers was 14.5%.

The conference program featured three keynote addresses delivered by distinguished leaders in both academic and industrial research. We were honored to have these prominent experts share their insights and groundbreaking work at ICSOC 2024. Their keynotes provided valuable perspectives, enriching the program with cutting-edge developments and trends in service-oriented computing and related fields:

- "The role of Service Computing in addressing challenges that arise from the adoption and convergence of critical technologies" by Surya Nepal (CSIRO Data61, Australia)
- "Sustainable services" by Barbara Pernici (Polytechnic University of Milan, Italy)
- "Infrastructure as a Service at Scale: The Journey to Zero-Toil Maintenance at LinkedIn" by Samir Tata (LinkedIn, USA)

We express our heartfelt gratitude to all individuals, institutions, and sponsors who supported ICSOC 2024. We thank all authors and participants for their insightful contributions and discussions. Special appreciation goes to the members of the Senior Program Committee, the international Program Committee, and external reviewers for their dedication to a rigorous and robust reviewing process. Our sincere thanks also extend to area chairs Farouk Toumani, Xumin Liu, Naouel Moha, and Cinzia Cappiello for their exceptional support throughout the review process. This high-quality program would not have been possible without the expertise and commitment of our PC members, especially our Senior PC members, and the tireless efforts of external reviewers. Their collective efforts helped make ICSOC 2024 a resounding success.

We are thankful to the ICSOC Steering Committee for entrusting us with organizing the 22nd edition of this prestigious conference. Special thanks go to our Steering Committee Liaison Chair, Boualem Benatallah, for his unwavering encouragement and commitment to ensuring the conference's success and smooth organization. Our gratitude also goes to the Organizing Committee members and all who contributed to the event's success. We are also grateful for the unwavering support, continuous guidance, and collaborative spirit of the General Chairs, Khalil Drira and Mohamed Jmaiel. We are particularly indebted to the local arrangements team from the University of Sfax, Tunisia, for their excellent organization of all conference-related, social, and co-located events. Additionally, we acknowledge the prompt and professional support from Springer, who published these proceedings as part of the Lecture Notes in Computer Science series.

We congratulate all authors whose papers appear in these proceedings. These works reflect the current state of the art in service-oriented computing research and practice, and we hope they inspire and stimulate further exploration.

In addition, we extend special thanks to the workshop organizers for promoting service-oriented computing (SOC) research to broader domains.

Most importantly, we appreciate all authors and participants of ICSOC 2024 for their invaluable insights and discussions. We anticipate that the ideas generated during this conference will lead to further innovations benefiting scientific, industrial, and social communities.

December 2024

Walid Gaaloul
Michael Sheng
Qi Yu
Sami Yangui

Organization

General Chairs

Khalil Drira	LAAS-CNRS, France
Mohamed Jmaiel	University of Sfax, Tunisia

Program Committee Chairs

Walid Gaaloul	Telecom sudParis, France
Michael Sheng	Macquarie University, Sydney, Australia
Qi Yu	Rochester Institute of Technology, USA

Proceedings Chair

Sami Yangui	LAAS-CNRS, France

Workshop Chairs

Slim Kallel	University of Sfax, Tunisia
Claudia Raibulet	Vrije Universiteit Amsterdam, Netherlands

Demonstration Chairs

Amel Bennaceur	Open University, UK
Saoussen Cheikhrouhou	University of Sfax, Tunisia

Phd Symposium Chairs

Ismail Bouassida	University of Sfax, Tunisia
Nora Faci	University of Lyon, France

Tutorial/Panel Chairs

Leila Ben Ayed	University of Manouba, Tunisia
Mohamed Sellami	Telecom SudParis, France
Elisa Yumi Nakagawa	University of São Paulo, Brazil

Publicity Chairs

Balsam Alkouz	University of Sydney, Australia
Hayet Brabra	Telecom Sudparis, France
Hatem Hadj Kacem	University of Sfax, Tunisia

Moez Krichen	Albaha University, Saudi Arabia
Zheng Jason Song	University of Michigan-Dearborn, USA
Deng Zhao	China University of Geosciences, Beijing, China

Web Chair

Fairouz Fakhfakh	University of Kairouan, Tunisia

Steering Committee

Boualem Benatallah	Dublin City University, Ireland
Athman Bouguettaya	The University of Sydney, Australia
Winfried Lamersdorf	University of Hamburg, Germany
Massimo Mecella	Sapienza Università di Roma, Italy
Antonio Ruiz Cortez	University of Sevilla, Spain
Jian Yang	Macquarie University, Australia
Liang Zhang	Fudan University, China

Senior Program Committee

Marco Aiello	University of Stuttgart, Germany
Boualem Benatallah	Dublin City University, Ireland
Salima Benbernou	Université de Paris, France
Athman Bouguettaya	University of Sydney, Australia
Carlos Canal	University of Malaga, Spain
François Charoy	Université de Lorraine-LORIA-Inria, France
Flavio De Paoli	Universita' di Milano-Bicocca, Italy
Schahram Dustdar	TU Wien, Austria
Hakim Hacid	Zayed University, United Arab Emirates
Mohad-Saïd Hacid	Université Lyon 1, France
Brahim Medjahed	University of Michigan-Dearborn, USA
Massimo Mecella	Sapienza University of Rome, Italy
Claus Pahl	Free University of Bozen-Bolzano, Italy
Cesare Pautasso	University of Lugano, Switzerland
Manfred Reichert	University of Ulm, Germany
Manuel Resinas	University of Sevilla, Spain
Antonio Ruiz-Cortés	University of Seville, Spain
Lionel Seinturier	University of Lille, France
Michael Q. Sheng	Macquarie University, Australia
Jianwen Su	University of California, Santa Barbara, USA
Stefan Tai	TU Berlin, Germany
Zhongjie Wang	Harbin Institute of Technology, China
Shangguang Wang	Beijing University of Posts and Telecommunications, China
Mathias Weske	HPI/University of Potsdam, Germany
Lina Yao	University of New South Wales, Australia

Jian Yang — Macquarie University, Australia
Jianwei Yin — Zhejiang University, China
Liang Zhang — Fudan University, China

Program Committee

Takoua Abdellatif — University of Carthage, Tunisia
Imen Abdennadher — University of Sfax, Tunisia
Lizy Abraham — Waterford Institute of Technology, Ireland
Rui Abreu — INESC-ID & U.Porto, Portugal
Simone Agostinelli — Sapienza University of Rome, Italy
Marco Aiello — University of Stuttgart, Germany
Abdulatif Alabdulatif — Qassim University, Saudi Arabia
Alessandro Aldini — University of Urbino "Carlo Bo", Italy
Abdullah Alfazi — University of Adelaide, Australia
Ahoud Alhazmi — Macquarie University, Australia
Shaukat Ali — Oslo Metropolitan University, Norway
Hamid Alinejad Rokny — University of New-South Wales, Australia
Abdulwahab Aljubairy — Umm Al-Qura University, Saudi Arabia
Asma Alkalbani — University of Technology and Applied Sciences, Oman
Mohammad Allahbakhsh — Ferdowsi University of Mashhad, Iran
Eman Abdullah Alomar — Stevens Institute of Technology, USA
Moayad Alshangiti — University of Jeddah, Saudi Arabia
Andreas Andreou — Cyprus University of Technology, Cyprus
Vasilios Andrikopoulos — University of Groningen, The Netherlands
Paolo Arcaini — National Institute of Informatics, Japan
Danilo Ardagna — Politecnico di Milano, Italy
Ala Arman — Sapienza University of Rome, Italy
Yacine Atif — Skövde University, Sweden
Salma Azzouzi — University Ibn Tofail, Morocco
Marcos Baez — Bielefeld University of Applied Sciences, Germany
Muneera Bano — CSIRO, Australia
Luciano Baresi — Politecnico di Milano, Italy
Johanna Barzen — University of Stuttgart, Germany
Amin Beheshti — Macquarie University, Australia
Faiza Belala — University of Constantine 2, Algeria
Khalid Belhajjame — Université Paris-Dauphine, France
Leila Ben Ayed — University of Manouba, Tunisia
Ali Ben Mrad — University of Sfax, Tunisia
Boualem Benatallah — Dublin City University, Ireland
Salima Benbernou — Université Paris Cité, France
Amel Bennaceur — Open University, England
Nadia Bennani — Université de Lyon, France
Djamal Benslimane — Université de Lyon 1, France
Federico Bergenti — Università degli Studi di Parma, Italy
David Bermbach — Technical University of Berlin, Germany

Javier Berrocal	University of Extremadura, Spain
Rodrigo Bonacin	CTI Renato Archer and FACCAMP, Brazil
Ismael Bouassida	Rodriguez University of Sfax, Tunisia
Juan Boubeta-Puig	University of Càdiz, Spain
Athman Bouguettaya	The University of Sydney, Australia
Hayet Brabra	Télécom SudParis, France
Lars Braubach	City University of Bremen, Germany
Uwe Breitenbücher	Reutlingen University, Germany
Antonio Brogi	Università di Pisa, Italy
Antonio Bucchiarone	University of L'Aquila, Italy
Alena Buchalcevova	University of Economics of Economics and Business, Czechia
Christoph Bussler Robert	Bosch LLC, USA
Cristina Cabanillas	University of Seville, Spain
Carlos Canal	University of Málaga, Spain
Cinzia Cappiello	Politecnico di Milano, Italy
Miriam Capretz	University of Western Ontario, Canada
Fabio Casati	ServiceNow, USA
Faten Chaabane	University of Gabes, Tunisia
Mariam Chaabane	University of Sfax, Tunisia
W. K. Chan	City University of Hong Kong, China
François Charoy	Université de Lorraine, France
Sotirios Chatzis	Cyprus University of Technology, Cyprus
Sanjay Chaudhary	Ahmedabad University, India
Saoussen Cheikhrouhou	University of Sfax, Tunisia
Feifei Chen	Deakin University, Australia
Chi-Hung Chi	CSIRO, Australia
Rolland Colette	Université Paris1 Panthéon-Sorbonne, France
Marco Comuzzi Ulsan	National Institute of Science and Technology, South Korea
Javier Cubo	Universidad Internacional de la Rioja, Spain
Carlos E. Cuesta	Universidad Rey Juan Carlos, Spain
Alexandre da Silva Veith	Nokia Bell Labs, Belgium
Jinen Daghrir	Ubotica Technologies, Ireland
Hoa Khanh Dam	University of Wollongong, Australia
Florian Daniel	Université de Nantes, France
Valeria De Castro	Universidad Rey Juan Carlos, Spain
Flavio De Paoli	Università Milano Bicocca, Italy
Martina De Sanctis	Gran Sasso Science Institute, Italy
Andrea Delgado	Universidad de la República, Uruguay
Shuiguang Deng	Zhejiang University, China
Oliver Denninger	FZI Research Center for Information Technology, Germany
Niranjana Deshpande	Rochester Institute of Technology, USA
Amine Dhraief	University of Manouba, Tunisia
Daniele Di Pompeo	University of L'Aquila, Italy

Chen Ding	Toronto Metropolitan University, Canada
Elisabetta DiNitto	Politecnico di Milano, Italy
Hai Dong	RMIT University, Australia
Praveen Kumar Donta	Stockholm University, Sweden
Fadoua Drira	University of Sfax, Tunisia
Khalil Drira	LAAS-CNRS, France
Yucong Duan	Hainan University, China
Schahram Dustdar	Vienna University of Technology, Austria
Gregorio Diaz	University of Castilla-La Mancha, Spain
Joyce El Haddad	Université Paris-Dauphine, France
Rik Eshuis	Eindhoven University of Technology, The Netherlands
Ralph Ewerth	Leibniz Information Centre, Germany
Onyeka Ezenwoye	Augusta University, Georgia
Nora Faci	Université de Lyon 1, France
Georgios Fakas	Uppsala University, Sweden
Fairouz Fakhfakh	University of Sfax, Tunisia
Xiu Susie Fang	Donghua University, China
Marcelo Fantinato	University of Sao Paulo, Brazil
Sheik Mohammad Mostakim Fattah	Curtin University, Australia
Sebastian Feld	Delft University of Technology, Germany
Yimeng Feng	Macquarie University, Australia
Zhiyong Feng	Tianjin University, China
Pablo Fernandez	University of Seville, Spain
Afonso Ferreira	IRIT-CNRS, France
George Feuerlicht	University of Technology, Australia
Bernd Freisleben	University of Marburg, Germany
Jonas Fritzsch	University of Stuttgart, Germany
Xiang Fu	Hofstra University, USA
Gangadharan G. R.	IBM, India
Walid Gaaloul	Télécom sudParis, France
Wafa Gabsi	University of Sfax, Tunisia
Jose Garcia-Alonso	University of Extremadura, Spain
José Maria Garcia	Universidad de Sevilla, Spain
Ilche Georgievski	University of Stuttgart, Germany
Efstratios Georgopoulos	University of Peloponnese, Greece
Azadeh Ghari Neiat	Deakin University, Australia
Chirine Ghedira	University of Lyon, France
Faiza Ghozzi	University of Sfax, Tunisia
Laura Gonzalez	Universidad de la República, Uruguay
Mohamed Graiet	University of Monastir, Tunisia
Paul Greenfield	CSIRO, Australia
Daniela Grigori	Université Paris-Dauphine, France
Georg Grossmann	University of South Australia, Australia
Mohammed Karim Guennoun	École Hassania des Travaux Publics, Morocco

Nawal Guermouche	LAAS-CNRS, France
Besma Guesmi	Ubotica Technologies, Ireland
Sam Guinea	Politecnico di Milano, Italy
Mohad-Saïd Hacid	Université de Lyon 1, France
Hatem Hadj Kacem	University of Sfax, Tunisia
Majid Haghparast	University of Jyvaskyla, Finland
Jun Han	Swinburne University of Technology, Australia
Chihab Hanachi	Université Toulouse 1, France
Qiang He	Swinburne University of Technology, Australia
Herodotos Herodotou	Cyprus University of Technology, Cyprus
Brahim Hnich	University of Monastir, Tunisia
Bing Huang	University of Sydney, Australia
Baldomero Imbernon	Universidad Católica de Murcia, Spain
Fuyuki Ishikawa	National Institute of Informatics, Japan
Bahman Javadi	Western Sydney University, Australia
Imen Jegham	Ubotica Technologies, Ireland
Hai Jin Huazhong	University of Science and Technology, China
Mohamed Jmaiel	University of Sfax, Tunisia
Afef Jmal Maâlej	University of Sfax, Tunisia
Slim Kallel	University of Sfax, Tunisia
Salil Kanhere	The University of New South Wales, Australia
Sokratis Katsikas	Norwegian University of Science and Technology, Norway
Yousri Kessentini	University of Sfax, Tunisia
Nesrine Khabou	University of Sfax, Tunisia
Mehdi Khouja	University of Gabes, Tunisia
Kais Klai	Université de Sorbonne Paris Nord, France
Stefan Klikovits	Johannes Kepler University Linz, Austria
Grzegorz Kolaczek	Wroclaw University of Technology, Poland
Gerald Kotonya	Lancaster University, England
Philippe Lalanda	Université de Grenoble, France
Winfried Lamersdorf	University of Hamburg, Germany
Chung Lawrence	University of Texas at Dallas, USA
Alexander Lazovik	University of Groningen, The Netherlands
Young Choon Lee	Macquarie University, Australia
Leila Ben-Ayed	University of Manouba, Tunisia
Frank Leymann	University of Stuttgart, Germany
Dan Li	Sun Yat-sen University, China
Weiping Li	Peking University, China
Ying Li	Zhejiang University, China
Spyros Likothanassis	University of Patras, Greece
Mark Little	Red Hat Research, USA
Mingyi Liu	Harbin Institute of Technology, China
Xumin Liu	Rochester Institute of Technology, USA
Zhizhong Liu	Henan Polytechnic University, China
Lauri Lovén	University of Oulu, Finland

Yutao Ma	Central China Normal University, China
Leszek Maciaszek	Wroclaw University of Economics, Poland
Adnan Mahmood	Macquarie University, Australia
Maude Manouvrier	Université Paris-Dauphine, France
Philippe Massonet	CETIC, France
Afef Mdhaffar	University of Sfax, Tunisia
Massimo Mecella	Sapienza Università di Roma, Italy
Inmaculada Medina-Bulo	University of Cádiz, Spain
Brahim Medjahed	University of Michigan-Dearborn, USA
Imen Megdiche	INU J-F Champollion, France
Philippe Merle	Inria, France
Nizar Messai	Université de Tours, France
Mira Mezini	Technical University of Darmstadt, Germany
Tommi Mikkonen	Jyväskylä University, Finland
Sirine Miladi	Ubotica Technologies, Ireland
Roy Miles	Imperial College London, England
Sumaira Sultan Minhas	University of Manchester, England
Sajib Mistry	Curtin University, Australia
Hana Mkaouar	University of Sfax, Tunisia
Mohamed Wiem Mkaouer	University of Michigan-Flint, USA
Lars Moench	University of Hagen, USA
Enrique Moguel	University of Extremadura, Spain
Naouel Moha	Université du Québec, Canada
Daniel Moldt	University of Hamburg, Germany
David Moloney	Ubotica Technologies, Ireland
Francisco Moo-Mena	FMAT-UADY, Mexico
Andrea Morichetta	Technical University of Vienna, Austria
Mohamed Mosbah	Université de Bordeaux, France
Hamid Motahari	Macquarie University, Australia
Malek Mouhoub	University of Regina, Canada
Charaf Moulay El Hassan	University Ibn Tofail, Morocco
Mohammad Reza Mousavi	King's College London, UK
Michael Mrissa	University of Primorska, Slovenia
Juan Manuel Murillo Rodriguez	University of Extremadura, Spain
Rania Mzid	University Tunis El-Manar, Tunisia
Bahareh Nakisa	Deakin University, Australia
Nanjangud Narendra	Ericsson, India
Talal H. Noor	Taibah University, Saudi Arabia
Alex Norta	Tallinn University of Technology, Estonia
Guadalupe Ortiz	University of Cádiz, Spain
Claus Pahl	Free University of Bozen-Bolzano, Italy
George Pallis	University of Cyprus, Cyprus
Efi Papatheocharous	RISE Research Institutes of Sweden, Sweden

Mike Papazoglou	Tilburg University, The Netherlands
José Antonio Parejo Maestre	Universidad de Sevilla, Spain
Rebecca Parsons	University of Manchester, UK
Cesare Pautasso	University of Lugano, Switzerland
Mario Piattini	University of Castilla-La Mancha, Spain
Ernesto Pimentel	University of Málaga, Spain
Pierluigi Plebani	Politecnico di Milano, Italy
Seyedamin Pouriyeh	Kennesaw State University, USA
Víctor Casamayor Pujol	Technical University of Vienna, Austria
Ricardo Pérez-Castillo	University of Castilla-La Mancha, Spain
Lianyong Qi Qufu	Normal University, China
Qiang Qu	Shenzhen Institutes of Advanced Technology, China
M. Mustafa Rafique	Rochester Institute of Technology, USA
Claudia Raibulet	Università degli Studi di Milano-Bicocca, Italy
Enayat Rajabi	Dalhousie University, Canada
Manfred Reichert	University of Ulm, Germany
Wolfgang Reisig	Humboldt Universität zu Berlin, Germany.
Mouna Rekik	University of Sfax, Tunisia
Manuel Resinas	University of Seville, Spain
Stefanie Rinderle-Ma	Technical University of Munich, Germany
Norbert Ritter	University of Hamburg, Germany
Philippe Roose	Université de Pau et du Pays de l'Adour, France
Thatiane Rosa	University of São Paulo, Brazil
Stéphane Rubini	Université de Bretagne Occidentale, France
Antonio Ruiz-Cortés	University of Seville, Spain
Andreas S. Andreou	Cyprus University of Technology, Cyprus
Morteza Saberi	University of Technology Sydney, Australia
Subhash Sagar	Macquarie University, Australia
Diptikalyan Saha	IBM Research, India
Ashkan Sami	Shiraz University, Iran
Hitesh Sapkota	Amazon, India
Ina Schaefer	Karlsruhe Institute of Technology, Germany
Stefan Schulte	Technical University of Hamburg, Germany
Boris Sedlak	Technical University of Vienna, Austria
Aviv Segev	University of South Alabama, USA
Lionel Seinturier	Université de Lille, France
Mohamed Sellami	Télécom SudParis, France
Jun Shen	University of Wollongong, Australia
Michael Sheng	Macquarie University, Australia
Weishi Shi	University of North Texas, USA
Yanjun Shu	Harbin Institute of Technology, China
Sarah Siddiqui	CSIRO, Australia
Frank Singhoff	Université de Brest, France
Zheng Song	University of Michigan-Dearborn, USA
Sandro Speth	University of Stuttgart, Germany

Ioannis Stamelos	Aristotle University, Greece
Jianwen Su	University of California at Santa Barbara, USA
Chang-Ai Sun	University of Science and Technology Beijing, China
Hedi Tabia	Université Paris-Saclay, France
Stefan Tai	Technical University of Berlin, Germany
Chouki Tibermacine	Université de Montpellier, France
Adel N. Toosi	University of Melbourne, Australia
Farouk Toumani	Université Clermont Auvergne, France
Hai Nam Tran	Université de Bretagne Occidentale, France
Michele Tucci	University of L'Aquila, Italy
Mariem Turki	University of Gabes, Tunisia
Willem-Jan van den Heuvel	Tilburg University, The Netherlands
Genoveva Vargas-Solar	University of Lyon, France
Monica Vitali	Politecnico di Milano, Italy
Mingxue Wang	Huawei, Ireland
Shangguang Wang	Beijing University of Posts and Telecommunications, China
Shuang Wang	Southeast University, Bangladesh
Xianzhi Wang	University of Technology Sydney, Australia
Zhongjie Wang	Harbin Institute of Technology, China
Benjamin Weder	University of Stuttgart, Germany
Jun Wei	Chinese Academy of Sciences, China
Sebastian Werner	Technical University of Berlin, Germany
Mathias Weske	University of Potsdam, Germany
Hanchuan Xu	Harbin Institute of Technology, China
Jiuyun Xu	China University of Petroleum, China
Jian Yang	Macquarie University, Australia
Sami Yangui	LAAS-CNRS, France
Lina Yao	University of New South Wales, Australia
Jianwei Yin	Zhejiang University, China
Sira Yongchareon	Auckland University of Technology, New Zealand
Tetsuya Yoshida	Nara Women's University, Japan
Jian Yu	Auckland University of Technology, New Zealand
Qi Yu	Rochester Institute of Technology, USA
Dong Yuan	University of Sydney, Australia
Elisa Yumi Nakagawa	University of São Paulo, Brazil
Munazza Zaib	Macquarie University, Australia
Bechir Zalila	University of Sfax, Tunisia
Gianluigi Zavattaro	University of Bologna, Italy
Muhammad Zawish	South East Technological University, Ireland
Uwe Zdun	University of Vienna, Austria
Liang Zhang	Fudan University, China
Wei Emma Zhang	University of Adelaide, Australia
Xuyun Zhang	Macquarie University, Australia
Yang Zhang	Macquarie University, Australia
Jianjun Zhao	Kyushu University, Japan

Weiliang Zhao Macquarie University, Australia
Zhangbing Zhou CUG Beijing, China
Christian Zirpins Karlsruhe University of Applied Sciences, Germany

Additional Reviewers

Afrin, Mahbuba
Alkalbani, Asma
Aloulou, Hamdi
Baccari, Yosr
Baravkar, Siddhi
Ben Amor, Lamia
Bennani, Mohamed Taha
Benzin, Janik-Vasily
Boucebsi, Rachida
Chakraborty, Tuhin
Chen, Qian
Chen, Wei
De Palma, Giuseppe
Dridi, Charaf Eddine
Ebrahimi, Elmira
Ehrendorfer, Matthias
Fan, Shujia
Garfatta, Ikram
Guo, Lucas
Hoang, Anh-Tu
Islam, Muhammad
Kanneganti, Sai Krishna Deepak
Kaur, Karamjit
Kerdoudi, Mohamed Lamine
Khouja, Mehdi
Kormiltsyn, Aleksandr
Kotonya, Gerald
Lertpongrujikorn, Pawissanutt
Li, Zhengquan
Liu, Hanwen
Liu, Ji
Mahmud, Md. Redowan
Meflah, Wided
Morgan, Rebecca
Mottakin, Khairul
Mukhtiar, Noorain
Naeem, Muhammad
Rekik, Mouna
Riad, Helal
Sarkar, Arupa
Segu Nagesh, Sanjay
Singh, Anuradha
Sober, Michael
Souifi, Lotfi
Stricker, Fabian
Strutzenberger, Diana
Telikani, Akbar
Tibermacine, Okba
Trentin, Matteo
Wang, Huan
Warnakulasooriya, Kolitha
Wijethilake, Kasun Eranda
Wu, Qiancheng
Wu, Tong
Yang, Yihong
Zhang, Alan
Zhang, Yuning
Zhong, Weiyi
Zhou, Xu

Contents – Part I

Edge and IoT

Efficient and Dependency-Aware Placement of Serverless Functions on Edge Infrastructures 3
    Luciano Baresi, Giovanni Quattrocchi, and Inacio Gaspar Ticongolo

POSEIDON: Efficient Function Placement at the Edge Using Deep Reinforcement Learning 21
    Prakhar Jain, Prakhar Singhal, Divyansh Pandey, Giovanni Quatrocchi, and Karthik Vaidhyanathan

ABBA-VSM: Time Series Classification Using Symbolic Representation on the Edge 38
    Meerzhan Kanatbekova, Shashikant Ilager, and Ivona Brandic

An Energy-Efficient Partition and Offloading Method for Multi-DNN Applications in Edge-End Collaboration Environments 54
    Zhiqing Yang, Xiang He, Teng Wang, and Zhongjie Wang

Crowdsourcing Task Assignment with Category and Mobile Combined Preference Learning 69
    Yue Ma, Xiaofeng Gao, and Guihai Chen

Federated Learning as a Service for Hierarchical Edge Networks with Heterogeneous Models 85
    Wentao Gao, Omid Tavallaie, Shuaijun Chen, and Albert Zomaya

Optimizing Traffic Allocation for Multi-replica Microservice Deployments in Edge Cloud 100
    Hokun Park, Hyungjun Kim, Donggyun Kim, Gyujeong Lim, and Heonchang Yu

An Event-B Based Approach for Horizontally Scalable IoT Applications 116
    Yassmine Gara Hellal, Lazhar Hamel, and Mohamed Graiet

Efficient Provisioning of IoT Energy Services 125
    Amani Abusafia, Athman Bouguettaya, and Abdallah Lakhdari

Attention-Driven Conflict Management in Smart IoT-Based Systems 133
    Christson Awanyo and Nawal Guermouche

Benchmarking Deep Learning Models for Object Detection on Edge
Computing Devices... 142
    *Daghash K. Alqahtani, Muhammad Aamir Cheema,
    and Adel N. Toosi*

Generative AI

LLM Enhanced Representation for Cold Start Service Recommendation 153
    *Dunlei Rong, Lina Yao, Yinting Zheng, Shuang Yu, Xiaofei Xu,
    Mingyi Liu, and Zhongjie Wang*

Combining Generative AI and PPTalk Service Specification for Dynamic
and Adaptive Task-Oriented Chatbots 168
    *María Jesús Rodríguez-Sánchez, Zoraida Callejas, Angel Ruiz-Zafra,
    and Kawtar Benghazi*

Automated Generation of BPMN Processes from Textual Requirements...... 185
    Quentin Nivon and Gwen Salaün

Plug-and-Play Performance Estimation for LLM Services without Relying
on Labeled Data.. 202
    *Can Wang, Dianbo Sui, Hongliang Sun, Hao Ding, Bolin Zhang,
    and Zhiying Tu*

UELLM: A Unified and Efficient Approach for Large Language Model
Inference Serving 218
    *Yiyuan He, Minxian Xu, Jingfeng Wu, Wanyi Zheng, Kejiang Ye,
    and Chengzhong Xu*

Service-Oriented Requirements Elicitation Through Systematic
Questionnaire Design: A Problem-Driven GenAI Approach 236
    *Julie Rauer, To Kim Bao Pham, Sam Supakkul, Tom Hill,
    and Lawrence Chung*

Assessing Large Language Models Effectiveness in Outdated Method
Renaming 253
    *Ali Ben Mrad, Abdoul Majid O. Thiombiano, Mohamed Wiem Mkaouer,
    and Brahim Hnich*

Service Security and Privacy

DynaEDI: Decentralized Integrity Verification for Dynamic Edge Data 263
    Qiang He, Jiyu Yang, Feifei Chen, Cong Tian, Yanhui Li, and Yun Yang

Heterogeneous Multi Relation Trust for SIoT Service Recommendation...... 281
    *Geming Xia, Chaodong Yu, Linxuan Song, Wei Peng, Yuze Zhang,
    and Hongfeng Li*

A Context-Aware Service Framework for Detecting Fake Images 296
    Muhammad Umair, Paramvir Singh, and Athman Bouguettaya

Bias Exposed: The BiaXposer Framework for NLP Fairness 312
    Yacine Gaci, Boualem Benatallah, Fabio Casati,
    and Khalid Benabdeslem

FlowShredder: A Protocol-Independent in-Network Security Service
in the Cloud 327
    Bin Song, Bin Sun, Qiang Fu, and Hao Li

Processes and Workflows

HiGPP: A History-Informed Graph-Based Process Predictor for Next
Activity 337
    Jiaxing Wang, Chengliang Lu, Yifeng Yu, Bin Cao, Kai Fang,
    and Jing Fan

From Visual Choreographies to Flexible Information Protocols 354
    Tom Lichtenstein, Amit K. Chopra, Munindar P. Singh,
    and Mathias Weske

Architectural Elements of Decentralized Process Management Systems 370
    Kai Grunert, Janis Joderi Shoferi, Lucas Gold, Wolf Rieder,
    and Axel Küpper

LLM-Based Business Process Documentation Generation 381
    Rui Zhu, Quanzhou Hu, Lijie Wen, Leilei Lin, Honghao Xiao,
    and Chaogang Wang

Author Index 391

Contents – Part II

Cloud Computing

Cost-Aware Dynamic Cloud Workflow Scheduling Using Self-attention and Evolutionary Reinforcement Learning 3
    Ya Shen, Gang Chen, Hui Ma, and Mengjie Zhang

LARE-HPA: Co-optimizing Latency and Resource Efficiency for Horizontal Pod Autoscaling in Kubernetes 19
    Donggyun Kim, Hyungjun Kim, Eunyoung Lee, and Heonchang Yu

STORELESS: Serverless Workflow Scheduling with Federated Storage in Sky Computing.. 35
    Sashko Ristov, Mika Hautz, Philipp Gritsch, Stefan Nastic, Radu Prodan, and Michael Felderer

Not Best but Fair: Achieving a Fair Service Deployment Through Sky Computing for Latency-Sensitive Applications 45
    Weijia Shi, Baokang Zhao, and Huan Zhou

QoS and SLA

Integrated QoS- and Vulnerability-Driven Self-adaptation for Microservices Applications 55
    Matteo Camilli, Fabio Luccioletti, Raffaela Mirandola, and Patrizia Scandurra

SLO-Aware Task Offloading Within Collaborative Vehicle Platoons 72
    Boris Sedlak, Andrea Morichetta, Yuhao Wang, Yang Fei, Liang Wang, Schahram Dustdar, and Xiaobo Qu

Client-Specific Homogeneous Service Composition at Runtime for QoS-Critical Tasks.. 87
    Zhengquan Li, Long Cheng, and Zheng Song

Network SLO-Aware Container Orchestration on Kubernetes Clusters 96
    Angelo Marchese and Orazio Tomarchio

Microservice

CSMO: The Cross-Supervision Method for Microservice Optimization through Decentralized Data Management 107
    Suxiang Wu, Ying Li, Xinzhou Zhu, Meng Xi, and Jianwei Yin

BOAM: A Business Oriented Identification Approach of Microservices
Within Legacy Systems.. 123
   Brahim Mahmoudi, Imen Trabelsi, Dalila Tamzalit, Naouel Moha,
   and Yann-Gaël Guéhéneuc

Motif-Based Linearizing Graph Transformer for Web API
Recommendation 138
   Xin Zheng, Guiling Wang, Yuqi Zhang, Boyang Han, and Jian Yu

Leveraging a Microservice Architecture, Access Control
and Interoperability Patterns to Manage Privacy-Related User Consents...... 146
   Selena Lamari, Nadjia Benblidia, Chouki Tibermacine,
   Christelle Urtado, and Sylvain Vauttier

Service Recommendation

A Toolchain for Checking Domain- and Model-Driven Properties of Jolie
Microservices.. 161
   Saverio Giallorenzo, Fabrizio Montesi, Marco Peressotti,
   Florian Rademacher, Sabine Sachweh, and Philip Wizenty

GSL-Mash: Enhancing Mashup Creation Service Recommendations
Through Graph Structure Learning 176
   Sihao Liu, Mingyi Liu, Tianyu Jiang, Shuang Yu, Hanchuan Xu,
   and Zhongjie Wang

Emerging Technologies and Approaches

Circuit Scheduling Policies on Current QPUs: QCRAFT Scheduler.......... 195
   Jaime Alvarado-Valiente, Javier Romero-Álvarez, Jorge Casco-Seco,
   Enrique Moguel, Jose Garcia-Alonso, and Juan M. Murillo

MuSS: Multimodal Satellite Service for Unsupervised Land-Cover
Classification 210
   Yassine Gacha, Olfa Besbes, and Takoua Abdellatif

HSC: An Artificial Intelligence Service Composition Dataset from
Hugging Face... 225
   Xiao Wang, Dunlei Rong, Hanchuan Xu, Xiangdong He,
   and Zhongjie Wang

Service Composition

Choreography-Defined Networks: A Case Study on DoS Mitigation 243
   Saverio Giallorenzo, Jacopo Mauro, Andrea Melis, Fabrizio Montesi,
   Marco Peressotti, and Marco Prandini

Racing the Market: An Industry Support Analysis for Pricing-Driven
DevOps in SaaS 260
  Alejandro García-Fernández, José Antonio Parejo,
  Francisco Javier Cavero, and Antonio Ruiz-Cortés

Compositio Prompto: An Architecture to Employ Large Language Models
in Automated Service Computing 276
  Robin D. Pesl, Carolin Mombrey, Kevin Klein, Denesa Zyberaj,
  Ilche Georgievski, Steffen Becker, Georg Herzwurm, and Marco Aiello

Composing Smart Data Services in Shop Floors Through Large Language
Models 287
  Jerin George Mathew, Flavia Monti, Donatella Firmani,
  Francesco Leotta, Federica Mandreoli, and Massimo Mecella

Blockchain

A Query Language to Enhance Security and Privacy of Blockchain as a
Service (BaaS) 299
  Nasrin Sohrabi, Norrathep Rattanavipanon, and Zahir Tari

Blockchain Based Efficient Pairing-Free Certificateless Authentication
Scheme for Vehicular Ad-hoc Network 314
  Meiju Yu, Rula Sa, Jin Zhang, Yi Zhao, Qi An, and Qiaomei Gao

A Blockchain-Enhanced Framework for Privacy and Data Integrity
in Crowdsourced Drone Services................................. 323
  Junaid Akram and Ali Anaissi

Towards an Automated Verification Approach for ERC-Based Smart
Contracts 331
  Rim Ben Fekih, Mariam Lahami, Mohamed Salem El Eze, Salma Bradai,
  and Mohamed Jmaiel

Industry Papers

Weather-Conditioned Multi-graph Network for Ride-Hailing Demand
Forecasting.. 341
  Mengjin Liu, Yuxin Zuo, Yang Luo, Daiqiang Wu, Peng Zhen,
  Jiecheng Guo, and Xiaofeng Gao

BIS: NL2SQL Service Evaluation Benchmark for Business Intelligence
Scenarios 357
  Bora Caglayan, Mingxue Wang, John D. Kelleher, Shen Fei, Gui Tong,
  Jiandong Ding, and Puchao Zhang

How Do Infrastructure-as-Code Practitioners Update their Provider
Dependencies? An Empirical Study on the AWS Provider 373
   Mahi Begoug and Ali Ouni

Author Index 389

Edge and IoT

Efficient and Dependency-Aware Placement of Serverless Functions on Edge Infrastructures

Luciano Baresi[1], Giovanni Quattrocchi[1], and Inacio Gaspar Ticongolo[1,2](✉)

[1] Politecnico di Milano, Dipartimento di Elettronica, Informazione e Bioingegneria, Milano, Italy
{luciano.baresi,giovanni.quattrocchi,inacio.ticongolo}@polimi.it
[2] Universidade Eduardo Mondlane, Departamento de Matematica e Informatica, Maputo, Mozambique

Abstract. Serverless computing is a promising paradigm for deploying and managing applications on edge infrastructures. It provides small granularity and high flexibility by decomposing applications into lightweight functions. Although this modularity facilitates efficient resource allocation and function placement on edge nodes, complex dependencies among functions pose significant challenges to their effective management. Existing research has explored various optimization techniques for serverless computing platforms, but dependency-aware function placement remains an open challenge. In this paper, we propose *PLUTO*, an efficient solution for the placement of serverless functions that supports complex dependencies. First, we present an optimal non-linear formulation of the placement problem. Then, we introduce a heuristic approach, derived from the optimal formulation, that ensures efficiency as the number of functions increases. An extensive empirical evaluation against state-of-the-art solutions shows that *PLUTO* significantly reduces the overall delay and memory consumption by up to 85% and 78%, respectively.

Keywords: Serverless functions · Edge computing · Function dependencies · Placement

1 Introduction

Serverless computing represents a promising approach to deploy and manage applications on edge infrastructures. By breaking applications into discrete isolated components, also known as *functions*, serverless architectures offer small granularity and high flexibility [3,6]. This fine-grained modularity allows serverless platforms to allocate resources efficiently and place function instances onto edge topologies characterized by resource-constrained nodes and workload fluctuations [16]. However, complex function dependencies (i.e., functions that depend on other functions) complicate the management of serverless applications [14]. In particular, the placement of functions onto edge nodes should depend not only on resource availability and proximity to users but also on the dependencies among functions. For example, an e-commerce application consists of numerous serverless functions deployed at the edge to deliver real-time product recommendations even when the workload fluctuates. These functions depend on others, for example, to calculate prices and allow for user personalization. The management of fluctuating workloads on edge nodes requires efficient provisioning of limited resources, but also a deep understanding of how functions are invoked and interact among them [15].

Serverless computing has been widely investigated in recent years [7,19,20]. Some approaches study dynamic resource provisioning to optimize edge node utilization [22], while others propose solutions based on probabilistic and machine learning techniques to minimize function management overhead (e.g., cold start) [10,24]. Despite these different efforts towards improving serverless computing platforms, handling function dependencies on resource-constrained edge nodes remains an open challenge [15,25].

This paper proposes *PLUTO*, a solution for the placement of functions on the edge that supports (complex) dependencies among functions. *PLUTO* is based on the computational model of *NEPTUNE* [5], a state-of-the-art solution for managing applications at the edge, and provides three main contributions: (i) a non-linear formalization of the optimization problem that considers the placement of functions with their dependencies onto edge nodes, (ii) a heuristic algorithm based on this formalization for its efficient usage, and (iii) an extensive empirical evaluation of *PLUTO* based on three benchmark applications and a comparison against state-of-the-art solutions. Our experiments demonstrate the benefits of *PLUTO*, and show a reduction of overall memory delay and consumption by up to 85% and 78%, respectively, compared to competitors.

The rest of the paper is organized as follows. Section 2 formulates the optimization problem and the proposed heuristic. Section 3 presents the evaluation and discusses the results obtained. Section 4 surveys the related work, and Sect. 5 concludes the paper.

2 *PLUTO*

PLUTO is based on the computational model of *NEPTUNE* [5], which considers dependencies only for dynamic resource allocation (and not for function placement). In *NEPTUNE*, an application consists of a set of serverless functions F whose dependencies are represented as a directed acyclic graph $DAG(F, E)$, where the nodes are the functions, and the edges represent their dependencies (or invocations). A function f can invoke another function f' $m_{f,f'}$ times. For example, a function f that calculates the distance between two points of interest might call another function f' twice to retrieve the geographical coordinates of both items, thus having $m_{f,f'} = 2$. The set of all dependencies of a function f is defined as D_f. Each function call can be executed either *sequentially* or *in parallel*. Sequential invocations require synchronous interactions with the other functions, and the caller must wait for the termination of each invocation. Parallel invocations are executed concurrently, and the caller only needs to wait for the slowest invocation. *NEPTUNE* supports two types of functions: *entrypoint* and *invoked* functions. Both types of functions can be called by other functions; however, *entrypoint* can be also directly called by users.

The edge topology T is represented as another graph, where N is the set of nodes (or servers), the edges are the links between them, and $\delta_{i,j}$ denotes the network delay from node i to node j. When a user aims to issue a request, we assume that s/he connects to the closest node. The workload for a given entrypoint function f on node i is denoted as $\lambda_{f,i}$, and defines the number of requests received within a set time window. These data are used by *PLUTO* to formulate the efficient placement of function instances on edge nodes. We begin by formulating a non-linear optimization problem and then propose a heuristic to obtain approximations of the optimal solution in a timely manner.

2.1 Optimization Problem

Given that edge nodes are resource-constrained and might not be able to handle all of the incoming workload, each node may forward requests to other nearby nodes in the network.

Thus, the placement problem is twofold. We need to (i) decide where function instances are to be instanced to handle the workload, and (ii) define *routing policies*, that is, for each node, define how to distribute the workload across the other nodes (and function instances). Additionally, the presence of vertical scaling capabilities [23] (as in *NEPTUNE*), lets us impose that only one instance of a function f (abbreviated as f instance from now on) can be hosted on each node.

Decision Variables. The formulation includes three main decision variables: $x_{f,i,j}$, $y_{f,i,f^s,j}$, and $z_{f,i,f^p,j}$. The first variable represents how the workload is routed within the network. More formally $x_{f,i,j} \in [0,1] \subseteq \mathbb{R}$ decides the fraction of workload $\lambda_{f,i}$ at node i for the f instance to be routed to node j. Given a sequential dependency between f and f', variable $y_{f,i,f',j} \in [0,1] \subseteq \mathbb{R}$ represents how sequential calls are handled within the network. Thus, $y_{f,i,f',j}$ decides the fraction of sequential invocations to be served by an f instance deployed on node i to an f' instance deployed on node j. Similarly, for parallel invocations, variable $z_{f,i,f',j}$ determines the fraction of parallel invocations to be served by an f instance deployed on node i to an f' instance deployed on node j. Finally, an additional variable $c_{f,i}$ computed using x, y, and z defines whether an f instance should be placed at node i, that is, whether some f requests should be handled on node i, either as direct or routed user calls, or as invocations by other functions (the formal definition of c can be found in the Appendix as Eq. 9).

Objective Function. The objective of this formulation is to minimize the overall delay, which consists of four components: (i) D_{user}, the delay caused by routing user requests among different nodes; (ii) D_{seq}, the delay from sequential invocations when the caller and the callee functions are not placed on the same node; (iii) D_{par}, the delay from parallel invocations when the caller and the callee functions are not placed on the same node; and (iv) D_{cold}, the time required to create and place functions on nodes if they do not already exist.

The complete MILP (Mixed Integer Linear Programming) formulation of the objective function can be found in the Appendix (Sect. A.1).

Constraints. Our formulation is subject to a set of constraints. First, each function has an input parameter θ_f that specifies the maximum forwarding delay allowed. This means that if a function instance is placed on a node, the delay between the nodes that forward (a fraction of) the workload and the node receiving it must be within the allowed limit to ensure timely execution. Second, each function has a parameter m_f that defines the amount of memory required for its execution. The total memory required by all function instances placed on a node must not exceed the node's memory capacity. This ensures that each node can handle the functions allocated to it without running out of memory. Third, each function f has a parameter $u_{f,i}$ that defines the average CPU cores consumed by an instance of f at node i. To avoid resource contention, the total CPU cores consumed by the function instances on a node must not exceed the CPU cores available on that node. Fourth, routing and invocation policies must be defined for all nodes in the topology and function instances. This means that the system must establish how function instances are routed and invoked across the nodes to maintain an efficient and organized network.

The complete MILP formulation of the constraints can be found in the Appendix (Sect. A.2).

2.2 Placement Algorithm

The formulation described above is non-linear. Given the need for timely decisions on edge nodes, we developed a heuristic to efficiently obtain approximate, yet reasonable results. The proposed heuristic is organized into two main steps. First, it places all entrypoints close to the sources of user-generated workload to optimize routing delays. Then, it places invoked functions to minimize the delay caused by inter-function calls.

Placement of Entrypoint Functions. The goal of this step is to compute variable $x_{f,i,j}$, which represents the routing policies for distributing the workload that enters the system through entrypoints across nodes. Note that, when a node is designated to handle part of the workload for a given function f, an instance of that function must be placed on that node.

Algorithm 1 presents the pseudo-code for placing entrypoints. Procedure EntrypointFunctionPlacement starts by sorting the entrypoints according to their set delay thresholds θ_f to ensure that functions with stricter delays are placed closer to users (line 2). For each function, the placement process begins by considering the workload to be handled by each node (lines 3–6). Starting with the node that receives the workload, function instances are placed iteratively until all requests are handled (line 7).

In line 8, procedure PlaceInstances takes as input a function, a node where the function instance should be placed, and the total number of requests that the instance should handle. It returns the number of requests that the placed instance (if any) will handle from the total number of requests. If the node does not have sufficient memory or CPU resources to handle at least one request (lines 17–18), the procedure returns 0, indicating that no requests will be handled and no instance will be placed. If the selected node has sufficient resources, the procedure calculates the needed cores to serve the requests and updates the memory available on the node (lines 15–23). If the node can serve all requests, the procedure updates the available CPU cores and returns the input number of requests (lines 24–26). If the node does not have enough cores to serve all unhandled requests, the fraction of the workload it can serve is calculated and returned, and the available cores are set to 0 (lines 27–30). Note that in this way, when a function instance is placed on $node_i$, either all the necessary resources to handle the expected workload or all the available ones are allocated. This strategy reduces the number of function instances needed, thus optimizing the delay caused by cold starts.

After executing PlaceInstances, variable x is updated with the percentage of the workload to route from $node_i$ to the considered node (line 9), the number of requests to handle is updated (line 10), and the next node to consider is the closest to $node_i$, among those not considered yet (line 11). This process is repeated until all the workload for entrypoints is served (if possible).

Placement of Invoked Functions. The goal of this step is to place invoked functions f' on the nodes. This involves computing variables $y_{f,i,f',j}$ or $z_{f,i,f',j}$ depending on whether function f' is called by f sequentially or in parallel, respectively.

Algorithm 2 presents the pseudo-code for doing it. This procedure takes as input a node $node_i$, a function f already placed on $node_i$, and a function f' called by f and to be placed on $node_i$ or nearby. In lines 2–14, the algorithm computes the amount of requests $\omega_{f,i}$ processed by the f instance placed on $node_i$. If f is an entrypoint (line 3), the procedure iterates through all nodes in N and adds to the workload $\omega_{f,i}$ the user workload ($\lambda_{f,j}$) sent by $node_j$ to the f instance placed on $node_i$, using the routing policies (lines 4–7). This is represented by variable $x_{f,j,i}$ computed by procedure EntrypointFunctionPlacement.

Next, if f is called by any other function $\bar{f}$ as a dependency (i.e., $f \in D_{\bar{f}}$), the procedure iterates through all nodes in N and further adds to the workload $\omega_{f,i}$ the amount of requests sent to the f instance on $node_i$ by any $\bar{f}$ instance multiplied by factor $m_{\bar{f},f}$ (lines 8–14), that is, the number of times each invocation of $\bar{f}$ invokes f.

Then, the procedure calculates the amount of invocation produced by the f instance on node i to be processed by f' instances, which is $\omega_{f,i}$ multiplied by the dependency multiplier $m_{f,f'}$ (line 15). Similarly to how entrypoints are placed,

Algorithm 1. Placement of entrypoint functions

```
 1: procedure ENTRYPOINTFUNCTIONPLACEMENT()
 2:     F_sorted ← sortby(F.entrypoints, θ_f)
 3:     for f ∈ F_sorted do
 4:         for node_i ∈ N do
 5:             reqToHandle ← λ_{f,i}
 6:             node_j ← node_i
 7:             while reqToHandle > 0 do
 8:                 handledReq ← PLACEINSTANCES(f, node_j, reqToHandle)
 9:                 x_{f,i,j} ← handledReq / λ_{f,i}
10:                 reqToHandle ← reqToHandle − handledReq
11:                 node_j ← node_i.nextClosestNode()
12:             end while
13:         end for
14:     end for
15: end procedure
16: procedure PLACEINSTANCES(f, node_i, reqToHandle)
17:     if node_i.availableMemory < m_f or node_i.availableCPU < u_{f,i} then
18:         return 0
19:     else
20:         neededCores ← reqToHandle ∗ u_{f,i}
21:         diffCores ← node_i.availableCores − neededCores
22:         node_i.availableMemory ← node_i.availableMemory − m_f
23:         c_{f,i} ← 1
24:         if diffCores ≥ 0 then
25:             node_i.availableCores ← diffCores
26:             return reqToHandle
27:         else
28:             handledReq ← node_j.availableCores / u_{f,i}
29:             node_j.availableCores ← 0
30:             return handledReq
31:         end if
32:     end if
33: end procedure
```

this workload is iteratively assigned to f' instances until all requests are handled (lines 16–26). Specifically, procedure PlaceInstances is called iteratively to handle f' placement (line 18).

If the dependency type between f and f' is sequential (line 19), variable $y_{f,i,f',j}$ is updated with the fraction of requests handled (line 20). For parallel dependencies, variable $z_{f,i,f',j}$ is updated similarly (line 22). The number of remaining requests to be handled is updated (line 24), and the next node considered is the closest to $node_i$ and not considered yet (line 25). This process is repeated until all the workload of invoked functions is served.

Placement. The main procedure of *PLUTO* is shown in Algorithm 3. First, procedure EntrypointFunctionPlacement is called to handle the initial placement

Algorithm 2. Placement of invoked functions

```
 1: procedure INVOKEDFUNCTIONPLACEMENT(node_i, f, f')
 2:     ω_{f,i} ← 0
 3:     if f ∈ F.entrypoints then
 4:         for node_j ∈ N do
 5:             ω_{f,i} ← ω_{f,i} + λ_{f,j} * x_{f,j,i}
 6:         end for
 7:     end if
 8:     for f̄ ∈ F do
 9:         if f ∈ D_{f̄} then
10:             for node_j ∈ N do
11:                 ω_{f,i} ← ω_{f,i} + ω_{f̄,j} * m_{f̄,f} * (y_{f̄,j,f,i} + z_{f̄,j,f,i})
12:             end for
13:         end if
14:     end for
15:     reqToHandle ← ω_{f,i} * m_{f,f'}
16:     node_j ← node_i
17:     while reqToHandle > 0 do
18:         handledReq ← PLACEINSTANCES(f', node_j, reqToHandle)
19:         if dependencyType(f, f') == SEQUENTIAL then
20:             y_{f,i,f',j} ← handledReq / (ω_{f,i} * m_{f,f'})
21:         else
22:             z_{f,i,f',j} ← handledReq / (ω_{f,i} * m_{f,f'})
23:         end if
24:         reqToHandle ← reqToHandle − handledReq
25:         node_j ← node_i.nextClosestNode()
26:     end while
27: end procedure
```

of entrypoints (line 1). Next, the entrypoints are sorted in topological order and stored in F_{topo} to ensure that functions are handled in the correct order (line 2).

The algorithm then iterates over each function f in F_{topo} until it is empty. For each function f, it further iterates over its sequential dependencies f'. For each node $node_i$ sorted by available resources, if an instance of function f is already placed on $node_i$ ($c_{f,i} == 1$), the algorithm calls procedure InvokedFunctionPlacement to place an instance of function f' at the appropriate node (lines 3–10).

After handling the sequential dependencies, the algorithm proceeds to manage parallel dependencies in a similar manner (lines 11–17). By handling sequential dependencies first, they are placed as close as possible to the caller functions since they impose more stringent constraints on function placement.

Finally, once all its dependencies are placed, f is removed from F_{topo} (line 18) and all its dependencies are prepended to the data structure, avoiding duplicates (line 19). This approach ensures that function placement is completed in topological order.

Algorithm 3. *PLUTO*

1: ENTRYPOINTFUNCTIONPLACEMENT()
2: $F_{topo} \leftarrow topologicalOrder(F.entrypoints)$
3: **while** $F_{topo}.size() > 0$ **do**
4:     **for** $f' \in D_f.sequential$ **do**
5:         **for** $node_i \in sortByAvailableResource(N)$ **do**
6:             **if** $c_{f,i} == 1$ **then**
7:                 INVOKEDFUNCTIONPLACEMENT($node_i$, f, f')
8:             **end if**
9:         **end for**
10:     **end for**
11:     **for** $f' \in D_f.parallel$ **do**
12:         **for** $node_i \in sortByAvailableResource(N)$ **do**
13:             **if** $c_{f,i} == 1$ **then**
14:                 INVOKEDFUNCTIONPLACEMENT($node_i$, f, f')
15:             **end if**
16:         **end for**
17:     **end for**
18:     $F_{topo}.remove(f)$
19:     $F_{topo}.prependAll(D_f)$
20: **end while**

Example. Figure 1 illustrates a simple placement example. The figure shows an application DAG with four functions (f_1, f_2, f_3, and f_4), obtained as user input or with an automatic approach, along with the network delays between nodes $\delta_{i,j}$ in milliseconds (shown as labels on the dashed lines). Function f_1 is the entrypoint function that sequentially invokes f_2. In turn, f_2 invokes f_3 and f_4 in parallel. For simplicity, we assume that all dependency multipliers $m_{f,f'}$ be equal to 1 and set the function delay requirements θ_f high enough to have no impact. In this scenario, node 1 receives 100 requests for f_1 ($\lambda_{f1,1} = 100$).

Following Algorithm 3, *PLUTO* first places the entrypoint function f_1 as close to the users as possible. In this example, node 1 has sufficient CPU cores and memory to handle the entire workload of f_1, so an f_1 instance is placed on node 1 (step ❶ in the figure).

After placing f_1, *PLUTO* considers f_2, the only dependency of f_1. Initially, *PLUTO* attempts to place f_2 on node 1, based on the placement from step ❶. However, while node 1 has enough resources to place an instance of f_2, it can only handle half of the invocations from the f_1 instance on node 1. Consequently, *PLUTO* looks for the closest node to node 1 in terms of delay, which is node 2, and places an instance of f_2 there. As a result (step ❷ in the figure), two instances of f_2 are placed: one on node 1, which receives 50 requests from the f_1 instance on node 1, and another on node 2, which handles the remaining 50 requests.

Next, *PLUTO* addresses the dependencies of f_2, namely f_3 and f_4 (step ❸ in the figure). Since node 1 is fully utilized by the placed instances, the algorithm places an instance of f_3 on node 2, which is set to receive all 50 invocations from the f_2 instance on node 2 and 30 from node 1, fully utilizing the resources of node 2. With 20 invocations from the f_2 instance on node 1 still to be handled, *PLUTO* places an f_3 instance on node 3, the only node with available resources. Finally, an instance of f_4 is also placed on node 3 to handle all 50 invocations from each of the f_2 instances.

3 Evaluation

To evaluate the performance of *PLUTO*, we answered the following two research questions. **RQ1:** How does *PLUTO* perform compared to state-of-the-art solutions under fluctuating workloads? **RQ2:** How does *PLUTO* perform compared to state-of-the-art solutions when the capacities of nodes vary?

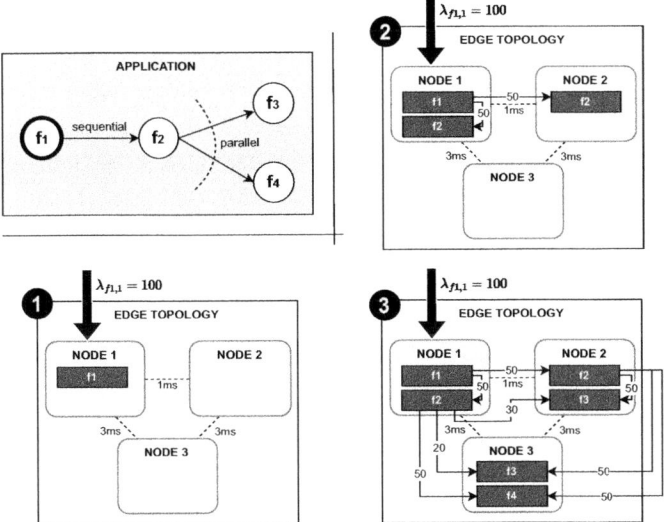

Fig. 1. Example of *PLUTO* Placement.

The first research question aims to evaluate the robustness and adaptability of *PLUTO* in handling variable workloads compared to other leading solutions. The second research question seeks to understand the effectiveness of *PLUTO* in scenarios where the capacity of nodes changes. Varying node capacities can significantly impact the performance of edge computing systems. By comparing *PLUTO* to state-of-the-art solutions, our aim is to determine its ability to optimize resource allocation and maintain low latency, even as nodes' resources change.

3.1 Experimental Setup

We compared *PLUTO* with two state-of-the-art solutions: *NEPTUNE* [4] and *HEU* [25]. *NEPTUNE* employs a Mixed Integer Linear Programming approach to place functions on edge nodes. *NEPTUNE*'s placement does not consider function dependencies, and its main goal is to minimize network delay and the cost of resources. *NEPTUNE* serves as a baseline to quantify the importance of handling function dependencies in this context. *HEU* is a heuristic designed to optimize the overall delay of function executions on edge nodes and considers function dependencies. Unlike *NEPTUNE* and *PLUTO*, which operate based on aggregate workload, *HEU* processes requests individually. This means that instead of periodically updating the overall placement based on the incoming workload, *HEU* either forwards each request to an existing instance or to a newly created one and considers function dependencies in the process.

Table 1. Results with varying workload.

	hotel reservation			sockshop			complex app		
	NEP	HEU	PLU	NEP	HEU	PLU	NEP	HEU	PLU
D_{net}	887	101	241	488	79	239	3776	3756	1807
D_{cold}	702	1338	702	3465	9592	3465	3222	22554	3222
D_{pl}	110	30	1	126	55	1	476	294	4
D	1699	1469	944	4079	9726	3705	7474	26604	5033
M_{all}	2048	3026	2374	1515	3168	1811	12500	36137	14910

We ran all the experiments on a MacBook Pro equipped with 4 cores and 16GB of RAM and running macOS Ventura (version 13.2.1). The experiments were carried out through a simulator[1] on an edge topology of 10 nodes with capacity between 1 and 16 cores and with between 2 and 32GB of memory. The network delay between nodes was randomly set between 1 and 5 milliseconds (ms) and kept constant during the experiments.

The experiments involved three applications: *hotel reservation*[2], *sockshop*[3], and *complex app*. The first two are well-known state-of-the-art benchmarks. *hotel reservation* is a serverless application that mimics a hotel website and includes 4 functions with two entrypoints. Its DAG has an average out-degree of 3 edges and an in-degree of 1 edge. All the dependent functions are invoked sequentially. *sockshop* is an e-commerce application whose micro-services were converted to serverless functions in a recent work [4]. It comprises 7 functions including 5 entrypoints and has an average out-degree of 6 edges and an in-degree of 1 edge.

---
[1] The code and the full dataset of the experiments is available at https://doi.org/10.5281/zenodo.12789199.
[2] https://github.com/vhive-serverless/vSwarm/tree/main/benchmarks/hotel-app.
[3] https://github.com/microservices-demo/microservices-demo.

One-third of the invocation is sequential, and two-thirds are parallel. *complex app* [5] includes 25 functions with 6 entrypoints, a 2-edge out-degree, 1-edge in-degree, and the number of sequential and parallel invocations is balanced (50% each). For all three applications, we considered a cold start time equal to 90% of their average response time, as suggested by Daw et al. [10].

We carried out the evaluation by measuring the overall network delay $D_{net} = D_{user} + D_{seq} + D_{par}$), the cold start delay (D_{cold}), the placement time (D_{pl}), that is, the time to compute a new placement, the total delay ($D = D_{net} + D_{cold} + D_{pl}$), and the total memory consumption M_{all}. All delays have been measured in milliseconds, while memory in MB. Each experiment was run 5 times and we report averaged values.

3.2 Performance with Workload Variation (RQ1)

Table 1 shows the average results obtained by the three approaches when varying the workload from 0 users to 200 by adding 1 user at each step of the experiment. Figure 3 shows the behavior of the approaches when dealing with *complex app*.

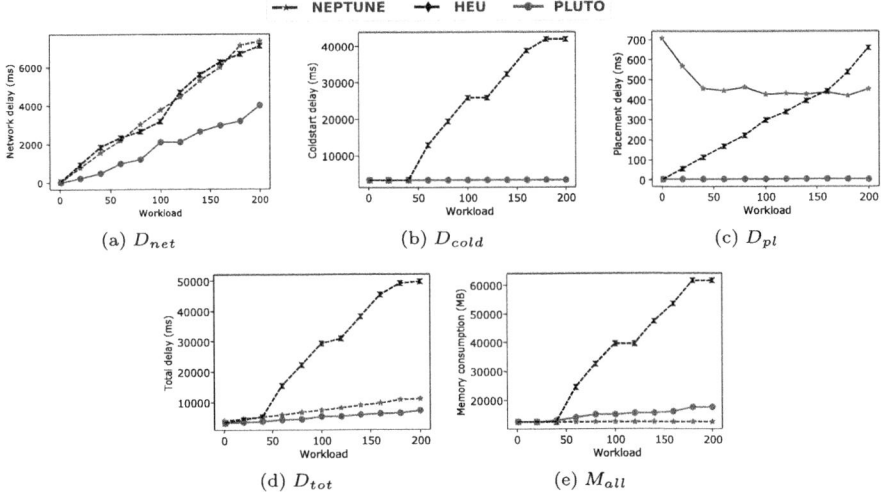

Fig. 2. Comparison with varying workload and application *complex app*.

The results show that *PLUTO* (PLU in the table) significantly reduces the total delay (D) compared to both *HEU* and *NEPTUNE* (NEP in the table). With application *hotel reservation*, *PLUTO* reduces D by 44.44% compared to *NEPTUNE* and by 35.73% compared to *HEU*. With application *sockshop*, *PLUTO* achieves a 9.17% reduction in total delay compared to *NEPTUNE* and a 61.91% reduction compared to *HEU*. With application *complex app* (see Fig. 2d), where dependencies are more frequent and intricate, the reduction is even more substantial: a 32% improvement against *NEPTUNE* and more than an 80% reduction against *HEU*.

When examining the delay-related metrics in isolation, we observe that *HEU* achieves the lowest D_{net} for smaller applications but doubles the network delay compared to *PLUTO* in *complex app*, showcasing the scalability of our approach (see Fig. 2a). *NEPTUNE*, on the other hand, yields the worst results in all three applications.

As for cold starts, *NEPTUNE* and *PLUTO* allocate a similar number of functions across the three applications (though placed on different nodes), resulting in the same D_{cold}. However, *HEU* suffers significantly from cold starts, consistently showing the worst results with an extremely high number of created instances for *complex app* (see Fig. 2b).

The results related to placement time (D_{pl}) indicate that *PLUTO* is the fastest in computing solutions. *NEPTUNE*, which employs an optimization problem, is the slowest, while *HEU* achieves intermediate results. This behavior can be attributed to the complexity of *NEPTUNE*'s solution (although it does not consider dependencies) and the fact that *HEU* operates on a per-request basis. As the workload increases, the placement time for *HEU* can exceed that of *NEPTUNE* (see Fig. 2c).

Table 2. Results with varying node capacities.

	hotel reservation			sockshop			complex app		
	NEP	HEU	PLU	NEP	HEU	PLU	NEP	HEU	PLU
D_{net}	945	22	75	965	41	113	8506	5437	3613
D_{cold}	702	834	702	3465	6048	3465	3222	41282	3222
D_{pl}	64	64	1	140	97	1	432	519	4
D	1711	920	778	4570	6186	3579	12160	47238	6839
M_{all}	2048	2432	2048	1515	2273	1515	12500	60813	12969

Lastly, in terms of total memory consumption (M_{all}), *PLUTO* shows a balanced performance, consuming slightly more memory than *NEPTUNE* but significantly less than *HEU*. For example, with *complex app*, *PLUTO*'s memory consumption is 19.28% higher than *NEPTUNE* but 58.76% lower than *HEU* (see Fig. 2e).

3.3 Performance with Node Capacity Variation (RQ2)

We also investigated the impact of node capacity on the performance of the approaches. We varied the processing power of the nodes from 1 to 16 cores and the memory from 2GB to 32GB by adding 1 core and 2GB of memory, respectively, at each step of the experiment, while fixing the number of nodes to 10 and the workload to 200 requests. The average results are summarized in Table 2 and illustrated in Fig. 3 for *complex app*, which shows the most interesting results.

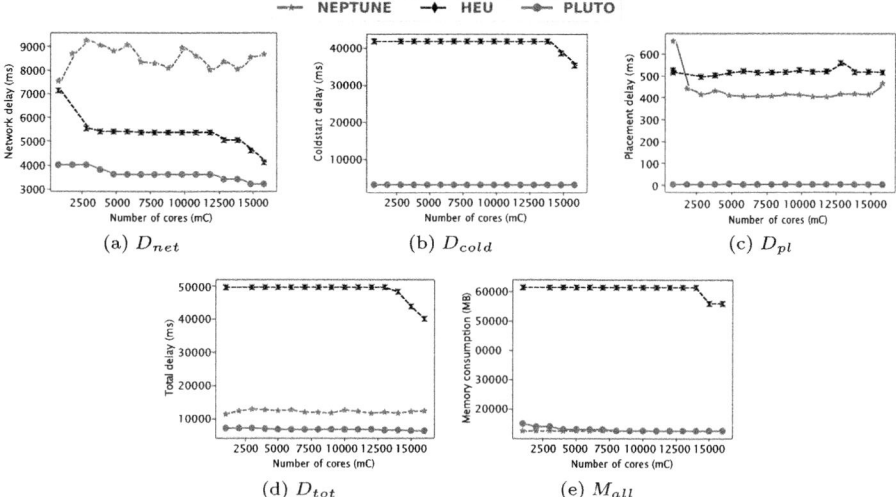

Fig. 3. Comparison with varying node capacity and application *complex app*.

As expected, we observed that the most powerful nodes that receive user calls result in lower delays and overall memory consumption (as shown in Fig. 3). Intuitively, larger nodes reduce the frequency of routing since multiple function instances can coexist on the same node that receives the workload. In general, the results confirm our findings from **RQ1**. *PLUTO* consistently achieves the lowest total delay (D) across all applications. In particular, the most significant performance improvement was measured for *complex app* (see Fig. 3d), where the delay is reduced by 85.52% and 78.67% compared to *HEU* and *NEPTUNE*, respectively. In terms of network delay (D_{net}), *PLUTO* outperforms the competitors with *complex app* (see Fig. 3a). However, *HEU* is the most efficient for applications *hotel reservation* and *sockshop*, at the cost of creating a significant number of additional function instances. Consequently, D_{cold} for *HEU* increases by an order of magnitude higher than *NEPTUNE* and *PLUTO*, and the computation time (D_{pl}) decreases with the size of the application (see Fig. 3c). The memory consumption results align with our observations from the previous section.

In general, *PLUTO* shows balanced and efficient performance in various metrics, applications, and experiments. Unlike our approach, *NEPTUNE* does not consider dependencies in its placement formulation, preventing it from efficiently optimizing delays and memory consumption. *HEU* tends to spread multiple instances across nodes, complicating the management of cold starts, and increases the overall usage of resources compared to *PLUTO*.

4 Related Work

Serverless functions have been a widely used means to deploy applications on edge frameworks, and their placement has been studied thoroughly, but existing solutions are still partial.

For example, Baresi et al. [4] propose NEPTUNE, a comprehensive framework for managing serverless functions at the edge that minimizes the overall network delay and the resources utilization cost. Chaudhry et al. [8] present an approach to manage functions on the edge and reduce their end-to-end response time and energy consumption. Abdelaal et al. [1] propose a heuristic algorithm to optimize function placement to jointly guarantee load balance, and minimize bandwidth, energy consumption, and placement cost. Mahmoudi et al. [19] exploit machine learning to tackle function placement and optimize system performance and resource usage while guaranteeing desired response times. Ding et al. [13] propose Pod-placement, a kubernetes-oriented microserice placement model to minimize the cost of resource usage and communication while meeting microservice instances deadline. Pod-placement, not only considers dynamic resource allocation, but also manages the shared dependency libraries between microservices instances. Although the relevance and importance of these approaches, none of them considers function dependencies while placing them on available nodes.

Elgamal et al. [14] investigate cost minimization through function fusion and placement. They identify the to-be-fused functions and where to place them: on the cloud or on edge nodes. They consider function dependencies, but only in the context of function fusion, and not for placement. A similar approach is proposed by Pelle et al. [21], which automates the deployment of functions, and decides where to place the functions (cloud or edge) according to resource availability and latency requirements. Other approaches [2,5,6] exploit dependencies for provisioning resources to functions to meet desired response times or for cold start mitigation [10].

When considering placement approaches that take function dependencies into account, existing techniques ignore the complexity of these dependencies. The approaches [11,12,17,18] propose function placement algorithms to minimize the overall application's execution time, but they do not distinguish between sequential and parallel invocations. He et al. [15] propose a novel greedy-based approach for deploying microservices with complex dependencies on edge nodes, but the authors only consider sequential executions. [9] propose heuristic function placement solutions to reduce memory consumption while guaranteeing serverless workflow Service Level Objective(SLO) by maximizing memory sharing for serverless workflows. Although they consider sequential and parallel invocations, their model ignores the number of times a function invokes other functions given a single call, the sequence of parallel invocations, and the network delay between nodes. Xu et al. [25] propose an efficient heuristic algorithm, along with its approximation, for placing serverless functions that depend on both functions and states on edge frameworks. They model applications as complex DAGs and consider the number of times a function invokes other functions. They also consider sequential and parallel invocations, but they tend to create too many function instances. This increases cold starts and memory consumption, particularly in scenarios with complex dependencies.

5 Conclusions

This paper presents *PLUTO*, a placement solution for serverless functions that considers dependencies. The complete formulation we propose in the paper is not linear, and the cost of computing placements would be excessive. This is why *PLUTO* is based on heuristics that allow us to both compute placements with acceptable delays and obtain results that outperform other state-of-the-art approaches. The assessment conducted by simulating three benchmark applications on a network of 10 nodes shows that *PLUTO* achieves reductions of up to 85% in overall delay and 78% in memory consumption.

Our future work comprises a further refinement of the heuristics, the management of dynamically changing edge topologies, and additional assessment with real-world, more complex, edge applications.

A Appendix

A.1 Objective Function

We define D_{user} as follows:

$$D_{user} = \sum_{f}^{F} \sum_{i}^{N} \sum_{j}^{N} x_{f,i,j} * \lambda_{f,i} * \delta_{i,j} \tag{1}$$

Intuitively, for each request routed from node i to node j in set N, the delay is equal to $\delta_{i,j}$.

D_{seq} is defined as:

$$D_{seq} = \sum_{f}^{F} \sum_{i}^{N} \sum_{j}^{N} \sum_{f'}^{S_f} y_{f,i,f',j} * m_{f,f'} * \omega_{f,i} * \delta_{i,j} \tag{2}$$

where S_f is the set of functions that are invoked by f sequentially and $\omega_{f,i}$ is the total amount of requests handled by f on node i. $\omega_{f,i}$ includes two main terms: i) the user requests when f is an *entrypoint* function, and ii) sequential and parallel calls to the f instance deployed on node i executed by the set of functions (D_f) that depends on f. Thus, $\omega_{f,i}$ is defined as follows:

$$\omega_{f,i} = \sum_{j}^{N} x_{f,j,i} * \lambda_{f,j} + \sum_{f'}^{D_f} \sum_{j}^{N} m_{f',f} * \omega_{f',k} * (y_{f',j,f,i} + z_{f',j,f,i}) \tag{3}$$

Note that such definition is recursive and can be unrolled since the set of function dependency D_f of f is empty when f is a starting node of the application DAG (the base case of the recursion). Similarly, D_{par} is defined as:

$$D_{par} = \sum_f^F \sum_i^N \sum_j^N \max_{f' \in P_f} (z_{f,i,f',j} * m_{f,f'} * w_{f,i} * \delta_{i,j}) \qquad (4)$$

where P_f is the set of functions that are invoked by f in parallel. Intuitively, instead of summing up all invocation delays, we only consider the maximum one. Finally, D_{cold} is defined as:

$$D_{cold} = \max_{f \in F}(coldstart_f * p_f) \qquad (5)$$

where $coldstart_f$ is the time to boot an instance of function f as measured during a profiling phase, and p_f is a boolean variable that is 1 if there is at least one function instance of f to be deployed on a node where an instance of f was not already running, and 0 otherwise.

The above formulae lead us to the following objective function:

$$minimize D_{user} + D_{seq} + D_{par} + D_{cold} \qquad (6)$$

A.2 Constraints

Our formulation is subject to a set of constraints. First, each function is characterized by an input parameter θ_f, that is, the maximum forwarding delay allowed for function f. This means that if the values of $x_{f,i,j}$, $y_{f,i,f',j}$, and $y_{f,i,f',j}$ are greater than 0, the delay between nodes i and j should be less than or equal to θ_f. Thus,

$$\begin{cases} x_{f,i,j} * \delta_{i,j} \le x_{f,i,j} * \theta_f \\ y_{f,i,f',j} * \delta_{i,j} \le y_{f,i,f',j} * \theta_f \\ z_{f,i,f',j} * \delta_{i,j} \le z_{f,i,f',j} * \theta_f \end{cases} \qquad (7)$$

$$\forall f \in F, \forall f' \in F, \forall i \in N, \forall j \in N$$

Second, the sum of the memory required by the function instances placed on a node cannot exceed its capacity.

$$\sum_f^F m_f * c_{f,i} \le M_i \quad \forall i \in N \qquad (8)$$

where m_f is the memory required by function f and $c_{f,i}$ indicates whether an instance of function f should be placed on node i and it is defined as follows:

$$c_{f,i} = \begin{cases} 1 & \text{if } \sum_j^N \left(x_{f,j,i} + \sum_{f'}^F (y_{f',j,f,i} + z_{f',j,f,i}) \right) > 0 \\ 0 & \text{otherwise} \end{cases} \qquad (9)$$

$$\forall j \in N, \forall f \in F$$

In essence, an instance of f is placed on a node i if some requests of f are forwarded to i either as direct user requests (if f is an entrypoint) or if invoked by other functions on i.

Third, to avoid resource contention, we must consider the amount of CPU cores available U_i on each node i, and the average CPU cores consumed $u_{f,i}$ by the f instance on node i. More formally,

$$U_i \geq \sum_j^N \sum_f^F (x_{f,j,i} * \lambda_{f,j} * u_{f,i} + \omega_{f,j} * \sum_{f'}^{D_f} m_{f,f'} * u_{f',i} * (y_{f,j,f',i} + z_{f,j,f',i}))$$
$$\forall i \in N \tag{10}$$

Fourth, routing and invocation policies must be defined for all the nodes in the topology and functions:

$$\sum_j^N x_{f,i,j} = 1, \ \sum_j^N y_{f,i,f',j} = 1, \ \sum_j^N z_{f,i,f',j} = 1 \tag{11}$$
$$\forall f \in F, \forall f' \in F, \forall i \in N, \forall j \in N$$

References

1. Abdelaal, M.A., Ebrahim, G.A., Anis, W.R.: Efficient placement of service function chains in cloud computing environments. Electronics **10**(3), 323 (2021)
2. Akhtar, N., Raza, A., Ishakian, V., Matta, I.: COSE: configuring serverless functions using statistical learning. In: IEEE INFOCOM 2020-IEEE Conf. on Computer Communications, pp. 129–138. IEEE (2020)
3. Baldini, I., et al.: Serverless computing: current trends and open problems. Res. Adv. Cloud Comput. 1–20 (2017)
4. Baresi, L., Hu, D.Y.X., Quattrocchi, G., Terracciano, L.: Neptune: a comprehensive framework for managing serverless functions at the edge. ACM Trans. Auton. Adapt. Syst. **19**(1), 1–32 (2024)
5. Baresi, L., Quattrocchi, G., Ticongolo, I.G.: Dependency-aware resource allocation for serverless functions at the edge. In: International Conference on Service-Oriented Computing, pp. 347–362. Springer (2023)
6. Bhasi, V.M., Gunasekaran, J.R., Thinakaran, P., Mishra, C.S., Kandemir, M.T., Das, C.: Kraken: adaptive container provisioning for deploying dynamic DAGs in serverless platforms. In: Proceedings of the ACM Symposium on Cloud Computing, pp. 153–167 (2021)
7. Cassel, G.A.S., et al.: Serverless computing for internet of things: a systematic literature review. Futur. Gener. Comput. Syst. **128**, 299–316 (2022)
8. Chaudhry, S.R., Palade, A., Kazmi, A., Clarke, S.: Improved QoS at the edge using serverless computing to deploy virtual network functions. IEEE Internet Things J. **7**(10), 10673–10683 (2020)
9. Cheng, D., Yan, K., Cai, X., Gong, Y., Hu, C.: SLO-aware function placement for serverless workflows with layer-wise memory sharing. IEEE Trans. Parallel Distrib. Syst. 1074–1091 (2024)

10. Daw, N., Bellur, U., Kulkarni, P.: Xanadu: mitigating cascading cold starts in serverless function chain deployments. In: Proceedings of International Middleware Conference, pp. 356–370 (2020)
11. De Maio, V., Bermbach, D., Brandic, I.: TAROT: spatio-temporal function placement for serverless smart city applications. In: International Conference on Utility and Cloud Computing, pp. 21–30. IEEE (2022)
12. Deng, S., et al.: Dependent function embedding for distributed serverless edge computing. IEEE Trans. Parallel Distrib. Syst. **33**(10), 2346–2357 (2021)
13. Ding, Z., Wang, S., Jiang, C.: Kubernetes-oriented microservice placement with dynamic resource allocation. IEEE Trans. Cloud Comput. **11**(2), 1777–1793 (2022)
14. Elgamal, T., Sandur, A., Nahrstedt, K., Agha, G.: Costless: optimizing cost of serverless computing through function fusion and placement. In: Symposium on Edge Computing (SEC), pp. 300–312. IEEE (2018)
15. He, X., Tu, Z., Wagner, M., Xu, X., Wang, Z.: Online deployment algorithms for microservice systems with complex dependencies. IEEE Trans. Cloud Comput. **11**(2), 1746–1763 (2022)
16. Kjorveziroski, V., Filiposka, S., Trajkovik, V.: IoT serverless computing at the edge: a systematic mapping review. Computers **10**(10), 130 (2021)
17. Lv, W., et al.: Graph-reinforcement-learning-based dependency-aware microservice deployment in edge computing. IEEE Internet Things J. **11**(1), 1604–1615 (2023)
18. Mahgoub, A., et al.: SONIC: application-aware data passing for chained serverless applications. In: USENIX Annual Technical Conference, pp. 285–301 (2021)
19. Mahmoudi, N., Lin, C., Khazaei, H., Litoiu, M.: Optimizing serverless computing: introducing an adaptive function placement algorithm. In: Proceedings of the International Conference on Computer Science and Software Engineering, pp. 203–213 (2019)
20. Nabil, E.I., Hästbacka, D., Pahl, C., Taibi, D.: Platforms for serverless at the edge: a review. In: International Workshops of ESOCC, pp. 29–40. Springer (2021)
21. Pelle, I., Paolucci, F., Sonkoly, B., Cugini, F.: Latency-sensitive edge/cloud serverless dynamic deployment over telemetry-based packet-optical network. IEEE J. Sel. Areas Commun. **39**(9), 2849–2863 (2021)
22. Pinto, D., Dias, J.P., Ferreira, H.S.: Dynamic allocation of serverless functions in IoT environments. In: International Conference on Embedded and Ubiquitous Computing, pp. 1–8 (2018)
23. Quattrocchi, G., Incerto, E., Pinciroli, R., Trubiani, C., Baresi, L.: Autoscaling solutions for cloud applications under dynamic workloads. IEEE Trans. Serv. Comput. 804–820 (2024)
24. Vahidinia, P., Farahani, B., Aliee, F.S.: Mitigating cold start problem in serverless computing: a reinforcement learning approach. IEEE Internet Things J. **10**(5), 3917–3927 (2023)
25. Xu, Z., et al.: Stateful serverless application placement in MEC with function and state dependencies. IEEE Trans. Comput. **72**(9), 2701–2716 (2023)

POSEIDON: Efficient Function Placement at the Edge Using Deep Reinforcement Learning

Prakhar Jain[1(✉)], Prakhar Singhal[1], Divyansh Pandey[1], Giovanni Quatrocchi[2], and Karthik Vaidhyanathan[1]

[1] Software Engineering Research Center, International Institute of Information Technology, Hyderabad, India
{prakhar.jain,prakhar.singhal}@research.iiit.ac.in,
divyansh.pandey@students.iiit.ac.in, karthik.vaidhyanathan@iiit.ac.in
[2] Politecnico di Milano, Dipartimento di Elettronica, Informazione e Bioingegneria, Milan, Italy
giovanni.quattrocchi@polimi.it

Abstract. Edge computing allows for reduced latency and operational costs compared to centralized cloud systems. In this context, serverless functions are emerging as a lightweight and effective paradigm for managing computational tasks on edge infrastructures. However, the placement of such functions in constrained edge nodes remains an open challenge. On one hand, it is key to minimize network delays and optimize resource consumption; on the other hand, decisions must be made in a timely manner due to the highly dynamic nature of edge environments. In this paper, we propose *POSEIDON*, a solution based on Deep Reinforcement Learning for the efficient placement of functions at the edge. *POSEIDON* leverages Proximal Policy Optimization (PPO) to place functions across a distributed network of nodes under highly dynamic workloads. A comprehensive empirical evaluation demonstrates that *POSEIDON* significantly reduces execution time, network delay, and resource consumption compared to state-of-the-art methods.

Keywords: Edge Computing · Serverless · Function Placement · Deep Reinforcement Learning

1 Introduction

Edge computing has emerged as a promising solution to address the limitations of centralized cloud systems, particularly in terms of reducing latency and operational costs. This paradigm shift enables computational tasks to be processed closer to the data source, thereby enhancing the performance and efficiency of applications [12]. In this decentralized framework, edge nodes, by their nature,

---

P. Singhal and D. Pandey—These authors contributed equally to this work.

are often constrained in terms of resources such as processing power, memory, and storage. Additionally, the workload on these nodes can be highly fluctuating, with varying demands depending on user activities and their dynamic geographical location. This inherent variability necessitates a flexible and efficient approach to managing applications running on edge nodes [24].

Recently, the serverless paradigm has emerged as a suitable solution for managing applications in edge computing infrastructures [15]. Serverless allows developers to deploy applications as a collection of discrete, self-contained functions that are designed to be lightweight and stateless [22]. In the context of edge computing, such functions can be quickly moved across nodes to adapt to the mobility of users and the shifting demands of applications.

Despite the advantages, dynamically placing serverless functions in edge nodes presents significant challenges [17]. Ideally, functions should be placed as close to users as possible to minimize network delays and optimize resource consumption. However, resource-constrained edge cannot always host all necessary functions and the mobility of users and the heterogeneity of functions in terms of CPU and memory requirements further complicate the problem. Moreover, such a dynamic environment requires timely decisions to cope with fluctuating workloads [3]. In the literature, most of the work exploits combinatorial optimization techniques, such as Integer Programming formulations, to solve the placement problem effectively [2,6,7]. While these methods are capable of producing optimal solutions, they are often complex and time-consuming, resulting in slow solution generation. Some approaches have proposed custom heuristics as an alternative [9], but these methods have been demonstrated to produce significantly lower quality placements compared to optimization-based approaches [3].

In this context, we introduce $POSEIDON$[1], a novel solution that utilizes Deep Reinforcement Learning [8] (DRL) to optimize the placement of serverless functions at the edge. $POSEIDON$ specifically leverages Proximal Policy Optimization [19] (PPO) to distribute functions across a network of nodes, effectively managing highly dynamic workloads. After determining the placement, $POSEIDON$ uses a simplified Mixed Integer Linear Programming (MILP) problem to optimize traffic routing across the different function instances. The proposed method aims to reduce network delays, improve resource consumption, and produce timely solutions compared to existing state-of-the-art techniques.

The high-dimensional nature of the placement problem and continuous state space render classical RL algorithms impractical. Traditional RL typically relies on discrete state-action spaces, which are unsuitable for complex scenarios such as edge computing. DRL overcomes this limitation by using neural networks to approximate complex mappings from states to actions or action probabilities, enabling efficient and scalable learning in high-dimensional state spaces. Moreover, being known for its ability to capture intricate interactions between states and actions, DRL is well-suited to handle real-world environments that are complex and dynamic, requiring flexible and adaptive learning methods [8,11].

---

[1] https://github.com/sa4s-serc/poseidon.

We evaluated *POSEIDON* through a comprehensive comparison with state-of-the-art solutions. Our extensive empirical evaluation demonstrated that *POSEIDON* is almost 16 times faster than the state-of-the-approach with respect to decision time with almost comparable cost and delay to the state-of-the-art.

The rest of the paper is organized as follows. Section 2 presents the problem and introduces our solution. Section 3 details the DRL solution and the MILP formulation. Section 4 presents the empirical evaluation of *POSEIDON* and the comparison against the state-of-the-art. Section 5 describes some relevant work and concludes with Sect. 6.

2 Problem and Solution Overview

In *POSEIDON*, an edge topology is defined as a graph where N is the set of nodes and the edges are the links between them. Each pair of nodes i and j is characterized by δ_{ij}, representing the network delay between them. F is the set of functions that could be deployed on the edge topology. We assume that users can connect to any of the nodes in N based on their geographical proximity to the closest one. Thus, for each function f and node i, the incoming workload for a function f to node i is defined as $w_{f,i}$, representing the number of requests for f arriving at node i. Since each node is resource-constrained and cannot host all functions, we assume that each node can route the requests to any other (nearby) node j. Thus, the problem *POSEIDON* tackles is twofold:

1. Deciding whether an instance of function f should be placed on node i (*placement*);
2. Deciding how the workload incoming to any node i for function f should be routed to any other node j (*routing policies*).

2.1 Solution Overview

To address these problems, *POSEIDON* leverages DRL for placement and a MILP formulation for routing policies. The goal of *POSEIDON* is to minimize both (i) the overall network delay, i.e., the latency while serving function requests, and (ii) the cost of running the function instances. The former goal focuses on placing functions as close to users as possible to minimize routing delays. The latter goal aims to use the minimum number of nodes to serve all the workload with minimal overhead. *POSEIDON* ensures a balance between these conflicting objectives using a user-defined trade-off. *POSEIDON* works in three phases and its architecture is shown in Fig. 1.

The *placement phase*, detailed in Sect. 3.1, is dedicated to computing the function placement. To achieve this, *POSEIDON* organizes the functions F into a queue q_F, prioritized by their specific criteria such as frequency of requests or resource requirements. Then, a DRL agent considers each function one at a time, starting with the highest priority. For each function, the agent computes

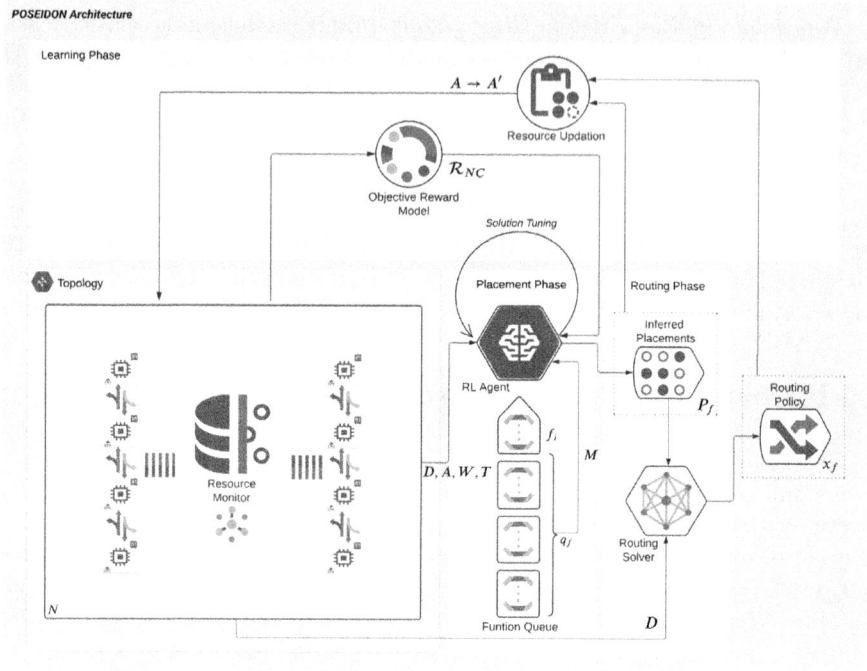

Fig. 1. *POSEIDON* architecture.

a placement vector, a boolean vector $\mathbf{c}_i^f$, which indicates whether a function f should be placed on node i. The agent leverages comprehensive information from the topology, including inter-node delays, available hardware resources, and function parameters such as memory requirements. It also considers the workload of the function instance, reflecting the traffic of function requests at each node. This information is used to infer an optimal function placement that satisfies our objectives.

In the *routing phase*, the function placement determined by the agent is used to compute the routing policies, as detailed in Sect. 3.2. In this phase, every node i could host an active function instance and/or route a portion of the requests to another node j with a previously placed f instance. This is done by computing matrix $\mathbf{x}_{i,j}^f$, where each value is a real number between 0 and 1 that represents the fraction of the workload incoming to node i for function f that should be routed to node j. To compute the routing policies, *POSEIDON* utilizes the generated function placements to formulate a MILP problem. The constraints of this problem ensure that all function requests are redirected to nodes with a running instance of the function. The objective is to minimize the network delay of function requests and the cost of running the functions, thereby aligning with the overall solution objective.

In the *learning phase*, the state of the topology is updated, and a reward $\mathcal{R}$ is calculated, as detailed in Sect. 3.3. This reward mechanism ensures that the DRL agent learns to place the functions in a manner that minimizes both the total network delay and the operational costs of the function instances.

Table 1. Inputs, Outputs and Reward Variables

Component	Symbol	Description
Topology Data		
Inter-Node Delay	$\delta_{i,j}$	Network delay between node i and node j
Available node memory	m_i	Available memory on node i
Available node cores	k_i	Available CPU cores on node i
Function Data		
Function Workload	$w_{f,i}$	Workload for function f on node i
Function memory	m_f^R	Memory required by function f
Function cores	$k_{f,i}^R$	Average CPU cores required by instances function f on node i
Monitored Data		
Total Delay	T	Total network delay
Total Cost	C	Total cost of running placed functions
Output Data		
Placement vector	$c_{f,i}$	Boolean decision variable representing whether function f is placed on node i.
Routing policy	$x_{f,i,j}$	Real decision variable representing the fraction of f workload incoming into node i to be routed to node j

3 POSEIDON

This section details the three phases of *POSEIDON*. To facilitate the read, we included the most important variables used in our formulation in Table 1.

3.1 Function Placement

POSEIDON uses five vectors to represent the state of the topology, D, A, W, M, T. D is the delay vector where each element is the inter-node delay $\delta_{i,j}$, A is the available resources, W is the workload of the current function f, M encodes the parameters of the current function and T denotes the cumulative delay of the topology. The delay vector D can be represented as:

$$D = \begin{bmatrix} \delta_{1,1} \ldots \delta_{1,n} \; \delta_{2,1} \ldots \delta_{2,n} \; \ldots \ldots \; \delta_{n,1} \ldots \delta_{n,n} \end{bmatrix}$$

with $\delta_{i,i} = 0$ (i.e., local communications do not have delays) and $\delta_{i,j} = \delta_{j,i}$ (i.e., delay is symmetric) for any node i and j.

The available resources in the topology A, consist of the available memory m_i and available CPU cores k_i of each node i. This variable captures the available hardware resources at each node and is updated after placing each function instance to account for the resources consumed by the placed functions. Formally,

$$A = \begin{bmatrix} k_1 & m_1 & k_2 & m_2 & \ldots & k_n & m_n \end{bmatrix}$$

The workload of the current function f, which is denoted by W, is composed of the function workload at each node i denoted by $w_{f,i}$. Such data helps determine whether a function needs to be placed on a specific node based on the amount of function requests being received by it. The function parameters are passed into the state vector in the form of a vector M consisting of $m_f^R, m_\mu^R, m_\sigma^R$ where the latter two represent the mean and standard deviation of the resource requirements required by the remaining functions in q_F. These guide the placement decisions while keeping track of the resource requirements of the remaining functions.

$$M = \begin{bmatrix} m_f^R & m_\mu^R & m_\sigma^R \end{bmatrix}$$

The total network delay T of the topology initially set to 0 is continuously monitored and updated after placing each function f as follows:

$$T = T + \sum_i^N \sum_j^N x_{f,i,j} * w_{f,i} * \delta_{i,j}$$

where $x_{f,i,j}$ is the routing variable for routing requests of function f from node i to j and is computed after the second phase, as described in Sect. 3.2

Feeding the cumulative total delay to the agent helps it learn to minimize the delay effectively based on the existing network delay of the system.

The DRL agent implemented in *POSEIDON* system employs a policy gradient method known as Proximal Policy Optimization (PPO) to learn an optimal policy π. This policy maps a given state $s \in \mathcal{S}$ of the topology (i.e., the execution environment) to an action $c \in \mathcal{A}$, where $\mathcal{A} \in \{0,1\}^N$ represents the action space of the agent. This action space comprises of a set of boolean values for each node, indicating whether a function instance should be placed on the corresponding node or not. The state s exists within a continuous state space and encapsulates environmental information that affect the placement of the function and is formally defined as a feature vector as follows:

$$s = \begin{bmatrix} D & A & W & M & T \end{bmatrix}^\top$$

Since s is high dimensional and in a continuous state space it is difficult to model the placement problem with RL methods such as Q-Learning which requires tabulation and hence impractical to store and update the table, the need for DRL arises. The agent consists of a neural network that takes $\mathcal{S}$ as input and estimates a policy π^* which infers actions $\mathcal{A}^*$. These actions are used to compute the reward $\mathcal{R}$ for the agent after a suitable routing policy is computed, as mentioned in Sect. 3.3.

3.2 Routing Policies

Function placement is not sufficient to minimize the total network delay of the system because a node with the running instance of the function may not be able to handle the heavy workload expected in edges networks. In such cases, the need to route a certain fraction of function requests to other available nodes arises which would prevent overloading the node with user requests. To handle the routing of function requests, the objectives are formulated as a Mixed Integer Programming problem where the constraints are defined as follows:

$$P_f = \{i \mid c_{f,i} = 1, i \in N\} \quad \forall f \in F \qquad (1)$$

where P_f is the set of chosen nodes for placing a function. Thus, the following constraint ensures that all the f workload from node i are routed only to the nodes that belong to P_f.

$$\sum_j^{P_f} x_{f,i,j} = 1 \quad \forall i \in N, \forall f \in F \qquad (2)$$

Algorithm 1. Update state after placing function f

Require: A, M, q_F, P_f
1: **for** each $i \in P_f$ **do**
2: $\quad m_i \leftarrow m_i - m_f^R$
3: $\quad k_i \leftarrow k_i - \sum_j^N w_{f,j} * x_{f,j,i} * k_{f,i}^R$
4: **end for**
5: $pop(q_F)$
6: $f = \textbf{peek}(q_F)$

On the contrary, the following equation states that no fraction of f workload should be routed from any node i to a node j that does not belong to P_f.

$$x_{f,i,j} = 0 \quad \forall i \in N, \forall f \in F, \forall j \notin P_f \qquad (3)$$

For each node j that host a function f, the required CPU cores to handle the total workload forwarded to the node should be lower than the available cores on that node. This is given by:

$$\sum_i^N x_{f,i,j} * w_{f,i} * k_{f,j}^R \leq k_j \quad \forall f \in F, \forall j \in P_f \qquad (4)$$

The objective of the problem is to minimize the network delay of the placed function. The network delay T_f for a specific function f is defined as:

$$T_f = \sum_i^N \sum_j^N x_{f,i,j} * w_{f,i} * \delta_{i,j} \tag{5}$$

3.3 State Update and Solution Tuning

Placing a function f in the environment updates the state space as defined in Algorithm 1.

Based on the updated state of the community, the reward $\mathcal{R}$ is calculated to facilitate the parameter updates and solution tuning (Algorithm 2). Solution tuning involves training on the current state s of the system to improve the DRL agent. The reward model for the environment is designed to ensure that the agent comprehends the objectives of the problem and refines the policy π^*. The agent receives different types of rewards based on its decisions. The network delay and the system's operational cost are incorporated into a reward term, formulated to be minimized by the agent to improve it's performance. Given the conflicting nature of minimizing network delay and system cost, a user-defined trade-off parameter α is introduced as coefficient of trade off with value in range $(0, 1)$ where increasing α corresponds to increasing weightage of cost

---

Algorithm 2. Episodic reward calculation after placing function f

1: **Input:** T, C, $T_{\min}$ (minimum observed total network delay), $T_{\max}$ (maximum observed total network delay), $C_{\min}$ (minimum observed cost) $C_{\max}$ (maximum observed cost)
2: **Output:** T' (normalized total network delay), C' (normalized cost), $\mathcal{R}$ (reward)
3: Calculate T' and C' using:

$$T' = 2\left(\frac{T - T_{\min}}{T_{\max} - T_{\min}}\right) - 1 \quad C' = 2\left(\frac{C - C_{\min}}{C_{\max} - C_{\min}}\right) - 1$$

4: **if** size(P_f) = 0 or $m_i < 0$ or $k_i < 0$ or $RoutingSolver.STATUS$ == $INFEASIBLE$ **then**
5:     $\mathcal{R} = \mathcal{R}_{penalty}$
6: **else**
7:     $\mathcal{R} = \mathcal{R}_{NC}$
8: **end if**
9: Update $T_{\min}$, $T_{\max}$, $C_{\min}$, and $C_{\max}$.
10: $UpdateState(A, M, f, P_f)$
11: **if** q_F is empty **then**
12:     Return Reward and end episode
13: **else**
14:     Return Reward and repeat the process.
15: **end if**

minimization objective and decreasing α corresponds to increasing weightage of delay minimization objective. Mathematically, the reward term is defined as:

$$\mathcal{R}_{NC} = -(\alpha C' + (1-\alpha)T') \tag{6}$$

where T' and C' are normalized values of the total network delay and the system's cost, respectively. Normalization is employed to linearly scale these terms between $[-1,1]$, ensuring equal upper and lower bounds for both objectives. This solves the scaling problem for different units, thereby maintaining a balanced consideration of both network delay and cost (line 3 of Algorithm 2). The maximum processing times, denoted as T_{max} is computed based on the edge-case scenario. This scenario assumes a complete cyclic routing, wherein each request must traverse through all nodes before being processed, whereas T_{min} is set to zero reflecting case where all requests can directly be served without need of routing any to other nodes.

$\mathcal{R}_{NC}$ is not sufficient to guide the agent for the objectives of *POSEIDON*. The agent may attempt to exploit the system by not placing the functions on any nodes, or it may make invalid decisions, such as placing functions on nodes with insufficient compute power or generating placements that result in infeasible mixed-integer programming (MIP) solutions during the routing phase. To discourage such undesirable behavior, the agent receives a a negative reward for each invalid placement decision made by the agent which involves violating compute resource, violating memory resources and violating routing constraint represented by $R_{Penalty}$ (line 5 of Algorithm 2), strictly guiding it away from these solutions.

$$R_{Penalty} = N(\Omega_i)$$

where Ω_i denotes an invalid placement decision.

4 Evaluation

The objective of the experiments is to evaluate the effectiveness and efficiency of our approach by answering the following questions:

RQ1. How does *POSEIDON* compare to state-of-the-art solutions in terms of delay and cost?
RQ2. How does *POSEIDON* perform with respect to decision time compared to state-of-the-art solutions?
RQ3. How does solution tuning in *POSEIDON* mitigate invalid placements?

4.1 Experimental Setup

Execution Environment: We implemented a simulated edge environment using the Gymnasium by providing the specifications of the nodes and functions as inputs to the simulation. Function requests were sampled using the Cabspotting [13] dataset, wherein the node delays between the nodes were predefined. The DRL agent was configured to learn within the Gymnasium environment[2], employing the Proximal Policy Optimization (PPO) algorithm, as implemented by the Stable-Baselines3 library[3]. The routing solver was integrated into the system using the Linear Solver provided by Google's OR-Tools. The *POSEIDON* was trained for 50 workload distributions at different timesteps and then evaluated on 150 different workload samples. Our simulation was run on an Ubuntu 23.04 machine with 16 GB RAM, powered by a 4.6 GHz 12th Gen Intel i7 processor, and an Nvidia RTX 3060 GPU with 6 GB VRAM.

Experiment Candidates: We evaluated *POSEIDON*[4] by performing four simulations this was done by placing different number of functions on 5 nodes equipped with 50, 50, 50, 25, 100 cores and memory capacities of 100, 100, 200, 50, 500 GB. The first two simulations, with $\alpha = 0$ and $\alpha = 0.5$, involved placing a *small payload* of 4 functions with memory requirements of 50, 10, 10, 10 GB whereas the third and the fourth simulation with $\alpha = 0$ and $\alpha = 0.5$ respectively involved placing a *large payload* of 10 functions with memory requirements of 10 GB each on the same set of nodes as described earlier. For each simulation, the agent was trained using 50 workloads for 2000 timesteps, with each timestep lasting 100 s. The data used for training came from the *Cabspotting* [13] dataset. The purpose of these simulations was to assess *POSEIDON*'s efficiency in not only minimizing the cost and delay but the decision time as well.

1. *CR-EUA* : Criticality-Awareness Edge User Allocation [9]: an allocation strategy tailored for safety-critical, low-latency applications where meeting strict performance and reliability requirements is paramount. This approach aims to maximize the number of requests processed at the highest level of criticality by intelligently assigning edge resources to the most critical tasks. By prioritizing requests based on their criticality levels, CR-EUA ensures that applications requiring immediate attention receive the necessary computational resources to function optimally.

2. *VSVBP* (Variable Sized Vector Bin) [6]: a placement and routing approach designed to optimize resource utilization in edge computing networks. It works by maximizing the number of allocated service requests while minimizing the number of active edge nodes, thereby reducing operational costs and energy consumption. The method ensures that the response times of deployed services stay within acceptable limits by efficiently distributing workloads across the available resources. VSVBP models the resource allocation problem as a variable-sized bin packing issue, which makes it ideal for scenarios where both performance and cost-effectiveness are critical

---

[2] https://gymnasium.farama.org.
[3] https://github.com/hill-a/stable-baselines.
[4] https://github.com/sa4s-serc/poseidon.

3. *NEPTUNE* [2,3]: a solution designed for optimal placement of serverless functions on edge nodes using MIP with the goal of minimizing both network latency and resource utilization. NEPTUNE optimizes the placement of functions by considering factors like network delay and minimizing the number of active nodes to reduce operational costs. After the initial placement, it uses a second optimization step to reduce service disruptions. Further, NEPTUNE also generates routing policies that direct traffic to the appropriate nodes, balancing the workload and minimizing inter-node delays, while ensuring functions are only terminated after they complete their current tasks.

Evaluation Metrics. To measure the effectiveness and efficiency of the approach, we use three different metrics: *i)* Total Delay: this represents the sum of the delay for each of the function requests in the topology, *ii)* Cost: this accounts for the total cost of running the function instances on the nodes, *iii)* Decision time: this metric evaluates how quickly the placement and routing of functions are determined, reflecting the computational efficiency of the approach.

4.2 Delay and Cost Analysis (RQ1)

To compare the effectiveness of *POSEIDON* for cost and delay, we evaluated *POSEIDON* with four different simulations as mentioned in Sect. 4.1. We can see from the Tables 2 and 3 and Figs. 2 and 3 that when $\alpha = 0$ in case of both *large* and *small payload* the average delay is very low but the average cost is high for both *POSEIDON* and NEPTUNE. This is expected because for $\alpha = 0$ both *POSEIDON* and NEPTUNE try to minimize the delay and the cost is not considered a critical factor leading to the high average cost. Also both *POSEIDON* and NEPTUNE outperform the other approaches when it comes to delay for similar average costs. VSVBP and CR-EUA exhibit higher delays because they prioritize maximizing resource utilization and processing the most critical tasks. This focus on handling critical requests often leads to resource overloading, increasing processing times. On increasing α from 0 to 0.5, averaging over *small* and *large* payloads, the average costs are much lower, dropping by 77.74 % for *POSEIDON* and 71.52% for NEPTUNE, the average delays increases by 24.9 times for *POSEIDON* and 33.69 times for NEPTUNE, as both approaches try to find a balance between the delay and the cost. Albeit overall, *POSEIDON* has a lower cost and higher delay than NEPTUNE. Even though *POSEIDON* is not as optimal as NEPTUNE but is comparable to NEPTUNE. CR-EUA and VSVBP exhibit higher costs than *POSEIDON* because they prioritize processing the maximum number of requests, which requires allocating additional resources. Moreover, the stability of *POSEIDON* can be attributed to its use of PPO, which is known for its robustness and ability to produce stable policies. The training of the DRL agent ensures that that *POSEIDON* learns to handle varying conditions in a controlled manner.

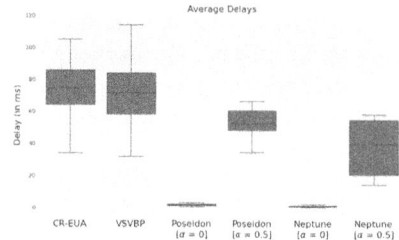
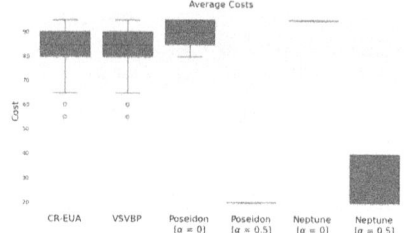

(a) Box plot depicting the delay while using each of the different approaches

(b) Box plot depicting the cost while using each of the different approaches

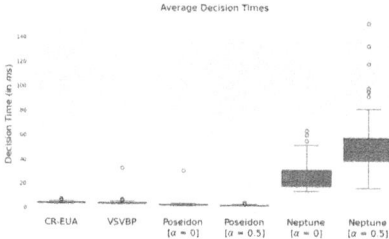

(c) Box plot depicting the average decision time while using each of the different approaches

Fig. 2. Effectiveness of the approaches with respect to various metrics for the *small payload*

4.3 Decision Time Analysis (RQ2)

To evaluate the efficiency of *POSEIDON* with respect to decision time compared to other approaches, we ran four different simulations as mentioned in 4.1 we can see from the Tables 2 and 3 and Figs. 2c and 3c *POSEIDON* demonstrates consistent decision times for $\alpha = 0$ and $\alpha = 0.5$ for both the *small payload* and *large payload* whereas for NEPTUNE the decision time is higher. This can be attributed to the fact that *POSEIDON* divides the solution into two parts: i) the DRL agent solves the placement problem and has a very small number of parameters, which enables faster decision-making with regards to placements, and ii) the routing solver which solves the routing problem uses MILP but has fewer constraints than NEPTUNE making *POSEIDON* 16.43 times faster. This also further highlights the scalability challenges incurred by NEPTUNE due to the computational complexity of solving the MILP problem with too many constraints. The other approaches, CR-EUA and VSVBP show comparable decision times to *POSEIDON* but mostly give sub-optimal solutions with respect to cost and delay.

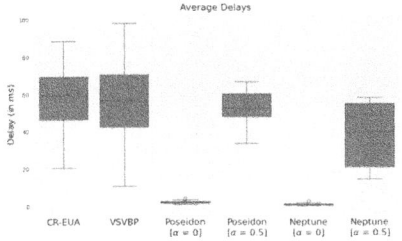
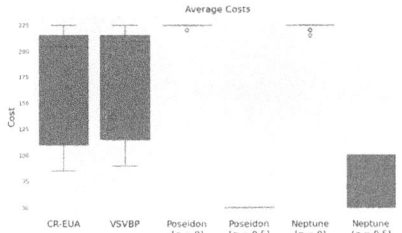

(a) Box plot depicting the delay while using each of the different approaches

(b) Box plot depicting the cost while using each of the different approaches

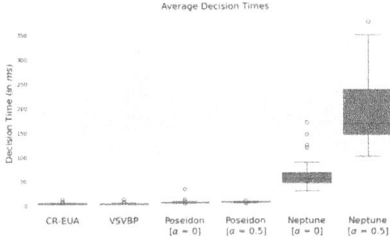

(c) Box plot depicting the average decision time while using each of the different approaches

Fig. 3. Effectiveness of the approaches with respect to various metrics for the *large payload*

Table 2. Comparison of *POSEIDON* with Other Approaches for *small payload* $\alpha = 0$ and $\alpha = 0.5$

Metric	Poseidon		Neptune		CR-EUA	VSVBP
	$\alpha = 0$	$\alpha = 0.5$	$\alpha = 0$	$\alpha = 0.5$		
Average Delay (in ms)	1.9420	53.1460	1.1060	38.7830	74.4574	71.6157
Average Cost	90.7000	20.2000	95.9500	26.4000	85.8500	85.1000
Average Decision Time (in ms)	3.1	2.4	26	52.1	4.5	4.5

4.4 Impact of Solution Tuning (RQ3)

Figure 4 shows the cumulative number of invalid placements performed by the agent against the iterations of the solution tuning cycle. The graph shows a converging curve, which can be correlated with the agent's overall improvement over the iterations as it learns to avoid invalid placements, which can be attributed to $R_{Penalty}$ (refer Sect. 3). We observe an average decrease of 49.13% in the aggregated number of invalid placements per workload's tuning iteration, indicating a strong positive learning trend.

Table 3. Comparison of *POSEIDON* with Other Approaches for *large payload* $\alpha = 0$ and $\alpha = 0.5$

Metric	Poseidon		Neptune		CR-EUA	VSVBP
	$\alpha = 0$	$\alpha = 0.5$	$\alpha = 0$	$\alpha = 0.5$		
Average Delay (in ms)	2.3156	51.8161	1.1744	37.6083	57.0778	54.1870
Average Cost	227.3333	50.5556	226.5000	66.6667	167.7222	178.1667
Average Decision Time (in ms)	7.3	7.3	61.7	190.6	4.7	4.6

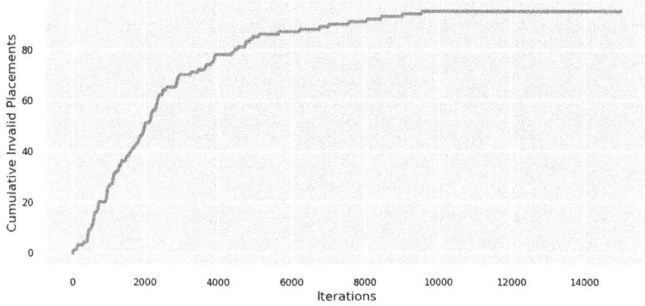

Fig. 4. Cumulative count of invalid placements versus iterations of solution tuning for *small payload* ($\alpha = 0$).

4.5 Threats to Validity

Threats to *Construct Validity* concern the use of controlled experimental setup and simulations. To this end, we ensured that we used workloads and configurations as close to the real-world scenario as possible. Specifically, we utilized the *Cabspotting* dataset [13] to train and test *POSEIDON*. However, it is important to note that while our simulations provide a controlled environment for evaluation, further experiments in real-world are necessary to fully assess the practical applicability and effectiveness of our findings.

Threats to *Internal Validity* concern the use of a static number of nodes for placements. In practice, the DRL agent needs to be retrained if there is a change in the topology, such as the addition or removal of a node. Although we can train the DRL agent to minimize the occurrence of invalid or infeasible placements, the nature of machine learning means that we cannot guarantee that the agent will always produce valid placements. Therefore, it is essential to have an external system in place to verify the placement decisions made by the DRL agent, ensuring their correctness and feasibility.

Threats to *External Validity* of our approach concern the generalizability and scalability of our approach. Although our approach has been applied to two different scenarios with 4 functions and 10 functions, respectively, the techniques used in the approach are scalable to a larger number of functions. This is further validated by the results as demonstrated in Sect. 4.3. As regards to the generalizability, the approach can be integrated to any MEC system as long as it provides with mechanisms to monitor the function parameters as well as to perform routing and placement.

5 Related Work

Deploying applications on edge infrastructures has increasingly become the preferred method to meet the rising demand for low-latency applications [21]. Thus, the placement of such applications and their request routing in edge systems has become a primary research focus [17] since existing solutions dedicated to cloud-computing often neglect the unique challenges of the edge context [5] such as managing the geographical distribution of computing nodes, maintaining low network latency, and coping with resource constrained nodes [15]. Numerous studies have tackled the challenges of placement and routing in edge computing [16,18]. A common approach involves framing the problem of service placement and workload routing as a *Integer Programming* problem [6,7].

For example, NEPTUNE [2] utilizes a MILP formulation to place serverless functions on edge nodes. Given computed placement and routing policies, NEPTUNE optimizes resources using vertical scaling controllers based on control-theory [4,14]. Compared to NEPTUNE, *POSEIDON* shares similar objectives but employs Reinforcement Learning for computing placements. This allows for timely computation of new placements and better adaptation to dynamic and fluctuating environments, such as edge computing. We view our approach as complementary to NEPTUNE: *POSEIDON* can be embedded within NEPTUNE communities to determine placements, while a simplified version of NEPTUNE can then be used to compute routing policies based on these placements.

Unlike *POSEIDON*, which reduces latency by placing applications closer to users, Ma et al. [10] focus on maximizing edge node utilization using MILP without considering network delays as we do. Liu et al. [9] address network delays by prioritizing requests based on criticality and response times, although the approach doesn't explicitly aim to minimize delays. *POSEIDON* does not explicitly consider the criticality of functions. However, one can prioritize critical application by affecting the ordering mechanism of functions employed in our RL-based approach. Finally, Tong et al. [20] utilize Mixed Nonlinear Integer Programming to maximize served requests in a hierarchical MEC network. The main benefit of *POSEIDON* compared to ones based on combinatorial optimization is to provide solutions in an efficient and timely manner which allow to better cope with edge nomadic users and highly-fluctuating workloads.

Raza et al. [1] present COSE, a framework that uses Bayesian Optimization to find the optimal resource configuration and placement for serverless applications, minimizing cost while meeting performance objectives. COSE provides an efficient, non-combinatorial, solution to the problem; however, compared to *POSEIDON*, it focuses on cloud architectures and does not consider the intrinsic characteristics of edge topologies.

Xu et al. [23] propose an adaptive function placement framework utilizing a Markov Decision Process to optimize serverless computing performance across terminal devices, edge nodes, and cloud data centers. The framework supports adaptation in real-time to allocate functions dynamically, aiming to minimize execution costs while maintaining performance satisfaction. Compared to the *POSEIDON*, the approach does not consider memory requirements, network delay among edge nodes, and routing times, which are central for edge computing. Moreover, while the approach aim to optimize the utilization of the available devices, *POSEIDON* also minimizes the overall network delay.

6 Conclusions

In this work, we presented *POSEIDON*, a novel approach that combines Deep Reinforcement Learning and traditional optimization (MILP), for placing serverless functions in edge infrastructures. Our evaluation demonstrate that *POSEIDON* makes near-optimal decisions with respect to cost and delay while providing low decision time. Our future work includes exploiting workload predictions to proactively place function instances and anticipate resource saturation. Moreover, we plan to use cooperative multi-agent approaches to further parallelize the decision taken by our DRL framework.

References

1. Ali, R., Nabeel, A., Isahagian, V., Ibrahim, M., Lei, H.: Configuration and placement of serverless applications using statistical learning. IEEE Trans. Netw. Serv. Manag. **20**(2), 1065 – 1077 (2023)
2. Baresi, L., Hu, D.Y.X., Quattrocchi, G., Terracciano, L.: NEPTUNE: network- and GPU-aware management of serverless functions at the edge. In: Proceedings of the International Symposium on Software Engineering for Adaptive and Self-Managing Systems, pp. 144–155. ACM (2022)
3. Baresi, L., Hu, D.Y.X., Quattrocchi, G., Terracciano, L.: NEPTUNE: a comprehensive framework for managing serverless functions at the edge. ACM Trans. Auton. Adapt. Syst. **19**(1), 1–32 (2024)
4. Baresi, L., Quattrocchi, G.: Towards vertically scalable spark applications. In: Proceedings of the Parallel Processing Workshops, vol. 11339, pp. 106–118. Springer (2018)
5. Bellendorf, J., Mann, Z.Á.: Classification of optimization problems in fog computing. Elsevier Future Gener. Comput. Syst. **107**, 158–176 (2020)
6. Lai, P., et al.: Optimal edge user allocation in edge computing with variable sized vector bin packing. In: Pahl, C., Vukovic, M., Yin, J., Yu, Q. (eds.) ICSOC 2018. LNCS, vol. 11236, pp. 230–245. Springer, Cham (2018). https://doi.org/10.1007/978-3-030-03596-9_15
7. Lai, P., et al.: Cost-effective app user allocation in an edge computing environment. IEEE Trans. Cloud Comput. **10**(3), 1701–1713 (2022)
8. Lillicrap, T.P., et al.: Continuous control with deep reinforcement learning (2019)
9. Liu, E., Zheng, L., He, Q., Xu, B., Zhang, G.: Criticality-awareness edge user allocation for public safety. IEEE Trans. Serv. Comput. **16**(1), 221–234 (2023)
10. Ma, Z., et al.: Towards revenue-driven multi-user online task offloading in edge computing. IEEE Trans. Parallel Distrib. Syst. **33**(5), 1185–1198 (2022)

11. Mnih, V., et al.: Human-level control through deep reinforcement learning. nature **518**(7540), 529–533 (2015)
12. Pham, Q., et al.: A survey of multi-access edge computing in 5G and beyond: fundamentals, technology integration, and state-of-the-art. IEEE Access **8**, 116974–117017 (2020)
13. Piorkowski, M., Sarafijanovic-Djukic, N., Grossglauser, M.: A parsimonious model of mobile partitioned networks with clustering. In: Proceedings of the International Communication Systems and Networks and Workshops, pp. 1–10. IEEE (2009)
14. Quattrocchi, G., Incerto, E., Pinciroli, R., Trubiani, C., Baresi, L.: Autoscaling solutions for cloud applications under dynamic workloads. IEEE Trans. Serv. Comput. (2024)
15. Raith, P., Nastic, S., Dustdar, S.: Serverless edge computing - where we are and what lies ahead. IEEE Internet Comput. **27**(3), 50–64 (2023)
16. Raith, P., Rausch, T., Dustdar, S., Rossi, F., Cardellini, V., Ranjan, R.: Mobility-aware serverless function adaptations across the edge-cloud continuum. In: Proceedings of the International Conference on Utility and Cloud Computing, pp. 123–132. IEEE (2022)
17. Russo, G.R., Cardellini, V., Presti, F.L.: Serverless functions in the cloud-edge continuum: challenges and opportunities. In: Proceedings of the International Conference on Parallel, Distributed and Network-Based Processing, pp. 321–328. IEEE (2023)
18. Russo, G.R., Mannucci, T., Cardellini, V., Presti, F.L.: Serverledge: decentralized function-as-a-service for the edge-cloud continuum. In: Proceedings of the International Conference on Pervasive Computing and Communications, pp. 131–140. IEEE (2023)
19. Schulman, J., Wolski, F., Dhariwal, P., Radford, A., Klimov, O.: Proximal policy optimization algorithms (2017)
20. Tong, L., Li, Y., Gao, W.: A hierarchical edge cloud architecture for mobile computing. In: Proceedings of the International Conference on Computer Communications, pp. 1–9. IEEE (2016)
21. Vierhauser, M., Wohlrab, R., Rass, S.: Towards cost-benefit-aware adaptive monitoring for cyber-physical systems. In: Proceedings of the Conference on Communications and Network Security, pp. 1–6. IEEE (2022)
22. Wen, J., Chen, Z., Jin, X., Liu, X.: Rise of the planet of serverless computing: a systematic review. ACM Trans. Softw. Eng. Methodol. **32**(5), 1–61 (2023)
23. Xu, D., Sun, Z.: An adaptive function placement in serverless computing. Cluster Comput. **25**(5), 3161–3174 (2022)
24. Zhang, X., Debroy, S.: Resource management in mobile edge computing: a comprehensive survey. ACM Comput. Surv. **55**(13s), 1–37 (2023)

ABBA-VSM: Time Series Classification Using Symbolic Representation on the Edge

Meerzhan Kanatbekova[✉][iD], Shashikant Ilager[✉][iD], and Ivona Brandic[✉][iD]

TU Wien, Vienna, Austria
{meerzhan.kanatbekova,shashikant.ilager,ivona.brandic}@tuwien.ac.at

Abstract. In recent years, Edge AI has become more prevalent with applications across various industries, from environmental monitoring to smart city management. Edge AI facilitates the processing of Internet of Things (IoT) data and provides privacy-enabled and latency-sensitive services to application users using Machine Learning (ML) algorithms, e.g., Time Series Classification (TSC). However, existing TSC algorithms require access to full raw data and demand substantial computing resources to train and use them effectively in runtime. This makes them impractical for deployment in resource-constrained Edge environments. To address this, in this paper, we propose an Adaptive Brownian Bridge-based Symbolic Aggregation Vector Space Model (ABBA-VSM). It is a new TSC model designed for classification services on Edge. Here, we first *adaptively* compress the raw time series into symbolic representations, thus capturing the changing trends of data. Subsequently, we train the classification model directly on these symbols. ABBA-VSM reduces communication data between IoT and Edge devices, as well as computation cycles, in the development of resource-efficient TSC services on Edge. We evaluate our solution with extensive experiments using datasets from the UCR time series classification archive. The results demonstrate that the ABBA-VSM achieves up to 80% compression ratio and 90–100% accuracy for binary classification. Whereas, for non-binary classification, it achieves an average compression ratio of 60% and accuracy ranging from 60–80%.

Keywords: Edge Computing · EdgeAI · Time Series Classification · Data Compression · Symbolic Representation

1 Introduction

The number of Internet of Things (IoT) devices worldwide is anticipated to experience a significant increase, nearly doubling from 15.9 billion in 2023 to over 32.1 billion by 2030, according to data from Statista (2023). They produce a massive amount of data, and it is expected to reach around 85 zettabytes (ZB) by 2025 [1,2,23]. All these are driven by the widespread utilization of IoT technology and services across various industries, from environmental monitoring [22] to smart city management [10]. Many of the IoT applications leverage Machine Learning (ML) algorithms in their pipeline to provide data-driven smart services. Traditionally, IoT data has been transmitted to, stored, and processed in the cloud [21]. However, the growing demand for latency-sensitive application services and privacy requirements has introduced a new paradigm called Edge AI. Edge AI provides limited computing resources to design and deploy applications at the network Edge [8,15,16].

Among many ML algorithms, Time Series Classification (TSC) is a widely applicable popular method that predicts a class label of a given Time Series (TS). TSC has various real-world applications in many domains, such as smart city management tasks [10], and environmental monitoring [22], among others.

The state-of-the-art TSC algorithms primarily focus on accuracy, demonstrating the capability to achieve high levels of accuracy across different datasets. However, these algorithms face a challenge in classifying large datasets in resource-constrained environments such as *Edge*. First, off-the-shelf TSC algorithms require sending full raw data from IoT to Edge devices. This is infeasible in the Edge environment since communication between IoT and Edge devices is expensive, some studies have shown that communication costs up to 80% of energy in IoT devices [2]. Moreover, Edge devices often have limited computing and memory resources to process the raw data and train new TSC models [3]. Furthermore, data from many applications has to be processed in near real-time [8]. Thus, it is necessary to develop a resource-efficient TSC method to handle the growing volume of IoT data generated and to manage Edge applications efficiently.

In response to these challenges, various strategies have been proposed to optimize the data processing at Edge [3,7,8]. For instance, in [3], authors propose data compression at the IoT level and train the ML model on reconstructed data at the Edge. While such a method solves the problem of high data traffic between IoT and Edge, Edge's memory and computation constraints remain challenging. Consequently, Symbolic Representation (SR) [11,12] methods offer an alternative approach to reduce the data size of numerical time series data and perform analytics on reduced data. The SR is a lossy data compression technique that partitions raw data into segments (chunks) and encodes them by symbols, creating a string of symbols. If required, symbols could be reconstructed back to the original time series with a controllable error rate. Contrary to classical compression methods, SR preserves data semantics, allowing us to do data analytics directly on symbols.

In this work, we explore how we can leverage SR to develop a time series classification model that is directly trained on symbols. While some works [20] have explored symbolic methods for TSC using SAX-VSM, such approaches do not apply to adaptive (streaming IoT data) compression and latency-constrained applications. Our approach is feasible in an environment where IoT devices can compress the data and transfer the reduced data to the Edge, thus reducing communication and storage costs between IoT and Edge, and processing costs at the Edge.

Therefore, we propose ABBA-VSM (Adaptive Brownian Bridge-based symbolic Aggregation Vector Space Model), an adaptive approach for TSC using SR. It consists of two main components: compression and classification. We first present the adaptive time series compression inspired by the Brownian bridge to reduce the size of the raw TS [6], followed by encoding the compressed data as a string of symbols. Second, the Vector Space Model (VSM) is constructed to build a TSC model. Finally, the ABBA-VSM outputs the TSC model trained to classify the next set of data points. Our approach is adaptive to the non-stationary data, dynamically adapts to create accurate symbols, and provides an algorithm for TSC, which is directly trained on symbols.

In summary, the **key contributions** of the paper are:

– We propose a new adaptive symbolic time series classification model for latency-constrained Edge applications, exploring its impact on memory and computation constraints.
– We empirically evaluate the proposed method on real-world datasets and compare it to non-adaptive baseline approaches.
– Our extensive experiments demonstrate that ABBA-VSM achieves 90–100% accuracy for binary classification datasets and achieves reasonable accuracy for multi-class classification.

The rest of the paper is organized as follows. Section 2 provides an overview of the existing symbolic TSC methods. Section 3 describes the real-world application scenario. Section 4 explains the proposed ABBA-VSM method in detail. Section 5 describes the experimental design and datasets used. Section 6 discusses the empirical results. Finally, Sect. 7 presents the concluding remarks and potential future work.

2 Related Work

Multiple techniques exist for TS reduction and classification, but only a few are designed to represent TS data symbolically. Here, we will provide an overview of existing symbolic data compression methods and symbolic time series classification algorithms, which are summarized in Table 1.

The TSC techniques can be broadly categorized into two groups: *full* time series-based methods and *feature-based* methods [9]. *Full* time series-based methods use a pointwise comparison of TS, for instance, with 1-NN Euclidean Distance (ED) or 1-NN Dynamic Time Warping (DTW). While these techniques are well suited for short TS, they are inefficient for long and noisy TS. Whereas *feature-based* techniques compare features

Table 1. Comparison of most relevant works that use symbolic representation for TS classification

Algorithm	Adaptive reduction	Symbol generation	Classification on the Edge
SAX-VSM [20]	×	✓	×
BOSS [17]	×	✓	×
WEASEL [19]	×	✓	×
MrSQM [13]	×	✓	×
ABBA-VSM	✓	✓	✓

or segments generated from full TS. The common approach within this *feature-based* group is the Bag-Of-Patterns (BOP) model [9]. Such models are built by breaking up a TS into segments representing discrete features, creating a bag of words from these features, and finally, building a histogram of feature counts as a basis for classification.

Most BOP models employ Symbolic Aggregate Approximation (SAX) and Symbolic Fourier Approximation (SFA), which are commonly used methods for creating linear segments from TS [9,14]. SAX partitions TS into segments of fixed length and then represents each segment by the mean of its values (i.e., a piece-wise constant approximation). In contrast, SFA converts TS into symbolic representations using Fourier coefficients [18].

The Bag of Symbolic Fourier Approximation Symbols (BOSS) algorithm is based on the SFA method, which involves approximating the original data using the Discrete Fourier Transform and then discretizing the resulting coefficients using a technique called Multiple Coefficient Binning [17]. Multiple Representations Sequence Miner (MrSQM) offers four different feature selection strategies, including random feature selection, pruning the all-subsequence feature space, and random sampling of features [13]. Word ExtrAction for time SEries cLassification (WEASEL) is a TSC method that creates a large SFA words feature space, filters it with Chi-square feature selection, then trains a logistic regression classifier [19]. Symbolic Aggregate Approximation Vector Space Model (SAX-VSM) is a TSC method that creates a feature space of SAX words and then builds a classifier by building the weight matrix of SAX words [20].

While these methods showcase the diversity in feature extraction and symbolic classification techniques for TS, they often fail to capture the changing trends in the data during real-time TS compression.

3 System Model

In this section, we provide a high-level overview of our approach, ABBA-VSM, as depicted in Fig. 1. ABBA-VSM has two main components, a **compressor** and a **classifier**. The **compressor** (e.g., IoT device) adaptively reduces TS up to linear segments (1) and transfers the resulting segments to Edge. The **classifier** (e.g., Edge device), receives the transmitted data, encodes the linear segments as a string of symbols (2), and by applying the sliding window technique, it creates a bag of words (3), which we call as *ABBA words*, and finally, it builds a classifier model to predict labels (4).

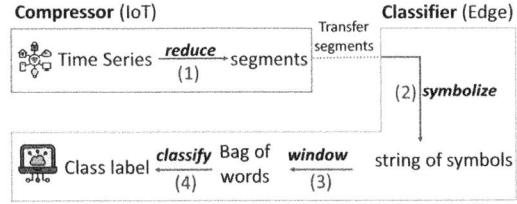

Fig. 1. A high-level view of our system model

Compressor: Let us consider IoT devices as compressors. The IoT device sources a TS, denoted as

$$T = [(x_1, y_1), ..., (x_N, y_N)] \qquad (1)$$

where x_i and y_i are values and timestamps, respectively. Then, it reduces the TS by creating a polygonal chain of linear pieces, where each piece is bounded by the timestamp length and squared Euclidean distance error, according to the compression step in ABBA [6]. These linear pieces are defined as $P = [p_1, p_2, ..., p_n]$, where each linear piece $p_j = (len_j, inc_j)$ is a tuple of time step length and increment value, and with $n \leq N$. For simplicity, from now on we will refer to these linear pieces as segments. To mitigate misclassification issues, the compressor waits until all segments corresponding to a particular class are generated before sending a collection of segments to the classifier. By creating such segments, the raw data T is converted into highly compressed data in the form of segments P.

Classifier: The classifier receives the segments $P = [p_1, p_2, ..., p_n]$ and clusters them to centers $C = [c_1, c_2, ..., c_k]$ with $k \leq n$ [6]. Then, each cluster is symbolized using the alphabet $A = [a_1, a_2, ..., a_k]$; thus, segments corresponding to the same cluster receive the same character as the cluster. Once we get the string of symbols representing the TS, we apply the windowing technique to create a *bag of words*. Unlike traditional windowing methods that apply a sliding window to the original TS [17], this paper proposes the application of a sliding window on compressed data, i.e., on a string of symbols. This approach facilitates the compression of raw TS at IoT without being influenced by sliding window characteristics (size and step). Then, we apply distance measure techniques to classify the labels of these bags of words.

4 Methodology

We have provided a high-level description of the proposed symbolic TSC in Sect. 3. Here, we present detailed methodologies for constructing ABBA-VSM, consisting of the two main parts: `compressor` and `classifier`. For `compressor`, we use the Adaptive Brownian Bridge Aggregation (ABBA) technique, a continuous-time stochastic process that restricts Brownian motion to trajectories and converges to a given terminal state, enabling efficient data compression applications [6]. By adaptively reducing the TS to linear segments, ABBA method demonstrates the ability to preserve the shape characteristics of TS better than other approaches like SAX and 1d-SAX representations. The key insight is that the segments can be modeled as a random walk with pinned start and end points, resembling a Brownian bridge. This allows for creating parameter-free (namely *adaptive*) segments except for the choice of a reduction tolerance. Once the TS is reduced to segments, we transfer them to the Edge and encode them as a string of symbols.

For `classifier`, we construct a Vector Space Model (VSM) using the string of symbols. VSM is a model that represents TS (in our case, symbolized TS)

Algorithm 1. ABBA-VSM Training

1: **procedure** ABBA-VSM TRAINING(training data, RT, C_type, W_size, W_step)
2:     $corpus \leftarrow$ empty_list
3:     **while** True **do**
4:         $sample \leftarrow$ get_data_from(training data)
5:         $segments \leftarrow$ reduction(sample, RT)
6:         $string \leftarrow$ cluster(segments, C_type)
7:         $windowed\_string \leftarrow$ window(string, W_size, W_step)
8:         $ABBA\_words \leftarrow$ create_bag_of_words(W_string)
9:         $labelled\_ABBA\_words \leftarrow$ label_words_by_class(ABBA_words)
10:        append $labelled\_ABBA\_words$ to corpus
11:     **end while**
12:     $training\_weight\_matrix \leftarrow$ apply_tf_idf_vectorizer(corpus)
13: **end procedure**

Algorithm 2. ABBA-VSM Testing

1: **procedure** ABBA-VSM TESTING(unlabeled data, RT, C_type, W_size, W_step)
2:     $segments \leftarrow$ reduction(unlabeled data, RT)
3:     $string \leftarrow$ cluster(segments, C_type)
4:     $windowed\_string \leftarrow$ window(string, W_size, W_step)
5:     $ABBA\_words \leftarrow$ create_bag_of_words(W_string)
6:     $testing\_weights \leftarrow$ apply_tf_idf_vectorizer(words)
7:     $class\_label \leftarrow$ cosine_similarity(training_weights, testing_weights)
8: **end procedure**

as vectors in a multi-dimensional space. A VSM allows efficient similarity comparisons, from which a classification algorithm can be developed. Unlike classical Machine Learning models, which often require extensive training on large datasets (mainly on original TS) and involve significant computational power and memory, operations performed in VSM, such as similarity measurement, require fewer computational resources. A step-by-step description of methodology is described below and implemented in Algorithms 1 and 2.

4.1 Compressor: Transforming Numerical Time Series Into Segments

A time series compression method at IoT level involves a single step: *reduce*.
Reduce: We start by considering the time series T in line 5 of Algorithm 1. Then, ABBA adaptively partitions T into n segments P with $n < N$ in line 5 Algorithm 1. Each segment in P consists of two values, the length of the time steps of each segment as $len_i := x_i - x_{i-1} \geq 1$ and increment in value as $inc_i := y_i - y_{i-1}$. The reduced time series is defined as follows,

$$\tilde{T} = [(len_1, inc_1), ..., (len_n, inc_n)] \in \mathbb{R}^{2 \times n} \quad (2)$$

The method is an adaptive compression as the Euclidean distance between T and $\tilde{T}$ is bounded by a user-defined reduction tolerance (RT) value [6]. Reducing raw TS into segments helps reduce the communication cost between IoT and Edge. It is important to note that we choose to create segments (P) on the IoT device and generate symbols on the Edge device. This distribution of computational tasks is necessary because symbols are needed at the Edge device, and creating symbols from segments (P) requires running a clustering algorithm for all new segments generated, which might be computationally infeasible for many IoT devices. Nevertheless, segments are already highly compressed TS, significantly reducing the communication costs between the IoT and Edge devices.

4.2 Classifier: A Symbolic Approach

The computational complexity of ABBA compression is $O(N)$ where N is the number of data points in T. While clustering operations are relatively efficient for Edge environments, they can be computationally intensive for resource-constrained IoT devices. Thus, clustering followed by symbolization and then the construction of *training* and *testing* are performed at `classifier` part of ABBA-VSM on the Edge.

Symbolize: Similar tuples from $\tilde{T}$ in Eq. 2 form clusters, each encoded as a single character, allowing all segments that belong to the same cluster to be assigned one symbol in line 6 of Algorithm 1. For this, tuple values (len_i, inc_i) are separately normalized by their standard deviations σ_{length} and σ_{inc}, respectively. Based on the empirical observations we conducted, the classification accuracy error between various clustering methods was negligible. Thus, for final empirical evaluation, we consider a sorting-based [4] and the k-means algorithm. K-means clustering requires the number of clusters to be known beforehand, whereas the sorting-based method is adaptive, using the user-defined clustering tolerance CT [4].

Finally, each tuple in the sequence $\tilde{T}$ in Eq. 2 is replaced by the symbol of the cluster it belongs to, resulting in the string of symbols $S = [s_1 s_2 ... s_n] \in A^n$.

ABBA-VSM Training: To create *ABBA words* from a string of symbols in S, we apply the sliding window technique as shown in line 7 of Algorithm 1. Compared to the traditional sliding window technique that is applied on time series before the compression, we propose to use the sliding window on symbolically compressed TS, i.e., on the string of symbols. Such a technique allows the adaptive compression of the original TS, forming Brownian bridges, without being affected by the sliding window dimensions. The sliding window dimensions can be pre-defined by the user. A *term* corresponding to one window defines a single *ABBA word*, a collection of ABBA words from one training sample forms a *labeled bag of words* in line 9. Then, a set of bags form *corpus* in line 10. Once all samples in training data are encoded as bags of *ABBA words*, we group the labeled words to corresponding class labels and create a *weight matrix*. This matrix defines the weights of all words in a corpus and is built as follows:

(a) *Representation:* Let d_i, D be a document that represents an individual class and a corpus, respectively.

(b) *Term Frequency(TF):* For each word t_j in document d_i, the TF_{ij} is the number of times t_j appears in d_i, i.e.,

$$TF_{ij} = \frac{\text{number of times } t_j \text{ appears in } d_i}{\text{total number of terms in } d_i}$$

(c) *Inverse Document Frequency (IDF):* The IDF_j quantifies a word's importance by calculating the logarithmic ratio of the total number of documents $|D|$ to the number of documents that include the term t_j.

$$IDF_j = log(\frac{|D|}{\text{number of documents containing } t_j})$$

(d) *TF-IDF*: By taking the product of TF_{ij} and IDF_j, we calculate the importance of term t_j in document d_i as $W_{ij} = TF_{ij} * IDF_j$.

(e) *Vector Representation:* Now each document d_i can be represented as vector $v_i = (W_{i_1}, W_{i_2}, ..., W_{i_{|T|}})$. The rows are individual ABBA words in the *weight matrix* (line 12 of Algorithm 1), and columns represent the class labels.
Testing: To classify an unlabeled TS, ABBA-VSM transforms it into a frequency vector w using the same steps that were used for training lines 2-6 of Algorithm 2. Then, it computes *cosine similarity* values between frequency vector w and v_i, with i representing weight vectors for different class labels:

$$similarity(w, v_i) = \frac{w \cdot v_i}{\|w\| \cdot \|v_i\|}$$

The unlabeled TS is assigned to the class label whose vector has the highest cosine similarity value (line 7 in Algorithm 2).

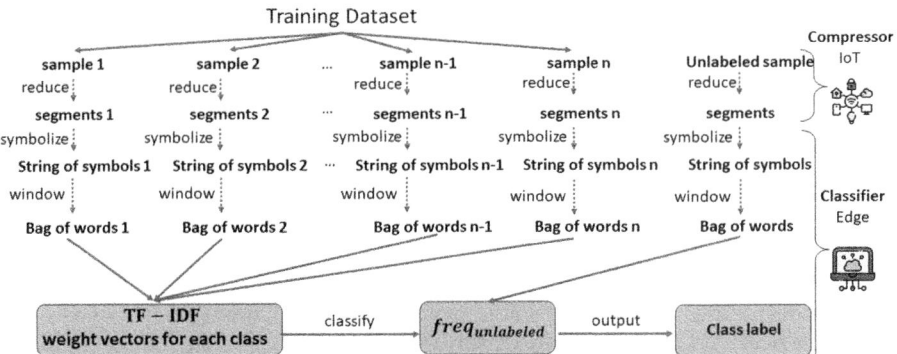

Fig. 2. Building ABBA-VSM with training time series dataset and testing on unlabeled data.

To further illustrate the whole process of symbolic classification, we provide a visual representation of the ABBA-VSM in Fig. 2. As depicted, during the training phase, each TS sample is reduced and segmented by the ABBA method, with each segment being symbolized as a character to construct a string of symbols corresponding to the TS. Subsequently, this string of symbols is windowed to generate a bag of ABBA words. To build a classification model, the $TF - IDF$ approach is applied to each ABBA word, resulting in a weight matrix where rows represent individual ABBA words and columns denote class labels. For the classification of unlabeled samples, a similar technique is employed. A bag of ABBA words is built for a new sample, which is then transformed into a frequency vector. This vector is compared using cosine similarity to determine the class label.

5 Performance Evaluation

In this section, we evaluate the performance of our proposed ABBA-VSM, a time series classification algorithm based on approximating time series into symbols. We perform a range of experiments to assess its performance and to gain insights into both compression and classification results.

5.1 Metrics

We present an evaluation framework for the ABBA-VSM algorithm. This framework encompasses a dual approach, incorporating both compression-based and classification-based metrics to assess the algorithm's performance across different dimensions. For compression-based metrics, we focus on quantifying the efficiency of the compression algorithm. First, the **compression ratio** (CR) measures the data reduction ratio achieved by the algorithm. A higher compression ratio implies more efficient compression, requiring less storage and providing potentially faster processing times. More formally,

$$CR = 1 - \frac{Size\,of\,compressed\,data}{Size\,of\,original\,data}$$

To overcome the complexity of storage measure in Python, we used a similar approach as in [7] by assuming that the size of the original data is the length of the uncompressed float value multiplied by 4 (4 bytes to store numerical value), and the size of compressed data is the length of the compressed string (assuming 1 byte to store symbols/character).

Conversely, for classification-based metrics, we focus on determining the algorithm's effectiveness in achieving **classification accuracy** (Acc) with compressed data. A higher accuracy score signifies the algorithm's capability to maintain classification performance even with compressed data. Accuracy is calculated as:

$$Acc = \frac{Number\,of\,correctly\,classified\,samples}{Total\,number\,of\,samples} \times 100\%$$

5.2 Hyper-Parameter Selection

We conducted an exhaustive experiment involving multiple hyperparameters, each playing a crucial role in shaping the performance of our classification model. These hyperparameters include *reduction tolerance (RT)*, which establishes the threshold for considering data changes insignificant during compression; *cluster type (Ctype)*, defining the clustering method for symbolic representation; *clustering tolerance (CT)*, defining the dimension of cluster in sorting-based ABBA clustering; *word size (Wsize)*, determining the length of ABBA words; *window step (Wstep)*, specifying the stride for moving the sliding window along the compressed data; *cluster size (Csize)*, utilized in k-means based ABBA; and *train-test split (Tsize)*, governing the proportion of samples allocated for model training and testing. Our study meticulously investigates the influence of these hyperparameter configurations on classification accuracy, with the ultimate goal of pinpointing the combination that optimally enhances accuracy. To ensure thorough exploration while avoiding excessive complexity, we define a well-structured search space for hyperparameters, encompassing a diverse range of values. This strategic selection of the search space strikes a balance between comprehensive exploration and computational feasibility, ensuring that our analysis yields robust and meaningful insights into the impact of hyperparameters on classification accuracy. Table 2 lists the search space for each hyperparameter.

Table 2. Hyperparameters and search space considered in the evaluation.

Param.	Search Space
RT	{0.001, 0.005, 0.01, 0.05, 0.1, 0.3, 0.5, 0.7}
$Ctype$	{k_means, sorting_based}
CT	{0.001, 0.005, 0.01, 0.05, 0.1, 0.3, 0.5, 0.7}
$Wsize$	{2,3,4,5,6,7,8,9,10}
$Wstep$	{1,2,3,4}
$Csize$	{2,3,4,5,6,7,8}
$Tsize$	{0.05, 0.1, 0.2, 0.3, 0.4}

5.3 Application Datasets

In our study, we analyze a variety of datasets from the UCR Time Series Classification Archive [5]. These datasets are from different domains, such as classifying unicellular algae, examining beef spectrograms, and distinguishing between Robusta and Arabica coffee beans. Each dataset has varying numbers of classes, adding complexity to our analysis. For example, the Beef dataset includes five beef spectrograms, while the Fish dataset covers seven fish types. Table 3 provides an overview of 19 selected datasets used for experiments. We selected similar datasets as in [20] to establish a comparison baseline.

Table 3. Selected Time Series Datasets from UCR archive.

Dataset	# classes	Shape
Adiac	37	(731,1,176)
Beef	5	(60,1,470)
CBF	3	(930,1,128)
Coffee	2	(56,1,286)
ECG200	2	(200,1,96)
Face All	14	(2250,1,131)
Face Four	4	(112,1,350)
Fish	7	(350,1,463)
Gun Point	2	(200,1,150)
Lightning2	2	(121,1,637)
Lightning7	7	(143,1,319)
OliveOil	4	(60,1,570)
OSU Leaf	6	(442,1,427)
Syn. Control	6	(600,1,60)
Swedish Leaf	15	(1125,1,128)
Trace	4	(200,1,275)
Two Patterns	4	(5000, 1,128)
Wafer	2	(7164,1,152)
Yoga	2	(3300,1,426)

5.4 Implementation

To implement ABBA-VSM, we extended the fABBA 1.2.1 framework [4] for the compression part, with modifications as required. Next, ABBA-VSM training and testing algorithms are implemented in Python and evaluated on an Intel(R) Core(TM) i7-8550U CPU @ 1.80GHz machine. We emulate the compressor (IoT device) and classifier (Edge device) locally on a single node.

6 Results and Discussion

In this section, we evaluate ABBA-VSM using the metrics defined in Section 5. In addition, we compare our result with baselines and perform sensitivity analysis of hyperparameters.

6.1 Main Results

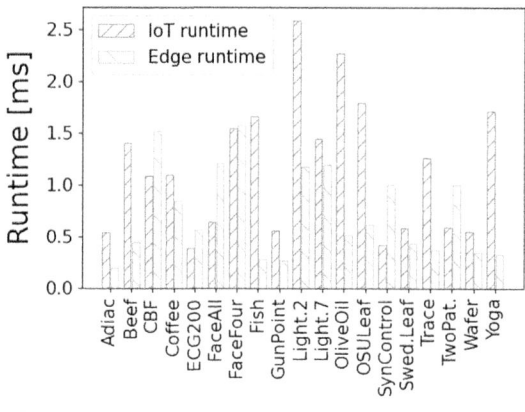

Fig. 3. The total runtime overhead at compressor (IoT) and classifier (Edge) for each dataset.

Our primary focus is to build the classification model using compressed data, emphasizing the need to achieve the best classification accuracy while maintaining a high compression ratio. Figure 4 demonstrates the change in compression ratio with varying reduction tolerance. For both binary and multiclass classification datasets, we observe the increase in compression ratio with the increase in reduction tolerance. The average compression ratio for binary classification datasets is 80–90%, whereas for multiclass, it is 50–60%, shown in Figs. 4a and 4b, respectively.

As depicted in Fig. 3, the runtime overhead of Edge is considerably lower compared to IoT. This disparity can be attributed to the Edge operating on already compressed time series (TS) data, while IoT processes the original uncompressed TS.

Moreover, we compared the classification accuracy of our proposed ABBA-VSM model against several state-of-the-art baseline classifiers in [20], such as 1NN classifiers based on Euclidean distance and Dynamic Time Warping (DTW), Fast-Shapelets pattern, Bag of Patterns (BoP) and SAX-VSM. 1NN classifiers use Euclidean distance to provide a straightforward approach for classifying TS by measuring the closest neighbor in the feature space, while DTW

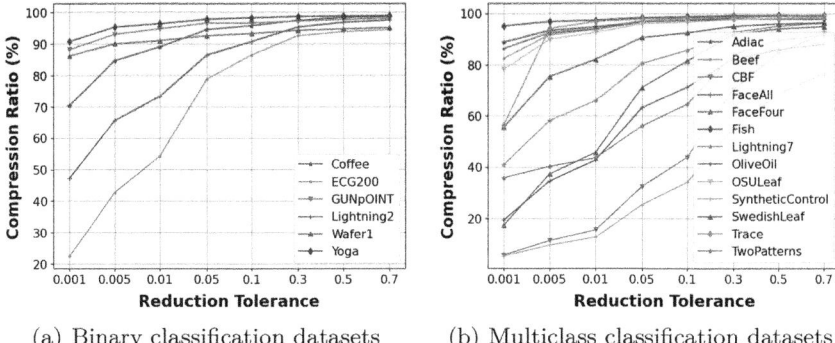

Fig. 4. Average compression ratio with varying reduction tolerance. For binary classification datasets in (a) the compression ratio gradually increases with the increase of reduction tolerance. In contrast, multiclass data in (b) compression ratio converges to linear much faster.

additionally adapts to variations in TS length. Fast-Shapelets detect unique patterns in TS, focusing on the most significant segments. In contrast, the BoP converts TS into symbolic representations, which streamlines classification through the analysis of pattern frequencies. Additionally, SAX-VSM integrates SAX with VSM.

The Results Demonstrate That Our Model Outperforms All Baseline Methods on Binary Classification Datasets. For instance, on binary classification datasets such as ECG200, GunPoint, and Lightning2, ABBA-VSM achieved the highest performance with an accuracy of 100%. In contrast, for Coffee and Wafer datasets, it performed as well as SAX-VSM by showing 90–100% accuracy. In multi-class classification scenarios, the accuracy varies depending on the number of class labels; however, here, ABBA-VSM performed as well as baselines, with the exception of the Face All dataset, where it recorded the lowest accuracy at nearly 40%.

Table 4 summarizes and compares the classification accuracy against the baselines given in [20]. In summary, our results demonstrate that ABBA-VSM is suitable in IoT and Edge environments for the development of Edge AI services utilizing classification services.

6.2 Sensitivity Analysis

We present the outcomes of exhaustive experiments with various hyperparameters, each playing a crucial role in shaping the classification model's performance. To identify the relevant combination of hyperparameter values, we consider classification accuracy results above a threshold value of 80%.

Reduction Tolerance: An increase in reduction tolerance leads to a decrease in the number of segments, consequently increasing the compression ratio and

Table 4. Comparison of classification accuracy (in the range of [0, 1], with 1 indicating 100% accuracy) of ABBA-VSM against baselines from [20].

Dataset	Type	1NN Euclidian	1NN DTW	Fast Shapelets Pattern	Bag of Patterns	SAX VSM	ABBA-VSM sorting	ABBA-VSM k-means
Adiac	multi	0.61	0.61	0.49	0.57	0.62	0.5	0.45
Beef	multi	0.53	0.53	0.55	0.57	0.97	1.00	1.00
CBF	multi	0.85	1.00	0.95	0.99	1.00	0.79	0.7
Coffee	binary	0.75	0.82	0.93	0.96	1.00	1.00	1.00
ECG200	binary	0.88	0.77	0.77	0.86	0.86	1.00	1.00
FaceAll	multi	0.71	0.81	0.60	0.78	0.79	0.39	0.27
FaceFour	multi	0.78	0.83	0.91	0.99	1.00	1.00	1.00
Fish	multi	0.78	0.83	0.80	0.93	0.98	1.00	1.00
GunPoint	binary	0.91	0.91	0.94	0.97	0.99	1.00	1.00
Lightning2	binary	0.75	0.87	0.70	0.84	0.80	1.00	0.90
Lightning7	multi	0.57	0.73	0.60	0.53	0.70	0.9	0.79
Olive Oil	multi	0.87	0.87	0.79	0.77	0.9	0.86	0.8
OSU Leaf	multi	0.52	0.59	0.64	0.76	0.89	0.7	0.6
Syn.Control	multi	0.88	0.99	0.92	0.96	0.99	0.67	0.6
Swed.Leaf	multi	0.79	0.79	0.73	0.80	0.75	0.7	0.7
Trace	multi	0.76	1.00	1.00	1.00	1.00	1.00	1.00
Two Patterns	multi	0.91	1.00	0.89	0.87	1.00	0.9	0.86
Wafer	binary	0.99	0.98	1.00	1.00	1.00	0.99	0.9
Yoga	binary	0.83	0.84	0.75	0.83	0.84	0.71	0.67

reducing the storage demand. This raises the question of whether ABBA-VSM can achieve better classification accuracy with a higher compression ratio. Among all sets of hyperparameter value combinations for binary classification, the reduction tolerance value $RT = 0.1$ achieved the accuracy threshold more frequently than the rest of the RT values. This is followed by tolerance ranges of $RT = \{0.3, 0.5\}$. However, for multiclass datasets, the accuracy exceeding the threshold is achieved with even higher tolerances, such as $RT = \{0.3, 0.5, 0.7\}$, and can be seen in Fig. 4. This evaluation shows us that RT can have a lower bound at 0.3 to achieve the accuracy threshold.

Cluster Type: In the binary classification case, the sorting-based clustering method outperformed k-means with an average accuracy improvement of 0.12, as seen in Table 4. However, both methods showed similar performance when dealing with multiclass datasets, with accuracy differences ranging only from 0.05 to 0.1. This suggests that the choice between sorting-based and k-means clusterings depends on the dataset's characteristics, especially on the number of classes involved.

Test Size: Nearly 80% of datasets with more than 20% test size performed lower than accuracy threshold. On the other hand, almost 90% of datasets with a test size less than 10% showed accuracy between 80–100%. This indicates that our method requires more data samples for training.

Training and Test Time: We observed that sorting-based clustering outperformed k-means clustering across all datasets in terms of computational efficiency. Specifically, when considering binary classification datasets, the k-means algorithm exhibited a notable increase in training time, ranging from 1.5x-2x more compared to sorting-based clustering. For multiclass datasets, k-means required approximately 0.5x-0.7x times more time than sorting-based clustering. For example, the FaceAll data required an average training time of 7.5 s for sorting-based clustering and 13.5 s for k-means-based clustering.

Window step and word size: For both binary and multiclass datasets, we did not observe a significant classification accuracy change in different window steps and word sizes. Thus, to reduce the computational time, larger values for window step and word size, i.e., within the range $\{3, 4\}$ and $\{7, 8, 9, 10\}$, can be considered, respectively.

Clustering tolerance: This hyperparameter is active when using *sorting-based* clustering selection. While half of the binary classification datasets achieved the accuracy threshold with values between $CT = \{0.001, 0.005, 0.01, 0.05, 0.1\}$, the remaining half achieved with $CT = \{0.1, 0.3, 0.5, 0.7\}$. In approximately 80% of multiclass datasets, the accuracy threshold is not met. This discrepancy can be attributed to the limited size of the training dataset, as indicated by experimental findings.

7 Conclusion and Future Works

We proposed ABBA-VSM, a symbolic time series classification method designed for resource-constrained Edge environments. Our proposed approach trains a Vector Space Model (VSM) classification model on a bag of words (i.e., compressed and symbolized time series data) and tests the model on unlabeled symbolic data. ABBA-VSM demonstrates 90–100% classification accuracy on binary classification datasets while achieving up to 80% compression ratio. In the future, we plan to explore the ABBA-VSM model for multivariate time series.

Acknowledgements. This research has been partially funded through the projects: Transprecise Edge Computing (Triton), Austrian Science Fund (FWF), DOI: 10.55776/ P36870; Trustworthy and Sustainable Code Offloading (Themis), FWF, DOI: 10.55776/ PAT1668223 and Satellite-based Monitoring of Livestock in the Alpine Region (Virtual Shepherd) funded by Austrian Research Promotion Agency (FFG) Austrian Space Applications Programme (ASAP) 2022 # 5307925.

References

1. Alam, T.: A reliable communication framework and its use in internet of things (IoT). Authorea Prepr. (2023)
2. Aslanpour, M.S., Toosi, A.N., Gaire, R., Cheema, M.A.: WattEdge: a holistic approach for empirical energy measurements in edge computing. In: Service-Oriented Computing: 19th International Conference, ICSOC 2021, Virtual Event, November 22–25, 2021, Proceedings 19, pp. 531–547. Springer (2021)

3. Azar, J., Makhoul, A., Barhamgi, M., Couturier, R.: An energy efficient IoT data compression approach for edge machine learning. Futur. Gener. Comput. Syst. **96**, 168–175 (2019)
4. Chen, X., Güttel, S.: An efficient aggregation method for the symbolic representation of temporal data. arXiv EPrint arXiv:2201.05697. The University of Manchester, UK (2022)
5. Dau, H.A., et al.: Hexagon-ML: the UCR time series classification archive (October 2018)
6. Elsworth, S., Güttel, S.: ABBA: adaptive Brownian bridge-based symbolic aggregation of time series. Data Min. Knowl. Disc. **34**(4), 1175–1200 (2020)
7. Hofstätter, D., Ilager, S., Lujic, I., Brandic, I.: SymED: adaptive and online symbolic representation of data on the edge. In: Cano, J., Dikaiakos, M.D., Papadopoulos, G.A., Pericàs, M., Sakellariou, R. (eds.) Euro-Par 2023: Parallel Processing, pp. 411–425. Springer Nature Switzerland, Cham (2023)
8. Ilager, S., De Maio, V., Lujic, I., Brandic, I.: Data-centric edge-AI: a symbolic representation use case. In: 2023 IEEE International Conference on Edge Computing and Communications (EDGE), pp. 301–308. IEEE (2023)
9. Lin, J., Khade, R., Li, Y.: Rotation-invariant similarity in time series using bag-of-patterns representation. J. Intell. Inf. Syst. **39**, 287–315 (2012)
10. Liu, S., Tan, C., Deng, F., Zhang, W., Wu, X.: A new framework for assessment of park management in smart cities: a study based on social media data and deep learning. Sci. Rep. **14**(1), 3630 (2024)
11. Malinowski, S., Guyet, T., Quiniou, R., Tavenard, R.: 1d-SAX: a novel symbolic representation for time series. In: International Symposium on Intelligent Data Analysis, pp. 273–284. Springer (2013)
12. Middlehurst, M., Schäfer, P., Bagnall, A.: Bake off redux: a review and experimental evaluation of recent time series classification algorithms. Data Min. Knowl. Discovery 1–74 (2024)
13. Nguyen, T.L., Ifrim, G.: MrSQM: fast time series classification with symbolic representations. arXiv preprint arXiv:2109.01036 (2021)
14. Pham, N.D., Le, Q.L., Dang, T.K.: HOT a SAX: a novel adaptive symbolic representation for time series discords discovery. In: Intelligent Information and Database Systems: Second International Conference, ACIIDS, Hue City, Vietnam, March 24-26, 2010. Proceedings, Part I 2, pp. 113–121. Springer (2010)
15. Rosero-Montalvo, P.D., István, Z., Tözün, P., Hernandez, W.: Hybrid anomaly detection model on trusted IoT devices. IEEE Internet Things J. **10**(12), 10959–10969 (2023)
16. Sabovic, A., Aernouts, M., Subotic, D., Fontaine, J., De Poorter, E., Famaey, J.: Towards energy-aware tinyML on battery-less IoT devices. Internet of Things **22**, 100736 (2023)
17. Schäfer, P.: The boss is concerned with time series classification in the presence of noise. Data Min. Knowl. Disc. **29**, 1505–1530 (2015)
18. Schäfer, P., Högqvist, M.: SFA: a symbolic fourier approximation and index for similarity search in high dimensional datasets. In: Proceedings of the 15th International Conference on Extending Database Technology, pp. 516–527 (2012)
19. Schäfer, P., Leser, U.: Fast and accurate time series classification with weasel. In: Proceedings of the 2017 ACM on Conference on Information and Knowledge Management, pp. 637–646 (2017)
20. Senin, P., Malinchik, S.: SAX-VSM: interpretable time series classification using SAX and vector space model. In: 2013 IEEE 13th International Conference on Data Mining, pp. 1175–1180. IEEE (2013)

21. Shukla, S., Hassan, M.F., Tran, D.C., Akbar, R., Paputungan, I.V., Khan, M.K.: Improving latency in internet-of-things and cloud computing for real-time data transmission: a systematic literature review (SLR). Cluster Comput. 1–24 (2023)
22. Tung, T.M., Yaseen, Z.M., et al.: A survey on river water quality modelling using artificial intelligence models: 2000–2020. J. Hydrol. **585**, 124670 (2020)
23. Vailshery, L.S.: IoT connections worldwide from 2022 to 2023, with forecasts from 2024 to 2033. In: Technology and Telecommunications. Statista (2024)

An Energy-Efficient Partition and Offloading Method for Multi-DNN Applications in Edge-End Collaboration Environments

Zhiqing Yang, Xiang He, Teng Wang, and Zhongjie Wang[✉]

Faculty of Computing, Harbin Institute of Technology, Harbin, China
{yangzhiqing, willtynn}@stu.hit.edu.cn, {hexiang, rainy}@hit.edu.cn

Abstract. Deep Neural Networks (DNNs) have emerged as the preferred solution for Internet of Things (IoT) applications, owing to their remarkable performance capabilities. However, the inherent complexity of DNNs presents significant challenges for IoT devices that are constrained by limited computational power and battery life. To adeptly navigate the demands of intricate inference tasks, edge computing is leveraged, enabling collaborative inference of DNNs between IoT devices and edge servers. However, existing research rarely focus simultaneously on the power consumption of IoT devices, the latency of collaborative inference and the cost of edge servers. Moreover, current research seldom takes into account the deployment of multiple DNN applications on IoT devices, a critical factor for adapting to increasingly complex edge-end collaborative environments. This research focuses on optimizing the inference power consumption of multiple DNN applications deployed on IoT devices in larger-scale edge-end collaboration environments, under the constraints of maximum End-to-End latency and the cost of edge servers. To address this issue, we propose the Greedy Genetic Algorithm, which leverages a combination of greedy strategy and Genetic Algorithm. The performance of our proposed method is extensively evaluated through experiments, demonstrating its superiority in achieving lower inference power consumption with fewer iterations compared to existing solutions.

Keywords: DNN inference · Edge Computing · DNN Partitioning and Offloading · Energy Efficiency · Greedy Genetic Algorithm

1 Introduction

Deep Learning (DL) approaches have become increasingly popular in a variety of Industrial Internet of Things (IIoT) applications [2]. Owing to the constrained computational capabilities inherent in IoT devices, they are ill-equipped independently infer complex DNN applications. Consequently, a prevalent approach in current research is to leverage edge servers to alleviate the computational burden, which denoted as the edge computing paradigm [7].

This paradigm situates computation in close proximity to data originators, which serves to diminish End-to-End (E2E) latency and bolster privacy safeguards [12]. Furthermore, for IoT devices that are predominantly powered by batteries, edge computing can markedly curtail computational energy consumption, thereby conferring a significant advantage in terms of device maintenance frequency [1,10]. Against this backdrop, the partitioning and offloading of DNNs have emerged as a significant research direction [5]. This approach optimizes the utilization of computational resources by offloading different parts of the DNN model to IoT devices and edge servers, effectively reducing E2E latency and the power consumption of IoT devices.

In IIoT scenarios, imposing cost constraints on edge servers involved in collaborative inference is an important consideration [13]. However, existing research does not fully address the edge-device collaboration issue, failing to adequately consider the interrelationship between the power consumption of IoT devices, maximum E2E latency, and the cost of edge servers. For example, [8] overlooks the impact of end device power consumption and server costs. Meanwhile, [4] employs a weighted aggregation of various factors for multi-objective optimization, a method that requires recalibrating parameters through iterative experimentation tailored to the nuances of each application scenario.

Additionally, most studies focus on deploying a single DNN application for each IoT devices [8,11]. However, as IIoT smart systems become increasingly sophisticated, a single DNN model can no longer meet the diverse and demanding requirements of tasks, necessitating the collaborative operation of multiple complex DNN models. Moreover, the number of IoT devices is gradually increasing, making support for multiple applications and larger-scale IoT devices also crucial. However, formulating the partition offloading strategy commonly framed as a Mixed-Integer Nonlinear Programming (MINLP) problem, which recognized as belonging to the NP-Hard class [9]. This problem is not only highly complex but also comes with an enormous search space. When supporting multiple applications and larger-scale IoT devices, the search space expands further, exacerbating the complexity of the problem. This makes generating strategies for DNN model partitioning and offloading even more challenging. Therefore, an efficient solving algorithm is necessary.

Motivated by the above, this paper proposed the Greedy Genetic Algorithm (GGA). This algorithm combines a greedy strategy with Genetic Algorithms (GA) to tackle the issue of energy-efficient partitioning and offloading (EPOMA) for multiple DNN applications within cooperative edge environments. The GGA is designed with a comprehensive consideration of the interdependencies among the power consumption of IoT devices, the maximum E2E latency, and the costs associated with edge servers. It facilitates the deployment of a greater number of IoT devices, each capable of hosting multiple DNN applications, thereby enhancing the integration and application of deep learning technologies in the IIoT. The novelties of our proposed approach are the following:

– We introduce an optimization problem that seeks to minimize the inference power consumption of multiple DNN applications across IoT devices, subject to constraints on maximum E2E latency and edge server costs. The formulation of this problem incorporates a broader spectrum of IoT devices and edge servers, with the flexibility to deploy multiple DNN applications on each IoT device. The holistic power consumption of the IoT devices is utilized as the key performance indicator for this optimization endeavor.
– This paper presents the GGA algorithm to address the optimization problem we have proposed, which utilizing a greedy strategy to reduce the problem space, thereby enabling the achievement of lower inference power consumption with fewer iterations.
– The efficacy of GGA has been substantiated through rigorous numerical experimentation. The findings reveal that the GGA surpasses current methodologies with respect to energy efficiency. Additionally, the effectiveness of the greedy strategy has been corroborated through ablation experiments.

The remainder of this paper is structured as follows. Section 2 provides a summary of the relevant literature. Section 3 defines the energy-efficient Multi-DNN application partition and offloading problem in edge-end collaboration environment. Section 4 introduces our proposed algorithm to tackle this problem. The methodologies and results of our experimental evaluation of the algorithm are detailed in Sect. 5. Finally, Sect. 6 synthesizes the findings of this study and posits avenues for future inquiry and advancement.

2 Related Work

In IIoT scenarios, there are several aspects that can be optimized in the collaborative inference of DNNs between IoT devices and edge servers, including the energy consumption, E2E latency, edge server costs, and data transmission volume. However, existing works often fail to consider all these factors appropriately. In this section, we review some of the algorithms from recent years based on the optimization objectives and summarize the factors they consider.

In terms of reducing task offloading latency, [8] proposed an improved particle swarm genetic algorithm (IPSGA) to achieve the optimal offloading strategy. The algorithm uses the variable acceleration coefficient with the number of iterations and the inertia weight with the success rate as the feedback parameters to improve the particle swarm optimization algorithm, and the GA is improved with the adaptive crossover probability and the adaptive mutation probability, aiming to minimize task offloading latency while considering the limitations of computing resources. [3] proposed a joint method by a self-adaptive DNN partition with cost-effective resource allocation to facilitate collaborative computation between IoT devices and edge servers, which can be proved to ensure the overall rental cost within an upper bound above the optimal solution while guaranteeing the latency for DNN-based task inference.

The research previously introduced has achieved efficient DNN inference, which is significant for the collaborative reasoning of edge devices. However, for

IoT devices powered by batteries, the pursuit of the fastest inference speed may lead to unnecessary energy consumption, thereby increasing the maintenance frequency of the devices.

In the realm of multi-objective optimization, a multi-objective optimization problem was proposed in [11], which jointly considers offloading decisions, allocation of communication and computation resources to minimize latency and cost. This study introduced a particle swarm optimization (PSO) based computation offloading (PSOCO) algorithm to obtain the Pareto-optimal solutions to the multi-objective optimization problem, while this method did not take into account energy consumption. [6] presented a container-based DNN partitioning placement and resource allocation strategy, which takes into account the varying processing capabilities, memory, and battery levels of heterogeneous IoT devices, aiming to simultaneously optimize E2E latency, service probability, and energy consumption. In [4], researchers jointly optimized the design of task partitioning and offloading to minimize the cost for each mobile edge device, including computational latency, energy consumption, and the price paid to servers. [14] designed a Deep Neural Network partitioning and Task Offloading (DPTO) algorithm based on Deep Reinforcement Learning, jointly optimizing the energy and latency issues of DNN partitioning and task offloading. However, this method did not consider the cost of the edge servers.

Although the aforementioned multi-objective optimization algorithms have incorporated the main optimization factors, the concurrent optimization of several objectives can engender superfluous complexity within the algorithms themselves. When applied to real-world settings with a substantial number of devices and intricate scenarios, these algorithms are prone to encountering protracted solution durations and the arduous task of identifying the global optimum.

In the IIoT scenario, the pursuit of minimal E2E latency is not always necessary. Different DNN applications, depending on the usage scenario, can meet real-time requirements as long as they do not exceed a certain E2E latency threshold. Moreover, the cost of edge servers is also a factor that cannot be ignored to ensure the feasibility and economic viability of the solution.

Therefore, our work considers minimizing the overall inference power consumption of multiple DNN applications on IoT devices under the constraints of maximum E2E latency and edge server costs. By adhering to the maximum E2E latency constraints, different DNN applications are enabled to meet their respective real-time requirements, which is of significant importance for extending the maintenance cycle and improving overall energy efficiency of devices.

3 Problem Modelling

This section provides a detailed exposition of the problem scenario, with meticulous modeling of the various factors involved in the problem, including multiple DNN applications, a range of IoT devices, several edge servers, the power consumption of IoT devices, E2E latency, and the cost of edge servers, all aimed at optimizing the power consumption across all IoT devices.

DNN Applications. For all DNN applications, each application corresponds to a DNN model. Let $\mathbb{D} = \{D_1, D_2, ..., D_n\}$ denote N different DNN models in the environment, where $D_i = <F_{D_i}, M_{D_i}, Data_{D_i}^{input}, Data_{D_i}^{result}>$

- $F_{D_i} = \{f_1, f_2, ..., f_{l_{D_i}}\}$ represents the floating point operations(FLOPs) for each layer.
- $M_{D_i} = \{m_1^{D_i}, m_2^{D_i}, ..., m_{l_{D_i}}\}$ represents the memory requirement for computation for each layer.
- $Data_{D_i}^{input} = \{s_1^{D_i}, s_2^{D_i}, ..., s_{l_{D_i}}^{D_i}\}$ is the size of input data for each layer.
- $Data_{D_i}^{result}$ is the size of result data.

and l_{D_i} denotes the layer number of D_i. Furthermore, this paper utilizes the torchstat library to perform an analysis on each DNN model, thereby obtaining three key attributes: the FLOPs for each layer, the memory requirements for computation and the size of the input data.

In this paper, our focus is on the impact of CPU and memory on inference performance. Therefore, we solely consider these two types of resources. The floating point operations per second (FLOPS) of a CPU can be calculated by Eq. 1, where $cores$ denotes the number of CPU cores, $cycles/second$ signifies the number of cycles per core per second, and $FLOPs/cycle$ represents the number of floating-point operations per cycle per core[1]. Furthermore, for the sake of analysis, we consider the system to be quasi-static, with the wireless channels remaining unchanged during DNN applications inferencing [8].

$$FLOPS = cores \times \frac{cycles}{second} \times \frac{FLOPs}{cycle} \qquad (1)$$

Edge Servers. Let $\mathbb{E} = \{E_1, E_2, ..., E_s\}$ denote S edge servers in the environment, where $E_i = <FLS_i^{edge}, Mem_i^{edge}, num^{core}, P_i^{core}, P_i^{mem}, P_i^{traffic}>$. In this notation, FLS_i^{edge} represent the FLOPS of edge servers, Mem_i^{edge} indicates the maximum available memory, num^{core} is the core number, P_i^{core}, P_i^{mem} and $P_i^{traffic}$ represent the price per core-second of CPU, the price per MB-second of memory and the price per Mbps per second of traffic, respectively.

IoT Devices. Let $\mathbb{I} = \{I_1, I_2, ..., I_k\}$ denote K IoT devices in the environment, where $I_i = <FLS_i^{end}, P_i^I, P_i^M, P_i^T, Mem_i^{end}, B_i, Dep_i, ML_i, MC_i>$, v denotes the number of DNN applications will deploy on IoT device I_i.

- FLS_i^{end} represent the FLOPS of I_i.
- P_i^I, P_i^M, P_i^T represents the idle power, max power, transmitting power of I_i.
- Mem_i^{end} is the maximum available memory of I_i.
- $B_i = \{B_{i,1}, B_{i,2}, ..., B_{i,s}\}$ is the bandwidth to edge servers.
- $Dep_i = \{a_1^i, a_2^i, ..., a_v^i\}$ is the set of DNN applications to be deployed on I_i.
- $ML_i = \{l_1^i, l_2^i, ..., l_v^i\}$ is the maximum latency for each application.
- $MC_i = \{c_1^i, c_2^i, ..., c_v^i\}$ is the maximum inference cost for each application.

---
[1] https://en.wikipedia.org/wiki/FLOPS.

End to End Latency. For the j-th DNN application with $l_{a_j^i}$ layers on IoT device I_i, we selects the partition point p_j^i, where the initial p_j^i layers of the DNN task are processed locally, while the subsequent layers from $p_j^i + 1$ to $l_{a_j^i}$ are processed in a selected edge server, assume that $pos_j^i = x$, indicating that we have chosen edge server E_x for this task.

The E2E latency can be expressed as $T_{a_j^i}^{total}$, as shown in Eq. 2. This includes the local execution time $T_{a_j^i}^{I_i}$, the execution time on the edge server $T_{a_j^i}^{E_x}$ and the data transmission time between IoT device and edge server $T_{a_j^i}^{tran}$.

$$T_{a_j^i}^{total} = T_{a_j^i}^{I_i} + T_{a_j^i}^{E_x} + T_{a_j^i}^{tran} \tag{2}$$

After the application a_j^i is partitioned, the computational latency for offloading to IoT device I_i and edge server E_x represented by $T_{a_j^i}^{I_i}$ and $T_{a_j^i}^{E_x}$, respectively, which can be calculated by Eq. 3 and 4, where f_{la} represents the FLOPs of layer la in a_j^i, $\theta_{I_i}^{a_j^i}$ and $\theta_{E_x}^{a_j^i}$ represents the percentage of computational resources allocated for application a_j^i on IoT device and edge server, respectively.

$$T_{a_j^i}^{I_i} = \sum_{la=1}^{p_j^i} \frac{f_{la}}{FLS_i^{end} \theta_{I_i}^{a_j^i}} \tag{3}$$

$$T_{a_j^i}^{E_x} = \sum_{la=p_j^i+1}^{l_{a_j^i}} \frac{f_{la}}{FLS_x^{edge} \theta_{E_x}^{a_j^i}} \tag{4}$$

$T_{a_j^i}^{tran}$ represent the time required for intermediate data transmission to the edge server and result data transmission to the IoT device, which can be computed by Eq. 5, where T_{ex} represents the latency associated with establishing network connections, data link transmission, and so on.

$$T_{a_j^i}^{tran} = \frac{s_{p_j^i}^{a_j^i} + Data_{a_j^i}^{result}}{B_{i,x}} + T_{ex} \tag{5}$$

Edge Server Cost. Let $C_{a_j^i}$ represent the computation, memory, and data transmission cost of layers $p_j^i + 1$ to l of model a_j^i on edge server E_x, each calculated by multiplying the respective prices by the time duration, which can be expressed as Eq. 6, where m_{la} represents the memory requirement for computation of layer la.

$$C_{a_j^i} = T_{a_j^i}^{E_x}(P_x^{core} num^{core} \theta_{E_x}^{a_j^i} + \sum_{la=p_j^i}^{l_{a_j^i}} m_{la}^{a_j^i}) + T_{a_j^i}^{tran} B_{i,x} \tag{6}$$

IoT Devices Energy Consumption. Let $E_{a_j^i}$ represent the energy consumption of inference from layer 1 to p_j^i of model a_j^i on end device I_i and the energy consumption of uploading the intermediate output data of the model to edge server E_x, each obtained by multiplying the corresponding power with time. which can be expressed as Eq. 7.

$$E_{a_j^i} = T_{a_j^i}^{I_i}(P_i^I + P_i^M \theta_{I_i}^{a_j^i}) + (\frac{s_{p_j^i}^{a_j^i}}{B_{i,x}} + T_{ex})P_i^T \quad (7)$$

Optimization Problem. We consider minimizing the energy consumption of all IoT devices under constraints of maximum E2E latency, edge server cost, computational capacity and memory resources. To achieve this, it is necessary to optimize the partition points of each DNN application, the location where the model is to be offloaded, the allocation of CPU resources for edge servers and IoT devices, represented by P, POS, θ_E and θ_I, respectively. The optimization problem is formulated as follows:

$$\min_{P,POS,\theta_E,\theta_I} \sum_{i=1}^{k}\sum_{j=1}^{v} E_{a_j^i} \quad (8)$$

$$\text{s.t.} \quad C_{a_j^i} \leq c_j^i, \quad T_{a_j^i}^{total} \leq l_j^i \quad i=1,\ldots,k, \quad j=1,\ldots,v \quad (9)$$

$$\sum_{j=1}^{v} \theta_{I_i}^{a_j^i} \leq 1 \quad i=1,\ldots,k \quad (10)$$

$$\sum_{j=1}^{v}\sum_{la=1}^{p_j^i} m_{la}^{a_j^i} \leq Mem_i^{end} \quad i=1,\ldots,k \quad (11)$$

$$\sum_{i=1}^{k}\sum_{j=1}^{v} Ind(pos_j^i,x)\theta_{E_x}^{a_j^i} \leq 1, \quad x=1,\ldots,s \quad (12)$$

$$\sum_{i=1}^{k}\sum_{j=1}^{v}\sum_{la=p_j^i+1}^{l_{a_j^i}} Ind(pos_j^i,x)m_{la}^{a_j^i} \leq Mem_x^{edge}, \quad x=1,\ldots,s \quad (13)$$

$$0 \leq \theta_{I_i}^{a_j^i}, \theta_{E_x}^{a_j^i} \leq 1, \quad 1 \leq pos_j^i \leq s, \quad 0 \leq p_j^i \leq l_{a_j^i} \quad (14)$$

where Eq. 9 represents the cost constraints for edge servers across various applications and the maximum E2E latency constraints for each application. Equation 10 and 11 indicate the computational capacity and memory constraints for IoT devices, respectively. Additionally, Eq. 12 and 13 address the computational and memory capacity constraints for edge servers, respectively. The indicator function $Ind(pos,x)$ returns 1 when the offloading position p_j^i of DNN model a_j^i is equal to x, and returns 0 when x does not equal to pos.

4 Proposed Algorithm

In this section, we describe our proposed GGA. The algorithm flowchart is shown in Fig. 1. The key advantage of our algorithm is that during the GA iteration process, a portion of the optimization variables is solved using a greedy strategy, which narrows down the problem space and makes the search more efficient. Consequently, it becomes easier to find the optimal solution during iterations.

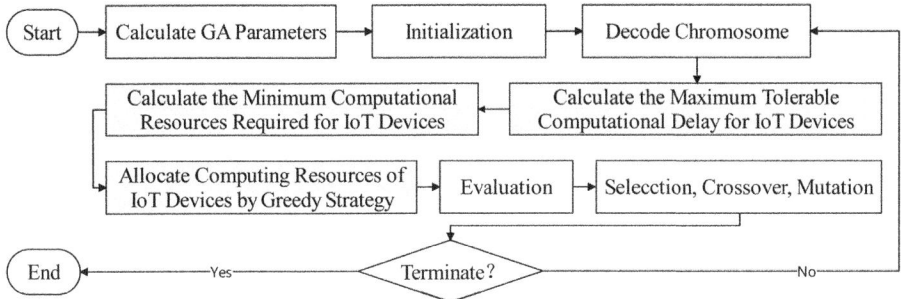

Fig. 1. Overall of Greedy Genetic Algorithm.

To transform the constrained optimization problem into an unconstrained one, we employ the penalty function method, which is commonly used in intelligent optimization algorithms to constrain the objective function. The fitness function is used to evaluate the performance of heuristic algorithms. After each iteration, the fitness value is calculated for all individuals in the population to assess the quality of a single chromosome. The fitness function F can be represented by Eq. 15, where the fitness function consists of the objective function plus the penalty function, and ρ represents the penalty coefficient.

$$Fit = \sum_{i=1}^{k}\sum_{j=1}^{v}(E_{a_j^i} + \rho(\max(0, C_{a_j^i} - c_j^i)$$
$$+ \max(0, T_{a_j^i}^{total} - l_j^i) + \max(0, \sum_{j=1}^{v}\sum_{la=1}^{p_j^i} m_{la}^{a_j^i} - Mem_i^{end}) \quad (15)$$
$$+ \max(0, \sum_{i=1}^{k}\sum_{j=1}^{v}\sum_{la=p_j^i+1}^{l_{a_j^i}} Ind(pos_j^i, x) m_{la}^{a_j^i} - Mem_x^{edge})))$$

Algorithm 1 shows the process of our proposed Greedy Genetic Algorithm, the initial population size of the genetic algorithm is denoted as GA_{ps}, which can be expressed by Eq. 16. The maximum number of iterations for the genetic algorithm, GA_{maxi}, can be represented by Eq. 17.

$$GA_{ps} = 100 + 100(Dep^{num}/30) \quad (16)$$

$$GA_{maxi} = 50 + 2Dep^{num} \qquad (17)$$

Algorithm 1. Greedy Genetic Algorithm

Input: DNN set D, IoT devices set I, Edge servers set E.
Output: The optimal strategy $best_x$.
1: Calculate $Dep^{num}, GA_{ps}, GA_{maxi}$;
2: Initialize chromosome populations, $best_x$, $GA_i = 1$;
3: **while** $GA_i \leq GA_{maxi}$ **do**
4:     Decode P, POS, θ_E from chromosome;
5:     Calculate T_I^{max}, R_I^{min};
6:     **if** sum(R_I^{min}) < 1 **then**
7:         Initialize list $tempR$;
8:         **for** $r_i \in R_I^{min}$ **do**
9:             Append $\sqrt{r_i}/sum(T_I^{max})$ to $tempR$;
10:        **end for**
11:        **if** all elements in $tempR$ no less than the corresponding element in R_I^{min} **then**
12:            $R_I = tempR$;
13:        **else**
14:            $R_I = $ Normalize(R_I^{min});
15:        **end if**
16:     **else**
17:        $R_I = $ Normalize(R_I^{min});
18:     **end if**
19:     Calculate Fit;
20:     Update $best_x$ as the best chromosome;
21:     Selecting the next generation of chromosome individuals;
22:     Execute two point crossover;
23:     Execute uniform variation;
24:     $GA_i = GA_i + 1$;
25: **end while**
26: **return** $best_x$

The process of initializing the GA population begins with tallying the number of DNN applications for deployment on all IoT devices, which denoted by Dep^{num}. Subsequently, we generate the partition points P, offloading positions POS and the proportion of CPU resource allocation on edge server θ_{E_x} according to constraints 14 for all Dep^{num} applications, these elements are then concatenated into a vector, encoded by Gray code, to form an initial chromosome. This procedure is repeated GA_{ps} times to fully initialize the GA population.

During each iteration, chromosome decoding provides the partition points, the offloading positions, and the percentage of server computational resource allocation for each DNN application. By applying Eqs. 4 and 5 in conjunction with Constraint 9, the maximum permissible computational latency for applications on IoT devices is ascertained, which denoted by T_I^{max}. Subsequently, Eq. 3 is employed to deduce the minimum proportion of computational resources that need to be allocated to the IoT devices, which denoted by R_I^{max}. With Eqs. 7 and 3 in mind, it shows that the value of $E_{a_j^i}$, given fixed partition points, offloading locations, and server computational resource distribution ratios for DNN applications, is dependent on the IoT device's computational resource allocation ratio, $\theta_{I_i}^{a_j^i}$, as $\theta_{I_i}^{a_j^i}$ increases, $E_{a_j^i}$ decreases.

Therefore, to minimize the power consumption of IoT devices, it is necessary to maximize the computing resources of IoT devices, ideally reaching 100%. Computational resources are redistributed based on the maximum tolerable latency for each application and are assessed against the minimum required allocations. If the new allocation suffices, the final distribution is made in proportion. Otherwise, the minimum allocations are normalized to yield a holistic offloading strategy and resource allocation plan for all models.

5 Experimental Evaluation

This section presents the experiment design and the experiment results to evaluate the performance of GGA. We evaluate the performance of all competing algorithms in terms of fitness value based on the resource allocation solutions found by the respective algorithms.

5.1 Experimental Setup

Simulation Environment. In our simulation experiments, we emulated the Raspberry Pi 4B with 1G and 4G memory versions. Their computing capabilities, idle power, maximum power and transmission power were evaluated by solving a set of dense linear algebraic equations with N variables using the Gaussian elimination method provided by the Linear system package.

We considered simulating the 2-core, 4G memory instance of Alibaba Cloud's Edge Node Service, with the CPU of E5-2680 v3 (Haswell), and we refer to their documentation to calculate the costs of CPU, memory, and public network bandwidth per second, and we determined the computing capability of instances by Eq. 1. The configurations are shown in Table 1.

In addition, we employ prevalent DNN models in the experiment encompass ResNet18, ResNet50, VGG11, VGG16, AlexNet, and GoogleNet [4,15]. Each DNN implementation is derived from the torchvision.models standard library and has been carefully scrutinized using the torchsummary function within ptflops to acquire comprehensive details, including the architecture, computational intensity, and inter-layer data transmission. On each IoT device, one of ResNet18, ResNet50, VGG11, or VGG16 is executed in conjunction with AlexNet and GoogleNet. Consequently, three DNN applications are inferred on each IoT device at the same time.

Experimental Strategy. This paper compares GGA to three baseline methods: IPSGA [8], PSOCO [11] and GA. The IPSGA is based on PSO algorithm,

Table 1. Configurations of IoT Devices and an Edge Server

Device	Computing capability (GFLOPS)	Memory (GB)	Idle Power (W)	Trans. Power (W)	Max. Power (W)
Raspberry Pi 4B(1G)	9.92	1	2.9	3.1	7.9
Raspberry Pi 4B(4G)	9.69	4	2.8	3.0	8.2
Edge Server	80	4	-	-	-

where during the PSO iteration, a subset of particles are treated as chromosomes. Subsequently, the application of GA iterations facilitates the discovery of superior particles, which in turn augments the overall search capability of the algorithm. PSOCO also based on the PSO algorithm, has been empirically demonstrated to surpass the performance of the GA within the context of the scenarios presented in their corresponding scholarly work. As our algorithm is an enhancement based on GA, it is appropriate to use GA as a control in ablation studies, thereby incorporating it into the baseline comparisons.

Since the aforementioned algorithms all require random initialization of the starting solutions, to enhance the reliability of the experimental results and minimize errors, we conduct the experiments three times with fixed random seeds of 1, 2, and 3, respectively. We then take the best solution from these three trials to evaluate the performance of the algorithms.

Experiment Setting. The GGA and GA algorithms are initialized with a mutation rate set to 0.001 and a tournament size of 5. The IPSGA and PSOCO algorithms, which are tailored to address distinct optimization issues and scenarios, require parameters that diverge from those outlined in their original publications. Through rigorous experimental evaluation, the IPSGA algorithm has been calibrated with the following parameters: $w = 0.65$, $c1 = 1$, $c2 = 0.5$, $ga_{mini} = 10$, $ga_{maxi} = 20$, $ga_{ps}^{min} = 5$, $ga_{ps}^{max} = 10$, $ga_{num}^{max} = 10$, and $ga_{num}^{min} = 5$. The PSOCO algorithm, on the other hand, has been fine-tuned with parameters of $w = 0.65$, $c1 = 1$, and $c2 = 0.5$.

All algorithms use the same number of iterations and initial solution scale, as determined by Eq. 16 and 17, and set the penalty coefficient $\rho = 1e5$. Taking into account the IIoT scenarios and the limited computational capabilities of edge devices, the maximum E2E latency for the ResNet18, ResNet50, VGG11, and VGG16 are limited to 3 s, with a edge server cost capped at 5e-5. For the AlexNet and GoogleNet, the maximum E2E latency is limited to 1 s, with a edge server cost capped at 3e-5.

5.2 The Impact of the Number of End Devices

To validate the effectiveness of GGA under a larger number of IoT devices, the experiment sets up IoT devices to increase from 5 to 100 units, while controlling the server resources to three instances of edge servers. The bandwidth between IoT devices and the servers are set at 150Mbps. The iteration processes with 5 and 100 IoT devices are shown in Fig. 2(a) and Fig. 2(b), respectively.

Figure 2(a) indicates that when there are only 5 IoT devices, PSOCO, IPSGA, GA, and GGA can all identify partitioning and offloading strategies with relatively low power consumption. However, Fig. 2(b) and Fig. 2(c) evident that as the number of IoT devices increases, only GA and GGA remain effective. PSOCO and IPSGA become trapped in local optima, resulting in strategies that do not meet the maximum E2E latency or cost constraints.

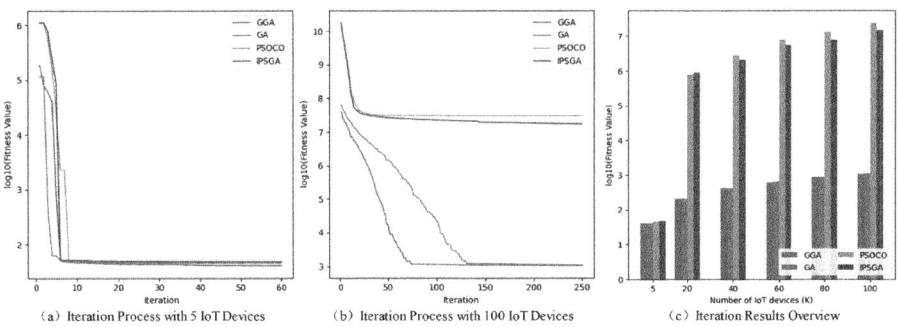

Fig. 2. Experimental results under different numbers of IoT devices.

Compared to GA, GGA can achieve the same performance with fewer iterations. Specifically, when there are 100 IoT devices, GGA reaches the same performance as GA after 250 iterations in just 139 iterations, reducing the number of iterations by 44.4%. After 250 iterations, the strategy generated by GGA has lower power consumption than that of GA, with values of 1052.57 and 1089.29, respectively, representing a 3.37% reduction in power consumption. This demonstrates that notwithstanding an escalation in the quantity of IoT devices, our greedy strategy can still effectively reduce the search space, thereby finding better solutions in fewer iterations.

5.3 The Impact of Link Bandwidth

To validate the effectiveness of GGA under different network bandwidth conditions, the server resources are controlled to consist of three edge server instances, with 50 IoT devices. The network bandwidth is increased from 100 Mbps to 300 Mbps. The iteration process at 100Mbps and 300Mbps is shown in Fig. 3(a) and Fig. 3(b), respectively, indicated that IPSGA and PSOCO, when dealing with 50 IoT devices, cannot find the global optimal solution even with increased network bandwidth. In contrast, GGA and GA are capable of escaping local optima.

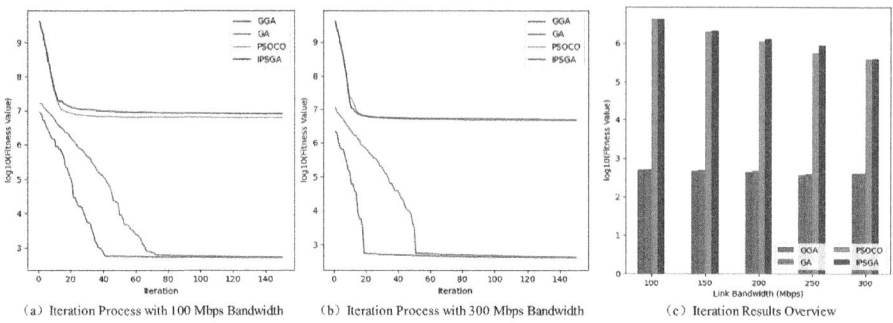

Fig. 3. Experimental Results Under Different Link Bandwidth.

From Fig. 2(c), it is evident that as the link bandwidth increases from 100 to 250 Mbps, the total energy consumption gradually decreases. However, when the bandwidth reaches 300 Mbps, the total energy consumption begins to rise. This is because higher bandwidth leads to increased data transmission costs, and due to cost constraints, the algorithms tend to split the DNN model data at layers with less transmission, resulting in increased computational tasks on the IoT devices and consequently higher power consumption.

Compared to GA, GGA requires fewer iterations to achieve the same effect. Specifically, at a bandwidth of 250 Mbps, GGA reaches the performance of GA's 150th iteration after just 110 iterations, reducing the number of iterations by 26.6%. Moreover, under the same number of iterations, the strategy generated by GGA has lower energy consumption than that of GA, with values of 405.46 and 416.10, respectively, representing a 2.55% reduction in energy consumption. This demonstrates that our greedy strategy can still effectively reduce the search space under different bandwidth, thereby finding better solutions in fewer iterations.

5.4 The Impact of Edge Server Computing Resources

To verify the effectiveness of GGA when server resources vary, such as in situations of abundance or scarcity, the number of edge servers is increased from 1 to 5, with 50 IoT devices, and the bandwidth between IoT devices and servers are set at 150 Mbps. The iteration processes with 1 and 5 edge servers are shown in Fig. 4(a) and Fig. 4(b), respectively, indicated that IPSGA and PSOCO, when dealing with 50 IoT devices, cannot find the global optimal solution even with increased edge servers. In stark contrast, the GGA and GA algorithms have demonstrated an adeptness at eluding local optima, thereby showcasing their potential for uncovering more efficient solutions.

From Fig. 4(c), we can observe that after the number of edge servers increases to 3, due to the cost constraints of each application, more abundant computational resources do not lead to a significant reduction in the power consumption of the end devices. Compared to GA, GGA can achieve the same effect with fewer

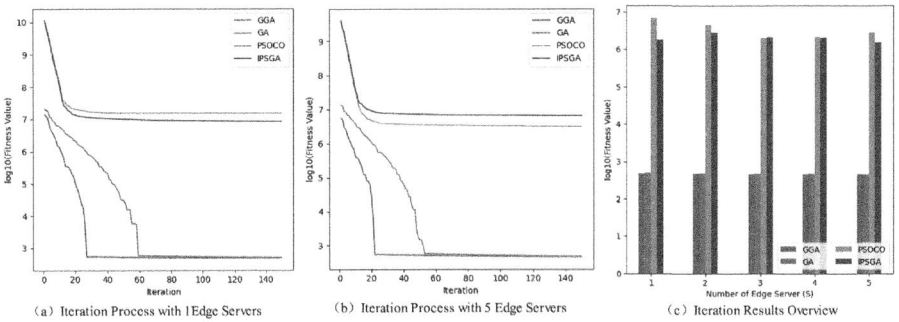

Fig. 4. Experimental results under different number of edge servers.

iterations. Specifically, when there are 3 edge servers, GGA reaches the performance of GA's 150th iteration after just 107 iterations, reducing the number of iterations by 28.6%. Moreover, under the same number of iterations, the strategy generated by GGA has lower power consumption than that of GA, with values of 459.40 and 471.88, respectively, representing a 2.64% reduction in power consumption. This proves that our greedy strategy can still effectively reduce the search space under different computational resource conditions, thereby finding better solutions in fewer iterations.

6 Conclusion and Future Work

This paper introduces an optimization problem within the scope of the IIoT, focusing on the minimization of inference power consumption for multiple DNN applications across an extensive array of IoT devices. This problem is addressed under the constraints of maximum E2E latency and the costs associated with edge server utilization. To tackle this issue, the GGA is proposed, which harnesses the iterative process of genetic algorithms to determine the partitioning points for DNN applications and the corresponding offloading strategies. Subsequently, a greedy strategy is implemented for the allocation of computational resources to IoT devices, thereby effectively condensing the search space. The experimental outcomes indicate that the GGA is superior to the baseline algorithm, as it reduces the energy consumption of IoT devices in a significantly reduced number of iterations.

Potential future research endeavors may involve refining problem modeling, and based on the proposed partitioning and offloading method, supporting deployment strategies for multiple instances of the same DNN application, instead of being limited to a single instance.

Acknowledgements. Research in this paper is supported by the National Natural Science Foundation of China (62372140), and the Postdoctoral Science Foundation of Heilongjiang Province, China (LBH-Z23145).

References

1. Abrar, M., Ajmal, U., Almohaimeed, Z.M., Gui, X., Akram, R., Masroor, R.: Energy efficient UAV-enabled mobile edge computing for IoT devices: a review. IEEE Access **9**, 127779–127798 (2021)
2. Chang, Z., Liu, S., Xiong, X., Cai, Z., Tu, G.: A survey of recent advances in edge-computing-powered artificial intelligence of things. IEEE Internet Things J. **8**(18), 13849–13875 (2021)
3. Dong, C., Hu, S., Chen, X., Wen, W.: Joint optimization with DNN partitioning and resource allocation in mobile edge computing. IEEE Trans. Netw. Serv. Manage. **18**(4), 3973–3986 (2021)
4. Gao, M., Shen, R., Shi, L., Qi, W., Li, J., Li, Y.: Task partitioning and offloading in DNN-task enabled mobile edge computing networks. IEEE Trans. Mob. Comput. **22**(4), 2435–2445 (2023)
5. Kakolyris, A.K., Katsaragakis, M., Masouros, D., Soudris, D.: Road-runner: Collaborative DNN partitioning and offloading on heterogeneous edge systems. In: 2023 Design, Automation & Test in Europe Conference & Exhibition (DATE), pp. 1–6 (2023)
6. Kim, T., Park, H., Jin, Y., Lee, S.S., Lee, S.: Partition placement and resource allocation for multiple DNN-based applications in heterogeneous IoT environments. IEEE Internet Things J. **10**(11), 9836–9848 (2023)
7. Kong, L., et al.: Edge-computing-driven internet of things: a survey. ACM Comput. Surv. **55**(8), 1–41 (2022)
8. Li, C., Chai, L., Jiang, K., Zhang, Y., Liu, J., Wan, S.: DNN partition and offloading strategy with improved particle swarm genetic algorithm in VEC. IEEE Trans. Intell. Veh. 1–11 (2023)
9. Liu, G., et al.: An adaptive DNN inference acceleration framework with end-edge-cloud collaborative computing. Futur. Gener. Comput. Syst. **140**, 422–435 (2023)
10. Liu, J., Pang, Y., Ding, H., Cai, Y., Zhang, H., Fang, Y.: Optimizing IoT energy efficiency on edge (EEE): a cross-layer design in a cognitive mesh network. IEEE Trans. Wireless Commun. **20**(4), 2472–2486 (2021)
11. Luo, Q., Li, C., Luan, T.H., Shi, W.: Minimizing the delay and cost of computation offloading for vehicular edge computing. IEEE Trans. Serv. Comput. **15**(5), 2897–2909 (2022)
12. Nain, G., Pattanaik, K., Sharma, G.: Towards edge computing in intelligent manufacturing: past, present and future. J. Manuf. Syst. **62**, 588–611 (2022)
13. Wang, P., Xu, J., Zhou, M., Albeshri, A.: Budget-constrained optimal deployment of redundant services in edge computing environment. IEEE Internet Things J. **10**(11), 9453–9464 (2023)
14. Zhang, J., Ma, S., Yan, Z., Huang, J.: Joint DNN partitioning and task offloading in mobile edge computing via deep reinforcement learning. J. Cloud Comput. **12**(1), 116 (2023)
15. Zhang, X., Mounesan, M., Debroy, S.: EFFECT-DNN: energy-efficient edge framework for real-time DNN inference. In: 2023 IEEE 24th International Symposium on a World of Wireless, Mobile and Multimedia Networks (WoWMoM), pp. 10–20 (2023)

Crowdsourcing Task Assignment with Category and Mobile Combined Preference Learning

Yue Ma, Xiaofeng Gao[✉], and Guihai Chen

MoE Key Lab of Artificial Intelligence, Department of Computer Science and Engineering, Shanghai Jiao Tong University, Shanghai 200240, China
ma_yue@sjtu.edu.cn, {gao-xf,gchen}@cs.sjtu.edu.cn

Abstract. The rapid growth of mobile networks and widespread mobile device usage has brought mobile crowdsourcing (MCS) for location-sensitive services into focus, particularly for spatial task assignments. However, current research often overlooks the combined impact of users' category and mobile preferences, resulting in suboptimal task assignments. Additionally, the inherent heterogeneity among users is frequently ignored, failing to represent the true dynamics of the MCS ecosystem. To address these gaps, we propose a comprehensive framework, *Task Assignment with User Preference and Heterogeneity*, consisting of two key components: the Category and Mobile Combined Preference (CAMP) model and the Preference-Aware Task Assignment mechanism. The CAMP model predicts users' combined category and mobile preferences using attention mechanisms to extract insights from sparse historical data. In parallel, the Preference-Aware Task Assignment mechanism introduces three novel algorithms that account for user preference and capacity heterogeneity. Extensive experiments on real-world datasets demonstrate the effectiveness and efficiency of the proposed methods.

Keywords: Task assignment · Mobile crowdsourcing · Preference learning · Attention mechanism

1 Introduction

In recent years, mobile crowdsourcing (MCS) has become a key component of the Internet of Things (IoT) [8], enabling users with mobile connectivity to complete a variety of location-based tasks [23]. A central challenge in MCS is *task assignment*—allocating large-scale spatial tasks to users [17]. Task assignment involves matching tasks with distinct features, such as category and location, to users based on factors like serviceable distance and personal preferences. This matching process is managed by the MCS platform, which acts as an intermediary between task publishers and users. Publishers post jobs with specific criteria, and the platform connects them with suitable users based on their historical task records, including category, location, and completion time. There are many existing works on task assignment that attempt to maximize the number of assigned tasks [10], maximize the profit of platform [23], or maximize the utility of platform [9]. The fundamental assumption in all of these works is that users are willing to accomplish the tasks assigned to them. In practice, this assumption may oversimplify users' complex behaviors [5]. Actually, if a user is not engaged, he or she may not finish the assigned task honestly and on time, which cannot ensure the quality of the task result. Furthermore, users' history records are typically scant, the desired category and mobile information are captured only when the user accomplishes a task. As a result, properly profiling user preferences based on sparse records is difficult. We develop an end-to-end model to capture users' dynamic interest patterns to address these difficulties.

In the meantime, the majority of works on task assignment separately evaluate users' category preference and mobile preference [22,24]. Note that traditional assignment models infer user preferences based on previous task-performance patterns or explicit feedback [12]. On the contrary, in MCS, in addition to the metric of the users' category preferences, we must also take into account the mobile information of historical task records, as tasks must be completed in a particular location within a valid time. Users have their own mobile preferences and prefer to complete tasks in the vicinity of their frequent locations. In order to properly assign tasks, it is necessary to consider both the category preference and mobile preference of users.

There are some works to model users' POI (Point-of-Interest) preference for task assignment [4,25]. Nonetheless, when the user's task records are numerous, it is challenging for the model to encode all POIs. Therefore, we apply Geohash [1] to divide the crowdsourcing area into different geo-zones and use users' check-ins in geo-zones as their spatial information, which could significantly alleviate the sparseness of POI information. Moreover, the mobile preference of users is generally periodic [15]. Consequently, only a small subset of previous check-ins are highly relevant to the user's next visit, and the successive check-ins would weaken the signals of related parts. The context of check-in, e.g., temporal information when a user is performing a task, can provide some hints to the way of modeling periodic interest.

In this paper, we propose a *Task Assignment with Category and Mobile Combined Preference* framework for task assignment in MCS. Specifically, the framework contains two components: 1) **C**ategory **a**nd **M**obile Combined **P**reference (CAMP) model; and 2) Preference-Aware Task Assignment. In the CAMP component, we learn contextual features of task records and jointly predict the probability distribution of users' category and mobile preferences. In the task assignment component, we propose three preference-aware task assignment algorithms based on predicting preference and considering user capacity heterogeneity.

2 Related Work

There are numerous investigations on MCS task assignment [17]. Kazemi and Shahabi [6] categorized the MCS based on the publishing mode: *server assigned tasks* (SAT) mode [24] and *worker selected tasks* (WST) mode [4], in which tasks are assigned by the MCS server or chosen by users, respectively. The majority of previous research employed SAT mode, in which the MCS server was responsible for task assignment, but they did not consider whether the task matched users' preferences. Here, our model follows SAT mode and considers user preferences.

Recent research has investigated the variety of user preferences. Mavridis et al. [12] used skills to model user preferences, so there was no ambiguity regarding the user's preference. ETA2 [22] and HCTD [24] inferred user preferences from historical task-performing patterns. ETA2 [22] utilized a novel method of semantic analysis to infer user expertise, and then assigned tasks and estimated truth based on the inferred expertise. HCTD [24] incorporated temporal dynamics in preference inference, which constructed two 3-D tensors about recent and historical task-performing data, as well as two context matrices that provided supplementary information, but assumed that location information had no impact on preference.

Moreover, Ji et al. [4] proposed a task recommendation model based on the prediction of users' mobile trajectories, employing a recurrent neural network to obtain the mobile patterns of users and predict their next destination. Zhu et al. [25] employed a translation-based recommendation (Trans) model to learn mobile preferences from users' historical task-performing data, and they proposed greedy and optimal algorithms based on mobile preferences for task assignment to trade off efficiency and effectiveness. Miao et al. [14] proposed a framework, Task Assignment with Federated Preference Learning, that performed task assignment based on user preferences while maintaining the data decentralized and private in each platform center. However, this work did not consider that the user's long- and short-term preferences are different and simply models one aspect of the user's category preference.

3   Problem Formulation

In this section, we introduce the necessary preliminaries and present the formal definition of our problem.

Definition 1 (Spatial Task). *The spatial task set is denoted by S. Each spatial task $s \in S$ is characterized by $s = \langle c_s, l_s, p_s, e_s \rangle$, where c_s is the task category, l_s is the location where s will be performed, p_s is the publication time, and e_s is the expiration time.*

We use Geohash-5 [1] $GH = \{g_1, g_2, \cdots, g_{|GH|}\}$ to express spatial information as geo-zones, and each task's location only belongs to one geo-zone, i.e., $\forall s \in S, \exists g_i \in GH, l_s \in g_i$. Here we select Geohash-5 to divide the crowdsourcing area, because the size of the geo-zones is suitable for the following experiential datasets, and the length of the geo-zones is about as large as the serviceable distance of users. Besides, the number of geo-zones is significantly smaller than the number of POIs, which can effectively mitigate the data sparseness. In the following, we use users' check-ins in geo-zones as their location records. Moreover, temporal features are represented by day of the week and hourly slot, where we have 7 days in a week $W = \{w_1, w_2, \cdots, w_7\}$ and 24 hourly slots in a day $H = \{h_1, h_2, \cdots, h_{24}\}$. After that, ser u_i's task record at the t-th time step is $R_t^u = (c_t^u, g_t^u, h_t^u, w_t^u)$. In our work, each feature has a unique ID and is represented by a learned embedding.

Definition 2 (User). U *is the user set. A user* $u \in U$ *with* $\langle l_u, sd_u, b_u, R^u \rangle$, *has a location* l_u, *a serviceable distance* sd_u, *a capacity* b_{u_i} *(i.e., u can perform at most b_{u_i} tasks, users' capacities are heterogeneous), and a task record* $R^u = \{R_1^u, R_2^u, \cdots\}$ *ordered by timestamps. The task record at t-th timestamp is* $R_t^u = (c_t^u, g_t^u, h_t^u, w_t^u)$ *including task category, location, hourly slot, and day of the week.*

Definition 3 (Spatial Task Assignment). *Given a set of users U and a set of spatial tasks S, we define A as a spatial task assignment that consists of a set of tuples (u, s), in which a spatial task s is assigned to user u while satisfying the spatio-temporal constraints of both the users and the tasks.*

Definition 4 (Preference-Aware Spatial Task Assignment). *Given a set of online users U with recorded data (i.e., historical task records) and a set of spatial tasks S at the current time instance, our problem is to find a spatial task assignment A that maximizes the number of completed tasks by considering users' preference and heterogeneity, i.e.,*

$$\max |A^S| \tag{1}$$

where $|A^S|$ denotes the number of completed tasks in task assignment A.

4 Methodology

4.1 Framework Overview

In this section, we introduce the details of the proposed framework *Task Assignment with Category and Mobile Combined Preference* (as shown in Fig. 1), which contains a combined preference learning component (in Sect. 4.2) and a task assignment component (in Sect. 4.3). In the preference learning component, we propose an end-to-end model—CAMP, which includes long-term and short-term preference learning with attention mechanisms. In the task assignment component, we design three preference-aware task assignment algorithms to achieve effective task assignment.

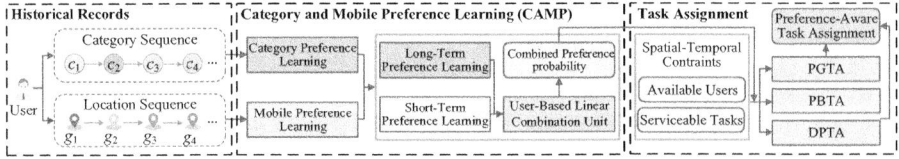

Fig. 1. Framework Overview

4.2 Category and Mobile Combined Preference Learning

Category and Mobile Combined Preference (CAMP) contains category and mobile preference learning two parts, which mainly consist of the feature embedding module, the long-term preference learning module, the short-term preference learning module, and the user-based linear fusion unit, respectively.

The Feature Embedding. For the task record $R^u = \{R_1^u, R_2^u, \cdots\}$ of user u, we learn the latent feature of user u and the contextual feature $(c_t^u, g_t^u, h_t^u, w_t^u)$ of every record R_t^u. For each timestamp t, the original information is continuous, which is difficult to embed. Therefore, we map the raw timestamps into discrete hours. Thus, each hour h_t^u is represented as a one-hot 24-dimensional vector, where the non-zero entry denotes the hour index. Similarly, user ID u, category c_i, geo-zone g_i, and day of week w_i are also represented as one-hot vectors, where the non-zero entry denotes the index. Intuitively, the sparsity increases with the user number, categories, geo-zones, and time slots, which will degrade the prediction model's efficiency. Therefore, we transform them into D^u, D^c, D^g, D^h, and D^w dimensional dense vectors: $\boldsymbol{v}^u$, $\boldsymbol{v}^c$, $\boldsymbol{v}^g$, $\boldsymbol{v}^h$, and $\boldsymbol{v}^w$, respectively.

The Long-Term Preference Learning. The long-term task record $LR^u = \{R_1^u, R_2^u, \cdots, R_L^u\}$ of a user u reflects the general task preference of the user, so we utilize it to learn the long-term preference. Here, we apply the attention mechanism by similarity computation between the latent vectors of user u and category/geo-zone to learn the importance of each category/geo-zone. To learn the latent vector of each category/geo-zone, we consider the contextual information, such as the hourly slot h_i and day of the week w_i. Meanwhile, the importance of each category/geo-zone is calculated with attention mechanisms. The long-term preference of u is designed as the weighted summarization of the concatenated vectors of categories/geo-zones in the long-term task record.

To learn the high-level representations of the categories in the long-term sequence of each user, we utilize the nonlinear transformation to capture the latent vector for each category/geo-zone. Furthermore, we consider the context information, such as the day of the week and the hourly slot. Here, the fusion feature of each category is calculated as follows:

$$e_t^c = ReLU(\boldsymbol{W}_c[\boldsymbol{v}_t^c; \boldsymbol{v}_t^h; \boldsymbol{v}_t^w] + \boldsymbol{b}_c) \tag{2}$$

where $\boldsymbol{W}_c$ and $\boldsymbol{b}_c$ are the weights and the corresponding bias parameters. The fused feature e_t^g of each geo-zone is calculated similarly to e_t^c in Eq. (2).

To learn the long-term preferences of users, we leverage the attention mechanism to calculate the summarization of contextual features of categories/geo-zones in the long-term task record. We use the embeddings of users learned by the embedding layer to measure the similarity between users' preferences and the latent vectors of task records. In this way, we can learn the user's long-term preference by fusing the latent vectors of categories/geo-zones with different weights. Here, the importance of each category/geo-zone is calculated as the normalized similarity between the latent vector of user u and the categories/geo-zones. Taking the category-level sequence as an example, the long-term category representation of user u is as follows:

$$a_t^c = \frac{\exp(\boldsymbol{u}^\top)e_t^c}{\sum_t \exp(\boldsymbol{u}^\top)e_t^c}, \boldsymbol{u}_l^c = \sum_t a_t[\boldsymbol{v}_t^c; \boldsymbol{v}_t^h; \boldsymbol{v}_t^w] \qquad (3)$$

where $[\boldsymbol{v}_t^t; \boldsymbol{v}_t^h; \boldsymbol{v}_t^w]$ represents the concatenation of embedding vectors of the tuple (c_t^u, h_t^u, w_t^u) of each category, a_i^c denotes the importance of each category, and $\boldsymbol{u}_l^c$ is the final representation of the long-term category preference of user u. Following that, $\boldsymbol{u}_l^c$ is fed into a fully connected layer to calculate the long-term category preference probability p_{lc}^u. Likewise, we could get the long-term mobile preference probability p_{lg}^u.

The Short-Term Preference Learning. We leverage a Transformer encoder block and a LSTM block to learn the short-term preferences of users. The input sequences contain user ID, category/geo-zone, and time information.

Firstly, for the short-term task record $SR^u = \{R_1^u, R_2^u, \cdots, R_S^u\}$ of user u, the latent vectors of user u and the tuple (c_t^u, g_t^u, h_t^u) of every record R_t^u are represented by the feature embedding. For short-term preference learning, only hourly patterns of user behavior are considered, not daily patterns.

To better learn the short-term preferences of different users, we combine the embeddings of users and time as context information for category-level and location-level sequences. After that, the combined vectors of categories $[\boldsymbol{v}_t^c; \boldsymbol{v}^u; \boldsymbol{v}_t^h]$ and geo-zones $[\boldsymbol{v}_t^g; \boldsymbol{v}^u; \boldsymbol{v}_t^h]$ are fed into the self-attention mechanism of Transformer encoder [18] to learn the multi-perspective relations of the short-term sequences with contextual information. The calculation of the category-level sequence is defined as follows:

$$\boldsymbol{x}_t^c = [\boldsymbol{v}_t^c; \boldsymbol{v}^u; \boldsymbol{v}_t^h], \boldsymbol{q}_t^c = \text{Transformer}(\boldsymbol{x}_t^c) \qquad (4)$$

where Transformer is a Transformer encoder block, and $\boldsymbol{q}_t^c$ is the new representation for the user's category record at t. Similarly, we could get the presentation $\boldsymbol{q}_t^g$ for location records.

Following that, the LSTM model [3] to learn the category-level and location-level preferences. First, we concatenate the original embedding $\boldsymbol{x}_t^c$ and the output of the Transformer encoder $\boldsymbol{q}_t^c$ to retain more information hidden in the original embeddings. Following that, we input the vectors into the basic LSTM block. By taking the category-level sequence as an example, we model user short-term category preference as follows:

$$\boldsymbol{o}_t^c = [\boldsymbol{x}_t^c; \boldsymbol{q}_t^c], \boldsymbol{u}_s^c = \text{LSTM}([\boldsymbol{o}_1^c, \cdots, \boldsymbol{o}_S^c]) \qquad (5)$$

where $\boldsymbol{u}_s^c$ is the final output of LSTM. Moreover, the output vectors are fed into a fully connected layer to obtain the short-term category preference $\boldsymbol{p}_{sc}^u$ and mobile preference $\boldsymbol{p}_{sg}^u$.

User-Based Linear Fusion Unit. In real-world scenarios, when selecting the next task, different users show different dependencies on long-term and short-term preferences. However, many researchers in the literature always neglect this important factor. Here, we integrate the results of long- and short-term preference learning modules with a user-based linear fusion unit in the output layer. Specifically, to learn the personalized preferences for different users, we learn the personalized weights over long- and short-term modules for different users. We compute the preference score of the next category by the linear combination of $\boldsymbol{p}_{lc}^u$ and $\boldsymbol{p}_{sc}^u$ as follows:

$$\hat{\boldsymbol{p}}_c^u = \text{softmax}(\alpha^u \cdot \boldsymbol{p}_{lc}^u + (1-\alpha^u) \cdot \boldsymbol{p}_{sc}^u) \qquad (6)$$

where $\boldsymbol{p}_{lc}^u$ represents the output for the next category obtained from the long-term preference learning. $\boldsymbol{p}_{sc}^u$ is the output of the category-level short-term preference learning, respectively. α^u is the specific weight for user u that will be learned by our model. Similarly, $\hat{\boldsymbol{p}}_g^u$ can be obtained. $\hat{\boldsymbol{p}}_c^u$ and $\hat{\boldsymbol{p}}_g^u$ would be used as the preference probabilities for tasks in the following task assignment stage.

Model Optimization. So far, we have introduced our solutions to capture users' preferences at different levels. The loss function is defined as the cross-entropy of the prediction and the ground truth. The loss of task category prediction is:

$$\mathcal{L}_{cat} = -\sum_{i=1}^{|C|} p_c^i \log(\hat{p}_c^i) + (1-p_c^i)\log(1-\hat{p}_c^i) \qquad (7)$$

where $|C|$ is the number of all category candidates, p_c^i is the variable indicating whether the task category is c_i, and $\hat{p}_c^i$ is the probability for the category candidate. Likewise, we could get the loss of all geo-zones $\mathcal{L}_{geo}$.

The whole loss is formulated as the loss for category and geo-zone attributes:

$$\mathcal{L} = \mathcal{L}_{cat} + \mathcal{L}_{geo} + \lambda\|\Theta\|^2 \qquad (8)$$

where λ denotes the L_2 regularization coefficient.

Category and Mobile Combined Preference Probability. According to Eq. (6), we could get $\hat{\boldsymbol{p}}_c^u$ and $\hat{\boldsymbol{p}}_g^u$ by the CAMP model, which are u's category and mobile preference probabilities, respectively. Following that, we could get u's preference probability of task s with category c_s and location l_s ($l_s \in g_s$), i.e.,

$$p(u,s) = \hat{\boldsymbol{p}}_c^u(c_s) + \hat{\boldsymbol{p}}_g^u(g_s) \qquad (9)$$

4.3 Preference-Aware Task Assignment

In this section, we first define the available user set for each task and the serviceable task set for each user. Due to users' capacity heterogeneity, we state the Preference-Aware Spatial Task Assignment is a special case for Maximum Weighted b-Matching. Moreover, we propose three preference-aware task assignment algorithms that utilize the preference score of each task by CAMP model.

Problem Redefinition. Due to the constraints of users' serviceable distances and tasks' valid time, we should filter users and tasks based on constraints.

Definition 5 (Available User Set and Serviceable Task Set) *Given a user set U and a task set S, the available user set for s and the serviceable task set for u are denoted as $AU(s)$ and $ST(u)$, respectively. $AU(s)$ ($\forall u \in AU(s), s \in S$) and $RT(u)$ ($\forall s \in ST(u), u \in U$) must satisfy the following two conditions:*

(1) $d(l_u, l_s) < sd_u$, and
(2) $t_{now} + d(l_u, l_s)/sp_u < e_s$, where $d(l_u, l_s)$ is the distance between l_u and l_s.

Definition 6 (Weighted b-Matching). *Given a graph $G = (V, E)$ and a function $b(\cdot)$ that maps each vertex to a natural number, a b-matching is a subset of edges M such that at most $b(v)$ edges in M are incident on each vertex v. An edge in M is matched, and an edge not in M is unmatched. If the edges have weights w, then the weight of a b-matching M is the sum of the weights of the matched edges, and the maximum weighted b-matching problem seeks to compute a b-matching M with maximum weight.*

Lemma 1. *Preference-Aware Spatial Task Assignment is a special case for Maximum Weighted b-Matching.*

The Preference-Aware Spatial Task Assignment problem is now converted into a special case of the Maximum Weight b-Matching problem, and then we could apply GREEDY algorithm [13] and b-SUITOR algorithm [7] to solve it.

Preference-Aware Greedy Task Assignment (PGTA) Algorithm. At first, the PGTA algorithm sorts edges in a non-increasing order of weights. During each iteration, the algorithm greedily chooses the edge e with the largest weight. If $M + e$ is a b-matching, add e to M. Finally, we can obtain the final b-matching M. The GREEDY algorithm is a 1/2-approximation algorithm for the maximum weight b-matching problem [13]. The running time of the PBTA algorithm is $O(|S||U|\log(|S||U|))$.

Preference-Aware b-Suitor Task Assignment (PBTA) Algorithm. The b-SUITOR algorithm, designed by Khan et al. [7], computes a 1/2-approximate weighted b-matching; indeed, it computes a matching identical to the one obtained by the GREEDY algorithm, provided weight ties are consistently broken in both algorithms. This algorithm is a generalization of the SUITOR algorithm [11] based on proposals, similar to the algorithms for the stable marriage problem and its variations (here the stable fixtures problem). Vertices can propose to their heaviest neighbors, and these proposals may be reciprocated or annulled by other vertices. Two vertices are matched when they propose to each other.

The original b-SUITOR algorithm uses $db(v)$ to track the times of v's proposal annulled by a neighbor and updates $b(v)$ to be $db(v)$ for the next iteration. In order to reduce the computation of updating, we use $r(v)$ to track the times of active proposals that v has made, the modified algorithm still maintains the

Algorithm 1: Preference-Aware b-SUITOR Task Assignment (PBTA)

Input: Graph $G = (V = V^U \cup V^S, E, w, b)$
Output: A b-matching M

1    $Q \leftarrow V;\ Q' \leftarrow \emptyset;\ P \leftarrow \emptyset;\ T \leftarrow \emptyset;\ r \leftarrow 0;$ // Initialize
2   **while** $Q \neq \emptyset$ **do**
3   **for** *each vertex $v \in Q$ in any order* **do**
4   **while** $r(v) < b(v)$ **do**
5             $x = \arg\max_{a \in N(v) \setminus T(v)} \{w(v,a) : w(v,a) > w(v, P(v).last)\};$
6   **if** $x \neq$ NULL **then**
7                $y = P(x).last;$ // The lowest suitor
8   **if** $y \neq$ NULL **then**
9                    $P(x).romove(y);\ Q' = Q' \cup y;\ r(y) = r(y) - 1;$ // Annul proposal
10             $P(x).insert(v);\ T(u).insert(x);$ // v makes a proposal to x
11             $r(v) = r(v) + 1;$ // The times of active proposals that v has made
12   **else**
13   break;   // There is no eligible neighbor for v
14      $Q = Q';\ Q' = \emptyset;$
15 Get the final b-matching M by P;
16 **return** M;

same result. The modified b-SUITOR algorithm is named the Preference-Aware b-SUITOR Task Assignment (PBTA) Algorithm as shown in Algorithm 1.

The PBTA algorithm maintains a priority queue P to track the active proposals. The queue $P(v)$ consists of the suitors of a vertex v, i.e., those neighbors of v currently have an active proposal to v. The operation $P(v).insert(x)$ adds a vertex x to $P(v)$, and $P(v).remove(x)$ removes it. The array $T(v)$ contains the vertices that v has proposed. We keep track of the lowest weight of a proposal received by a vertex v (made by a suitor of v) in $P(v).last$. If v has received fewer than $b(v)$ proposals, this value is NULL.

During the iteration, it collects vertices whose proposals are annulled in a set Q' that would be processed in the next iteration. For each vertex $v \in Q$, while $r(v)$ is smaller than $b(v)$ and $N(v)$ has not been exhaustively searched, the algorithm finds *eligible* neighbors to propose to. A neighbor x is an *eligible* neighbor of v if it holds fewer than $b(x)$ proposals, or v can beat the lowest suitor $P(x).last$. If v cannot beat this suitor, it considers its next heaviest neighbor. But if x has fewer than $b(x)$ proposals, or if v can beat the lowest offer that x has, then v proposes to x and becomes a suitor of x. In the latter case, v annuls the lowest-weight proposal of x, say from a vertex y, and y has to make another proposal in the next iteration. $P(x).last$ is also updated. After each vertex $v \in Q$ is processed, Q and Q' are updated for the next iteration. The running time of the PBTA algorithm is $O(|S||U|\log\beta)$, where $\beta = \max_{u \in U} b_u$.

Distance-Based Preference-Aware Task Assignment (DPTA) Algorithm. Users are more likely to perform nearby tasks [16,24], and travel cost is a critical factor when users choose which tasks to perform. We compute the travel cost between a user u and a task s, denoted as $d(l_u, l_s)$. Here, we propose a Distance-based Preference-Aware Task Assignment (DPTA) algorithm that uses travel costs to discount user-task preference. Specifically, DPTA modifies PBTA by resetting the weight $w(v^u, v^s)$ of each edge (v^u, v^s) to $f(u,s) \cdot p(u,s)$, where $f(u,s) = 1 - \min\{1, d(l_u, l_s)/sd_u\}$.

5 Experiments

5.1 Datasets and Experiment Settings

We conduct evaluations on the real-world datasets crawled from Foursquare [21], which are widely used in the MSC task assignment [24,25]. The public Foursquare check-in datasets were collected from New York City (NYC) and Tokyo (TKY). The check-in records are collected from April 2012 to February 2013. Each record contains a user ID, POI ID, venue category name, GPS, and timestamp. In the following experiments, for each user, we set the records in chronological order based on the timestamp of each record. Since there are too many venue categories, 417 [21], we manually merge these subcategories into 10 categories and use them to represent the task categories. To ensure a fair comparison, we filter out users with less than 20 records. Following that, we take the first 80% check-ins as the training set, and the latter 20% as the test set.

The key parameters in our model include: the embedding dimensions of latent vectors for user D^u, category D^c, geo-zone D^g, day of week D^w, and hourly slot D^h. We set the dimensions as follows: $D^u = 32$, $D^c = 64$, $D^g = 64$, $D^h = 24$, and $D^w = 8$. The batch size is set to 100, the learning rate is set to 0.0001, and the dropout rate is set to 0.5. At the same time, the l_2 penalty is set to 10^{-5} to alleviate overfitting. The length of the short-term sequence is set to 20.

5.2 Experiments on Category Preference Learning

Evaluation Methods. The methods are as follows:

1) TD: TD [24] models users' preferences by Tensor decomposition approach.
2) HCTD: HCTD [24] models users' temporal preferences by History-based Context-aware Tensor Decomposition.
3) CAMP: The category preference learning part of CAMP is detailed in Sect. 4.2.

Metrics. To evaluate the accuracy of category preference learning, we use P@K (Precision, $K \in \{1,2,3\}$) as the evaluation metrics. This metric counts the proportion of times when the categories of ground-truth tasks are ranked among the top-K predictions.

Table 1. Category Preference Learning Performance

Model	Dataset					
	Foursquare-NYC			Foursquare-TKY		
	P@1	P@2	P@3	P@1	P@2	P@3
TD	0.3617	0.5532	0.6689	0.5026	0.6520	0.7317
HCTD	0.3624	0.5799	0.7197	0.5015	0.7073	0.8219
CAMP	**0.3722**	**0.5975**	**0.7341**	**0.5109**	**0.7193**	**0.8432**

Results. The performance comparison between our method and the benchmarks is shown in Table 1. We can observe that the three metrics of CAMP are superior to the two baselines, TD and HCTD. As we can see, our method CAMP achieves the best performance on category preference learning in terms of P@1, P@2, and P@3, which demonstrates the efficacy and validity of CAMP for category preference learning. Moreover, the accuracy of Foursquare-TKY is much higher than that of Foursquare-NYC among all models, so we conjecture that Tokyo users' category preferences have stronger regularities than New York users.

5.3 Experiments on Mobile Preference Learning

Evaluation Methods. The methods are as follows:

1) LSTM: LSTM [3] applies recurrent neural network (RNN) to learn users' sequential behaviors based on check-in location sequences.
2) DeepMove: DeepMove [2] learns user preference using RNNs for historical sequence and current sequence.
3) PLSPL: PLSPL [20] uses user-based attention and LSTMs for long- and short-term interests, respectively.
4) CAMP: The mobile preference learning part of CAMP is detailed in Sect. 4.2.

Results. The performance comparison between our method and the benchmarks is shown in Table 2. Among the baseline models, LSTM and Transformer have the worst performances because they do not incorporate the context information. For Foursquare-NYC and Foursquare-TKY, our CAMP model is better

Table 2. Mobile Preference Learning Performance

Model	Dataset					
	Foursquare-NYC			Foursquare-TKY		
	P@1	P@2	P@3	P@1	P@2	P@3
LSTM	0.4784	0.6821	0.7757	0.4529	0.6345	0.7251
DeepMove	0.4922	0.6911	0.7875	0.4652	0.6440	0.7353
PLSPL	0.4955	0.6981	0.7943	0.4750	0.6566	0.7449
CAMP	**0.4973**	**0.6995**	**0.7935**	**0.4769**	**0.6582**	**0.7464**

Table 3. Parameter Settings

Parameter	Values
$|S|$	500, 1000, 1500, **2000**
$|U|$	500, **1000**, 1500, 2000
$sd\ (km)$	1, 2, **3**, 4, 5
b	1, **2**, 3, 4, 5

than other models. DeepMove and PLSPL are the best two baselines, and similarly to CAMP, both of them extract information from long-term and short-term sequences separately. Due to the Transformer encoder block learning the dependencies between vectors and extracting transition patterns, CAMP performs marginally better than PLSPL and DeepMove.

5.4 Experiments on Task Assignment

Here we study the performance of task assignments only on Foursquare-TKY, due to space limitations. Table 3 shows our parameter settings, where the default values of parameters are in bold.

Evaluation Methods. We study the following algorithms.

1) PAR-Greedy [19]: The task assignment algorithm selects user-task pairs with the maximum utility increase.
2) PTA [24]: The task assignment algorithm with users' temporal preferences calculated by the HCTD method.
3) PGTA: Greedy algorithm with users' preference calculated by CAMP model.
4) PBTA: PBTA algorithm with users' preferences calculated by CAMP model.
5) PBTA_C: PBTA considers users' category preferences only.
6) PBTA_M: PBTA considers users' mobile preferences only.
7) DPTA: Modifies PBTA by resetting the edge weights with travel costs.

Metrics. The three main metrics are compared among the above algorithms, i.e., the number of assigned tasks, the assignment success number, and the mean distance cost. The assignment success number refers to how many tasks a user completes with the same category in the subsequent three tasks [24]. The mean distance cost is the average distance between the user and the assigned tasks.

Effect of $|S|$. First, we study the effect of the number of tasks $|S|$, as shown in Fig. 2. With the increase of $|S|$, a user can access more available and interested tasks with less competition, so both the number of assigned tasks and the assignment success number show an increased trend. In Fig. 2(a), the number of assigned tasks assigned by b-Suitor methods is slightly higher than that of greedy-based methods, which could find better assignment results. As depicted in Fig. 2(b), the assignment success numbers of PAR-Greedy and PBTA_M are relatively low, because they only consider mobile information. Meanwhile, PBTA performs better than PBTA_C and PBTA_M in terms of assignment success numbers, indicating that ignorance of the combined action of two part preferences would negatively impact assignment efficiency. Moreover, DPTA exhibits obvious advantages on the assignment success number and the mean distance cost in Fig. 2(b)- 2(c).

Effect of $|U|$. Next, we evaluate the effect of user number $|U|$. In Fig. 3(a), the number of assigned tasks increases with the increase of $|U|$. In Fig. 3(b), the

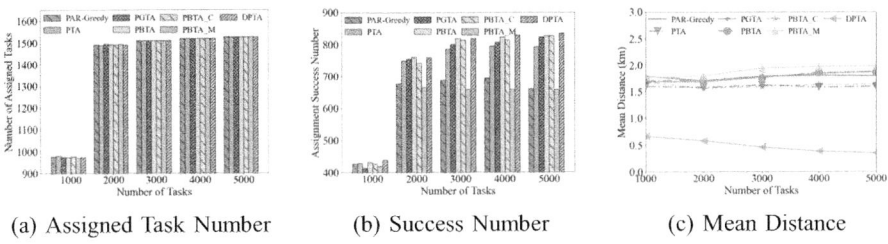

Fig. 2. Performance of Task Assignment: Effect of Number of Tasks $|S|$

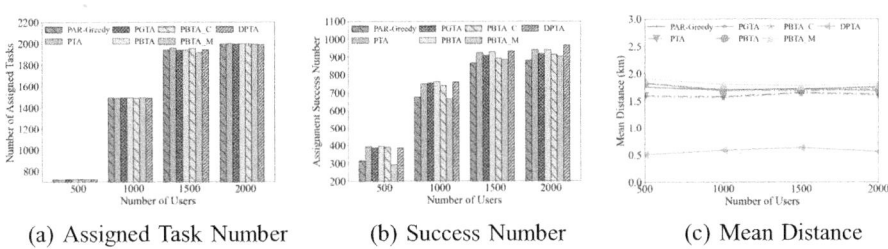

Fig. 3. Performance of Task Assignment: Effect of Number of Users $|U|$

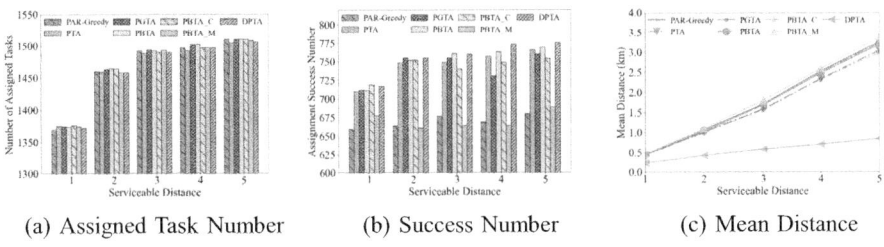

Fig. 4. Performance of Task Assignment: Effect of Serviceable Distance sd

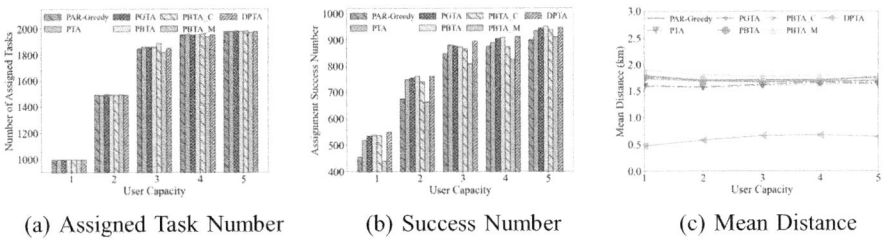

Fig. 5. Performance of Task Assignment: Effect of User Capacity b

assignment success number decreases as the number of users increases because all algorithms prioritize improving the assignment number, and all category preference based algorithms maintain a high assignment success number. Moreover, PBTA and DPTA maintain the highest assignment success numbers compared with baselines. In Fig. 3(c), the mean distance cost shows a slow downward trend, as the number of users increases. Besides, DPTA shows distinctive advantages in terms of the mean distance cost.

Effect of sd**.** We study the effect of users' serviceable distance sd. As shown in Fig. 4(a), the number of assigned tasks increases as sd increases, since users are more likely to be assigned their available tasks. In Fig. 4(b), when sd increases, the assignment success number rises slowly. Moreover, the performance of DPTA is best on assignment success numbers in most cases. In Fig. 4(c), as sd increases, the mean distance cost of each method shows a clear upward trend, because users can choose tasks that are farther away but have higher preference scores.

Effect of b**.** We finally evaluate the effect of the capacity b of users. As shown in Fig. 5(a), the number of assigned tasks increases as b increases, since users could choose more available tasks with a larger b. According to Fig. 5(b), when b increases, the assignment success numbers of all methods significantly increase. In Fig. 5(c), as b increases, the mean distance cost shows a slow downward trend except for DPTA. Furthermore, DPTA significantly outperforms other baselines in terms of assignment success number and mean distance cost, demonstrating the effectiveness of our proposed approach.

6 Conclusion

In this paper, we address the *Preference-Aware Spatial Task Assignment* in MCS, optimizing task assignment by considering user preferences. We propose a framework, *Task Assignment with Category and Mobile Combined Preference*, consisting of two components: the CAMP model and Preference-Aware Task Assignment. The CAMP model predicts users' category and mobile preferences by leveraging both long- and short-term data. The task assignment component introduces three algorithms—PGTA, PBTA, and DPTA—that prioritize users with higher preference scores while considering capacity heterogeneity. Experiments on real datasets demonstrate the effectiveness of our approach.

Acknowledgment. This work was supported by the National Natural Science Foundation of China [U23A20309, 62272302, 62172276, 62372296]; Shanghai Municipal Science and Technology Major Project [2021SHZDZX0102]; and CCF-DiDi GAIA Collaborative Research Funds for Young Scholars [202404].

References

1. Geohash (2008). https://web.archive.org/web/20080305102941/, http://blog.labix.org/2008/02/26/geohashorg-is-public/
2. Feng, J., et al.: Deepmove: predicting human mobility with attentional recurrent networks. In: WWW, pp. 1459–1468 (2018)
3. Hochreiter, S., Schmidhuber, J.: Long short-term memory. Neural Comput. **9**(8), 1735–1780 (1997)
4. Ji, Y., Mu, C., Qiu, X., Chen, Y.: A task recommendation model in mobile crowdsourcing. In: WCMC, pp. 1–12 (2022)
5. Karaliopoulos, M., Koutsopoulos, I., Titsias, M.: First learn then earn: optimizing mobile crowdsensing campaigns through data-driven user profiling. In: MobiHoc, pp. 271–280 (2016)
6. Kazemi, L., Shahabi, C.: Geocrowd: enabling query answering with spatial crowdsourcing. In: SIGSPATIAL, pp. 189–198 (2012)
7. Khan, A., et al.: Efficient approximation algorithms for weighted b-matching. SISC **38**(5), S593–S619 (2016)
8. Kong, X., Liu, X., Jedari, B., Li, M., Wan, L., Xia, F.: Mobile crowdsourcing in smart cities: technologies, applications, and future challenges. IoT-J **6**(5), 8095–8113 (2019)
9. Li, Y., Li, H., Huang, X., Xu, J., Han, Y., Xu, M.: Utility-aware dynamic ridesharing in spatial crowdsourcing. TMC **23**(2), 1066–1079 (2024)
10. Ma, Y., Gao, X., Bhatti, S.S., Chen, G.: Clustering based priority queue algorithm for spatial task assignment in crowdsourcing. TSC **17**(2), 452–465 (2024)
11. Manne, F., Halappanavar, M.: New effective multithreaded matching algorithms. In: IPDPS, pp. 519–528 (2014)
12. Mavridis, P., Gross-Amblard, D., Miklós, Z.: Using hierarchical skills for optimized task assignment in knowledge-intensive crowdsourcing. In: WWW, pp. 843–853 (2016)
13. Mestre, J.: Greedy in approximation algorithms. In: Azar, Y., Erlebach, T. (eds.) ESA 2006. LNCS, vol. 4168, pp. 528–539. Springer, Heidelberg (2006). https://doi.org/10.1007/11841036_48
14. Miao, H., et al.: Task assignment with efficient federated preference learning in spatial crowdsourcing. TKDE **36**(4), 1800–1814 (2024)
15. Rahmani, H.A., Aliannejadi, M., Baratchi, M., Crestani, F.: A systematic analysis on the impact of contextual information on point-of-interest recommendation. TOIS **40**(4), 1–35 (2022)
16. To, H., Ghinita, G., Shahabi, C.: A framework for protecting worker location privacy in spatial crowdsourcing. Proc. VLDB Endow. **7**(10), 919–930 (2014)
17. Tong, Y., Zhou, Z., Zeng, Y., Chen, L., Shahabi, C.: Spatial crowdsourcing: a survey. VLDBJ **29**(1), 217–250 (2020)
18. Vaswani, A., et al.: Attention is all you need. In: NIPS, pp. 6000–6010 (2017)
19. Wang, J., et al.: Hytasker: hybrid task allocation in mobile crowd sensing. TMC **19**(3), 598–611 (2019)
20. Wu, Y., Li, K., Zhao, G., Qian, X.: Personalized long-and short-term preference learning for next poi recommendation. TKDE **34**(4), 1944–1957 (2022)
21. Yang, D., Zhang, D., Zheng, V.W., Yu, Z.: Modeling user activity preference by leveraging user spatial temporal characteristics in LBSNs. TSMC **45**(1), 129–142 (2015)

22. Zhang, X., Wu, Y., Huang, L., Ji, H., Cao, G.: Expertise-aware truth analysis and task allocation in mobile crowdsourcing. TMC **20**(3), 1001–1016 (2019)
23. Zhao, Y., et al.: Profit optimization in spatial crowdsourcing: effectiveness and efficiency. TKDE **35**(8), 8386–8401 (2023)
24. Zhao, Y., Zheng, K., Yin, H., Liu, G., Fang, J., Zhou, X.: Preference-aware task assignment in spatial crowdsourcing: from individuals to groups. TKDE **34**(7), 3461–3477 (2022)
25. Zhu, C., Cui, Y., Zhao, Y., Zheng, K.: Task assignment with spatio-temporal recommendation in spatial crowdsourcing. In: APWeb-WAIM, pp. 264–279 (2022)

Federated Learning as a Service for Hierarchical Edge Networks with Heterogeneous Models

Wentao Gao[1(✉)], Omid Tavallaie[1,2], Shuaijun Chen[1], and Albert Zomaya[1]

[1] School of Computer Science, The University of Sydney, Sydney, Australia
{wentao.gao,shuaijun.chen,albert.zomaya}@sydney.edu.au
[2] Department of Engineering Science, University of Oxford, Oxford, UK
omid.tavallaie@eng.ox.ac.uk

Abstract. Federated learning (FL) is a distributed Machine Learning (ML) framework that is capable of training a new global model by aggregating clients' locally trained models without sharing users' original data. Federated learning as a service (FLaaS) offers a privacy-preserving approach for training machine learning models on devices with various computational resources. Most proposed FL-based methods train the same model in all client devices regardless of their computational resources. However, in practical Internet of Things (IoT) scenarios, IoT devices with limited computational resources may not be capable of training models that client devices with greater hardware performance hosted. Most of the existing FL frameworks that aim to solve the problem of aggregating heterogeneous models are designed for Independent and Identical Distributed (IID) data, which may make it hard to reach the target algorithm performance when encountering non-IID scenarios. To address these problems in hierarchical networks, in this paper, we propose a heterogeneous aggregation framework for hierarchical edge systems called HAF-Edge. In our proposed framework, we introduce a communication-efficient model aggregation method designed for FL systems with two-level model aggregations running at the edge and cloud levels. This approach enhances the convergence rate of the global model by leveraging selective knowledge transfer during the aggregation of heterogeneous models. To the best of our knowledge, this work is pioneering in addressing the problem of aggregating heterogeneous models within hierarchical FL systems spanning IoT, edge, and cloud environments. We conducted extensive experiments to validate the performance of our proposed method. The evaluation results demonstrate that HAF-Edge significantly outperforms state-of-the-art methods.

Keywords: Federated Learning as a Service (FLaaS) · Model Heterogeneity · Edge Computing · IoT Networks

1 Introduction

Federated learning (FL) [21] is a distributed learning algorithm designed for privacy-aware applications. Without compromising the user's privacy, FL aggregates trained local models to build a new global model [23]. In each training round, all client devices receive the global model from the cloud server, train it using local data, and send the updated model back to the server for building a new global model in the aggregation process (Fig. 1). Compared with traditional centralized training, FL alleviates concerns about direct data violation [12], as the client's original data is never transmitted to the server in the training process. In recent years, Machine Learning as a Service (MLaaS) has gained widespread attention, proved by the increasing demand for cloud-based machine learning platforms and large-scale analytics across various industries [28]. However, the concerns of widely collecting privacy data have also grown [8]. FL, as a decentralized machine learning, has the capability to face the challenges of privacy concerns. In 2020, Nicolas et al. proposed Federated Learning as a Service (FLaaS) for permission and privacy management [13]. In recent years, FL has been applied in various applications such as healthcare systems [2], prediction maintenance for Internet of Things (IoT) devices [7], and edge networks [20,24].

Data heterogeneity among client devices is one of the major challenges in FL [17]. In practical FL scenarios, the client's data is highly dependent on user behavior. As a result, training data on clients' devices may have significantly different distributions [10]. This phenomenon is called non-Independent and Identical (non-IID) distributed data, which has a significant impact on the global model's performance [4,18]. Device heterogeneity in the computational hierarchy is another existing problem of FL. Most proposed FL frameworks require all participants to use the same model architecture regardless of their computational resources. However, in practical FL scenarios such as Google Gboard [30], mobile clients could have various hardware configurations [14]. In this setting, running the same model on all client devices is challenging, if it is not impossible. Devices with low computational resources are incapable of finishing the training process on time [14], which increases the average time for a training round as the server can perform the model aggregation when it receives trained models from all devices.

To address these research problems, various methods have been proposed to aggregate heterogeneous models within conventional Federated Learning (FL) systems [22]. However, most of these methods cannot reach the target performance when encountering non-IID data [17]. In this paper, we introduce an aggregation method for heterogeneous models in three-level hierarchical FL frameworks (IoT/edge/cloud) called **HAF-Edge**. In this computational hierarchy, IoT devices are clustered based on some specific requirements (data/hardware configurations), such as the facilities in a smart city or industry of IoT. Each cluster is connected to an edge server that receives the trained models and aggregates them to create an edge-aggregated model. All edge servers are connected to a cloud server that receives edge-aggregated models with different structures. The cloud server performs the second level of aggregation by using knowledge sharing and based on similarity in structures of different models to build a global model for each edge server. HAF-Edge not only leverages the advantages of hierarchical federated learning, potentially reducing the need for

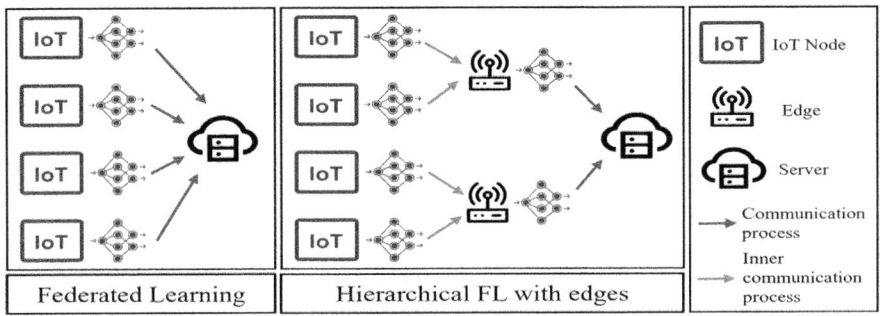

Fig. 1. Comparison between vanilla FL and Hierarchical FL

the Internet to aggregate trained IoT models at the edge [25], but also addresses the challenge of aggregating edge models with different settings at the cloud level. By connecting a cluster of IoT nodes with the same setting to an edge server using local communication technologies (e.g., Bluetooth or Zigbee), the need for using the Internet in creating edge-aggregated models is eliminated [25] (reduces communication cost). HAF-Edge addresses the challenge of **aggregating heterogeneous models at the cloud by adopting a strategy called MaxCommon** [27] in hierarchical edge networks. At the cloud level, we extract parts of the knowledge from different model settings to enhance the global model's aggregation process. Our experimental results demonstrate that **models trained with IID data tend to have a greater distance from the global model compared to scenarios where non-IID data is used.** Based on this observation, we propose a distance-based weighting aggregation approach and apply it to the aggregation process at the edge level to improve performance for applications with non-IID data. The main contributions of our work are summarized as follows:

- 1) To the best of our knowledge, HAF-Edge is the first attempt to resolve the challenge of aggregating heterogeneous models in hierarchical federated learning architecture with two levels of aggregations (edge and the cloud).
- 2) A distance-based weighting aggregation approach is proposed, which makes HAF-Edge enables to achieve a better performance facing non-IID data compared to the state-of-the-art FL frameworks.
- 3) We perform extensive sets of experiments on two public datasets (MNIST [15] and FMNIST [29]). The evaluation results show that HAF-Edge achieved a better performance compared to state-of-the-art methods.

2 Related Works

FL [21] is a decentralized model training method that was proposed for training neural networks in a distributed fashion without sharing the user's data.

However, the existence of non-IID data among client devices in practical FL scenarios is one of the most important problems that reduces the performance of the global model [32]. In vanilla FedAvg, only data volume is considered in the aggregation process. As a result, in practical FL scenarios with non-IID data, regardless of data distribution, the same weighting coefficient is considered for trained models of two client devices that had data with the same size but with completely different labels. Broadly aggregating the models trained with low-quality data can have a serious impact on the performance of the global model in FL [6]. Some proposed methods start to shift the focus to the quality of client data or models. FAIR proposed in [6] improves the performance of the global model by filtering the local models with low quality.

In practical IoT FL scenarios, the expected local model architecture may differ among client devices due to heterogeneous hardware configurations, tasks, and personal demands [11,17,31]. To address these challenges, FedMD [16] has been proposed based on knowledge distillation [9]. However, in the methods using knowledge distillation, a public dataset is created, which can compromise client data privacy. In contrast to knowledge distillation, some methods aggregate common layers of heterogeneous models to share learned features among participants, such as MaxCommon [27] and Rank-Based Lora Aggregation [5]. MaxCommon targets heterogeneous model architectures and refines the aggregation of local updates to specific layers rather than entire models. By aggregating as many common layers as possible from different clients' models, MaxCommon maximizes knowledge sharing. The method employs data quantity-based aggregation to merge common layers from various clients' updates, ensuring that a client's model with a larger training dataset contributes more to the aggregated common layers. However, this approach does not consider the distribution of local training data.

Hierarchical federated learning (Fig. 1) is realized by introducing hierarchical clustering steps into FL [3], where client devices are clustered according to specific requirements to avoid sending trained models directly to the cloud server for aggregation. A common three-level structure in FL is the client-edge-cloud model [19]. In this model, edge servers aggregate the received local updates from clients and then send the aggregated updates to the cloud server, which subsequently aggregates the updates from the edges to create a new global model. In hierarchical FL, IoT devices are connected to edge servers rather than directly to the cloud server (the cloud server communicates only with edge servers). One apparent advantage of hierarchical FL compared to conventional FL networks is the reduction in communication costs. By aggregating local updates within clusters first, the number of updates sent to the cloud server is minimized. Communication costs between IoT devices and edge servers are typically lower than that for the communication between IoT devices and the cloud server as local network communication technologies (e.g., Bluetooth or Zigbee) are utilized to connect IoT devices to edge servers [25]. Additionally, hierarchical federated learning can reduce communication latency as the aggregation process for the local network is placed at the edge [1].

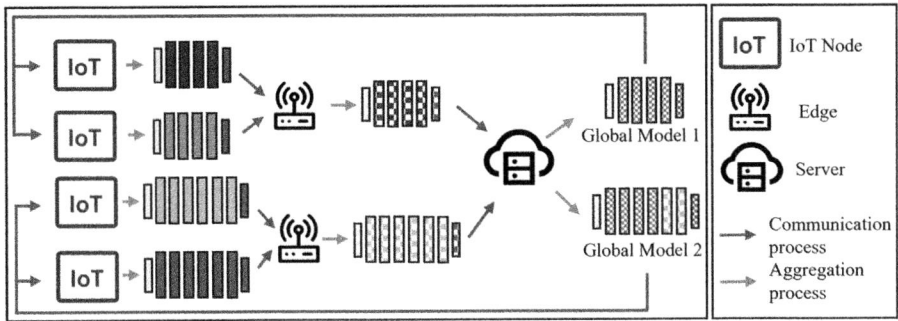

Fig. 2. Entire process of HAF-Edge, where orange and blue arrow represents inner aggregation and communication process, respectively. (Color figure online)

3 Framework Design

By employing HAF-Edge, client devices are clustered based on their model architectures to ensure that IoT devices with identical model architectures are grouped into the same cluster. Each cluster of IoT devices is connected to an edge server which aggregates local models and forwards the edge-aggregated model to the cloud server. Then, edge-aggregated models with heterogeneous architectures are aggregated in the cloud by using the MaxCommon strategy. Subsequently, the cloud server distributes the updated global models with distinct architectures to corresponding edge servers. Edge servers then propagate these new global models to the IoT devices within their clusters, guaranteeing synchronized updates across edge servers and client devices (Fig. 2).

The distance-based weighting is implemented at the edge server to enable the weights of the contribution from client devices depending on the quality of training data instead of quantity so that **HAF-Edge can achieve better performance in the scenarios involving non-IID data compared to FedAvg and MaxCommon Strategy**. The distance-based weighting guarantees that local models trained with IID data have a greater contribution to the edge-aggregated model. The detailed steps of HAF-Edge for one completed round after clustering client devices based on their model architectures are:

– First step, in each cluster, the client devices train the models with their local data and send the trained local models to the edge server.
– Second step, each edge server aggregates the trained local models from the client devices and then forwards the edge-aggregated model to the cloud server.
– Third step, the cloud server applies MaxCommon strategy on edge-aggregated models with different architectures to **create several new heterogeneous global models**.
– Fourth step, the cloud server transmits new global models to the matching edge servers. Then each edge server distributes the received new global model to the connected client devices.

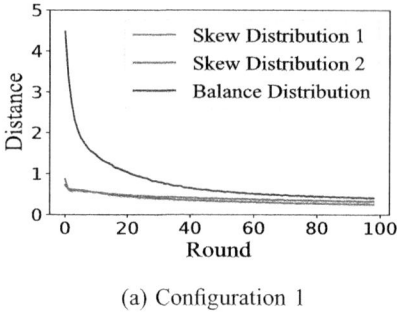 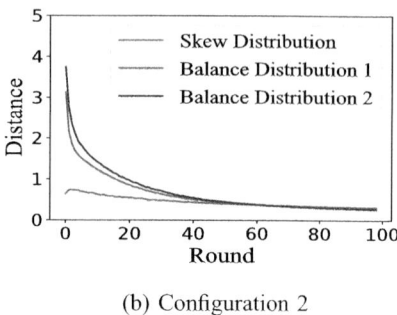

(a) Configuration 1   (b) Configuration 2

Fig. 3. The changing curves of Euclidean distance between client model and global model per communication round on three clients with varied data distribution.

3.1 Distance-Based Weighting

In HAF-Edge, we use the Euclidean distance-based weighting method to reduce the impact of non-IID data. In FL, under the non-IID scenario, the Euclidean distance of clients trained with skewer data distribution is lower than the models trained with balanced distributed data due to the neural network having to update more weights to capture more detailed client data features. We conducted an experiment with two different configurations:

- Configuration 1: In total three participants, one participant has balanced distributed data while the rest have skewed distributed data, data volume are the same across these devices.
- Configuration 2: In total three participants, two participants have balanced distributed data while the other has skewed distributed data, data volume are the same across these devices.

Configuration 1 represents the scenario in which the number of client devices with non-IID data exceeds the number of client devices with IID data in the aggregation process. Conversely, configuration 2 indicates that there are more client devices with IID data. The Euclidean distance metric can be employed to quantify the disparity between the two models. In the Euclidean distance [26]:

$$d(p,q) = \sqrt{(p_1 - q_1)^2 + (p_2 - q_2)^2 + (p_3 - q_3)^2 + \cdots + (p_n - q_n)^2}, \quad (1)$$

where $d(p,q)$ is the Euclidean distance between p and q, p and q are matrices in n dimensions. FedAvg is utilized to aggregate three local models from client devices in both Configuration 1 and Configuration 2. The distance between the local models of three client devices and the aggregated global model from the previous round is calculated using the Euclidean distance metric.

Figure 3 shows the changing curve of the Euclidean distance between client models and the global model by communication rounds. In both configurations, the Euclidean distance to the global model of local models trained with skewed

Table 1. Declaration of notations

Notation	Definition
L_k^t	A local model from client k at round t
E_i^t	An edge-aggregated model from edge server i at round t (the aggregated model from edge server i contains i layers in total)
N_k	The total number of data used for training in client k
l_i^j	Layer j from E_i
X_i	A set of edge servers whose aggregated models contain layer i
K_i	The set of client devices connected to edge server i
Gl_i^t	A global layer i at round t
G_i^t	A global model for edge server i at round t

data is lower than the local models from the client devices having balanced data. The distance between the local models trained with IID data to the global model decreases from **3.1–4.4 to 0.27–0.4**, and for the models with non-IID data decreases from **0.5–0.9 to 0.24–0.31**, which **verified our insight that regardless of whether the client's data is evenly distributed, the model trained with data in less non-IIDness has a higher Euclidean distance** to the global model compared with the models trained with higher data non-IIDness. Based on this observation, we propose a Euclidean distance-based weighting aggregation:

$$\frac{d(L_j^t, G_i^{t-1})}{\sum_{k \in K_i} d(L_k^t, G_i^{t-1})}, \qquad (2)$$

where K_i is the set of client devices connected with edge server i, client j belongs to K_i. L_j^t is the local model from client j at round $t(t > 1)$. G_i^{t-1} is the global model for edge server i (the aggregated model from edge server i contains i layers in total) at round $t - 1(t > 1)$. If local models are trained with data in less non-IIDness, by applying Eq. 2 can assign these models a higher weight coefficient for aggregation.

3.2 Edge Aggregation

The IoT devices connected to the same edge server have an identical model architecture. The model-level aggregation can be used at edge servers. In the initial round, the cloud server did not generate the aggregated global models. Hence, the aggregation based on the quantity of data is implemented at edge servers for the first round. The edge-aggregated model E_i^1 at the first communication round from edge server i is shown as:

$$E_i^1 = \sum_{k \in K_i} \frac{N_k}{\sum_{k \in K_i} N_k} L_k^1, \qquad (3)$$

where N_k is the total number of data used to train the local model in the client k. After receiving edge-aggregated models, the cloud server creates new global

Algorithm 1. The Aggregation at Edge Servers. K_i is the set of client devices connected with edge server i. L_k^t is the local model from client k at round t. N_k is the number of data used for training in client k. G_i^t is the global model from the cloud server for edge server i at round t. E_i^t is the edge-aggregated model from edge server i at round t. t is the round counter.

1: **if** $t = 1$ **then**
2: $\quad E_i^t = \sum_{k \in K_i} \frac{N_k}{\sum_{k \in K_i} N_k} L_k^t$
3: **else**
4: $\quad E_i^t = \sum_{k \in K_i} \frac{d(L_k^t, G_i^{t-1})}{\sum_{k \in K_i} d(L_k^t, G_i^{t-1})} L_k^t$
5: **end if**
6: **return** E_i^t
---

models with different architectures by aggregating common layers from various edge-aggregated models. New global models are distributed to matching edge servers. The edge server propagates the received new global model to connected client devices. Hence, starting from the second round, the distance-based weighting aggregation is applied at the edge server. The edge-aggregated model E_i^t at round $t (t > 1)$ from edge server i is:

$$E_i^t = \sum_{k \in K_i} \frac{d(L_k^t, G_i^{t-1})}{\sum_{k \in K_i} d(L_k^t, G_i^{t-1})} L_k^t. \tag{4}$$

Algorithm 1 shows the aggregation process at edge servers.

3.3 Cloud Aggregation

MaxCommon strategy is adopted to aggregate the models from different edge servers at the cloud server. MaxCommon strategy is a layer-level aggregation. Hence we define a function:

$$l_j^i = Extract(E_i^t, j), \tag{5}$$

to extract layer j from edge-aggregated model E_i^t. Then, the cloud server aggregates the common layers extracted from distinct edge-aggregated models:

$$Gl_i^t = \sum_{x \in X_i} \frac{\sum_{k \in K_x} N_k}{\sum_{x \in X_i} \sum_{k \in K_x} N_k} l_i^x, \tag{6}$$

where Gl_i^t is the global layer i after aggregating at round t, X_i is a set of edge servers whose aggregated models contain layer i. K_x is the set of client devices connected to edge server x, N_k is the total number of data used for training in the client k. l_i^x is layer i from E_x^t.

After aggregating the common layers from various edge-aggregated models, these global layers are combined to create several global models with heterogeneous architectures based on the requirements of different edge servers. The formula to combine the global layers is shown as:

$$G_i^t = Gl_1^t \oplus Gl_2^t \oplus Gl_3^t \oplus \cdots \oplus Gl_i^t, \tag{7}$$

where G_i^t is the global model for edge server i at round t, and there are i layers in total. Algorithm 2 shows the aggregation process at the cloud servers. Table 1 shows notations used in our paper.

Algorithm 2. The Aggregation at Cloud Server. n is the number of layers contained by the edge server with the highest layer count. X_i is a set of edge servers whose aggregated models contain layer i. E_x^t is an edge-aggregated model from edge server x at round t. l_i^x is layer i from E_x^t. Gl_i^t is the global layer i. K_x is the set of client devices connected to edge server x. N_k is the total number of data used for training in the client k. G_i^t is the global model for edge server i. t is the round counter.

1: **for** $i = 1, 2, 3, \ldots, n$ **do**
2:     **for** $x \in X_i$ **do**
3:         $l_i^x = Extract(E_x, i)$
4:     **end for**
5:     $Gl_i^t = \sum_{x \in X_i} \frac{\sum_{k \in K_x} N_k}{\sum_{x \in X_i} \sum_{k \in K_x} N_k} l_i^x$
6: **end for**
7: **for** $i = 1, 2, 3, \ldots, n$ **do**
8:     $G_i^t = Gl_1^t \oplus Gl_2^t \oplus Gl_3^t \oplus \cdots \oplus Gl_i^t$
9: **end for**
10: **return** $G_1^t, G_2^t, G_3^t, \ldots, G_n^t$

---

4 Implementation and Evaluation

In our study, we evaluate the effectiveness of HAF-Edge using MNIST and FMNIST which are recognized as benchmarks in FL systems for image classification applications by comparing its performance with two baselines: vanilla FedAvg [21] and MaxCommon strategy [27]. The TensorFlow library of Python is used for implementation. In our experiment, we use heterogeneous models with different numbers of dense layers. Table 2 represents the foundation model structure. The x-nn represents the model which has x number of dense layers except the output layer. As an example, 1nn and 5nn represent models that have 1 dense layer and 5 dense layers, respectively. To verify the effectiveness of our method, three different scenarios are applied to evaluate the performance of HAF-Edge. Table 3 shows the detailed settings of three experiment scenarios.

Table 2. Fundamental x-nn model architecture.

Layer	Output Shape	Activation	Parameters
Input	(784,)	None	0
Dense	(200,)	ReLU	157,000
...			
Dense	(10,)	Softmax	2,010

1NN and 3NN models are used in Scenario 1 and Scenario 2. In Scenario 3, 5 different model architectures from 1NN to 5NN are employed. To generate non-IID training sets for the client devices in three scenarios, MNIST and FMNIST datasets are sorted according to labels and partitioned into several subsets based on the required number of non-IID client devices in different scenarios, and each subset is regarded as one non-IID client. The client device with IID data contains all labels in three scenarios.

4.1 Experiment Setup

We use test accuracy and convergence speed as evaluation metrics. The test accuracy is the accuracy of the global model on the test set, and the convergence speed is the number of communication rounds needed for methods to reach the target test accuracy of the global model. FedAvg and MaxCommon strategy are used as baselines, where FedAvg is applied to different clusters of client devices grouped by their model architectures to obtain global models with various architectures, and MaxCommon strategy is applied to client devices without clustering, the common layers are extracted and aggregated to create heterogeneous global models.

4.2 Evaluation Results

For Scenario 1, Fig. 4a and Fig. 4b present the test accuracy trends of global 1NN and 3NN models aggregated by HAF-Edge, FedAvg and MaxCommon strategy using MNIST dataset. The convergence speed of HAF-Edge is faster than that of FedAvg and MaxCommon strategy. The global 1NN model trained by HAF-Edge reaches **80%** accuracy **25** rounds faster than FedAvg and **30** rounds faster than

Table 3. Basic settings of three scenarios

Scenario	Number of Model Architectures	Client Number per Edge	Client Data Volume	IID Clients : Non-IID Clients in Each Edge
1	2	6	6000	1:5
2	2	60	600	1:5
3	5	11	1200	1:10

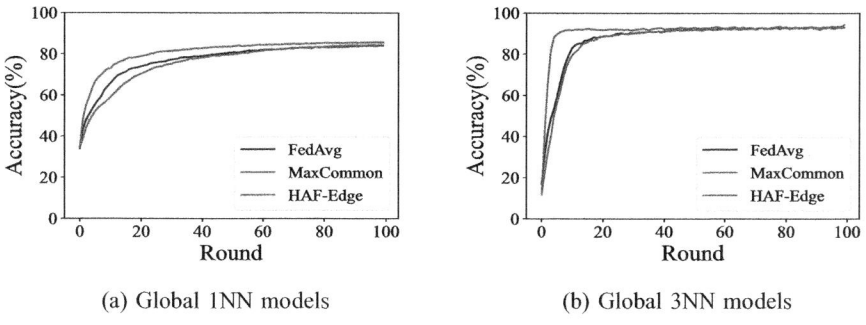

Fig. 4. Evaluating HAF-Edge, FedAvg, and MaxCommon strategy for Scenario 1 (2 edge servers, 6 clients for each edge server) using MNIST dataset.

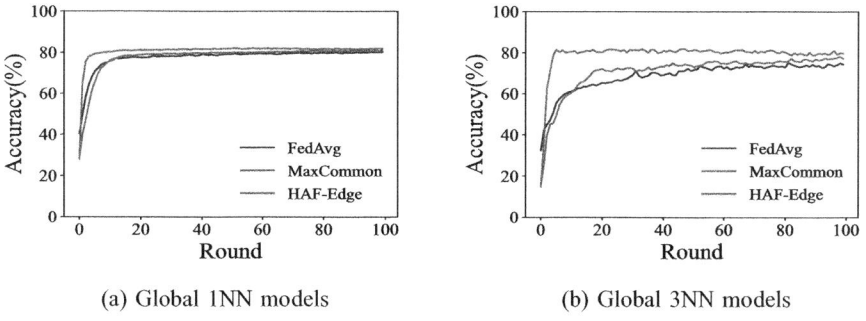

Fig. 5. Evaluating HAF-Edge, FedAvg, and MaxCommon strategy for Scenario 1 (2 edge servers, 6 clients for each edge server) using FMNIST dataset.

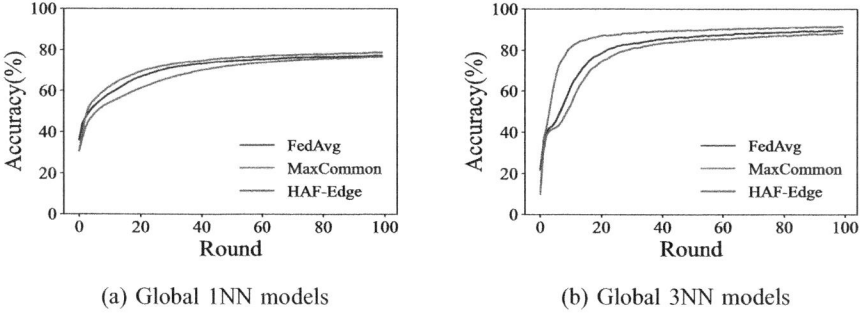

Fig. 6. Evaluating HAF-Edge, FedAvg, and MaxCommon strategy in Scenario 2 (2 edge servers, 60 clients for each edge server) with 1NN and 3NN models for the MNIST dataset.

MaxCommon strategy. Moreover, HAF-Edge achieves 85% accuracy, whereas FedAvg and MaxCommon strategy only reaches 84% with global 1NN models in 100 rounds. Figure 5a and Fig. 5b show the test accuracy trends of global

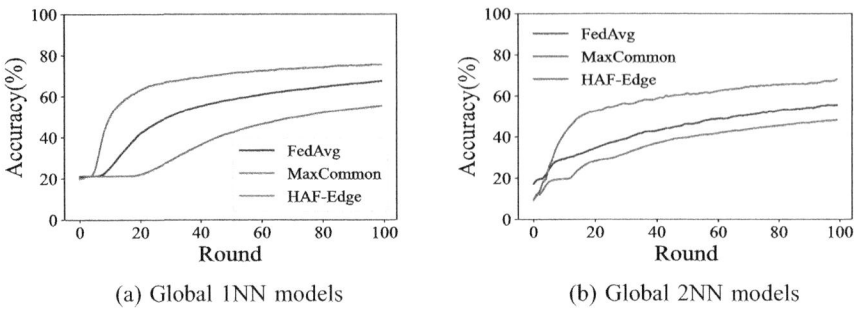

Fig. 7. Evaluating HAF-Edge, FedAvg, and MaxCommon strategy in Scenario 3 (5 edge servers, 11 clients for each edge server) with 1NN and 2NN models for the MNIST dataset.

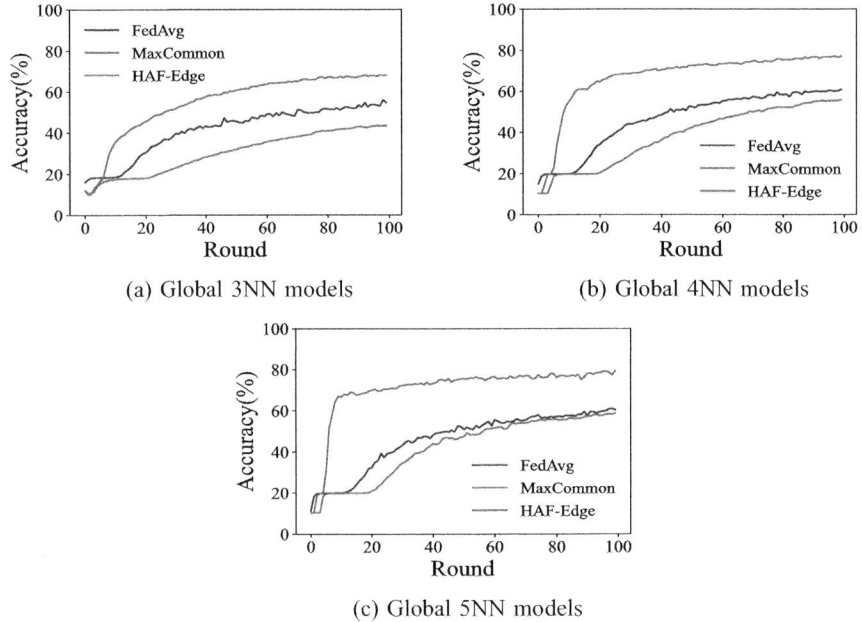

Fig. 8. Evaluating HAF-Edge, FedAvg, and MaxCommon strategy for Scenario 3 (5 edge servers, 11 clients for each edge server) with global 3NN, 4NN, and 5NN models.

1NN and 3NN models aggregated by HAF-Edge, FedAvg, and MaxCommon strategy using FMNIST dataset. HAF-Edge has a faster convergence speed and higher maximum accuracy on both global 1NN and 3NN models compared to FedAvg and MaxCommon strategy. The global 1NN model trained by HAF-Edge reaches **80%** accuracy **73** rounds faster than FedAvg and **47** rounds faster than MaxCommon strategy. The maximum accuracy of the global 1NN model trained by HAF-Edge is around **1%** higher than those trained by FedAvg and

MaxCommon strategy in 100 rounds. The maximum accuracy of 3NN global models trained by FedAvg and MaxCommon strategy is **75%** and **78%** in 100 rounds, respectively. However, the maximum accuracy of the 3NN global model trained by HAF-Edge is **80%**.

For Scenario 2, the test accuracy curves of global 1NN, and 3NN models aggregated by HAF-Edge, FedAvg, and MaxCommon strategy using the MNIST dataset are shown in Fig. 6. Even though the number of client devices in each edge is increased compared to Scenario 1, the global 1NN model and 3NN model trained by HAF-Edge achieve better performance on both convergence speed and test accuracy. The maximum accuracy of the global 1NN model trained by HAF-Edge is **78%**, which is **1%** higher than that of FedAvg and **2%** higher than that of MaxCommon strategy. The global 3NN model trained by HAF-Edge achieves **91%** accuracy, and global 3NN models trained by FedAvg and MaxCommon strategy reach **89%** and **88%** accuracy, respectively.

For Scenario 3, the number of edge servers and model architecture types is increased compared to Scenario 1 and Scenario 2. Figures 7 and 8 present the test accuracy trends for 5 different global models (1NN, 2NN, 3NN, 4NN, 5NN). MNIST dataset is used in Scenario 3. The results of HAF-Edge are better in both test accuracy and convergence speed compared to the FedAvg and MaxCommon strategies. In all cases, the models trained by HAF-Edge can achieve at least **10%** accuracy higher than models trained by FedAvg and MaxCommon. For the 5NN model, the maximum accuracy of HAF-Edge is about **80%**, while the best performance of both FedAvg and MaxCommon reach to 60% accuracy.

5 Conclusion

Non-IID data and model heterogeneity are two important challenges of FLaaS. In this paper, we present HAF-Edge, a three-level hierarchical federated learning where client devices with the same model settings are clustered and connected to an edge server that aims to solve these problems. In HAF-Edge, MaxCommon strategy is adopted at the cloud server to extract and aggregate common layers from models with different architectures. A distance-based weighting aggregation is proposed and applied at edge servers to reduce the impact of data non-IIDness, which is based on our observation that the Euclidean distance between local models trained with IID data and the global model is larger compared with the local models trained with non-IID data. We also evaluate the performance of HAF-Edge based on MNIST, FMNIST datasets under multiple scenarios. The results indicate that HAF-Edge outperforms FedAvg and MaxCommon Strategy under scenarios with non-IID data and heterogeneous models.

References

1. Abad, M.S.H., Ozfatura, E., Gunduz, D., Ercetin, O.: Hierarchical federated learning across heterogeneous cellular networks. In: ICASSP 2020-2020 IEEE International Conference on Acoustics, Speech and Signal Processing (ICASSP), pp. 8866–8870. IEEE (2020)
2. Antunes, R.S., André da Costa, C., Küderle, A., Yari, I.A., Eskofier, B.: Federated learning for healthcare: systematic review and architecture proposal. ACM Trans. Intell. Syst. Technol. (TIST) **13**(4), 1–23 (2022)
3. Briggs, C., Fan, Z., Andras, P.: Federated learning with hierarchical clustering of local updates to improve training on non-IID data. In: 2020 International Joint Conference on Neural Networks (IJCNN). pp. 1–9. IEEE (2020)
4. Chen, S., et al.: Optimization of federated learning's client selection for non-IID data based on grey relational analysis (2024). https://arxiv.org/abs/2310.08147
5. Chen, S., Tavallaie, O., Nazemi, N., Zomaya, A.Y.: RBLA: rank-based-LoRA-aggregation for fine-tuning heterogeneous models in flaas (2024). https://arxiv.org/abs/2408.08699
6. Deng, Y., et al.: Fair: quality-aware federated learning with precise user incentive and model aggregation. In: IEEE INFOCOM 2021-IEEE Conference on Computer Communications, pp. 1–10. IEEE (2021)
7. Hard, A., et al.: Federated learning for mobile keyboard prediction. arXiv preprint arXiv:1811.03604 (2018)
8. Hesamifard, E., Takabi, H., Ghasemi, M., Wright, R.N.: Privacy-preserving machine learning as a service. Proc. Priv. Enhancing Technol. (2018)
9. Hinton, G., Vinyals, O., Dean, J.: Distilling the knowledge in a neural network. arXiv preprint arXiv:1503.02531 (2015)
10. Hsieh, K., Phanishayee, A., Mutlu, O., Gibbons, P.: The non-IID data quagmire of decentralized machine learning. In: International Conference on Machine Learning, pp. 4387–4398. PMLR (2020)
11. Kairouz, P., et al.: Advances and open problems in federated learning. Found. trends® mach. learn. **14**(1–2), 1–210 (2021)
12. Kirienko, M., et al.: Distributed learning: a reliable privacy-preserving strategy to change multicenter collaborations using AI. Eur. J. Nucl. Med. Mol. Imaging **48**, 3791–3804 (2021)
13. Kourtellis, N., Katevas, K., Perino, D.: FLaaS: federated learning as a service. In: Proceedings of the 1st Workshop on Distributed Machine Learning, pp. 7–13 (2020)
14. Lai, F., Zhu, X., Madhyastha, H.V., Chowdhury, M.: Oort: Efficient federated learning via guided participant selection. In: 15th USENIX Symposium on Operating Systems Design and Implementation (OSDI 21), pp. 19–35. USENIX Association (Jul 2021). https://www.usenix.org/conference/osdi21/presentation/lai
15. LeCun, Y., Cortes, C., Burges, C.J.: MNIST handwritten digit database (2010). http://yann.lecun.com/exdb/mnist/
16. Li, D., Wang, J.: FedMD: heterogenous federated learning via model distillation. arXiv preprint arXiv:1910.03581 (2019)
17. Li, T., Sahu, A.K., Talwalkar, A., Smith, V.: Federated learning: challenges, methods, and future directions. IEEE Signal Process. Mag. **37**(3), 50–60 (2020)
18. Li, X., Huang, K., Yang, W., Wang, S., Zhang, Z.: On the convergence of FedAvg on non-IID data. arXiv preprint arXiv:1907.02189 (2019)

19. Liu, L., Zhang, J., Song, S., Letaief, K.B.: Client-edge-cloud hierarchical federated learning. In: ICC 2020 - 2020 IEEE International Conference on Communications (ICC), pp. 1–6 (2020)
20. Lu, X., Zheng, H., Liu, W., Jiang, Y., Wu, H.: POP-FL: towards efficient federated learning on edge using parallel over-parameterization. IEEE Trans. Serv. Comput. **17**(2), 617–630 (2024)
21. McMahan, B., Moore, E., Ramage, D., Hampson, S., Arcas, B.A.y.: Communication-efficient learning of deep networks from decentralized data. In: Proceedings of the 20th ICAIS, vol. 54. PMLR (2017)
22. Meng, Q., Zhou, F., Ren, H., Feng, T., Liu, G., Lin, Y.: Improving federated learning face recognition via privacy-agnostic clusters. arXiv preprint arXiv:2201.12467 (2022)
23. Nazemi, N., et al.: ACCESS-FL: agile communication and computation for efficient secure aggregation in stable federated learning networks. arXiv preprint arXiv:2409.01722 (2024)
24. Qu, Y., Yu, S., Gao, L., Sood, K., Xiang, Y.: Blockchained dual-asynchronous federated learning services for digital twin empowered edge-cloud continuum. IEEE Trans. Serv. Comput. **17**(3), 836–849 (2024)
25. Rana, O., et al.: Hierarchical and decentralised federated learning. In: 2022 Cloud Continuum, pp. 1–9. IEEE (2022)
26. Smith, K.: Precalculus: A Functional Approach to Graphing And Problem Solving. Jones & Bartlett Publishers (2013)
27. Wang, K., et al.: FlexiFed: personalized federated learning for edge clients with heterogeneous model architectures. In: Proceedings of the ACM Web Conference 2023, pp. 2979–2990. WWW '23, Association for Computing Machinery, New York, NY, USA (2023)
28. Weng, Q., et al.: MLaaS in the wild: workload analysis and scheduling in large-scale heterogeneous GPU clusters. In: 19th USENIX Symposium on Networked Systems Design and Implementation (NSDI 22), pp. 945–960. USENIX Association, Renton, WA (Apr 2022). https://www.usenix.org/conference/nsdi22/presentation/weng
29. Xiao, H., Rasul, K., Vollgraf, R.: Fashion-MNIST: a novel image dataset for benchmarking machine learning algorithms. arXiv preprint arXiv:1708.07747 (2017). https://arxiv.org/abs/1708.07747
30. Xu, Z., et al.: Federated learning of gboard language models with differential privacy. In: Proceedings of the 61st Annual Meeting of the Association for Computational Linguistics (Volume 5: Industry Track), pp. 629–639. Association for Computational Linguistics (2023)
31. Ye, M., Fang, X., Du, B., Yuen, P.C., Tao, D.: Heterogeneous federated learning: state-of-the-art and research challenges. ACM Comput. Surv. **56**(3), 1–44 (2023)
32. Zhao, Y., Li, M., Lai, L., Suda, N., Civin, D., Chandra, V.: Federated learning with non-IID data. arXiv preprint arXiv:1806.00582 (2018)

Optimizing Traffic Allocation for Multi-replica Microservice Deployments in Edge Cloud

Hokun Park, Hyungjun Kim, Donggyun Kim, Gyujeong Lim, and Heonchang Yu[✉]

Department of Computer Science and Engineering, Korea University, Seoul, South Korea
{hokunpark98,ledzep0830,kdonggyun97,gjlim2485,yuhc}@korea.ac.kr

Abstract. Microservice architecture enhances scalability and flexibility by decomposing a single application into loosely coupled, independently deployable components. Unlike monolithic services, microservices require frequent inter-component communication and are deployed with multiple replicas primarily to ensure quick response times to varying user requests. However, existing studies have not adequately addressed the challenges inherent in multi-replica environments, leading to suboptimal performance. To address these challenges, we propose a latency-aware replica placement method and traffic allocation strategy that minimizes communication overhead among replicas while achieving load balancing. These issues are especially critical in edge-cloud environments with diverse and high inter-node latencies, leading to QoS degradation. The experimental results show significant reductions of up to 81% in the 99th percentile tail latency compared to existing techniques.

Keywords: Edge-Cloud · Microservice · Multi-replica · QoS

1 Introduction

Contemporary web services and user-facing applications are moving from monolithic architectures to Microservices Architectures (MSA) [13]. Unlike traditional monolithic structures, MSA enhances scalability and flexibility by decomposing a single application into loosely coupled, independently deployable components [15]. This architecture aligns well with the strengths of containers. Containerization of microservices facilitates service deployment and improves management efficiency by leveraging the characteristics of containers, such as resource isolation, rapid startup, and efficient resource management, making it suitable for cloud-native environments [7]. Uber, Netflix, and eBay are prominent examples of companies that have adopted MSA in their containerized environments.

Edge computing is increasingly used as an infrastructure technology for services that require low latency, as it positions services closer to end users, thereby reducing communication overhead and improving Quality of Service (QoS) [12].

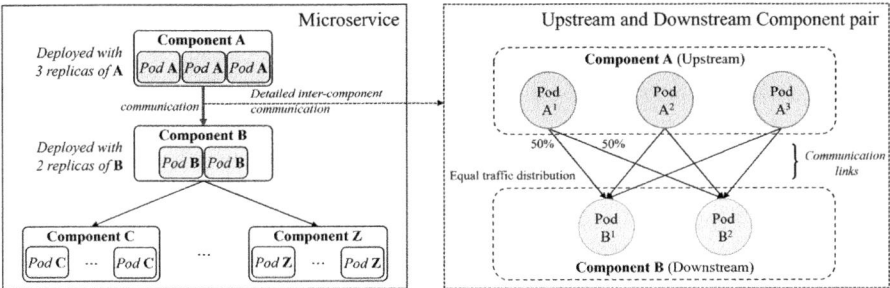

Fig. 1. Inter-Component Communication in a K8s Environment

However, deploying numerous containerized microservices across distributed nodes complicates management [4]. Kubernetes[1](K8s), a container orchestration tool, is widely used to address this issue. K8s automates the deployment and management of containerized applications. However, the default K8s scheduling policy focuses on resource fairness and does not consider communication overhead among microservice components [1]. As a result, QoS degradation due to communication overhead becomes inevitable, especially when microservices are deployed in geographically distributed edge-cloud environments.

Existing studies have primarily focused on minimizing communication overhead between components, assuming each is deployed with a single replica [5,6,11]. Traffic localization (Localization) reduces communication overhead by placing frequently communicating components on the same node. Some studies using this approach have utilized the Istio[2] service mesh to monitor communication frequency and data transmission size, aiming to move high-communication components to the same or adjacent nodes, thus minimizing overhead and reducing bandwidth consumption [3,8,9,14].

However, microservice components are typically deployed with multiple replicas to ensure scalability, fault tolerance, and resource efficiency. This indicates that existing studies provide solutions based on assumptions that deviate from actual service environments. For example, auto-scaling replicas is a commonly used technique to ensure Service Level Agreements (SLAs), which are based on response times [2], by adjusting the number of replicas according to changes in user requests. This functionality, built into K8s, highlights the widespread use of multi-replica deployments in service operations.

In single-replica environments, there is only one communication path for each pair of upstream and downstream components. In contrast, in multi-replica environments, the number of possible communication paths for each component pair increases to the product of the number of replicas of each component, as shown in Fig. 1. This variability in communication paths introduces an additional dimension to consider: the cost associated with different paths, even for the same

---

[1] https://kubernetes.io/.
[2] https://istio.io/.

pair of components. If this unique characteristic of multi-replica environments is not taken into account, the following issues arise:

1. **Increased average response times** when replicas are placed on nodes with high inter-node latency.
2. **Increased tail-latency** due to equal traffic distribution among replicas, irrespective of inter-node latency differences.
3. **Increased processing delays** due to overloading when traffic is concentrated on a single path, while other replicas' resources remain underutilized.

To our best knowledge, OptTraffic [16] is the only study focused on multi-replica environments. OptTraffic achieves load balancing and bandwidth efficiency by allocating traffic and migrating replicas based on upstream and downstream replica counts. However, OptTraffic shows minimal performance improvement when inter-node communication is frequent. This indicates that OptTraffic's performance heavily depends on replica placement. It prioritizes load balancing by enforcing fair traffic distribution to remote nodes, a problem that worsens with significant inter-node latency variation. Specifically, OptTraffic performs well when the global-to-local ratio of upstream and downstream replicas is balanced. However, with a large disparity in this ratio, frequent inter-node communication leads to minimal latency reduction. Overall, OptTraffic is unsuitable for edge-cloud environments where inter-node latency is variable and resource constraints are tighter than in cloud data centers, making it difficult to control the global-to-local ratio effectively.

We propose a novel approach that combines latency-aware replica placement and traffic allocation strategies to improve QoS by reducing 99th percentile tail-latency (P99 latency) in multi-replica microservice deployments within edge-cloud environments. Our main contributions are as follows:

Latency-Aware Replica Placement. We group replicas based on service demand and select nodes with sufficient resources and low inter-node latency for optimal placement, thereby reducing communication overhead.

DAG representation of inter-component communication. We model inter-component communication as a directed acyclic graph (DAG) and formulate the traffic allocation problem as a Minimum-Cost Flow Problem.

Latency-Aware Traffic Allocation for Multi-replica Environments. Using the network simplex algorithm, we find the optimal solution that minimizes P99 latency, balances the load, and improves QoS. We implement a prototype and conduct experiments on K8s. The results demonstrate that the proposed approach reduces P99 latency by an average of 32% compared to the default K8s scheduler, Localization, and OptTraffic.

2 Motivation

In this section, we empirically demonstrate the issues of increased response time, tail-latency, and processing delays in multi-replica environments, as mentioned

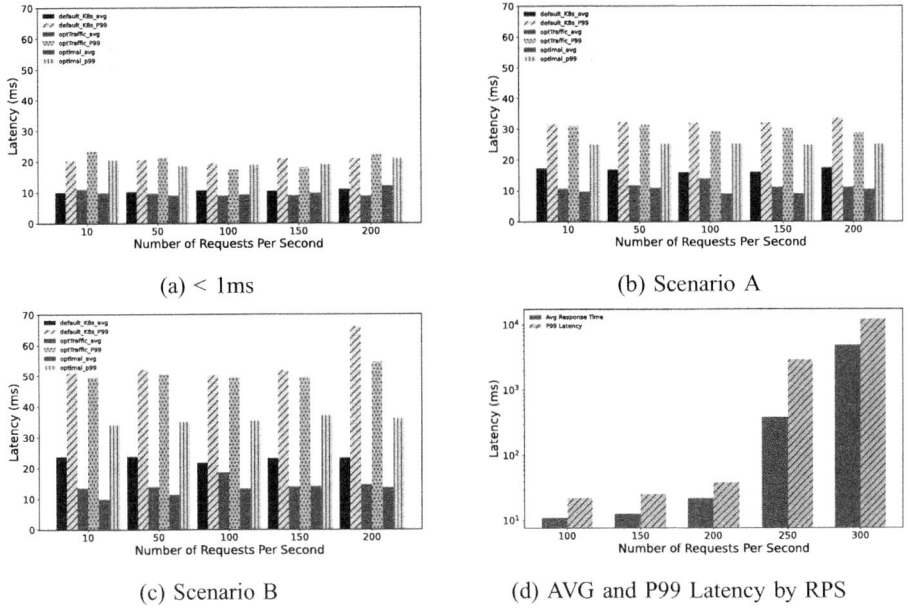

Fig. 2. Average and P99 Latency Under Different Scenarios

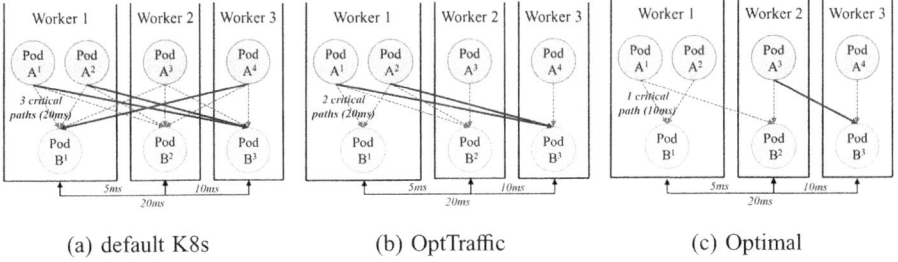

Fig. 3. Communication Path Comparison in Scenario A

above, under various load and inter-node latency conditions. The latency conditions among nodes in Scenario A and Scenario B are detailed in Sect. 4.1.

2.1 The Impact of Inter-Node Latency on Average Response Time

We measured the average response time based on the inter-node latencies among the nodes in which replicas are placed. Replicas are deployed on worker nodes as shown in Fig. 3. Figure 2(a) shows when the inter-node latencies are less than 1 ms, the communication overhead among replicas is low, resulting in the shortest average response time and P99 latency. Figure 2(b) shows the evaluation results in Scenario A, and Fig. 2(c) shows the evaluation results in Scenario B. In Scenario B, the inter-node latency is increased by ×2 compared to Scenario A. When the inter-node latency is increased by ×2, the default K8s showed an increase in average response time by 33%–44% and P99 latency by 57%-97%. OptTraffic exhibited an increase in average response time by 28%–106% and P99 latency by 59%–89%, as shown in Fig. 2(c). Therefore, to improve QoS, a replica placement strategy that considers inter-node latency is required.

2.2 The Impact of Traffic Allocation Strategy on P99 Latency

Figure 3 illustrates the critical paths for the default Kubernetes (K8s), Opt-Traffic, and the optimal traffic allocation strategy. Compared to default K8s, OptTraffic reduced the average response time by 35% on average, while the P99 latency was reduced by 6% on average, as shown in Fig. 2(c). Despite these improvements, QoS degraded, particularly under high inter-node latency conditions. This is due to OptTraffic's *padding stage*, which maintains the critical path's length similar to the default K8s scheduler, as shown in Fig. 3. First, OptTraffic employs a *local-first* strategy to reduce inter-node communication and bandwidth consumption. The *padding stage* is then used for load balancing, but the critical path, closely related to P99 latency, remains largely unchanged as shown in Fig. 2. These results indicate the necessity of a novel approach to optimizing the critical path.

2.3 The Impact of Overloading Replicas on Processing Delays

When all traffic is allocated to the nearest replica to minimize network overhead from inter-node communication, it results in that replica handling all the processing tasks. This leads to overloading of the replica when the load exceeds a certain level. Consequently, the overloaded replica experiences resource shortages, leading to increased processing delays. As shown in Fig. 2(d), when the requests per second (RPS) increased from 100 to 300, the average response time rose from 11 ms to 4890 ms, and the P99 latency increased from 22 ms to 12250 ms. This significant increase in both P99 latency and average response time demonstrates that such a traffic allocation policy, although intended to reduce inter-node communication delays, overlooks the available resources of replicas and leads to degraded QoS. To prevent these issues, it is essential to balance the load among replicas, taking into account their resource availability.

3 Proposed Approach

3.1 Overall Design

To address the aforementioned challenges, we propose a *replica placement method* and *traffic allocation strategy* that minimize inter-node communication overhead while ensuring load balancing among replicas. The main goal is to improve QoS by reducing P99 latency in multi-replica microservice deployments in edge-cloud.

Latency-Aware Replica Placement Method: When replicas of communicating components are placed on nodes with high inter-node latency, communication

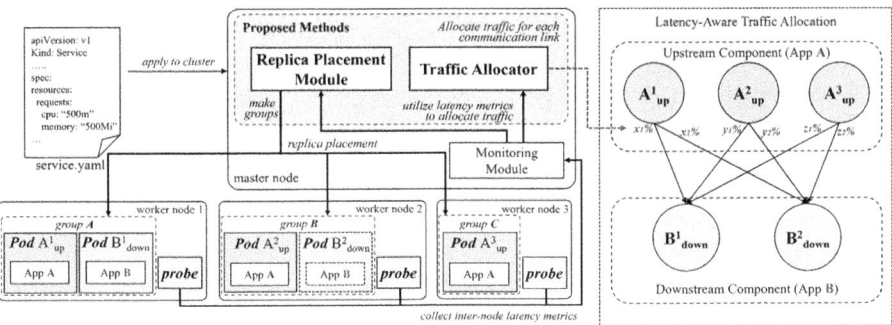

Fig. 4. Overall System Architecture

overhead increases significantly. This causes an increase in the average response time of user requests. To mitigate this issue, we propose a replica placement method that considers inter-node latency.

Latency-Aware Traffic Allocation Strategy: As discussed in Sects. 2.2 and 2.3, the high P99 latency is caused by the critical path having high inter-node latency and the processing delays due to overload, which can degrade QoS. To mitigate these issues, a traffic allocation strategy that allocates traffic in an appropriate proportion for each communication link is proposed, minimizing communication overhead while ensuring load balancing.

Figure 4 illustrates the architecture of our proposed system. The *Replica Placement Module* groups the replicas of a requested service based on the average number of replicas for each component. These groups are placed on worker nodes with sufficient resources and lowest inter-node latency. The *Monitoring Module* collects inter-node latency metrics and monitors the available node resources in the cluster. The *Traffic Allocator* uses the latency metrics and constructs a DAG to identify pairs of upstream and downstream components, then efficiently allocates traffic for each communication link to reduce P99 latency and balance the load among replicas.

3.2 Replica Placement

To prevent high average response times due to inter-node latency, we proposed a group-based replica placement method. We measured the inter-node latency by deploying network probes[3] on all worker nodes. These probes send ping traffic to all nodes every 15 s. And Prometheus[4] collected the latency metrics. A service deployment request includes the resource requirements and the number of replicas for each component of the service. Based on these metrics, the average number of replicas per component is calculated to determine the number of groups. Then, nodes for each group are selected. This approach can prevent QoS

---

[3] https://github.com/prometheus/blackbox_exporter.
[4] https://prometheus.io/.

Algorithm 1. Generating Groups Based on Average Replicas

// Let C denote the set of all components in the microservice.
// Each component $c_i \in C$ is represented as $C = \{c_0, c_1, \ldots, c_m\}$
// Each replica $r_{i,k} \in c_i$ is represented as $r = \{r_{i,0}, r_{i,1}, \ldots, r_{i,n}\}$
1: **Input:** C
2: $avgReplicas \leftarrow \text{CALAVGNUMBEROFREPLICAS}(C)$
3: Initialize $groups$ as an empty list
4: **for** each c_i in C **do**
5:     **for** each $r_{i,k}$ in c_i **do**
6:         Assign $r_{i,k}$ to $groups[i \mod avgReplicas]$
7:     **end for**
8: **end for**
9: **Output:** $groups$

---

degradation due to high inter-node communication overhead and reduce the risk of service interruption due to node failure.

Problem Formulation: The set of all worker nodes in the cluster are denoted as N, where $n_i \in N$. The available CPU of n_i is denoted as n_i^{cpu}, and the available memory is denoted as n_i^{mem}. The set of all groups are denoted by G, where $g_j \in G$. The inter-node latency between nodes where g_j and g_k are placed is represented as $Latency(g_j, g_k)$. Each group g_j consists of replicas $\{r_{j,0}, r_{j,1}, \ldots, r_{j,m}\}$. The CPU and memory requirements of each replica $r_{j,l}$ within g_j are denoted as $r_{j,l}^{cpu}$ and $r_{j,l}^{mem}$, respectively. Let $z_{g_j}^{n_i} \in \{0,1\}$ be an indicator of whether g_j is placed on n_i. If g_j is placed on n_i, then $z_{g_j}^{n_i} = 1$; otherwise, $z_{g_j}^{n_i} = 0$. The objective is to minimize the total latency among the nodes where the groups are placed. The problem can be formulated as follows:

$$\text{Minimize} \sum_{g_j \in G} \sum_{g_k \in G} latency(g_j, g_k) \tag{1}$$

Subject to:

$$\sum_{n_i \in N} z_{g_j}^{n_i} = 1 \quad \forall g_j \in G \tag{2}$$

$$z_{g_j}^{n_i} + z_{g_k}^{n_i} \leq 1 \quad \forall g_j, g_k \in G, g_j \neq g_k \tag{3}$$

$$n_i^{cpu} \geq g_j^{cpu}, \quad g_j^{cpu} = \sum_{r_{j,l} \in g_j} r_{j,l}^{cpu}, \quad \text{if } z_{g_j}^{n_i} = 1 \tag{4}$$

$$n_i^{mem} \geq g_j^{mem}, \quad g_j^{mem} = \sum_{r_{j,l} \in g_j} r_{j,l}^{mem}, \quad \text{if } z_{g_j}^{n_i} = 1 \tag{5}$$

Algorithm 2. LARP

// Let W denote the set of all worker nodes in the cluster.
// Each worker node $w_i \in W$ is represented as $W = \{w_0, w_1, \ldots, w_m\}$

1: **Input:** $groups, W$
2: Sort $groups$ based on resource requirements in descending order
3: Initialize $nodeAssignments$ as an empty list
4: **for** each w_i in W **do**
5:     **if** $groups[0]$ can be placed on w_i **then**
6:         Initialize $nodeAssignment$ as an empty list
7:         Copy $groups$ to $tempGroups$ and Copy W to $tempW$
8:         Remove $groups[0]$ from $tempGroups$ and Remove w_i from $tempW$
9:         Sort $tempW$ by lowest latency to w_i
10:         **for** each w_j in $tempW$ **do**   // $w_i \neq w_j$
11:             **for** each $group_k$ in $tempGroups$ **do**   // $group_k \neq groups[0]$
12:                 **if** $group_k$ can be placed on w_j **then**
13:                     Append $(group_k, w_j)$ to $nodeAssignment$
14:                     Remove $group_k$ from $tempGroups$
15:                     break
16:                 **end if**
17:             **end for**
18:         **end for**
19:         **if** all groups are placed **then**
20:             CALCULATEAVERAGELATENCY($nodeAssignment$)
21:             Append $nodeAssignment$ to $nodeAssignments$ with avgLatency
22:         **end if**
23:     **end if**
24: **end for**
25: **if** $nodeAssignments$ is not empty **then**
26:     Select the assignment with lowest avgLatency as $bestNodeAssignment$
27: **else**
28:     Wait for suitable nodes
29: **end if**
30: **Output:** $bestNodeAssignment$

Latency-Aware Replica Placement Algorithm (LARP): We addressed the problem formulated above using a greedy approach to solve it in polynomial time. Algorithm 1 shows the process of generating groups. First, in line 2, the number of groups is calculated based on the average number of replicas. Then, in lines 4–8, the replicas of each component are sequentially assigned and allocated to groups. For example, if Component A has three replicas and Component B has two replicas, two groups are created. The resulting Group 1 has three replicas made up of two A and one B, and Group 2 has one replica of A and one of B.

Based on the groups generated in Algorithm 1, Algorithm 2 selects suitable worker nodes to place these groups. In Algorithm 2, in lines 4–24, a node is found where the group with the highest resource requirements can be placed. Then, starting with the node that has the lowest latency to the initially selected node, lines 6–18 check if the remaining groups can be accommodated. This involves

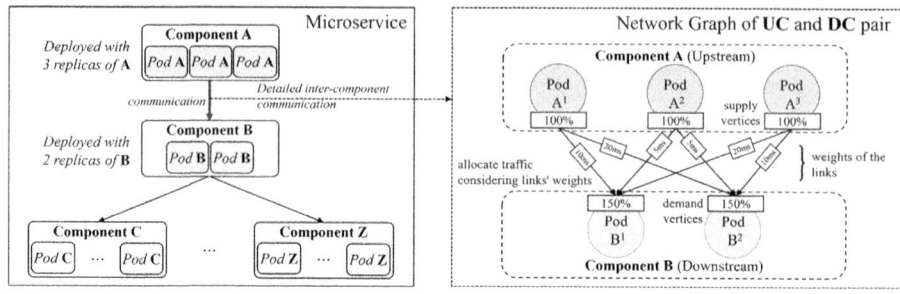

Fig. 5. Example of Network Graph

iterating through the remaining worker nodes and attempting to place each of the remaining groups on the node with the lowest latency relative to the initially selected node. If all the groups can be placed, in lines 19–22, the average latency among the selected nodes is calculated and the node assignments are recorded along with the average inter-node latency. Finally, in lines 25–26, the nodes with the lowest average inter-node latency are selected for placing each group. If there are no suitable nodes, the algorithm waits for suitable nodes to become available.

3.3 Traffic Allocation Strategy

The traffic allocation strategy allocates traffic for each communication link among replicas. This strategy reduces P99 latency in edge-cloud environments with varying inter-node latency. To achieve this, we formulate the traffic allocation problem as a *Minimum-Cost Flow Problem* (MCFP) [10], which involves finding the optimal flow with the minimum cost in a *network graph*, as shown in Fig. 5. A supply vertex supplies to the flow, while a demand vertex consumes from the flow. The supply vertex and the demand vertex are connected to each other by links, which have weights and capacities. The objective is to find an appropriate flow proportion for each communication link to minimize communication overhead while ensuring load balancing.

Problem Formulation: For each pair of deployed components, the set UC represents the replicas of upstream components, with each replica denoted as $uc_i \in UC$. Similarly, the set DC represents the replicas of downstream components, with each replica denoted as $dc_j \in DC$. The communication link between uc_i and dc_j is denoted as (uc_i, dc_j). The $Flow(uc_i, dc_j)$ indicates the proportion of traffic allocated to (uc_i, dc_j).

Figure 5 illustrates an example of a *network graph* for a pair of A and B components. In a component pair, the supply vertices are $\forall uc_i \in UC$, and the demand vertices are $\forall dc_j \in DC$. Since each uc_i cannot send traffic exceeding 100%, the flow $Flow(uc_i, dc_j)$ for each link (uc_i, dc_j) ranges from 0% to 100%. Eq. (6) finds an appropriate proportion for each link that minimizes communication overhead using the cost function $Latency(\text{uc}_i, \text{dc}_j)$:

$$\text{Minimize} \sum_{\text{uc}_i \in UC} \sum_{\text{dc}_j \in DC} Flow(\text{uc}_i, \text{dc}_j) \cdot Latency(\text{uc}_i, \text{dc}_j) \quad (6)$$

Flow conservation is captured by *Eq.* (7) and *Eq.* (7), ensuring the sum of the flow supplied by each uc_i equals the sum of the flow consumed by each dc_j. The required flow is satisfied by *Eq.* (7), ensuring that all traffic generated by the upstream components is fully received by each dc_j. Additionally, the load is balanced because each dc_j receives the same proportion of traffic.

$$\sum_{\text{dc}_j \in DC} Flow(\text{uc}_i, \text{dc}_j) = 100\,(\%), \quad \forall \text{uc}_i \in UC \quad (7)$$

$$\sum_{\text{uc}_i \in UC} Flow(\text{uc}_i, \text{dc}_j) = \frac{|UC|}{|DC|} \times 100\,(\%), \quad \forall \text{dc}_j \in DC \quad (8)$$

Capacity constraints are imposed by *Eq.* (9), restricting each traffic flow to be between 0 and 100%:

$$0 \leq Flow(\text{uc}_i, \text{dc}_j) \leq 100\,(\%) \quad (9)$$

Latency-Aware Traffic Allocation Algorithm (LATA): Algorithm 3 demonstrates the traffic allocation strategy. We utilized Istio, a widely-used service mesh, to determine the dependencies among components and represent them as a DAG. In line 3, *componentPairs* demonstrates upstream and downstream component as pairs of the service. Line 7 enforces the constraint from Eq. (7), and line 8 enforces the constraint from Eq. (8). Lines 9–10 retrieve the inter-node

---

Algorithm 3. LATA

//DAG represents the relationships among components.
1: **Input:** DAG
2: $componentPairs \leftarrow \text{CREATECOMPONENTPAIRS}(DAG)$
3: Initialize $allComponentFlows$ as an empty list
4: **for** each $pair$ in $componentPairs$ **do**
5:    $UC \leftarrow \text{GETUPSTREAMCOMPONENT}(pair)$
6:    $DC \leftarrow \text{GETDOWNSTREAMCOMPONENT}(pair)$
7:    $UCsend \leftarrow Calculate\ by\ Eq.\ (7)$
8:    $DCrecv \leftarrow Calculate\ by\ Eq.\ (8)$
9:    $linkWeights \leftarrow \text{GETALLINTERNODELATENCY}(UC, DC)$
10:    $netGraph \leftarrow \text{MAKENETGRAPH}(UC, DC, UCsend, DCrecv, linkWeights)$
11:    $flow \leftarrow \text{MINCOSTFLOW}(netGraph)$
12:    Append the $flow$ to $allComponentFlows$
13: **end for**
14: **Output:** $allComponentFlows$

Table 1. Scenario A

node	WN1	WN2	WN3	WN4
WN1	–	5 ms	20 ms	40 ms
WN2	5 ms	–	10 ms	25 ms
WN3	20 ms	10 ms	–	5 ms
WN4	40 ms	25 ms	5 ms	–

Table 2. Scenario B

node	WN1	WN2	WN3	WN4
WN1	–	10 ms	40 ms	80 ms
WN2	10 ms	–	20 ms	50 ms
WN3	40 ms	20 ms	–	10 ms
WN4	80 ms	50 ms	10 ms	–

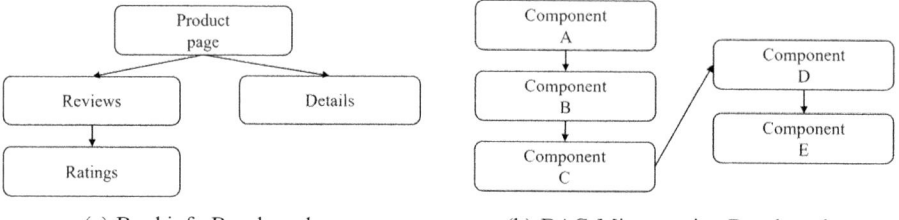

(a) Bookinfo Benchmark   (b) DAG Microservice Benchmark

Fig. 6. Architecture of Bookinfo and DAG microservice benchmark

latencies between the worker nodes where the UC and DC replicas are placed and assign these latencies as links' weights in the *network graph*, as shown in Fig. 5. Line 11 solves Eq. (6), which represents the MCFP, utilizing the network simplex algorithm and finds the optimal traffic allocation proportions for each link.

4 Experimental Results

4.1 Experimental Setup

To evaluate our proposed approach, we created a K8s cluster consisting of one master node and four worker nodes. Each physical node has 4 cores of CPU and 8 GB of memory. To simulate a geographically distributed edge-cloud environment, we configured varying latencies among the worker nodes. We used the Linux traffic control utility, tc[5], to apply different network delays. Tables 1 and 2 present the specific latency configurations for each scenario.

For our experiments, we utilized two benchmarks: Istio Bookinfo benchmark and DAG microservice benchmark (illustrated in Fig. 6). All components of both services were configured with resource limits of 500 millicores of CPU and 500 MB of memory. Each component was set to have 3-5 replicas. The DAG microservices were implemented using Python's FastAPI framework, handling end-user requests sequentially from A to E. Requests to each service were sent

---
[5] https://man7.org/linux/man-pages/man8/tc.8.html.

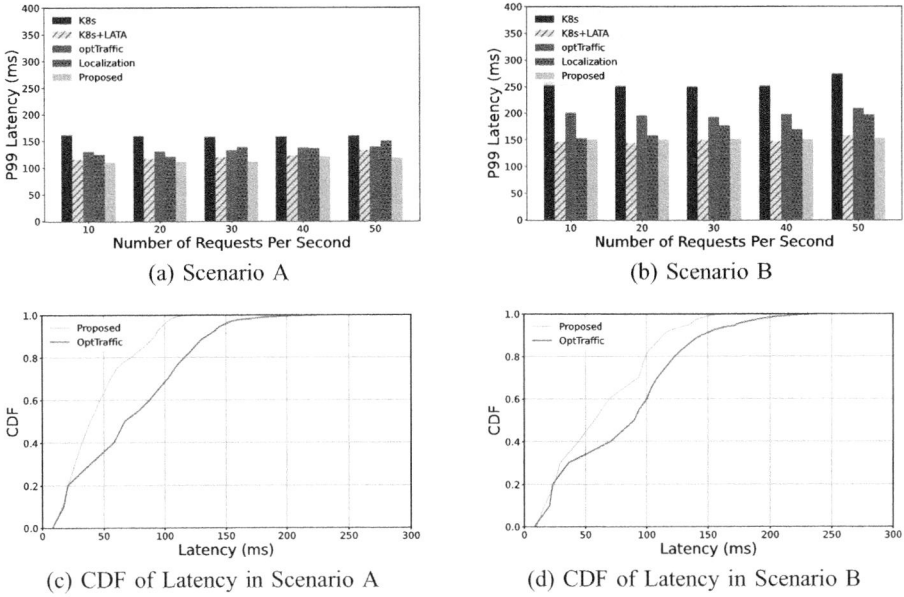

Fig. 7. Bookinfo Benchmark

using the stress testing tool wrk2[6]. To measure the response time, we conducted our experiment 10 times and calculated the mean value.

We compared our approach with existing methods, including the default K8s, Localization, and OptTraffic. For Localization, inter-communicating components were placed on the same node whenever possible or on adjacent nodes if resources were insufficient. To demonstrate the efficiency of LATA itself, we also included a default K8s replica placement with improved traffic management using LATA as another candidate for our comparison.

To demonstrate the effectiveness of our approach compared to OptTraffic, we configured the experiments to ensure that $|global\ ratio - local\ ratio| \leq 1$. Note that this setup highly favors OptTraffic by minimizing inter-node communication, placing it in an optimal state. The *global ratio* is defined as $\frac{|UC|}{|DC|}$, while the *local ratio* represents the ratio of UC to DC replicas deployed on each worker node. By maintaining a similar global-local ratio, we reduce the likelihood of situations where OptTraffic's enforced load balancing would lead to increased inter-node communication and higher latency, ensuring a fair comparison.

4.2 Bookinfo Benchmark

Figure 7 shows the experimental results under various scenarios and RPS using the Bookinfo benchmark. In Fig. 7(a) and Fig. 7(b), Localization exhibits similar performance to our approach at lower RPS. However, as RPS increases, its

---

[6] https://github.com/giltene/wrk2.

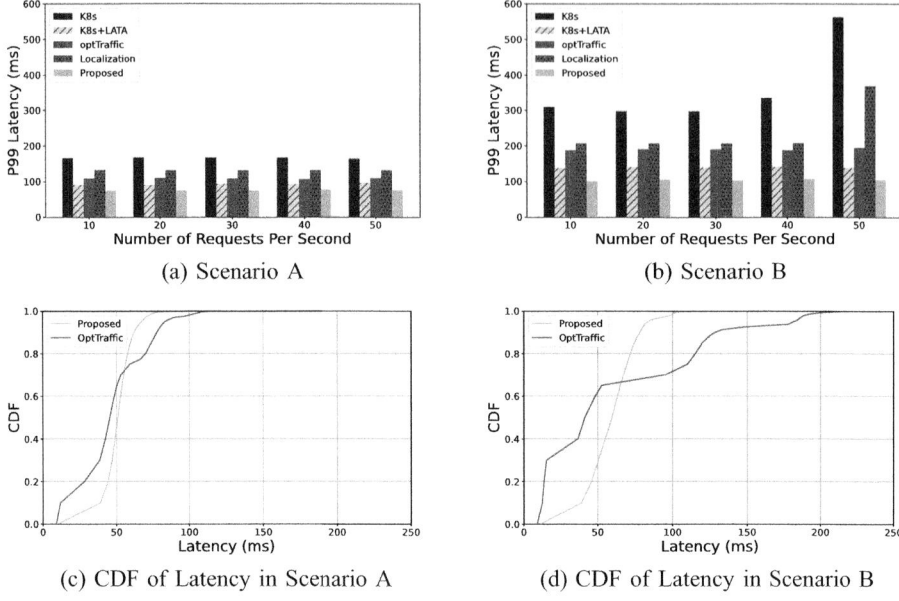

Fig. 8. DAG Microservice Benchmark

performance degrades due to shared resource contention caused by most component replicas being placed on the same worker node, leading to increased P99 latency. Notably, in Fig. 7(b), our approach reduces P99 latency by an average of 25% compared to OptTraffic. The reasoning is that OptTraffic focuses on reducing inter-node communication bandwidth without accounting for inter-node latency, leading to relatively high P99 latency during the padding stage (Sect. 2.2) while our approach does consider inter-node latency. Furthermore, as shown in Fig. 7(c) and Fig. 7(d), our approach not only decreases P99 latency but also reduces the average request response time by 9% and 23%, respectively.

4.3 DAG Microservice Benchmark

To analyze the performance of services with more complex topologies, we conducted experiments using the DAG microservice benchmark. As microservice topology becomes more complex, Localization fails to place relevant communicating replicas in the same node due to node resource limitations. This results in higher inter-node communication and increased P99 latency, as shown in Fig. 8(a) and Fig. 8(b). In contrast, our approach demonstrated a reduction of 48%-72% in P99 latency compared to Localization, 43%-46% compared to OptTraffic, and 67%-81% compared to default K8s in Scenario B. Moreover, the default K8s with LATA (K8s + LATA) demonstrated better performance and is second only to our proposed method, showing that LATA can be effective when applied to different placement strategies.

As shown in Fig. 8(d), our approach reduced the average request response time by 4% compared to OptTraffic. OptTraffic's superior performance in the lower 65th percentile is due to its traffic allocation strategy, which focuses on minimizing inter-node communication rather than overall communication overhead, unlike our approach. Our proposed approach improves P99 latency and average response time in edge-cloud environments with diverse inter-node latencies compared to existing methods. These results emphasize that our approach significantly enhances QoS by effectively considering multi-replica deployments in edge-cloud environments, which are not sufficiently accounted for in existing methods.

5 Related Works

Single-Replica Environments: NetMARKS [14] monitors communication between components using Istio Service Mesh, calculates node suitability scores and then replaces components to the nodes with the highest scores. Nautilus [6] uses a microservice mapper to reduce communication overhead by first partitioning microservices based on communication frequency and data transfer size, and then placing them on appropriate nodes. Marchese et al. [8,9] considers the available resources of nodes and communication overhead during placement, and evicts components if better nodes are found after the initial placement. However, these approaches assume a single-replica environment. When deployed in a multi-replica environment, these approaches lead to QoS degradation due to K8s' inefficient traffic allocation strategy.

Multi-replica Environments: OptTraffic [16] addresses multi-replica scenarios by allocating traffic based on the number of replicas for each pair of microservice components. First, OptTraffic reduces cross-machine traffic by using a local-first strategy to allocate as much traffic as possible to replicas on the same node, without exceeding the *global ratio*. Then, padding is used to distribute the remaining traffic to achieve load balancing. Additionally, frequently communicating component pairs are identified and migrated to closely match the *global* and *local ratios*. However, OptTraffic did not consider inter-node latency, making it ineffective at reducing tail-latency in edge-cloud environments.

6 Conclusion

In this work, we proposed a latency-aware replica placement method (LARP) and a latency-aware traffic allocation strategy (LATA) to reduce average response time and 99th percentile tail-latency in edge-cloud environments. We implemented a prototype, conducted experiments on K8s, and compared our approach with default K8s, Localization, OptTraffic, and default K8s with LATA. The results showed that our approach improves 99th percentile tail-latency and average response time compared to the other techniques.

In our future work, we plan to focus not only on reducing communication overhead within the cluster but also on developing traffic scheduling techniques that minimize end-to-end response time by considering the distance to end users.

Acknowledgments. This research was supported by the MSIT(Ministry of Science, ICT), Korea, under the National Program for Excellence in SW, supervised by the IITP(Institute of Information & communications Technology Planing & Evaluation) in 2024(2023-0-00044).

This research was supported by the MSIT(Ministry of Science and ICT), Korea, under the ICAN(ICT Challenge and Advanced Network of HRD) support program(IITP-2024-RS-2022-00156439) supervised by the IITP(Institute for Information & Communications Technology Planning & Evaluation).

References

1. Ahmad, I., AlFailakawi, M.G., AlMutawa, A., Alsalman, L.: Container scheduling techniques: a survey and assessment. J. King Saud Univ. Comput. Inform. Sci. **34**(7), 3934–3947 (2022)
2. Amazon Web Services: What is a service level agreement (sla)? (2024). https://aws.amazon.com/what-is/service-level-agreement/, Accessed 25 July 2024
3. Cao, L., Sharma, P.: Co-locating containerized workload using service mesh telemetry. In: Proceedings of the 17th International Conference on emerging Networking EXperiments and Technologies, pp. 168–174 (2021)
4. Carrión, C.: Kubernetes scheduling: taxonomy, ongoing issues and challenges. ACM Comput. Surv. **55**(7), 1–37 (2022)
5. Centofanti, C., Tiberti, W., Marotta, A., Graziosi, F., Cassioli, D.: Latency-aware kubernetes scheduling for microservices orchestration at the edge. In: 2023 IEEE 9th International Conference on Network Softwarization (NetSoft), pp. 426–431. IEEE (2023)
6. Fu, K., et al.: Qos-aware and resource efficient microservice deployment in cloud-edge continuum. In: 2021 IEEE International Parallel and Distributed Processing Symposium (IPDPS), pp. 932–941. IEEE (2021)
7. Gannon, D., Barga, R., Sundaresan, N.: Cloud-native applications. IEEE Cloud Comput. **4**(5), 16–21 (2017)
8. Marchese, A., Tomarchio, O.: Extending the kubernetes platform with network-aware scheduling capabilities. In: International Conference on Service-Oriented Computing. pp. 465–480. Springer (2022). https://doi.org/10.1007/978-3-031-20984-0_33
9. Marchese, A., Tomarchio, O.: Application and infrastructure-aware orchestration in the cloud-to-edge continuum. In: 2023 IEEE 16th International Conference on Cloud Computing (CLOUD), pp. 262–271. IEEE (2023)
10. Orlin, J.: A faster strongly polynomial minimum cost flow algorithm. In: Proceedings of the Twentieth annual ACM symposium on Theory of Computing, pp. 377–387 (1988)
11. Santos, J., Wauters, T., Volckaert, B., De Turck, F.: Towards network-aware resource provisioning in kubernetes for fog computing applications. In: 2019 IEEE Conference on Network Softwarization (NetSoft), pp. 351–359. IEEE (2019)
12. Shi, W., Cao, J., Zhang, Q., Li, Y., Xu, L.: Edge computing: vision and challenges. IEEE Internet Things J. **3**(5), 637–646 (2016)

13. Singh, V., Peddoju, S.K.: Container-based microservice architecture for cloud applications. In: 2017 International Conference on Computing, Communication and Automation (ICCCA), pp. 847–852. IEEE (2017)
14. Wojciechowski, Ł., et al.: Netmarks: network metrics-aware kubernetes scheduler powered by service mesh. In: IEEE INFOCOM 2021-IEEE Conference on Computer Communications, pp. 1–9. IEEE (2021)
15. Xiao, Z., Wijegunaratne, I., Qiang, X.: Reflections on soa and microservices. In: 2016 4th International Conference on Enterprise Systems (ES), pp. 60–67. IEEE (2016)
16. Zhu, X., et al.: On optimizing traffic scheduling for multi-replica containerized microservices. In: Proceedings of the 52nd International Conference on Parallel Processing, pp. 358–368 (2023)

An Event-B Based Approach for Horizontally Scalable IoT Applications

Yassmine Gara Hellal[1]((✉)) , Lazhar Hamel[2,3] , and Mohamed Graiet[2]

[1] Faculty of Sciences of Monastir, University of Monastir, Monastir, Tunisia
garayesmine@gmail.com
[2] Department of Computer Science, ISIMM, University of Monastir, Monastir, Tunisia
lazhar.hamel@isimm.rnu.tn, mohamed.graiet@isimm.u-monastir.tn
[3] Efrei Research Laboratory, EFREI Paris, Pantheon Assas University, Villejuif, France

Abstract. The applications are being growingly executed on IoT systems. Such systems may involve devices that often rely on limited power sources, processing capabilities and shut down for prolonged durations to maximize energy efficiency. They do not possess the means to forge reliable and direct communications with the Internet. Establishing horizontally scalable applications is not always assured in IoT systems. In this paper, we propose a model to verify horizontally scalable IoT applications. Three verification axes are considered: Architectural, Intermediation, and Horizontal Scalability. Thus, we adopted the Event-B formal method to incrementally develop our model, taking advantage of its refinement features. We also engaged proof obligations to accurately verify the model and then leveraged the ProB animator for its validation.

Keywords: IoT Applications · Architectural Verification · Intermediation · Horizontal Scalability · low-power · Event-B

1 Introduction

The Internet of Things (IoT) [1] refers to a global network of devices that are embedded with internet connectivity and Cloud technology [2], to permit the development of applications through the exchange, storage and process of data.

Significantly, the applications are intended to run on IoT networks. An IoT network [3] may be characterised by limits with suboptimal transmission speed and includes numerous devices [3] that have tight limits in terms of energy, processing capabilities and remain unreachable for long periods to save their available power. Such devices do not have enough power to communicate directly with the Internet in a reliable manner. They participate in Internet communications with the help of larger intermediary devices acting as shared caches [4] or gateways. An intermediary device occurs in IoT systems to assist the devices that are unable to communicate, while preserving their functionalities and keeping the interfaces between them intact [4]. An intermediary forwards requests and relays back responses on behalf of IoT devices, while making namespace and protocol translations. However, the number of IoT devices has rapidly grown, up to billions. Thereby, an intermediary (e.g., shared cache) may experience contention issues due to the limited amount of devices it can aid at the same time.

To address the mentioned issues, we propose an approach for horizontally scalable applications that may be executed on IoT systems. The approach consists of formally modeling and verifying IoT application and its horizontal scalability mechanism, to prevent communication inconsistencies during its execution. The major contribution of this work is a model that tackles three verification axes: Architectural, Intermediation and Horizontal Scalability.

The verification is divided into many levels. Hence, we opt for the Event-B [5] formal method for its ability to perform complex problem decomposition through its refinement capabilities. The use of a formal method is nowadays a necessity to eliminate ambiguities and ensure the safety properties are held, thereby creating a reliable and mathematically grounded model for IoT applications. We provide a rigorous reasoning on the correctness of our model at each refining stage by discharging proof obligations [6]. The validation of our model is achieved through the use of ProB animator.

The following sections organize the present paper: In Sect. 2 we expose our motivations. Section 3 presents existing related works. Our formal model is introduced in Sect. 4. Section 5 explains the verification approach. Finally, we submit the conclusion and highlight future works in Sect. 6.

2 Motivations and Problem Statement

This section presents a healthcare application as a practical demonstration of our approach. Its objective is to deliver timely alerts of emerging health risks, which ensure proactive patient care. As depicted in Fig. 1, the application is intended to run on an IoT system that incorporates two Low-power and Lossy Networks [3]. The first embraces constrained devices (*Temp_Sen*, *Resp_Sen*) that are designed with strict limits on resources. Besides, they enter deep sleep mode for extended intervals, while remaining primed for quick reactivation when needed. The second holds a group of constrained (*EMG_Sen*) and unconstrained devices (*Analyzer*, *FES_Act*) with further limits arising from the network. These devices encapsulate a set of resources. Each service is a resource, but not every resource is a service [7]. Based on this understanding, the following items (1–4) are referred to as resources in a general sense. But they can be specifically identified as medical services.

1. *Electromyography (EMG) Sensing Service*: offered by the *EMG_Sen*.
2. *Respiratory Rate Sensing Service*: hosted on the *Resp_Sen*.
3. *Temperature Sensing Service*: supplied by the *Temp_Sen*.
4. *Functional Electrical Stimulation (FES) Service*: hosted on the *FES_Act*.

As the application runs, IoT devices interact seamlessly to monitor health metrics of the *Patient* (e.g. Respiratory Rate). For example, the *Analyzer* device reaches out to the *EMG_Sen* to inquire about the resource *'Electromyography Sensing Service'* it manages. The *EMG_Sen* operates under severe constraints and frequently turns into a full power-off state. Therefore, it typically falls short in establishing direct communication with the *Analyzer*, which exploits a robust protocol stack like *HTTP*. In this scenario, the *Intermediary1* must step in to orchestrate effective protocol translations. Accordingly, it conveys a representation of the captured resource on behalf of the *EMG_Sen*. The

Analyzer is responsible for aggregating the data sourced from the *EMG_Sen*, *Resp_Sen* and *Temp_Sen* that reveal respiratory rate and so on. Once aggregated, the Cloud service evaluates these reading based on a threshold to ascertain whether an imminent danger is established. For instance, if the Electromyography (EMG) signal amplitude falls below 10–20 μV range for some muscles during voluntary contraction, the Cloud will immediately trigger the *'Functional Electrical Stimulation Service'* to avoid deterioration of muscle activity, atrophy or even complete paralysis in critical scenarios.

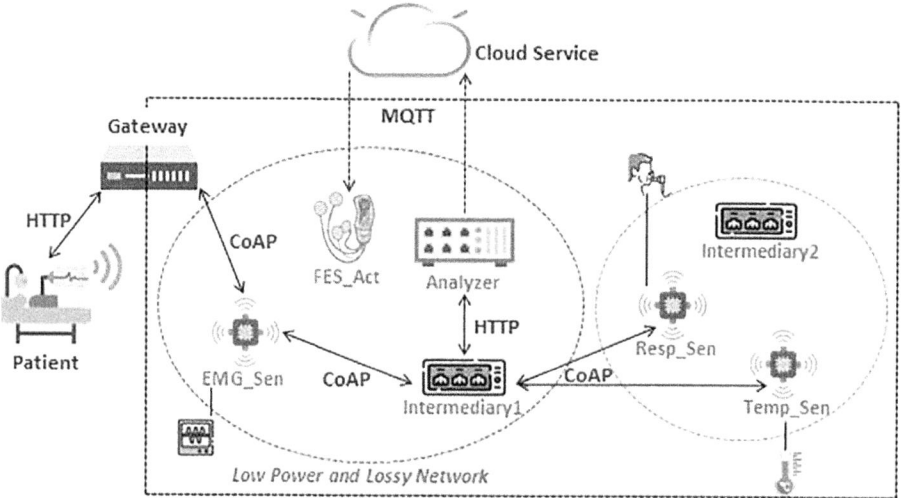

Fig. 1. IoT Healthcare Application System

In this context, we propose an Event-B model that covers :

- **Architectural Verification:** It verifies the design of IoT systems.
- **Intermediation Verification:** It checks whether the intermediaries are correctly behaving toward assisting IoT devices.
- **Horizontal Scalability Verification:** It integrates the horizontal scaling mechanism to improve the system while verifying that as it scales, it continues to function correctly and efficiently.

3 Related Work

This section provides an overview of the existing research in this area.

In [8] the authors suggested a rigorous approach to mathematically model the architecture of IoT systems and to express the behavior of devices within them. In [9] an enhanced time behavior protocol is introduced to specify and verify the timed interaction behaviors in IoT systems. The protocol integrates time consumption constraints and time-related operators, enabling effective modeling of real-time components. In

[10] an automated MUD profiles and a model-based methodology are devised to detect behavioral failures by exploiting proper formalisms. The profiles are validated through the use of a semantic framework. In [11] a novel mechanism is proposed to allow event-triggered state updates and to verify non-interference requirements in smart IoT device ensembles. Besides, other methodologies articulated with timed process algebra [12], temporal logic of actions [13] and others [14], check the correctness of IoT events that are manifested in terms of MQTT, CoAP and trickle communications. The key demerit in the stated works is that they do not analyze the scalability requirements.

In this work, we overcome the limits of existent works by introducing a novel approach that combines the modeling and verification of the three requirements: Architectural, Intermediation and Horizontal Scalability. Our model takes advantage of using event-B that combines proof and model checking techniques. The use of Event-B in our approach is chosen because it is an integrative method providing tools that cover the whole cycle of the systems development from the requirement specification to the code generation. Further, our approach (1) addresses IoT systems that appear with notable limits (e.g., low-power) in the architectural level (2) considers the role of intermediaries in the intermediation level, (3) verifies the horizontal scaling in IoT systems.

4 The Proposed Horizontally Scalable IoT Application Model

This section presents our Event-B model for the verification of horizontally scalable IoT applications. As illustrated in Fig. 2, our model comprises three verification levels: Architectural, Intermediation and Horizontal Scalability.

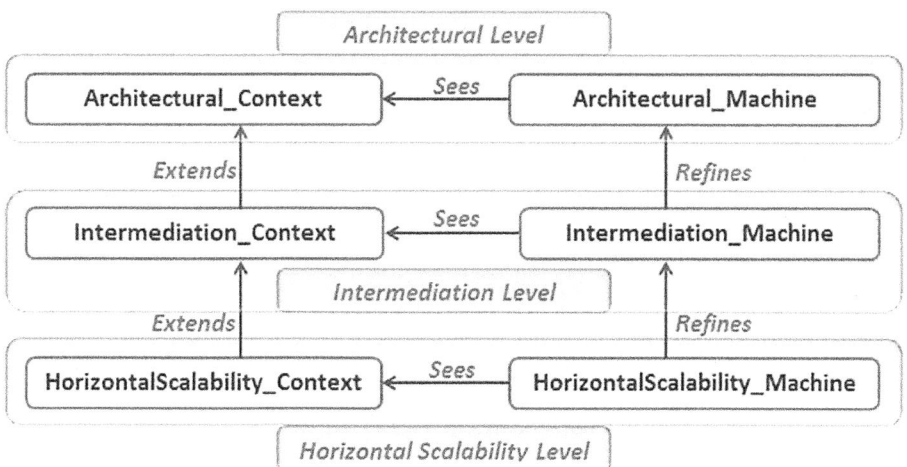

Fig. 2. An Incremental Model for Horizontally Scalable IoT Applications

4.1 Modeling the Architectural Requirements

Initially, we specify the foundational components that shape the design of IoT systems. To do so, we benefit from the Event-B method to generate the *"Architectural_Context"* (Fig. 3), where we define IoT components as SETS called *IoTSys*, *Networks* and *Devices*. The connections between these sets are articulated in the AXIOMS clause, where the types of constants are explicitly assigned.

Table 1. Architectural Requirements

AR1 An IoT system incorporates a set of Low-Power and Lossy Networks *LLN*.
AR2 A *LLN* consists of certain limits arising from the network, plus a set of devices that are classified as highly-constrained (*high*), quite-constrained (*quite*), unconstrained (*uncst*) and intermediary (*inter*) devices.
AR3 A device is associated to one *LLN* that encompasses at least two constrained devices (*high* and/or *quite*) and one intermediary. $card(high) + card(quite) \geq 2 \wedge card(inter) \neq \emptyset$.
AR4 The vast majority of devices in a *LLN* should be constrained.

CONTEXT Architectural_Context	MACHINE Architectural_Machine
SETS	**SEES** Architectural_Context
IoTSys Networks Devices ...	**VARIABLES**
CONSTANTS	*sys net llnDv* ...
SysNet NetDev DevLev ...	**INVARIANTS**
	inv1 : $sys \subseteq IoTSys$
	inv2 : $net = SysNet^{-1}[sys]$
	inv3 : $llnDv \in net \cap NetGenre[\{LLN\}]^{-1} \leftrightarrow Devices$
AXIOMS	inv4 : $\forall l \cdot l \in dom(llnDv) \Rightarrow$
axm1 : $finite(IoTSys)$	$card(NetDev[\{l\}]^{-1} \cap DevLev[\{high\}]^{-1}) +$
$\wedge finite(Devices) \wedge finite(Networks)$	$card(NetDev[\{c\}]^{-1} \cap DevLev[\{quite\}]^{-1}) \geq 2$
axm2 : $Genre = \{LLN, CNN\}$	$\wedge NetDev[\{l\}]^{-1} \cap DevLev[\{inter\}]^{-1} \neq \emptyset$
axm3 : $SysNet \in Networks \rightarrowtail IoTSys$	inv5 : $\forall l \cdot l \in dom(llnDv) \Rightarrow$
axm4 : $NetGenre \in Networks \rightarrow Genre$	$card(NetDev[\{l\}]^{-1} \cap DevLev[\{uncst\}]^{-1}) <$
axm5 : $Lev = \{high, quite, uncst, inter\}$	$card(NetDev[\{l\}]^{-1} \cap DevLev[\{high\}]^{-1}) +$
axm6 : $NetDev \in Devices \rightarrowtail Networks$	$card(NetDev[\{l\}]^{-1} \cap DevLev[\{quite\}]^{-1})$
axm7 : $DevLev \in Devices \rightarrow Lev$	
END	**END**

Fig. 3. The Event-B *Architectural_Context* and *Architectural_Machine*

The *"Architectural_Context"* is seen (clause **SEES**) by *"Architectural_Machine"* (see Fig. 3) that defines in INVARIANTS certain variables to model the dynamic parts of IoT systems. As depicted, we have introduced the variables *sys* and *net* to model the subset of IoT systems and the networks within it (*inv1*, *inv2*). To each *LLN* network, we have affiliated its devices designated by the total relation *llnDv* (*inv3*).

Table 2. Intermediation Requirements and Rules

IR1 A device must be responsible for at least one *resource* and employs at least one *protocol*.
IR2 A device cannot sustain only *CoAP*, if it's not associated with systems that follow REST[7].
IR3 If a device is *high* or (*quite* & does not employ *Bundle protocols* [15] or *CoAP*)
  $\Rightarrow$ An *intermediary* of the same network must support the device.
IR4 If a device is *quite* & employs *Bundle protocols* and/or *CoAP* & belongs to *LLN*
  $\Rightarrow$ The interaction will be satisfied without the aid of an *intermediary*.

CONTEXT Intermediation_Context
EXTENDS Architectural_Context
SETS
Protocols Resources ...
AXIOMS
axm1 : *ConnectDev* $\in$ *Devices* $\leftrightarrow$ *Devices*
axm2 : *DevRsc* $\in$ *Devices* $\leftrightarrow\!\!\!\rightarrow$ *Resources*
axm3 : *ProtEmploy* $\in$ *Devices* $\leftrightarrow$ *Protocols*
axm4 : *IntermedCapacity* $\in$ *Devices* $\rightarrow$ $\mathbb{N}1$
axm5 : $\forall e \cdot (e \in dom(ProtEmploy) \setminus dom(DevRsc)) \Rightarrow ProtEmploy(e) \neq CoAP$ **END**

Fig. 4. The Event-B *Intermediation_Context*

AR3 and **AR4** (see Table 1) are correspondingly enclosed in *inv4* and *inv5*. In fact, they confront the density of the fulfilled *LLN* clusters, while monitoring the amount and genre of devices within them. The devices that belong to other kinds of networks (e.g., Constrained Node Networks *CNN*) are modeled in a similar way, but their formalization is hidden for better readability.

4.2 Modeling the Intermediation Requirements

The refined *"Intermediation_Context"* adds the following constants. *ConnectDev* denotes the (*client, server*) pairs (*axm1*). *axm2* establishes a total surjective relation that links a specific resource to its corresponding device, ensuring that each device hosts at least one resource, as outlined in **IR1** presented in Table 2. **IR1** is also modeled in *axm3* that expresses the protocols employed by each device. **IR2** is specified in *axm5*. Finally, *IntermedCapacity* reveals the intermediary capacity (*axm4*). The above context is seen by *"Intermediation_Machine"* where we declare *InterResp* (*InterResp* $\in DevLev\,[\{inter\}]^{-1} \rightarrow \mathbb{N}$) that indicates the amount of devices supported by a given *intermediary*. The boolean *Intermediating* is set to TRUE when an *intermediary* intervenes in an IoT communication. Finally, the *NewIntermediating* indicates that a new *intermediary* must be duplicated if it is evaluated to TRUE.

4.3 Modeling the Horizontal Scalability Requirements

In this section, we extend the previously developed formalization with the horizontal scalability mechanisms to formally model horizontally scalable IoT applications.

The horizontal scalability mechanisms are two operations: *'DuplicateIntermediary'* and *'ConsolidateIntermediary'*. To do so, we create the *"HorizontalScalability_Context"* to define the constant *newCopy* that correlates each original *intermediary* to its copy, while covering **HSR1**. The context is seen by *"HorizontalScalability_Machine"*, where we define the variable *duplicatedInter* that refers to new duplicated *intermediaries*.

Table 3. Horizontal Scalability Requirements

HSR1 A copy and its original *intermediary* should possess similar capabilities and deliver comparable speed.
HSR2 If the request on an *intermediary* exceeds its offered *capacity*, it should be possible to duplicate the *intermediary* in the future.
HSR3 If the request on an *intermediary* subpar relative to its offered *capacity*, it should be possible to remove its useless copies.

When *NewIntermediating* of the above event is set to TRUE, it means that all the *intermediaries* are saturated and the event *'DuplicateIntermediary'* should be activated (see Fig. 5). This event enables duplicating new *intermediaries* while covering **HSR2** (see Table 3). The *grd1* and *grd2* detect the saturated *intermediary* and select a new copy that has similar capabilities of the saturated one. Once triggered (*act1*), a *new intermediary* is immediately duplicated to manage the growing workload. The event *'ConsolidateIntermediary'* (Fig. 5) removes the useless *intermediaries* from the system, whenever these copies are under-provisioned (**HSR3**).

DuplicateIntermediary $\widehat{=}$	**ConsolidateIntermediary** $\widehat{=}$
ANY saturated dup	**ANY** liberated
WHERE	**WHERE**
grd1: $saturated \in ran(newCopy) \land saturated \in$ $dom(InterResp) \land newIntermediating = TRUE$ $\land InterResp(saturated) - threshold(saturated) >$ $IntermedCapacity(saturated)$ $\times (card(dom(duplicatedInter)) + 1)$	grd1: $liberated \in dom(InterResp)$
	grd2: $liberated \in ran(duplicatedInter)$
	grd3: $InterResp(liberated) <$ $IntermedCapacity(liberated)$
	THEN
grd2: $dup \in newCopy[\{saturated\}]^{-1}$	act1: $duplicatedInter :=$ $duplicatedInter[\{liberated\}]^{-1}$ $\vartriangleleft duplicatedInter$
THEN	
act1: $duplicatedInter(dup) := saturated$	
END	**END**

Fig. 5. The events *'DuplicateIntermediary'* and *'ConsolidateIntermediary'*

5 Proof Obligations Based Verification

In light of the strong mathematical foundation that Event-B offers, it becomes straightforward to apply formal reasoning and proofs (POs) to verify the consistency of our

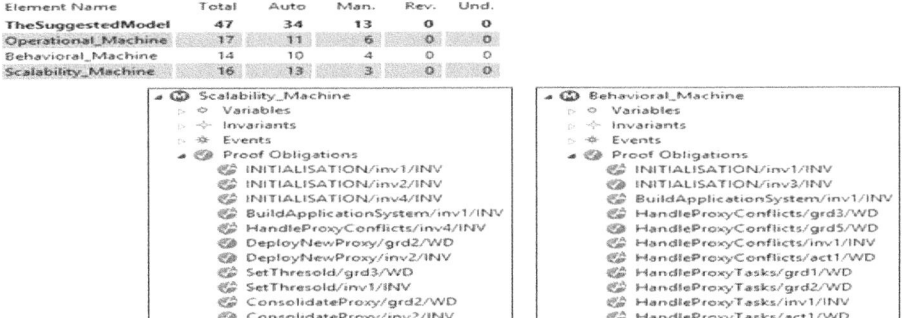

Fig. 6. POs of the *Horizontal Scalability Model* and proof statistics

suggested model. POs are represented by *hypotheses* → *goal*, which indicates that if the hypotheses are correct, and the conclusion is likewise correct. Indeed, vigorous tools assist the proof process to ensure that the events related to three levels do not falsify the 19 invariants. Effectively, our checked model has generated a total of 47 POs. 34 of them are automatically discharged (denoted by the green "A" symbol) through the utilization of the automatic prover (3O sec to all proofs). The latter fails to discharge the remaining proofs due to the extensive number of steps required, and not on account of their difficulty. To finish discharging these proofs, we ultimately resorted to the interactive prover and guided it to discover the appropriate steps and rules to apply. Figure 6 displays proof statistics and some POs of the Horizontal Scalability level.

6 Conclusion

To conclude, this paper introduced a robust approach to ensure the reliability of IoT applications while emphasizing three axes: architectural, intermediation, and horizontal scalability. By offering a formal foundation and employing proof obligations, this work contributes to the evolution of resilient IoT systems without compromising their stability. Our solution provides a pathway for the developers to systematically verify IoT applications, thereby addressing potential challenges early in the development process. Future work will involve expanding our model to account for mobility in IoT systems, where dynamic topologies and intermittent connectivity amplify reliability challenges.

References

1. Sadeghi-Niaraki, A.: Internet of Thing (IoT) review of review: bibliometric overview since its foundation. Futur. Gener. Comput. Syst. **143**, 361–377 (2023)
2. Burak Cinar and Jasmin Praful Bharadiya: Cloud computing forensics; challenges and future perspectives: a review. Asian J. Res. Comput. Sci. **16**(1), 1–14 (2023)
3. Bormann, C., et al. RFC 7228: Terminology for constrained-node networks (2014)
4. Shelby, Z., et al.: The Constrained Application Protocol (CoAP). RFC 7252 (June 2014)

5. Abrial, J.R.: Modeling in Event-B: system and software engineering. Cambridge University Press (2010)
6. Abrial, J.-R., et al.: Rodin: an open toolset for modelling and reasoning in Event-B. Int. J. Softw. Tools Technol. Transfer **12**, 447–466 (2010)
7. Fielding, R.T.: Architectural Styles and the Design of Network-based Software Architectures; Doctoral dissertation (2000)
8. Yassmine, G.H., et al.: A Formal Modeling and Verification Approach for IoT-Cloud Resource-Oriented Applications. In: 2024 IEEE 24th International Symposium on Cluster, Cloud and Internet Computing (CCGrid), pp. 347–356 (2024)
9. Jia, Y., Zhang, Z., Cao, X., Wang, H.: Formal specification and verification of timing behavior in safety-critical IoT systems. In: Arabnia, H.R., Deligiannidis, L., Tinetti, F.G., Tran, Q.-N. (eds.) Advances in Software Engineering, Education, and e-Learning. TCSCI, pp. 459–470. Springer, Cham (2021). https://doi.org/10.1007/978-3-030-70873-3_32
10. Hamza, A., et al.: Verifying and monitoring iots network behavior using MUD profiles. IEEE Trans. Dependable Secure Comput. **19**(1), 1–18 (2020)
11. Pasqua, M., Miculan, M.: Behavioral equivalences for AbU: verifying security and safety in distributed IoT systems. Theoret. Comput. Sci. **998**, 114537 (2024)
12. Suresh Kumar, N., Santhosh Kumar, G.: Abstracting IoT protocols using timed process algebra and SPIN model checker. Cluster Comput. **26**(2), 1611–1629 (2023)
13. Shkarupylo.V., et al.: On the aspects of IoT protocols specification and verification. In 2019 IEEE International Scientific-Practical Conference Problems of Infocommunications, Science and Technology (PIC S&T), pp. 93–96. IEEE (2019)
14. Hofer-Schmitz, K., Stojanović, B.: Towards formal verification of IoT protocols: a Review. Comput. Netw. **174**, 107233 (2020)
15. Persampieri, L.: Unibo-BP: an innovative free software implementation of Bundle Protocol Version 7 (RFC 9171). Master's thesis in Computer Science Engineering (2023)

Efficient Provisioning of IoT Energy Services

Amani Abusafia[(✉)], Athman Bouguettaya, and Abdallah Lakhdari

The University of Sydney, Sydney, NSW 2000, Australia
{amani.abusafia,athman.bouguettaya,abdallah.lakhdari}@sydney.edu.au

Abstract. We propose a QoE-based framework for providing energy services. The provisioning is constrained by the fluctuating availability of energy providers, coupled with the super provider's limited reward budget. We present a new Linear Programming (LP) formulation for QoE-based energy service provisioning. We use GLPK solver to find the optimal service composition by leveraging providers' preferences. A set of experiments were conducted to evaluate the effectiveness of our approach.

Keywords: wireless power transfer · IoT Services · Energy Services · QoE

1 Introduction

Energy-as-a-Service, i.e., EaaS is the *transfer of wireless power* to nearby IoT devices [1]. For instance, a smartshirt (i.e., energy provider) may offer their spare energy to a closeby smartwatch (i.e., energy consumer). The spare energy may be harvested from renewable resources, e.g., kinetic movement [2], or body heat [3]. Energy services is an eco-friendly solution that provides *spatial-freedom* in charging IoT devices [4]. Energy services may be delivered using "Over-the-Air" charging technologies [5]. For instance, a device developed by Energous can charge up to three watts within five meters[1]. These technologies are inefficient in energy transfer, though future advancements are expected to enhance the amount of transferred energy [6]. Recent studies propose using central sources for wireless charging [7]. However, they require high-frequency magnetic fields that may pose health risks [8]. Therefore, recent studies proposed to crowdsource energy services from multiple, lower-energy sources as a safer alternative [9,10].

The energy service environment consists of confined areas, i.e., microcells, where people often gather, such as coffee shops and theaters. In a microcell, IoT devices share energy as services. The Energy Service Oriented Architecture (SOA) uses three key entities: service *providers*, service *consumers*, and *super providers* [4]. In this architecture, providers announce their services, and consumers request energy. The super provider, such as a microcell owner, coordinates the distribution of energy services between providers and consumers. This paper focuses on the perspective of the super-provider.

Super-providers may *improve their consumers' experience* by using energy services [11,12]. Several case studies by "air-charge" found that offering wireless

---

[1] energous.com.

energy services positively impacted customers' *Quality of Experience (QoE)*[2]. In the context of energy services, consumers' QoE is defined as the consumers' *cumulative satisfaction* with the received energy services *over time* [12]. This research focuses on provisioning energy to provide consumers with the best QoE.

Ensuring energy consumers' QoE is challenging due to *the resistance and lack of commitment from providers* [13]. Providers may resist due to the critical nature of energy or their preferences, e.g., resisting provisioning in the morning. Rewards may be used to overcome providers' resistance [13]. However, they do not ensure their commitment to provisioning [14]. The *uncertainty* in provider behavior may lead to real-time recompositions when a participating provider fails to commit. Finding nearby energy services to replace failed ones in real-time is not guaranteed, which may negatively impact consumers' QoE [14,15].

Existing QoE-based energy-service composition approaches often overlook the *uncertain availability* of providers [11,12]. They also assume that a super provider has an *unlimited budget* for incentives. However, allocating an unlimited budget is unrealistic [16]. This study addresses the challenges of uncertain provider availability and the budget constraints of super providers. Traditional resource allocation algorithms are ineffective as they do not account for providers' uncertainty. They also do not consider the super provider's context-sensitive perspective [11,12]. For example, a super provider might prioritize smaller, high-revenue requests. This might involve allocating a larger budget for time slots with high-profit consumers and lower energy demands.

We propose an efficient energy service provisioning framework to maximize QoE. Our framework allocates uncertain available energy services while adhering to the super provider's perspective and limited budget. Our framework leverages the probabilistic preferences and flexibility of providers to cope with time and budget constraints. We formulate the problem of QoE-based energy provisioning as a Linear Programming (LP) problem. Our formulation considers the constraints of service provisioning and super provider budget to provide optimal solutions in terms of QoE and rewards. In this regard, a GLPK solver model was used to solve the LP problem. The main contributions of this paper are:

- A QoE-based energy services provisioning framework.
- A binary linear formulation of the energy provisioning problem.

2 System Model

We adopt the energy service and request definitions from [1]. Additionally, we adopt the QoE model from [11]. The problem formulation is outlined below.

2.1 Problem Definition

Given energy demand in a microcell $ED = <d_1, d_2, ..., d_n>$ within a time window $W = <t_1, t_2, ..., t_n>$, an importance model $IM = <im_1, im_2, ..., im_n>$,

---
[2] air-charge.com.

reward budget RB, and a group of m energy providers $P = p_1, p_2, ..., p_m$, each provider can submit a set of Expression of Interest (EoI) services $S = s_1, s_2, ..., s_k$. These services may vary in quality or time slots and are derived from each provider's probabilistic conditional preference network $PCP\text{-}Net$. Energy providers register their services based on (1) the energy amount ($s.a$), (2) temporal provision preferences ($s.d$), (3) availability probability ($s.ap$), and (4) the expected reward per unit $s.ru$. The super provider uses their importance model IM, reward budget RB, and the providers' services $P.S$ to assign services to slots. This allocation approach seeks to maximize QoE by minimizing the gap between energy demand ED and allocated services $P.S$, while adhering to the reward budget RB and importance model IM. We reformulate the QoE-based service provisioning problem into a time-constrained resource allocation problem. The objective is to effectively allocate the most aligned energy services based on their spatial and temporal characteristics, provider preferences, the importance model, and the energy required in each time slot. We use the following assumptions to formulate the problem.

- The energy amount of a service is fixed within the time window.
- Providers and consumers are static during service provisioning.
- The computation of the importance model (IM), rewards budget (RB), and energy demand (ED) are out of the scope of this work and are given as input.
- The total energy demand (ED) deterministic.
- There is no energy loss during the sharing process.

3 Energy Service Composition Framework

We present the energy service provision framework designed to compose energy services while ensuring consumers QoE and considering the super provider's reward budget (RB) and importance model (IM). The framework seeks to enhance QoE by minimizing the gap between the required energy and the allocated services while adhering to the reward budget. The framework is structured into three steps: (1) generation of providers' service Expressions of Interest (EoI), (2) service composition, and (3) assessment of QoE and costs. Below, we provide a detailed discussion of each step:

3.1 Energy Services Expression of Interest (EoI) Generation

In the first step, the framework generates each provider's set of Expressions of Interest (EoI) to offer energy service based on their probabilistic conditional preference network, $PCP\text{-}Net$. $PCP\text{-}Net$ is used to rank and generate a description of the services, their price per energy unit, and their availability. As previously mentioned, providers may have multiple preferences for provisioning. This allows them to be available at various time slots or offer different services. However, they may favor specific times over others, such as morning slots over evening ones. Intuitively, assigning providers to their most preferred slots typically requires fewer rewards. Therefore, prioritizing providers' preferences can help the super provider minimize the needed rewards.

A provisioning model based on CP-Net was developed to capture the preferences of service providers [11]. This model uses Conditional Preference Networks (CP-Net) to organize and rank the providers' preferences. However, CP-Net cannot show detailed information about the likelihood or uncertainty of preferences [17]. To address this, the model was extended using a Probabilistic Conditional Preference Network (PCP-Net), which can represent preferences with probabilities, allowing it to handle uncertainty in preferences. A PCP-Net graph represents the dependencies between attributes and assigns probabilities to different preference orders. Each node in the graph corresponds to an attribute, and the connections (arcs) show how one attribute influences the preference for another. To compute the probability of an outcome o in PCP-Net, we can use the following equation:

$$p(o) = P(u_0) \times \prod_{i=1}^{n} P(u_i \mid \text{Parents}(u_i)) \qquad (1)$$

where:

- $P(u_0)$ is the probability of the root attribute.
- $P(u_i \mid \text{Parents}(u_i))$ is the conditional probability of an attribute u_i given its parent attributes.

This equation calculates the probability of an outcome by considering how each attribute depends on its parents. In our context, we present each provider's provisioning preferences using a PCP-Net. Generating the energy services' Expression of Interest (EoI) for each provider involves several key steps. First, the provider's PCP-Net is traversed to capture the dependencies and preferences within the network. An induced graph is generated based on each provider's PCP-Net, representing their preferences. Following this, the probability of each possible outcome is computed using Eq. 1.

3.2 Energy Services Composition

This step focuses on composing the most aligning energy services to maximize QoE and adhere to the reward budget. Our composition method leverages flexible providers with multiple provisioning preferences, assigning them to the most critical time slots if within budget. For instance, if a provider offers services in two slots, the service is allocated to the most important slot within budget constraints. If that slot doesn't need the service, it is assigned to the next available slot. Additionally, the method uses providers' *PCP-Net* to choose services with a higher likelihood of availability. We employ a linear programming technique for efficient service composition [18]. Next, we present the problem formulation as a linear programming problem and then discuss the service composition approach.

LP Formalization of Energy Service Composition: We approach the problem of Quality of Experience (QoE)-based energy provisioning using Linear Programming (LP) formulation [18]. This method allows us to define objective functions and constraints for optimizing energy service allocations.

Decision Variables: The decision variables indicate whether a specific provider is assigned to a particular time slot. For each provider, the binary decision variable is set to 1 if the provider is assigned to a time slot and 0 otherwise.

Objective Function: The goal of the LP formulation is to maximize the total allocated energy across all providers and time slots while considering the probability of each provider's availability. This optimization seeks to maximize the Quality of Experience (QoE) by selecting providers who can offer the most energy at the right time, considering their preferences.

Constraints: The following constraints are applied:

- **Binary Decision Constraint**: Each decision to assign a provider to a time slot is binary: 'yes' (1) or 'no' (0), with no intermediate values.
- **Single Slot Assignment**: To ensure that no provider is assigned to multiple time slots simultaneously, each provider is limited to a single time slot.
- **Energy Demand Constraint**: The total energy allocated to a time slot must meet, but not exceed, its demand, ensuring the energy matches the slot's needs and prevents over-allocation.
- **Unit Price Constraint**: The cost per unit of energy from each provider must not exceed the reserved price for the time slot, ensuring energy is purchased at the super provider's preferred rate.
- **Budget Constraint per Slot**: The total cost of allocating energy for each time slot must stay within its allocated budget.
- **Total Budget Constraint**:
  The total energy cost across all time slots must stay within the overall budget, ensuring total expenses do not exceed the super provider budget.

3.3 Energy Services Provisioning Composition

We present our proposed energy service composition approach. The goal is to allocate the most certain energy services to maximize QoE and adhere to the reward budget. Our composition approach utilizes flexible providers, i.e., providers with multiple provisioning preferences, to assign them to the most important time slots if it is within the budget. We use our LP formulation and several solvers to compose the optimal services. Algorithm 1 describe the energy service composition approach.

4 Experiments Results

We evaluate our proposed energy service composition (EC) using GLPK solver (EC-GLPK) [18]. We compare our composition approach using GLPK solver (EC-GLPK) with a baseline traditional resource allocation algorithm, namely, first-come first-served allocation (*Greedy1*). In Greedy1, time slots and services are processed based on their start time. We also compared our approach with the *Demand-based* method proposed by [12]. In the Demand-based algorithm, slots and services are sorted based on energy, and the allocation starts with the

Algorithm 1. Energy Services Provisioning

Input: Time Window (W), Importance Model (IM), Energy Demand (ED), Rewards Budget (RB), Providers (P)
Output: energy composition ($energy\_comp$), Quality of Experience (QoE), Cost (C)
1: Generate and filter services S submitted by P
2: Define LP problem to maximize the objective
3: Create binary decision variables $x[i][j]$ for Providers (P) and time slots in W
4: Set objective: Maximize the product of the provided energy service amount (a) and the availability probability (ap)
5: Define the constraints of the problem
6: Solve LP problem to obtain $energy\_comp$
7: Compute QoE and C of $energy\_comp$
8: **return** $energy\_comp$, QoE, C

Table 1. Experiments Variables

Variables	Value
Total Energy Requests for coffee shop 1 in April	16830
Energy Services	10000
Duration of All Energy Services	5–30 min
Duration of Energy Requests	5–30 min
Provided Energy	5–100 mAh
Requested Energy	5–100 mAh
Number of time slots	8
Providers' preferences	1–4

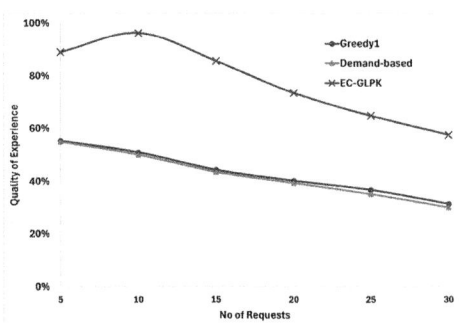

Fig. 1. The average of QoE

least flexible providers. However, we modified the assumptions demand approach to account for the fact that flexible providers may be unavailable for all time slots. We evaluate the effectiveness of each approach by measuring the quality of experience and cost. We utilized a real dataset generated from an app developed in [19,20]. Table 1 presents the statistics of the used dataset. We tested the approaches under different settings by fixing the number of services and incrementally increasing the requests' number over the time window W. Each experiment was repeated 3000 times, using the average values for each approach.

The first experiment compared the QoE of the proposed approach with the other approaches. As mentioned earlier, a higher QoE for a composition indicates greater consumer satisfaction from the super provider's perspective. Figure 1 shows the average QoE in the microcell for each approach. In this experiment, 15 services were randomly selected out of 340 for each run. Our proposed approach *EC-GLPK* outperforms all other approaches. This is because our approach uses linear programming solvers to compose the services. In general, solvers surpass resource allocation algorithms because of their guaranteed optimality [18]. Typically, solvers can find an optimal solution to an optimization problem, whereas priority-based allocation may not always lead to an optimal solution.

The second experiment evaluated the cost $\mathcal{C}$ of allocating services using the resulting composition of each approach. The cost is the sum of the rewards paid by the super provider to encourage providers to offer their services. The proposed approach demonstrated a lower cost compared to other methods. This is due to the linear programming solvers constantly searching for optimal solutions, ensuring that when multiple services are available, the one with the lowest reward is selected. In contrast, other resource allocation methods select any service that meets the super provider's constraints. The corresponding figure was removed due to page limitations.

5 Related Work

Energy services have been proposed as alternative methods to charge IoT devices [4,21]. Several studies have tackled challenges related to the energy consumers' [1,15,22]. A time-based composition approach was proposed to allocate services for a single consumer [1]. The approach uses partial services and a fractional knapsack algorithm to maximize the provided energy. A heuristic approach proposed the replacement or tolerance of intermittent energy services [22]. The approach predicts temporary disconnections in services based on crowd mobility patterns. Other studies proposed allocating energy services using a modified maximum flow algorithm [9]. Other research has focused on challenges from the provider's perspective [13,23]. For instance, a context-aware incentive model was proposed to overcome resistance to offering energy services [13]. Recent studies have approached these challenges from a super provider's perspective. A QoE model was proposed as an indicator for assigning services to requests [12]. Another study introduced QoE-based composition using CP-Net to represent providers' temporal provision preferences [11]. Another study proposed a trust model to evaluate the providers' provisioning commitment before selecting services [14]. However, these QoE-based composition approaches do not account for providers' uncertain availability or the limited budget of the super provider.

6 Conclusion

We proposed an efficient QoE-aware energy service-provisioning framework. We capture providers' fine-grained provisioning preferences and availability using PCP-Net . A QoE-driven composition approach to effectively allocate energy services while considering the super provider constraints was proposed. Our approach uses linear programming to formulate the energy-provisioning problem. We used GLPK solver to compose services. We conducted a set of experiments to assess the effectiveness of the proposed framework.

Acknowledgment. This research was supported by Australian Research Council grants LE220100078 and DP220101823. Statements herein are the sole responsibility of the authors.

References

1. Lakhdari, A., Bouguettaya, A., Neiat, A.G.: Crowdsourcing energy as a service. In: Pahl, C., Vukovic, M., Yin, J., Yu, Q. (eds.) ICSOC 2018. LNCS, vol. 11236, pp. 342–351. Springer, Cham (2018). https://doi.org/10.1007/978-3-030-03596-9_24
2. Pan, Q., et al.: A nonresonant and frequency up-conversion motion converter for footstep energy harvesting. IEEE/ASME Trans. Mechatr (2024)
3. Zhao, Z., Youfan, H.: Textile triboelectric nanogenerator: Future smart wearable energy-integration technology. Adv, Materials Technologies (2024)
4. Abusafia, A., et al.: Service-based wireless energy crowdsourcing. Springer, In ICSOC (2022)
5. Yang, P., et al.: Energy loss prediction in iot energy services. In: IEEE ICWS, pp. 371–381. IEEE (2023)
6. Feng, H., et al.: Advances in high-power wireless charging systems: overview and design considerations. TTE **6**(3), 886–919 (2020)
7. Iyer, V., et al.: Charging a smartphone across a room using lasers. IMWUT **1**(4), 1–21 (2018)
8. Baikova, E.N., et al.: Study on electromagnetic emissions from wireless energy transfer. In: IEEE PEMC, pp. 492–497. IEEE (2016)
9. Abusafia, A., et al.: Flow-based energy services composition. IEEE TSC (2023)
10. Lakhdari, A., Bouguettaya, A.: Fairness-aware crowdsourcing of iot energy services. In: Hacid, H., Kao, O., Mecella, M., Moha, N., Paik, H. (eds.) ICSOC 2021. LNCS, vol. 13121, pp. 351–367. Springer, Cham (2021). https://doi.org/10.1007/978-3-030-91431-8_22
11. Abusafia, A., et al.: Quality of experience optimization in iot energy services. In: ICWS. IEEE (2022)
12. Abusafia, A., Bouguettaya, A., Lakhdari, A.: Maximizing consumer satisfaction of iot energy services. In: ICSOC. Springer (2022). https://doi.org/10.1007/978-3-031-20984-0_28
13. Abusafia, A., et al.: Incentive-based selection and composition of iot energy services. In: IEEE SCC, pp. 304–311. IEEE (2020)
14. Abusafia, A., et al.: Context-aware trustworthy iot energy services provisioning. In: ICSOC, pp. 167–185. Springer (2023). https://doi.org/10.1007/978-3-031-48424-7_1
15. Lakhdari, A., et al.: Elastic composition of crowdsourced iot energy services. EAI Mobiquitous (2020)
16. Faccia, A., Pandey, V.: Business planning and big data, budget modelling upgrade through data science. In: ISE, pp. 21–25 (2021)
17. Fidha, S.E., Amor, N.B.: Probabilistic weighted CP-nets. In: Neves-Silva, R., Jain, L.C., Howlett, R.J. (eds.) Intelligent Decision Technologies. SIST, vol. 39, pp. 159–169. Springer, Cham (2015). https://doi.org/10.1007/978-3-319-19857-6_15
18. Vanderbei, R.J., et al.: Linear programming. Springer (2020)
19. Yan, P., et al.: Monitoring efficiency of iot wireless charging. In: IEEE Percom (2023)
20. Yang, P., et al.: Towards peer-to-peer sharing of wireless energy services. In: ICSOC. Springer (2022). https://doi.org/10.1007/978-3-031-26507-5_38
21. Kaswan, A., et al.: A survey on mobile charging techniques in wireless rechargeable sensor networks. IEEE Comm. Surv. Tutorials **24**(3), 1750–1779 (2022)
22. Lakhdari, A., Bouguettaya, A.: Fluid composition of intermittent iot energy services. In: SCC, pp. 329–336. IEEE (2020)
23. Abusafia, A., Bouguettaya, A.: Reliability model for incentive-driven iot energy services. In: Mobiquitous, Germany, p. 1. EAI (2020)

Attention-Driven Conflict Management in Smart IoT-Based Systems

Christson Awanyo(✉) and Nawal Guermouche

LAAS-CNRS, University of Toulouse, INSA, Toulouse, France
{kjbcawanyo,nguermou}@laas.fr

Abstract. In the rapidly evolving landscape of Internet of Things (IoT)-based systems, which are becoming increasingly complex and interconnected, conflict resolution emerges as a pivotal challenge. The proliferation of cohabiting systems that rely on the mutual use of IoT devices results in a corresponding increase in potential conflicts. This requires the development of a highly effective, run-time, and dynamic conflict management framework. Traditional approaches to conflict resolution often struggle to adapt to dynamic and complex environments. This paper introduces a novel attention-based conflict resolution model that dynamically resolves conflicts by focusing on critical system aspects. By integrating real-time contextual and historical data, the model optimizes conflict resolution, enhancing responsiveness and adaptability. Extensive experiments validate the approach, showing significant improvements in addressing IoT conflicts.

Keywords: IoT · Conflict Resolution · Attention Model · Dynamic Systems · Large Scale IoT Systems · Smart City

1 Introduction

The rapid growth of IoT systems, driven by advancements in Artificial Intelligence (AI), is significantly improving efficiency and quality of life, particularly in smart cities that rely on interconnected systems. However, as these systems expand in complexity and scale, managing their interactions and dependencies becomes more challenging. These systems often operate independently, each pursuing its own objectives, can fulfill various and concurrent invocations on IoT services within a shared environment, which can lead to *conflicts*. A conflict arises when simultaneous invocations of IoT services at the same time result in an undesirable situation [14].

Conflict detection has been extensively explored in the literature [6,15,16]. However, conflict resolution remains pivotal for maintaining operational efficiency, safety, and consistency. Mainly, there are two approaches to resolving conflicts in IoT systems. The first category concerns static approaches where potential conflicts within a system are identified and addressed through static analysis [2,5,6], conducted during the design phase. This analysis detects conflicts before system deployment, allowing early resolution. Identified conflicts are addressed by modifying operational policies, such as reconfiguring rules or adjusting workflows, ensuring smooth and conflict-free operation. Resolving conflicts early improves system efficiency and reliability, significantly reducing the likelihood of issues during execution. However, static resolution, despite its goal of managing all potential conflicts, encounters significant challenges. It must exhaustively consider all possible interactions to detect potential conflicts, a task that is highly complex and often unfeasible in dynamic and constantly evolving IoT environments. The second category is fulfilled on the fly [1,18], where conflicts are detected and resolved during run-time, taking reactive actions based on predefined rules [15], ontology [4], or matrix factorization [3]. This approach enables the system to adapt and respond to issues as they occur, ensuring continuous and smooth operation despite the presence of conflicting events or conditions. However, these approaches remain rigid and unsuitable within complex, open, and dynamic systems and lack of real-time adaptability.

In recent years, attention mechanisms [17], inspired by human cognitive processes, have gained significant prominence in AI. They enable AI models to selectively focus on the most relevant parts of input data, thereby improving efficiency and performance. This selective focus allows models to better capture context and dependencies, leading to more accurate and meaningful outcomes in various applications. Considering these recent advancements, in this paper, we propose a novel attention model-based conflict resolution approach for IoT systems. This model dynamically prioritizes and resolves conflicts by leveraging real-time contextual information and historical data, ensuring more effective and adaptive conflict management. By continuously learning from environmental changes, the model improves the system's responsiveness and adaptability, leading to more effective and efficient conflict resolution. The contribution of this paper can be summarized as follows: 1- We introduce a predictive approach that leverages attention mechanisms to address the IoT conflict resolution problem. 2- We develop a comprehensive and adaptive framework that integrates real-time contextual information and historical data, enhancing the accuracy and relevance of conflict resolution processes in IoT systems. 3- We validate our approach through comprehensive evaluations, showcasing its effectiveness.

This paper is organized as follows. Section 2 provides a comprehensive review of related works. In Sect. 3, we formalize the problem we address. Section 4 presents the proposed attention model-based approach. Section 5 details the experiments we conducted and presents the results. Finally, Sect. 6 concludes the paper.

2 Related Work

Conflicts in IoT systems are classified into three categories: *Rule-based*, *Application-based*, and *Ontology-based* [14]. Rule-based conflicts arise from contradictory automation policies [13,15]. Application-based conflicts occur when multiple IoT applications contend for access to the same device or exert divergent effects on either the device itself or its surrounding environment [8,12]. Ontology-based conflicts are detected using ontologies, a structured framework that establishes semantically enriched relationships and properties among diverse entities [4]. Various detection methods have been proposed, including conflict classification through predefined rule relationships [16], knowledge graphs to analyze IoT service effects [7], and probabilistic approaches [9]. Architectures such as watchdog systems for real-time conflict detection in smart cities have also been developed [10]. While these works focus on conflict detection, resolving conflicts is essential for maintaining system functionality. Static methods like SOTERIA [2] translate IoT code into intermediate representations to identify conflicts during system design. It is done through three key stages: translating platform-specific IoT source code into an intermediate representation (IR), deriving a state model from the IR, and performing model checking to verify the desired properties. [5] presented HOMEGUARD which detects Cross-App Interference threats among IoT applications. IoTMon [6] analyzes physical interactions and generates risk mitigation strategies. These static approaches, though valuable, are constrained by their inability to fully capture the complexities and variability of dynamic IoT-based systems, particularly in environments characterized by intricate interactions and dependencies. Several dynamic and on-the-fly approaches have been introduced to address the limitations of static methods in managing the dynamic nature of IoT systems. One approach employs a Natural Language Processing (NLP) model to analyze service actions in real-time based on user-defined privacy preferences, automatically blocking conflicting actions to maintain privacy [1]. Another method, CityResolver, leverages Integer Linear Programming (ILP) and Signal Temporal Logic (STL) to resolve conflicts by continuously monitoring system states and identifying optimal solutions. However, CityResolver encounters scalability challenges in large systems and does not account for contextual factors during conflict resolution [11]. A preference-based conflict resolution framework for multi-resident smart homes uses temporal proximity and matrix factorization (SVD) to aggregate user preferences over time, enhancing contextual relevance [3]. However, it is limited to non-critical conflicts, suffers from computational complexity, and struggles to adapt to sudden changes in preferences, reducing its scalability and effectiveness in dynamic environments. To overcome the aforementioned limitations, we propose a novel approach for run-time conflict resolution that leverages attention mechanisms combined with adaptive learning algorithms. Our approach relies on attention mechanisms to dynamically prioritize and focus on the most critical conflict patterns. By integrating adaptive learning, our system continuously refines its conflict resolution strategies, improving both accuracy and efficiency over time. This approach not only improves responsiveness and effectiveness but also ensures that the system evolves and adapts to changing conditions and emerging patterns.

3 Problem Formulation

We define the conflict resolution problem in IoT-based systems. Consider an IoT service $\mathcal{S}$ that performs actions $A = \{a_1, a_2, \ldots, a_n\}$ and interacts with services $\{SR_1, SR_2, \ldots, SR_m\}$. Each service SR_j submits a request r_j defined as:

$$r_j = [a_j, w_j, st_j, et_j, t_j],$$

where a_j is the action, w_j is the weight preference (with $w_j \in [0,1]$ and $\sum_{j=1}^{m} w_j = 1$), st_j and et_j are the desired start and end times, and t_j is the request timestamp.

The goal of conflict resolution is to prioritize actions for execution and determine which to delay, maximizing utility and minimizing conflicts. This is modeled as an optimization problem where each request r_j is assigned a binary variable x_j (with $x_j = 1$ for execution and $x_j = 0$ for delay). The objective is to maximize total utility:

$$\text{Maximize} \sum_{j=1}^{m} U_j \cdot x_j$$

where U_j is the utility of each request. To prevent simultaneous execution of conflicting requests, the constraint $x_j + x_k \leq 1$ is applied for conflicting requests r_j and r_k (denoted $C(r_j, r_k) = 1$).

4 Attention-Based Conflict Resolution

Given a set of requests, the objective is to identify a subset that avoids conflicts, while maximizing the total utility. This involves a detailed evaluation of each request's utility and its contribution to the overall system performance. The goal is to develop an optimization strategy that achieves the highest combined benefit. By effectively managing conflicts and optimizing utility, we can significantly enhance the system's efficiency and effectiveness in achieving its operational goals. In this context, we propose an attention-based model (Fig. 1) that dynamically prioritizes and resolves conflicts through iterative refinement, leading to more precise outcomes. The attention mechanism adapts to varying complexities and system changes, providing a scalable solution. The model has four steps: 1) Request Encoding, 2) Attention Encoder, 3) Request Selection, and 4) Request Filtering.

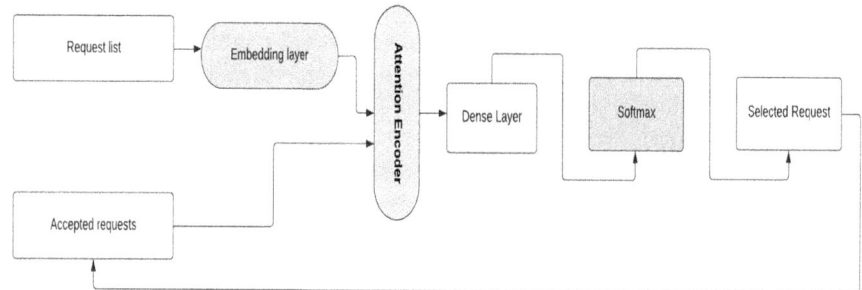

Fig. 1. Attention-based model architecture for conflict resolution

4.1 Request Encoding

The initial step involves representing each request, which is crucial for effective processing. Each request $r_j = [a_j, w_j, st_j, et_j, t_j]$ is represented as a vector capturing key attributes for effective processing. This vector is passed through an embedding layer, transforming it into a higher-dimensional space to capture complex relationships. This improves the model's ability to detect patterns, resolve conflicts, and process diverse requests, enhancing overall system performance.

4.2 Attention Encoder

The attention encoder assigns varying levels of importance to different parts of the input data, enabling the model to focus on the most relevant features. Given an input sequence $X = \{x_1, x_2, \ldots, x_n\}$, it computes attention scores α_i using a query-key compatibility function. The softmax function ensures the scores sum to one:

$$\alpha_i = \frac{e^{q \cdot k_i}}{\sum_{j=1}^{n} e^{q \cdot k_j}}, \quad \text{Attention}(Q, K, V) = \sum_{i=1}^{n} \alpha_i v_i$$

where Q, K, and V denote the query, key, and value matrices, respectively. In our approach, attention encoding is used to generate an updated representation of each request, incorporating both the context and the presence of other requests. This enables a more comprehensive understanding of each query. The resulting representation is then used to calculate the probability of each request being selected.

4.3 Request Selection

Requests are transformed to extract key features. The embedded query vectors pass through dense layers, refining feature representations for decision-making. These features are then processed by a softmax layer:

$$\text{softmax}(z_i) = \frac{e^{z_i}}{\sum_j e^{z_j}}$$

where z_i is the input for the i-th request. The softmax function converts logits $\{z_i\}$ into a probability distribution, summing to one. This distribution reflects the model's confidence in each request's selection based on priority and timing.

4.4 Request Filtering

We perform filtering after each selection to mask out any conflicting requests from the remaining pool. Given a set of requests that have already been selected

$\mathcal{R}$, the filtering is accomplished by applying for each request r_i a mask M, which is defined as:
$$M(r_i) = \begin{cases} 0 & \text{if } C(r_i, r_j) = 1 \, \forall r_j \in \mathcal{R}, \\ 1 & \text{otherwise} \end{cases}$$

5 Experimental Evaluation

5.1 Dataset and Model Training

We compiled a comprehensive dataset specifically crafted to simulate conflicts within smart city systems. This dataset includes a variety of requests, each assigned distinct weights. The dataset covers a range of potential actions, varying from 2 to 20, to capture a broad spectrum of scenarios. Conflicts are identified through an analysis of these requests and their interactions. This dataset enables thorough evaluations, allowing us to test and assess the system's performance across a diverse array of actions and services.

We utilize the Adaptive Moment Estimation (Adam) optimization method, known for its effectiveness and faster convergence in large-scale problems.

5.2 Comparative Study

The evaluation examines how optimality evolves according to the number of services capable of sending requests and the number of options (i.e.,possible actions). As the number of options increases, the likelihood of conflicts rises. To assess our approach, we compare its optimality Opt_{app} against the optimal solution U_{opt}: $Opt_{app} = \frac{U_{app}}{U_{opt}}$, where U_{app} is the utility of accepted requests, defined as the sum of their weights: $U_{app} = \sum_{r_i \in \mathcal{SR}} w_i$.

Figure 2 illustrates how optimality evolves with changes in the number of services and the number of possible options.

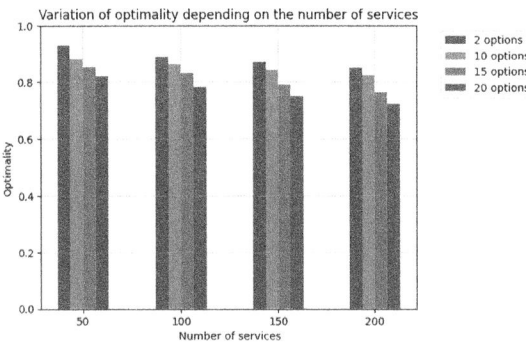

Fig. 2. Variation of optimality according to the number of possible options and services

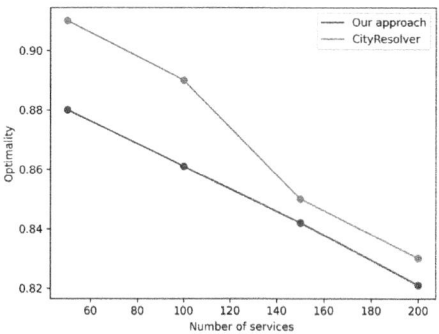 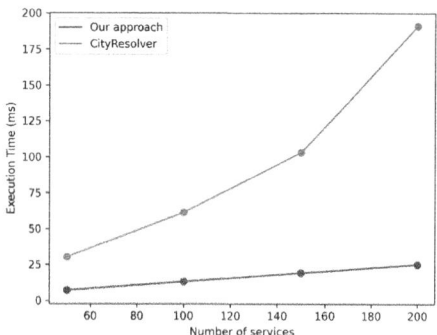

Fig. 3. Variation of the optimality according to the number of services

Fig. 4. Evaluation of the execution time according to the number of services

The results show that the model remains notably stable under varying conditions. Although a slight decrease in optimality is observed as either the number of services or execution options increases, this reduction is minimal. This demonstrates the robustness and adaptability of our model to generalize effectively across diverse scenarios, reinforcing its potential applicability in dynamic and huge environments.

Additionally, we performed a comparative study to evaluate the effectiveness of our approach in relation to the *CityResolver* [11] method. CityResolver offers a conflict resolution solution utilizing Integer Linear Programming and Signal Temporal Logic, tailored for open IoT systems.

Optimality: Figure 3 compares the optimality of our approach with CityResolver, with the exact approach serving as the 100% benchmark.

While CityResolver shows higher initial optimality, its performance decreases as the number of services grows. In contrast, our attention model maintains a narrower optimality gap. This suggests that our approach is particularly effective in managing an increasing number of services, likely due to its enhanced ability to handle complex dependencies and contextual information.

Scalability and Time Performance: Figure 4 clearly shows that our approach scales more effectively compared to the ILP-based approach. This highlights our model's superior ability to handle larger and more complex service environments efficiently.

6 Conclusion

In this paper, we presented a novel conflict resolution approach for IoT systems that leverages attention models to dynamically prioritize and resolve conflicts. Our method offers enhanced adaptability, scalability, and contextual sensitivity, making it suitable for large-scale IoT systems where dynamic conflict management is essential. Our comprehensive evaluation demonstrates that the attention model consistently maintains stable optimality and high performance as the number of services increases, underscoring its effectiveness in managing complex service conflicts. Future work will extend the model to consider the direct and indirect impacts of resolutions on targeted, requesting, and cohabiting systems, providing a comprehensive understanding of resolution effects. We will also conduct tests on larger datasets and scenarios to further validate its performance.

References

1. Babun, L., Celik, Z.B., McDaniel, P., Uluagac, S.: Real-time analysis of privacy-(un)aware iot applications. Proc. Priv. Enhancing Technol. **2021**, 145–166 (2021). https://doi.org/10.2478/popets-2021-0009
2. Celik, Z.B., McDaniel, P., Tan, G.: Soteria: automated IoT safety and security analysis. In: 2018 USENIX Annual Technical Conference (USENIX ATC 2018), pp. 147–158. USENIX Association, Boston, MA (Jul 2018)
3. Chaki, D., Bouguettaya, A.: Dynamic conflict resolution of iot services in smart homes. In: Hacid, H., Kao, O., Mecella, M., Moha, N., Paik, H. (eds.) ICSOC 2021. LNCS, vol. 13121, pp. 368–384. Springer, Cham (2021). https://doi.org/10.1007/978-3-030-91431-8_23
4. Chaki, D., Bouguettaya, A., Mistry, S.: A conflict detection framework for iot services in multi-resident smart homes, pp. 224–231 (Oct 2020). https://doi.org/10.1109/ICWS49710.2020.00036
5. Chi, H., Zeng, Q., Du, X., Yu, J.: Cross-app interference threats in smart homes: categorization, detection and handling. In: Proceedings - 50th Annual IEEE/IFIP International Conference on Dependable Systems and Networks, DSN 2020, pp. 411–423 (Jun 2020). https://doi.org/10.1109/DSN48063.2020.00056
6. Ding, W., Hu, H.: On the safety of iot device physical interaction control, pp. 832–846 (Oct 2018). https://doi.org/10.1145/3243734.3243865
7. Huang, B., Dong, H., Bouguettaya, A.: Conflict detection in iot-based smart homes. CoRR abs/ arXiv: 2107.13179 (2021)
8. Igaki, H., Nakamura, M.: Modeling and detecting feature interactions among integrated services of home network systems. IEICE Trans. **93-D**, 822–833 (2010). https://doi.org/10.1587/transinf.E93.D.822
9. Luo, H., Wang, R., Li, X.: A rule verification and resolution framework in smart building system, pp. 438–439 (Dec 2013). https://doi.org/10.1109/ICPADS.2013.74
10. Ma, M., Preum, S.M., Tarneberg, W., Ahmed, M.Y., Ruiters, M., Stankovic, J.A.: Detection of runtime conflicts among services in smart cities. 2016 IEEE International Conference on Smart Computing (SMARTCOMP), pp. 1–10 (2016)
11. Ma, M., Stankovic, J., Feng, L.: Cityresolver: A decision support system for conflict resolution in smart cities, pp. 55–64 (April 2018). https://doi.org/10.1109/ICCPS.2018.00014
12. Nakamura, M., Igaki, H., Matsumoto, K.i.: Feature interactions in integrated services of networked home appliances (July 2005)
13. Perumal, T., Sulaiman, M., Datta, S.K., Ramachandran, T., Leong, C.: Rule-based conflict resolution framework for internet of things device management in smart home environment, pp. 1–2 (10 2016). https://doi.org/10.1109/GCCE.2016.7800444

14. . Pradeep, P., Kant, K.: Conflict detection and resolution in iot systems: a survey. IoT **3**(1), 191–218 (2022). https://www.mdpi.com/2624-831X/3/1/12
15. Pradeep Kumar, P., Pal, A., Kant, K.: Automating conflict detection and mitigation in large-scale iot systems (April 2021). https://doi.org/10.1109/CCGrid51090.2021.00063
16. Sun, Y., Wang, X., Luo, H., Li, X.: Conflict detection scheme based on formal rule model for smart building systems. IEEE Trans. Hum.-Mach. Syst. **45**, 1–13 (2014). https://doi.org/10.1109/THMS.2014.2364613
17. Vaswani, A., et al.: Attention is all you need (2023)
18. n Wang, Q., Hassan, W., Bates, A., Gunter, C.: Fear and logging in the internet of things (Jan 2018). https://doi.org/10.14722/ndss.2018.23291

Benchmarking Deep Learning Models for Object Detection on Edge Computing Devices

Daghash K. Alqahtani[1(✉)], Muhammad Aamir Cheema[2], and Adel N. Toosi[1,2]

[1] The University of Melbourney, Melbourne, VIC, Australia
daghash.alqahtani@student.unimelb.edu.au, adel.toosi@unimelb.edu.au
[2] Monash University, Melbourne, VIC, Australia
Aamir.Cheema@monash.edu

Abstract. Modern applications, such as autonomous vehicles, require deploying deep learning algorithms on resource-constrained edge devices for real-time image and video processing. However, there is limited understanding of the efficiency and performance of various object detection models on these devices. In this paper, we evaluate the performance of several state-of-the-art object detection models, including YOLOv8 (Nano, Small, Medium), EfficientDet Lite (Lite0, Lite1, Lite2), and SSD (SSD MobileNet V1, SSDLite MobileDet), on popular edge devices such as the Raspberry Pi 3, 4, and 5 (with and without TPU accelerators), as well as the Jetson Orin Nano. We collect key performance metrics, including energy consumption, inference time, and Mean Average Precision (mAP). Our findings highlight models with lower mAP such as SSD MobileNet V1 are more energy-efficient and faster in inference, whereas higher mAP models like YOLOv8 Medium generally consume more energy and have slower inference, though with exceptions when accelerators like TPUs are used. Among the edge devices, Jetson Orin Nano stands out as the fastest and most energy-efficient option for request handling, despite having the highest idle energy consumption.

Keywords: Deep Learning · Object Detection Models · Performance evaluation · Inference Time · Energy Efficiency · Accuracy · Edge

1 Introduction

Object detection is crucial in computer vision for identifying and locating objects in images or videos. It helps organizations optimize and automate processes and has diverse applications in fields like autonomous vehicles, surveillance, retail, healthcare, agriculture, manufacturing, sports analytics, environmental monitoring, and smart cities. In autonomous vehicles, for example, object detectors enable precise recognition of pedestrians, obstacles, and other vehicles to ensure safe operation and facilitate route planning. These capabilities highlight the significant value of object detection in enhancing the performance and safety of automated systems [2].

The field of object detection is marked by continuous technological progress, with ongoing refinement of detection algorithms to improve accuracy and speed in complex environments. The emergence of *edge computing* enables real-time object detection on devices like smartphones, drones, and Internet of Things (IoT) devices, reducing latency and cloud dependence. However, significant challenges remain in developing robust object detection systems for edge computing due to constrained resources and varying energy requirements. Researchers and industries must select appropriate models and edge devices to balance accuracy, processing speed, and energy consumption.

In this paper, we aim to evaluate the performance of most popular deep learning models for object detection including YOLOv8 (Nano, Small, Medium), EfficientDet Lite (Lite0, Lite1, Lite2), and SSD (SSD MobileNet V1, SSDLite MobileDet) across prominent edge devices like the Raspberry Pi 3, 4, and 5 with/without TPU accelerators, and Jetson Orin Nano, collecting key metrics such as energy consumption, inference time, and accuracy. Additionally, we provide insights for deploying these models on the investigated edge devices.

Our **key contributions** include the development of object detection applications as web services using Flask-API, deployed across various edge devices. We evaluate the models' accuracy using the FiftyOne[1] tool, reporting the mean Average Precision (mAP) on the COCO dataset for each model-device combination. Additionally, we perform automated performance tests using Locust[2] to generate workload, measuring and reporting key metrics such as energy consumption and inference time.

2 Target Edge Devices and Object Detection Models

2.1 Edge Devices

Our experimental setup includes various edge devices to evaluate the performance of object detection models as Table 1 shows. The devices tested are Raspberry Pi 3 Model B+, Raspberry Pi 4 Model B and Raspberry Pi 5. These devices are selected for their popularity and affordability. To enhance computational power for deep learning tasks, we equip these Raspberry Pi models with Google Coral USB Accelerators (TPUs). For high-performance comparison, we include the NVIDIA Jetson Orin Nano. This allow us to compare devices with CPUs, TPUs, and GPUs.

2.2 Object Detection Models and Frameworks

We evaluate various object detection models, including YOLOv8 [14] in different sizes (nano, small, medium), SSD [11] models like MobileNet V1 and SSDLite MobileDet, and EfficientDet Lite (0, 1, 2) [13] for embedded devices. Using frameworks like PyTorch, TensorFlow Lite, and TensorRT, we deploy these models on

---

[1] https://voxel51.com/fiftyone/.
[2] https://locust.io/.

Table 1. Edge Devices, Models and Frameworks.

Edge Device	RAM	YOLOv8 Framework	EfficientDet Framework	SSD Framework
Raspberry Pi 3 Model B+	1 GB	PyTorch	TFLite	TFLite
Raspberry Pi 4 Model B	4 GB	PyTorch	TFLite	TFLite
Raspberry Pi 5	4 GB	PyTorch	TFLite	TFLite
Pi 3 Model B+ with TPU	1 GB	TFLite	TFLite	TFLite
Pi 4 Model B with TPU	4 GB	TFLite	TFLite	TFLite
Pi 5 with TPU	4 GB	TFLite	TFLite	TFLite
Jetson Orin Nano	4 GB	TensorRT	TensorRT	TensorRT

different edge devices, as detailed in Table 1, optimizing performance for devices with CPUs, TPUs, and GPUs.

3 Performance Evaluation

3.1 Metrics

- **Inference Time:** This metric measures the time taken by each model from receiving the input image to producing detection results, excluding pre-processing or post-processing steps. We report the inference time in milliseconds for each model on each device, averaging over a series of test images for consistent and reliable measurements.
- **Energy Consumption:** This metric evaluates the energy efficiency of each model on different edge devices. First, we measure the base energy consumption (BE) of the devices in an idle state for five minutes without running any computations. Next, we measure the total energy consumption (TE) for five minutes while running an object detection model under stress using requests generated by Locust. Reported in milliwatt-hours (mWh), we consider two versions of the Energy Consumption, 1) total energy consumption per request and 2) energy consumption per request excluding the base energy. The total energy consumption per request is measured as $\frac{TE}{NR}$. The total energy consumption per request excluding the base energy is determined by subtracting the base energy consumption from the total energy consumption and dividing this difference by the number of requests (NR) processed, as follows: $\frac{TE-BE}{NR}$. These metrics are calculated on a per-request basis, as energy consumption varies with the number of processed requests within each five-minute interval, which can differ depending on the model. Evaluating on a per-request basis is crucial for a fair comparison across the different platforms, as it precisely indicates the amount of energy consumed for each request.
- **Model Evaluation Using COCO Dataset:** To determine the capabilities and accuracy of the YOLOv8, EfficientDet Lite, and SSD models, we use the COCO validation dataset of 5,000 images. The open-source FiftyOne tool facilitates visualization, access to COCO data resources, and model evaluation. It calculates model accuracy by comparing detected objects to ground

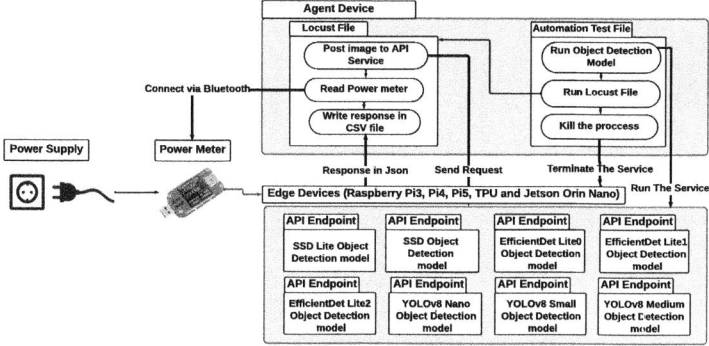

Fig. 1. Experimental Software and Hardware Setup.

reference data. Accuracy is evaluated using four metrics: *Precision, Recall, F1 score*, and *COCO mean Average Precision (mAP)*.

3.2 Experimental Procedure

The procedure for evaluating the object detection models involved several steps as Fig. 1 presents. First, the base energy consumption for each device was measured by running an energy reader Python script on a separate device for five minutes without any computational load. Second, the Locust file was used to send requests sequentially, with each new request sent immediately after the previous response, for five minutes, during which the total energy consumption was measured using the energy reader script, and the average inference time was calculated from the responses along with the number of requests. All this data was automatically written to a CSV file by the Locust file. Next, to automate the testing, a bash script on the agent device ran the object detection service on the edge device, followed by the Locust file. Upon completion, the script terminated the service and proceeded to the next model, ensuring consistent testing across all devices. Experiments were repeated three times for each model on each device, with the average values used for the final analysis. Finally, the accuracy measurement involved separate Python scripts to calculate mAP.

3.3 Experimental Results

This section presents the experimental results for each metric individually. For further details, including comparisons between metrics using 2D plots and trade-offs illustrated with 3D plots, please refer to our full technical report [1].

Energy Consumption: Pi3 devices generally exhibit higher energy consumption per request compared to Pi4 and Pi5 models, indicating an improvement in energy efficiency in the newer models. The addition of TPUs consistently

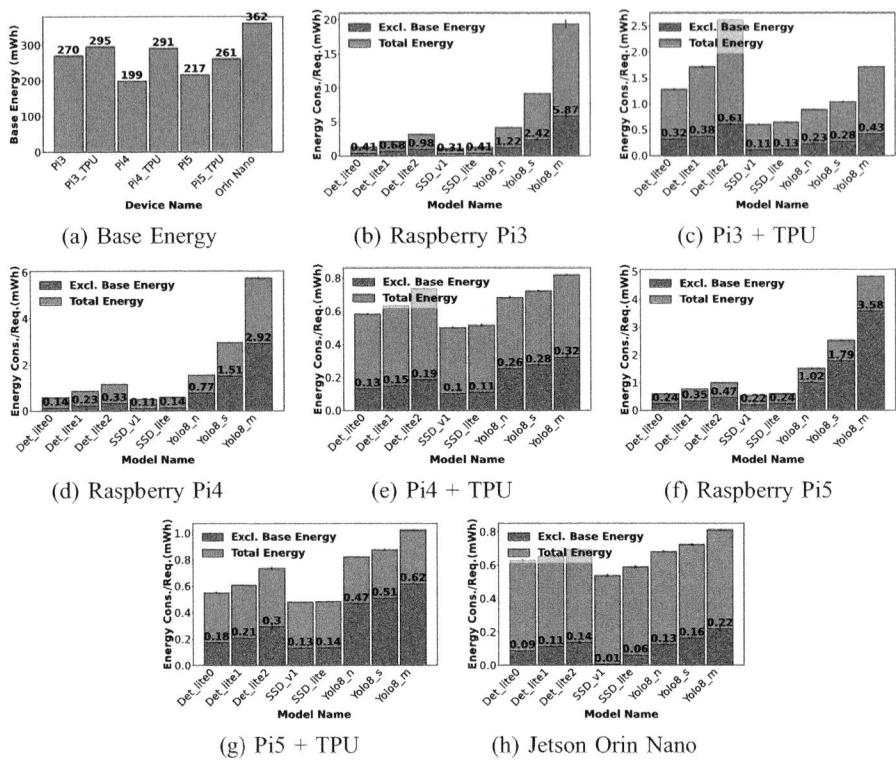

Fig. 2. Base Energy and Energy Consumption per Request excluding the base energy/Total Energy consumption per request for different edge devices.

reduces the energy consumption per request for object detection tasks across all Pi models, particularly in Pi4 and Pi5. However, it is important to note that the addition of TPU has increased the base energy consumption of these devices by 9%, 46%, and 20% for Pi 3, 4, and 5, respectively. Among all the models tested, YOLO8_m has the highest energy consumption per request, while SSD_v1 consumes the lowest energy per request.

Inference Time: The measurements, reported in milliseconds, reveal distinct performance patterns across these platforms as presented in Fig. 3. SSD_v1 exhibits the most rapid inference times when deployed across various edge devices. The incorporation of TPU, substantially enhances the performance of the evaluated models. Conversely, YOLO8_m generally demonstrates the slowest inference times among the tested configurations.

Accuracy: The mAP on the Raspberry Pi devices varied across model sizes is shown in Fig. 4. YOLO8_m demonstrates consistently superior accuracy compared to other evaluated models across various device platforms. Conversely,

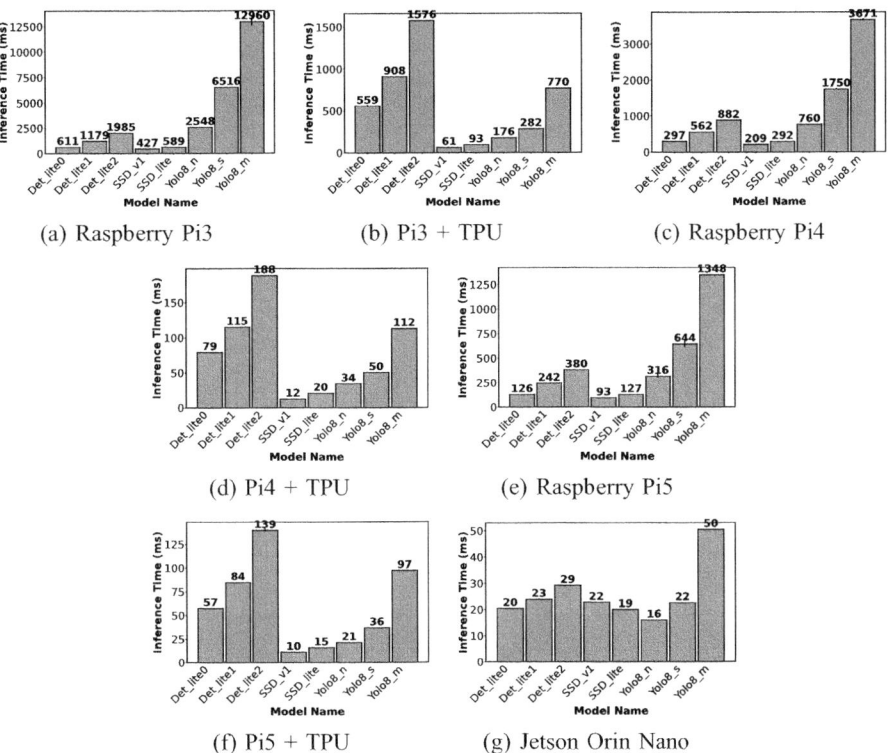

Fig. 3. Inference Time per request for different edge devices.

the SSD_v1 model often exhibits the lowest mAP among the tested models. The use of TPU accelerators on the Pi devices yields similar accuracy levels for the Det_lite and SSD model families, but results in a reduction in accuracy for the YOLO8 models. Jetson Orin Nano exhibits comparable accuracy patterns for the YOLO8 models to the other setups, but shows a slightly lower mAP for the remaining models in comparison to the Raspberry Pi and TPU-equipped configurations. The variation in accuracy of the same model across devices is due to the underlying frameworks, as shown in Table 1.

4 Related Work

This section provides an overview of the relevant research on deep learning models for edge computing devices and compares it with our work as Table 2 depicts. To the best of our knowledge, our work is unique due to its comprehensive evaluation of various object detection models and edge devices.

Several other studies have investigated various object detection models, notably focusing on YOLO variants, with Bulut et al. [4] assessing lightweight

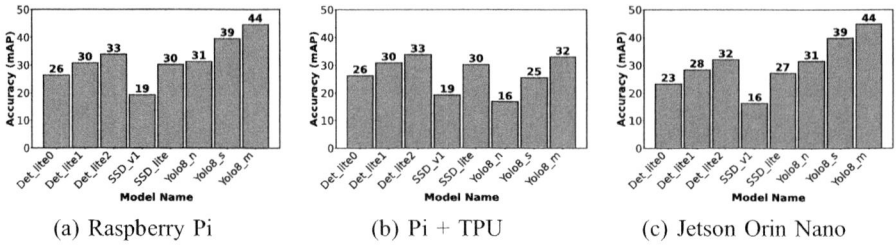

Fig. 4. Accuracy (mAP) for different edge devices.

models such as YOLOv5-Nano, YOLOX-Nano, YOLOv6-Nano, and YOLOv7-Tiny. Galliera and Suri [7] explore YOLOv5 within the context of deep learning accelerators for low-latency decision-making, while Lema et al. [10] evaluate YOLOv3, YOLOv5, and YOLOX. In parallel, Cantero et al. [5] examine SSD models alongside CenterNet, and Faster R-CNN. Kang and Somtham [9] and Zagitov et al. [15] evaluate SSD variants such as MobileNetV2 SSD in conjunction with YOLO models, while Chen et al. [6] deploy SSD-MobileNets to study performance improvements. Furthermore, Kamath and Renuka [8], Cantero et al. [5] and Zagitov et al. [15] include EfficientDet in their analysis. Additionally, Baller et al. [3] present DeepEdgeBench to assess MobileNetV2. Lastly, Magalhães et al. [12] evaluate RetinaNet ResNet-50 across heterogeneous platforms.

Table 2. Comparison of Studies Based on Device Architectures and Key Criteria.

Study	CPU	TPU	GPU	YOLOv8	EfficientDet	SSD	Infer Time	Energy Cons.	mAP
Cantero et al. [5]	✓	✓			✓	✓	✓		
Kamath and Renuka [8]	✓				✓		✓		✓
Kang and Somtham [9]		✓	✓			✓	✓	✓	✓
Baller et al. [3]	✓	✓	✓			✓	✓	✓	✓
Bulut et al. [4]			✓				✓	✓	✓
Chen et al. [6]	✓					✓	✓		✓
Zagitov et al. [15]	✓		✓	✓	✓	✓	✓		✓
Galliera and Suri [7]		✓	✓				✓		✓
Lema et al. [10]		✓	✓				✓	✓	✓
Magalhães et al. [12]		✓	✓				✓	✓	✓
Our Work	✓	✓	✓	✓	✓	✓	✓	✓	✓

5 Conclusions

In this paper, we evaluated the performance of deep learning object detection models, including YOLOv8 (Nano, Small, Medium), EfficientDet Lite (Lite0, Lite1, Lite2), and SSD (SSD MobileNet V1, SSDLite MobileDet), on edge devices like Raspberry Pi 3, 4, and 5 (with/without TPU accelerators) and Jetson Orin Nano. We collected the mAP metric and assessed the models' performance in terms of inference time and energy consumption.

Our evaluation reveals a trade-off between accuracy, energy consumption, and inference time. The SSD_v1 model had the lowest energy consumption and fastest inference time but was the least accurate. Jetson Orin Nano was the fastest and most energy-efficient device for YOLOv8 models without compromising accuracy. However, converting SSD and EfficientDet_Lite models to TensorRT framework reduced their accuracy. Edge TPU accelerator improved the performance of SSD and EfficientDet Lite models without affecting accuracy but significantly decreased the accuracy of YOLOv8 models.

References

1. Alqahtani, D.K., Cheema, A., Toosi, A.N.: Benchmarking deep learning models for object detection on edge computing devices. arXiv preprint arXiv:2409.16808 (2024)
2. Balasubramaniam, A., Pasricha, S.: Object detection in autonomous vehicles: Status and open challenges. arXiv preprint arXiv:2201.07706 (2022)
3. Baller, S.P., Jindal, A., Chadha, M., Gerndt, M.: Deepedgebench: benchmarking deep neural networks on edge devices. In: 2021 IEEE International Conference on Cloud Engineering (IC2E), pp. 20–30. IEEE (2021)
4. Bulut, A., Ozdemir, F., Bostanci, Y.S., Soyturk, M.: Performance evaluation of recent object detection models for traffic safety applications on edge. In: Proceedings of the 2023 5th International Conference on Image Processing and Machine Vision, pp. 1–6 (2023)
5. Cantero, D., Esnaola-Gonzalez, I., Miguel-Alonso, J., Jauregi, E.: Benchmarking object detection deep learning models in embedded devices. Sensors **22**(11), 4205 (2022)
6. Chen, C.W., Ruan, S.J., Lin, C.H., Hung, C.C.: Performance evaluation of edge computing-based deep learning object detection. In: Proceedings of the 2018 VII International Conference on Network, Communication and Computing, pp. 40–43 (2018)
7. Galliera, R., Suri, N.: Object detection at the edge: off-the-shelf deep learning capable devices and accelerators. Proc. Comput. Sci. **205**, 239–248 (2022)
8. Kamath, V., Renuka, A.: Performance analysis of the pretrained efficientdet for real-time object detection on raspberry pi. In: 2021 International Conference on Circuits, Controls and Communications (CCUBE), pp. 1–6. IEEE (2021)
9. Kang, P., Somtham, A.: An evaluation of modern accelerator-based edge devices for object detection applications. Mathematics **10**(22), 4299 (2022)
10. Lema, D.G., Usamentiaga, R., García, D.F.: Quantitative comparison and performance evaluation of deep learning-based object detection models on edge computing devices. Integration **95**, 102127 (2024)
11. Liu, W., et al.: SSD: single shot multibox detector. In: Leibe, B., Matas, J., Sebe, N., Welling, M. (eds.) ECCV 2016. LNCS, vol. 9905, pp. 21–37. Springer, Cham (2016). https://doi.org/10.1007/978-3-319-46448-0_2
12. Magalhães, S.C., dos Santos, F.N., Machado, P., Moreira, A.P., Dias, J.: Benchmarking edge computing devices for grape bunches and trunks detection using accelerated object detection single shot multibox deep learning models. Eng. Appl. Artif. Intell. **117**, 105604 (2023)

13. Tan, M., Pang, R., Le, Q.V.: Efficientdet: scalable and efficient object detection. In: Proceedings of the IEEE/CVF Conference on Computer Vision and pattern recognition, pp. 10781–10790 (2020)
14. Ultralytics: Home (2024). https://docs.ultralytics.com/
15. Zagitov, A., Chebotareva, E., Toschev, A., Magid, E.: Comparative analysis of neural network models performance on low-power devices for a real-time object detection task. Computer **48**(2) (2024)

Generative AI

LLM Enhanced Representation for Cold Start Service Recommendation

Dunlei Rong[1], Lina Yao[2,3], Yinting Zheng[4], Shuang Yu[1], Xiaofei Xu[1], Mingyi Liu[1], and Zhongjie Wang[1(✉)]

[1] Faculty of Computing, Harbin Institute of Technology, Harbin, China
21B903066@stu.hit.edu.cn, {yushuang,xiaofei,liumy,rainy}@hit.edu.cn
[2] Csiro's Data61, Sydney, Australia
lina.yao@data61.csiro.au
[3] University of New South Wales, Sydney, Australia
[4] School of Economics and Finance, South China University of Technology, Guangzhou, China
202130072104@mail.scut.edu.cn

Abstract. With the rise of service globalization and the advent of LLMs, users are becoming increasingly active on the internet to discover services and engage in social interaction. Instead of browsing through vast amounts of information, users prefer to interact directly with smart devices for decision-making and recommendations. However, there are two main challenges in this process: firstly, user needs are often ambiguous, with different functionalities potentially being described in similar terms. Secondly, the internet hosts a large number of services and requirements, complicating the process of service composition. To address the first challenge, this paper proposes the Graph Self-Attention Transformer (GSAT) model, which enhances representation from both semantic and topological perspective. From topological perspective, it integrates local features by walking through the historical records of mashups, uses graph self-attention module on this records, and employs an attention mechanism on all mashups to capture global features. From semantic perspective, it enhances mashup and API descriptions with the help of LLMs. To verify the effectiveness in solving the second challenge, This paper partitions the ProgrammableWeb dataset under and evaluates the GSAT performance under the cold-start setting. This paper compares GSAT with traditional methods and several LLMs, including BERT, T5, LLaMA and ChatGPT. The experiments show that GSAT effectively distinguishes between mashups and achieves state-of-the-art (SOTA) performance.

Keywords: Service Recommendation · LLM · Service Representation

1 Introduction

Web 2.0 is characterized by structured web pages, vast amounts of services, and personalized user experiences. During this era, users input keywords based on their preferences to retrieve the most relevant pages and fulfill their needs. With the advent of Web 3.0 and the emergence of LLMs, a shift from a structure-based to a semantic-based internet becomes possible. In the Web 3.0 era, users leverage natural language to express their needs, and API services are represented in natural language format on the internet. Therefore, developers collect user needs and design service recommendation systems to find the most relevant services. However, past research in service computing has highlighted the inherent ambiguity of user needs, as users themselves may not always have a clear understanding of their own needs. Thus, in the Web 3.0 era, it is crucial to develop service recommendation systems that can effectively understand the semantics of user needs and services.

Service recommendation involves selecting relevant services from a vast repository and combining them into a cohesive service combination. Traditional service recommendation methods considered the associations between mashups and API services and proposed various matching approaches. However, these methods typically rely on static representation techniques, such as Word2Vec, to encode APIs and mashups. They rarely design approaches from the perspective of enhancing representations by semantic and structural features integration and often ignore the analysis of the impact of different encoding methods, which is crucial for the cold start service recommendation.

Language models have been employed in text mining tasks [1] [2], and the emergence of ChatGPT marks a significant step toward general artificial intelligence, encouraging various fields to explore how LLMs can be used to solve problems. In service computing, [3] utilizes the zero-shot capabilities of LLMs, prompting LLMs to uncover implicit relationships between knowledge step-by-step, constructing a service knowledge graph, and addressing issues such as the diversity and complexity of domain knowledge and the lack of annotations for services. [4] proposes the "plan, generate, and match" approach, which uses

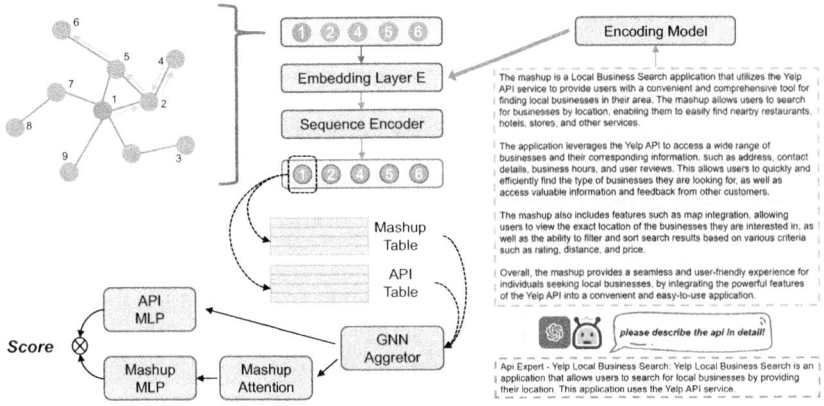

Fig. 1. Overall Model Framework

LLMs to generate scientific workflows and provides user suggestions. However, the application of LLMs to service recommendation remains relatively rare.

This paper proposes the GSAT model, which enhances service representation from both semantic and topological perspectives, as shown in Fig. 1. From a topological perspective, this paper uses two modules, graph self-attention and mashup-attention, to integrate neighbor and global information. First, a random walk algorithm is performed on the service invocation graph, and the node sequences are encoded using a sequential neural network model to integrate multi-step neighbor features. Subsequently, a graph self-attention module is employed to integrate the features of neighboring nodes. Through these two steps, GSAT captures local features and better distinguishes the distances between different mashups. Additionally, observations indicate implicit relationships between mashups, even when there is a long distance between them [5]. Therefore, this paper introduces a mashup-attention mechanism to integrate global features. From a semantic perspective, this paper compares multiple embedding methods, including word2vec, BERT, and OpenAI Text Embedding3-Small. However, some of the mashup descriptions are poor and ambiguous, making it difficult for traditional method to distinguish them effectively. Notably, LLMs are trained on massive amounts of unsupervised text and possess the capability in commonsense knowledge reasoning. Moreover, past research has shown that LLMs are good at expanding textual concepts [6] [7]. Therefore, this paper introduces LLM, including LLaMA and ChatGPT, to encoding descriptions of mashups and APIs and explores the potential for using LLMs for direct prediction. As platform providers strive to offer multiple high-quality API services for new mashups, this paper focuses on service recommendation effectiveness in a cold start environment.

In summary, the contributions of this paper are as follows:

This paper proposes the GSAT model, which enhances representation from both semantic and topological perspectives, achieving better differentiation of representations for mashups and obtaining promising results.

This paper employs multiple embedding methods to comprehensively explore the impact of semantic encoding and structural integration on model performance, providing a deep analysis.

This paper uses ChatGPT for representation enhancement and introduces several strong baselines for comparison. It provides an initial exploration of the application of LLMs in the service recommendation.

The structure of this paper is as follows: Sect. 2 reviews related work, Sects. 4 presents the proposed methodology, Sect. 5 discusses the experimental design and model performances, and Sect. 6 is the conclusion.

2 Related Work

2.1 Service Recommendation

Service recommendation involves invoking multiple web services to form a solution that meets the functional requirements of a mashup. It focuses on the association between mashups and web services. [8] proposes a multi-layer attention mechanism that mines functional associations between mashups and APIs based on API tags and considers non-functional associations by evaluating service quality. [9] addresses the long-tail effect in service recommendation by reordering APIs based on user interests after analyzing the historical API sequence. [10] models the functional and structural associations between APIs and mashups separately and performs representation fusion. [11] emphasizes social associations between users, considering factors such as the number of items interacted with by users and social trust. [12] comprehensively considers QoS and user trust, proposing a three-layer social service recommendation model. [13] constructs a hypergraph using API tag information and service interaction information, explicitly representing neighbor information in the hypergraph to capture higher-order relationships between APIs and mashups. Most methods adopt separate modeling of APIs and mashups, performing representation fusion before prediction. This paper conducts feature fusion during the representation process and focuses on the associations between mashups.

2.2 Service Representation

Service representation is a foundational step in service recommendation. In many cases, the textual descriptions of user requirements and services are unclear, making it difficult to generate representations and accurately identify their relationships [14] [15]. [16] addresses the cold start problem by constructing a hypergraph based on user and item interaction history, and using a multi-layer perceptron to encode users and items separately. [17] uses BERT to encode mashups and APIs, integrating replaced token detection (RTD) and contrastive learning methods to train BERT and attention models. [18] proposes constructing invocation graphs based on service and API classifications, utilizing graph neural networks for encoding, and feeding them into a dual-channel GRU for feature fusion to enhance representation. [19] jointly performs missing label prediction to enhance multi-label service recommendation. [20] introduces a dynamic graph neural network model (DYSR) to address service evolution and mitigate the semantic gap between services and mashups. While many works highlight the importance of service tags in distinguishing API functions, not all APIs have service tags, and incorrect annotation issues are also prevalent. Moreover, labeling services in new datasets is a manually intensive task. This paper explores the impact of various encoding methods on service recommendation models and demonstrates that encoding only API descriptions can also achieve good results.

3 Problem Definition

Firstly, this paper provides definitions for several concepts, and then describes service recommendation. This paper defines mashups as $MS = \{m_1, m_2, \ldots, m_M\}$, where $m_i = \{name, description, enhanced - description\}$. In this concept, $name$ is the name of the mashup, $description$ is the natural language description of the mashup, and *enhanced-description* represents the enhanced representation obtained by concatenating the mashup's name and description and inputting them into ChatGPT. This paper defines service set as $S = \{s_1, s_2, \ldots, s_N\}$, where $s_j = \{name, description, enhanced-description, \{tag_1, tag_2, \ldots, tag_t\}\}$. The definition is similar to that of the mashup, but tag represents the API's functional tags. This paper defines invocation as $R = \{r_{i,j} | i \in [0, M], j \in [0, N]\}$, where $r_{i,j} = (m_i, s_j)$ represents mashup m_i invokes s_j.

Based on the above concepts, this paper defines the service recommendation problem as follows: Given any mashup m_i, the service recommender should select the top-k APIs from S that can meet the functional requirements of the mashup:

$$S_i = f(m_i, S) = \{s_{i,1}, s_{i,2}, \cdots, s_{i,k}\}. \tag{1}$$

4 Method

To integrate the semantic and structural features of nodes, this paper proposes the GSAT model, as shown in Fig.1. It first performs random walks on the invocation graph for all nodes and uses a sequential neural network for feature fusion. Then, a graph self-attention transformer is utilized to integrate all two-hop neighbor features. To integrate global features, this paper designs a mashup self-attention mechanism. Finally, mashups and APIs are input into specific MLPs to obtain the final representations. Additionally, this paper employs LLMs to enhance representation. Specifically, this paper first prompts ChatGPT to enhance before encoding the mashup and API descriptions, then inputs the newly encoded descriptions into the GSAT. The paper also designs prompts for direct prediction by ChatGPT and the T5 model and outlines a method for fine-tuning the T5 model. The detailed process is as follows.

Before encoding mashups and APIs, this paper first constructs an invocation graph based on R. The invocation graph is a bipartite graph that includes both mashup and API nodes, with no relationships between mashup nodes. Then this paper adopts a random walk algorithm on this graph to obtain node sequences $n_i = \{node_i, node_1, node_2, \ldots, node_n\}$ for all mashups and APIs, and encodes the node sequential using a sequence encoder:

$$h_i = SeqEnc(n_i) \tag{2}$$

Seq-Enc($\cdot$) can be any sequential model. This paper uses Bi-GRU, however, Bi-GRU models exhibit locality when sequences are too long. In the future, they can be replaced by other models, such as transformers.

To gain a comprehensive understanding of the local environment, this paper proposes the graph self-attention module to capture relationships between neighboring nodes within one step. This module is similar to the Graph Attention Network (GAT) but utilizes a self-attention mechanism. Specifically, this paper defines mashup and api embedding table as $E \in \mathbb{R}^{(M+N) \times d}$, the attention weights as $W_q, W_k, W_v \in \mathbb{R}^{d \times d}$, and the weight adjustment parameter

$a_T \in \mathbb{R}^{2d}$. The first-order neighbors of node i in the invocation graph are defined as $neighbor(i)$. The GSAT model can be described as follows:

$$e_{i,u} = h_i W_u, u \in [k, q, v] \tag{3}$$

$$\alpha_{i,j} = \begin{cases} RELU([e_{i,k}||e_{j,q}]a_T), & j \in neighbor(i), \\ 0, & else \end{cases} \tag{4}$$

Then, a softmax operation is applied to α, and the aggregated features of neighboring nodes are used to form new node representations $e'_i \in E'$. It is noteworthy that the computation process of GSAT is similar to the node attention in [21], but this paper operates solely on the invocation graph without involving hypergraphs.

Api_Name: Envato Api_Description: The Envato API allows developers to access and search Envato's market information, retrieve user details, get Envato market stats, and check on the Envato forums from their own applications. Api_Tags: [eCommerce, Marketplace]	ChatGPT Prediction Prompt Design: This is the name and description of the mashup: <Mashup> This is the probable apis the mashup may call in the future: <Api1> <Api2> ......
Mashup_Name: Api Expert - Yelp Local Business Search Mashup_Description: Yelp Local Business Search is an application that allows users to search for local businesses by providing their location. This application uses the Yelp API service.	<Api10> you should select the most 10 probable apis the mashup may call in the future and sort them from high to low according to the probability, Please think step by step.

Fig. 2. ChatGPT Prediction Prompt Design

Some studies emphasize the effectiveness of implicit relationships among all mashups. Intuitively, mashups with similar topological structures and semantics are likely to be similar. To gain this global perspective, this paper adopts a mashup self-attention mechanism. Specifically, for any mashup embedding $e_{m,i} \in E'$:

$$e_{m,i} = Self-Attention(e_{m,i}) \tag{5}$$

The mashup self-attention is a standard self-attention network, but is applied only among mashup embeddings. This paper uses a two-layer mashup self-attention. The obtained representations of mashups and APIs are then separately input into Mashup-MLP and API-MLP models to obtain the final representations. Mashup-MLP and API-MLP have similar structures, consisting of three-layer perceptron architectures. The degree of matching between APIs and mashups is calculated using vector dot products:

$$score = e_{m,i} \odot e_{a,j} \tag{6}$$

$score \in [0,1]$ represents the probability of mashup i invokes API j. This paper uses Multi-Label Soft Margin loss function to train the GSAT model.

To investigate the impact of LLMs, this paper employs two approaches. The first method involves enhancing representations using LLMs. Specifically, as depicted in Fig. 1, this paper designs prompting phrases where a LLM regenerates descriptions of mashups and APIs. These regenerated descriptions are then encoded and input into the GSAT model.

The second approach involves direct prediction by the LLMs. The designed prompt is shown in Fig. 2. Due to the limited input length for LLMs and to improve computational efficiency, the paper first extracts 30 candidate APIs from S using a efficiently parameterized model. The LLMs then rank and select from these 30 candidate APIs.

5 Experiment

This section first introduces the dataset, evaluation metrics, and comparison methods, then analyzes the model's performance from multiple perspectives.

This paper uses the ProgrammableWeb dataset[1]. The dataset totally contains 8654 mashups and 12562 APIs. However, many APIs are not invoked, and some mashups are obsolete without invoking any APIs. Therefore, this paper filters the active mashups and APIs, resulting in 6424 mashups, 1216 APIs and 10778 invocations. The source code is: https://github.com/Dunlei-Rong/GSAT.

Many previous methods randomly sample invocations and split them into training, validation, and test datasets. However, in most cases, users do not provide API examples when making requests, which more closely resembles a cold-start environment-an aspect we focus on. To better simulate this cold-start scenario, this paper adopts the following approach for dataset partitioning: it extracts part of mashups that invoke multiple APIs, uses one of the invocations as an example for training, and the remaining invocations as the test set. After excluding the instances from the test set, the remaining invocations are divided into training and validation sets at a 3:1 ratio. Only the invocations from the train set are used to construct the invocation graph, which is then used in the validation and test process. This paper uses Precision (P@K) and Normalized Discounted Cumulative Gain (NDCG@K) to evaluate the accuracy of GSAT in API recommendations, with $K = [1, 5, 10]$.

To compare the effectiveness of the model, this paper selects four classic yet effective methods from recent SOTA papers in service recommendation. Additionally, it introduces methods using LLM, such as LLaMA and ChatGPT. Next, this paper will introduce these methods separately:

---

[1] It is available at https://github.com/HIT-ICES/Correted-ProgrammableWeb-dataset.

Table 1. Performance Comparison Red, yellow, and green indicate the optimal, second-best, and third-best performance, respectively. The data in the table are the average results under five random seeds.

		MAP@1	MAP@5	MAP@10	NDCG@1	NDCG@5	NDCG@10
BERT .4	MF	0.158	0.350	0.453	0.229	0.421	0.482
	MGSR	0.003	0.008	0.011	0.004	0.008	0.011
	NGCF	0.005	0.023	0.038	0.009	0.023	0.031
	HHAN	0.000	0.002	0.004	0.000	0.002	0.002
	GSAT	0.096	0.145	0.193	0.137	0.178	0.201
PreBERT .4	MF	0.158	0.360	0.433	0.229	0.427	0.472
	MGSR	0.001	0.005	0.01	0.001	0.004	0.007
	NGCF	0.006	0.026	0.044	0.010	0.026	0.036
	HHAN	0.000	0.002	0.004	0.000	0.002	0.002
	GSAT	0.097	0.113	0.121	0.141	0.147	0.15
OpenAI .4	MF	0.152	0.157	0.165	0.219	0.225	0.231
	MGSR	0.001	0.004	0.007	0.002	0.004	0.006
	NGCF	0.058	0.141	0.181	0.080	0.144	0.167
	HHAN	0.011	0.016	0.035	0.023	0.020	0.033
	GSAT	0.174	0.369	0.444	0.252	0.454	0.496
Word2vec .4	MF	0.150	0.234	0.269	0.220	0.311	0.334
	MGSR	0.000	0.004	0.007	0.000	0.004	0.006
	NGCF	0.006	0.024	0.04	0.010	0.023	0.032
	HHAN	0.002	0.031	0.035	0.003	0.019	0.019
	GSAT	0.172	0.368	0.416	0.253	0.451	0.482
User-Similarity		0.041	0.079	0.091	0.062	0.098	0.107
Popularity		0.027	0.067	0.088	0.040	0.080	0.091
T5		0.113	0.215	0.218	0.177	0.251	0.132
T5+w/o		0.166	0.366	0.394	0.249	0.415	0.258
LLaMA		0.037	0.076	0.077	0.058	0.080	0.055
ChatGPT Prediction		0.149	0.354	0.394	0.220	0.372	0.291

Table 2. Comparison on BERT Embedding

Bert Setting	MAP@1	MAP@5	MAP@10	NDCG@1	NDCG@5	NDCG@10
Hattention	0.15	0.229	0.233	0.227	0.32	0.322
Random Walk	0.078	0.177	0.241	0.144	0.231	0.274
GSAT	0.096	0.145	0.193	0.137	0.178	0.201
MF	0.158	0.35	0.453	0.229	0.421	0.482

Frequence: It sorts all APIs based on their usage frequency.

User-Similarity: It identifies a set of mashups most similar to the current mashup based on invocations, then sorts all APIs according to the frequency of their usage across this mashups set.

Matrix factorization(MF): It uses a two-layer linear neural network to encode mashups and APIs respectively. Then it performs an element-wise dot product between mashups and APIs, and ranks all APIs based on the resulting scores.

NGCF [22]: It leverages neighborhood information from the interaction graph and embeddings of mashups and APIs, propagating information and integrating features through multiple neural network layers.

MGSR [21]: It proposes a new GNN and uses a hierarchical attention mechanism that combines a node-level and a motif-level attention mechanisms.

HHAN [13]: It exploits the user-API interaction data and additional API attribute information, aggregates the neighbor information on the heterogeneous hypergraph to capture the high-order relationships between APIs and users.

T5 [23]: A unified text-to-text transformer model, this paper designs prompts to help the T5 model score each API.

LLaMA: LLaMA is an open-source large language model that demonstrates remarkable performance across various natural language processing tasks. [24] indicates that LLaMA has the capability to decode the representation space of recommendation sequences. This paper adopts the method from [24] for model pre-training.

ChatGPT [25]: ChatGPT is a state-of-the-art language model designed for natural language understanding and generation tasks. It generates human-like text based on input prompts, making it suitable for various applications. This paper also designs prompts for it to recommend.

The experiments utilize an NVIDIA 3090 with 24 GB of memory. The source code is implemented based on PyTorch 2.3.0 with CUDA 11.8. Let dim denote the input dimension, which is determined by the embedding model. The embedding dimensions for BERT, pretraing BERT, Word2Vec and OpenAI Text Embedding3-Small(openai) are 768, 768, 300, 1236, respectively. The embedding dimension is kept as dim during training, except in the Mashup MLP and API MLP, which are three-layer MLPs with the input and output dimension equals to dim, but with the hidden dimension equals to $dim/2$. All activation functions used in this paper are ReLU.

5.1 Results Comparison

The experimental results are shown in Table 1. This paper employs various encoding methods. "BERT" refers to the use of the BERT-Base-Uncased model, "PreBERT" indicates the BERT-Base-Uncased model pre-trained on the dataset with contrastive learning tasks, "OpenAI" denotes the use of the OpenAI Text Embedding 3-Small model, and "Word2Vec" refers to the encoding with 300-dimensional Word2Vec vectors. It is evident that GSAT achieves overall optimal performance when using OpenAI and Word2Vec encoding, and sub-optimal performance with BERT encoding, demonstrating the model's representational generalization. The latest SOTA models did not perform well under this experimental setup. In the cases of MGSR and HHAN, the models consider structural characteristics, but the scenario in this paper is more similar to a cold start environment, which poses challenges for models that require extensive neighbor node features.

Although the GSAT model achieves SOTA performance across the entire experiment, it performs worse than MF under BERT embedding settings. To understand this phenomenon, this paper conducts an additional experiment under BERT settings, with results shown in Table 2. Considering the embedding features, Word2Vec assigns fixed representations to words, whereas in this paper, averaging word embeddings in sentences is used, disregarding sentence structure features. Consequently, similar Mashups have similar sentence representations. In contrast, BERT considers not only word embeddings but also sentence structure, resulting in dissimilar sentence representations for Mashups with different structural patterns. Observing the dataset, many Mashups share similar word expressions but differ in sentence structures and selected APIs. Considering the method design, MF directly inputs Mashup and API vectors into a multi-layer perceptron for dot product operations, making it sensitive to mashup similarities. Thus, BERT provides better initial discriminability than Word2Vec for the MF method. GSAT adopts a multi-step representation fusion strategy, particularly the random walk module, which aggregates similar neighbors to enhance differentiation among different types of mashups. However, BERT's sentence-level differentiation structure is compromised by neighbor integration. As shown in Table 2, after ablating the mashup-attention or random walk module, the model's performance on the BERT setting significantly improves compared to the original model. Additionally, NGCF, another method based on neighbor similarity computation, demonstrates relatively good results on OpenAI and Word2Vec embeddings but performs poorly on BERT and PreBERT embeddings, further substantiating the findings of this paper.

The performance of the non-pretrained T5 model is poor. However, significant improvements are observed after applying contrastive learning, achieving third-best results in certain metrics.

Unfortunately, the performance of LLaMA is not satisfactory. Analysis reveals that the LLaMA model tends to repeat recommendations and, in many cases, outputs meaningless characters. In future work, this paper will focus on optimizing the LLaMA prompts and exploring alternative fine-tuning strategies.

Additionally, although ChatGPT does not achieve the best prediction results, its explanations are reasonable from a human perspective. This is discussed in detail in the case study of Sect. 5.5.

5.2 Experimental Performance of ChatGPT-Enhanced Representation

To further explore the effectiveness of the GSAT model, this paper examines two perspectives, following the principles of model design: 1) from a semantic perspective, this paper uses ChatGPT to generate more detailed mashup and API descriptions; 2) from a topological perspective, giving that many mashup descriptions have high similarity but different functionalities, this paper randomly shuffles mashup descriptions, relying solely on the topological features of mashups for prediction. However, this operation also renders semantic-based matching completely ineffective. The experimental results are shown in Table 3. In this table, "One-Hot" represents encoding all mashups using one-hot encoding and mapping them with a multilayer perceptron, "Shuffle" refers to randomly shuffling all mashup representations, and "ChatGPT" denotes descriptions enhanced by ChatGPT. All descriptions, except for One-Hot, are encoded using OpenAI Text Embedding3-Small.

Table 3. ChatGPT Enhenced Representation Performance

	MAP@1	MAP@5	MAP@10	NDCG@1	NDCG@5	NDCG@10
One-Hot	0.168	0.361	0.431	0.247	0.450	0.496
Shuffle	0.166	0.399	0.482	0.243	0.488	0.533
Nomal	0.179	0.385	0.442	0.264	0.422	0.518
Shuffle+ChatGPT	0.166	0.399	0.478	0.245	0.497	0.542
ChatGPT	0.166	0.399	0.476	0.245	0.495	0.537

By comparing One-Hot, Normal, and ChatGPT, it can be observed that as the semantics of the representation become richer, the model's performance improves significantly. This indicates the semantic representation capability of GSAT. Comparing Shuffle and Normal shows that, despite losing the original semantic representation, the method of increasing the disparity between similar mashup representations and highlighting topological features achieves significant improvement. Furthermore, comparing Shuffle+ChatGPT and ChatGPT reveals that even when solely relying on ChatGPT to increase the disparity between representations while completely ignoring semantics, there is still a slight performance improvement. This demonstrates the model's advantage in integrating topological structures and suggests that future efforts should focus on balancing both semantic and topological aspects to further enhance model performance.

Comparative analysis shows that Normal achieves a substantial advantage in MAP@1 and NDCG@1. Even the one-hot encoding, which weakens representation capabilities, still outperforms other methods. However, for the other four metrics, both Normal and One-Hot perform poorly. This suggests that the Normal approach excels in head predictions but has weak generalization capabilities for other APIs, indicating a significant long-tail effect compared to other methods. From other comparisons, both semantic enhancement and topological structure enhancement can noticeably suppress the long-tail effect.

5.3 Ablation Experiment

The functional modules of GSAT are divided into two parts: Random Walk + graph self-attention transformer, which capture local node features, and mashup self-attention, which captures global semantic relevance features. This paper conducts ablation studies by removing these two modules separately, and the results are shown in Table 4. Apart from the improvement in NDCG@5 when the Random Walk module is removed, other metrics show considerable declines. This experiment confirms the effectiveness of these two modules.

Table 4. Ablation Result /$Random - Walk$ refers to retaining only the mashup-attention structure, /$Mashup - Attention$ refers to retaining only the random walk and graph self-attention.

	MAP@1	MAP@5	MAP@10	NDCG@1	NDCG@5	NDCG@10
/Random-Walk	0.150	0.230	0.230	0.227	0.321	0.321
/Mashup-Attention	0.142	0.350	0.406	0.229	0.439	0.470
Whole	0.179	0.385	0.442	0.264	0.422	0.518

5.4 Representation Clustering Analysis

To explore the effect of the GSAT model on enhancing node representations, this paper selects representations from different modules, performs PCA for dimensionality reduction, and then conducts clustering. The number of clusters is set to 6, and the results are shown in Fig. 3. Figure 3a illustrates the node distribution encoded by OpenAI, where all mashup nodes are aggregated within a small range, showing no significant separation. Figure 3b displays the node distribution after local representation enhancement, with all nodes exhibiting an initial discrete state. Figure 3c shows the node distribution after global enhancement, where three categories of nodes are distant from the densely distributed nodes and exhibit clearer boundaries, demonstrating the GSAT model's ability to provide personalized representations. The results of the Word2Vec representation are slightly less distinct compared to the OpenAI results, but show a more distinct discrete state than the initial state. Under the BERT representation, the GSAT model performs the weakest, as the clustering results under BERT representation do not show significant differentiation compared to the initial state.

5.5 ChatGPT Prediction Case Study

Figure 4 is a prediction example from ChatGPT. The mashup requires creating an application that can monitor social media account followers, involving sites such as Twitter and YouTube. ChatGPT finds Twitter but does not find

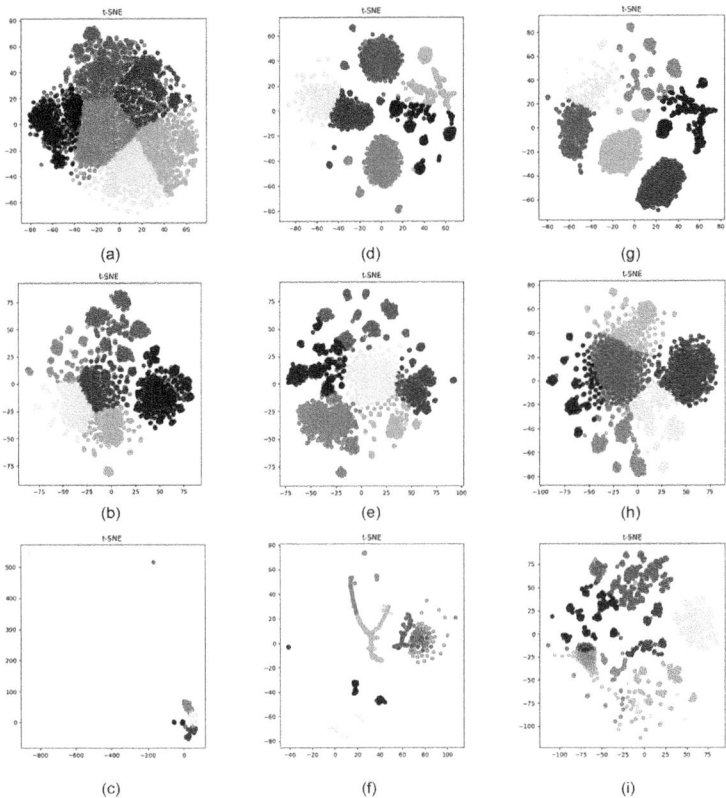

Fig. 3. Representation Clustering Analysis panels (a), (b) and (c) show the results under the OpenAI setting, panels (d), (e) and (f) show the results under the Word2Vec setting, and panels (g), (h) and (i) show the results under the BERT setting.

Mashup:

Social Mirror: monitors popular [English language] Twitter accounts , Facebook pages , YouTube channels offers basic visualizations posting activities observed social media accounts follower engagement.

ChatGPT Prediction:

1. Bittrex (Statistics, Monitoring, Cryptocurrency, Accounts, Payments, Prices)
2. Twitter (Blogging, Social)
3. Oracle NetSuite (Customer Relationship Management, Enterprise)

GroudTruth:

1. Twitter (Blogging, Social)
2. YouTube (Media, Video)

Fig. 4. ChatGPT Prediction Case Study

YouTube, as this option is not present in the top 30 APIs generated by the SOTA model. Additionally, ChatGPT ranks the account monitoring API "Bitterex" first. This API clearly meets the mashup's requirements but is not included in the ground truth labels. The third recommended application by ChatGPT is "Oracle NetSuite", a customer relationship management API, which also evidently fits the follower monitoring needs of the mashup. Therefore, ChatGPT's predictions are valid, but the performance evaluation process is limited by the ground truth. Addressing such evaluation bias is one of the future development directions in the field of service recommendation.

6 Conclusion

This paper proposes the GSAT model, which integrates local structural features and global structural features to enhance node representation. To analyze the impact of different representation method on models, this paper designs four representation methods: OpenAI, Word2Vec, BERT, and pre-trained BERT, demonstrating the effects of different representations on models and conducting analysis. The paper also explores how to incorporate LLM into service recommendation and discusses future development directions.

Acknowledgements. The research in this paper is partially supported by the National Key Research and Development Program of China (No.2021YFF0900900), Key Research and Development Program of Heilongjiang Providence (2022ZX01A28), the Postdoctoral Fellowship Program of CPSF (GZC20242204), and the Postdoctoral Science Foundation of Heilongjiang Province, China (LBH-Z23161).

References

1. Zhang, Y., et al.: When large language models meet citation: A survey. arXiv preprint arXiv:2309.09727 (2023)
2. Zhang, Y., Wang, Y., Sheng, Z., Mahmood, A., Zhang, W.E., Zhao, R.: Hybrid data augmentation for citation function classification. In: 2023 International Joint Conference on Neural Networks (IJCNN). IEEE, pp. 1–8 (2023)
3. Yu, S., Huang, T., Liu, M., Wang, Z.: Bear: revolutionizing service domain knowledge graph construction with LLM. In: International Conference on Service-Oriented Computing. Springer, pp. 339–346 (2023)
4. Gu, Y., Cao, J., Guo, Y., Qian, S., Guan, W.: Plan, generate and match: Scientific workflow recommendation with large language models. In: International Conference on Service-Oriented Computing. Springer, pp. 86–102 (2023)
5. Liao, G., Deng, X., Wan, C., Liu, X.: Group event recommendation based on graph multi-head attention network combining explicit and implicit information. Inf. Proce. Manage. **59**(2), 102797 (2022)
6. Wei, W., et al.: Llmrec: large language models with graph augmentation for recommendation. In: Proceedings of the 17th ACM International Conference on Web Search and Data Mining, pp. 806–815 (2024)
7. He, X., et al.: Explanations as features: Llm-based features for text-attributed graphs. arXiv preprint arXiv:2305.19523, vol. 2, no. 4, p 8 (2023)

8. Boulakbech, M., Messai, N., Sam, Y., Devogele, T.: Deep learning model for personalized web service recommendations using attention mechanism. In: International Conference on Service-Oriented Computing. Springer, pp. 19–33 (2023)
9. Kermany, N.R., Pizzato, L., Yang, J., Xue, S., Wu, J.: Pd-srs: personalized diversity for a fair session-based recommendation system. In: International Conference on Service-Oriented Computing. Springer, pp. 331–339 (2022)
10. Wang, X., Xi, M., Yin, J.: Functional and structural fusion based web api recommendations in heterogeneous networks. In: IEEE International Conference on Web Services (ICWS). IEEE **2023**, 91–96 (2023)
11. Ma, L.: Expoev: enhancing social recommendation service with social exposure and feature evolution. In: 2023 IEEE International Conference on Web Services (ICWS). IEEE, pp. 105–111 (2023)
12. Zhang, S., Zhang, D., Wu, Y., Zhong, H.: Service recommendation model based on trust and qos for social internet of things. IEEE Trans. Serv. Comput. (2023)
13. Mai, J., Tang, M., Xie, F., Liao, L.: Third-party api recommendation based on heterogeneous hypergraph attention networks. In: 2023 IEEE International Conference on Web Services (ICWS). IEEE, pp. 545–552 (2023)
14. Zhang, Y., et al.: Towards employing native information in citation function classification. Scientometrics, 1–21 (2022). https://doi.org/10.1007/s11192-021-04242-0
15. Zhang, Y., Wang, Y., Sheng, Q.Z., Mahmood, A., Emma Zhang, W., Zhao, R.: Tdm-cfc: towards document-level multi-label citation function classification. In: Web Information Systems Engineering–WISE 2021: 22nd International Conference on Web Information Systems Engineering, WISE 2021, Melbourne, VIC, Australia, October 26–29, 2021, Proceedings, Part II 22. Springer, pp. 363–376 (2021)
16. Wu, H., et al.: Feature matching machine for cold-start recommendation. IEEE Trans. Serv. Comput. (2023)
17. Wang, X., Zhou, P., Wang, Y., Liu, X., Liu, J., Wu, H.: Servicebert: a pre-trained model for web service tagging and recommendation. In: International Conference on Service-Oriented Computing. Springer, pp. 464–478 (2021)
18. Xu, S., Xiang, Q., Fan, Y., Yan, R., Zhang, J.: Exploiting category information in sequential recommendation. In: International Conference on Service-Oriented Computing. Springer, pp. 51–66 (2023)
19. Chen, W., Liu, M., Tu, Z., Wang, Z.: Tagtag: a novel framework for service tags recommendation and missing tag prediction. In: International Conference on Service-Oriented Computing. Springer, pp. 340–348 (2022)
20. Liu, M., Tu, Z., Xu, H., Xu, X., Wang, Z.: Dysr: a dynamic graph neural network based service bundle recommendation model for mashup creation. IEEE Trans. Serv. Comput. (2023)
21. Zheng, X., et al.: H-mgsr: a hierarchical motif-based graph attention neural network for service recommendation. In: IEEE International Conference on Web Services (ICWS). IEEE vol. 2023, pp. 553–562 (2023)
22. Wang, X., He, X., Wang, M., Feng, F., Chua, T.S.: Neural graph collaborative filtering. In:Proceedings of the 42nd International ACM SIGIR Conference on Research and Development in Information Retrieval, pp. 165–174 (2019)
23. Raffel, C., et al.: Exploring the limits of transfer learning with a unified text-to-text transformer. J. Mach. Learn. Res. **21**(140), 1–67 (2020)
24. Yang, Z., et al.: Large language model can interpret latent space of sequential recommender. arXiv preprint arXiv:2310.20487 (2023)
25. Floridi, L., Chiriatti, M.: Gpt-3: Its nature, scope, limits, and consequences. Mind. Mach. **30**, 681–694 (2020)

Combining Generative AI and PPTalk Service Specification for Dynamic and Adaptive Task-Oriented Chatbots

María Jesús Rodríguez-Sánchez[(✉)], Zoraida Callejas, Angel Ruiz-Zafra, and Kawtar Benghazi

University of Granada, Granada, Spain
{mjesusrodriguez,zoraida,angelr,benghazi}@ugr.es

Abstract. In recent years, chatbots have become increasingly prevalent in various business domains, providing services such as booking flights, making hotel reservations, and scheduling appointments. These systems, known as task-oriented chatbots, initiate a conversation to collect the necessary data and subsequently invoke a specific web service to complete the task. Traditionally, they operate on the basis of predefined rules or are trained with specific task data. While effective, this approach is often rigid and lacks adaptability to the evolving peculiarities of individual businesses. For instance, a chatbot designed for general restaurant reservations will request common data such as the number of diners or reservation time, but may fail to accommodate specific preferences such as terrace seating, buffet options, or karaoke availability.

To address the limitations of traditional task-oriented chatbots, we propose an innovative approach leveraging generative AI and a novel service specification concept called PPTalk. This approach enables chatbots to dynamically introduce business-specific elements into conversations, enhancing their adaptability to the unique characteristics of each business. We have developed a proof of concept to demonstrate the feasibility and effectiveness of our proposal, obtaining highly positive results.

Keywords: openAPI · chatbot · adaptive dialogue · LLM

1 Introduction

The significance and integration of chatbots in businesses have seen substantial growth in recent years. As users may interact with their own words, they break the communication barriers between companies and their customers, enhancing customer service and operational efficiency [4]. These systems support companies in offering services that are more easily accessible to a broader audience.

Task-oriented chatbots maintain a conversation aimed at fulfilling a particular task, such as booking a flight or making a reservation. Currently, these systems can have dialogue flows configured during the design phase that are either tailored to the specificities of the particular services or designed to provide a general conversation (e.g. for the common aspects related in booking a flight, such as origin or destination). Both approaches have several limitations, including the need for system developers to update the rules or models when services change and the requirement to adapt the system when new functionalities, possibly related to web services, are introduced [2]. Thus resulting in intrinsically closed dialogue systems that cannot invoke services which are not considered during the design phase. This limitation leads to a lack of scalability and makes it impossible to add new functionalities without incurring significant costs in terms of time and money. Moreover, the predefined dialogue flows in these systems involve asking users the same questions in each interaction, without adapting to the specific requirements of each business's service. For instance, consider a task-oriented conversational system designed for restaurant bookings. Initially, the system is configured to handle reservations for specific dates, times, and party sizes at a given restaurant. However, if the restaurant introduces new dining experiences, such as private dining rooms or special event bookings, the chatbot may not immediately support inquiries related to these new offerings.

Recently, Large Language models (LLMs) have appeared as an alternative to traditional rule and intent-based approaches. As they have been trained with massive amounts of language data, they provide very advanced natural language understanding and generation capabilities, which make them very fitted for question answering and open-domain conversation tasks. However, their usage to develop task-oriented chatbots is still not solved, as it requires that LLMs circumscribe their conversational capabilities to particular domains and are able to invoke specific services.

In this paper we focus on service capabilities to address these issues. Our fundamental contributions are: (1) the definition of a new type of conversational service specification, (2) the definition of a novel process for automatic dialogue generation that invokes a conversational service, (3) a chatbot for restaurant businesses as a proof-of-concept with very positive results.

On the one hand, we contribute the OpenAPI Specification (OAS) named PPTalk, which is used to endow chatbots with the capability to engage in dynamic and adaptive slot-filling dialogues to obtain the necessary pieces of data to invoke the services. On the other hand, we provide a process for the automatic generation of dialogues based on conversational services and LLMs. Unlike state-of-the-art approaches, in our approach LLMs are not the chatbot per se, but are used to improve the main phases involved during conversation: understanding what the user wants to do (intent recognition, e.g., if they want to book a table or cancel a reservation), identifying which parameters need to be requested (e.g., the number of diners and the time), determining when a necessary piece of information has been provided (entity recognition), managing the interaction to decide how to request them (slot-filling), and generating system responses with as much variation as possible through natural language generation.

Thus, our proposal provides further control over the chatbot behaviour. When LLMs are used to manage the interaction in a single step (generating a direct system response for a user input), they constitute a black box; whereas following our process, the conversational interaction between customers and the business is more explainable and manageable.

The rest of the paper is structured as follows. Section 2 presents the related work, Sect. 3 describes our proposal for the dynamic generation of task-oriented chatbots, Sect. 4 presents a proof-of-concept and the evaluation conducted. Finally, Sect. 5 presents the conclusions and outlines future work.

2 Related Work

Previous attempts to automate dialogue management using APIs to enhance the scalability of conversational systems, such as in [11], have resulted in low-quality dialogues and lack explicit integration into web services. With the emergence of LLMs, chatbots are able to understand more complex inputs, producing more sophisticated dialogues. For example, the ShoppingGPT [14] proposal demonstrates the effective use of GPT models for enhancing product recommendations, improving its ability to understand and respond to user input through multi-turn dialogues. However, challenges include reliance on high-quality training data and risks of generating unsafe or toxic content. Approaches such as state machine-based models [15], which manage multi-turn and multi-intent conversations through hierarchical state transitions, offer a more structured control over dialogue management without relying on large amounts of training data. However, these systems tend to be closed and inflexible, as the questions are predefined as transitions between states in the code itself, limiting the chatbot's ability to dynamically adapt to new scenarios. Thus, there is a need to investigate approaches that allow to exploit the benefits of LLMs, while retaining control over the generated responses, obtaining better results than traditional pre-trained models like BERT [7].

A first step in this direction is to study prompting strategies to influence the output generated by the model [5]. Creating effective and broadly applicable prompt strategies is complex [17], the reported challenges include the difficulty of choosing and formulating the right instructions to achieve the desired effects. For example, [16] proposes a process to iteratively prototype prompts to enhance user experience, while studies as [12] designs prompts or frameworks [8,9] to successfully satisfy NLU tasks, for example, slot-filling.

LLMs are best suited for open-domain conversations, adequately adapting them to task-oriented or domain-specific scenarios is still an open research issue. In [10] the authors introduce a domain-specific language (DSL) based on YAML to define task-oriented dialogue system modules, compiled into structured prompts. However, the DSL is specific to the proposal, requiring developer definition and not utilizing existing business service specifications like OpenAPI, resulting in a closed system with non-reusable modules. Similarly, in the work of Kalia et al. [6], the Quark system formalizes chatbot interactions through goals and commitments, but also suffers from limitations in flexibility, as it depends on predefined business processes that restrict adaptability to new services or dynamic requirements.

The aim of our proposal is to address these open issues by focusing on service capabilities and automated and dynamic dialogue generation based on the services specification. Taking as a reference the article [1], where automation levels for service development are established, our proposal would be positioned at level 3, where the discovery of services is fully automatic, approaching even level 4, as both discovery and invocation of services are performed automatically, the service specification is built in a guided way through a simple user interface, and services can be added and removed without affecting the automatic dialogue generation. The control over the responses provided by the chatbot, as they are written by the service provider themselves, avoids sending inappropriate responses. Thanks to the use of LLMs as a tool to fulfill NLU tasks such as slot filling or intent recognition, the aim is to achieve high-quality output by appropriately selecting the prompts to be used with the model.

3 Proposal for Dynamic Task-Oriented Chatbot Generation

This section presents our approach for creating dynamic and adaptive task-oriented chatbots. We introduce the Plug, Play, and Talk Service Specification, our extended OAS for chatbots, and the process of automatic dialogue generation that builds the conversation using these specifications.

3.1 Extended OpenAPI Specification for Chatbots: Plug, Play and Talk Service Specification

To seamlessly integrate services with chatbots, we have extended the OAS for the proposed PPTalk services with the elements highlighted in blue in Fig. 1.b). These elements are: *1)* the *Question* concept, which contains the questions the chatbot can ask to request a property or parameter, *2)* the *Tag* concept, which allows services to be classified into tags representing business characteristics, *3) DataField*, a conceptual abstraction that encapsulates all data elements that are either passed to an endpoint method (*Parameters*) or required within a request or response body (*Properties*), and *4) DiscriminativeParameter*, necessary parameters with a value property that defines a business characteristic.

A service consists of operations, which can be GET, POST, PUT, or DELETE. For our purposes, we focus on GET and POST operations. GET operations include parameters that may be defined for internal service operations (*InternalParameter*) or are provided by the user (*UserInputParameter*). A *UserInputParameter* can be categorized as *DiscriminativeParameter*. POST operations also contain schemas with properties that must be requested to the user.

Matching the PPtalk Specification and Chatbot Elements. Figure 1 shows with discontinuous lines how each element in the PPTalk specification metamodel (Fig. 1.b) corresponds to elements in the chatbot metamodel (Fig. 1.a):

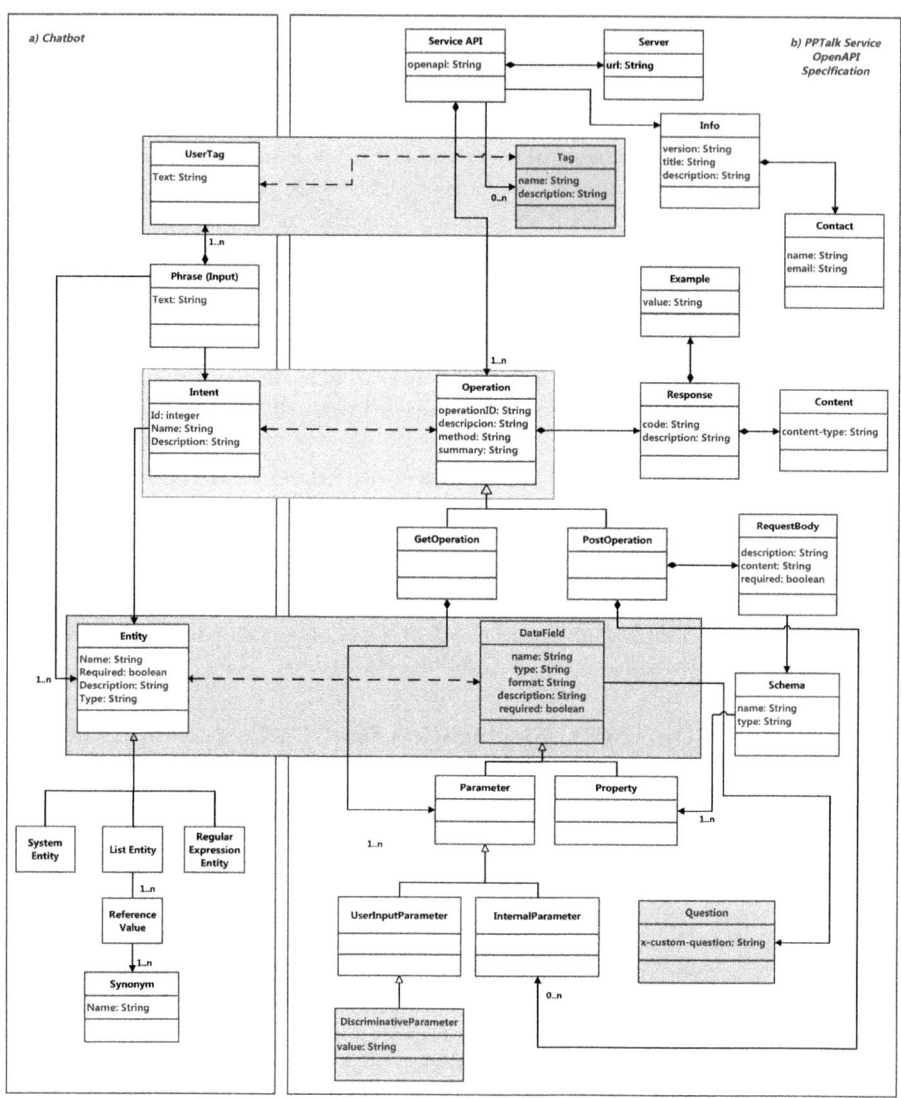

Fig. 1. Interconnection between both meta models

1. **Intent → Operation**: In a conversational system, intents represent the user's goals or desired actions, while operations in a web service specification define the actions the backend service can perform. Formally, let I be the set of user intents and O the set of operations defined in OAS. We define a function IntToOp that maps each intent to a corresponding operation based on their names or synonyms:

$$\text{IntToOp} : I \to O \tag{1}$$

such that

$$\text{IntToOp}(i) = o \quad \text{if} \quad \text{match}(\text{name}(i), \text{name}(o)) = \text{true} \quad (2)$$

where name(x) returns the name of x, and match(a, b) is a function that returns true if a and b are the same or synonyms.

2. **Entity → DataField**: In natural language processing systems and chatbots, entities (or slots) are pieces of information required to provide an appropriate response. Similarly, in a web service specification, DataFields represent the values passed to the endpoint method to execute a specific operation, or define specific data points required in a request or response body.

To perform the matching between entities and datafields, we define a function $EntToD$ that is defined formally as follows: let E be the set of entities and D the set of DataFields in the OAS:

$$\text{EntToD} : E \to D \quad (3)$$

such that

$$\text{EntToD}(e) = d \quad \text{if} \quad e \in \text{entities}(d) \quad \text{or} \quad \text{match}(e, d) = \text{true} \quad (4)$$

The function match(e, d) identifies and extracts relevant information from the input text that corresponds to a DataField d.
entities(d) is the set defined as follows:

$$\text{entities}(d) = \{e \in E \mid \text{match}(e, d) = \text{true}\} \quad (5)$$

3. **UserTag → Tag**: In a conversational system, user tags can be conceptually understood as names or adjectives extracted from the user's initial input to identify their preferences, needs, or intentions. These tags help the system understand and categorize user requirements effectively. Tags within the OAS serve as descriptive labels that categorize different aspects or features of services offered by an API.

Formally, let T be the set of tags within the OAS and UT the set of user tags. We define a function UserTagToTag:

$$\text{UserTagToTag} : UT \to T \cup \{\emptyset\} \quad (6)$$

such that

$$\forall ut \in UT, \text{UserTagToTag}(ut) = \begin{cases} t & \text{if} \quad \exists t \in T \quad \text{where} \quad \text{match}(ut, t) = \text{true} \\ \emptyset & \text{otherwise} \end{cases}$$

$$(7)$$

where match(ut, t) verifies if a user tag matches a tag in the OAS.

3.2 Dynamic Dialogue Building Process

The proposed chatbot building process, shown in Fig. 2, dynamically generates and manages the dialogues from PPTalk service specifications following the steps explained below. Some of the phases described (intent detection, slot filling, dialogue enhancement, and question generation) involve prompting a pre-trained LLM. To facilitate understanding, we illustrate each step with an example in which the chatbot responds to the user's input: *"I want to eat in a vegetarian restaurant in Granada."*. Table 1 lists the specific prompts that can be used for this example.

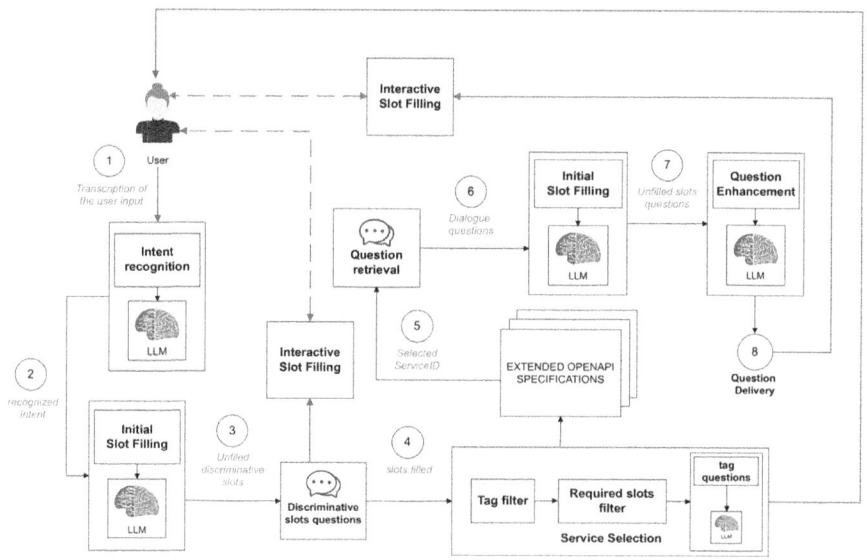

Fig. 2. Dialogue building with PPTalk services

Intent Recognition. When the chatbot receives a request to perform a task, it first detects the user's intent (in our example, the intent is *BookRestaurant*). To do so, it treats intent detection as a classification problem, using the prompt specified in Table 1. Once the *intent* is detected, we perform a string split to identify the verb in the intent, aiming to find synonyms.

Initial Slot Filling. The slot filling task is performed using the initial user input and the LLM with the prompt specified in Table 1. For the service selection task, it is necessary to fill the discriminative parameters to make the selection as close as possible to the user's preferences. Once the service is selected and the parameter information is retrieved (data fields required to complete a task and corresponding questions), the system performs slot filling to execute that specific operation with the data required by the selected service. Figure 3, highlighted in orange, shows how the initial input fills the discriminative parameter ['foodtype': 'vegetarian'] and the selected service parameter ['area': 'Granada'].

Table 1. Chatbot tasks and corresponding LLM prompts.

Chatbot Task	LLM Prompt
Intent Recognition	"You are a chatbot in the restaurant domain, and your task is to determine the intent behind a user's input or query. Below is a list of intents related to the restaurant domain: BookRestaurant, RestaurantInformation, FindRestaurant, OrderFood. Given the input 'I', determine the intent of the user based on the provided intents, return a JSON with only one. Consider that users often want to make reservations when specifying a type of restaurant."
Slot Filling	"Forget the information provided in our previous interactions. Provided the prompt: P, these previous inputs during the conversation: $UserAnswers$ and the API specification: $PPTalkService$, which contains an endpoint called "$Intent$" with a list of parameters, give me a JSON list with the slots and the values that are given in the prompt directly. If no value given, assign the value NULL. The key of the dictionary is the parameter name and the value is the parameter value."
Discriminative tags question generation	"Provide an informal question that can be answered with yes or no to understand someone's preference regarding a parameter with this tag when selecting a restaurant: "$tagName$""
Question improvement	"Provided the question $Question$ in the scope of restaurant booking, give me only one alternative question"

Interactive Slot Filling. All questions are associated with a data field, which in turn is linked to an entity required to perform an operation in the service. When a question or set of questions is sent to the user, a question-response interaction is created. This interaction fills the slots that could not be completed transparently using LLM prompting, as shown in Fig. 3 in green colour, allowing the user to perform the slot filling task interactively.

Service Selection. If several services correspond to the discriminative parameters (in the example, several services correspond to restaurants with the same type of food and price range), the system asks the user for their preferences based on other tags (e.g. availability of terrace). This way, the chatbot can select the service that best suits the user's needs following the algorithm specified in Algorithm 1.

Algorithm 1. Optimized Service Selection Algorithm

Input:
// Services with matching tags and number of coincidences.
tagServices: Dictionary<ServiceID, Float>
// Discriminative parameters
slots: Dictionary<String, String>
Output: selected_services: List<ServiceID>
1: $max\_value \leftarrow$ max(tagServices.values())
2: $max\_keys \leftarrow \{key \mid$ tagServices$[key] = max\_value\}$
3: // Resolve tie based on user preferences if needed
4: **if** len(max_keys) > 1 **then**
5:     $selected\_services \leftarrow []$
6:     **for** service_id **in** max_keys **do**
7:         $doc \leftarrow$ restaurant_sv.find_one($\{"\_id" :$ ObjectId($service\_id$)$\}$)
8:         **if** doc **and** 'paths' **in** doc **then**
9:             $params \leftarrow doc["paths"]["/bookrestaurant"]["get"]["parameters"]$
10:             **for** param **in** params **do**
11:                 $param\_name \leftarrow param["name"]$
12:                 $param\_value \leftarrow param["schema"]["value"]$
13:                 **if** $param\_name\ ==\ "pricerange"$ **and** $param\_value\ ==\ slots["pricerange"]$ **then**
14:                     $selected\_services$.append($service\_id$)
15:                 **else if** $param\_name\ ==\ "food"$ **and** $param\_value\ ==\ slots["food"]$ **then**
16:                     $selected\_services$.append($service\_id$)
17:                 **end if**
18:             **end for**
19:         **end if**
20:     **end for**
21: **else**
22:     $selected\_services \leftarrow [max\_keys[0]]$
23: **end if**
24: // Randomly select if no matches found
25: **if** ($selected\_services == []$) **then**
26:     $selected\_services \leftarrow [$random.choice(list(tagServices.keys()))$]$
27: **end if**
28: **return** $selected\_services$

These three stages (intent recognition, discriminative slot filling and service selection) are depicted in Fig. 4.

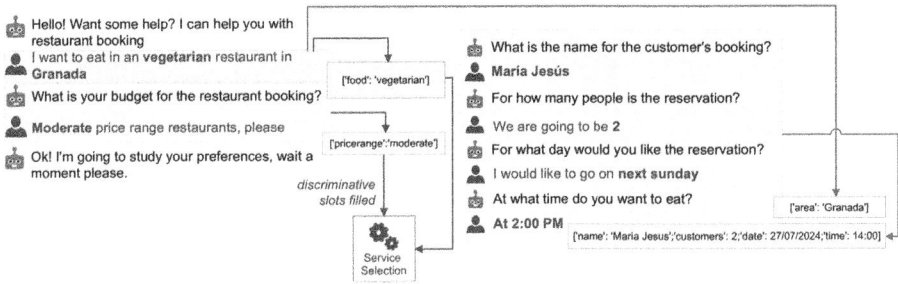

Fig. 3. Initial and Interactive Slot Filling

Question Retrieval. The OAS of the selected service returns the questions that must be asked to the user to gather the information required for the specific service (for example, [date, "On what date would you like to make the reservation", time, "At what time would you like to reserve?", diners, "For how many people do you want the reservation?"]).

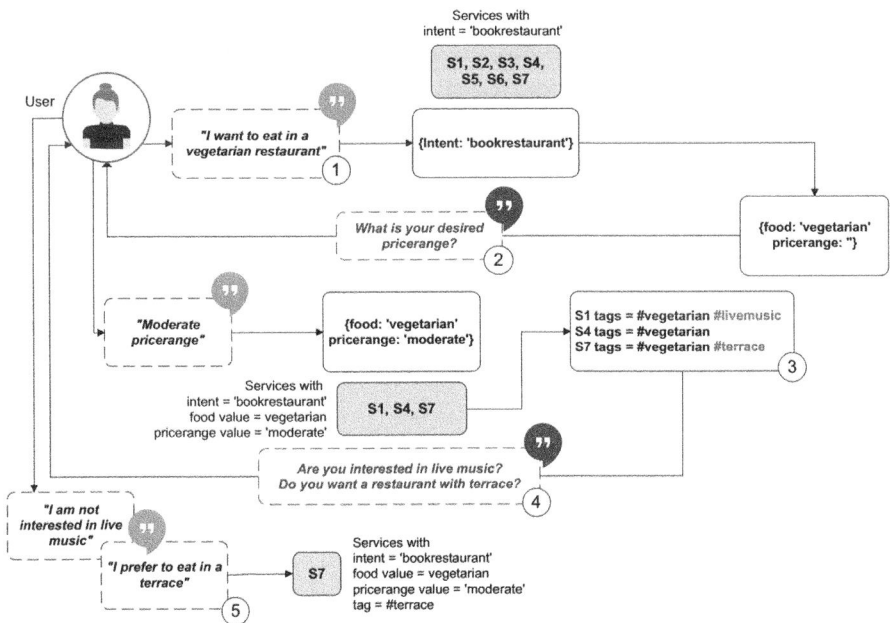

Fig. 4. Intent Recognition, Discriminative Slot Filling, and Service Selection Processes

Question Enhancement. With the help of the LLM, the system detects slots that are already filled and improves the questions for the slots that were not completed with the initial input to avoid making unnecessary calls to the model and thus make the dialogue less monotonous (for example, as an alternative to the question "On what date would you like to make the reservation?" it suggests "What specific date would you prefer for booking your reservation?").

Question Delivery. The updated set of questions is used to generate the system's response, focusing on slots that have not yet been completed (for example, [date, "What specific date would you prefer for booking your reservation?", time, "What specific time would you prefer to make the reservation?", diners, "How many individuals would you like the reservation to be made for?"]) This sequential process ensures an organized and interactive dialogue between the conversational system and the user. However, the system allows the user to provide values for multiple slots in a single turn (for example, the input "I want a table for two for tomorrow evening" would simultaneously fill the date, time, and diners slots), thus facilitating interaction.

3.3 Dynamic Service Integration

In our approach, web services can be dynamically added to the chatbot during its operation phase. The proposal includes a transformation mechanism through which a standard OpenAPI specification can be converted into a PPTalk specification. Figure 5 illustrates the two ways by which a service provider can add their specifications to the system: 1) uploading an existing OAS specification or 2) creating a new OAS specification. If the service has an OAS specification, it can be uploded and will be prompted to provide the discriminative parameter values and business tags through a simple form.

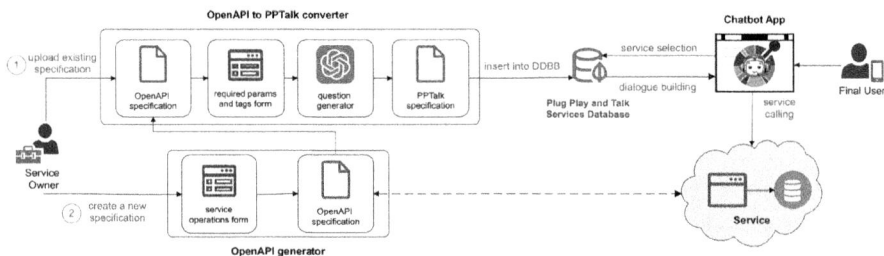

Fig. 5. PPtalk Specification addition to the system

Using LLM, questions are automatically generated for all parameters with the prompt: *"I am developing a chatbot that users can employ to Intent in the domain Domain. Generate just a question without format that the chatbot can use to ask the user for Parameter"* These questions are included in the resulting PPTalk specification.

If the service does not have an OAS specification, service providers can fill in a form with the service characteristics. A valid OAS is automatically generated through a user-friendly process that requires no prior knowledge, simplifying the creation and integration of PPTalk specifications. The service provider can transform this generated specification into PPTalk using the transformation process.

4 Proof of Concept and Evaluation

To validate the feasibility and effectiveness of our approach, we have developed a proof-of-concept system specifically focusing on a chatbot designed for restaurant bookings within a dynamic shopping mall environment, and conducted an evaluation with simulated users.

Consider a scenario where a shopping mall has a spacious food court that hosts a variety of restaurants, each with specific features that set them apart. For instance, some restaurants offer all-you-can-eat buffets, others have karaoke areas, and some have outdoor terraces.

Additionally, these restaurants have the ability to evolve and adapt, incorporating new services they did not previously offer. For example, a restaurant might start offering live music to enhance the customer experience, or add a drink service to complement their food offerings. Likewise, over time, new restaurants may open and others may close.

To allow the chatbot to adapt to the specificities of each restaurant and the possible changes introduced in their services, several applications have been developed using Flask and GPT 3.5 as the pre-trained LLM: *1)* a chatbot[1] capable of engaging in a dialogue with users, using one of the PPTalk Specifications integrated into the system; *2)* an application for transforming OAS into PPTalk Specification and managing them[2]; *3)* an API[3] that enables the insertion, editing, deletion, and retrieval of PPTalk specifications from our database, facilitating the efficient management of these specifications.

We have tested this setting with three services[4] that we have developed in Python, and their specifications have been added to the MongoDB of our system, where the PPTalk Specifications are stored. Although the services perform the same action (booking), they are designed to be diverse; for example, two of them allow the client to eat in the terrace, one of them allow pets and has smoking area. Additionally, two of them offer vegetarian food to ensure correct discrimination between them according to user preferences.

---

[1] https://github.com/mjesusrodriguez/chatbot_mono.
[2] https://github.com/mjesusrodriguez/openapitopptalk.
[3] https://github.com/mjesusrodriguez/pptalk.
[4] https://github.com/mjesusrodriguez/bookrestaurant1,
  https://github.com/mjesusrodriguez/bookrestaurant2,
  https://github.com/mjesusrodriguez/bookrestaurant3.

Figure 6 shows the example explained in Sect. 3, implemented in an operational chatbot called Chat-PPT. In Fig. 6a), the user types the initial input *'I want to eat in a vegetarian restaurant'* and the system, upon detecting the intent (*BookRestaurant*), requests the discriminative parameters that were not collected in the first slot-filling task (in this case the price range). Discriminative parameters (type of food and price range) are used to perform the initial filtering of services corresponding to the selected intent. In our setting, the three services include the *BookRestaurant* operation, and thus correspond to the user's intent. However, only two of them support the selected combination of type of food and price range. Figure 6b) shows how tag questions are asked in order to select one of the two. The questions posed to the user ask about the properties each service has defined in its tags that may match additional user's needs or preferences. In this case the user wants to eat in a restaurant that has smoking area, so the selected service will be the one shown in the image.

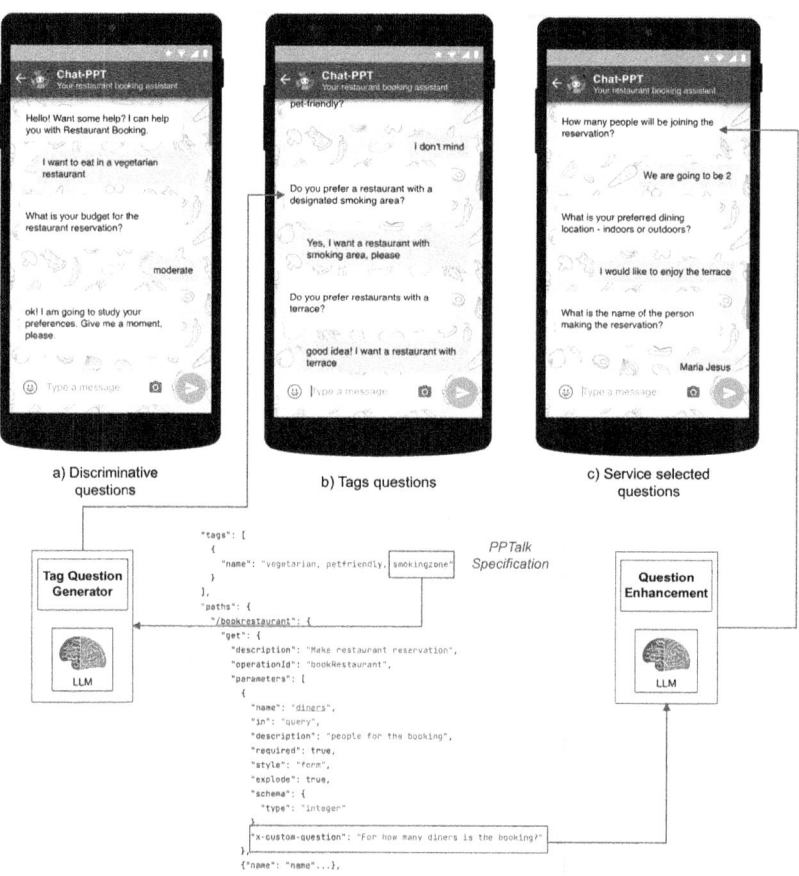

Fig. 6. Chat-PPT chatbot with the PPTalk Specification

Once the service is selected, the parameters that were not filled in the second slot-filling task, but are required to invoke the service (e.g. the number of diners) are directly asked to the user in what we call *Interactive Slot Filling* as shown in Fig. 6c). This process uses the questions written in the service after improving them with the LLM so that they are not posed verbatim as indicated in the specification in every conversation.

Thus, until now we have demonstrated with the development of a functional chatbot the applicability of our proposal, showcasing the adaptability of the chatbot's dialogues to the specificity of the services and also the possibility of integrating new services or modifying existing ones during the chatbot's operation time. To the best of our knowledge, our proposal is innovative and there is no gold standard to compare it with.

Nevertheless, to contribute additional evaluation results, we also underwent an evaluation of the quality of the dialogues generated to show that the chatbot does not ask unnecessary or redundant questions, and that the number of conversation turns is well balanced to identify the users' preferences but at the same time allow an efficient access to services that does not require a lengthy dialogue.

In order to do so, we have developed an automatic method to generate conversations with a simulated user. This is a widely used method in the conversational systems domain in order to optimise the evaluation processes and obtain a comprehensive number of interactions.

Table 2. Summary of dialogue system evaluation results

Evaluated Aspect	Result
Average incidence of unnecessary questions	0.28
Redundancy in questions	None
Average number of turns per conversation	6.06
Percentage of slots filled initially by the user	30.01%
F1 Score	0.78

This method exploits the pre-trained BERT model presented in [3] that is finetuned for question-answering. This model is adjusted with question-answer data to enhance its performance in extracting answers from a given context or paragraph. In our case, for each conversation, we select as context a random task from the CamRest676 dataset [13], a well-recognized dataset for evaluating task-oriented dialogue systems in restaurant booking domain. Each task in this corpus represents a user objective (e.g. making a reservation at a restaurant with a particular price range). Then, an initial user input is generated to match the context following a variety of scenarios, from more informative inputs providing several entities to more concise phrases that lack important pieces of information.

To generate a response to specific booking questions, such as the phone number, number of diners, or the date and time of the reservation, rules have been established for the simulated user to provide an appropriate answer. Following this method, we have generated fifty conversations between the proposed chatbot and the simulated user.

For each conversation, we record the entire dialogue, the number of turns, the result of the slot-filling task at the end of the dialogue, and the selected PPTalk service for the conversation. Our proposal allows the user to express complex queries that can fill multiple slots in a single turn. For this reason, we have also recorded the number of slots filled with the user's initial prompt, so there will be no need to request this information later.

Table 2 highlights the system's effectiveness in simulated dialogues. The low incidence of unnecessary questions and the absence of redundant queries demonstrate efficient slot-filling with minimal turns (6 to 10), suitable for gathering essential booking details. In the first turn, users fill 30.01% of the slots, enhancing dialogue efficiency. This is partly due to the CamRest676 dataset's context, which does not include specific booking details such as the day or time. The number of slots varies per service, customized for each owner. The F1 score, calculated with the help of a human that fills the slots properly, shows balanced precision and recall, with an F1 score of 78% in correctly identifying instances.

5 Conclusions

We have presented a novel approach to build dynamic and adaptive task-oriented chatbots combining PPTalk services specification and generative AI.

The PPTalk OpenAPI specification enhances traditional OpenAPI by adding elements like user questions and tags, which facilitate dynamic dialogue generation, as service providers can easily modify services and their elements and chatbots can adapt immediately to such changes. This method allows generating conversations in operation time based on PPTalk specifications, tailoring interactions to user needs and preferences, thereby improving user experience and system efficacy. We also contribute an implementation in the restaurant domain that demonstrates the practicality and effectiveness of our approach, showcasing its scalability and adaptability.

The integration of generative AI with the PPTalk service specification marks a significant advancement in the development of task-oriented chatbots, overcoming many limitations of both traditional rule and intent based systems and one-step extreme-to-extreme LLM based conversations. By exploiting pre-trained LLMs in several steps of the dialogue management process, our approach enables the creation of dynamic and adaptive conversational agents that can seamlessly incorporate new services without extensive reprogramming or retraining, while providing more control over the interactions generated.

Future work will focus on extending the application of PPTalk specifications to other domains, fine-tuning LLMs for specific tasks, verifying client-provided data for type and range accuracy, and transitioning to a microservices-based architecture to further improve scalability and flexibility.

Acknowledgments. This publication is part of the R&D&I project GOMINOLA supported by the Spanish Ministry of Science and Innovation (refs. PID2020-118112RB-C21 and PID2020-118112RB-C22), financed by MCIN/AEI/10.13039/501100011033.

References

1. Aiello, M.: A challenge for the next 50 years of automated service composition. In: Service-Oriented Computing, pp. 635–643 (2022). https://doi.org/10.1007/978-3-031-20984-0_45
2. Brabra, H., Báez, M., Benatallah, B., Gaaloul, W., Bouguelia, S., Zamanirad, S.: Dialogue management in conversational systems: a review of approaches, challenges, and opportunities. IEEE Trans. Cogn. Dev. Syst. 783–798 (2022). https://doi.org/10.1109/TCDS.2021.3086565
3. Devlin, J., Chang, M.W., Lee, K., Toutanova, K.: Bert: pre-training of deep bidirectional transformers for language understanding. In: North American Chapter of the Association for Computational Linguistics (2019). https://doi.org/10.48550/arXiv.1810.04805
4. Følstad, A., Brandtzæg, P.B.: Chatbots and the new world of HCI. Interactions **24**, 38–42 (2017). https://doi.org/10.1145/3085558
5. Hou, Y., Tamoto, H., Miyashita, H.: "My agent understands me better": integrating dynamic human-like memory recall and consolidation in LLM-based agents. In: Extended Abstracts of the CHI Conference on Human Factors in Computing Systems, pp. 1–7 (2024). https://doi.org/10.48550/arXiv.2404.00573
6. Kalia, A.K., Telang, P.R., Xiao, J., Vukovic, M.: Quark: a methodology to transform people-driven processes to chatbot services. In: Service-Oriented Computing, pp. 53–61 (2017). https://doi.org/10.1007/978-3-319-69035-3_4
7. Labruna, T., Brenna, S., Magnini, B.: Dynamic task-oriented dialogue: a comparative study of llama-2 and bert in slot value generation. In: Proceedings of the 18th Conference of the European Chapter of the Association for Computational Linguistics: Student Research Workshop, pp. 358–368 (2024). https://doi.org/10.18653/v1/2023.eacl-srw.16
8. Labruna, T., Magnini, B.: Addressing domain changes in task-oriented conversational agents through dialogue adaptation. In: Conference of the European Chapter of the Association for Computational Linguistics (2023). https://doi.org/10.18653/v1/2023.eacl-srw.16
9. Mok, J., Kachuee, M., Dai, S., Ray, S., Taghavi, T., Yoon, S.: LLM-based frameworks for API argument filling in task-oriented conversational systems. In: Proceedings of the 2024 Conference of the North American Chapter of the Association for Computational Linguistics: Human Language Technologies (vol. 6: Industry Track), pp. 419–426 (2024). https://doi.org/10.18653/v1/2024.naacl-industry.36
10. Sánchez Cuadrado, J., Pérez-Soler, S., Guerra, E., De Lara, J.: Automating the development of task-oriented llm-based chatbots. In: Proceedings of the 6th ACM Conference on Conversational User Interfaces. CUI '24, New York, NY, USA (2024). https://doi.org/10.1145/3640794.3665538
11. Vaziri, M., Mandel, L., Shinnar, A., Siméon, J., Hirzel, M.: Generating chat bots from web api specifications. In: Proceedings of the 2017 ACM SIGPLAN International Symposium on New Ideas, New Paradigms, and Reflections on Programming and Software, pp. 44–57 (2017). https://doi.org/10.1145/3133850.3133864

12. Wei, J., Kim, S., Jung, H., Kim, Y.H.: Leveraging large language models to power chatbots for collecting user self-reported data. Proc. ACM Hum.-Comput. Interact. **8**(CSCW1) (2024). https://doi.org/10.1145/3637364
13. Wen, T.H., et al.: A network-based end-to-end trainable task-oriented dialogue system, 438–449 (2017). https://doi.org/10.48550/arXiv.1604.04562
14. Yu, R., Guan, Y., Zhan, Y.: Shoppinggpt: A gpt-based product recommendation dialogue system, 501–509 (2023). https://doi.org/10.1109/PRML59573.2023.10348314
15. Zamanirad, S., Benatallah, B., Rodriguez, C., Yaghoubzadehfard, M., Bouguelia, S., Brabra, H.: State machine based human-bot conversation model and services. Adv. Inf. Syst. Eng. 199–214 (2020). https://doi.org/10.1007/978-3-030-49435-3_13
16. Zamfirescu-Pereira, J., et al.: Herding AI cats: lessons from designing a chatbot by prompting gpt-3. In: Proceedings of the 2023 ACM Designing Interactive Systems Conference, pp. 2206–2220 (2023). https://doi.org/10.1145/3563657.3596138
17. Zamfirescu-Pereira, J., Wong, R.Y., Hartmann, B., Yang, Q.: Why johnny can't prompt: How non-AI experts try (and fail) to design LLM prompts. In: Proceedings of the 2023 CHI Conference on Human Factors in Computing Systems. CHI '23, New York, NY, USA (2023). https://doi.org/10.1145/3544548.3581388

Automated Generation of BPMN Processes from Textual Requirements

Quentin Nivon[(✉)] [iD] and Gwen Salaün [iD]

Univ. Grenoble Alpes, CNRS, Grenoble INP, Inria, LIG, 38000 Grenoble, France
{quentin.nivon,gwen.salaun}@inria.fr

Abstract. Modelling and designing business processes has become a crucial activity for companies in the last 20 years. As a consequence, multiple workflow modelling notations were proposed. Business Process Modelling Notation (BPMN) is one of them and is now considered as the *de facto* standard for process modelling. The BPMN notation offers a rich syntax that requires a certain level of expertise before being able to write correct and well-structured processes corresponding to some expected requirements. The BPMN modelling phase can thus be tedious and error-prone if carried out by non-experts. The main goal of the approach presented in this paper is to help users modelling BPMN processes. To do so, the approach takes as input the requirements of the user in a textual format informally describing the tasks and their ordering constraints, and generates as output a BPMN process satisfying them. The solution has been implemented as a tool that was applied on a large number of examples for evaluation purposes.

1 Introduction

Developing and controlling business processes has become a major activity for companies, since this is crucial in order to improve productivity and reduce costs. A first and mandatory step in that direction is the modelling and the design of business processes. Several workflow-based notations have emerged for processes, one of them being the Business Process Modelling Notation (BPMN) [9]. BPMN has become the standard notation for modelling business processes, and many graphical tools have been developed for supporting BPMN modelling.

The BPMN syntax is quite rich and offers a large number of constructs. There is therefore a need to learn the BPMN notation in order to be able to write syntactically and semantically correct processes. Modelling business processes with BPMN thus remains a tedious and error-prone task for non-experts. Moreover, the existing modelling tools allow a lot of freedom in the design of the processes, and do not systematically provide integrated solutions for asserting their correctness.

The approach proposed in this paper aims at helping users during the BPMN modelling phase. To do so, it takes as input a textual description of the process. From these textual requirements, the approach automatically generates the corresponding BPMN process. This solution is useful for non-experts since it provides a way to specify BPMN processes without mastering the intricacies of the notation. It is also helpful for experts because it simplifies the modelling step by generating BPMN processes automatically, thus avoiding the burden of graphically writing the entire workflow step by step.

More precisely, the textual description is converted into its corresponding BPMN process in three main steps. In the first step, the capabilities of GPT-3.5[1] are used to extract the tasks and their ordering constraints from the description written by the user. To provide interpretable results, GPT-3.5 was fine-tuned in order to make it capable of converting the textual ordering constraints into an internal format similar to regular expressions [11]. Each expression returned by GPT-3.5 is then transformed into its corresponding abstract syntax tree [13]. In a second step, several operations are applied on the generated abstract syntax trees in order to gather the task ordering constraints that they contain into a single abstract syntax tree. Finally, the resulting abstract syntax tree is translated into a BPMN process and returned to the user. The whole approach is fully automated by a tool that was applied on multiple descriptions written by several users (novices or experts) to measure the quality of the generated results.

Section 2 introduces several notions on which the approach relies. Section 3 provides a description of the different steps necessary to transform text to BPMN. Section 4 describes the tool support and some experimental results used to validate the approach. Section 5 compares the solution to related work, and Sect. 6 concludes this paper.

2 Preliminaries

2.1 BPMN

BPMN 2.0 (BPMN, as a shorthand, in the rest of this paper) was published as an ISO/IEC standard in 2013 and is nowadays extensively used for modelling and developing business processes. This paper focuses on activity diagrams including the BPMN constructs related to control-flow modelling and behavioural aspects.

Specifically, the node types event, task, and gateway, and the edge type sequence flow are considered. Start and end events are used, respectively, to initialize and terminate processes. A task represents an atomic activity that has exactly one incoming and one outgoing flow. A sequence flow connects two nodes executed one after the other in a specific execution order. Gateways are used to control the divergence and convergence of the execution flow. In this work, the two main kinds of gateways used in activity diagrams are considered, namely, exclusive and parallel gateways. Gateways with one incoming branch and multiple outgoing branches are called splits, e.g., split parallel gateway. Gateways with one outgoing branch and multiple incoming branches are called merges, e.g., merge parallel gateway. A parallel gateway creates concurrent flows for all its outgoing branches or synchronizes concurrent flows for all its incoming

---
[1] https://www.openai.com/.

branches. An exclusive gateway chooses one out of a set of mutually exclusive alternative incoming or outgoing branches. Such gateways can also be used to represent repetitive behaviours (i.e., loops).

2.2 Textual Requirements

In this work, the user must provide as input a textual representation of a business process that is going to be generated. This description is informal, in the sense that no prerequisite is required to be able to write a valid description. In this description, the user describes in natural language the tasks that the process should contain, along with their ordering constraints. For instance, if two tasks must be executed one after the other in the final process, this should be stated in the description. To improve the results, the user is advised to name the tasks that should appear in the process. However, this is not mandatory for the approach to work.

Running Example. The following description, in which the tasks that should appear in the resulting process have been named, describes the opening of a bank account: "First, the banker either *CreateProfile (CP)* for the user, or, if it is not needed, he *RetrieveCustomerProfile (RCP)* which triggers the system to perform the *AnalyseCustomerProfile (ACP)* task. Then, the user executes the task *ReceiveSupportDocuments (RSD)* so that the system can start *UpdateInfoRecords (UID)* and perform a *BackgroundVerification (BV)*. If the verification finds missing or incorrect information, the system *RequestAdditionalInfo (RAI)* to the user, who has to *ReceiveSupportDocuments (RSD)* again. Otherwise, the process ends with *CreateAccount (CA)*." As the reader can see, the specification is rather informal, except that names are given to the tasks that should appear in the process. Also, the specification can be written in various styles, with or without context around the important information. It is worth noting that the acronyms written between parenthesis are not mandatory, and are just presented here to shorten the size of the future examples.

2.3 Task Ordering Constraints

To generate a BPMN process from a textual description, one of the intermediate steps consists in extracting tasks ordering constraints or dependencies from the text. Several works, such as [6], make use of sequential constraints written as couples to represent ordering constraints between tasks. However, such constraints are limited in the sense that they only allow one to represent sequence and parallelism. In this work, not only sequential and parallel constraints are supported, but also exclusive choices, and looping behaviours. Although allowing a greater expressiveness, these new constraints require a more powerful language than couples of tasks. The language chosen in this approach to capture the supported subset of the BPMN syntax can be seen as a variant of the language of regular expressions. This language defines several usual operators, such as the '|' operator which symbolises an exclusive choice, the '&' operator which symbolises the parallelism (i.e., two elements that can be executed simultaneously), or the '<'

operator which symbolises the sequential dependency (i.e., an element must be executed before another one). This language also has a loop operator '*' that encloses element that can be repeated. Moreover, as in BPMN, loops are split into two parts. The first part, that is necessarily executed, is represented inside a loop using the '+' operator. It corresponds to the part of a BPMN loop that is located between the exclusive merge gateway and the exclusive split gateway. The second part, that is optionally executed, is represented inside a loop using the '?' operator. It corresponds to the part of a BPMN loop that is located between the exclusive split gateway and the exclusive merge gateway. It is worth noting that these two loop operators are used internally but can not appear in the generated expressions. Finally, the operator ',' is used to list elements that are constrained to each other. Expressions written in this language must obey the rules of the following Backus-Naur Form (BNF) grammar:

$$\langle E \rangle ::= \ \mathtt{t} \ | \ (\langle E \rangle) \ | \ \langle E_1 \rangle \ \langle op \rangle \ \langle E_2 \rangle \ | \ (\langle E_1 \rangle) *$$
$$\langle op \rangle ::= \ \text{'|'} \ | \ \text{'\&'} \ | \ \text{'<'} \ | \ \text{','}$$

where $\mathtt{t}$ is a terminal symbol representing the name of a task. This language has priority between operators ('|' > '&' > '<' > ',' > '*') and is right-associative. It is worth noting that this language suffices to capture the subset of the BPMN syntax supported in this work.

Example. Let us consider the textual description proposed in the example of Sect. 2.2. By analysing it, one can generate three expressions capturing all the tasks ordering constraints that it contains: (i) $(RCP < ACP) \ | \ CP$, (ii) $(RCP, ACP, CP) < (RSD < (UIR, BV))$ and (iii) $(UIR, BV) < ((RAI < RSD) \ | \ CA)$. As an illustration, expression (i) means that either RCP should be executed before ACP, or CP is executed alone.

2.4 Abstract Syntax Tree

Due to the properties of the language presented above (priority of operators, right associativity, ...), abstract syntax trees (ASTs) were chosen to represent and manipulate the expressions written in this language. Indeed, abstract syntax trees are suitable to represent hierarchical priorities between operators while allowing powerful recursive computations. An abstract syntax tree is a regular tree representing the abstract syntactic structure of a text written in a formal language.

Definition 1. *(Tree) A tree is a set of nodes S_N and edges S_E where $S_E \subseteq S_N \times S_N$. An edge between two nodes is represented as $n \to n' \in S_E$. A tree has exactly one root node that has no incoming transition, i.e., $\exists! n \in S_N$ such that $\forall n_p \in S_N, \nexists e_p = n_p \to n \in S_E$. The other nodes have exactly one predecessor, i.e., $\forall n_i \in S_N \setminus \{n\}, \exists! n_{i-1}, n_{i-1} \neq n_i$, such that $n_{i-1} \to n_i \in S_E$. Finally, each node can have 0, 1, or several successor nodes.*

Example. Figure 1 presents the ASTs generated from the expressions corresponding to the running example. As the reader can see, the priority between the operators of the expressions is represented by the hierarchy of nodes in the corresponding AST. For instance, in Fig. 1(a), nodes RCP and ACP are below a '$<$' node meaning that they are both in sequence. Moreover, their position (i.e., RCP on the left and ACP on the right) is important as it indicates the direction of the sequential dependency (i.e., if RCP is executed before ACP or the opposite). Finally, the '$<$' node is below the '$|$' node, meaning that there is a mutual exclusion between both RCP and ACP and the node CP.

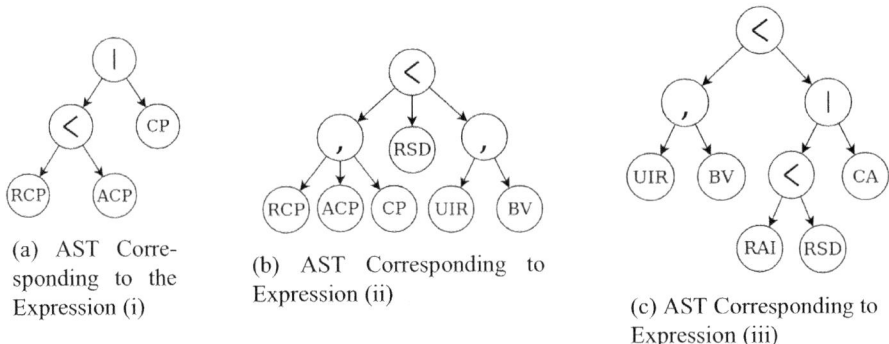

(a) AST Corresponding to the Expression (i)

(b) AST Corresponding to the Expression (ii)

(c) AST Corresponding to Expression (iii)

Fig. 1. ASTs Corresponding to the Expressions of Sect. 2.3

2.5 GPT

Inferring ordering constraints from a textual description is not an easy task, as it requires complex mechanisms to understand the structure of the text, extract its components (i.e., the tasks), and discover the multiple relationships connecting them. In this work, Large Language Models (LLMs) are used to perform this analysis, and more precisely, the GPT model. GPT, which stands for Generative Pre-trained Transformer, is an open-access generative model developed by OpenAI, and freely accessible through the well-known website ChatGPT. GPT, and more precisely its "3.5-turbo-0125' version, is used in this work for its natural language processing capabilities, that are helpful to produce expressions corresponding to the language presented in Sect. 2.3.

3 Core of the Approach

The approach proposed in this paper starts by submitting the textual requirements of the user to a fine-tuned version of GPT and asks it to convert them into expressions corresponding to the language defined in Sect. 2.3. Each resulting expression is then parsed and mapped to its corresponding AST. When multiple expressions are returned by GPT, and thus multiple ASTs are generated, it is not straightforward to compute the corresponding BPMN process. This is due to the fact that the generated BPMN process should contain all the information scattered among the generated ASTs. To merge this information, the solution proposed in this paper consists in analysing the generated ASTs in order to produce a single AST containing all the information of the original ones. This AST can then be converted to its equivalent BPMN process. Figure 2 illustrates these multiple steps, which are detailed in the rest of this section, except for the parsing and mapping of the expressions to their corresponding ASTs, which is straightforward.

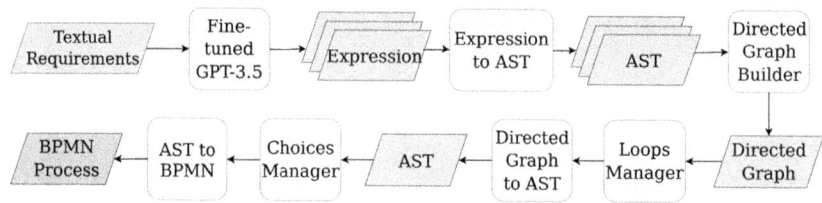

Fig. 2. Overview of the Approach

3.1 Fine-Tuned GPT 3.5

The standard version of the GPT 3.5 model has no knowledge about the expected output language defined in Sect. 2.3. Thus, it is not straightforward for it to generate expressions corresponding to this language. One of the opportunities of GPT is to allow fine-tuning in order to increase its capabilities in precise fields. Roughly speaking, fine-tuning is an approach consisting in improving a model by training it on new data. Often, fine-tuning becomes a tedious task as adjusting hyper-parameters and providing sufficient data can be rather complex and time-consuming. Hopefully, GPT proposes intuitive and easy-to-follow fine-tuning options, which do not require large amount of data to get started. This phase, which can be repeated at any time to improve the quality of the results, has for now been performed on four hundred examples. It is worth noting that the fine-tuning was performed on the version 3.5 of GPT, as more recent models (such as GPT-4, GPT-4-o or GPT-4-turbo) are not yet available for fine-tuning. The training examples provided to GPT consist of three elements. The first one is a system prompt, which describes the expected behaviour of GPT (i.e., the fact that GPT should extract task ordering constraints from the textual requirements given as input) and the shape that its output should take. The second one is a user prompt usually corresponding to the question asked by the user (i.e., the textual requirements here). The last one is an assistant prompt, corresponding to the answer that GPT should provide. For the system prompt and the assistant prompt, the expected output is a set of expressions corresponding to the language defined in Sect. 2.3. Once training and validation data are given to GPT, the fine-tuning process starts automatically. When the fine-tuning finishes, it outputs a new version of the model that can be used by its owner. After this fine-tuning phase, the generated model was able to transform textual requirements into expressions. It is worth noting that, for a single textual description, GPT may generate several expressions to represent all the task ordering constraints that it found. It is for instance the case for the description "A before C, B before C, B before D" that can not be represented with a single expression. It requires at least two expressions, such as $(A, B) < C$ and $B < D$. Indeed, a single expression, such as $(A, B) < (C, D)$ would add the unnecessary constraint $A < D$.

3.2 Directed Graph Construction

To gather the information scattered in the generated ASTs, the first step consists in building the skeleton of the process-to-be. This is done by extracting the sequential constraints stored in the ASTs, in order to build a unique directed graph comprising all of them. This extraction is performed by a classical depth-first search algorithm, which traverses each original AST and creates couples of tasks (T_1, T_2) for each node of the AST containing a '<' operator. Once this algorithm terminates, the generated couples are analysed by another algorithm in charge of generating a directed (possibly cyclic) graph corresponding to the extracted sequential constraints. The generated graph is then transitively reduced using classical algorithms [1].

Example. Let us consider the ASTs shown in Fig. 1. The first algorithm extracts the following couples from them: (RCP, ACP), (RCP, RSD), (ACP, RSD), (CP, RSD), (RSD, UIR), (RSD, BV), (BV, RAI), (BV, CA), (UIR, RAI), (UIR, CA), (RAI, RSD). From these couples, the second algorithm generates the directed cyclic graph given in Fig. 3. It is worth noting that some sequential constraints, such as (RCP, RSD), have been suppressed by the transitive reduction algorithm.

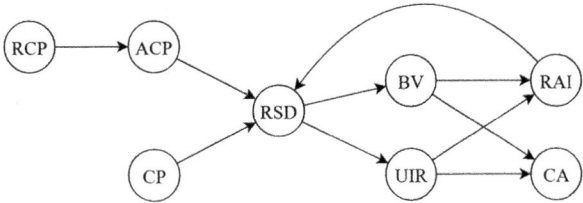

Fig. 3. Directed Cyclic Graph Corresponding to the ASTs in Fig. 1

3.3 Loops Management

The directed graph generated in the previous step may be cyclic, which indicates loops in the process-to-be. As such structures generate complexity in the graph, they are removed from the graph (i.e., the graph is made acyclic), and all the information required to recreate them is stored in internal structures. In BPMN, a loop can be represented using four elements: its entry nodes, its exit nodes, its mandatory paths, and its optional paths. The entry nodes are the first reachable nodes of the graph belonging to the loop. The exit nodes are the first reachable nodes of the loop having at least one child node not belonging to the loop. Finally, the mandatory (resp. optional) paths are all the paths starting with the entry (resp. exit) nodes and ending with an exit (resp. entry) node. The computations of these four elements is presented below.

(i) To identify the entry node(s) of the loop, the graph is traversed in a depth-first way. During the traversal, each node is analysed to detect whether it belongs to a loop or not. If that is the case, it is marked as entry point and the exploration stops for the current branch.
(ii) Similarly to step (i), the exit nodes are computed using a depth-first traversal of the graph. For each node belonging to the loop, the algorithm checks whether it has at least one child node that does not belong to the loop. If that is the case, the current node is marked as exit point and the exploration stops for the current branch.
(iii) Similarly to the previous steps, a depth-first traversal of the graph between the entry (resp. exit) node(s) and the exit (resp. entry) node(s) suffices to compute all the mandatory (resp. optional) paths.

Once these elements are computed, the graph is made acyclic by removing all the incoming transitions of the entry node(s) of the loop coming from nodes belonging to the loop.

Example. Figure 4 depicts the four steps presented above. Figure 4(a) presents the result of the computation of the entry nodes on the graph in Fig. 4(b). *RSD* is the first reachable node of the graph belonging to a loop. Thus, it is tagged as entry node of the loop. Figure 4(b) shows the result of the computation of the exit nodes on the graph of Fig. 3. Both *BV* and *UIR* have a child node that does not belong to the loop (*CA*), and both are at equal distance of the entry node. Thus, they are both tagged as exit nodes of the loop. Figure 4(c) describes the result of the computation of the mandatory paths of the loop, which are all the paths starting from the entry node and ending with an exit node. In this case, there are two paths: (*RSD, BV*) and (*RSD, UIR*). Figure 4(d) illustrates the result of the computation of the optional paths of the loop, which are all the paths starting from an exit node and ending with the entry node. For the given example there is only one path: (*RAI, RSD*). Finally, the graph is made acyclic by removing the transition between *RAI* and *RSD*.

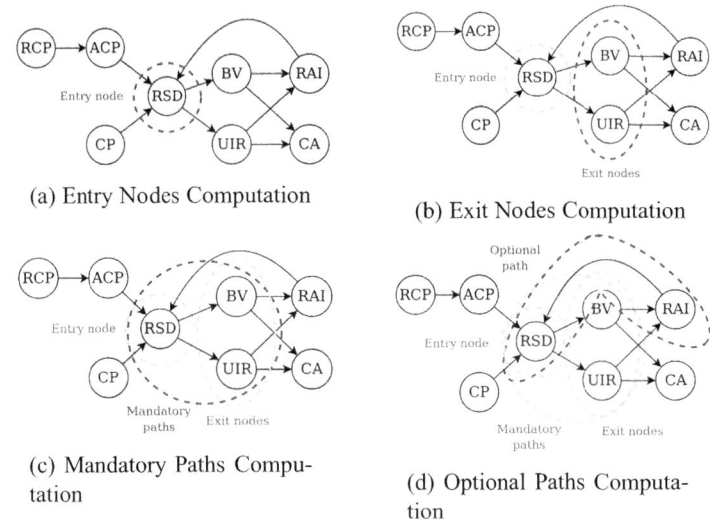

Fig. 4. Graph Loops Management

3.4 Directed Graph to AST

The next step consists in converting the directed graph into its corresponding AST. To do so, the graph is traversed in a depth-first way. During this traversal, each task of the graph is examined to know whether it has already been added to the AST or not. If not, all the ancestor (resp. successor) nodes of this task in the graph are retrieved. Among them, only the closest ones already added to the AST are kept. This computation returns the nodes of the AST after (resp. before) which the current task should be placed. They are called the *left-bounding nodes* (resp. *right-bounding nodes*). It is worth noting that the AST may already contain nodes between the left-bounding nodes and the right-bounding nodes of the task to insert. As these nodes are not bounding nodes, they are not constrained with regards to the task to insert. Consequently, the task to insert will be put in parallel of them in the AST. If the task is the entry node of a loop, the loop is entirely generated and added to the AST at the position where the current task should have been inserted.

Example. Let us consider the AST shown in Fig. 5(a). This AST already contains tasks *RCP*, *ACP*, *RSD*, *BV*, *UIR*, *RAI* and *CA*. The loop containing *RSD*, *BV*, *UIR* and *RAI* has been replaced by a "..." node for brevity. The next task to add is *CP*. By analysing the graph in Fig. 3, one can see that *CP* has no ancestor and five successors: *RSD*, *BV*, *UIR*, *RAI* and *CA*. As it has no ancestor, it consequently has no left-bounding node. On the other hand, the analysis of the AST shows that the closest successor already in it is *RSD*. Thus, the right-bounding node of *CP* is *RSD*. As *RSD* belongs to a loop to which *CP* does not belong, the right-bounding node of *CP* becomes the root node of the loop, i.e., the '*' node. This means that *CP* must be put on the left of this '*' node. As one can see, there are already two nodes on the left of the '∗' node, RCP and ACP. These nodes are not constrained to CP (otherwise they would be bounding nodes), and will thus be put in parallel of it. To preserve the sequential constraint between them, they will also be placed under a new '<' node. The result of this insertion is shown in Fig. 5(b).

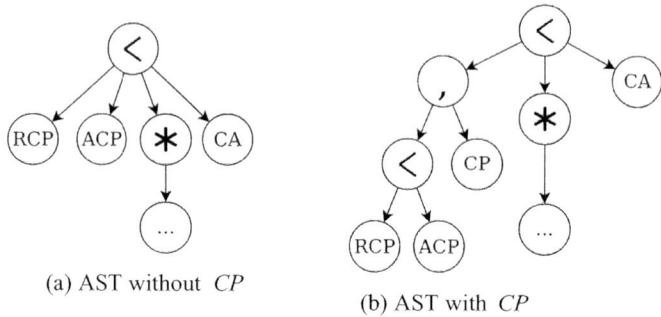

(a) AST without CP

(b) AST with CP

Fig. 5. Illustration of the AST Generation Process

3.5 Choices Management

The AST generated in the previous step is almost complete. The only constraints that have not been managed yet are the eventual exclusive choices between the tasks. For each exclusive choice between two tasks, the AST undergoes a modification depending on its structure. The three possible modifications are listed below.

(i) The two tasks do not yet belong to the tree. In this case, the two tasks are put below a '|' node which is put in parallel of the whole tree.
(ii) One of the two tasks already belongs to the tree. In this case, the two tasks are put below a '|' node, which is inserted at the position of the task already belonging to the tree, thus replacing it.
(iii) Both tasks already belong to the tree. In this case, they have a least common ancestor that should be a ',' node (otherwise they are already constrained and can consequently not be mutually exclusive). This ',' node is thus simply replaced by a '|' node to represent the exclusive choice between the two tasks.

Example. Figure 6(b) shows the result of adding the exclusive choice constraints to the AST of Fig. 6(a). As the reader can see, either RCP and ACP can be chosen or CP, as required by the original textual description. The original constraints also state that after UIR and BV, the process should contain an exclusive choice executing either CA or RAI followed by RSD. This constraint, although not visible in the AST, is implicitly present in it. Indeed, at the end of the mandatory part of a loop, one can either execute the optional part that goes back to the beginning, or leave the loop. Here, after UIR and BV, one can either perform RAI and restart the loop with RSD, or leave it and execute CA. Thus, one has to make a "choice" between RAI followed by RSD and CA.

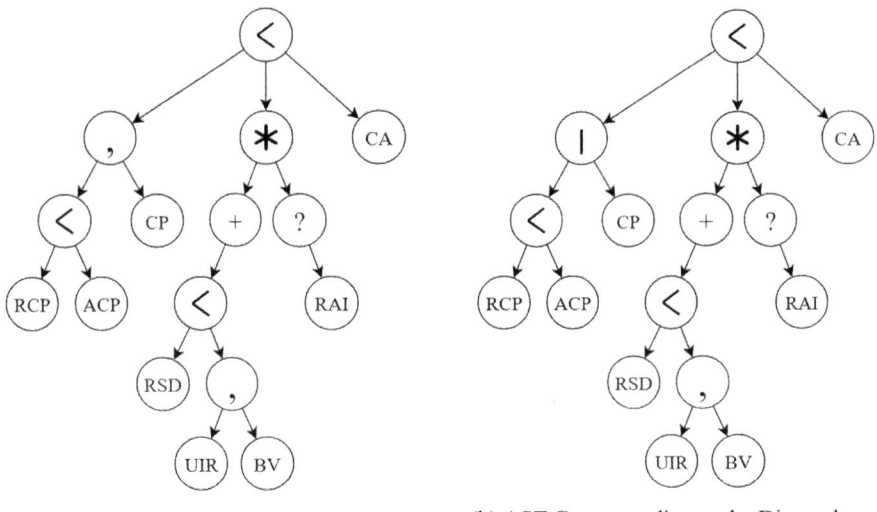

(a) AST Corresponding to the Directed Graph in Figure 3

(b) AST Corresponding to the Directed Graph in Figure 3 with Choices

Fig. 6. Choices Management

3.6 AST to BPMN

At this step of the approach, the AST resulting from the former steps is complete, meaning that it contains all the information of the original constraints stated by GPT. Thus, it is ready to be converted into its equivalent BPMN process. To do so, the transformation patterns presented in Table 1 are applied recursively on the nodes of the AST in a bottom-up fashion. Concretely, the deepest nodes of the AST (i.e., the task nodes) are the first being generated. Then, these tasks are connected together by applying the appropriate pattern. This generates a BPMN sub-process that will be connected to other sub-processes by recursively applying the patterns on their parent nodes up to the root.

Example. The BPMN process in Fig. 7 shows the result of the transformation of the AST presented in Fig. 6(b). This process was obtained by applying first the sequential pattern to tasks RCP and ACP, then the choice pattern to task CP and the freshly generated sub-process containing RCP and ACP in sequence, and so on until reaching the root of the AST. It is worth noting that the ordering constraints of the AST are respected, as are the textual requirements presented in the example of Sect. 2.3.

Table 1. Transformation Patterns from AST to BPMN

Pattern	AST	BPMN
(1) Sequential Pattern	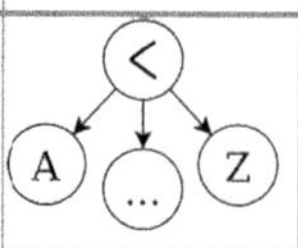 < → A, ..., Z	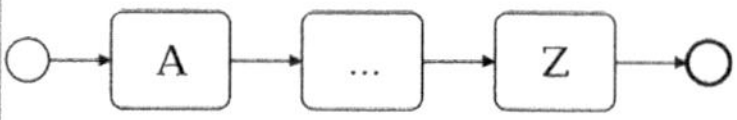 A → ... → Z
(2) Parallel Pattern	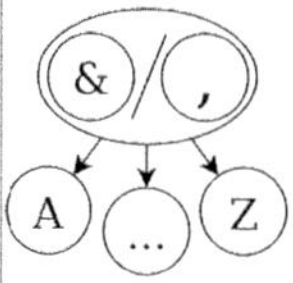 &/, → A, ..., Z	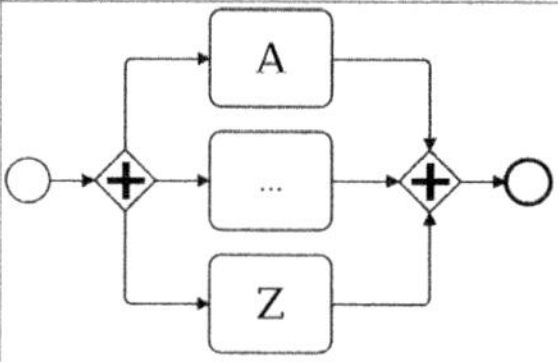 parallel gateway with A, ..., Z
(3) Choice Pattern	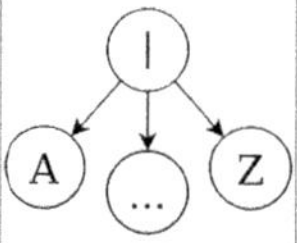 | → A, ..., Z	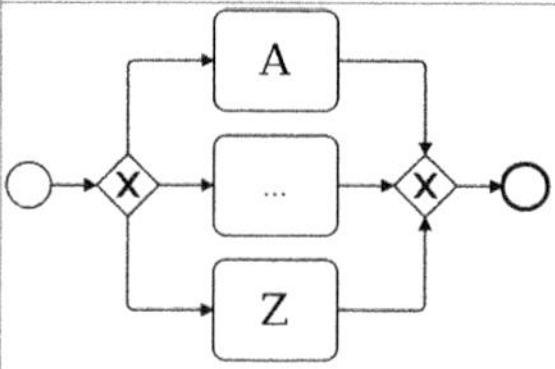 exclusive gateway with A, ..., Z
(4) Loop Pattern	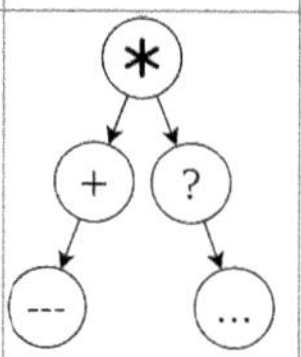 * → +, ? → ---, ...	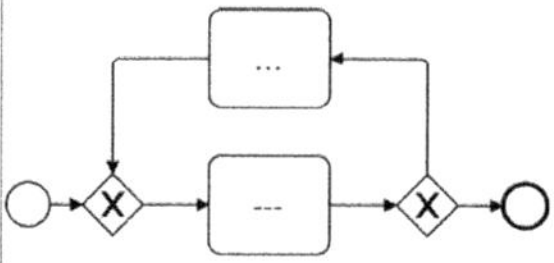 loop with ---

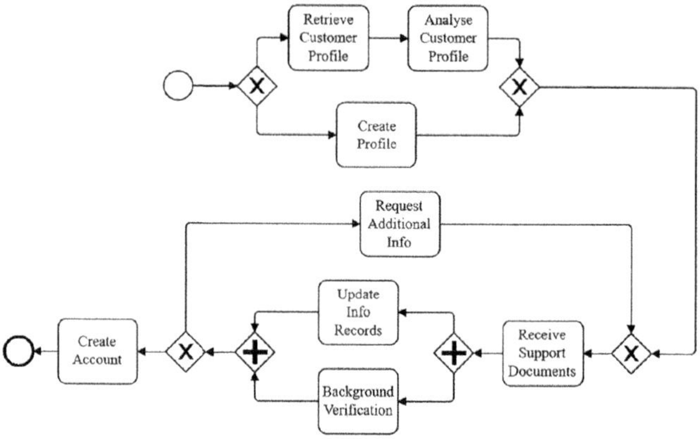

Fig. 7. BPMN Process Generated from the AST in Fig. 6(b)

4 Tool and Experiments

This approach has been entirely implemented and validated by a tool written in Java. To facilitate its usage, the Java code has been embedded in the backend of a web server which is freely available online[2]. The implementation details are given in Fig. 8. The user writes his textual description on the web application that is developed in HTML, CSS, JavaScript and makes use of JQuery, Ajax and BootStrap. The description is then transmitted to the backend written in NodeJS, which asks the Java program to send description to GPT. The expressions returned by GPT are transformed into their corresponding ASTs, which are eventually converted into the resulting BPMN process. This process is finally rendered by bpmn.io[3], and displayed in the web application.

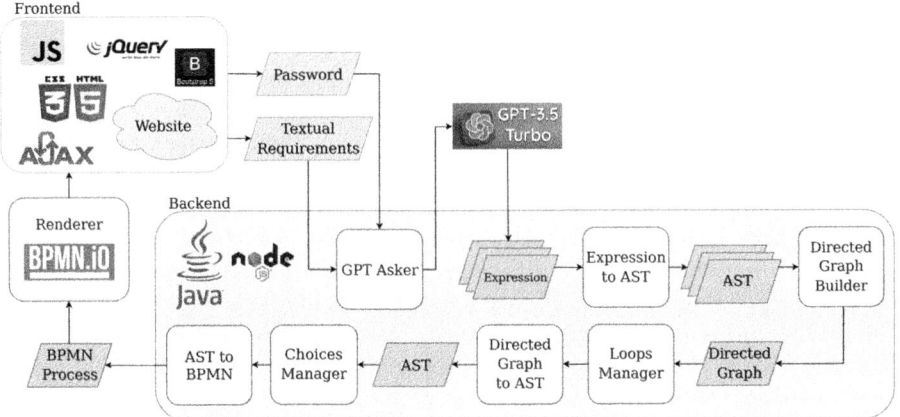

Fig. 8. Overview of the Toolchain

This approach was tested and validated on 200 descriptions from various sources. 25% come from the literature (PET dataset [3], proceedings, ...). The remaining 75% were handcrafted by 9 users (5 experts and 4 novices) who experimented the tool. All these examples contain tasks which were named beforehand. Experiments were also conducted on raw descriptions (i.e., without names for tasks) and showed a 24% loss of accuracy. This is mainly due to the fact that GPT often misses tasks in the description, or does not detect implicit loops. It is also worth noting that, for these 200 examples, GPT returned syntactically correct expressions with regards to the grammar defined in Sect. 2.3. The central part of these experiments consisted in comparing the tool proposed in this approach to other tools coming from the literature, and to LLMs directly. To the best of our knowledge, only one tool is recent enough and available online: ProMoAI [14]. Our tool was also compared to the LLMs Gemini [4] and GPT-4-turbo [5]. ProMoAI was used as is, while the two LLMs were given the simple instruction *"I want you to generate the BPMN process corresponding to the description provided between curvy brackets: {Lorem ipsum dolor sit amet,*

---

[2] https://quentinnivon.github.io/pages/givup.html.
[3] https://bpmn.io/.

consectetur adipiscing elit.}". These experiments aimed at assessing both the accuracy of the result and the time taken by the tools to generate the BPMN process.

The results, presented in Table 2, are split into three different groups. The first group, labelled with a tick, represents the processes that were considered as valid by the two experts who analysed the results, called reviewing experts. Here, the notion of validity relies on the correspondence between the expected process and the generated one. In other words, a process is considered as valid if it corresponds exactly to the expectations of the reviewing experts, and thus to the textual requirements. The second group, labelled with a question mark, represents the processes that were considered as ambiguous by the reviewing experts. Such processes are considered as ambiguous because, according to their textual description, one may generate several valid processes. As a choice has to be done, one of these possible processes is generated, which may not correspond to the expectations of the expert. For this reason, they belong to the group of ambiguous processes. For instance, a simple sentence such as *"I want A and B and C"* does not state how A, B, and C are related to each others. Thus, putting them in sequence, in parallel or partially in sequence and in parallel remains correct with regards to the description. Similarly, a sentence such as *"I want A before B or C before D"* can be interpreted as a choice between A before B and C before D, or as a sequence executing first A, then B or C, and finally D. For this reason, such processes have been separated from the others, but remain considered as valid. The third and last group, labelled with a cross, represents the processes that were considered as invalid by the reviewing experts. Such processes are at least partially non-compliant with the textual description. It is for instance the case when a non-ambiguous constraint is missing (e.g., two tasks are not put in sequence although they should be), or erroneous (e.g., two tasks are put in an exclusive choice instead of one after the other). Invalid processes are generated when GPT is not able to extract a constraint stated textually, or when it misinterprets it.

Table 2. Experimental Results

Tool/Model	✓	?	✗	Avg. Exec. Time (s)
Our tool	**78.5%**	8%	13.5%	**4.07**
ProMoAI	50%	8.7%	41.2%	24.7
Gemini	32.2%	8.1%	59.7%	8.32
GPT-4-turbo	66.6%	21.1%	**12.2%**	19.2

The results of these experiments, provided in Table 2, showed that our tool obtains the best results both in terms of generation quality (with 78.5% of well-formed processes) and execution time (with an average execution time of 4.07 s). Without much surprise, the execution time of this approach grows as the textual description grows, and as the number of generated expressions increases. Regarding the 13.5% incorrect processes, a deeper analysis shows that they are usually close to the expected process, with very few missing or erroneous constraints. Rather surprisingly, GPT-4-turbo obtained very good results, especially with regards to its low failure percentage. It also greatly outperformed Gemini which obtained the worst results of these experiments. However, the results obtained by the LLMs must be handled with care as they are very probably overrated. Indeed, to the best of our knowledge and experiments, LLMs are, for now, not capable of generating directly the XML code of a BPMN process correctly. For this reason, the LLMs were asked to generate a textual representation of the BPMN process, which was then visually analysed by the reviewing experts and used to compute the score of these models. As generating the exact XML code adds an additional difficulty layer for the LLM, it is likely that the results shown in Table 2 would be lower.

5 Related Work

In [10], the authors propose a solution for modelling BPMN processes from natural language. To do so, they design a Domain-Specific Language (DSL) along with its corresponding grammar to manage textually the dependencies that may exist between the elements of the process-to-be. Once the user has written a specification that is compliant with the proposed grammar, the DSL parser extracts traces from it. These traces are then transformed into a BPMN model with the help of a process mining algorithm. The goal of our approach is similar, in the sense that it also aims at generating a BPMN process from a textual input. The main difference between their approach and ours is that we allow textual descriptions written in natural language while they require a description that is compliant with their grammar, and must be learned before use.

In [16], the authors give insights of how LLMs could be used within the Business Process Management lifecyle. For each step, namely *identification, discovery, analysis, redesign, implementation* and *monitoring*, they synthesise how LLMs could be used jointly with human interactions to improve the quality of the result or lower the time needed to perform the step. The work presented in [15] presents a theoretical approach aiming at extracting a business process from a natural language specification with the help of LLMs. In this work, the authors propose to use sentence level and text level analysis to infer activities and dependencies from a specification in natural language. In both works, the focus is made on partial extraction of data (activities, actors, dependencies) that requires a human intervention in a second phase in order to obtain a business process. In our case, we propose to automatically generate a complete BPMN process from a textual description, without any human intervention.

In [12], the authors perform a series of question/answer exchanges with a chatbot enhanced with natural language processing capabilities. The goal of these iterations is to create or improve process models. In particular here, the authors state that a fully integrated conversational modelling toolchain would include task extraction, logic extraction, BPMN layout creation and BPMN refinement capabilities, but they restrict their focus on the extraction of tasks. The authors also provide several metrics about the quality of the results returned by several well-known LLMs. In [2], the authors propose a technique to transform a natural language specification into some formatted output that is understandable by a computer. To do so, they make use of in-context learning, that gives the opportunity of guiding the dialog towards the desired output. In both papers, the authors end up with pieces of processes (tasks, participants, ...), which have to be put together manually, while our approach automatically provides a BPMN process in which the information extracted from the specification is represented.

In [8], the authors make use of subject-verb-object techniques to extract tasks and participants from the specification, and search for gateway-related keywords to extract information about gateways. From this information, they build an internal spreadsheet format corresponding to the execution sequence of the process, which is finally converted to BPMN. This approach requires partially formatted text in the sense that non-verbal sentences, or sentences without keywords (i.e., "if" for choices) are not likely to be recognised. Also, only sequential composition and choices seem to be supported. In our approach, the input text does not need to be formatted, and parallelism and loops are supported. In [7], the authors make use of a DSL to pre-train a LLM on the BPMN semantics. By doing so, they are able to extract tasks and relationships between them from natural language descriptions. However, the supported syntax is restricted to exclusive and parallel gateways with two paths and loops are not considered. In our approach, such elements are supported.

6 Concluding Remarks

The main goal of the approach proposed in this paper is to automatically convert a textual description into its corresponding BPMN process. To do so, tasks and constraints are extracted from the textual requirements and represented as ASTs. These ASTs are then analysed, modified and recomposed through several steps in order to obtain a single AST containing all the information of the original textual description. Finally, this AST is converted to its corresponding BPMN process and shown to the user. The approach has been implemented, tested and validated by both experts of the BPMN community and novice users.

This work offers several axes of improvements. The main one being to use the GPT-4 model (and/or derivatives) instead of GPT-3.5, which will be done as soon as this model becomes available for fine-tuning. Using a more recent model is very likely to improve significantly the quality of the generated expressions, and thus the generated process. Similarly, increasing the fine-tuning training set would enlarge the proportion of natural language understood by the model, thus limiting its mistakes and increasing the quality of the resulting process. Another possibility could be to extend this work with model checking driven by a temporal logic property written in text.

References

1. Aho, A.V., Garey, M.R., Ullman, J.D.: The transitive reduction of a directed graph. SIAM J. Comput. **1**(2), 131–137 (1972)
2. Bellan, P., Dragoni, M., Ghidini, C.: Extracting business process entities and relations from text using pre-trained language models and in-context learning. In: Proceedings EDOC'22, pp. 182–199. Springer International Publishing (2022)
3. Bellan, P., van der Aa, H., Dragoni, M., Ghidini, C., Ponzetto, S.P.: PET: an annotated dataset for process extraction from natural language text tasks. In: International Conference on Business Process Management. Lecture Notes in Business Information Processing, vol. 460, pp. 315–321. Springer (2022)
4. Team, G., et al.: Gemini: A Family of Highly Capable Multimodal Models (2024)
5. Achiam, J., et al.: GPT-4 Technical Report (2024)
6. Falcone, Y., Salaün, G., Zuo, A.: Semi-automated modelling of optimized BPMN processes. In: Proceedings of SCC'21, pp. 425–430. IEEE (2021)
7. Fill, H.G.: Conceptual modeling and large language models: impressions from first experiments with ChatGPT. In: Proceedings EMISAJ'23, pp. 1–15 (2023)
8. Honkisz, K., Kluza, K., Wiśniewski, P.: A concept for generating business process models from natural language description. In: Proceedings KSEM'18, pp. 91–103 (2018)
9. ISO/IEC. International Standard 19510, Information technology – Business Process Model and Notation (2013)
10. Ivanchikj, A.: From text to visual bpmn process models: design and evaluation. In: Proceedings of MODELS'20, pp. 229–239. Association for Computing Machinery (2020)
11. Kleene, S.C.: Representation of events in nerve nets and finite automata. Automata Stud. 3–41 (1951)
12. Klievtsova, N., Benzin, J.V., Kampik, T., Mangler, J., Rinderle-Ma, S.: Conversational process modelling: state of the art, applications, and implications in practice. In: Proceedings BPM'23, pp. 319–336. Springer Nature Switzerland (2023)
13. Knuth, D.E.: The Art of Computer Programming, vol. 2: Seminumerical Algorithms. Addison-Wesley, Reading, MA (1969)
14. Kourani, H., Berti, A., Schuster, D., van der Aalst, W.M.: ProMoAI: Process Modeling with Generative AI (2024)
15. Sintoris, K., Vergidis, K.: Extracting business process models using natural language processing (NLP) techniques. In: Proceedings KSEM'17, pp. 135–139 (2017)
16. Vidgof, M., Bachhofner, S., Mendling, J.: Large Language Models for Business Process Management: Opportunities and Challenges (2023)

Plug-and-Play Performance Estimation for LLM Services without Relying on Labeled Data

Can Wang, Dianbo Sui, Hongliang Sun, Hao Ding, Bolin Zhang(✉), and Zhiying Tu(✉)

Harbin Institute of Technology, Harbin, Heilongjiang, China
{23B903072,21B903094,dinghao}@stu.hit.edu.cn,
{suidianbo,brolin,tzy_hit}@hit.edu.cn

Abstract. Large Language Model (LLM) services exhibit impressive capability on unlearned tasks leveraging only a few examples by in-context learning (ICL). However, the success of ICL varies depending on the task and context, leading to heterogeneous service quality. Directly estimating the performance of LLM services at each invocation can be laborious, especially requiring abundant labeled data or internal information within the LLM. This paper introduces a novel method to estimate the performance of LLM services across different tasks and contexts, which can be "plug-and-play" utilizing only a few unlabeled samples like ICL. Our findings suggest that the negative log-likelihood and perplexity derived from LLM service invocation can function as effective and significant features. Based on these features, we utilize four distinct meta-models to estimate the performance of LLM services. Our proposed method is compared against unlabeled estimation baselines across multiple LLM services and tasks. And it is experimentally applied to two scenarios, demonstrating its effectiveness in the selection and further optimization of LLM services.

Keywords: Generative AI as a Service · Large Language Model · Performance Estimation · Service Selection · Optimization Tuning

1 Introduction

Large language models (LLM) have the capability to understand and generate natural language text, making them valuable tools for a variety of natural language processing tasks such as text generation, translation [23], summarization [29], question answering [9], and more. LLM services, such as OpenAI LLM API[1], allow users to conveniently solve their tasks by interacting with LLM in a flexible conversational manner, without needing to know whether the LLM has been trained on these tasks or not.

---
[1] OpenAI publishes LLM services through https://openai.com/blog/openai-api.

This remarkable capability is realized through the paradigm of In-Context Learning (ICL) [3], which enables the LLM to generalize rapidly only employing a few labeled examples without requiring additional training. However, such a paradigm is not flawless. Many studies have revealed such a reality: ICL is highly sensitive to task and context [22,32]. ICL can demonstrate significant advantages in certain tasks when using appropriate LLM services and contexts, such as solving entity linking tasks with the Phi-2 service. But it can be virtually ineffective in other scenarios, like solving web-question tasks with the Llama-7B service[2]. Therefore, in the face of different tasks and contexts, it is both challenging and necessary to estimate the performance of LLM services in advance.

To estimate the LLM services' performance, typical solutions use labeled data to invoke LLM services [17,27], which necessitate collecting labels and testing them for each task. However, generally purposed LLM services address a wide range of natural language tasks and most of these tasks are not human-labeled. Especially in domain-specific tasks that require expertise, such as medical or law text understanding, the high cost of annotation poses a significant challenge. Another solutions avoiding labeled data by exploiting the information within the LLM during inference, potentially requiring the LLM's architecture and parameters to be open [12,16,18,20]. These approaches have limitations for LLM services that only provide usage access without disclosing internal information, and in practice, extracting internal information on a large number of heterogeneous LLM services is also a time-consuming and laborious work.

Building on this, we explore a more practical and appealing idea to estimate the performance of LLM services, which can be "plug-and-play" for various LLM services and unlabeled tasks in different contexts. In detail, we explore the common relationship between the semantic features exhibited during the invocation of LLM services and performance. We find two useful features, negative log-likelihood and perplexity, which rely solely on the answers generated during LLM service invocation, but can reflect the performance potential of the LLM service on the current task and context. Then, we propose our meta-model based approach tightly integrated with the ICL paradigm: for a quick and reliable performance estimation, only the answers of the LLM service to a few examples are needed. Our novel training and inference approach using linear interpolation makes the meta-model effective and generalizable, which can be used for a wide range of different LLM services and unlabeled tasks without retraining.

The contributions of this paper are:

- We explore the common phenomenon exhibited during the invocation of LLM services, and select the available features based on their relevance.
- We propose a method for LLM service performance estimation that is able to reach low-error estimates at little cost on various unlabeled tasks, which can be applied to most LLM services that do not know the internal information.

---

[2] We conducted experiments to prove this. For more detailed information about this paper, including the dataset, hyperparameter settings, etc., please see: https://github.com/WangCan1178/Plug-and-Play-Estimation.

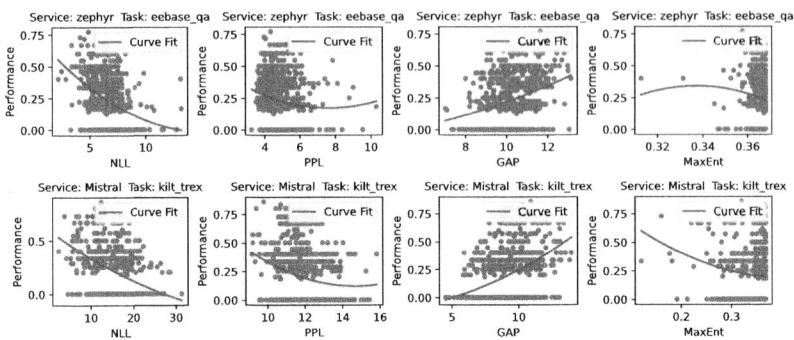

Fig. 1. Distribution of the four features and the LLM service performance, as well as the fitting curve (from two randomly selected task invocation results).

– We verify the effectiveness of our method in two scenarios: the selection of LLM services and the further optimization for few-shot tasks of LLM services, proving that it can be helpful in various future works.

2 Pilot Experiments

This section describes the phenomenon we observe when LLM services are invoked to perform ICL. Specifically, we mainly explore the following two research questions: **RQ1**: What features can be extracted on unlabeled task when invoking LLM services through ICL paradigm? **RQ2**: How to select appropriate features to reflect the performance of LLM services?

2.1 Experiment Setup

In the pilot experiments, we select the top 5 generative LLM services according to the downloads of hugging face model library (https://huggingface.co/models), which have different sizes and structures. Besides, we choose a representative benchmark dataset: CROSSFIT [30], a benchmark to study the generalization capability of LLMs, containing 160 different few-shot NLP tasks. Given that our method is based on ICL and few-shot tasks, we don't use datasets for common NLP tasks that LLM services may have seen the data during training. We sample examples from the training dataset of each task, constitute the context of the unlabeled data, and invoke the LLM service on the testing dataset. And F1-score [26] is used to calculate the accuracy of the generation on unlearned tasks, reflecting the performance of LLM service when invoked.

2.2 What Features Can Be Extracted on Unlabeled Task? (RQ1)

To answer the RQ1, we survey LLM services on the market and find that almost all of them provide (top-few) word-list probabilities of the reasoned answer. We

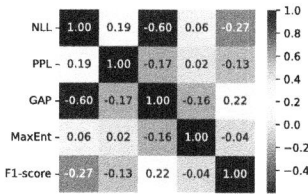

Fig. 2. Pearson correlation coefficient of features and LLM services performance.

use this probability to come up with the following usable features. A intuitive illustration of their strong correlation can be observed in Fig. 1, by fitting the distribution between these features and performance on these tasks.

Negative Log-likelihood (NLL). We treat the process of the LLM service invocation as a generation task. NLL can be used for measuring how well LLM fit on the dataset, which can be obtained from each generated sequence as following:

$$nll(x) = -\sum_{t=1}^{|x|} \log P(x_t \mid x_{<t}; \theta) \tag{1}$$

where x is the output sequence of the LLM service with parameter θ, and $P(x_t \mid x_{<t})$ is the maximum probability assigned at t-th token. The smaller the value, the more confident about the generated sentence.

Perplexity (PPL). Perplexity reflects the likelihood of a LLM having seen and learned (in other word, be pretrained on) this data before. It is calculated based on the probability that the LLM reconstructs the input sequence.

$$ppl(x) = \exp\left(-\sum_{t=1}^{|x|} \log P(\tilde{x}_t \mid x_{<t}; \theta)\right) \tag{2}$$

Its calculation is similar to NLL, except the predicated token x_t is replaced by the input token $\tilde{x}_t$ in the conditional probability. The smaller the value, the more likely it is that the LLM has seen and learned the generated sentence.

GAP. GAP is defined as the difference between the probability of the most likely token (i.e., the first ranked token) and the probability of the second most likely token (i.e., the second ranked token) in the probability distribution generated for the current word.

$$gap(x) = \sum_{t=1}^{|x|} P(x_t - x_{t\_sec} \mid x_{<t}; \theta) \tag{3}$$

GAP takes into account the effect of potentially possible answers. And the bigger the value, the more accurate about the generated sentence.

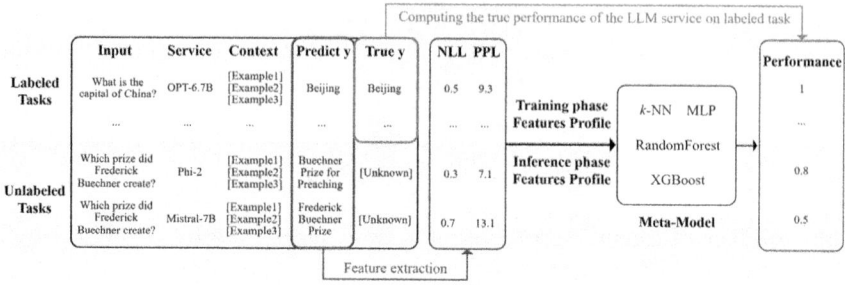

Fig. 3. Procedure of our meta-model based LLM service performance estimation.

Maximum Entropy (MaxEnt). Entropy is an indicator to measure the uncertainty about the generated tokens. Preliminary experiments [10] show that simply taking the maximum token entropy significantly outperforms other aggregation methods such as averaging or taking the minimum.

$$MaxEnt(x) = \max_{t \in |x|} \mathcal{H}(x_t \mid x_{<t}; \theta) \quad (4)$$

where $\mathcal{H}(x_t \mid x_{<t}; \theta)$ is the entropy of the current token calculated from its probability. The smaller the value, the more certain about the generated sentence.

2.3 How to Select Appropriate Features to Reflect the Performance of LLM Services? (RQ2)

Based on the proposed features in Sect. 2.2, we can compute the correlation between these features and the LLM services performance, in units of tasks. Pearson correlation coefficient is used as the indicator of measurement. And F1-score is used to calculate the accuracy of the generation on unlearned tasks, reflecting the performance of LLM service. Figure 2 shows the overall correlations by simply taking the average over all results. These features can constitute different combinations that reflect the LLM service performance. According to the theory of correlation and collinearity [1,14], we expect to select combinations that are strongly correlated with the performance, but not strongly correlated with other features. Thus, we define a score to this end as followed.

$$Score(F) = \sum_{f_i, f_j \in F} corr(f_i, F1) - corr(f_i, f_j) \quad (5)$$

where $F = \{f_1, f_2, ... f_n\}$ is a combination of different features, and $corr(f_i, f_j)$ denotes the correlation between the feature f_i and f_j, without repeating calculating $corr(f_j, f_i)$. Through this score, we find the best combination of features is $F = \{NLL, PPL\}$, denoting these two features can reflect the performance of LLM service best from two different aspects.

3 Methodology: LLM Services Performance Estimation

In this section, we first illustrate the definition of LLM services performance estimation problem in Subsect. 3.1. Then, the meta-model based method we proposed is introduced in Subsect. 3.2, detailing its novel training and inference process in Subsect. 3.3. The whole procedure of the proposed meta-model based method is shown as shown in Fig. 3.

3.1 Problem Definition

In this paper, we focus on estimating performance of LLM services on unlearned and unlabeled tasks. Our goal can be formalized as investigating how to quickly and cheaply estimate the performance $\widehat{per}_{T,C}^{S}$ of ICL, given a LLM service S, an unlearned and unlabeled task $T = \{x^{(1)}, \ldots, x^{(n)}\}$, with the context C.

Absolute error is used to measure the effectiveness of our method, defined as $|per_{T,C}^{S} - \widehat{per}_{T,C}^{S}|$, where $per_{T,C}^{S}$ is the true performance of the LLM service S invoked to handle the same task T with C. We explore performance estimation on a broad LLM service market $\{S_i\}_{i=1}^{I}$, a wide range of natural language tasks $\{T_j\}_{j=1}^{J}$ and different contexts $\{C_k\}_{k=1}^{K}$. Therefore, the final mean abstract error (MAE) is calculated by the following method, using the average absolute error:

$$MAE = \frac{1}{I}\frac{1}{J}\frac{1}{K} \sum_{i \in I} \sum_{j \in J} \sum_{k \in K} |per_{T_j,C_k}^{S_i} - \widehat{per}_{T_j,C_k}^{S_i}| \qquad (6)$$

In different subsequent works, several of the terms in the Eq. 6 can be fixed to simplify the calculation. Such as selecting the most appropriate LLM service for a specific fixed task with a given context, it only needs to minimize the average error of all LLM services.

3.2 Meta-Model Based Method

Meta-model[3] refers to a high-level model that does not predict the data directly, but makes the final prediction or decision by combining and analyzing the prediction results of other base models. In our proposed method, the meta-model is able to accept the features from generated answers when invoking the LLM service, and to estimate the performance when inference.

For efficiency, we choose meta-models with simple structures containing much fewer parameters than LLM, which are easy to train and have fast inference speed. Four meta-models with different architectures are selected: *k*-**Nearest Neighbors** (*k*-NN), which estimates the performance of the LLM service by measuring the similarity of features between samples [8]. **Multilayer Perceptron** (MLP), which estimates the performance of LLM service by the probability propagation between neurons [24]. **RandomForest**, which estimates the performance of LLM service by bagging multiple weak Learners [2]. **eXtreme Gradient Boosting** (XBoost), which estimates the performance of LLM service by boosting multiple weak Learners [6].

---
[3] Extend from metamodeling(https://wikipedia.org/wiki/Metamodeling).

3.3 Training and Inference

The goal of the training phase is to obtain a good meta-model M, which must possess sufficient generalization capability to be applied across a wide range of LLM services and open-domain tasks. It is satisfied through three required inputs: a set of LLM services $\{S_i\}_{i=1}^{I}$, a set of labeled tasks $\{T_j^{labeled}\}_{j=1}^{J}$, and a set of contexts $\{C_k\}_{k=1}^{K}$ sampled from the respective task. These three inputs can be arbitrarily combined to obtain the results of invocations of different LLM services under various tasks and contexts. As mentioned in Sect. 2, we can extract the useful meta-model features $nll_{T_j^{labeled}, C_k}^{S_i}$ and $ppl_{T_j^{labeled}, C_k}^{S_i}$ of the series of invocations, as well as the true performance $per_{T_j^{labeled}, C_k}^{S_i}$ demonstrated.

A key problem is that different scale sizes of tasks result in different dimensions of features. We borrow the idea of profile [11], and map the features to the same dimension d by linear interpolation. It is defined as follows, where D is the dataset size of the current task $T_j^{labeled}$, and f_n is the n-th index of the features such as $nll_{T_j^{labeled}, C_k}^{S_i}$ or $ppl_{T_j^{labeled}, C_k}^{S_i}$.

$$f_n = liner(f_{\lfloor |D| \times n/d \rfloor}, f_{\lceil |D| \times n/d \rceil}) \tag{7}$$

In this way, by continuously reducing the difference between the estimated performance $\widehat{per}_{T_j^{labeled}, C_k}^{S_i}$ and the true performance $per_{T_j^{labeled}, C_k}^{S_i}$, the meta-model gradually converges to the point where it can estimate the LLM service performance on different unlearned tasks.

In the inference phase, a partial subset of the unlabeled task $T^{*unlabeled} \subseteq T^{unlabeled}$ is selected, and the estimated LLM service S is invoked with the context C for inference. Using the same method as in the training phase, the features $nll_{T^{*unlabeled}, C}^{S}$ and $ppl_{T^{*unlabeled}, C}^{S}$ and are obtained and mapped to a d dimensional space. Then, the trained meta-model M is applied and the estimated performance of LLM service is obtained as defined.

$$\widehat{per}_{T^{*unlabeled}, C}^{S} = M(nll_{T^{*unlabeled}, C}^{S}, ppl_{T^{*unlabeled}, C}^{S}) \tag{8}$$

In summary, our trained meta-model achieves estimation on a wide range of unlabeled tasks and contexts, by exploring the relationship between the features exhibited during LLM service invocation and its performance.

4 Experiments

In this Section, we first introduce the baseline methods, including methods using both labeled and unlabeled data. Then in Subsect. 4.2, the details of our experiments are presented. The main results are given in Subsect. 4.3, demonstrating the effectiveness and practicality of our approach. Finally, we conduct an ablation study to show the impact of features and the number of unlabeled samples used to make estimations.

4.1 Baselines

We design the following baselines that do not involve LLM internal information to compare with our method, which allows LLMs to be used as black-box services.

Sample Accuracy of Labeled Examples. (Sample^n) It is straightforward to estimate the performance of LLM services exhibited in different tasks by labeling the few data [27]. This method samples n examples from the dataset of the task $T^{unlabeled}$ to label, and calculate the accuracy of these n examples as the performance of the whole task, which we call it Sample^n. According to the law of large numbers, the more sample examples are labeled, the closer the estimated accuracy is to the true performance, at the cost of more expensive labeling costs. When estimating LLM service performance, we want our method to be able to approximate the accuracy of Sample^n without using labeled data.

$$\widehat{per}_{T,C}^S(\text{Sample}^n) = \frac{1}{n}\frac{1}{K}\sum_{i=1}^{n}\sum_{k\in K} per_{x^{(i)},C_k}^S$$

where $per_{x^{(i)},C}^S$ is the true performance of the LLM service S invoked on the labeled sample $x^{(i)}$ sampled from the unlabeled task T dataset.

Average Accuracy on the Training Dataset (AvgTrain). Similarly, the average over all labeled tasks can also be used as a baseline for LLM service.

$$\widehat{per}_{T,C}^S(\text{AvgTrain}) = \frac{1}{J}\frac{1}{K}\sum_{j\in J}\sum_{k\in K} per_{T_j,C_k}^S$$

Average Threshold of Confidence (ATC). Another practical baseline approach is to obtain a threshold based on the confidence of LLM service on task-level [12], whereby the accuracy is predicted by the proportion of unlabeled instances where model confidence surpasses the threshold. And the average of the ATC obtained from the estimates of each seen task is used as a baseline.

$$\widehat{per}_{T,C}^S(\text{ATC}) = \frac{1}{J}\frac{1}{K}\sum_{j\in J}\sum_{k\in K} atc_{T_j,C_k}^S$$

where atc_{T_j,C_k}^S is the accuracy estimation of task T_j using the threshold of model confidence.

4.2 Experimental Details

We use the dataset mentioned in Sect. 2 because it provides enough few-shot NLP tasks to facilitate the study of performance of LLM services across tasks. Thirteen open-ended generation tasks are selected for our experiments. We combine the "train" and "dev" set to train our meta-model as labeled tasks. For each task, three examples are sampled from it at a time as context. And we conducted a total of 50 different sampling times to fully investigate the impact of context

Table 1. Experimental results (MAE) and variations (SD) for different LLM services performance estimation on our method and baselines.

LLM service	Llama-7B	Mistral-7B	OPT-6.7B	Phi-2	Zephyr-7B-β	Total
Baselines						
SAMPLE^8	7.98 ± 4.10	5.27 ± 1.34	10.23 ± 3.09	10.20 ± 3.79	4.74 ± 2.45	8.28 ± 4.25
SAMPLE^{16}	6.78 ± 2.82	4.12 ± 1.59	8.70 ± 2.75	9.22 ± 2.61	3.98 ± 1.49	6.12 ± 3.60
SAMPLE^{32}	4.15 ± 1.54	3.12 ± 0.94	6.24 ± 2.38	6.78 ± 2.41	3.10 ± 1.36	5.14 ± 2.84
AvgTrain	6.20 ± 2.70	5.74 ± 4.64	8.96 ± 3.71	8.60 ± 2.23	5.80 ± 2.48	6.74 ± 4.62
ATC	40.91 ± 10.24	38.82 ± 5.36	30.56 ± 11.42	31.10 ± 9.98	39.20 ± 9.02	39.82 ± 5.37
Meta Models						
3-NN	6.50 ± 2.50	7.30 ± 2.69	7.02 ± 2.63	7.42 ± 3.61	6.18 ± 0.23	7.30 ± 2.96
MLP	7.24 ± 5.60	5.30 ± 0.71	7.24 ± 0.82	6.58 ± 1.31	5.50 ± 1.44	5.30 ± 1.70
RandomForest	5.80 ± 0.99	**4.02 ± 1.61**	8.60 ± 1.60	**5.38 ± 1.46**	**4.04 ± 1.34**	**4.72 ± 1.61**
XGBoost	**4.76 ± 0.63**	5.42 ± 1.59	**6.17 ± 0.81**	5.44 ± 1.60	4.56 ± 1.17	5.42 ± 2.59

on the invocation of different LLM services. In total, we have experimented with executing 5 LLM services on 13 tasks with 50 contexts (3250 ICL settings).

We use 1000 unlabeled samples and 5-fold cross-validation to verify our method's effectiveness. The number of features d is set to 100, and the optimal hyperparameters are selected by grid search for each meta-model.

4.3 Main Results

In this subsection, we first compare the error of our proposed method and baselines. Then we demonstrate the effectiveness of our method in terms of the accuracy improvement of two subsequent works.

LLM Services Performance Estimation Performs all Unlabeled Baselines. Table 1 shows the MAE obtained by performance estimation on different LLM services. On all LLM services, our method performs better than the unlabeled baselines on average across the 13 tasks. And in the best case (XGBoost with OPT-6.7B), the meta-model's MAE is 31.1% lower than the best baseline method without labels.

Compared with method SAMPLE^n using labeled data, our method can mostly outperform the method with 16 samples, and sometimes even outperform the method with 32 samples. In particular, when not differentiated by LLM service, our model performs at a comparable level to sampling 64 samples(4.78 ± 2.10), which shows the high generalization of our method. The implication is that we can significantly save annotation costs to estimate the performance of different LLM services on a wide range of natural language tasks. Furthermore, note that the standard deviation of the best meta-model on the LLM performance estimation using our method is significantly smaller than that of the other method. It indicates the stability of our method, that is, it is almost unaffected by the sampled different unlabeled samples.

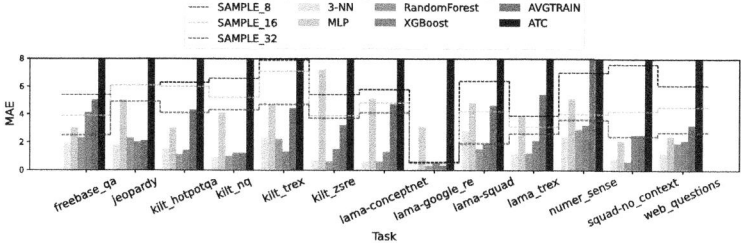

Fig. 4. Experimental results (MAE) for different tasks of the LLM services performance estimation (our method) and baselines.

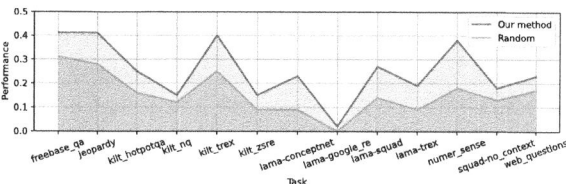

Fig. 5. Execution performance under the settings of our method and randomly selected services or contexts.

We also explore the performance of LLM service performance estimation on different tasks, and the results are presented in Fig. 4. It shows that in all 13 few-shot tasks, our best meta-model outperforms all baseline methods, including the previous best performing method $SAMPLE^{32}$. This may be due to the fact that the probability distribution of the results for the same task is similar, which leads to faster convergence and better performance of our method. It is more practical and attractive than estimating the LLM service performance on multiple tasks, because the performance estimation on a certain given task is more in line with the actual demands.

LLM Services Performance Estimation Helps the Subsequent Works.
To verify the practicality of our method, we conduct experiments of two common scenarios, applying LLM services performance estimation to subsequent works.

The first scenario considers the selection of services and contexts when the user invokes the LLM service to perform some unlearned task. We experiment with the best hyperparameters of the best meta-model architecture (RandomForest). Five LLM services and ten different contexts are randomly sampled for a total of 50 ICL settings. The estimation performance on different settings are given through the inference of the meta-model, which the best one are selected as the recommended service and context of our method. It is compared with the random selection of services and contexts that often happens in the actual invocation scenario, and the results shown in Fig. 5 are obtained.

In 13 different few-shot tasks, the selected services and contexts using our proposed LLM service performance estimation indeed exhibit stronger ICL capa-

Table 2. Fine-tuning effects on the low-performing tasks of LLM services selected by our method and all LLM services.

Task	kilt_zsre	lama-conceptnet	lama-google_re
Llama-7B	0.09 - 0.02	**0.06 + 0.09**	0.00 + 0.08
Mistral-7B	**0.12 + 0.13**	0.12 + 0.05	0.01 + 0.10
OPT-6.7B	0.04 + 0.05	0.09 + 0.02	0.01 + 0.02
Phi-2	0.03 + 0.06	**0.22 + 0.09**	0.00 - 0.01
Zephyr-7B-β	0.12 + 0.07	0.05 + 0.03	**0.02 + 0.11**

Table 3. Evaluation results (MAE) and variants (SD) of different features selected to use in our method.

LLM service	Llama-7B	Mistral-7B	OPT-6.7B	Phi-2	Zephyr-7B-β	Total
NLL only						
3-NN	8.22 ± 3.50	8.15 ± 3.29	7.02 ± 2.63	10.67 ± 4.64	8.82 ± 2.23	9.10 ± 4.37
MLP	9.23 ± 5.51	7.03 ± 4.25	8.51 ± 2.46	7.70 ± 3.27	7.47 ± 3.40	6.52 ± 3.86
RandomForest	7.85 ± 2.24	**6.11 ± 3.57**	9.00 ± 3.97	7.42 ± 2.34	**6.83 ± 3.57**	**6.90 ± 3.13**
XGBoost	**6.61 ± 1.90**	7.94 ± 2.55	**6.17 ± 3.24**	**7.32 ± 2.34**	6.97 ± 3.76	7.17 ± 4.05
PPL only						
3-NN	14.50 ± 4.78	9.23 ± 4.31	12.78 ± 3.79	11.45 ± 5.82	9.14 ± 2.56	11.68 ± 4.56
MLP	12.67 ± 6.34	11.95 ± 5.13	9.72 ± 2.89	14.79 ± 5.14	10.56 ± 4.60	9.19 ± 4.02
RandomForest	10.97 ± 5.67	9.85 ± 4.98	11.14 ± 5.42	10.06 ± 2.68	8.05 ± 3.99	11.21 ± 3.68
XGBoost	13.03 ± 5.22	10.67 ± 3.97	11.44 ± 3.57	11.00 ± 2.81	10.89 ± 3.32	14.36 ± 4.19

bility. This is undoubtedly appealing, as users can improve the performance of the current task by even up to 21% at no additional annotation cost.

Another scenario considers domain tasks that are difficult for all LLM services, such as lama-conceptnet (concept question with answer is a single word), which performs best with only an F1-score of 0.12. At this time, further optimization of the LLM service is necessary, and a common approach is to fine-tune the LLM's parameters, which is often laborious and resource-consuming. Our approach can help indicate which LLM service has a wider optimization space, and to make a better choice in advance.

The reason we believe that estimated performance can represent the optimization space is that the LLM services are always under-fitting and low-performaning on these tasks. The higher the estimated performance of the LLM service, the stronger its potential language modeling ability for the task, indicating it can perform best after further optimization. Similarly, we performed the experiments in different 50 settings, and use the difference of performance to indicate how much the LLM service has improved after fine-tuning, which is defined as $diff = per_{T,C}^{S_{fineturn}} - per_{T,C}^{S}$.

Table 2 presents the results (in the form of $per_{T,C}^{S} \pm diff$ to display the changes before and after fine-tuning) of further optimization on the three worst performing tasks. It is shown that the estimation of LLM service performance

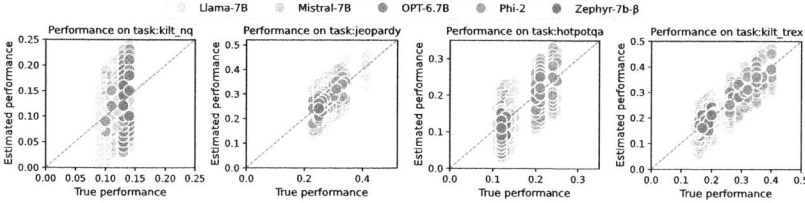

Fig. 6. True and estimated performance on four different tasks. The number of unlabeled samples is from 200 to 1600, sampling in the interval of 200. The more opaque the color, the more the unlabeled samples.

can subconsciously indicate the best suitable service for fine-turning. And it can provide useful guidance for further optimization of LLM services on low-performance tasks.

4.4 Ablation Study

We explore the influence of two important factors in our method. The effect of the different features selected on the results is shown in the Table 3, including NLL only and PPL only. Regardless of the meta-model architecture, using one feature alone resulted in larger estimation errors compared to using both features. This corroborates our idea that these two different features reflect the performance of LLM services from different perspectives.

Another ablation study for the number of unlabeled samples is performed on the best meta-model architecture RandomForest. And we chose the best parameters setting obtained by grid search for ablation study with the number of unlabeled samples: the depth of the tree is 10, the number of weak learners is 260, and the sampling ratio is 0.8.

For simplicity, we define $n = |T^{*unlabeled}|$ to represent the number of unlabeled samples that need to be used for the estimation of LLM service performance. And we performed experiments on all the tasks, reducing the average MAE from 6.30 for $n = 200$ to 2.52 for $n = 1600$. This effect is visually shown in Fig. 6, where increasing n achieves better estimations, despite the need to perform additional LLM service invocations on unlabeled samples. In practice, we recommend 400 unlabeled samples for a task, which can accurately estimate the LLM service performance on the basis of controlling the invocation cost.

5 Related Work

5.1 Language Model as a Service

Large language models represent the latest development of generative AI and have shown outstanding performance in the service field, due to their outstanding natural language understanding and representation capability [31]. It is shown to have an attractive capability to "learn" [3,7], that is, to perform unlearned tasks correctly given only a few labeled examples.

However, a rapidly growing number of LLM services have different costs and qualities, resulting in the heterogeneity of the execution performance of the same task [5]. On the one hand, many studies have explored the problem of LLM service selection and composition [21,25,28], to obtain a more affordable and accurate solution to the invocation of LLM services. On the other hand, the performance of LLM services also strongly depends on the choice of prompt templates and examples [22,32]. The selection [33] and enhancement of the prompts [15] have been widely discussed to enhance the performance and generalization of LLM services.

Among all these works, the estimation of the LLM service performance is key because it gives an indication that can be quantified and compared. And this indication can be used to give guidance in the selection of services, order of invocations, optimization of prompts, and so on.

5.2 LLM Performance Estimation

LLM performance estimation aims to estimate LLM performance on a specific task in advance. Unlike evaluation [4], performance estimation occurs before invocation and focuses on unlearned datasets (out-of-distribution predictions) [13].

Early work focused mainly on estimation based on labeled data, and it is a straightforward idea to take a subset of the dataset and design experiments or benchmarks for performance prediction [17,27]. However, these methods are limited by the representativeness of the data and the cost of annotation. In recent years, with the increasing interest in unsupervised learning [19], researchers explore how to utilize the LLM internal information for performance estimation [16,20]. These approaches can bypass the need for labeled data, estimating the performance by analyzing LLMs' hidden states or attention weights. approaches without labeled data are especially effective in domain tasks [12,18], which learn model confidence to improve the performance estimates for specific tasks. But these approaches require the model to disclose internal details and have limitations for most LLM services that are published in black-box form.

Previous studies provide us with rich experience and enlightenment to explore the LLM service performance estimation methods that do not rely on the labeled dataset. Our approach follows the idea of exploring the available features revealed when scaling on a wide range of unlearned unlabeled tasks, and based on this to estimate the service performance.

6 Conclusion

In conclusion, this paper presents a promising approach to addressing the challenge of estimating LLM service performance without labeled data, which can be conveniently applied in a "plug-and-play" manner to a variety of LLM services and tasks. By leveraging the meta-model based approach integrated with the ICL paradigm, our method offers accurate performance estimates that exceed baselines, facilitating informed decision-making in LLM service selection and optimization. Our work still has limitations that need to be explored, such as how to extend the method to larger models and more complex tasks, and how to leverage the ICL capabilities to enhance the generalization of meta-models. We believe that our contributions pave the way for the application of LLM services in practical scenarios, and we look forward to further research based on that.

Acknowledgments. The work is supported by the National Key R&D Program of China (Grant No.2022YFF0902703), the National Natural Science Foundation of China (Grant No.62472121), the National Natural Science Foundation of China (Grant No. 62306087), and the Special Funding Program of Shandong Taishan Scholars Project.

References

1. Bobrowski, L.: Collinearity models in the eigenvalue problem. In: Nguyen, N.T., Hoang, D.H., Hong, T.P., Pham, H., Trawiński, B. (eds.) Intelligent Information and Database Systems, pp. 402–409. Springer International, Cham (2018)
2. Breiman, L.: Random forests. Mach. Learn. **45**(1), 5–32 (2001). https://doi.org/10.1023/A:1010933404324
3. Brown, T.B., et al.: Language models are few-shot learners. In: Larochelle, H., Ranzato, M., Hadsell, R., Balcan, M., Lin, H. (eds.) Advances in Neural Information Processing Systems 33: Annual Conference on Neural Information Processing Systems 2020, NeurIPS 2020, December 6-12, 2020, virtual (2020). https://proceedings.neurips.cc/paper/2020/hash/1457c0d6bfcb4967418bfb8ac142f64a-Abstract.html
4. Chang, Y., et al.: A survey on evaluation of large language models. ACM Trans. Intell. Syst. Technol. (2024). https://doi.org/10.1145/3641289
5. Chen, L., Zaharia, M., Zou, J.: Frugalgpt: How to use large language models while reducing cost and improving performance. CoRR **abs/2305.05176** (2023). https://doi.org/10.48550/arXiv.2305.05176
6. Chen, T., Guestrin, C.: Xgboost: A scalable tree boosting system. In: Proceedings of the 22nd ACM SIGKDD International Conference on Knowledge Discovery and Data Mining. ACM (2016). http://dx.doi.org/10.1145/2939672.2939785
7. Chowdhery, A., el al.: Palm: Scaling language modeling with pathways. arXiv preprint arXiv:2204.02311 (2022)
8. Cover, T., Hart, P.: Nearest neighbor pattern classification. IEEE Trans. Inf. Theory **13**(1), 21–27 (1967). https://doi.org/10.1109/TIT.1967.1053964
9. Etezadi, R., Shamsfard, M.: The state of the art in open domain complex question answering: a survey. Appl. Intell. **53**(4), 4124–4144 (2023)
10. Fadeeva, E., el al.: Fact-checking the output of large language models via token-level uncertainty quantification (2024)
11. Fu, H.Y., Ye, Q., Xu, A., Ren, X., Jia, R.: Estimating large language model capabilities without labeled test data. In: Bouamor, H., Pino, J., Bali, K. (eds.) Findings of the Association for Computational Linguistics: EMNLP 2023, Singapore, December 6-10, 2023, pp. 9530–9546. Association for Computational Linguistics (2023). https://aclanthology.org/2023.findings-emnlp.639

12. Garg, S., Balakrishnan, S., Lipton, Z.C., Neyshabur, B., Sedghi, H.: Leveraging unlabeled data to predict out-of-distribution performance. In: The Tenth International Conference on Learning Representations, ICLR 2022, Virtual Event, April 25-29, 2022. OpenReview.net (2022)
13. Guillory, D., Shankar, V., Ebrahimi, S., Darrell, T., Schmidt, L.: Predicting with confidence on unseen distributions. In: Proceedings of the IEEE/CVF International Conference on Computer Vision, pp. 1134–1144 (2021)
14. Hall, M.A.: Correlation-based feature selection for machine learning. Ph.D. thesis, The University of Waikato (1999)
15. Haurum, J.B., Escalera, S., Taylor, G.W., Moeslund, T.B.: Which tokens to use? investigating token reduction in vision transformers. In: Proceedings of ICCV (2023)
16. Huang, H., et al.: Towards making the most of LLM for translation quality estimation. In: Liu, F., Duan, N., Xu, Q., Hong, Y. (eds.) Natural Language Processing and Chinese Computing Proceedings, Part I. Lecture Notes in Computer Science, vol. 14302, pp. 375–386. Springer (2023). https://doi.org/10.1007/978-3-031-44693-1_30
17. Kang, W., Ni, J., Mehta, N., Sathiamoorthy, M., Hong, L., Chi, E.H., Cheng, D.Z.: Do llms understand user preferences? evaluating llms on user rating prediction. CoRR **abs/2305.06474** (2023). https://doi.org/10.48550/arXiv.2305.06474
18. Kaur, R., Jha, S., Roy, A., Sokolsky, O., Lee, I.: Predicting out-of-distribution performance of deep neural networks using model conformance. In: 2023 IEEE International Conference on Assured Autonomy (ICAA), pp. 19–28 (2023)
19. Kryeziu, L., Shehu, V.: A survey of using unsupervised learning techniques in building masked language models for low resource languages. In: 11th Mediterranean Conference on Embedded Computing, MECO 2022, Budva, Montenegro, June 7-10, 2022, pp. 1–6. IEEE (2022)
20. Li, Z., Kamnitsas, K., Islam, M., Chen, C., Glocker, B.: Estimating model performance under domain shifts with class-specific confidence scores. In: Medical Image Computing and Computer Assisted Intervention–MICCAI 2022: 25th International Conference, Singapore, September 18–22, pp. 693–703. Springer (2022)
21. Lu, K., et al.: Routing to the expert: Efficient reward-guided ensemble of large language models. CoRR (2023)
22. Perez, E., Kiela, D., Cho, K.: True few-shot learning with language models. Adv. Neural. Inf. Process. Syst. **34**, 11054–11070 (2021)
23. Ranathunga, S., Lee, E.A., Skenduli, M.P., Shekhar, R., Alam, M., Kaur, R.: Neural machine translation for low-resource languages: a survey. ACM Comput. Surv. **55**(11), 229:1–229:37 (2023). https://doi.org/10.1145/3567592
24. Rumelhart, D.E., Hinton, G.E., Williams, R.J.: Learning representations by back-propagating errors. Nature **323**(6088), 533–536 (1986)
25. Sakota, M., Peyrard, M., West, R.: Fly-swat or cannon? cost-effective language model choice via meta-modeling. CoRR (2023)
26. Sasaki, Y.: The truth of the f-measure. Teach Tutor Mater (2007)
27. Singhal, P., Forristal, J., Ye, X., Durrett, G.: Assessing out-of-domain language model performance from few examples. arXiv preprint arXiv:2210.06725 (2022)
28. Wang, C., Zhang, B., Sui, D., Tu, Z., Liu, X., Kang, J.: A survey on effective invocation methods of massive llm services. ArXiv **abs/2402.03408** (2024)
29. Watanangura, P., Vanichrudee, S., Minteer, O., Sringamdee, T., Thanngam, N., Siriborvornratanakul, T.: A comparative survey of text summarization techniques. SN Comput. Sci. **5**, 47 (2024). https://doi.org/10.1007/s42979-023-02343-6

30. Ye, Q., Lin, B.Y., Ren, X.: Crossfit: A few-shot learning challenge for cross-task generalization in NLP. In: Moens, M., Huang, X., Specia, L., Yih, S.W. (eds.) Proceedings of the 2021 Conference on Empirical Methods in Natural Language Processing, Punta Cana, Dominican Republic, 7-11 November, 2021, pp. 7163–7189 (2021). https://doi.org/10.18653/v1/2021.emnlp-main.572
31. Yu, L., Chen, Q., Lin, J., He, L.: Black-box prompt tuning for vision-language model as a service. In: Proceedings of IJCAI (2023)
32. Zhao, Z., Wallace, E., Feng, S., Klein, D., Singh, S.: Calibrate before use: improving few-shot performance of language models. In: International Conference on Machine Learning, pp. 12697–12706. PMLR (2021)
33. Zhou, J., Li, F., Dong, J., Zhang, H., Hao, D.: Cost-effective testing of a deep learning model through input reduction. In: 31st IEEE International Symposium on Software Reliability Engineering, Coimbra, Portugal, October 12-15 (2020)

UELLM: A Unified and Efficient Approach for Large Language Model Inference Serving

Yiyuan He[1,2], Minxian Xu[1(✉)], Jingfeng Wu[1], Wanyi Zheng[3], Kejiang Ye[1], and Chengzhong Xu[4]

[1] Shenzhen Institute of Advanced Technology, Chinese Academy of Sciences, Shenzhen, China
{yy.he2,mx.xu,jf.wu2,wy.zheng,kj.ye}@siat.ac.cn
[2] Southern University of Science and Technology, Shenzhen, China
[3] Shenzhen University of Advanced Technology, Shenzhen, China
[4] State Key Lab of IoTSC, University of Macau, Macau, China
czxu@um.edu.mo

Abstract. In the context of Machine Learning as a Service (MLaaS) clouds, the extensive use of Large Language Models (LLMs) often requires efficient management of significant query loads. When providing real-time inference services, several challenges arise. Firstly, increasing the number of GPUs may lead to a decrease in inference speed due to a heightened communication overhead, while an inadequate number of GPUs can lead to out-of-memory errors. Secondly, different deployment strategies need to be evaluated to guarantee optimal utilization and minimal inference latency. Lastly, inefficient orchestration of inference queries can easily lead to significant Service Level Objective (SLO) violations. To address these challenges, we propose a Unified and Efficient approach for Large Language Model inference serving (UELLM), which consists of three main components: **1)** *resource profiler*, **2)** *batch scheduler*, and **3)** *LLM deployer*. The *resource profiler* characterizes resource usage of inference queries by predicting resource demands based on a fine-tuned LLM. The *batch scheduler* effectively batches the queries profiled by the *resource profiler* based on batching algorithms, aiming to decrease inference delays while meeting SLO and efficient batch processing of inference queries. The *LLM deployer* can efficiently deploy LLMs by considering the current cluster hardware topology and LLM characteristics, enhancing resource utilization and reducing resource overhead. UELLM minimizes resource overhead, reduces inference latency, and lowers SLO violation rates. Compared with state-of-the-art (SOTA) techniques, UELLM reduces the inference latency by 72.3% to 90.3%, enhances GPU utilization by 1.2× to 4.1×, and increases throughput by 1.92× to 4.98×, it can also serve without violating the inference latency SLO.

Keywords: Large Language Model Inference · Cloud Computing · Resource Management · Scheduling Algorithm

1 Introduction

The rapid development of deep learning has driven the emergence of large models, and technology companies are increasingly building large MLaaS clouds for model training and inference services. Due to the massive number of inference requests in MLaaS cloud services (e.g., trillions daily on Facebook, billions monthly on OpenAI [1]), most resources and costs are dedicated to inference services (e.g., up to 90% in AWS, 70% in Meta AI [2]). Moreover, inference services are often part of user-facing applications, thus they have strict latency requirements [3]. Additionally, different inference requests have different latency requirements. For example, 98% of inference services need to be served within 200 milliseconds, while recommendation services require responses in less than 100 milliseconds [4]. Although the serving time for LLM can be extended, reducing LLM inference latency remains a critical requirement to ensure a good user experience [5].

In a typical MLaaS workflow, developers use large datasets to train LLMs offline, then deploy multiple trained LLMs in the cloud to provide online inference services. Due to the increasing number of parameters in current LLMs, distributed deployment is required [6]. This means that LLMs need to be deployed on more hardware accelerators. However, the more hardware accelerators deployed simultaneously, the greater the communication latency between different hardware accelerators, which can increase inference latency and the rate of SLO violations. Additionally, owing to the sequential execution characteristics of LLM inference, multiple hardware accelerators can only work serially during inference. This implies that as more hardware accelerators are deployed, the waiting time increases, which in turn reduces the utilization rate.

To improve inference efficiency, batch processing[1] is often used. However, the majority of contemporary LLM architectures are based on Transformer [7]. The autoregressive characteristic of the self-attention layer in these architectures presents notable obstacles for model deployment and batching. Specifically, when generating a new token, the model needs to attend to the previous tokens. To reduce iterations, this requires the model to retain all information of the previous tokens and store it in memory [6]. For a particular inference computation, denote the batch size by b, the maximum length of input sequence by s, the maximum length of output sequence by n, the hidden dimension of the transformer by h, and the total number of transformer layers by l. The total number of bytes to store the Key-Value Cache (KV Cache) in peak is $4 \times blh(s+n)$ [8]. Thus, the size of the KV Cache grows with the batch size and the maximum length of output sequences. This means that processing requests with similar output lengths in a batch can reduce redundant KV Cache and calculation load.

In light of these challenges, we propose UELLM, which integrates batching requests and deploying LLMs efficiently. UELLM aims to maximize through-

---

[1] Batch processing represents the processing of inference requests with batches, which is different from batching as discussed in this article. Here, batching refers to the effective scheduling among batches and the efficient combination of requests within each batch.

put, reduce inference latency, and lower SLO violation rates. UELLM primarily consists of three components: *resource profiler*, *batch scheduler* and *LLM deployer*. The *resource profiler* mainly uses a fine-tuned LLM to predict the output length of each request and obtain the SLO for each request to facilitate subsequent scheduling. The *batch scheduler* optimizes the combination of inference requests within a batch based on predicted output sequence length and schedules them according to the SLO, reducing SLO violation rates and inference latency. The *LLM deployer* strategically deploys LLMs based on the network topology of the current hardware system and the specific characteristics of the LLMs, enhancing GPU utilization and reducing inference latency. Finally, UELLM runs a backend monitoring program to detect erroneous predictions and adjust the allocated memory size to improve accuracy. By integrating these components, UELLM optimizes memory usage and scheduling during inference. This integration leads to a reduction in latency and SLO violation rates, while also enhancing resource utilization when deploying Transformer-based LLMs for text generation on GPUs.

In summary, our key **contributions** are:

– We analyze the primary bottlenecks present in LLM inference services: **1)** the challenge of efficiently batching diverse inference requests, and **2)** the difficulty of effectively utilizing resources during LLM inference due to the extensive search space and diverse model structures.
– We propose UELLM, which can reasonably adjust batch combinations to reduce latency and resource overhead, improve throughput, and efficiently deploy LLMs, thereby increasing resource utilization, reducing latency, and minimizing resource overhead while meeting SLOs.
– We experimentally evaluate the effectiveness of UELLM on a realistic cluster. Compared with SOTA techniques, UELLM reduces the inference latency by 72.3% to 90.3%, enhances GPU utilization by $1.2\times$ to $4.1\times$, and increases throughput by $1.92\times$ to $4.98\times$, it can serve without violating the inference latency SLO.

2 Background and Motivation

In this section, we will introduce the relevant background information regarding LLMs and the phenomena that have motivated our design.

2.1 Background: Generative LLM Consumes Large Amount of Memory

Currently, Transformer-based generative LLMs (such as ChatGPT [9], Llama [2], ChatGLM [10], etc.) are autoregressive. They share the common characteristic of predicting the most probable token based on past tokens. When not using batch processing, the model generates one token at a time, requiring n iterations to generate a sequence of n tokens. Each iteration involves an input token traversing the model, which consists of a stack of transformer layers, including an attention layer, two normalization layers, and two feed-forward layers. The self-attention layer uses information from past tokens to generate the next token. Through the self-attention mechanism, the model can weight each word in the input sequence, focusing on important contextual information. During each step of the generation process, the attention mechanism needs to compute queries, keys, and values. To avoid recalculating each time, the previously generated keys and values can be cached. This caching mechanism significantly reduces computation during the generation phase and increases generation speed. However, since the KV Cache sequentially stores information about previous tokens, it expands as the model generates more tokens.

2.2 Motivation: LLM Inference Performance on Various Deployment Configurations

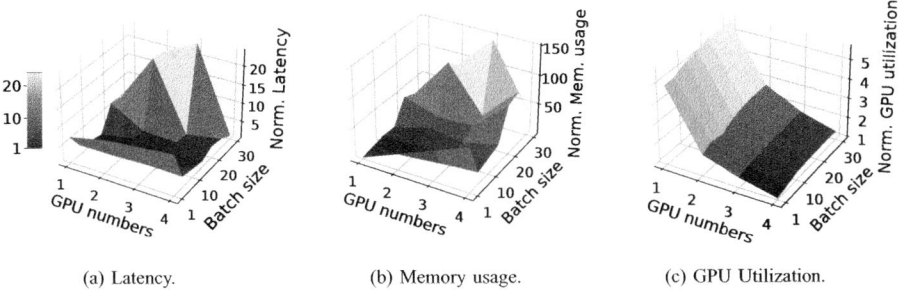

Fig. 1. Normalized latency, memory usage, and GPU utilization under different configurations of GPU numbers and batch sizes. Each metric is normalized to its minimum value.

Observation #1: Slight changes in deployment configurations can have a significant impact on LLM inference performance. With the development of large model technologies, the size and parameters of LLMs have increased. To deploy LLMs for inference services, it is essential to allocate a significant amount of memory. Nevertheless, the growth in the size of LLMs far outpaces the development of hardware, making it difficult for a single hardware accelerator (e.g., GPU) to support a LLM. Consequently, when deploying LLMs for inference tasks, it is a common practice to distribute the model across multiple hardware accelerators, thereby requiring a distributed deployment approach. To facilitate this, a device map is required to delineate the allocation of model layers to specific hardware accelerators. To ensure efficient subsequent inference, the device map must be finely tuned, as the inference performance of LLMs is highly sensitive to different deployment configurations. The process of a deployment configuration can be simplified as follows: **1)** determining the number of GPUs, and **2)** detailed adjustment of the device map to deploy each layer of LLM on the corresponding GPU. Determining the appropriate number of GPUs can be challenging, as merely increasing the number of GPUs may not always be advantageous, given that an excessive number of GPUs can escalate communication and synchronization costs among them. Figure 1 shows that a reasonable number of GPUs can improve GPU utilization by 4× and reduce latency by 20× compared to a poor GPU configuration. Even if the optimal number of GPUs is determined, fine-tuning the device map is required. Table 1 shows that a well-configured device map (last row in Table 1) has the potential to increase throughput significantly, doubling it compared to a poorly configured setup (increasing from 11.19 to 22.55 in terms of average throughput). Therefore, the inference performance of LLM is notably impacted by the model's deployment configurations.

Table 1. throughput variations of ChatGLM2-6B on two GPUs (GPU#0: Tesla V100 and GPU#1: RTX 3090). It shows average, maximum, and minimum throughput for different device maps.

Device map		Throughput (token/s)		
GPU#0	GPU#1	Average	Maximum	Minimum
layer 0-15	layer 16-32	11.19	11.58	10.84
layer 0-19	layer 20-32	13.09	13.48	12.61
layer 0-23	layer 24-32	14.85	15.45	14.09
layer 0-27	layer 28-32	17.23	18.00	16.16
layer 0-31	layer 32	**22.55**	**23.07**	**22.11**

2.3 Motivation: LLM Inference Performance on Various Batching Strategies

Observation #2: Batching multiple requests can reduce the SLO violation rate of LLM inference services under a large number of inference requests. When faced with a large number of inference requests, batching multiple requests can reduce the SLO violation rate of LLM inference services. This is because different requests can share weights, allowing multiple tokens to be generated in a single iteration through batching, thereby increasing the token generation rate and reducing the SLO violation rate. However, batching requests for LLM services requires addressing two key issues. **1)** Requests may arrive at different times. A simple batching strategy either makes earlier requests wait for later ones or delays incoming requests until earlier ones are processed, leading to significant queuing delays. **2)** Requests may have vastly different input and output lengths. Current batching techniques pad the inputs and outputs of requests to balance their lengths [6], but this strategy requires fine-tuning of the batched inference requests. Otherwise, it will lead to significant wastage of GPU computation and memory (see Sect. 2.3). Figure 1 shows the relationship between batch size, GPU numbers, latency, GPU utilization, and memory usage. It is evident that a well-configured combination of batch size and GPU numbers can reduce latency by nearly 20×(with the worst-case scenario involving offloading), improve GPU utilization by 5×, and reduce memory usage by 150×. Consequently, the default batch combination technique results in significant memory waste and low effective GPU utilization.

Given the background and our observations, they motivate us to design a comprehensive framework capable of efficiently deploying LLMs and effectively combining batches during inference, thereby improving system utilization and reducing inference latency.

3 Related Work

In this section, we will discuss the SOTA technologies focusing on model deployment resource allocation and inference request batching in LLM inference services, and their associated limitations.

3.1 Model Deployment

In the realm of model deployment resource allocation, Zhang et al. [4] proposed MArk, a service system designed for ML inference. MArk integrates IaaS and serverless computing to minimize costs while meeting SLOs. However, MArk primarily focuses on the effective deployment of small models, overlooking LLMs and the influence of device map on LLM deployment. In contrast, Wang et al. [1] presented Morphling, a rapid and nearly optimal auto-configuration framework for cloud-native model services. Morphling uses model-agnostic meta-learning to navigate large configuration spaces. Morphling quickly adapts the meta-model for new inference services by sampling a small number of configurations and utilizing it to find the best configuration. However, Morphling performs stress tests on each candidate configuration, resulting in additional computational burden and causing significant latency during LLM testing, rendering it unsuitable for scenarios with limited resources.

Moreover, there are some research studies that concentrate on the hardware aspect. Choi et al. [11] focused on the hardware layer and introduced a novel multi-model machine learning inference server scheduling framework. A crucial aspect of their proposal involves utilizing hardware support for the spatial partitioning of GPU resources. By implementing spatiotemporal sharing, they established a new GPU resource abstraction layer was created using configurable GPU resources. The scheduler assigns requests to virtual GPUs, known as gpulets, based on the optimal resource allocation. In order to reduce the expenses associated with cloud-based inference servers, the framework dynamically adjusts the number of GPUs required for a specific workload. Regrettably, Choi et al. solely focused on deploying small models (e.g., ResNet50, LeNet, VGG16) and did not consider the prevalent large models in the current landscape (e.g., ChatGLM [10], Llama [2]).

3.2 Model Inference

In the context of batching inference requests, the predominant system in use is the Triton Inference Server[2]. It provides simple dynamic scheduling and batch processing features. As previously mentioned in Sect. 2.3, getting the output length of the query before scheduling is crucial for reducing latency and enhancing resource utilization. Nevertheless, Triton Inference Server lacks a viable batch combination algorithm that takes into account SLOs and query output for scheduling. To address this problem, Jin et al. [6] presented S^3, which is a system-algorithm co-design framework that treats batch combination as a bin packing problem through sequence length prediction to maximize GPU utilization and achieve higher throughput. However, S^3 only considers predicted output length when scheduling requests, without accounting for SLOs and other metrics.

Some studies focus on the inference services of traditional machine learning models. Ali et al. [12] proposed BATCH, a framework designed to enhance the efficiency of machine learning services on serverless platforms by addressing the absence of batch processing support. The framework utilizes lightweight profiling techniques and analytical models to identify the optimal parameter configurations (i.e., memory size, batch size, and timeout) to improve system performance while meeting user-defined SLOs. However, BATCH uses exhaustive search methods for configuration, resulting in high time complexity and failing to meet real-time requirements. Clearly, due to the significant differences between LLMs and traditional machine learning models, these inference systems and studies are challenging to apply to more complex LLM inference systems. Wang et al. [13] proposed Tabi, the first inference system addressing the resource overhead in increasingly large language models. It is a multi-stage inference engine driven by individual query feedback and leverages the latest ML advancements to optimize LLM inference latency for classification tasks. However, Tabi is only optimized for discriminative models (such as text recognition models) within the service framework, i.e., non-generative LLMs (GPT [9], GLM [10]). Gunasekaran et al. proposed Cocktail [14], a cost-effective ensemble-based model service framework aimed at providing highly accurate predictions with minimal latency and reducing deployment costs in public cloud environments. Cocktail consists of two key components: **1)** a dynamic model selection framework that reduces the number of models in the ensemble while meeting accuracy and latency requirements, **2)** an adaptive resource management framework that employs a distributed proactive auto-scaling strategy to allocate resources efficiently to models. Although Cocktail focuses on model selection, it is more centered on ensemble learning rather than selecting individual models for inference. Seo et al. [15] proposed an SLO-aware inference scheduler for heterogeneous processors on edge platforms. While it addresses the issue of selecting appropriate model services for inference

---

[2] https://developer.nvidia.com/triton-inference-server.

tasks, the models discussed are only small traditional deep learning models and do not consider large models.

Our work, UELLM, is significantly different from S^3 and Morphling. **1)** Compared to S^3, firstly, S^3 recognizes the issues faced by batching but focuses solely on reducing inference latency and improving utilization. In contrast, UELLM considers factors like SLO in addition to those addressed by S^3 and proposes more diverse scheduling algorithms that support customization for different scheduling objectives. Secondly, S^3 does not consider efficient model deployment, whereas UELLM uses dynamic programming to optimize resource allocation during LLM deployment. Thirdly, while both S^3 and UELLM fine-tune LLMs for predicting output length, UELLM employs online learning, which is better suited for the real-time tasks faced by LLM inference services. **2)** Compared to Morphling, UELLM uses simpler and more varied deployment algorithms to efficiently deploy LLMs, whereas Morphling employs more complex and singular meta-learning to find the optimal deployment configuration. Additionally, Morphling generates multiple possible configurations and stress tests them simultaneously, greatly increasing system resource usage. In UELLM, only one configuration is generated at a time, and supports dynamic scaling.

4 System Design

In this section, we present the detailed design of UELLM, a unified LLM inference serving resource scheduling architecture comprising three main components: **1)** the *resource profiler*, **2)** the *batch scheduler*, and **3)** the *LLM deployer*. The primary framework is illustrated in Fig. 2.

4.1 Resource Profiler

Before scheduling, each request undergoes processing by the *resource profiler*, which consists of three primary modules: data collection, output length prediction, and resource profiling. For predicting the length of inference requests, we draw inspiration from S^3 [6] and fine-tune the large model ChatGLM3-6B [10] to categorize the output lengths. The model is fine-tuned on the representative Q&A dataset Alpaca[3], using questions as inputs and the token length of the answers as labels. Our observations indicate that the predictor accurately predicted the buckets with a precision of 99.51%. Furthermore, we evaluate our predictor on established datasets such as the Google Natural-Question dataset (See footnote 1) and the Alpaca GPT-4 dataset[4], where it consistently achieved an accuracy exceeding 80%.

---

[3] https://ai.google.com/research/NaturalQuestions.
[4] https://github.com/tatsu-lab/stanford_alpaca.

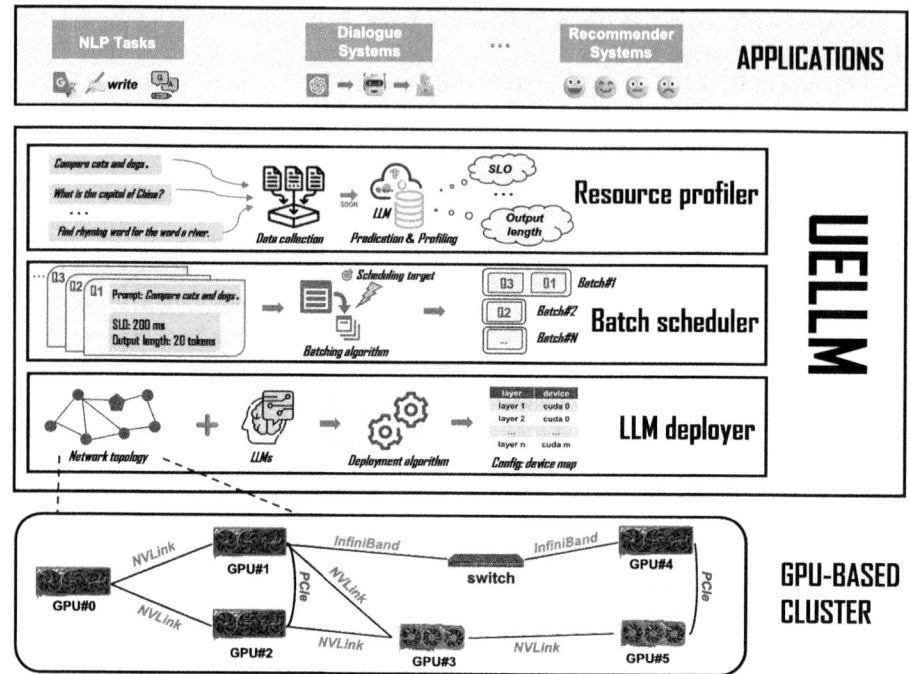

Fig. 2. The main framework and functional details of UELLM.

4.2 Batch Scheduler

Assume a $batch = \{q_1, q_2, ..., q_b\}$ contains b queries, where each query q_i indexed by i has input and output lengths denoted as $Input_i$ and $Output_i$. The premise of model batching is to ensure that the lengths of all inputs are equal. Hence, prior to making inferences, each query will be padded to $\max_{i=1}^{b}(Input_i)$ to achieve uniform length, leading to increased memory usage as a result of padding. During the inference phase, the model needs to populate all outputs in the batch to $O = \max_{i=1}^{b}(Output_i)$. Thus the total number of generated tokens during inference is $b \times O$. In contrast to the substantial memory consumption associated with generating a large KV Cache, the memory occupied by batching itself is minimal [5]. As Fig. 3 shows, there are three queries: $query\#1$, $query\#2$, $query\#3$ to be scheduled, the default batching will batching these queries into a single batch, which will require 6 paddings and 174 tokens. Notably, for $query\#2$ and $query\#3$, numerous redundant tokens are generated. While UELLM will batching the three queries into two batches: $batch\#2$ and $batch\#3$, requiring only 2 paddings, generating 74 tokens and reducing the number of redundant tokens significantly. Since the number of tokens is roughly proportional to the computational and memory overhead, this reduction diminishes inference latency and memory usage. The efficacy of UELLM is validated in Sect. 5.

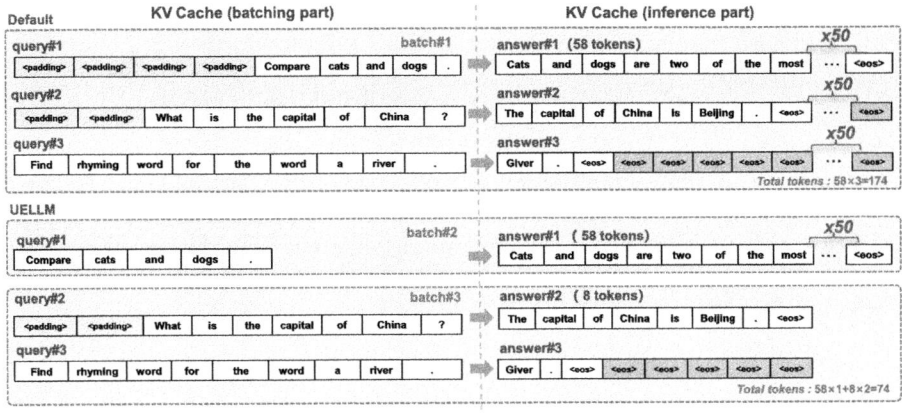

Fig. 3. Comparison between UELLM and the default batching algorithm. The comparison illustrates the utilization of the KV Cache in both the batching and inference stages for three queries. UELLM focuses on optimizing token usage, leading to a notable decrease in the overall number of tokens processed during inference in comparison to the default method.

In UELLM, the *batch scheduler* plays a crucial role in batching inference requests following profiling into suitable batch for subsequent LLM inference. The primary objective of the *batch scheduler* is to minimize latency, optimize memory usage, and prevent SLO violations during the batching process of these queries. To attain this objective, we introduced the SLO-ODBS algorithm 1, which is based on the resource utilization characteristics during LLM inference, while considering both the inference latency and SLO requirements. Furthermore, to prevent excessive delays and overhead caused by the algorithm's execution, we have streamlined its design while ensuring its effectiveness. SLO-ODBS receives a sequence of inference requests from the resource profiler and outputs batches. The algorithm can be divided into three stages: **1)** the initialization phase (lines 1–4), **2)** the combining single batches based on output phase (lines 5–19), and **3)** the sorting all combined batches (lines 20–23).

In stage **1)**, all requests are initially sorted in ascending order according to their SLO and a set of parameters is initialized.

In stage **2)**, we first maintain the properties of the current batch to be combined, denoted as $batch_c$: the current maximum latency L_{CM}, the current maximum output length O_{CM}, and the current maximum composite metric CM. Therefore, the total latency T_l can be defined as:

$$T_l = \sum_{i=1}^{N} ((SLO_i + L_{CM}) \times (|\text{batch}_c| + 1) \times L_1), \quad (1)$$

and total output length T_o can be denoted as:

$$T_o = \sum_{i=1}^{N} ((Length_i + O_{CM}) \times (|\text{bacth}_c| + 1) \times L_2). \quad (2)$$

Among them, N represents the number of queries in the $batch_c$ and $L1, L2$ represent the additional overhead due to parallel computing. Therefore, our optimization objective mainly considers two aspects: the total latency T_l and the total output length T_o. We use weights w_1 and w_2 to balance the importance of these two factors:

$$\max_{w_1, w_2} (w_1 \times T_l + w_2 \times T_o) \leq Threshold. \quad (3)$$

To optimize system performance, it is necessary to ensure that the total sum $Total$ of the batch does not exceed the threshold T after adding each request: Total $\leq$ T. This approach allows the request sequence to be reassembled into $batch_1, batch_2, ..., batch_n$.

Algorithm 1: SLO and Output-Driven Dynamic Batch Scheduler (SLO-ODBS)

Input: *requests*: A list of requests after profiling
Output: *batches*: A list of batch

1 **Procedure** SLO-ODBS(*requests*):
2    $sorted\_requests \leftarrow \text{sort}(requests)$; ▷ Sort by SLO in ascending order
3    $batches, batch_c \leftarrow \emptyset$;
4    $L_{CM}, O_{CM}, CM \leftarrow 0$;
5   **for** q *in* $sorted\_requests$ **do**
6       $T_l \leftarrow (q.SLO + L_{CM}) \times (len(batch_c) + 1) \times L1$;
7       $T_o \leftarrow (q.length - O_{CM}) \times (len(batch_c) + 1) \times L2$;
8       $Total \leftarrow w_1 \times Latency\_total + w_2 \times Length\_total$;
9   **if** $batch_c = \emptyset$ **or** $Total \leq Threshold$ **then**
10          $batch_c.append(q.index)$;
11          $L_{CM} \leftarrow \max(L_{CM}, q.SLO)$;
12          $O_{CM} \leftarrow \max(O_{CM}, q.length)$;
13          $CM \leftarrow \max(CM, w_1 \times q.length + w_2 \times q.SLO)$;
14   **else**
15          $batches.append(batch_c)$;
16          $batch_c \leftarrow \{q.index\}$;
17          $L_{CM} \leftarrow q.SLO$;
18          $O_{CM} \leftarrow q.length$;
19          $CM \leftarrow w_1 \times q.length + w_2 \times q.SLO$;
20   Dynamically adjust $batch\_size$ according to the value of CM;
21   **if** $batch_c \neq \emptyset$ **then**
22       $batches.append(batch_c)$;
23   **return** $batches$;

In stage **3)**, we combine the batches obtained in stage **2)** into a ready list $batches = \{batch_1, batch_2, ..., batch_n\}$ for subsequent batch processing.

Based on the SLO-ODBS algorithm, different scheduling objectives can be addressed by adjusting the values of w_1 and w_2. Specifically, when $w_1 = 0$, we developed the SLO Dynamic Batch Schedule (SLO-DBS) algorithm to reduce the SLO violation rate by efficiently arranging inference requests. Conversely, when $w_2 = 0$, we designed the Output-Driven Dynamic Batch Schedule (ODBS) algorithm to minimize inference latency by skillfully merging requests based on the predicted output length.

4.3 LLM Deployer

The *LLM deployer* mainly starts during the LLM deployment phase. It arranges the layers of the LLM according to the topology of the current system's hardware accelerators and the computational characteristics of each LLM layer. This process establishes a suitable device mapping to allocate each LLM layer to appropriate hardware accelerators, thereby achieving the objectives of enhancing hardware utilization and reducing latency. Specifically, it can be defined as follows: given a hardware network represented by a graph $G = (D, E)$, where $D = \{d_1, d_2, \ldots, d_n\}$ is a set of hardware devices, and E is the set of edges connecting the hardware. The large model llm_i has memory requirements $M(llm_i)$ and the number of required layers $Layer(llm_i)$. Each node d_i possesses the following attributes: $Memory(d_i)$ denotes the available memory at node d_i, and $performance(d_i)$ represents the computational capacity of node d_i. The objective is to find a device allocation scheme $S \subseteq D$ that minimizes processing time while satisfying memory constraint:

$$\sum_{i=1}^{|S|} \text{Memory}(d_i) \geq M. \tag{4}$$

It is straightforward to see that this problem is a dynamic programming problem. Based on this, we designed the HELR as shown in Algorithm 2. This algorithm is capable of ascertaining the most effective configuration for the deployment of an LLM, considering the current cluster node topology and the specific LLM intended for deployment. The algorithm is divided into three parts: **1)** the initialization phase (lines 1–2), **2)** the dynamic programming phase (lines 3–15), and **3)** the device map update phase (lines 16–19).

In stage **1)**, some necessary parameters are set and obtain the current model information and cluster topology structure.

In stage **2)**, a two-dimensional array dp is maintained, where $dp[mark][i]$ denotes the Minimal latency from the initial state to the device node d_i and $Performance(d)$ denotes processing performance of device d. The dynamic programming recurrence relation can be expressed as:

$$\text{dp}[mark][i] = \min_{1 \leq j \leq |S|} \left(dp[mark][i], dp[i][j] + Latency(E[i][j]) + p \times \frac{layers[i] \times m}{performance(i)} \right). \tag{5}$$

Therefore, our goal is to minimize latency:

$$\min_{1 \leq i \leq |S|} \left(dp[2^k - 1][i] + \sum_{j=1}^{|S|} \left(Latency(E[i][j]) + p \times \frac{layers[i] \times m}{performance(i)} \right) \right), \quad (6)$$

where $layers[i]$ represents the number of layers assigned to device node d_i, $Latency(E[i][j])$ represents the communication delay between device node d_i and d_j, and p adjusts processing performance-time relationship. The algorithm updates the array dp and the current state using Eq. (5).

In stage **3)**, the optimal allocation state $best\_state$ is recorded to ensure the best possible utilization of resources. The $Device\_map$ is then updated using the information from $layers$ and S. This update process ensures that the deployment configuration reflects the optimal state, leading to improved efficiency and performance in the subsequent stages.

Similar to the batch processing algorithm, different deployment objectives can be achieved by adjusting the values of a_1 and a_2 in the HELR algorithm. Due to the sequential nature of inference, deploying on the minimum number of GPUs possible can effectively improve GPU utilization. Therefore, to optimize GPU utilization, setting a_1 to 0 while updating the dp array can significantly

---

Algorithm 2: High-Efficiency Low-Latency Resource Allocation Algorithm (HELR)

Input: M: Memory requirement of LLM, $Layer(M)$: Number of layers in the large model M
$G(D, E)$: Graph representing the hardware platform, E: Connections between various nodes
D: Hardware device nodes, $Latency(E[i][j])$: Communication latency between node i and node j
$Performance(d)$: Processing performance of device d, $Memory(d)$: Available memory of device d
Output: $Device\_map$: Mapping of layers to devices

1 **Procedure** HELR($M, Layer(M), G(D,E), E, D, Latency(E[i][j]), Performance(d), Memory(d)$):
2   Initialize $best\_state \leftarrow \infty$, Initialize $Device\_map \leftarrow \emptyset$;
3   **for** each n from 1 to $|D|$ **do**
4   S_n is the subset of D with size n;
5   **if** the total memory of nodes in S_n is more than M **then**
6   skip to the next subset;
7   Initialize $dp[mark][i] \leftarrow \infty$;
8   **for** each $mark$ from 1 to $2^n - 1$ **do**
9   Sort the nodes in S_n in descending order by performance and memory;
10   Calculate the memory per layer $m \leftarrow \frac{M}{Layer(M)}$;
11   **for** each i from 1 to $|S_n|$ **do**
12   **for** each j from 1 to $|S_n|$ where $j \neq i$ **do**
                         // T is the memory reserved for KV Cache
13   Calculate the maximum layers assignable to node i:
                       $layers[i] \leftarrow \min(Layer(M), \frac{Memory(i)-T}{m})$;
14   Calculate the latency l using the formula:
                       $l = dp[i][j] + Latency(E[i][j]) + p \times \frac{layers[i] \times m}{Performance(i)}$;
15   Update $dp[mark][i] \leftarrow \min(dp[mark][i], l)$;
16          $current\_state \leftarrow \min(dp[2^n - 1][i] + \sum_{j=1}^{|S_n|}(Latency(E[i][j]) + p \times \frac{layers[i] \times m}{Performance(i)}))$;
17   **if** $current\_state < best\_state$ **then**
18              $best\_state \leftarrow current\_state$;
19   Update $Device\_map$ with $layers$ and nodes in S_n;
20   **return** $Device\_map$;

enhance utilization. This configuration of a_1 forms the High-Efficiency Resource Allocation (HE) algorithm, which is suitable for environments with limited resources. Conversely, to fulfill the minimum latency requirement without considering expenses, the weight of a_1 can be increased. For example, setting a_1 to 10:1 establishes the Low-Latency Resource Allocation (LR) algorithm, which prioritizes latency by assigning a high weight to a_1.

5 Implementation and Evaluations

5.1 Evaluation Setup

Testbed. We use a local cluster (consisting of 4 Nvidia RTX 3090 GPUs) as the test platform for conducting extensive experiments. To differentiate GPU performance in our experiments, we set different performance limits for the GPUs, as detailed in the Table 2.

ML Models. For the LLM inference service, we select the ChatGLM2-6B [10], which is currently stable and widely recognized, to perform inference tasks. As the ChatGLM2-6B model lacked batch inference capabilities at the time, we make adjustments to its inference code to enable batch processing for future experiments.

SLO. In our experiments, we define the SLO as the requirement for an inference request to receive a complete answer within a certain time frame. To better approximate real-world scenarios, we designed different SLOs for different inference requests, ranging from 1 s to 350 s, ensuring that each inference request's SLO is completely random.

Resource Monitoring. Furthermore, it is essential to maintain continuous real-time monitoring of individual GPUs within the cluster, focusing on metrics such as GPU utilization, GPU memory usage, and the execution time of inference programs. To achieve this, we utilized Nvidia's interfaces to develop a script capable of real-time monitoring of GPU information across the cluster.

Table 2. Cluster network topology. There are three different types of connections: 1) X = Self, 2) PIX = Connection traversing at most a single PCIe bridge, and 3) NODE = Connection traversing PCIe as well as the interconnect between PCIe Host Bridges within a NUMA node.

	GPU#0	GPU#1	GPU#2	GPU#3	Maximum power
GPU#0	X	PIX	NODE	NODE	350 W
GPU#1	PIX	X	NODE	NODE	300 W
GPU#2	NODE	NODE	X	PIX	250 W
GPU#3	NODE	NODE	PIX	X	150 W

5.2 Baselines and Metrics

Baselines. We construct three versions of the UELLM prototype on a local cluster: 1) UELLM-deploy (UD), which only uses the HELR model deployment algorithm. 2) UELLM-batch (UB), which uses the SLO-ODBS batching algorithm. 3) UELLM-all (UA), which employs both the HELR model deployment algorithm and the SLO-ODBS batching algorithm. Currently, there are almost no systems similar to ours, so we chose the current SOTA method Morphling (Mor) [1] and the batching algorithm in S^3 [6] as our baselines for comparison with UD, UB, and UA.

Metrics. We adopt four widely used metrics to evaluate performance: 1) **Latency**, denoting the time taken for the system to respond to a request, encompassing the duration from request initiation to the commencement of processing and result delivery. Lower latency enhances the user experience of LLM inference services. 2) **Throughput**, quantified by the number of tokens processed per second. Higher throughput means the system capacity to manage requests or data within a specific timeframe, thereby improving overall processing efficiency. 3) **GPU utilization**, where high utilization typically indicates efficient execution of computational tasks, while low utilization may suggest underutilized resources or bottlenecks necessitating further optimization. 4) **SLO violation**, a crucial metric for assessing user experience. A lower default rate generally signifies a stable and dependable service, leading to higher user satisfaction. Conversely, a high default rate can result in diminished user experience or even user attrition.

5.3 Experiment Analyses

To minimize randomness, each experiment was repeated 5 times, and each data point in Fig. 4 and Fig. 5 represents the average of these 5 trials. Before conducting the main experiments, we validated the effectiveness and advancement of the batching algorithms and LLM deployment algorithms by two comparisons: **1)** We compared SLO-ODBS, SLO-DBS, and ODBS with the default batching algorithm (FIFO) on scheduling metrics: latency and SLO violation rate. **2)** We compared LR, HE, and HELR with the baseline deployment algorithm, Basic Greedy Scheduling Algorithm (BGS), on deployment metrics: throughput and GPU utilization. Figure 4a and Fig. 4b show that under high request loads, by reasonably combining requests, SLO-ODBS reduces the number of iterations and memory overhead, maintaining low latency similar to the ODBS. At the same time, SLO-ODBS schedules requests according to SLOs, achieving a low SLO violation rate close to the SLO-DBS. Because HELR selects more reasonable resource allocation and deployment methods, Fig. 4c and Fig. 4d show that HELR maintains utilization close to HE while achieving throughput similar to the LR.

Figure 5 compares the differences between UELLM and the SOTA algorithms S^3 and Morphling across various metrics. Figure 5a illustrates the comparison of GPU utilization, showing the average results of the algorithms over five different time periods. It is observed that due to S^3 and UB focusing solely on batch scheduling, their GPU utilization is significantly lower compared to other baselines, indicating inefficiency in resource utilization. Morphling uses meta-learning

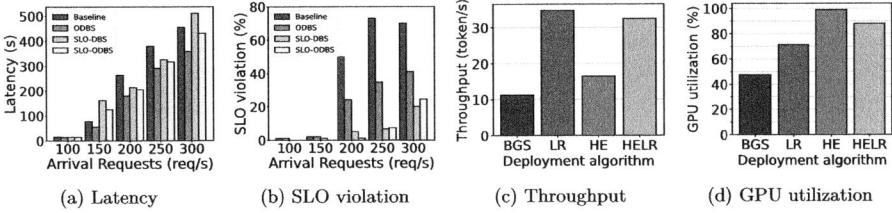

Fig. 4. Performance comparison of different batching algorithms and deployment algorithms. (a) Latency, (b) SLO violation under various batching algorithms, while (c) Throughput, and (d) GPU utilization under different deployment algorithms.

to search for the optimal configuration and conducts stress testing, while UA and UD use the HELR algorithm to select the best resource configuration based on the current node topology and model characteristics. Therefore, the results of these three are very close. Overall, UELLM can achieve deployment effects similar to Morphling with lower costs.

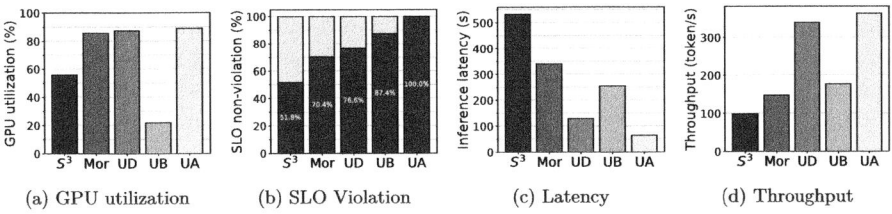

Fig. 5. Comparison results of various metrics between S^3, Morphling, UD, UB, and UA. Metrics include (a) GPU utilization, (b) SLO non-violation, (c) inference latency, and (d) throughput.

Figure 5b describes the comparison of SLO violation rates. UB, using only the SLO-ODBS batching algorithm with the default deployment algorithm, can meet the SLO for 87.4% of requests, serving as a baseline for analyzing the performance of the other four algorithms. Compared to UB, S^3 only considers memory optimization without considering the SLO of each request and deployment strategy, resulting in the poorest performance. The results of Morphling and UD are almost identical because both only consider deployment strategies without considering the SLOs of different requests. Although their inference delays are lower in Fig. 5d, they still have a higher SLO violation rate compared to UB. UA represents the optimal state of UELLM, considering both SLO and deployment strategy. Thus, in five experiments, UA meets the SLO for all requests, achieving the best performance. Overall, compared to S^3 and Morphling, UELLM optimizes the SLO violation rate by 29.6% to 48.2%.

Figure 5c and Fig. 5d describe the comparison of inference latency and throughput, both metrics indicating the inference speed of the system, and are thus discussed together. We use S^3 and Morphling as benchmarks to analyze the performance of the other three algorithms. Compared to Morphling, UD without the need for stress testing, which in turn reduces stress testing time, leading to lower overall inference latency and improved throughput. Compared to S^3, UD optimizes resource allocation, improving utilization and communication latency, significantly reducing inference latency. Compared to Morphling and S^3, UB uses the SLO-ODBS algorithm to optimize batch combinations, reducing iterations, lowering inference latency, and improving throughput. UA shows the best performance because it reduces latency and improves throughput from both reasonable batch combination and resource allocation dimensions. UA uses the HELR algorithm to optimize resource allocation and the SLO-ODBS algorithm to optimize batch combinations, achieving the best results in five experiments. Overall, compared to S^3 and Morphling, UELLM reduces the inference latency by 72.3% to 90.3% and improves throughput by 1.92× to 4.98×.

6 Conclusion

In this paper, we propose UELLM, a framework that integrates request batching and LLM deployment. UELLM is designed to maximize throughput, reduce inference latency, lower SLO violation rates, and minimize memory wastage. We introduce the HELR LLM deployment algorithm and the SLO-ODBS batching algorithm. The SLO-ODBS algorithm optimizes batch composition, while HELR optimizes resource utilization during deployment, ensuring that UELLM maintains high-quality service in terms of inference latency, throughput, and SLO violation rates. Our experiments demonstrate that UELLM outperforms the state-of-the-art in efficiently utilizing resources and reducing SLO violation rates. This approach has the potential to significantly enhance the efficiency and reliability of LLM-based inference services in cloud computing environments.

Acknowledgments. This work is supported by the National Natural Science Foundation of China (No. 62102408, 62072451, 92267105), Guangdong Basic and Applied Basic Research Foundation (No. 2024A1515010251, 2023B1515130002), Shenzhen Basic Research Program under grants JCYJ20240809180935001, and Shenzhen Industrial Application Projects of undertaking the National key R & D Program of China (No. CJGJZD20210408091600002).

Software Availability. The codes have been open-sourced to https://github.com/HYIUYOU/UELLM for research usage.

References

1. Wang, L., et al.: Morphling: fast, near-optimal auto-configuration for cloud-native model serving. In: Proceedings of the ACM Symposium on Cloud Computing (SoCC 21), 2021, pp. 639–653. https://doi.org/10.1145/3472883.3486987
2. Wu, C.-J., et al.: Sustainable ai: Environmental implications, challenges and opportunities. In: Proceedings of Machine Learning and Systems (MLSys 22), vol. 4, 2022, pp. 795–813 (2022)

3. Crankshaw, D., Wang, X., Zhou, G., Franklin, M.J., Gonzalez, J.E., Stoica, I.: Clipper: a Low-Latency online prediction serving system. In: 14th USENIX Symposium on Networked Systems Design and Implementation (NSDI 17), Mar. 2017, pp. 613–627. https://www.usenix.org/conference/nsdi17/technical-sessions/presentation/crankshaw
4. Zhang, C., Yu, M., Wang, W., Yan, F.: MArk: exploiting cloud services for Cost-Effective, SLO-Aware machine learning inference serving. In: 2019 USENIX Annual Technical Conference (USENIX ATC 19), Jul. 2019, pp. 1049–1062. https://www.usenix.org/conference/atc19/presentation/zhang-chengliang
5. Kwon, W., et al.: Efficient memory management for large language model serving with pagedattention. In: Proceedings of the 29th Symposium on Operating Systems Principles (SOSP 23), pp. 611–626 (2023)
6. Jin, Y., Wu, C.-F., Brooks, D., Wei, G.-Y.: s^3: increasing gpu utilization during generative inference for higher throughput. In: Advances in Neural Information Processing Systems (NeurIPS 23), vol. 36, 2023, pp. 18 015–18 027 (2023)
7. Vaswani, A., et al.: Attention is all you need. In: Advances in neural information processing systems (NeurIPS 17), vol. 30 (2017)
8. Sheng, Y., et al.: Flexgen: high-throughput generative inference of large language models with a single gpu. In: International Conference on Machine Learning (ICML 23). PMLR, pp. 31 094–31 116 (2023)
9. Brown, T., et al.: Language models are few-shot learners. In: Advances in Neural Information Processing Systems 33 (NeurIPS 20), vol. 33, 2020, pp. 1877–1901 (2020). https://proceedings.neurips.cc/paper_files/paper/2020/file/1457c0d6bfcb4967418bfb8ac142f64a-Paper.pdf
10. Du, Z., et al.: GLM: general language model pretraining with autoregressive blank infilling. In: Proceedings of the 60th Annual Meeting of the Association for Computational Linguistics (ACL 22), May 2022, pp. 320–335. https://aclanthology.org/2022.acl-long.26
11. Choi, S., Lee, S., Kim, Y., Park, J., Kwon, Y., Huh, J.: Serving heterogeneous machine learning models on Multi-GPU servers with Spatio-Temporal sharing. In: 2022 USENIX Annual Technical Conference (USENIX ATC 22), Jul. 2022, pp. 199–216. https://www.usenix.org/conference/atc22/presentation/choi-seungbeom
12. Ali, A., Pinciroli, R., Yan, F., Smirni, E.: Batch: machine learning inference serving on serverless platforms with adaptive batching. In: International Conference for High Performance Computing, Networking, Storage and Analysis (SC 20), pp. 1–15. IEEE (2020)
13. Wang, Y., Chen, K., Tan, H., Guo, K.: Tabi: an efficient multi-level inference system for large language models. In: Proceedings of the Eighteenth European Conference on Computer Systems (EuroSys 23), pp. 233–248 (2023). https://doi.org/10.1145/3552326.3587438
14. Gunasekaran, J.R., Mishra, C.S., Thinakaran, P., Sharma, B., Kandemir, M.T., Das, C.R.: Cocktail: a multidimensional optimization for model serving in cloud. In: 19th USENIX Symposium on Networked Systems Design and Implementation (NSDI 22), pp. 1041–1057, April 2022. https://www.usenix.org/conference/nsdi22/presentation/gunasekaran
15. Seo, W., Cha, S., Kim, Y., Huh, J., Park, J.: Slo-aware inference scheduler for heterogeneous processors in edge platforms. In: ACM Trans. Architecture Code Optim. (TACO 21) 18(4), 1–26 (2021)

Service-Oriented Requirements Elicitation Through Systematic Questionnaire Design: A Problem-Driven GenAI Approach

Julie Rauer[1]([✉]), To Kim Bao Pham[1], Sam Supakkul[2], Tom Hill[1], and Lawrence Chung[1]

[1] University of Texas at Dallas, 800 W. Campbell Road, Richardson, TX 75080-3021, USA
{jrr053000,Bao.PhamTo,tlh019200,Chung}@utdallas.edu
[2] NCR Voyix Corporation, 864 Spring St NW, Atlanta, GA 30308, USA
Sam.Supakkul@ncrvoyix.com

Abstract. Service-oriented requirements elicitation emphasizes understanding and addressing stakeholder needs. As a critical phase in software development, it relies heavily on clear and effective communication with stakeholders. One valuable tool for facilitating this communication is the questionnaire. However, the challenge lies in the fact that there are an infinite number of potential questions that could be asked. Often, critical questions are forgotten or omitted, leading to incomplete requirements. Additionally, wrong questions or poorly phrased questions can result in incorrect requirements. To address these challenges, we leverage GenAI to identify well-written, critical questions. In our proposed Problem-Driven GenAI Requirements Elicitation Process, question formulation and requirements gathering are systematic, iterative, incremental, and interleaving. Our approach focuses on the four key dimensions of Requirements Engineering (RE): Functional Requirements/Non-Functional Requirements, Problem/Solution, Product/Process, and Stakeholder. Taking the cross-product of these four dimensions, we delineate 24 distinct sectors. In order to ask the right questions and the right number of questions, we use GenAI to conduct experiments that systematically generate questions across these sectors. This process helps uncover critical questions for the development of Theia, an indoor navigation system designed for visually impaired individuals. As part of our evaluation, we compare student-generated questions for Theia with those created by ChatGPT 4.0, under the guidance of Requirements Engineers. The questions are then assessed based on desirable properties of questioning. In our limited studies, we find that our problem-driven GenAI approach reduces the occurrence of omitted and wrong questions by 54.45%, depending on the sector. We believe this approach is important as it helps narrow down the infinite number of potential questions and helps address critical questions.

Keywords: Service-Oriented Requirements Elicitation · RE Dimensions · Problem-Driven · Generative AI (GenAI) · Systematic Questionnaires

1 Introduction

Providing **good service** is important for just about any software system. So, we ask questions to find out what the stakeholders' needs are, then ask more questions to find out the requirements. During RE, we use a questionnaire for elicitation. It is crucial to understand that manual question construction is a complex process requiring training, expertise, and resources [2]. One important technique involves asking the 'right' questions to identify requirements [19,23]. However, this can be challenging because it's difficult to know what the 'right' question is. An essential question, can potentially cause project failure or even loss of life if not asked. For many years, poor software requirements gathering has been the leading cause of project failures, accounting for 39.03% in 2023 [10,14]. There are various concerns when developing service requirements: service stakeholders, responsibilities, service performance metrics, resolution of conflicting stakeholder service requirements, and stakeholder acceptance of service change [16]. Questionnaires [4] are used to validate the identified problems from engineers working on service oriented projects.

Our main focus, **Problem-Driven Service-Oriented Requirements Elicitation (SO-REL)**, is an essential activity since its output, the requirements, serve as the foundation upon which the application is built. To develop a comprehensive set of requirements, we ask questions and we have identify and use the four dimensions of RE. A dimension is a perspective; a particular attitude toward or way of regarding something; point of view.

Our **problem-driven approach** starts with asking questions about the problem. To gather a good set of requirements, we often need to change our perspective, **dimension**, look at many different points of view of the problem. We start SO-REL by getting the users point of view and asking questions. We create a questionnaire which addresses the **problem from every possible angle** that we can find, addressing dimensions. We ask for second opinions, follow-up questions, hoping that we'll see what others might have missed, **omissions**, or mistakes people have made, **commissions**. Forgotten or omitted questions are **omissions** and wrong questions are **commissions**.

An omission in questionnaire design occurs when a questionnaire does not contain enough questions belonging to a relevant dimension. For example, a questionnaire is created to survey the pedestrians about walking on campus at night. The purpose of the **questionnaire** is to determine the **problems** with walking at night and how to improve it for students on campus. Questions can range from Problem-NF (How do you feel about walking on campus at night?) to Solution-F (What features can improve the safety of pedestrians on campus at night?). If the questionnaire does not contain questions about Problem-Functional dimension, then there is an omission. Omissions causes purely captured sets of requirements, leading to a cascade of incompleteness errors in designs and implementations. The RE dimensions (Sect. 3) in our approach allow us to identify omissions in essential categories. The omission and commission problems are addressed by our problem-driven approach, but to effectively execute this approach would still require some ideas, skills and domain knowledge that are addressed by the use of GenAI.

We leverage **GenAI** to suggest quality questions by providing GenAI **desirable properties of questions**. We employ Experienced Requirements Engineers to generate ChatGPT questions with the hope that GenAI would reduce the time and cost of generating questionnaires. We find that this approach enables more comprehensive questionnaires, making them a more viable option for interviews. Using GenAI, we formulate open-ended questions to gain deeper understanding of the problem and mechanisms [12], then design and build a questionnaire. At this point we start defining the requirements, too.

This paper is organized as follows: Sect. 2 presents the Related Work, Sect. 3 is the Dimensions of RE, Sect. 4 is our Problem-Driven Approach (2 Composite patterns) and Proposed Requirements Elicitation Process (To-Be), Sect. 5 Experimentation, Sect. 6 Discussion, Sect. 7 Threats to Validity, and Sect. 8 Conclusion.

2 Related Work and Motivations

2.1 Problem-Driven

The problem-driven approach is the main motivation for this paper. Problems drive the concepts and steps; concepts are the dimensions. Questions are asked about the concepts. A problem-driven approach focuses on identifying and addressing specific problems as the primary driver of all subsequent actions and decisions. We break down our problem into smaller, more manageable sub-problems [21]. Each sub-problem focuses on a specific aspect of the main challenge and provides a more detailed understanding of what needs to be addressed. This approach ensures that the solutions developed are directly aligned with real-world needs and challenges.

2.2 Goals and Questions

The GQM (Goal/Question/Metric) approach is based upon the assumption that for an organization to measure in a purposeful way it must first specify the goals for itself and its projects, then it must trace those goals to the products, processes and resources [5]. Goals act as the criteria for the notion of "good enough" and drive the process of SO-REL, in terms of, among other things, questions that are tailored to the difficulties of blind individual and the services they might benefit from [19]. Software development requires a measurement mechanism for feedback and evaluation [5]. Measurement is a mechanism for creating a corporate memory and an aid in answering a variety of questions associated with the enactment of any software process [5].

2.3 Questionnaire

Questionnaire has long been mentioned in the SO-REL landscape. The questionnaire technique is thought of as more of a survey than an interview. The assumed difference is that prepared questionnaires are to be distributed to a large amount of people and allow them to respond by themselves. However, the definition of the questionnaire technique for our context refers to a questionnaire as a guide for an in person interview with stakeholders. This technique can also be referred as structured interview in literature. Questionnaire began gaining traction as a verbal reporting technique to observe knowledge [3]. Surveys on SO-REL techniques such as [11,15,18] pointed out both structured interview and questionnaire as effective SO-REL techniques. This makes questionnaire an important area of research to improve SO-REL. Recent work on SO-REL involving questionnaire such as [22] proposed a framework for questionnaire design based on socio-technical concepts. Another such work is a framework that was created for SO-REL using a questionnaire-driven approach, developing a focused, usable questionnaire to derive requirements [19]. These works proposed the structure and underlying theories for systematic questionnaire design for SO-REL, which our study aims to improve upon by utilizing GenAI. Overall, questionnaire is a traditional but effective technique which can benefit from adopting the recent advancements in GenAI technology.

2.4 GenAI in Requirements Engineering

Large language models (LLMs) have made a substantial impact across various domains, including requirements engineering. However, the understanding of their use, impact, and potential limitations in this field is still evolving and remains in its early stages. In our study of related work, we analyze the role of LLMs, such as ChatGPT, in requirements engineering-an essential area in software development that is rapidly advancing due to artificial intelligence. An exploration [8] into the use of ChatGPT in creating goal models, assessing how much knowledge ChatGPT retains about goal modeling, testing whether it can generate a complete goal model, and evaluating how immediate feedback affects the quality of the resulting models. An investigation [24] into the effectiveness of ChatGPT as a software development assistant across different phases of the software development lifecycle, particularly in student-led projects. An examination [26] of the potential of ChatGPT for automating software requirements engineering tasks by analyzing and evaluating the quality of questions generated by ChatGPT for eliciting software requirements. Here's an emphasis [17] on the importance of agile methodologies in software development, particularly the concept of user stories. The studies [1] explore the zero-shot learning capabilities of LLMs in three requirements classification tasks: functional/non-functional (FR/NFR) binary classification, NFR classification, and binary security requirement classification. This approach is noteworthy because it eliminates the need for training data typically required by other machine learning techniques. Another exploration [20] into the use of LLMs in requirements elicitation, leveraging prompt engineering to generate requirements based on a questionnaire created by researchers. These generated requirements are combined with expert-derived requirements and evaluated by a panel of experts.

3 Metamodel of Requirements Engineering

3.1 Requirements Engineering Dimensions

We have identified four Dimensions of RE and used them to discover questions and corresponding requirements. The dimensions include: Product/Process, P, Functional Requirements (FRs)/Non-Functional Requirements (NFRs), X, Problem/Solution, Y, and Stakeholder (Users/Developers/Owners), Z. The Sectors, N, are calculated by taking the cross product of the dimensions:

$$P * Q * Y * Z = N \tag{1}$$

P = 2, Q = 2, Y = 2, Z = 3, therefore, 2 * 2 * 2 * 3 = 24 sectors

3.2 Dimensions of Requirements Engineering: Metamodel Diagram

Asking questions, we rule things out, **identify constraints** on the dimensions. We uncover **new information** while trying to solve the problem. We try to get to what's actually wrong with the product and/or the process. Our creation, Dimensions of RE metamodel diagram is similar to an ontology. Ontology is the categories of essential individual concepts, relationships between the individual concepts, constraints on individual concepts, and constraints on the relationships between individual concepts.

Categories of essential individual Concepts and their Relationships: Goal/Problem: During SO-REL, the first step is identifying the problem that the software needs to solve. Problems typically represent challenges, gaps, or obstacles that prevent the current state (As-Is) from transitioning to a desired state (To-Be). A problem might be a deficiency (something lacking) or a difficulty (something that needs to be overcome). When a problem is identified, goals are often set as a response to this problem. Goals are specific objectives or outcomes that an individual or organization aims to achieve. The goal defines the desired state or the solution to the problem. Essentially, a goal is what you aim to achieve as a resolution to the identified problem. The phrase "problem is against or inhibits the goal" implies an obstacle where a problem prevents the achievement of a goal. **Stakeholder:** The relationship between the identified problem and the set goals guides the entire elicitation process. It determines the types of questions asked, the stakeholders involved, and the information that needs to be gathered. **Problem/Process:** In the context of software development, the relationship between a problem and a process is integral to finding effective solutions. The nature of the problem dictates the following: 1.) the type of processes needed, for example, our process is questioning, 2.) the resources required, ChatGPT, 3.) the stakeholders to be involved, Owners, Developers, Engineers, Subject Matter Experts (SMEs), and Users. For example, a problem of requirements for a software

Systematic Questionnaire Design: A Problem-Driven GenAI Approach 241

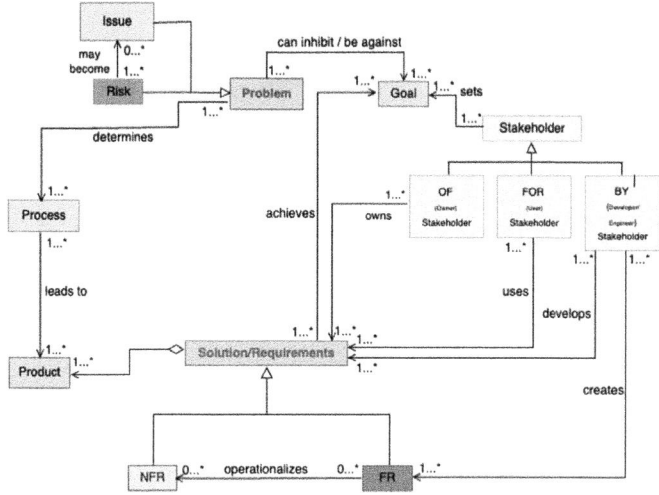

Fig. 1. Dimensions of Requirements Engineering: A Metamodel Diagram

system leads to a process that emphasizes incrementally questioning stakeholders, iteratively evaluating questions, subsequently interleaving questions and requirements gathering. Process involves executing the steps, monitoring progress, and making necessary adjustments. The effectiveness of a process is often judged by how well it addresses the problem it was designed to solve. Ultimately, the success of a process is measured by whether it resolves the problem or achieves the desired outcome, **Goal**. The end result should be that the problem no longer exists or is managed to an acceptable level, thanks to the effectiveness of the process.

Problem/Risk/Issue: Risks [13] represent potential obstacles that could impact the achievement of our goals, either positively or negatively. A risk is an uncertain event or condition that, if it materializes, could affect a project's objectives, outcomes, or performance. While risks are inherently uncertain and may not occur, they can evolve into issues. An issue is a risk that has materialized.

FR/NFR/Solution/Stakeholder: The goals derived from the problem help in formulating both FR and NFRs [9]. Functional requirements describe what the system should do (e.g., automate voice controls, obstacle detection), directly addressing the problem. For example, a functional requirement might state that the software must allow users to verbally ask for directions and generate a response providing verbal directions, one step at a time. NFRs define how the system performs certain functions, encompassing aspects such as usability and reliability. FR and NFRs guide the development of solutions. Stakeholders are people or groups who are affected by a software development project and have a vested interest in the outcome of the project. They might include Of-Stakeholder (owners), By-Stakeholder (developers, engineers), For-Stakeholder (users), etc.

Process/Product/Solution: Understanding these relationships helps in effectively navigating the complexities of SO-REL. It defines the sequence of actions and decision-making protocols that teams follow to move from concept to completion. The product is a composition of one-or-more similar products. There is one solution or set of requirements meeting stakeholder needs. The product is the end result of the software development process. Effective management of these interrelationships during SO-REL and questioning is crucial for delivering a successful solution.

4 Our Problem-Driven GenAI Approach

4.1 Problem-Driven Approach Two Composite Design Patterns

Problem (pink) and **Solution** (green) Composite Design Patterns; each a hierarchical tree structure with multiple levels. There are one or more questions in the graph. The parent or children ask one or more questions. Any problem node that is not associated with any question - omission error. If we have a question node not associated with any problem - commission error. **Key: Our problem-driven approach is an essential part of our solution because it helps narrow down the infinite number of potential questions.**

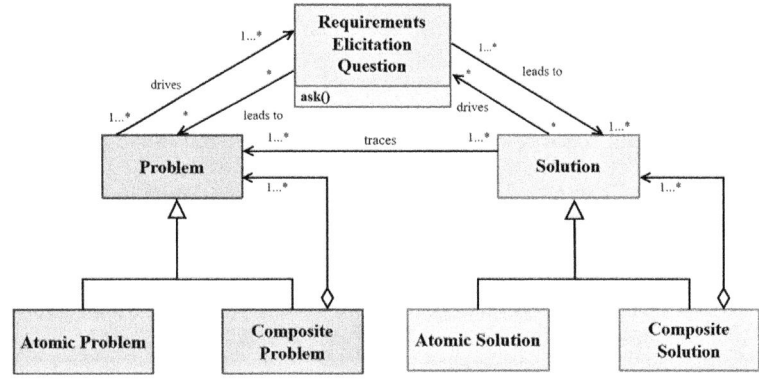

Fig. 2. Problem-Driven Approach - Composite Pattern Diagram

4.2 Proposed Problem-Driven GenAI SO-REL Process (To-Be)

We use our SO-REL process to systematically formulate a questionnaire and gather system requirements through structured, effective questioning of stakeholders. Our process emphasizes actively and iteratively asking targeted questions to draw out detailed, precise information that may not be immediately offered by the stakeholders. We incrementally add questions and requirements to our database.

4.3 Desirable Properties of Questions

Relevance: Make an idea, situation, or problem clear to someone by describing it in more detail or revealing relevant facts, provide question context. Exploring relevance and coherence for automated text scoring using multi-task learning [25]. **In-Depth:** Questions, Sub-Questions, 3 or more levels deep. **High-Value:** Meaningful questions, questions that have significance; questions that are likely to lead to answers that generate requirements and, ultimately, a success project outcome. When we ask questions that facilitate a new understanding - how something can be improved - those questions are deemed valuable. The answer provokes the generation of new/valuable requirements. **Understandable, Example Oriented:** Perceive the intended meaning of; interpret or view (something) in a particular way; Unambiguous. **Complete:** As complete as possible. **Well-Structured, Modularized:** Structure is the arrangement of - construct or arrange according to a plan; focus on the relationships between the parts or elements of the question complexities. Through understanding the problem/solution, give a pattern or organization to the question. **Begin with the end in mind - know the answer before you ask the question:** Try to know as many possible answers to the questions. **Adequate level or degree of granularity in questions, answers:** Ask follow-up questions. **Attitude: If I win - You win:** What helps you, helps me build a better software system. **Categorize:** Each question is part of a category - full coverage of a category; group questions based upon category; group questions based on open and closed. **Simplicity:** Make the questions as simple as possible, easy to understand, no big words. **Refinement:** Purified, clarified, unwanted elements having been removed by processing. **Precise:** Make the questions accurate, correct, exact. **Priority:** Assign priority to important sections of questions. **Timeliness of Questions:** Asking some questions continuously.

5 Experimentation

In order to determine if our approach does in fact reduce omissions and commissions, we conducted 2 experiments: 1 to establish the baseline omission and commission rate of questionnaires made without using this approach, and 1 to test the performance of our approach.

5.1 Experiment S (Students' Theia App Questionnaires)

Setup: In our first experiment, we want to measure the omission (omitted or left out questions) and commission (wrong questions) rates of questionnaires written

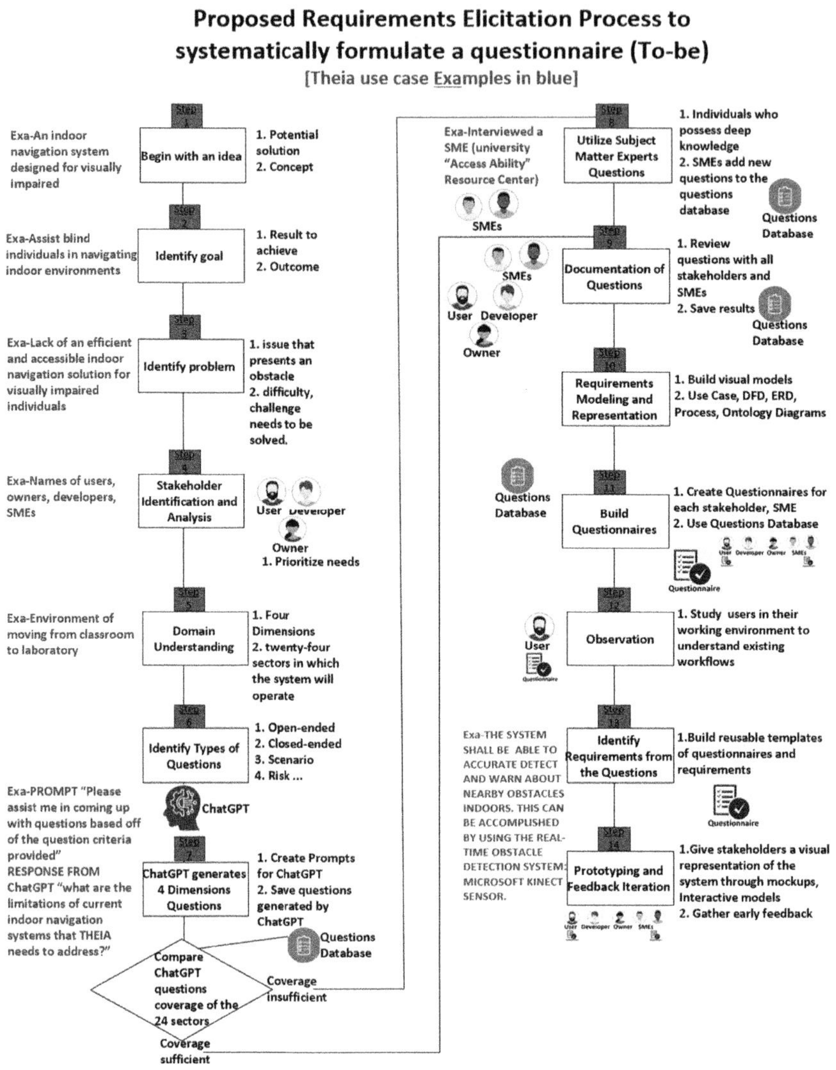

Fig. 3. Proposed Problem-Driven GenAI Requirements Elicitation Process to systematically formulate a questionnaire (To-Be). Using the Theia App example, we understand the problem we are trying to solve. We identify all the stakeholders who will have an interest in the system. Domain Understanding: recognizing the unique needs of visually impaired users, their limitations, and the challenges posed by indoor environments. We use ChatGPT to help us generate quality questions. We interleave question sessions and requirements gathering. Utilize SMEs, Subject Matter Experts, to come up with questions such as, "How did you become blind, from birth or in some other way?" This question can directly affect how the navigational system is built. Perform Requirements Modeling and Representation. Build Questionnaires: organize and prioritize questions in logical sections. Identify Requirements from the Questions. Please find the As-Is Diagram on Github with our other supporting documentation.

by students taking RE class. In order to do this, we evaluated 11 questionnaires from undergraduate and graduate RE courses at for their course project by mapping them against the sectors. The students receive training on RE and elicitation via questionnaire, but they do not receive training on the new approach. As part of the project assignment, the students are assigned the task of creating a questionnaire for requirements elicitation of stakeholders. In order to eliminate anomalies and improve quality, we only extracted questionnaires with an A grade, which resulted in 25 questionnaires. Then, we randomly picked 11 for evaluation. We by no means assume that university students are experts and that this experiment result is generalizable to the industry. The experiment is meant as a preliminary study that gives a reasonable benchmark on the omission and commission rate in elicitation questionnaires. We will have 2 PhD students in software engineering analyze the questionnaires and assign a value in a column of dimension of RE, with a total of 4 columns (Problem-Solution, FR-NFR, Product-Process, Of-By-For) for each question. There are two exceptions in the value assignment. The value in a column can be null if the question is not related to that dimension, or it could contain all the values in that dimension if the question is too general can be responded with any value. A null value on a question does not mean a question is invalid (i.e. "What is your name?" has a null value for all four dimensions). However, a question with more than one value per column is a commission, since it could be more specified. If a questionnaire does not have any questions in a combination, it is an omission.

We calculate the omission rate by looking at the coverage of the cross products. Combinations are split by stakeholders, meaning 8 sectors per stakeholder, so 8, 16, 24, and so on. Since the combinations with null values are considered valid but they are not in the combination coverage, we exclude them from the calculation. Questions that have double values in their combinations are counted as commissions. There are also commission from asking the question to the wrong stakeholder (i.e. asking an end user "What are the options of algorithms for implementing indoor navigation?").

Results: The pie chart in Fig. 4 is the summary of the combined questionnaires. There are a total of 360 questions, assigned into combinations. The most frequent categories are Solution-FR-Product-For at 16.4%, Problem-FR-Process-For at 12.1%, Problem-FR-Product-For at 9.7%, Problem-NFR-Process-For at 9.1%, and Solution-NFR-Product-For at 8.2%. The results highlight some patterns in the questionnaires. First, most of the questionnaires are aimed towards the For stakeholders, which are the users of the system. Secondly, Problem occupies the largest portion of the questions, even though Solution-FR-Product-For is the most frequent combination.

The more important finding in this experiment is the omission and commission rate of these questionnaires. Table 1 shows the detailed results of the experiment, and Table 2 shows the summary of the questionnaires, along with their average omission and commission rate. The lowest and highest omission

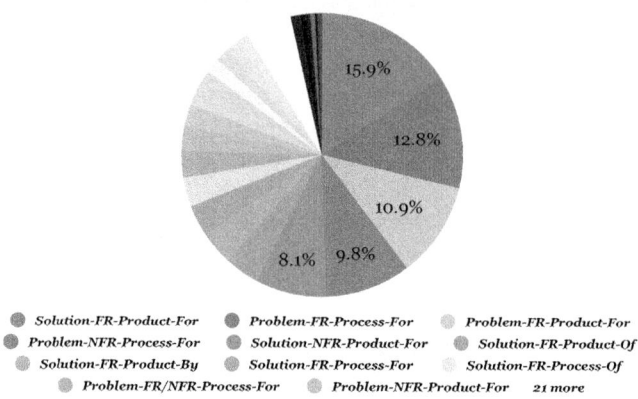

Fig. 4. Pie Chart of RE Domain Combination Distribution 2020 to 2023. The most frequent combinations have their percentage labeled

Table 1. Results of students' questionnaires. OR is Omission Rate, and CR is Commission Rate. Stakeholders column denotes who the questionnaire is designed for.

QID	No. Questions	Stakeholders	Omissions	OR	Commissions	CR
1	23	For-Of	8	50.00%	3	13.04%
2	32	For	2	25.00%	6	18.75%
3	16	For	3	37.50%	1	6.25%
4	15	For	4	50.00%	1	6.67%
5	34	For	2	25.00%	3	8.82%
6	6	For	4	50.00%	0	0.00%
7	52	For-Of-By	12	50.00%	11	21.15%
8	22	Of-By	9	56.25%	2	9.09%
9	24	For	4	50.00%	2	8.33%
10	74	For-Of-By	11	45.83%	15	20.27%
11	62	For-By	7	43.75%	2	3.23%

Table 2. Summary of experiment S's results

Average No. Questions	Average Omission Rate	Average Commission Rate
32.73	43.94%	10.51%

rates are 25% and 56.25%, while the lowest and highest commission rates are 0% and 21.15%.

5.2 Experiment T: Engineer-Driven GenAI Questionnaires for the Theia App

Setup: Using ChatGPT, at least 24 questions are generated and analyzed by experienced requirements engineers for each Stakeholder. There are 72 questions generated in total. Questions are generated for the Theia App. We decide to keep the question or throw it away. If the question is thrown away, then a new question is generated in its place. For example, if a question asks about security passwords then the question is thrown away because security passwords inhibit usability for blind individuals.

In Fig. 5, we prompt ChatGPT to provide questions and examples for clarity of the questions. Note: Desirable properties of questions are entered first. In the interest of space, the green prompt is shown only once. The green prompt example shows the engineer prompting ChatGPT as follows:

PROMPT for ChatGPT 4.0:

We are asking the User questions.
GOAL: To Help Blind Individuals, like Theia, Navigate Indoors Safely
PROBLEM: Amy, Blind Individual, falls down going to class
SOLUTION: Theia App - A Programmable Navigational Software System with Speech Recognition Commands
Usability is the primary non-functional requirement.
Please assist me in coming up with questions based off of the question criteria provided. Please provide examples for each question.
Ask questions about each Requirements Engineering sector:
Problem, Functional Requirement, Process

Fig. 5. Experiment T: Prompt instance for question generation for 24 sectors

Responses from ChatGPT are in blue and are all different. We can only show two responses from ChatGPT. The remaining responses are shown on Github.

Figure 6 Results: Q1: "What specific obstacles do you face when navigating indoors that you would like the Theia app to overcome?": Understanding these obstacles from the user's perspective is critical for developing a solution that truly meets their needs. It ensures that the app is designed to address practical, everyday difficulties, making it more effective and relevant. **Q2:** "What key functions should the app have to assist you in overcoming these obstacles?": This is crucial to ask a blind individual because it places their needs and preferences at the center of the design process. This question enables users to directly communicate their expectations, suggesting features they feel would help them navigate and overcome the specific challenges they encounter in daily life. **Q3:**

```
RESPONSE from ChatGPT 4.0:

PROBLEM:
    • Question: "What specific obstacles do you face when navigating indoors that you would like the THEIA app to help overcome?"
    • Example to Clarify: "For instance, do you find it difficult to locate doors, stairs, or elevators when you are in unfamiliar indoor
      environments? Are there specific types of obstacles like low furniture or overhanging objects that you frequently encounter?"
FUNCTIONAL REQUIREMENTS:
    • Question: "What key functions should the app have to assist you in overcoming these obstacles?"
    • Example to Clarify: "Imagine the app could give you verbal alerts when you approach a stairway or beep when you're near a door.
      Would specific alerts like these be helpful, or are there other functions like directional guidance or obstacle warnings that you would
      find more useful?"
PROCESS:
    • Question: "Can you describe how these functions would ideally work in sequence to guide you indoors?"
    • Example to Clarify: "For example, when you enter a building, how would you like the app to guide you? Should it first announce
      the layout of the foyer, then give directions to your desired location step by step? How should it alert you to immediate obstacles, and
      would you prefer continuous feedback or only notifications at key points?"
```

Fig. 6. Questions for User about the Problem, Functional Requirement & Process

"Can you describe how these functions will ideally work in sequence to guide you indoors?": This is important because it uncovers the practical user experience by asking blind individuals to think through the sequence of interactions. It ensures that the app is not only functionally complete but also easy to use.

```
RESPONSE from ChatGPT 4.0:

PROBLEM:
    • Question: "From a technical standpoint, what are the limitations of current indoor navigation systems that THEIA needs to address?"
    • Example to Clarify: "For example, some navigation systems struggle with real-time updating when a user deviates from a path or
      fails in environments with low connectivity. Have you identified similar technical challenges, and how significant are they in the
      context of our app?"
FUNCTIONAL REQUIREMENTS:
    • Question: "How will you design THEIA's features to improve upon these limitations?"
    • Example to Clarify: "Considering issues like delayed updates in route recalculations, how would you enhance the app's
      responsiveness? Would implementing faster processing algorithms or integrating more reliable sensors help improve these aspects?
      How would you approach these solutions from a design perspective?"
PRODUCT:
    • Question: "How do these features fit into the overall architecture of the app?"
    • Example to Clarify: "If we were to integrate advanced sensors for better accuracy and responsiveness, how would this integration
      affect the app's current architecture? Would this require a significant redesign of existing components, or could it be incorporated
      with minimal changes? How would these technical enhancements impact the app's performance and user experience?"
```

Fig. 7. Questions for Developer about the Problem, Functional Requirement & Product

Figure 7 Results: Q1: "From a technical standpoint, what are the limitations of current indoor navigation systems that the Theia App needs to address?": This question encourages developers to evaluate existing technologies and identify their shortcomings, such as inaccurate positioning, signal interference, or lack of real-time updates in indoor environments. They can clearly define what needs to be improved, providing a focused direction for development. **Q2:** "How will you design the Theia App features to improve upon these limitations?": This pushes developers to think beyond identifying problems and focus on designing practical, implementable solutions that directly address the limitations of current systems. This question helps the app meet the practical needs of visually impaired users.

Q3: "How do these features fit into the overall architecture of the app?": This question is crucial because it helps the proposed features have a design that fits seamlessly within the overall system architecture.

We have posted all of our work that we cannot show in this paper on Github There are Tables of Definitions, Questionnaires containing 72 questions plus examples for clarification: https://github.com/JulieRauer/Questionnaire.

6 Discussion

6.1 Evaluation of Our Problem-Driven GenAI Approach

Our problem-driven GenAI approach provides a systematic pathway for ensuring that complex problems are tackled effectively, resulting in questions and requirements that are relevant and comprehensive. The support of the Requirements Engineer's insights are essential. We find that our Problem-Driven GenAI questions significantly reduced the time and cost of generating questionnaires. However, ChatGPT is ineffective at understanding non-functional requirements and their practical applications. Our Problem-Driven GenAI Approach **weaknesses** lie in the lack of contextual sensitivity, irrelevance, and limited ability to handle non-functional requirements and ambiguity. We overcome these limitations by combining the strengths of GenAI with human expertise to ensure the process remains flexible, context-aware, and fully aligned with stakeholder needs.

6.2 GenAI Pros and Cons

The **strengths of GenAI** are efficiency and speed, GenAI can quickly generate large volumes of content or data, saving significant time compared to manual efforts. It is cost-effective, over time, using AI can reduce costs associated with labor-intensive tasks. Data analysis and insights: It can analyze vast amounts of data to provide insights and identify patterns that humans might miss. The primary **weaknesses of GenAI** is the **lack of understanding**, AI lacks true understanding and can generate outputs that are contextually inappropriate or nonsensical.

6.3 Omission (Omitted) vs. Commission (Wrong Questions)

We were able to obtain the omission and commission rates of questionnaires in experiment S, which gives us some insights into the nature between omission, commission and number of questions in a questionnaire. First, it seems that more questions in a questionnaire, the higher commission rate. This pattern makes sense, since if you ask more questions, there is a higher likelihood you would ask a wrong question. Second, omission rate seems to decrease with more questions, which means more questions reduce the likelihood of missing an important question. Since commission rate and omission rate have opposite relationships with number of questions, that must mean there is an ideal number of questions that minimizes both omission rate and commission rate. We intend to research this concept in future work through more experimentation.

7 Threats to Validity

Internal Validity: A threat to the internal validity of our study can be the maturation of the Theia project. The project is a long standing group assignment that lasts the whole semester. It is possible questionnaires produced by the later groups are better quality than the older ones due to maturation in teaching, communication, schedule and general skills of students. We try to address this threat as well as selection bias by randomize the selection of questionnaires from semesters ranging from 2020 to 2023.

External Validity: A factor that can affect our external validity is the skill level of the participants. Undergraduate and graduate students are not considered professional, therefore the findings using them as data might not be generalizable for industry settings. With the appropriate filters, the questionnaires in this study comes from students who have had training in software engineering and requirements engineering, giving a reasonable baseline of expected results. We believe that the questionnaires provide the study with concrete data, giving some sense of reality in the findings. The questionnaires are also concentrated on the running topic of the Theia project, allowing for extensive comparisons to other experiments.

8 Conclusion

This paper proposes and tests a novel approach to developing a questionnaire that supports the requirements elicitation process. Our Systematic Problem-Driven GenAI approach provides a structured framework, while its iterative, incremental, and interleaving aspects enable adaptability, gradual progress, and concurrent workflows.

Experiment T involves experienced engineers creating comprehensive ChatGPT-generated questionnaires, which are then compared to student-generated questionnaires. The student questionnaires had 43.94% omitted questions and 10.51% incorrect questions (those that did not meet the desired properties of quality questions). Unlike experienced engineers, students typically do not have the same vested interest in producing high-quality questionnaires, which likely leads to more omissions and errors. The comparison between the student and ChatGPT-generated questionnaires offers valuable insights into how experience, methodology, and the use of advanced AI tools affect the quality of requirements elicitation. Our comparative study revealed the following key insights. **Focused Questions**: By starting with a clearly defined problem and systematically breaking it down, our approach ensures that questions remain focused and relevant. **Reduced Complexity**: Decomposing the main problem into subproblems simplifies addressing complex challenges. **Thorough Exploration**: Using GenAI allows for comprehensive exploration, reducing the risk of missing critical questions or asking irrelevant ones. **Requirements Clarity**: The structured process results in clearly defined, well-documented requirements that are directly tied to solving specific aspects of the problem.

Leveraging GenAI in the requirements elicitation process is both relevant and timely, and we believe it is highly effective. Our proposed Problem-Driven GenAI Requirements Elicitation Process (SO-REL) significantly narrows down the infinite number of potential questions that could arise in software development by formulating questions across 24 distinct sectors. Through the use of ChatGPT, question quality improved, as reflected in our evaluation based on desirable properties, though further research is needed to confirm this.

By using ChatGPT to assist in crafting these questions, we believe the likelihood of asking incorrect questions is significantly reduced. Moreover, formulating questions across 24 sectors ensures that the chances of omitting important questions are minimized. Our goal was to ask sufficiently comprehensive and relevant questions across all 24 sectors, which we believe we have achieved.

Further research and experimentation will be necessary for validation. Future work will involve additional analysis to assess ChatGPT's efficiency in eliciting questions, its accuracy in capturing user needs, and its potential to improve communication among stakeholders. Moreover, we recognize the need for more in-depth research into the quality of questions as our study was limited in scope.

References

1. Alhoshan, W., Ferrari, A., Zhao, L.: Zero-shot learning for requirements classification: an exploratory study. Inf. Softw. Technol. **159**, 107202 (2023)
2. Arora, C., Grundy, J., Abdelrazek, M.: Advancing requirements engineering through generative AI: assessing the role of LLMs. In: Nguyen-Duc, A., Abrahamsson, P., Khomh, F. (eds.) Generative AI for Effective Software Development, pp. 129–148. Springer, Cham (2024). https://doi.org/10.1007/978-3-031-55642-5_6
3. Bainbridge, L.: Verbal reports as evidence of the process operator's knowledge. Int. J. Hum Comput Stud. **51**(2), 213–238 (1999)
4. Bano, M., Zowghi, D., Ikram, N., Niazi, M.: What makes service oriented requirements engineering challenging? A qualitative study. IET Softw. **8**(4), 154–160 (2014)
5. Basili, V.R.: Applying the Goal/Question/Metric paradigm in the experience factory. Softw. Qual. Assur. Meas. Worldwide Perspect. **7**(4), 21–44 (1993)
6. Belzner, L., Gabor, T., Wirsing, M.: Large language model assisted software engineering: prospects, challenges, and a case study. In: Steffen, B. (eds.) International Conference on Bridging the Gap between AI and Reality, pp. 355–374. Springer, Cham (2023). https://doi.org/10.1007/978-3-031-46002-9_23
7. Bencheikh, L., Höglund, N.: Exploring the efficacy of ChatGPT in generating requirements: an experimental study (2023)
8. Chen, B., et al.: On the use of GPT-4 for creating goal models: an exploratory study. In: 2023 IEEE 31st International Requirements Engineering Conference Workshops (REW), pp. 262–271. IEEE (2023)
9. Chung, L., Nixon, B.A., Yu, E., Mylopoulos, J.: Non-functional Requirements in Software Engineering, vol. 5. Springer, Cham (2012). https://doi.org/10.1007/978-1-4615-5269-7
10. Clancy, T.: The standish group report. Chaos report (1995)

11. Davis, A., Dieste, O., Hickey, A., Juristo, N., Moreno, A.M.: Effectiveness of requirements elicitation techniques: empirical results derived from a systematic review. In: 14th IEEE International Requirements Engineering Conference (RE 2006), pp. 179–188. IEEE (2006)
12. Haaland, I.K., Roth, C., Stantcheva, S., Wohlfart, J.: Measuring what is top of mind (No. w32421). National Bureau of Economic Research (2024)
13. Kolluri, K., Ahn, R., Hill, T., Rauer, J., Chung, L.: Identifying risks for collaborative systems during requirements engineering: an ontology-based approach. In: International Conferences on Software Engineering and Knowledge Engineering (2022)
14. Krasner, H.: The cost of poor software quality in the US: a 2020 report. Proc. Consortium Inf. Softw. QualityTM (CISQTM) **2** (2021)
15. Krosnick, J.A.: Questionnaire design. In: The Palgrave Handbook of Survey Research, pp. 439–455 (2018)
16. Lichtenstein, S., Nguyen, L., Hunter, A.: Issues in IT service-oriented requirements engineering. Australas. J. Inf. Syst. **13**(1) (2005)
17. Oswal, J.U., Kanakia, H.T., Suktel, D.: Transforming software requirements into user stories with GPT-3.5-: an AI-powered approach. In: 2024 2nd International Conference on Intelligent Data Communication Technologies and Internet of Things (IDCIoT), pp. 913–920. IEEE (2024)
18. Pacheco, C., García, I., Reyes, M.: Requirements elicitation techniques: a systematic literature review based on the maturity of the techniques. IET Software **12**(4), 365–378 (2018)
19. Rauer, J.R., Kolluri, K., Chung, L., Liu, C., Hill, T.: Eliciting smartphone app requirements for helping senior people: a questionnaire approach. In: 2021 IEEE 29th International Requirements Engineering Conference Workshops (REW), pp. 278–287. IEEE (2021)
20. Ronanki, K., Berger, C., Horkoff, J.: Investigating ChatGPT's potential to assist in requirements elicitation processes. In: 2023 49th Euromicro Conference on Software Engineering and Advanced Applications, pp. 354–361. IEEE (2023)
21. Supakkul, S., Chung, L.: Extending problem frames to deal with stakeholder problems: an agent-and goal-oriented approach. In: Proceedings of the 2009 ACM symposium on Applied Computing, pp. 389–394 (2009)
22. Wahbeh, A., Sarnikar, S., El-Gayar, O.: A socio-technical-based process for questionnaire development in requirements elicitation via interviews. Requirements Eng. **25**(3), 295–315 (2020)
23. Wang, M., Zeng, Y.: Asking the right questions to elicit product requirements. Int. J. Comput. Integr. Manuf. **22**(4), 283–298 (2009)
24. Waseem, M., Das, T., Ahmad, A., Liang, P., Fahmideh, M., Mikkonen, T.: ChatGPT as a software development bot: a project-based study. In: International Conference on Evaluation of Novel Approaches to Software Engineering. SCITEPRESS-Science and Technology Publications (2024)
25. Yang, Y., Zhong, J., Wang, C., Li, Q.: Exploring relevance and coherence for automated text scoring using multi-task learning. In: SEKE, pp. 323–328 (2022)
26. Yeow, J.S.N., Rana, M.E., Majid, N.A.A.: An automated model of software requirement engineering using GPT-3.5. In: 2024 ASU International Conference in Emerging Technologies for Sustainability and Intelligent Systems (ICETSIS), pp. 1746–1755. IEEE (2024)

Assessing Large Language Models Effectiveness in Outdated Method Renaming

Ali Ben Mrad[1,2(✉)], Abdoul Majid O. Thiombiano[3], Mohamed Wiem Mkaouer[4], and Brahim Hnich[2,3]

[1] Department of Computer Science, College of Computer, Qassim University, Buraydah, Saudi Arabia
a.benmrad@qu.edu.sa
[2] CES Lab, ENIS, University of Sfax, 3038 Sfax, Tunisia
[3] FSM, University of Monastir, 5000 Monastir, Tunisia
[4] University of Michigan-Flint, Flint, USA

Abstract. Identifying effective methods for automatic method renaming after code modifications is crucial for maintaining developer productivity and enhancing the performance of source code analysis tools. In this study, we focus on benchmarking the effectiveness of the ChatGPT large language model (LLM) in predicting new method names after code modifications. Leveraging a dataset of method code snippets along with their original and modified names, we conducted experiments on 116 samples to assess the prediction accuracy of ChatGPT. Using Jaccard similarity as the metric, we varied the similarity threshold to evaluate the classification performance of predicted names. However, the Jaccard similarity does not retain the magnitude or direction of the vectors, reflecting the strength and polarity of the similarity. In addition, it ignores the order and context of the words, which results in missing potential syntactic or semantic variations. To solve this problem, we propose another validation process which not only detects whether or not an LLM captured semantic changes of a method, but also its structural changes in order to be able to generate a suitable name for this given method. Our results indicate that ChatGPT achieves a high success rate in predicting method names, obtaining 98% (Resp. 94%) when the threshold is set to 0.5 for the Cosine (resp. Jaccard) similarity. For a threshold of 1 (maximum similarity), ChatGPT maintains a notable performance with 49% (Resp. 74%) Cosine (resp. Jaccard) similarity. This demonstrates the potential of ChatGPT for automating method renaming tasks in software development workflows.

Keywords: API Renaming · Benchmarking Large Language Models · Machine Learning · Natural Language Processing

1 Introduction

In service-oriented computing, services encapsulate specific functionalities or operations. Thus, keeping the names representative of their behaviors is challenging given the large set of code changes developers perform on a daily basis. Also, proper naming of services directly impacts the quality of service composition, as better service naming can help with their composability [11,17].

Existing scholarly endeavors in the domain of programming nomenclature bifurcate into technical and semantic analyses. On the technical forefront, studies have dissected structural properties like the length or stylistic conventions of names [2]. Conflicting evidence exists surrounding the impact of abbreviation usage on the ease of comprehension. Some research has addressed the use of single-letter names, concluding that even these can possess semantic weight [10]. In contrast, extended names are associated with variables of a wider scope [12] and are indicative of experienced developers [2]. In terms of nomenclatural style, there is an ongoing academic debate as to whether camelCase or snake_case holds distinct advantages [3,19].

Semantic-oriented research, on the other hand, scrutinizes the grammatical and part-of-speech classifications of the lexicon employed in the naming. Observations have been drawn from the study of renamings that transpire during the maintenance of programs, with one identified trend being that names typically adopt a more specialized focus via the incorporation of additional terms. Furthermore, the complete alteration of semantics has been observed when replacements occur within a name [15].

The question persists, how do developers practically engage in the process of choosing names? An illuminating investigation conducted by Feitelson et al. probed this question with experiments in which developers named objects within predetermined contexts. This research is distinguished by its generation of data that reflects the naming choices for identical objects by different developers, thereby unveiling intrinsic variability. Although diverse, these chosen names frequently shared structural and lexical commonalities. The study also proposed a tripartite model detailing the nomenclatural creation process, offering substantial insight into developers' behavior in naturalistic naming environments.

In this paper, we explore the ability of large language models (i.e., GPT3.5-175B Llama2-6.74B, and Mistral-instruct-v0.2-7.24B) to actually help developers better rename their methods. This research significantly differs from previous studies that simply try to guess the right name of a method given the source code body. Our paper tackles the problem of renaming methods in a novel way by mimicking what developers are actually experiencing on a daily basis: we benchmark large language models in a context where we are feeding as inputs the method name, along with the source code body, and finally a given code change inside the body. The main question is, weather the proposed change is significant enough to change the method behavior, and so, requires a major update on the method name. This scenario is actually what represents the difficult challenge that developers are facing regularly as they perform micro changes throughout their entire system. Our paper is so driven by the following research questions:

RQ1: What is the effectiveness of ChatGPT in predicting method names after code modifications, and how does this effectiveness vary depending on the complexity of renaming and semantic updates?

RQ2: What are the advantages and limitations of integrating ChatGPT predictions into automated method renaming processes, and what strategies exist to optimize this integration in software development workflows?

2 Methodology

The study examines method rename refactorings in open-source projects, identifying code changes that lead to renaming, and creates a data set of such changes. A corresponding negative set is gathered for changes that don't result in renaming. This enables the evaluation of large language models (LLMs) on their ability to predict if a code change will trigger a rename and suggest a new name. Traditional similarity measures like Jaccard are insufficient, so a new validation process is introduced to ensure LLMs understand both semantic and structural changes when renaming methods.

2.1 Data Extraction and Analysis

In this study, we use a database [14] containing information related to commits made to projects written in Java on GitHub. Among the database's tables, our study emphasized the following tables: *git_commit*, *rename_method*, *analyzed_form* and *analyzed_semantic*. Each row in *analyzed_method* holds information related to modifications made to a single in a given commit. However, the method's implementation is not provided. Nonetheless, information such as the method's old and new names, return types, arguments, and the method's commit hash was provided. In order to get the method's implementation we proceeded as follows:

- First of all, group code modifications by commit hash.
- Query GitHub's API to retrieve metadata related to 60 randomly selected commits. During this querying process, we randomly selected 60 commits because of GitHub's API rate limit which is 60 requests per hour. This process was repeated until we had a sufficient number of downloaded commits metadata.
- Given that each commit metadata has a *files* attribute which indicates the modified files, we only retained files with a "modified" status.
- Using a regex-based approach, we were able to extract old and new code from each file *patch* attribute.
- We discarded any commit whose date is prior to 2023, to minimize the data leakage that can potentially occur when LLMs were trained on these sets.

As a result, we generated JSON files that captured details for each method, including old and new signatures, arguments, return types, implementations, and commit hash. By the conclusion of this phase of our research, our dataset comprised 116 methods.

2.2 Evaluation Baselines

To assess ChatGPT's effectiveness, it was prompted to suggest a meaningful name for each modified based on an input composed of the method's old and new arguments, return types, implementations, and old name only. To avoid any confusion from the model, we provided ChatGPT one JSON document at a time. We also ran some tests with open-source Large Language Models (LLMs) such as Mistral-7B [9] and Llama 2-7B [1]. Leveraging quantization [4] on a T4 GPU and using the same approach as with ChatGPT, Mistral, and Llama were prompted on the same set of JSON documents to predict a name for the method after it has been modified. To measure how similar the predicted name is to the real new one, we have used **Jaccard index** [6] which measures the similarity between two sets based on the following formula:

$$J(A,B) = \frac{|A \cap B|}{|A \uplus B|} = \frac{|A \cap B|}{|A| + |B|} \text{ where } 0 \leq J(A,B) \leq 1 \tag{1}$$

We chose the Jaccard similarity coefficient, as it is effective in method comparison, as method names tend to be relatively small and composed of contiguous tokens. In this context, the Jaccard coefficient only accounts for the presence of elements in sets, disregarding their frequency. It is insensitive to the frequency of characters, sparsity of data, and lack of magnitude or direction. One of the main challenges of adopting the Jaccard similarity is its computational expense with larger datasets. However, in our context, we are comparing relatively smaller strings, and therefore, we did not experience any regression in the performance of our analysis.

2.3 Semantic-Driven Validation Process

Using the Jaccard similarity to measure the quality of predicted names by LLMs considers only the name's structure. It provides no way to confirm if an LLM really understood a method's code changes. To solve this problem, we propose another validation process which not only detects whether or not an LLM captured semantic changes of a method, but also its structural changes in order to be able to generate a suitable name for this given method.

The proposed validation process introduces an encoder-only method that will be used as an evaluator. To do so, we fine-tuned BGE-base-en-v1.5 [18], a BERT-based model [5] to learn word embeddings of methods name using the *rename_method* table from the database [16].

In order to create an association between a method's old name and its new name, we modeled our fine-tuning objective as information retrieval where the *query* would be the method's old name and the *response* its new name. Using up to 60 000 entries from the *rename_method* table, we created 60 000 pairs.

We then used these pairs to create a new vocabulary of 40 000 tokens for our model based on WordPiece [5] tokenization algorithm.

Using an Nvidia T4 GPU, Mixed Precision Training [13] and LoRA [8] applied on the embedding layers of the model, we fine-tuned BGE-base-en-v1.5 on this

Table 1. Accuracy Comparison of the Three LLMs Across Jaccard Coefficient Variants

Jaccard Coefficient	ChatGPT Accuracy	Mistral Accuracy	LLaMA Accuracy
>0.5	94%	91%	67%
>0.7	90%	78%	48%
>0.8	85%	65%	38%
>0.9	75%	49%	21%
= 1 (Maximum similarity)	74%	40%	6.5%

newly created vocabulary. The associated loss function to our modeling task is the multiple negatives ranking loss function [7] which is used to train embeddings for retrieval setups.

Using the evaluator model, we computed embeddings for each of the 116 methods real names, as well as their predicted counterparts by ChatGPT, Mistral and Llama 2-7B. And using the **cosine-similarity**, we came up with a score indicating to which extent did the LLMs captured the code changes of each method in their predicted new name.

$$\text{cosine similarity} = \frac{A \cdot B}{\|A\|\|B\|} = \frac{\sum_{i=1}^{n} A_i B_i}{\sqrt{\sum_{i=1}^{n} A_i^2} \sqrt{\sum_{i=1}^{n} B_i^2}} \qquad (2)$$

where A and B are embedding vectors. By thresholding the similarity measurements with the values $0.5, 0.7, 0.8, 0.9$ and 1 we performed a binary classification to measure each LLM accuracy. Naturally, a similarity score of 1 means that the LLM generated a string matching perfectly the method's real name. For instance, if a method's real name is *get_Age* then, the predicted name will also be *get_Age*.

3 Results

In this section, we present the results of our experiments aimed at evaluating the effectiveness of different language models (LLMs), including ChatGPT, Mistral, and LLaMA, in predicting method names after code modifications.

We evaluated the performance of three LLMs - ChatGPT, Mistral, and LLaMA - in predicting method names after code modifications. The results of this evaluation are summarized in Table 1. We observed a significant trend in the performance of the three LLMs as the Jaccard similarity threshold increased. At a Jaccard similarity threshold exceeding 0.5, ChatGPT surpassed the other LLMs in terms of precision, achieving an accuracy rate of 94%. Mistral also exhibited robust performance at this threshold, with a precision of 91%, while LLaMA demonstrated inferior results, achieving a precision of 67%. As we increased the similarity threshold to 0.7, we observed a decrease in performance for all LLMs. However, ChatGPT maintained its superiority with a precision of 90%, followed by Mistral with 78% precision and LLaMA with 48% precision.

At higher similarity thresholds of 0.8 and 0.9, we noted a significant decrease in precision for all LLMs. Nevertheless, ChatGPT sustained notable performance with precision rates of 85% and 75% respectively, surpassing the performance of Mistral and LLaMA by a considerable margin. Finally, at a maximal Jaccard similarity threshold (1), ChatGPT maintained a precision of 74%, while Mistral and LLaMA exhibited lower performances with precisions of 40% and 6.5% respectively. These results unequivocally demonstrate the superiority of ChatGPT in predicting method names after code modifications, underscoring its potential for automating method renaming tasks in software development workflows.

Furthermore, we conducted additional analysis to evaluate the performance of the three LLMs across different types of renaming and semantic updates. Table 2 illustrate the results of this experimentation.

In various renaming scenarios, ChatGPT consistently surpasses Mistral and LLaMA. For straightforward renames, ChatGPT achieves a precision of 35.71%, while Mistral scores 32.14%, and LLaMA only 7.14%. In more complex renames, ChatGPT excels with an impressive 85.36% precision rate, surpassing Mistral's 41.46% and LLaMA's mere 6.10%. Furthermore, ChatGPT shows strong performance in formatting and reordering renames, with precision rates of 66.66% and 33.33% respectively, while Mistral and LLaMA demonstrate significantly lower or non-existent performance in these areas. Regarding semantic updates, ChatGPT shows strength in predicting changes with a precision of 73.83%, while Mistral and LLaMA achieve 40.19% and 6.54% precision respectively. Notably, ChatGPT excels in predicting semantic updates, particularly "Change - Broaden", with a

Table 2. Accuracy of the Three LLMs with Rename Form Types and Rename Semantic Meaning Updates

Type	ChatGPT			Mistral			LLaMA		
	True	False	Acc	True	False	Acc	True	False	Acc
Rename form types									
Simple	10	18	35.71%	9	19	32.14%	2	26	7.14%
Complex	70	12	85.36%	34	48	41.46%	5	77	6.10%
Formatting	2	1	66.66%	0	3	0%	0	3	0%
Reordering	1	2	33.33%	0	3	0%	0	3	0%
Rename semantic meaning updates									
Preserve	4	5	44.44%	0	9	0%	0	9	0%
Change	79	31	73.83%	43	64	40.19%	7	100	6.54%
Change – Broaden	51	3	94.44%	22	32	40.74%	5	49	9.26%
Change – Narrow	23	14	62.16%	14	23	37.84%	0	37	0%
Change – Add	2	7	22.22%	3	6	33.33%	2	7	22.22%
Change – Remove	3	4	42.86%	4	3	57.14%	0	7	0%

precision of 94.44%. The findings highlight ChatGPT's capability in automating the process of renaming methods within software development workflows, offering significant insights for developers and practitioners.

Table 3. Accuracy of Method Name Prediction using the fine-tuned model

Cosine similarity	ChatGPT Accuracy	Mistral Accuracy	LLaMA Accuracy
>0.5	98%	92%	90%
>0.7	90%	70%	37%
>0.8	79%	52%	15%
>0.9	74%	41%	4%
=1	49%	26%	2%

The results obtained using the fine-tuned embedding model to evaluate semantically the different methods are shown in Table 3. Indeed, it measures to what extend the various LLMs understood the semantic and structural code changes of the method. Not surprisingly, the results correlate well with those found using Jaccard similarity. That is to say that ChatGPT presents superior capabilities compared these two other LLMs.

4 Conclusion and Future Work

This paper has presented a comprehensive comparison underlining 3 LLMs, namely, i.e., GPT3.5-175B, Llama2-6.74B, and Mistral-instruct-v0.2-7.24B, particularly for predicting a suitable method name for a given input code change to its body. The results obtained using Jaccard similarity measure and the fine-tuned embedding model confirm that ChatGPT presents superior capabilities compared to the two other LLMs.

In conclusion, the empirical assessment presented in this study contributes to the evolving landscape of language models' applications in API quality. The research opens avenues for further investigations qualitatively with testing the proposed solution in an industrial setting, in which we can survey developers about their reflections after adopting this solution as part of their quality assurance processes. Furthermore, our fine-tuned embedding model can also be provided as an API that can used to semantically evaluate method renaming.

References

1. Touvron, H.: LLaMA 2: open foundation and fine-tuned chat models (2023)
2. Alsuhaibani, R., Newman, C., Decker, M., Collard, M., Maletic, J.: On the naming of methods: a survey of professional developers. In: 2021 IEEE/ACM 43rd International Conference on Software Engineering (ICSE), pp. 587–599. IEEE (2021)

3. Amit, N., Feitelson, D.G.: The language of programming: on the vocabulary of names. In: 2022 29th Asia-Pacific Software Engineering Conference (APSEC), pp. 21–30. IEEE (2022)
4. Dettmers, T., Pagnoni, A., Holtzman, A., Zettlemoyer, L.: QLoRa: efficient fine-tuning of quantized LLMs (2023)
5. Devlin, J., Chang, M.W., Lee, K., Toutanova, K.: BERT: pre-training of deep bidirectional transformers for language understanding (2019). https://arxiv.org/abs/1810.04805
6. da F. Costa, L.: Further generalizations of the Jaccard index (2021)
7. Henderson, M., et al.: Efficient natural language response suggestion for smart reply (2017). https://arxiv.org/abs/1705.00652
8. Hu, E.J., et al.: LoRA: low-rank adaptation of large language models (2021). https://arxiv.org/abs/2106.09685
9. Jiang, A.Q., Sablayrolles, A.: Mistral 7B (2023)
10. Kashiwabara, Y., Onizuka, Y., Ishio, T., Hayase, Y., Yamamoto, T., Inoue, K.: Recommending verbs for rename method using association rule mining. In: 2014 Software Evolution Week-IEEE Conference on Software Maintenance, Reengineering, and Reverse Engineering (CSMR-WCRE), pp. 323–327. IEEE (2014)
11. Lucky, M.N., Cremaschi, M., Lodigiani, B., Menolascina, A., De Paoli, F.: Enriching API descriptions by adding API profiles through semantic annotation. In: Service-Oriented Computing: 14th International Conference, ICSOC 2016, Banff, AB, Canada, 10–13 October 2016, Proceedings 14, pp. 780–794. Springer, Cham (2016)
12. Mastropaolo, A., Aghajani, E., Pascarella, L., Bavota, G.: Automated variable renaming: are we there yet? Empir. Softw. Eng. **28**(2), 45 (2023)
13. Micikevicius, P., et al.: Mixed precision training (2018). https://arxiv.org/abs/1710.03740
14. Peruma, A.: A preliminary study of android refactorings. In: 2019 IEEE/ACM 6th International Conference on Mobile Software Engineering and Systems (MOBILESoft), pp. 148–149 (2019). https://doi.org/10.1109/MOBILESoft.2019.00030
15. Peruma, A., Mkaouer, M.W., Decker, M.J., Newman, C.D.: Contextualizing rename decisions using refactorings, commit messages, and data types. J. Syst. Softw. **169**, 110704 (2020)
16. Peruma, A., Mkaouer, M.W., Decker, M.J., Newman, C.D.: Contextualizing rename decisions using refactorings, commit messages, and data types. J. Syst. Softw. **169**, 110704 (2020). https://doi.org/10.1016/j.jss.2020.110704, http://www.sciencedirect.com/science/article/pii/S0164121220301503
17. Stocker, M., Zimmermann, O., Zdun, U., Lübke, D., Pautasso, C.: Interface quality patterns: communicating and improving the quality of microservices APIs. In: Proceedings of the 23rd European Conference on Pattern Languages of Programs, pp. 1–16 (2018)
18. Xiao, S., Liu, Z., Zhang, P., Muennighoff, N., Lian, D., Nie, J.Y.: C-Pack: packaged resources to advance general Chinese embedding (2024). https://arxiv.org/abs/2309.07597
19. Zhang, J., Zou, W., Huang, Z.: An empirical study on the usage and evolution of identifier styles in practice. In: 2021 28th Asia-Pacific Software Engineering Conference (APSEC), pp. 171–180. IEEE (2021)

Service Security and Privacy

DynaEDI: Decentralized Integrity Verification for Dynamic Edge Data

Qiang He[1,3], Jiyu Yang[2,3], Feifei Chen[4(✉)], Cong Tian[2], Yanhui Li[5], and Yun Yang[3]

[1] Huazhong University of Science and Technology, Wuhan, Hubei, China
hqiang@hust.edu.cn
[2] Xidian University, Xi'an, Shannxi, China
jiyuy2024@stu.xidian.edu.cn, ctian@mail.xidian.edu.cn,
jiyuyang@swin.edu.au
[3] Swinburne University of Technology, Melbourne, VIC, Australia
yyang@swin.edu.au
[4] Deakin University, Burwood, VIC, Australia
feifei.chen@deakin.edu.au
[5] Nanjing University, Nanjing, Jiangsu, China
yanhuili@nju.edu.cn

Abstract. In an edge computing environment, data can be cached on edge servers to enable fast data services for users. These edge data are subject to corruption and must be verified to ensure their integrity. Meanwhile, they are also subject to partial content changes over time. Existing Edge Data Integrity (EDI) schemes are designed to verify edge data as a whole. They fail to accommodate partially-identical edge data, and consequently, suffer from low verification accuracy in many real-world applications. This paper presents DynaEDI, a novel decentralized scheme capable of verifying the integrity of partially-identical edge data. At its core, DynaEDI generates pairing trees, a new tree structure, as data digests. Based on these data digests, edge servers can verify the integrity of their data through subtree-based content comparison between version-matched data blocks. In addition, DynaEDI reduces communication overhead by transmitting only the root nodes instead of complete trees for verification. Experimental results show that DynaEDI increases verification accuracy by up to 35% and reduces communication overhead by an order of magnitude, compared to benchmark schemes.

Keywords: edge data services · data integrity · edge computing

1 Introduction

Over the past decade, cloud computing has become the fundamental infrastructure for the majority of a wide range of mobile and IoT applications. However, its ability to power latency-sensitive applications, e.g., video streaming and online gaming, is limited by the high and often unstable network latency caused by

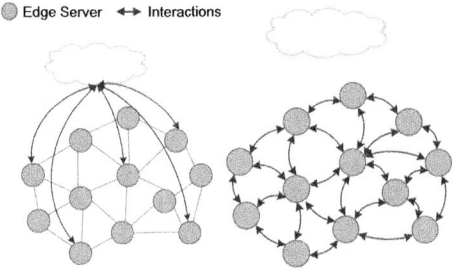
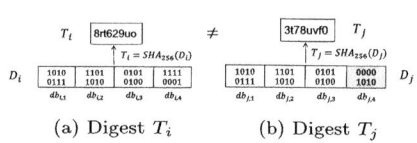

Fig. 1. EDI: Centralized vs. Decentralized.

Fig. 2. Digest comparison: data replica D_i vs. data variant D_j.

the long distance between users and the cloud [5]. Many mobile and IoT app vendors have turned to edge computing [25], a new computing paradigm that ensures low service latency by deploying edge servers at locations close to users, such as 5G base stations [6,13].

Edge Data Integrity. In the edge computing environment, content providers can cache popular data like viral videos on edge servers distributed close to users to enable fast data access [10,20,24], providing better user experiences and faster downloads compared to today's CDN [4]. Unfortunately, due to the lack of centralized data management and security assurance, these *edge data* are subject to corruption in the dynamic edge computing environment [16]. Data corruption can easily undermine users' quality of experience and threaten their security. This raises concerns about edge data integrity (EDI) [16]. Unlike cloud data integrity (CDI) which focuses on the integrity of one or a few data replicas stored in a central data center, EDI must inspect a much larger number of data replicas stored at geographically-distributed locations.

Existing Solutions. To tackle the EDI problem, some centralized integrity verification schemes have been proposed [16,17,27,28]. As shown in Fig. 1a, under these schemes, app vendors act as global controllers and interact with edge servers to verify the integrity of their data. Centralized control eases the interactions and coordination, but incurs excessive network traffic between edge servers and the cloud [15]. This contradicts a fundamental design objective of edge computing, i.e., to alleviate the traffic pressure on the backhaul network [11]. To avoid centralized control, a series of decentralized EDI schemes have emerged in recent years. As illustrated in Fig. 1b, they perform integrity verification through collaboration between edge servers [15,18].

Challenge I - Partially-Identical Content. Following the same assumption as existing work on cloud data integrity [3,12,21], decentralized EDI schemes like CooperEDI [15] and EdgeWatch [18] have commonly assumed that there are many identical edge data replicas in the system. Under this assumption, the integrity of a data item can be verified holistically by comparing its digest with the ground truth (the digests of correct replicas). However, this assumption is not always realistic. In real-world scenarios, edge data often share partially-identical content. For example, users often publish their videos on multiple social platforms to maximize profits. These social platforms often modify these videos for policy compliance, e.g., muting audio, blurring disturbing content, and adding content warnings for content moderation. They may also insert advertisements tailored to user interests into users' videos for advertising [8]. These video modifications generate massive partially-identical data across edge servers, which are referred to as *dynamic edge data* hereafter for ease of exposition. They do not share the same ground truth as a whole. Consequently, Existing EDI schemes that rely on comparison between supposedly-identical data replicas cannot properly verify the integrity of dynamic edge data. Figure 2 shows an instance where the last block of D_j is modified, leading to a digest different from D_i's. Compared with ground truth, T_j will be mistakenly identified as corrupted under existing decentralized EDI schemes when D_j is actually intact.

Challenge II - Communication Overhead. Another major advantage of decentralized EDI schemes over centralized ones is the reduced traffic over the backhaul network [15]. However, existing decentralized EDI schemes require many interactions between edge servers. These interactions generate traffic at the network edge and incur expenses. For example, AWS charges $0.01 for transferring every GB of data between edge servers within the same AWS Wavelength Zone [2]. Data transmissions across different AWS Wavelength Zones are even more expensive. Thus, decentralized EDI verification may not always be economical. In existing decentralized EDI schemes, edge servers transmit Merkle trees as data digests for integrity [15,18]. These Merkle trees are large when edge data are partitioned into small data blocks to enable fine-grained integrity verification. For example, a complete Merkle tree generated from 1,024 data blocks has 2,047 nodes in total.

Contributions. This paper presents DynaEDI, a new decentralized scheme for verifying the integrity of dynamic edge data. Under DynaEDI, edge servers 1) generate digests with pairing functions based on data blocks for block-level integrity verification; and 2) follow a new interaction protocol to verify the integrity of their dynamic data with greatly reduced communication overhead. In general, this paper makes the following main contributions.

- Compared with centralized EDI schemes, DynaEDI leverages the ability of edge servers to interact. All the operations, e.g., digest generation, transmission, and comparison, are performed by edge servers without centralized control. The entire verification procedure is carried out at the network edge, generating minimal backhaul network traffic.
- Compared with existing decentralized EDI schemes, DynaEDI enables verification of dynamic edge data that share the ground truth partially or in whole. The key is to enable edge servers to verify their data blocks against the same versions of data blocks cached by other edge servers (Sect. 3).
- DynaEDI employs a new data digest named the pairing tree to minimize the communication overhead incurred during the verification procedure (Sect. 4).

It generates tree digests with pairing functions instead of hash functions. Edge servers transmit only the root nodes Instead of transmitting entire trees for integrity verification. Compared with the predominant use of Merkle trees in data integrity verification, the use of pairing trees profoundly reduces the communication overhead incurred.

2 Related Work

As service providers like AWS and Alibaba roll out their edge computing infrastructure worldwide [1], app vendors can cache popular data like viral videos and software updates on edge servers for quick access. Ensuring the integrity of these data has become a prominent and urgent issue.

Cloud Data Integrity. Cloud data integrity (CDI) is one of the most crucial data security problems in the past decade [3,12]. Its key challenge is to verify the integrity of data stored in remote cloud storage without accessing the data. To verify the integrity of a data item D under a CDI scheme, a client preprocesses D to generate a data digest in advance and requests the cloud server to prove that D is not corrupted. The client verifies the response of the cloud server against the data digest to confirm the integrity of D.

EDI vs. CDI. In the edge computing environment, app vendors cache popular data on edge servers to ensure rapid data access for users [20]. This raises concern about edge data integrity (EDI), i.e., how to verify their integrity without accessing them [15,16,18]. EDI faces three main challenges that arise from its fundamental differences from CDI:

- Edge servers often suffer from constrained resources and cannot afford computationally expensive schemes like cloud servers [15].
- EDI involves inspecting a substantial number of data replicas, whereas CDI focuses on only a few data replicas [16].
- Edge servers are geographically distributed, rendering CDI schemes designed for centrally-managed cloud servers ineffective, if not entirely incapacitated [15].

Edge Data Integrity: Data Dynamics. EDI-V [16], the first EDI scheme, employs a centralized approach and focuses on reducing the computation overhead on edge servers. It was implemented in our experiments as a representative centralized EDI scheme (Sect. 5). Its limitation is obvious, i.e., excessive communication overhead over the backhaul network [15], which is shared by recent centralized EDI schemes like EDI-S [17], SIA [27] and DVA-P [28]. Several other EDI schemes employ a decentralized approach to verify edge data integrity through interactions between edge servers [15,18]. The key idea is to find correct data replicas as a ground-truth data quorum for integrity verification, similar to the concept of data block quorum under DynaEDI (Sect. 3), but at a higher level of granularity. As discussed in Sect. 1, the data cached on edge servers are often partially-identical. A replica of D becomes a data variant when it is modified. Consequently, these data variants cannot be verified against the replicas of D as a whole. This reduces the possibility of finding data quorums under existing decentralized EDI schemes and lowers their verification accuracy, as experimentally demonstrated in Sect. 5. To tackle this challenge, DynaEDI versions modified data blocks, allowing edge servers to find data block quorums instead of data quorums for integrity verification (Sect. 3).

Edge Data Integrity: Communication Overhead. The verification of dynamic cloud data has also been studied in the past decade. Wang et al. proposed a solution to verify whether the data blocks comprising a data item that intact based on Merkle tree [23]. Since then, the Merkle tree has been employed as the predominant data digest by many CDI and EDI schemes [9,26]. Under centralized EDI schemes, the communication overhead incurred is reasonable - N Merkle trees are transmitted from edge servers to the cloud server for verifying N edge data replicas. However, under decentralized EDI schemes [15,18], edge servers transmit massive Merkle trees to verify dynamic edge data. This incurs significant communication overhead, as experimentally illustrated in Sect. 5. To reduce the communication overhead, DynaEDI employs the new pairing tree instead of the Merkle tree to generate data digests (Sect. 4).

3 Verification Procedure

The verification procedure under DynaEDI consists of three main phases, i.e., Setup, Digest Collection, and Inspection.

Phase 1: Setup. In this phase, edge servers prepare for integrity verification. Specifically, edge servers generate a tree digest for each cached data item. When an edge server s_i needs to verify a data replica D_i. it needs the digest of D_i, denoted as T_i. When an edge server s_j responds to a request from s_i to verify D_i, it needs to provide s_i with T_j. DynaEDI does not dictate when these digests are generated. The timing can be determined by the app vendor domain specifically. When a data replica D_i is transmitted from the cloud s_i for caching, s_i can generate a digest from s_i immediately. Alternatively, s_i can generate digests from data replicas when it is idle. Another option is to generate T_i or T_j when D_i needs to be inspected for integrity. Here, we assume that data digests are ready before Phase 2. Merkle trees are often generated from data as digests for integrity verification [15,16,18]. DynaEDI follows the same idea and generates tree digests for integrity verification, one leaf node for each data block.

As discussed in Sect. 1, edge data are often partially identical. A data item modified from the original is referred to as a *data variant*. Under existing EDI schemes, an edge server cannot verify a data replica against a data variant by comparing their digests. As shown in Fig. 3, T_i, the tree digest generated from the original data item, differs from T_j, the digest of a data variant (one of its four data blocks was modified), in three of the nodes in their tree digests. However, with a closer look, we can see that the other three data blocks in D_i, i.e., $db_{i,1}$,

Algorithm 1: DIGEST-COLLECTION Message Generation

Input: $d_i.ID$ /* ID of data replica d_i in s_i */, $d_i.version[]$ /* collection of data block versions */
Output: DIGEST-COLLECTION
1 create a request message DIGEST-COLLECTION
2 DIGEST-COLLECTION.$ID \leftarrow d_i.ID$
3 DIGEST-COLLECTION.$version[] \leftarrow d_i.version[]$
4 **return** DIGEST-COLLECTION

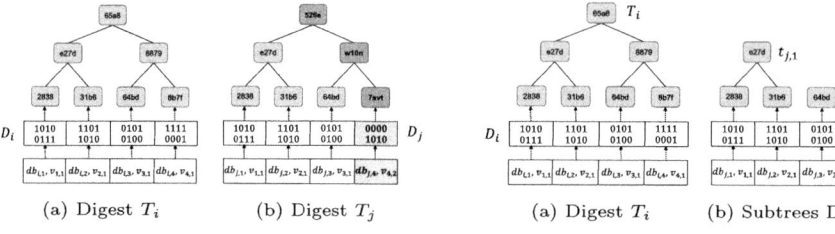

Fig. 3. Merkle tree digests generated from data variants.

Fig. 4. Subtree identification for verification.

$db_{i,2}$, and $db_{i,3}$, can still be verified against $db_{j,1}$, $db_{j,2}$, and $db_{j,3}$, which have not been modified. Under DynaEDI, data blocks are versioned when edge data are modified so that edge servers can verify their data blocks against the same versions of data blocks cached on other edge servers.

Phase 2: Digest Collection. In this phase, edge server s_i interacts with other edge servers in the system to find correct data as ground truth for comparison. The design of DynaEDI draws on Paxos [14] and Raft [19], two consensus protocols successfully implemented in various domains. These protocols facilitate consensus within potentially unreliable nodes in a decentralized system. A fundamental assumption underlying these protocols is that no more than half of the nodes in the system will experience concurrent failures. Under this assumption, Paxos and Raft allow a majority of the nodes to eventually reach a consensus when some nodes may fail temporarily. DynaEDI is designed under a similar assumption: given n replicas of a data block db_i cached on n edge servers in the system, a maximum of $\lceil \frac{n}{2} \rceil - 1$ of these data blocks are corrupted at the same time. That is, at least $\lceil \frac{n+1}{2} \rceil$ of these data blocks are correct and can be used as the ground truth to verify db_i. They constitute a *data block quorum*.

When an edge server s_i needs to verify the integrity of a data item d_i, it needs to find the ground truth for each of the data blocks. These ground-truth data blocks may be cached on other edge servers as part of a replica or a variant of d_i. Edge server s_i needs to query the edge servers in the system for the digests of these data blocks, following the steps below.

– **Step 2.1.** Edge server s_i broadcasts a DIGEST-COLLECTION message in the system. The message carries the ID of d_i, and the versions of the data blocks

---
Algorithm 2: DIGEST Message Generation

Input: DIGEST-COLLECTION /* received from s_i */, $d_j.version[]$ /* data block versions */, T_j /* tree digest of D_j */
Output: DIGEST /* collection of root nodes from subtrees */
1 check whether DIGEST-COLLECTION.ID matches $D_j.ID$
2 create a response message DIGEST
3 **for** v_i in DIGEST-COLLECTION.$version[]$ **do**
4   **if** $v_i \in d_j.version[]$ **then** add v_i to $commonVersion[]$
5   find root nodes of subtrees in T_i that include matched data blocks
6 **for** each subtree t_j **do** add $subtree.root.digest$ to DIGEST
7 **return** DIGEST

Algorithm 3: Digest Comparison

Input: DIGEST /* received from s_j */, T_i /* tree digest for D_i */
Output: INSPECTION-STATE /* comparison results */
1 **for** each data block db_i in D_i **do** /* initialization */
2   create $state_i$; set $state_i$ to **true**; add $state_i$ to INSPECTION-STATE
3 **for** each data block db_j **not** in DIGEST **do** change $state_j$ to **null** /* exclude data blocks with different versions in D_i and D_j */
4 **for** each *root* of subtree **in** DIGEST **do** /* start comparing each subtree in turn */
5   find the corresponding common subtree root *node* in T_i
6   **if** $node.digest == root$ **then** continue **else**
7   **function** Digest_Comparing(*node*, *root*)
8   **if** *node* is leaf node and *root* is leaf node **then**
9   change the *state* of *node* to **false**
10            $\{root.left, root.right\} \leftarrow P^{-1}(root)$ /* unfold node */
11             $left \leftarrow node.left$; $right \leftarrow node.right$
12   **if** $left.digest \neq root.left$ **then**
13   Digest_Comparing($left, root.left$)
14   **if** $right.digest \neq root.right$ **then**
15   Digest_Comparing($right, root.right$)
16 **return** INSPECTION-STATE
---

in d_i. In the meantime, it sets a *digest collection timeout* and waits for the responses from other edge servers. The pseudocode is demonstrated by Algorithm algorithm 1.

– **Step 2.2.** Upon the receipt of the DIGEST-COLLECTION message from s_i, each edge server, denoted as s_j, checks whether a replica of d_i or a variant of d_i (both denoted by d_j hereafter in this section for ease of exposition) is in its cache. If the answer is no, it ignores the message. Otherwise, from its own tree digest of d_j, s_j finds a minimum set of subtrees that include all the data blocks matching the versions of the data blocks in d_i. Figure 4 presents an example for illustration purposes. Then, s_j sends a DIGEST message to s_i as the response to its query. This message carries the set of subtrees s_j found. The pseudocode is shown by Algorithm algorithm 2.

Phase 3: Inspection. When s_i receives a DIGEST message from each edge server in the system or its digest collection timeout collapses, it inspects the received DIGEST messages to verify the integrity of d_i. Specifically, it compares each of the subtrees in the received DIGEST messages against the corresponding subtrees in T_i, its own tree digest generated from d_i in the Setup phase (Sect. 3). Given two subtrees $t_i \in T_i$ and $t_j \in T_j$, the comparison process consists of two main steps, as illustrated by Algorithm algorithm 3.

- **Step 3.1.** Edge server s_i compares $t_i.root$ and $t_j.root$. If they are identical, the corresponding subtrees are considered identical as well, indicating that the cached data blocks on s_i are correct, i.e., not corrupted. Otherwise, the comparison proceeds to Step 3.2.
- **Step 3.2.** Edge server s_i compares the nodes in t_i and t_j, and find the leaf node(s) in t_i not identical with the counter parts in t_j. The corresponding data blocks are potentially corrupted.

Through these subtree comparisons, s_i can 1) find a data block quorum for each of the data blocks in d_i; and 2) find out whether each of the data blocks in d_i matches the corresponding data block quorum, i.e., the majority of the corresponding data blocks in the replicas or variants of d_i cached in the system, as illustrated by Algorithm algorithm 4.

In this phase, s_i may not be able to receive sufficient subtrees as ground truth for verifying d_i. This happens when only a few replicas or variants of d are cached in the system. Edge server s_i can still complete Step 3. However, it can be easily inferred that the lack of sufficient ground truth will compromise the verification accuracy. In such cases, s_i can seek help from the cloud server with verification. This does not limit the application of DynaEDI in practice. The reasons are twofold. First, app vendors usually cache popular data on edge servers [20]. It is unlikely that an edge server cannot find sufficient ground truth for comparison. Second, decentralized EDI schemes like CooperEDI [15] and DynaEDI, are originally designed to inspect data items (replicas and variants) that are too many for cloud-based methods like EDI-V [16] to inspect.

Algorithm 4: Inspection

Input: INSPECTION-STATE set /* received from each s_j */
Output: verification result
1   **for** each data block db_i **in** D_i **do**
2   collect *state* from each INSPECTION-STATE
3   **if** # of **false** exceeds # of **true then return** ERROR
4   **else return** CORRECT /* distributed consensus protocol */

4 Pairing Tree for DynaEDI

As discussed above in Sect. 3, DynaEDI can verify the integrity of dynamic edge data with less communication overhead than CooperEDI. The key is to identify and transmit subtrees instead of whole trees for verification. However, as discussed in Sect. 1, transmitting large Merkle trees may still incur excessive communication overhead.

In Phase 3 (Sect. 3), the comparison between two subtrees t_i and t_j begins with their root nodes. If the root nodes are identical, the comparison ends in Step 3.1. Otherwise, the comparison proceeds to identify the leaf node(s) in t_i not identical with t_j, aiming to find out which data blocks in D_i may be corrupted in Step 3.2. If the root nodes are identical, Step 3.2 is not performed and the child nodes in t_j are not visited at all. In such cases, these child nodes were transmitted from s_j to s_i in Phase 2 for nothing and did not contribute to the integrity verification in Phase 3.

To overcome this limitation, DynaEDI employs a new tree structure named the *pairing tree* instead of the Merkle tree as data digests. It generates tree digests with Szudzik's pairing function [22] (for its well-known efficiency) instead of hash functions. A pairing function ($P : \mathbb{N} \times \mathbb{N} \to \mathbb{N}$) maps two inputs (usually non-negative integers) into a single output (an integer or another data type).

Definition: Pairing Tree. A pairing tree is a binary tree where each leaf node is the hash of a data block and each non-leaf node is the output of a pairing function with its child nodes as the inputs.

Pairing Tree Generation. As illustrated in Fig. 5, the generation of a pairing tree for a data item D goes through the following steps.

- **Step 4.1.** Compute the hash with a hash function like SHA-256 for each data block in D and incorporate the resulting hash into a corresponding leaf node in the pairing tree.
- **Step 4.2.** Create non-leaf nodes that represent the output of the pairing function for each pair of leaf nodes. Assign the results to the non-leaf nodes.
- **Step 4.3.** In a bottom-up manner, at each level of the tree, create non-leaf nodes as the output of the pairing function for each pair of previously created parent nodes at the same level.

Under DynaEDI, edge servers create pairing trees instead of Merkle trees in Phase 1 (Sect. 3) as data digests, and transmit subtrees in these pairing trees (referred to as *pairing subtrees* hereafter) in Phase 2, and verify data in Phase 3 based on these subtrees. The main differences are summarized below.

- In Phase 1, edge servers generate a pairing tree (instead of a Merkle tree) from each data item as the digest.
- In Phase 2 at Step 2.2, edge servers transmit only the root nodes of the pairing subtrees (instead of the entire pairing subtrees) to s_i in their responses to s_i's DIGEST-COLLECTION messages. The comparison proceeds when $t_i.root$ and $t_j.root$ are not identical.

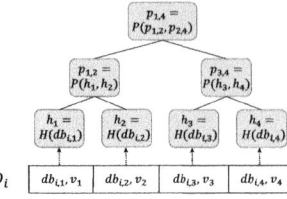
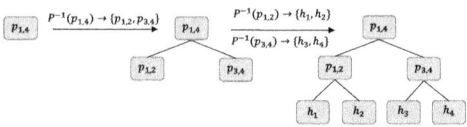

Fig. 5. Generating a pairing tree from a data item D_i comprised of four data blocks.

Fig. 6. Expanding a pairing tree T_j from its root node.

- In Phase 3 at Step 3.1, edge server s_i compares the root nodes of its pairing subtrees (instead of Merkle subtrees) against the root nodes of the received pairing subtrees (instead of Merkle subtrees). Next, in Phase 3 at Step 3.2, s_i expands t_j from $t_j.root$ with P^{-1}, the inverse function of P. It then inspects the other nodes in t_j to identify potentially-corrupted data blocks.

Inverse Pairing Function. An inverse pairing function P^{-1} is the inverse function for a pairing function P. Given a non-negative integer $z \in \mathbb{N}$, P^{-1} outputs a pair of integers $(x \in \mathbb{N}, y \in \mathbb{N})$ that fulfill $P(x,y) = z$. As discussed above, DynaEDI employs Szudzik's pairing function, which is capable of mapping a pair of non-negative integers to a *unique* non-negative integer:

$$P(x,y) = \begin{cases} y^2 + x & x \neq max(x,y) \\ x^2 + x + y & x = max(x,y) \end{cases} \quad (1)$$

The inverse Szudzik's pairing function below outputs the original pair of non-negative integers (x,y) taken by Szudzik's pairing function to produce z:

$$P^{-1}(z) = \begin{cases} \{z - \lfloor \sqrt{z} \rfloor^2, \lfloor \sqrt{z} \rfloor\} & z - \lfloor \sqrt{z} \rfloor^2 < \lfloor \sqrt{z} \rfloor \\ \{\lfloor \sqrt{z} \rfloor, z - \lfloor \sqrt{z} \rfloor^2 - \lfloor \sqrt{z} \rfloor\} & z - \lfloor \sqrt{z} \rfloor^2 \geq \lfloor \sqrt{z} \rfloor \end{cases} \quad (2)$$

Figure 6 presents an example that demonstrates the expansion of a pairing tree T_j from its root node $T_j.root$ for comparison with T_i under DynaEDI. Now, edge servers can transmit only the root nodes of their pairing subtrees. This minimizes the communication overhead, but comes with a price - edge servers need to expand the pairing subtrees at Step 3.1. Fortunately, the inverse Szudzik's pairing function (Eq. (2)) is highly efficient and does not incur significant computational overhead, as experimentally presented in Sect. 5.4.

5 Experimental Evaluation

We implement DynaEDI on a testbed system to evaluate its performance against three representative EDI schemes experimentally.

5.1 Experiment Settings

Testbed Setup. We build a testbed system consisting of 30 edge servers by deploying 30 virtual machines running on geographically dispersed physical machines. Each virtual machine is configured with 2 virtual CPUs (vCPUs) and 2GB of memory, running Ubuntu 22.04. We deploy an AWS p3.2xlarge EC2 instance with 8 vCPUs and 61GB memory in the AWS cloud as the application vendor's cloud server. Network testing showed that the latency between edge servers ranges between 5 and 10 milliseconds. Accordingly, the digest collection timeout is set at 100 milliseconds in Phase 2.1 (Sect. 3).

Benchmark Implementations. The following three baseline EDI schemes are implemented for comparison with DynaEDI.

- **EDI-V** [16]. This is a representative centralized EDI scheme. Its core idea is shared by many recent centralized EDI schemes, e.g., SIA [27] and DVA-P [28]. Under this scheme, the app vendor generates a verifiable Merkle hash tree (VMHT) for each version of data D. To verify the data variants of D, the cloud server sends a request to each edge server, asking for an integrity proof. To respond to the verification request, each edge server generates a subtree from its Merkle tree generated from data blocks sampled from its version of D. It then sends the root node to the cloud server as the integrity proof.
- **CooperEDI** [15]. This is the state-of-the-art decentralized EDI scheme. Its main idea is shared by EdgeWatch [18], another decentralized EDI scheme. Under this scheme, to verify the integrity of D, the edge servers storing the same version of D compare their data digests generated by the SHA-256 hash function. Then, they find the correct replicas that comprise a data quorum for D as the ground truth for comparison with D.
- **CooperEDI-MV**. This is a modified version of CooperEDI. It generates Merkle trees instead of SHA256 hashes as data digests, and versions data blocks to enable digest comparison between data replicas of the same version.

Data and Request Generation. In the experiments, a total of 100 most popular videos collected from TikTok over 15 d in December 2023 in four different geographic locations worldwide are cached on each of the 30 edge servers. The sizes of these video clips range between 5MB and 20MB (like most popular YouTube video clips [7]) unless specified otherwise. To simulate a variety of dynamic EDI scenarios, we randomly modify a proportion of the video clips in the system according to the *modification rate*, which ranges from 0 to 0.5 with a default value of 0.3. When a video clip is modified, a proportion of its data blocks are modified in the same way, according to the *modification degree*, which ranges from 0 to 0.5 with a default value of 0.3. Meanwhile, we corrupt a proportion of all the video clips according to the *corruption rate*, which ranges from 0 to 0.3 with a default value of 0.2. When corrupting a video clip, we randomly modify a proportion of its data blocks sized 512KB by default, according to the *corruption degree*, which ranges from 0 to 0.3 with a default value of 0.2. In each experiment, edge servers are randomly selected to initiate a total of 100 requests to verify randomly selected videos, and the average results are reported.

Table 1. Accuracy Comparison between four EDI schemes categorized as static and dynamic schemes based on their ability to handle dynamic edge data. (Modification Rate = 0.3, Modification Degree = 0.3, Corruption Rate = 0.2, Corruption Degree = 0.2.)

Scheme Category	Scheme	Accuracy	TP	TN	FP	FN
Static Scheme	EDI-V	92%	5%	87%	8%	0%
	CooperEDI	65%	3%	62%	5%	0%
Dynamic Scheme	CooperEDI-MV	100%	4%	96%	0%	0%
	DynaEDI	100%	4%	96%	0%	0%

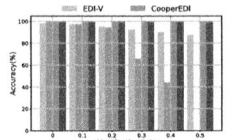
(a) vs. Modification Rate
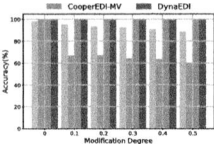
(b) vs. Modification Degree

Fig. 7. Accuracy evaluation. Default settings: modification rate = 0.3, modification degree = 0.3, corruption rate = 0.2, corruption degree = 0.2.

5.2 Accuracy

To find out whether DynaEDI can properly verify the integrity of dynamic edge data (Challenge I in Sect. 1), we evaluate its verification accuracy, measured by the percentage of data blocks correctly identified as corrupted or intact. Table 1 compares the verification accuracy achieved by different schemes under default settings. The following key findings can be drawn.

– EDI-V and CooperEDI (together referred to as static schemes hereafter) fail to verify some data blocks, the latter being more than the former, while CooperEDI-MV and DynaEDI (together referred to as dynamic schemes) manage to verify all the data blocks tested, and can fully tackle the first challenge discussed in Sect. 1. The reasons for EDI-V's failed cases and CooperEDI's failed cases are not entirely the same. Without the ability to match data block versions, they cannot distinguish data variants and both mistakenly identify modified (yet correct) data blocks as corrupted (Sect. 1). In addition, CooperEDI also failed the tests when the ground truth cannot be found for verification (Sect. 1).
– As dynamic schemes, CooperEDI-MV and DynaEDI both manage to verify all the tested video clips successfully, outperforming EDI-V and CooperEDI by 8% and 35%, respectively. This indicates the importance of versioning data blocks to accommodate data modifications in verification. However, CooperEDI-MV pays a much higher price - it incurs immensely more communication overhead than DynaEDI (Sect. 5.3).

Accuracy vs. Modification Rate. As analyzed above, the existence of data variants is the main reason why existing static EDI schemes suffer from poor verification accuracy. The modification rate dictates the number of data variants in the system. To evaluate its impact on the performance of DynaEDI, we vary the modification rate from 0 to 0.5 when setting up the experiments, and measure the accuracy achieved under different schemes. Figure 7a demonstrates the results. CooperEDI-MV and DynaEDI version data blocks based on their modifications. They can identify the right data blocks for verification. Thus, their performance is not impacted by the increase in the modification rate. However,

Table 2. Communication Overhead (KB). (Data Size = [5MB, 20MB].)

Scheme Category	Scheme	Overhead[a]
Static Scheme	EDI-V	445
	CooperEDI	140
Dynamic Scheme	CooperEDI-MV	1,331
	DynaEDI	128

[a] Data transfer from AWS cloud to the edge is 4×-8× more expensive than data transfer between edge servers [2]. Accordingly, its communication overhead is calculated as 5× of the later.

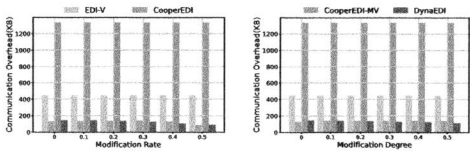

(a) vs. Modification Rate (b) vs. Modification Degree

Fig. 8. Communication overhead evaluation. Default settings: modification rate = 0.3, modification degree = 0.3, corruption rate = 0.2, corruption degree = 0.2.

it is not the case with EDI-V and CooperEDI. As the number of data variants in the system increases, they are more likely to mistake modified data blocks for corrupted data blocks. When the modification rate is 0.5, more than half of the video replicas in the system are modified or corrupted. As a result, CooperEDI cannot find a data quorum (Sect. 2) as the ground truth for verification and the verification fails. Thus, with the impact of the corruption rate piled on, CooperEDI's accuracy drops rapidly when the modification rate increases.

Accuracy vs. Modification Degree. The modification degree is the proportion of data blocks that are modified in a data item. To evaluate its impact on verification accuracy, we vary its value from 0 to 0.5 in the experiments. Figure 7b illustrates the results. Again, CooperEDI-MV and DynaEDI achieve a 100% accuracy consistently despite the increase in the modification degree. When the modification degree is 0, no data blocks are modified and there are no data variants in the system. The four schemes achieve the same accuracy as they did when the modification rate was 0. When the modification degree increases to 0.1, some of the data replicas are modified and become data variants. They "collaborate" with corrupted data replicas to stop edge servers from finding data quorums for verification under CooperEDI, dropping its accuracy to 0.65. As the modification degree increases further, more modified data blocks are mistakenly identified as corrupted data blocks by CooperEDI. Its accuracy decreases accordingly. This is also the reason for EDI-V's decreased accuracy.

5.3 Communication Overhead

To find out how much communication overhead DynaEDI can reduce (Challenge II in Sect. 1), we measure the amount of data that needs to be transmitted in the system to complete the verification of a video clip. Communication overhead is incurred in different ways under the four EDI schemes:

– **EDI-V.** Under EDI-V, communication overhead predominantly comes from the transmission of edge servers' integrity proofs (in the form of Merkle trees) to the cloud server.
– **CooperEDI.** Under CooperEDI, communication overhead is incurred when edge servers elect the leaders, exchange data digests to find data quorums and transmit data block digests to identify corrupted data blocks.
– **CooperEDI-MV.** Under CooperEDI-MV, communication overhead results from the exchange of data digests (i.e., Merkle trees) between edge servers.
– **DynaEDI.** DynaEDI's main communication overhead comes from transmitting the root nodes of pairing trees between edge servers in Phase 2.2 (Sect. 3).

Overall Comparison. Table 2 compares the average amount of data that needs to be transmitted to verify each video clip. It reveals the following key findings.

– Incurring communication overhead only at the network edge, CooperEDI and DynaEDI incur less communication overhead than EDI-V. This validates the advantage of decentralized EDI schemes discussed in Sect. 1.
– CooperEDI-MV incurs communication overhead that is an order-of-magnitude higher than other schemes, including EDI-V. It comes from its adoption of Merkle trees (instead of SHA-256 hashes) as data digests.
– DynaEDI incurs the least communication overhead, about 71.24%, 8.6%, and 90.38% less than EDI-V, CooperEDI, and CooperEDI-MV on average. This indicates that DynaEDI can tackle Challenge II (Sect. 1) effectively.

Communication Overhead vs. Modification Rate. Figure 8a demonstrates the communication overhead and impact of modification rate. The overall comparison is consistent with Table 2. Now, let us take a close look at the comparison between CooperEDI and DynaEDI, which incur much less communication overhead than EDI-V and CooperEDI-MV. DynaEDI is the winner in most cases except when the modification rate is 0.5. When the modification rate is 0.5, CooperEDI cannot find the ground truth for comparison in any of the test cases (Sect. 5.2). There are no subsequent interactions or data transmissions between the edge servers in these cases. Figure 8a tells us that DynaEDI's adoption of pairing trees as data digests can indeed reduce its communication overhead profoundly. When the modification rate increases, DynaEDI can accommodate the increased diversity in the data variants with 100% accuracy (as shown in Sect. 5.2) without additional communication overhead. This is a superior advantage in practice.

Communication Overhead vs. Modification Degree. Fig. 8b demonstrates the communication overhead with varying modification degree. DynaEDI is again the winner in the competition. As the modification degree increases, the proportion of data variants in the system increases. They constitute smaller data block quorums. The number of data digests transmitted between edge servers looking for data block quorums decreases accordingly. As a result, DynaEDI's communication overhead decreases. This shows the ability of DynaEDI to handle dynamic EDI scenarios involving substantial data modifications.

5.4 Further Evaluation

Performance vs. Data Size. As discussed in Sect. 1, data size plays a crucial role in communication overhead. To evaluate its impact, we conducted an experiment on five sets of video clips of different sizes. Figure 9 shows the results. It can be observed that an increase in data size incurs more communication overhead under all four schemes. With a fixed data block size of 512KB, a larger video clip will be partitioned into more data blocks. This facilitates fine-grained identification of corrupted data blocks, but increases the sizes of the Merkle trees transmitted between edge servers for verification under EDI-V and CooperEDI-MV, and consequently, the communication overhead. In the case of CooperEDI, edge servers have to transmit more data block digests to find corrupted data blocks. Under DynaEDI, edge servers transmit only the root nodes of matched pairing subtrees despite the sizes of their pairing trees. However, they need bigger tree nodes to host the values generated by pairing functions, including the root nodes. These bigger root nodes increase the communication overhead under DynaEDI. Specifically, when the data size range increases from [5MB, 20MB] to [80MB, 100MB], the average communication overhead under DynaEDI increases from 12.28KB to 122.64KB. This is comparable to CooperEDI, showing that DynaEDI can handle large data items with ease.

Computation Overhead: Merkle Tree vs. Pairing Tree. As discussed in Sect. 5.3, the advantage of DynaEDI in communication overhead comes from its transmissions of only the root nodes (instead of the entire pairing trees) between edge servers for verification. However, in Phase 3, edge servers need to expand the pairing subtrees from their root nodes in search for corrupted data blocks (Sect. 3). This computation takes time, which is the price DynaEDI pays to reduce communication overhead. To evaluate this computation overhead, we implement DynaEDI-M, a new version of DynaEDI that generates and transmits Merkle trees instead of pairing subtrees as data digests, and compare its per-verification computation time in Phase 3 against DynaEDI. Figure 10 demonstrates the results. DynaEDI and DynaEDI-M employ the same search method to traverse trees of the same size, which takes them the same amount of time to complete, as illustrated in Fig. 10a. The pink bars in the figure indicate the average tree expansion time in DynaEDI. It ranges between 0 milliseconds and about 11 milliseconds. When the modification degree increases, the differences between data replicas and data variants increase. In response to the DIGEST-COLLECTION messages from an edge server s_i in Phase 2 (Sect. 3), edge servers find fewer version-matched data blocks and as a result, transmit smaller pairing subtrees for verification. These smaller pairing subtrees take s_i less time to expand and search a pairing tree in Phase 3 (Sect. 3). Accordingly, we can observe a decrease in both the expansion time and search time in DynaEDI when the modification degree increases. When performing a root node comparison in Phase 3, an edge server s_i will expand the received pairing subtree to identify corrupted data blocks when the root nodes are not identical. When its data D_i is severely corrupted, s_i is more likely to need to expand received pairing subtrees.

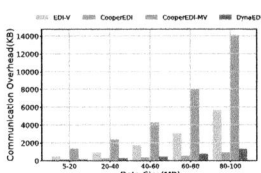 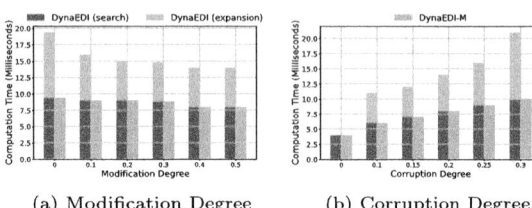

Fig. 9. Impact of Data Size. Default settings: modification rate = 0.3, modification degree = 0.3, corruption rate = 0.2, corruption degree = 0.2.

Fig. 10. Computation overhead: Merkle tree vs. pairing tree. Default settings: modification rate = 0.3, corruption rate = 0.2, data size = [5MB, 20MB]. The modification rate and corruption rate do not affect the computation time under DynaEDI or DynaEDI-M. They are thus not included in this experiment.

Accordingly, the average tree expansion time increases. Figure 10b demonstrates that this increase is linear to the increase in the corruption degree.

6 Conclusion

This paper presented DynaEDI, a new decentralized scheme for verifying the integrity of identical and partially-identical dynamic edge data. It implements a new interaction protocol that enables edge servers to transmit subtrees instead of complete trees as digests for verification. It employs new pairing trees instead of Merkle trees as data digests, allowing edge servers to transmit root nodes rather than complete subtrees for verification. As the first dynamic EDI scheme, DynaEDI increases verification accuracy by up to 35% and reduces communication overhead by an order of magnitude, compared to state-of-the-art schemes.

Our future work will focus on enhancing the security of the verification process, as the current scheme assumes that edge servers can honestly respond to integrity verification. However, in real-world scenarios, edge servers may act maliciously. Preventing and detecting malicious behavior during verification is an important topic for exploration.

Acknowledgment. This research was supported in part by the National Key R&D Program of China under Grant No. 2023YFB4502400, the Australian Research Council Discovery Projects under Grant No. DP200102491, DP230101790, and Linkage Projects under Grant No. LP210301393 and LP220100482. Feifei Chen is the corresponding author of this paper.

References

1. AWS Wavelength for media & entertainment (2021). https://d1.awsstatic.com/Wavelength2020/AWS-Wavelength-for-Media-Entertainment-SolutionBrief-Feb2021-Final.pdf
2. Amazon EC2 on-demand pricing (2023). https://aws.amazon.com/ec2/pricing/on-demand/
3. Ateniese, G., et al.: Provable data possession at untrusted stores. In: ACM Conference on Computer and Communications Security, pp. 598–609 (2007)
4. AWS: edge caching on AWS wavelength (2022). https://aws.amazon.com/blogs/media/metfc-edge-caching-on-aws-wavelength/
5. AWS: AWS wavelength features (2024). https://aws.amazon.com/wavelength/features/
6. Baresi, L., Quattrocchi, G., Ticongolo, I.G.: Dependency-aware resource allocation for serverless functions at the edge. In: Monti, F., Rinderle-Ma, S., Ruiz Cortés, A., Zheng, Z., Mecella, M. (eds.) Service-Oriented Computing: 21st International Conference, ICSOC 2023, Rome, Italy, November 28 – December 1, 2023, Proceedings, Part I, pp. 347–362. Springer Nature Switzerland, Cham (2023). https://doi.org/10.1007/978-3-031-48421-6_24
7. Che, X., Ip, B., Lin, L.: A survey of current YouTube video characteristics. IEEE Multimedia **22**(2), 56–63 (2015)
8. Google: Youtube advertising formats (2024). https://support.google.com/youtube/answer/2467968
9. Guo, W., et al.: Dynamic proof of data possession and replication with tree sharing and batch verification in the cloud. IEEE Trans. Serv. Comput. **15**(4), 1813–1824 (2022)
10. He, Q., Dong, Z., Chen, F., Deng, S., Liang, W., Yang, Y.: Pyramid: enabling hierarchical neural networks with edge computing. In: The Web Conference, pp. 1860—1870 (2022)
11. Hu, Y.C., Patel, M., Sabella, D., Sprecher, N., Young, V.: Mobile edge computing-a key technology towards 5G. ETSI White Paper **11**(11), 1–16 (2015)
12. Juels, A., Kaliski Jr, B.S.: PORs: proofs of retrievability for large files. In: ACM Conference on Computer and Communications Security, pp. 584–597 (2007)
13. Lai, P., et al.: Optimal edge user allocation in edge computing with variable sized vector bin packing. In: Pahl, C., Vukovic, M., Yin, J., Yu, Q. (eds.) Service-Oriented Computing: 16th International Conference, ICSOC 2018, Hangzhou, China, November 12-15, 2018, Proceedings, pp. 230–245. Springer International Publishing, Cham (2018). https://doi.org/10.1007/978-3-030-03596-9_15
14. Lamport, L.: Paxos made simple. ACM Sigact News **32**(4), 18–25 (2001)
15. Li, B., et al.: Cooperative assurance of cache data integrity for mobile edge computing. IEEE Trans. Inf. Forensics Secur. **16**, 4648–4662 (2022)
16. Li, B., He, Q., Chen, F., Jin, H., Xiang, Y., Yang, Y.: Auditing cache data integrity in the edge computing environment. IEEE Trans. Parallel Distrib. Syst. **32**(5), 1210–1223 (2021)
17. Li, B., He, Q., Chen, F., Jin, H., Xiang, Y., Yang, Y.: Inspecting edge data integrity with aggregate signature in distributed edge computing environment. IEEE Trans. Cloud Comput. **10**(4), 2691–2703 (2021)
18. Li, B., He, Q., Yuan, L., Chen, F., Lyu, L., Yang, Y.: EdgeWatch: collaborative investigation of data integrity at the edge based on blockchain. In: 28th ACM SIGKDD International Conference on Knowledge Discovery in Data Mining, pp. 3208–3218. ACM (2022)

19. Ongaro, D., Ousterhout, J.: In search of an understandable consensus algorithm. In: USENIX Annual Technical Conference, pp. 305–319 (2014)
20. Peng, J., et al.: MagNet: cooperative edge caching by automatic content congregating. In: The ACM Web Conference, pp. 3280–3288 (2022)
21. Shi, E., Stefanov, E., Papamanthou, C.: Practical dynamic proofs of retrievability. In: ACM SIGSAC Conference on Computer & Communications Security, pp. 325–336 (2013)
22. Szudzik, M.: An elegant pairing function. In: Wolfram Research (ed.) Special NKS 2006 Wolfram Science Conference, pp. 1–12 (2006)
23. Wang, Q., Wang, C., Ren, K., Lou, W., Li, J.: Enabling public auditability and data dynamics for storage security in cloud computing. IEEE Trans. Parallel Distrib. Syst. **22**(5), 847–859 (2011)
24. Xia, X., et al.: Graph-based optimal data caching in edge computing. In: Yangui, S., Bouassida Rodriguez, I., Drira, K., Tari, Z. (eds.) Service-Oriented Computing: 17th International Conference, ICSOC 2019, Toulouse, France, October 28–31, 2019, Proceedings, pp. 477–493. Springer International Publishing, Cham (2019). https://doi.org/10.1007/978-3-030-33702-5_37
25. Xia, X., Chen, F., He, Q., Grundy, J.C., Abdelrazek, M., Jin, H.: Cost-effective app data distribution in edge computing. IEEE Trans. Parallel Distrib. Syst. **32**(1), 31–44 (2020)
26. Zhang, Y., Xu, C., Liang, X., Li, H., Mu, Y., Zhang, X.: Efficient public verification of data integrity for cloud storage systems from indistinguishability obfuscation. IEEE Trans. Inf. Forensics Secur. **12**, 676–688 (2017)
27. Zhao, Y., Qu, Y., Chen, F., Xiang, Y., Gao, L.: Data integrity verification in mobile edge computing with multi-vendor and multi-server. IEEE Trans. Mob. Comput. **23**(5), 5418–5432 (2024)
28. Zhao, Y., Qu, Y., Xiang, Y., Shi, C., Chen, F., Gao, L.: Long-term over one-off: heterogeneity-oriented dynamic verification assignment for edge data integrity. IEEE Trans. Mob. Comput. **23**(5), 4601–4616 (2023)

Heterogeneous Multi Relation Trust for SIoT Service Recommendation

Geming Xia[✉], Chaodong Yu, Linxuan Song, Wei Peng, Yuze Zhang, and Hongfeng Li

National University of Defense Technology, Changsha 410003, China
xiageming@163.com

Abstract. With the rapid development of Internet of Things (IoT) technology, the deep integration of IoT devices and social networks has given rise to the field of Social Internet of Things (SIoT), where the significance of SIoT service recommendation is increasingly prominent. Given the heterogeneity and complexity of user interaction patterns in the SIoT service recommendation, as well as the abundance of user-centric semantic information, building an effective trust mechanism has become a key element in improving service quality and promoting successful interaction between users. In this paper, we propose a novel heterogeneous multi relation trust evaluation model (HMTrust). This model accurately captures the association patterns of users in multi-dimensional trust communities based on meta-paths. Subsequently, we introduce a two-layer attention mechanism to delve into the rich semantic features embedded within heterogeneous trust relationships, achieving a refined evaluation of trust relationships. Based on this evaluation result, we can effectively implement personalized SIoT service recommendation to meet the diverse needs of users. Experiments on real-world datasets show the advantages of our proposed HMTrust compared to existing baselines.

Keywords: Social Internet of Things · Service Recommendation · Heterogeneous Graph Neural Networks · Trust Evaluation

1 Introduction

As the Internet of Things (IoT) system becomes increasingly large and complex, it covers many fields such as smart home, smart city, smart medical care and etc. And it also gradually penetrates into people's daily social activities, giving birth to the emerging concept of Social Internet of Things (SIoT) [2]. In the SIoT environment, service recommendation is very important as the key link between user requirements and service resources. In the face of massive SIoT services and diversified user needs, accurately recommending services that meet users' preferences can greatly improve user experience. However, due to the openness

---

G. Xia and C. Yu—Contribute equally to this work and should be considered co-first authors.

and high heterogeneity of SIoT, the interaction between service providers, users and IoT devices is full of uncertainty. For example, users may intentionally provide a false rating [20] for malicious purposes, thus undermining a valid service recommendation. Therefore, in the process of SIoT service recommendation, the establishment of trust evaluation [23,27] mechanism is particularly important.

There are two major challenges in exploring the trust evaluation mechanism of SIoT service recommendation. The first challenge is to deeply explore the multi-dimensional trust attributes in SIoT service recommendations. Many past methods [7,11,12,28] are based on neural networks [3,6,10] for trust prediction. Due to the heterogeneity of SIoT environments and the complexity of interaction patterns between nodes, these methods tend to be limited to a few dimensions, thus ignoring the multifaceted nature of trust in SIoT. Even though some methods [28] take into account the semantic information in SIoT, they are only a simple concatenation of semantic knowledge embedding and node embedding. In this way, it fails to deeply explore the intricate internal relations and dependencies in SIoT heterogeneous environment. The second challenge is to effectively retain and leverage the rich node semantic information in SIoT service recommendations. Some past methods [1,5,8,13,14,16,18] are based on trust computing to aggregate multiple semantic data. However, the aggregating weights of these methods are mostly set based on experience. Even though some methods [7,12,28] employ the attention mechanism, they are limited by the finite trust dimension. This will lead to the loss of semantic information and the misjudgment of evaluation results.

In this paper, we propose a novel heterogeneous multi relation trust evaluation model (HMTrust). We comprehensively consider the heterogeneous network topology, users' trust relationship and the semantic background of multi-dimensional trust communities as the key trust characteristics in SIoT service recommendation. Specifically, HMTrust constructs intricate association patterns among users in multi-dimensional trust communities by using meta-path to deeply capture the multi-dimensional trust attributes of SIoT heterogeneous environment. We then introduce a two-layer attention mechanism to dynamically aggregate key trust characteristics in multi-dimensional trust communities and heterogeneous objects. We also design a trust-based SIoT service recommendation method to improve the personalized service recommendation experience for users.

The rest of the paper is organized as follows. Section 2 briefly describes the preliminary of trust in SIoT service recommendations. Section 3 introduces the heterogeneous multi relation trust evaluation method and the trust-based SIoT service recommendation method. Section 4 discusses the experimental results. Section 5 presents the related work. Section 6 concludes the paper.

2 Preliminary

Definition 1. SIoT Service Recommendation. This paper considers the problem of trust evaluation in SIoT Service Recommendation, which is modeled as a heterogeneous directed graph, denoted as $\mathcal{G} = (\mathcal{V}, \mathcal{E})$. $\mathcal{V} = \{v_1, ..., v_n\}$ is the object set and $\mathcal{E} = \{e_{i,j}, ..., e_{u,v}\}$ is the relationship set, respectively. And $\mathcal{G}$ is also with a object type mapping function $\phi: \mathcal{V} \to \mathcal{A}$ and a relationship type mapping function $\psi: \mathcal{E} \to \mathcal{R}$. $\mathcal{A}$ and $\mathcal{R}$ denote the set of predefined object types and relationship types in SIoT service recommendation, where $|\mathcal{A}| > 1$ and $|\mathcal{R}| > 1$.

Definition 2. Trust Meta-Path [17]. In SIoT service recommendation, heterogeneous objects can be connected through different semantic trust meta-paths. Trust meta-path Φ is defined as $\mathcal{A}_1 \xrightarrow{\mathcal{R}_1} \mathcal{A}_2 \ldots \xrightarrow{\mathcal{R}_n} \mathcal{A}_{n+1}$, which describes a composite relation $\mathcal{R} = \mathcal{R}_1 \diamond \mathcal{R}_2 \diamond \mathcal{R}_n$ between objects $\mathcal{A}_1$ and $\mathcal{A}_{n+1}$, where $\diamond$ denotes the composition operator on relations.

Definition 3. Trust Evaluation. Given $\mathcal{G}$, let $\mathcal{W} = \{\langle u, v \rangle, w_{u,v} | e_{u,v} \in \mathcal{E}\}$ be the set of observed trust relationships in SIoT service recommendation, where u, v are the trustor and trustee respectively. $w_{u,v}$ denotes the trustworthiness from u to v, which is typically application specific. For example, in Ciao [19], trustworthiness is simply divided into two types, trust and distrust. Trust evaluation is the design of a mapping $\mathcal{F}(\cdot)$ to evaluate the trustworthiness of the observed/unobserved trust relationship of the trustor-trustee pair, where $u, v \in \mathcal{V}$, $u \neq v$, and $e_{u,v} \notin \mathcal{E}$.

3 HMTrust: Proposed Framework

In this section, we first give a brief overview of the proposed method. And then we introduce the main components in detail. In order to effectively evaluate the trust relationship between heterogeneous users in SIoT service recommendation, we propose a novel model, which can fully mine the inherent characteristics of heterogeneous trust and effectively integrate various attributes of heterogeneous trust in SIoT, namely HMTrust. The structure of HMTrust is shown in Fig. 1, which consists of three main components, namely, meta-path based multi-dimensional trust community module, two-layer attention mechanism module and prediction module. At the meta-path based multi-dimensional trust community module, we generate users' embedding vector from three dimensions, namely, heterogeneous network topology, users' trust relationship and the semantic background of multi-dimensional trust community, which can be applied to modeling users' trust attributes. At the two-layer attention mechanism module, we model trustor trust and trustee trust to capture the asymmetry of trust. Then, we introduce the object-level attention mechanism and social attention mechanism to consider the aggregation and propagation rules of heterogeneous objects relationships and multi-dimensional trust community respectively. And we provide attention weights for various heterogeneous attributes and trust relationships. At the prediction module, the extracted potential factors are transformed into potential representations of trust relationships by introducing a full connection layer. The softmax function is then used to predict the probability of heterogeneous trust among users in SIoT service recommendation. Then we design a trust-based SIoT service recommendation model with the evaluated trust values.

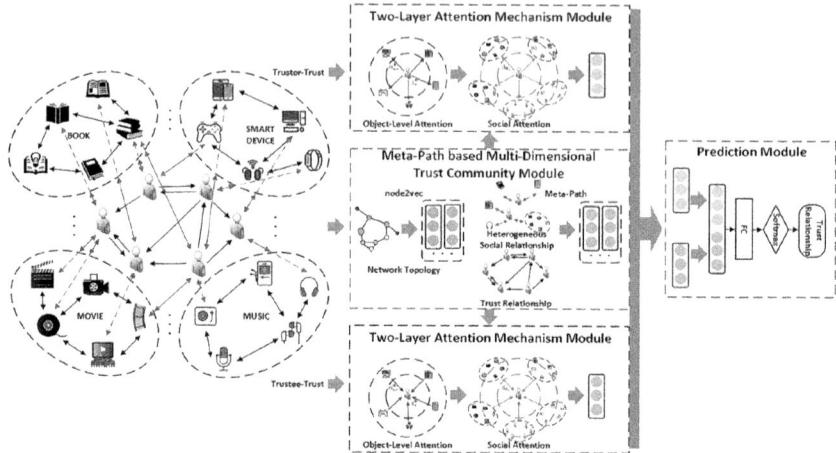

Fig. 1. The architecture of HMTrust, which is consist of three parts: 1) Meta-Path based Multi-Dimensional Trust Community Module: heterogeneous network topology, users' trust relationship and the semantic background of multi-dimensional trust community; 2) Two-Layer Attention Mechanism Module: hierarchical attention mechanism of object-level attention and social attention; 3) Prediction Module: evaluating the trust relationships between users.

3.1 Meta-Path Based Multi-Dimensional Trust Community Module

To gain a deeper understanding of the inherent characteristics of heterogeneous trust in SIoT service recommendation, we will obtain user embedding vectors to represent each user's pattern. We consider heterogeneous network topology, users' trust relationship and the semantic background of multi-dimensional trust community, which will serve as inputs to the two-layer attention mechanism module. For the heterogeneous network topology, we use graph embedding technology to map the topology information of the high-dimensional structure to the low-dimensional potential space in order to capture the network topology information. In particular, we use node2vec [5] to learn a representation vector for each object of $\mathcal{G}$ in SIoT. For the trust relationship, we use a one-hot encoding to transform it, so as to ensure the extensibility of the trust relationship. For semantic background of multi-dimensional trust community, we use meta-path to represent the complex relationship between heterogeneous objects. For example, in Ciao [19], the set of objects is $\langle user, category, product \rangle$. And the meta-path can be $\langle user_u - category_j - user_v \rangle$, $\langle user_u - product_k - user_v \rangle$, etc.

3.2 Two-Layer Attention Mechanism Module

Due to the asymmetric nature of social relationships between users in SIoT service recommendation, we consider to learn users' embedding by constructing trustor-trust and trustee-trust to capture relevant trust relationships. Trustor-trust refers to the trustworthiness given to others by the user, indicating the willingness of the user to trust others. Trustee-trust refers to the trustworthiness of the user observed by others, indicating the degree to which the user is trusted by others. The more trusted a user is, the higher its trustee-trust is.

When evaluating the trustworthiness of SIoT users, the users have heterogeneous social relationships. This will be divided into a number of multi-dimensional trust communities, and the trust relationship between communities has a certain role of reference, but each has different influences. For example, users' trust in the movie community can be used as a reference for the TV drama community, because movies and TV dramas are both film and television works and have certain similarities. However, the user's trust in the film community may have small affects to the trust relationship in the football community. We build multi-dimensional trust communities through meta-paths. The users generally have multiple meta-paths, and each meta-path contains multiple types of heterogeneous objects. By constructing object-level attention mechanism and social attention mechanism, we realize the trust fusion of heterogeneous objects and heterogeneous social relationships in SIoT service recommendation.

Firstly, we fuse the trust features of heterogeneous objects of a single trust community to eliminate the influence of heterogeneity object to the trust evaluation in SIoT service recommendation.

Trust of Heterogeneous Objects. Due to the heterogeneity of objects, different types of objects have different feature spaces. We project the features of different types of objects into the same feature space by designing type-specific transformation matrix Δ_ϕ. For the object u_i with a type ϕ_i, the projection process is shown in Eq. 1:

$$f_i' = \Delta_{\phi_i} \cdot f_i \qquad (1)$$

where f_i and f_i' are the original and projected embedding of object u_i, respectively.

Different types of neighbor objects may have different degrees of impact on trust. Therefore, in order to achieve the feature fusion of heterogeneous objects, we use the object-level attention mechanism [21] to learn the weights of various types of heterogeneous objects. For the given trust community Φ between users u and v, we construct an object-level attention matrix α_{uv}^Φ to represent the importance of heterogeneous object features on trust community Φ of user pairs $\langle u, v \rangle$. For each given trust community, we model the connection pattern of the trust community by building a deep neural network Υ_{object} [24] of object-level attention. Then, we input the heterogeneous graph structure information containing the trust community and the user's trust features into Υ_{object} to learn the importance of heterogeneous objects, and then normalize the object-level attention matrix α_{uv}^Φ through softmax function, as shown in Eq. 2.

$$\alpha_{uv}^\Phi = \frac{exp(\Upsilon_{object}(f_u', f_v'; \Phi))}{\sum_{i \in \Psi_u^\Phi}(exp(\Upsilon_{object}(f_u', f_k'; \Phi)))} \qquad (2)$$

where Ψ_u^Φ is the set of heterogeneous neighbor objects of user u of trust community Φ. And Υ_{object} is calculated in Eq. 3.

$$\Upsilon_{object}(f_u', f_v'; \Phi) = \sigma(\delta_\Phi^T \cdot [f_u' \otimes f_v']) \tag{3}$$

where σ is the activation function, δ_Φ^T is the object-level attention vector of trust community Φ, $\otimes$ is concatenate operation.

After obtaining the object-level attention matrix α_{uv}^Φ, we can perform feature aggregation on the heterogeneous objects on a single trust community to represent its specific semantic information. In trust aggregation, we construct the asymmetry of trust through trustor f and trustee $\overline{f}$, and aggregate the trust of trustor and trustee through the concatenate operation. And we introduce multiple attention mechanism to repeat object-level attention M times, so as to fully realize the feature aggregation of heterogeneous objects, as shown in Eq. 4.

$$z_u^\Phi = \prod_{m=1}^{M} \sigma(\sum_{i \in \Psi_u^\Phi} \alpha_{uv}^\Phi \cdot (f_i' \otimes \overline{f_i'})) \tag{4}$$

After completing the feature aggregation of heterogeneous objects in a single trust community, we further aggregate the trust features of multiple trust community of users, thereby eliminating the influence of heterogeneous social relationship to trust evaluation in SIoT service recommendation.

Trust of Heterogeneous Social Relationships. The social relationship represented by a single trust community can only reflect the trust feature of users from one aspect. In order to comprehensively learn the heterogeneous social relationship of users, we need to integrate the semantic information of multiple heterogeneous trust communities. Different meta-paths represent different semantic backgrounds of heterogeneous trust communities, and their importance will change with different trust requirements. We construct the social attention mechanism to represent the importance of the features of heterogeneous trust communities between user pairs $\langle u, v \rangle$. We construct deep neural networks $\Upsilon_{metapath}$ of social attention to capture various types of semantic information of heterogeneous social relationships. Then, we input the trust features containing a single trust community into $\Upsilon_{metapath}$ to learn the importance of heterogeneous social relationships. And then we obtain the social attention matrix β_Φ after normalization through softmax function, as shown in Eq. 5.

$$\beta_{\Phi_i} = \frac{exp(\frac{1}{|\mathcal{V}|} \sum_{k \in \mathcal{V}} \zeta^T \cdot tanh(W \cdot z_k^\Phi + b))}{\sum_{i=1}^{P} exp(\frac{1}{|\mathcal{V}|} \sum_{k \in \mathcal{V}} \zeta^T \cdot tanh(W \cdot z_k^{\Phi_i} + b))} \tag{5}$$

where W is the weight matrix, b is the bias matrix, P is the number of trust communities and ζ is the social attention vector.

Finally, we aggregate the trust features of heterogeneous trust communities through the social attention matrix β_Φ to obtain the final embedding Z of users, as shown in Eq. 6.

$$Z = \sum_{i=1}^{P} \beta_{\Phi_i} \cdot Z_{\Phi_i} \tag{6}$$

3.3 Prediction Module

In order to convert the learned user embeddings into potential factors of trust relationships in SIoT service recommendation, for a given user pair $\langle u,v \rangle$, we first concatenate the embeddings of users u and v. Then we fit them to a standard fully-connected (FC) layer followed by a softmax layer, as shown in Eq. 7. The overall process of HMTrust is shown in Algorithm 1.

$$\widetilde{y}_{uv} = \sigma(W_{fc} \cdot (Z_u \otimes Z_v)) \tag{7}$$

where $\widetilde{y}_{uv}$ is the predicted probability that the user pair $\langle u, v \rangle$ belongs to a trusted pair or a distrusted pair, W_{fc} is the weight matrix of FC layer.

Finally, we define the trust evaluation loss function by using cross entropy as shown in Eq. 8:

$$\mathcal{L} = -\frac{1}{|\mathcal{W}|} \sum_{(\langle u,v \rangle, w_{u \to v}) \in \mathcal{W}} y_{uv} log\widetilde{y}_{uv} + \lambda \cdot ||\Theta||_2^2 \tag{8}$$

where $\mathcal{W} = \{\langle u,v \rangle, w_{u \to v}\}$ is the set of observed trustor-trustee pairs and associated trust relationships, y_{uv} denotes the ground truth of trust relationship of user pair $\langle u, v \rangle$, Θ denotes all trainable model parameters, and λ controls the $L2$ regularization strength to prevent over-fitting. In particular, we employ the back propagation algorithm and Adam [9] optimizer to train the model.

3.4 Trust-Based SIoT Service Recommendation Model

In this section, we aim to implement reliable service recommendations to ensure the user's experience. Traditional service recommendation methods mainly focus on user behavior analysis and demand mining to construct user preferences. However, these methods often ignore the malicious information hidden in user interactions, thus limiting the effectiveness of recommendations. Therefore, in order to improve the accuracy and efficiency of the SIoT service recommendation, we suggest further integrating trust factors on the basis of user preference modeling, and propose a trust-based SIoT service recommendation model. This method not only considers the matching degree between the service and the user's preference, but also takes the trust score of the service provider as the key screening condition to enhance the reliability of the recommendation. We can use any prioritization optimization algorithm, such as genetic algorithm, knapsack algorithm, etc., to ensure the accuracy of recommendation while significantly improving the reliability of service recommendation and user satisfaction. Specifically, the algorithm first selects a group of candidate services based on user preferences, then sorts the candidate services carefully according to trust scores, and finally recommends the top-ranked services to users. In addition, the algorithm can also be designed as a multi-factor comprehensive decision-making mechanism, that is, comprehensively considering multiple factors affecting user preferences and trust score factors together as the factors to determine service recommendation. And we appropriately enhance the priority of trust score because the reliability

Algorithm 1. The overall progress of HMTrust.

Input: The graph topology $\mathcal{G}$ of SIoT service recommendation, the users' feature f, the trust community set(including heterogeneous social relationship and trust relationship) $\{\Phi_0, \Phi_1, ...\Phi_P\}$, the number of attention head M,

Output: Predicted Trust Relationship $\widetilde{y}_{uv}$.
1: **for** $\Phi_i \in \{\Phi_0, \Phi_1, ...\Phi_P\}$ **do**
2:    **for** $m = 1...M$ **do**
3:      Type-specific transformation $f_i^{'} = \Delta_{\phi_i} \cdot f_i$;
4:      **for** $v \in \mathcal{V}$ **do**
5:        Find the trust community based heterogeneous neighbor objects Ψ_u^Φ;
6:        **for** $i \in \Psi_u^\Phi$ **do**
7:          Calculate the object-level attention matrix
$$\alpha_{uv}^\Phi = \frac{exp(\Upsilon_{object}(f_u^{'},f_v^{'};\Phi))}{\sum_{i \in \Psi_u^\Phi}(exp(\Upsilon_{object}(f_u^{'},f_k^{'};\Phi)))};$$
8:        **end for**
9:      **end for**
10:      Concatenate the learned embedding from all attention head
$$z_u^\Phi = \prod_{m=1}^{M} \sigma(\sum_{i \in \Psi_u^\Phi} \alpha_{uv}^\Phi \cdot (f_i^{'} \otimes \overline{f_i^{'}}));$$
11:    **end for**
12:    Calculate social attention matrix β_Φ;
13:    Calculate final embedding $Z = \sum_{i=1}^{P} \beta_{\Phi_i} \cdot Z_{\Phi_i}$;
14: **end for**
15: Calculate predicted trust relationship $\widetilde{y}_{uv} = \sigma(W_{fc} \cdot (Z_u \otimes Z_v))$;
16: Calculate Cross-Entropy $\mathcal{L} = -\frac{1}{|\mathcal{W}|} \sum_{(\langle u,v \rangle, w_{u \to v}) \in \mathcal{W}} y_{uv} log \widetilde{y}_{uv} + \lambda \cdot ||\Theta||_2^2$;
17: Back propagation and update parameters in HMTrust;

of the service based on trust is the most important factor in determining the service experience. This ensures that the services ultimately recommended to the user are both tailored to their individual needs and have a high level of trust and reliability.

4 Evaluation

4.1 Dataset Description

We conduct experiments on two widely used real-world datasets, namely Epinions [19] and Ciao [19], where the basic information is summarized in Table 1.

Epinions and Ciao are derived from two product review websites. For each user, the dataset contains his profile, ratings, and trust relationships. For each rating, there is the product name and its category, the rating score, and the helpfulness of the rating. These two sites offer two levels of trustworthiness.

4.2 Experimental Settings

Baselines. We compare with some state-of-art baselines to verify the effectiveness of our proposed HMTrust, including three network embedding methods:

Table 1. Statistical Description of Datasets.

Dataset	Users	Categories	Objects	TR	Meta-path	Density
Epinions	7,152	27	137,224	360,000	UCU UOU	0.007
Ciao	7,376	9	6	318,280	UCU UOU	0.0059

* TR denotes Trust Relationships.

Deepwalk [16], Line [18], node2vec [5] and five graph neural network based methods: GCN [10], GAT [22], SLF [25], STNE [26], Guardian [11]. All experiments run 10 times to ensure statistical significance.

- **Deepwalk** [16]: A random walk based network embedding method is proposed. It generates the embedding of the sentence through skipgram [15].
- **Line** [18]: A method for large-scale information networks embedding is proposed. It uses edge sampling (alias algorithm) to prevent the problem caused by excessive gradient variance. And it improves the computational efficiency of second-order similarity based on negative sampling optimization.
- **node2vec** [5]: A network embedding method based on biased random walks is proposed. It uses two hyperparameters p and q to control the migration strategy, so as to realize the conversion between Depth First Search and Breadth First Search.
- **GCN** [10]: A semi-supervised graph convolutional network is proposed. It combines topological structure and vertex attribute information to learn the embedding representation of vertices in the graph.
- **GAT** [22]: A semi-supervised graph convolutional network is proposed and attention mechanisms on homogeneous graphs are considered.
- **SLF** [25]: A signed network embedding model is proposed. It correlates each type of social relationship with the combined effects of positive-negative sign potential factors and learns node embedding by minimizing the negative log-likelihood objective function.
- **STNE** [26]: A social trust network embedding model is proposed. It predicts social trust by considering the potential factors and trust transfer patterns of users.
- **Guardian** [11]: An end-to-end trust evaluation model is proposed. It predicts social trust by taking into account popularity factors and engagement factors.

Implementation Details. For all baselines, we use the source code published by their respective authors. For HMTrust, we implement our proposed framework by pytorch. We use the Xavier initializer [4] to initialize the parameters and Adam to optimize the model. We set the learning rate to 0.001, the L_2 normalization coefficient to 0.00001, the dimension of the social attention vector to 32, the number of attention heads M to 4, and the droupout ratio to 0.3. We use an early stop patience of 30. That is, if we confirm that the training loss has not decreased in 30 successive epochs, we stop the training. Since there are only observed trust relationships in Ciao datasets, a set of unlinked users with the same proportion is randomly selected as a negative instance set for training and testing.

We use **Accuracy** and **F1-Score**, which are two commonly used metrics in trust evaluation tasks, to measure the performance of our proposed HMTrust and baselines.

4.3 Performance Comparisons

Firstly, we conduct an experimental analysis of HMTrust to verify its effectiveness.

Effectiveness. For different datasets, we set the ratio of training set to test set to 90%: 10% to report the average results of different models.

Table 2. Quantitative results (%) on two datasets. (bold: best).

Datasets	Metrics	Deepwalk	Line	Node2vec	GCN	GAT	SLF	STNE	Guardian	HMTrust
Epinions	Accuracy	66.67	62.49	66.67	81.55	66.18	72.28	78.68	82.39	**83.29**
	F1-Score	40.01	46.74	40.00	78.20	40.63	58.44	71.91	75.94	**81.20**
Ciao	Accuracy	66.09	65.77	66.36	67.98	69.80	69.45	78.25	74.26	**83.43**
	F1-Score	51.37	47.50	51.72	49.09	59.73	52.45	74.40	63.86	**81.22**

As shown in Table 2, we can find that HMTrust consistently outperforms all baselines on SIoT datasets. Specifically, in terms of accuracy, HMTrust's improvement ranges for different baselines were 0.90% to 20.80% and 5.18% to 17.66% on Epinions, Ciao, respectively. In terms of the F1-Score, HMTrust's improvements across the two datasets ranged from 5.26% to 41.20% and 6.82% to 33.72% across different baselines. In particular, the performance improvement of HMTrust compared to Guardian further shows that the semantic background of heterogeneous trust communities can be fully considered by constructing meta-paths and introducing social attention, which can capture richer trust features than simple mean aggregation trust features, thus improving the performance of trust evaluation. Through the above analysis, we can find that the proposed HMTrust achieves the best performance on all data sets. The results show that it is very important to analyze the trust relationship between heterogeneous objects and heterogeneous trust communities in SIoT service recommendation.

4.4 Ablation Study

To test the effectiveness of each component, we conducted the experiment by comparing HMTrust with four variations. The variables are as follows: 1) Use deepwalk instead of node2vec to initialize the embedding of HMTrust, which is named HMT_{deep}; 2) Use line instead of node2vec to initialize the embedding of HMTrust, which is named HMT_{line}. 3) Remove the social attention layer of HMTrust and aggregates information only from the object-level attention layer, which is named HMT_{obj}, and 4) Removes the object-level attention layer of HMTrust and aggregates information only from the social attention layer, which is named HMT_{soc}.

Table 3. Comparisons of our HMTrust and its four variants on two datasets in terms of Accuracy (%) and F1-Score (%).

Datasets	Metrics	HMT_{deep}	HMT_{line}	HMT_{obj}	HMT_{soc}	HMTrust
Epinions	Accuracy	82.43	82.34	81.87	81.90	**83.29**
	F1-Score	80.65	80.34	79.77	79.80	**81.20**
Ciao	Accuracy	82.51	81.50	80.78	80.64	**83.43**
	F1-Score	80.23	78.82	77.91	76.05	**81.22**

From the results in Table 3, we can find that the results of HMTrust are always superior to its four variants, indicating the validity and necessity of fully considering heterogeneous network topology, users' trust relationship and the semantic background of heterogeneous trust community in the trust evaluation of SIoT. Compared with deepwalk and line, HMTrust uses node2vec to further expand and learn the weight of trust between users, thereby optimizing the ability of trust evaluation. By introducing object-level attention, HMTrust effectively assigns different attention values to neighboring heterogeneous objects, thus distinguishing their differences. It improves the ability to evaluate trust by assigning a higher recommendation trust weight value to meaningful neighbor objects. And heterogeneous social relationships constitute different trust communities. HMTrust divides trust communities through meta-path, and extracts the differences of heterogeneous trust communities through social attention, thus improving the recommendation trust ability of heterogeneous trust communities.

4.5 Parameter Analysis

We investigated the sensitivity of two main parameters on the Ciao datasets, including the number of attention heads and the final embedding dimension.

The Number of Attention Heads. To test the effectiveness of multiple attention heads, we studied the performance of HMTrust with different number of attention heads. The result is shown in Fig. 2a. Through experiments, we can find that the increase number of attention head will improve the performance of HMTrust. This is because the introduction of multiple attention can learn the trust characteristics and information of different dimensions in the heterogeneous environment of SIoT, which is conducive to the in-depth mining of the characteristics of heterogeneous objects and heterogeneous trust communities. However, with the increasing number of attention heads, the performance of HMTrust only improved slightly. The slight improvement in the performance of trust evaluation due to the large increase in computational overhead is not worth adopting.

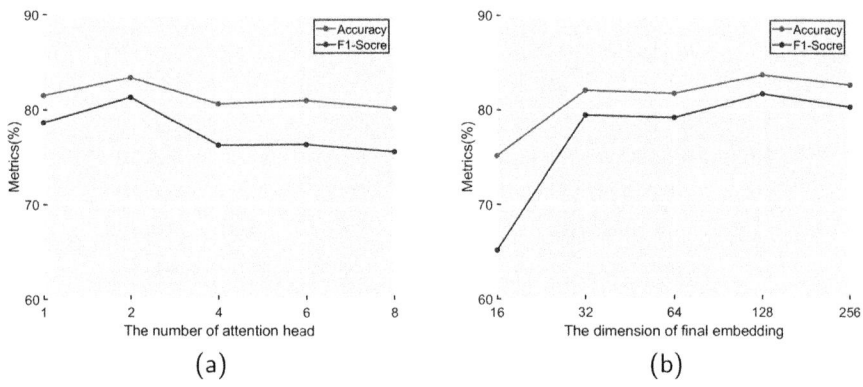

Fig. 2. The performance of sensitive parameters with different ratio.

Final Embedding Dimension. We tested the effect of the final embedding dimension and changed it from 16 to 256. The result is shown in Fig. 2b. We found that with the increase of the final embedding dimension, the accuracy and F1-Score of HMTrust first increased and then decreased. Through analysis, we can see that this is because the SIoT environment contains a large number of heterogeneous objects and heterogeneous trust communities, and appropriate dimensions are needed to encode key components in SIoT service recommendation, including heterogeneous network topology, users' trust relationships and the semantic background of heterogeneous trust communities. By increasing the embedding dimension, more useful trust characteristics can be included. But a too large dimension may introduce additional redundancy, which will affect the performance of trust evaluation.

5 Related Work

Existing trust evaluation methods can be roughly divided into two categories, including trust computing-based methods and neural network-based trust prediction methods.

Trust Computing-Based Methods. Trust computing mainly obtains the trust value of devices by aggregating the ratings of direct interactions and the recommendation ratings of referrals. OptimalTrust [13] generates trust quality by considering the user's social relationship, trust relationship, recommendation role, etc., so as to search for the best trust path. Ahlem [8] considers dynamics and similarity to calculate trust values, and combines the user's expertise level to optimize web service recommendations. OpinionWalk [14] designs discounting and combining operators to model trust propagation and aggregation. And it improves model efficiency with breadth-first search. Amani [1] optimizes energy supplier selection by taking into account suppliers' behavior and energy supply history and implementing context-aware trust computing based on service demand.

Neural Network-Based Trust Prediction Methods. As neural networks become increasingly capable, several studies have focused on using neural networks to improve the performance of trust evaluation. Guardian [11] considers the propagation, composition and asymmetry of trust when designing the GCN trust model. GAtrust [7] integrates graph structure, trust relationships, and node attributes to generate the embedding. And it introduces the attention mechanism to predict the reliability of the node. KGTrust [28] further considers the user's comment information to generate semantic knowledge embedding and node embedding to enrich the inherent characteristics of nodes and enhance the prediction of user's credibility.

To summarize, most of the studies mentioned above only calculate trust through simple weighted aggregation of multiple factors or predict trust through data mining. In contrast, our work is different from other works on two levels. The first contribution is related to adaptive weighted aggregation of multiple factors. We introduce a two-layer attention mechanism to adjust the weight of multiple factors, and deeply explore the rich semantics of heterogeneous trust. The second contribution is digging deeper into the underlying interaction patterns. We further consider the underlying patterns of semantic information. We model multi-dimensional trust community through meta-path, and further explored the deep association pattern in SIoT service recommendation.

6 Conclusion

In this paper, we propose a heterogeneous multi relation trust evaluation model, HMTrust. It comprehensively considers heterogeneous network topology, user trust relationship and the semantic background of trust communities in SIoT service recommendation. We build multi-dimensional trust communities among heterogeneous objects through meta-path. Then, we introduce a two-layer attention mechanism to capture complex interaction patterns and rich semantic information in multi-dimensional trust communities and heterogeneous objects in SIoT service recommendation. Experiments show that the performance of our proposed model is better than the existing models.

However, in the construction of multi-dimensional trust communities in this paper, the introduction of meta-path is manually set. And this paper doesn't take into account the time-varying of trust in highly dynamic networks, which may lead to the incorrect use of future interactions to infer past trust relationships. Thus it may reduce the performance of the model. In future work, we will consider the adaptive generation of meta-path and incorporating relevant temporal properties of trust into the model.

References

1. Abusafia, A., Bouguettaya, A., Lakhdari, A., Yangui, S.: Context-aware trustworthy iot energy services provisioning. In: 21st International Conference on Service-Oriented Computing (ICSOC) (2023)
2. Atzori, L., Iera, A., Morabito, G.: Siot: Giving a social structure to the internet of things, pp. 1193–1195. Communications Letters, IEEE pp (2011)
3. Chen, Y., Wu, L., Zaki, M.J.: Iterative deep graph learning for graph neural networks: Better and robust node embeddings. In: NIPS'20: Proceedings of the 34st International Conference on Neural Information Processing Systems (2020)
4. Glorot, X., Bengio, Y.: Understanding the difficulty of training deep feedforward neural networks. In: Proceedings of the International Conference on Artificial Intelligence and Statistics (2010)
5. Grover, A., Leskovec, J.: node2vec: scalable feature learning for networks. In: KDD '16: Proceedings of the 22nd ACM SIGKDD International Conference on Knowledge Discovery and Data Mining (2016)
6. Hamilton, W.L., Ying, R., Leskovec, J.: Inductive representation learning on large graphs. In: NIPS'17: Proceedings of the 31st International Conference on Neural Information Processing Systems (2017)
7. Jiang, N., Wen, J., Li, J., Liu, X., Jin, D.: Gatrust: A multi-aspect graph attention network model for trust assessment in osns. IEEE Transactions on Knowledge and Data Engineering pp. 5865–5878 (2023)
8. Kalaï, A., Zayani, C.A., Amous, I., Sedès, F.: Expertise and trust -aware social web service recommendation. In: 14th International Conference on Service Oriented Computing (ICSOC 2016) (2016)
9. Kingma, D.P., Ba, J.: Adam: A method for stochastic optimization. In: Proceedings of the International Conference on Learning Representations (2015)
10. Kipf, T.N., Welling, M.: Semi-supervised classification with graph convolutional networks. In: Proceedings of the International Conference on Learning Representations (2016)
11. Lin, W., Gao, Z., Li, B.: Guardian: Evaluating trust in online social networks with graph convolutional networks. In: IEEE INFOCOM 2020 - IEEE Conference on Computer Communications (2020)
12. Lin, W., Li, B.: Medley: Predicting social trust in time-varying online social networks. In: IEEE INFOCOM 2021 - IEEE Conference on Computer Communications (2021)
13. Liu, G., Wang, Y., Orgun, M.A., Lim, E.P.: Finding the optimal social trust path for the selection of trustworthy service providers in complex social networks. IEEE Transactions on Services Computing pp. 152–167 (2013)
14. Liu, G., Chen, Q., Yang, Q., Zhu, B., Wang, H., Wang, W.: Opinionwalk: An efficient solution to massive trust assessment in online social networks. In: IEEE INFOCOM 2017 - IEEE Conference on Computer Communications (2017)
15. Mikolov, T., Chen, K., Corrado, G., Dean, J.: Efficient estimation of word representations in vector space. In: Proceedings of the International Conference on Learning Representations (2013)
16. Perozzi, B., Al-Rfou, R., Skiena, S.: Deepwalk: online learning of social representations. In: KDD '14: Proceedings of the 20th ACM SIGKDD International Conference on Knowledge Discovery and Data Mining (2014)
17. Sun, Y., Han, J.: Mining heterogeneous information networks: a structural analysis approach. ACM SIGKDD Explorations Newsletter, pp. 20–28 (2012)

18. Tang, J., Qu, M., Wang, M., Zhang, M., Yan, J., Mei, Q.: Line: large-scale information network embedding. In: WWW '15: Proceedings of the 24th International Conference on World Wide Web (2015)
19. Tang, J., Gao, H., Liu, H., Sarma, A.D.: etrust: understanding trust evolution in an online world. In: KDD '12: Proceedings of the 18th ACM SIGKDD International Conference on Knowledge Discovery and Data Mining (2012)
20. Truong, N.B., Lee, G.M., Um, T.W., Mackay, M.: Trust evaluation mechanism for user recruitment in mobile crowd-sensing in the internet of things (article). IEEE Trans. Inform. Forensics Secur., 2705–2719 (2019)
21. Vaswani, A., et al.: Attention is all you need. In: Proceedings of the Conference and Workshop on Neural Information Processing Systems (2017)
22. Velickovic, P., Cucurull, G., Casanova, A., Romero, A., Liò, P., Bengio, Y.: Graph attention networks. In: Proceedings of the International Conference on Learning Representations (2018)
23. Wang, J., Jing, X., Yan, Z., Fu, Y., Witold, P., Laurence T, Y.: A survey on trust evaluation based on machine learning. ACM Computing Surveys pp. 107–143 (2020)
24. Wang, X., Ji, H., Shi, C., Wang, B., Ye, Y., Cui, P., Yu, P.S.: Heterogeneous graph attention network. In: Proceedings of WWW (2019)
25. Xu, P., Hu, W., Wu, J., Du, B.: Link prediction with signed latent factors in signed social networks. In: Proceedings of the ACM SIGKDD Conference on Knowledge Discovery and Data Mining (2019)
26. Xu, P., Hu, W., Wu, J., Liu, W., Du, B., Yang, J.: Social trust network embedding. In: 2019 IEEE International Conference on Data Mining (ICDM) (2019)
27. Yu, C., Xia, G., Wang, Z.: Trust evaluation of computing power network based on improved particle swarm neural network. In: 17th IEEE International Conference on Mobility, Sensing and Networking (MSN) (2021)
28. Yu, Z., et al.: Kgtrust: evaluating trustworthiness of siot via knowledge enhanced graph neural networks. In: 2023 World Wide Web Conference, WWW 2023 (2023)

A Context-Aware Service Framework for Detecting Fake Images

Muhammad Umair[✉][iD], Paramvir Singh[iD], and Athman Bouguettaya[iD]

The University of Sydney, Sydney, NSW 2006, Australia
{muhammad.umair,psin0239,athman.bouguettaya}@sydney.edu.au

Abstract. We propose a novel *context-based service framework* to detect *changes* in social media images using *image metadata*. In this service-oriented architecture, each image is abstracted as a *service*. This method is unique in its *exclusive* reliance on metadata tags, which serve as *non-functional* attributes of the *image service*. We employ a transformer model trained on a large image metadata corpus to identify *changes* in image services. The training process is meticulously designed to focus solely on the metadata of image services falling within the relevant *context*, ensuring high precision. This targeted training ensures that the models are finely tuned to detect even subtle modifications pertinent to their respective categories, thereby improving the reliability and effectiveness of the framework. In this regard, a state-of-the-art transformer model, BERT is first trained on this corpus and then fine-tuned on a fact-checked, context-based dataset. Experiments are conducted on a subset of the Multimodal C4 dataset. Results demonstrate that the model's effectiveness improves up to 20% when utilizing a context-based corpus, highlighting the value of targeted training in enhancing the accuracy of change detection.

Keywords: Fake images · image metadata · misinformation · fake news · BERT · BERTopic · fact-checking · MMC4 · Exif-BERT · disinformation · Exif2Vec

1 Introduction

Social media images are more than just visuals; they shape *perceptions*, influence culture, and connect people worldwide [25]. The widespread use of social media has turned images into powerful tools for communication, self-expression, and information sharing [8]. Whether it is showcasing personal moments on Instagram, breaking news on Twitter, sharing art on Pinterest, or documenting events on Snapchat, each type of image serves a unique *contextual* purpose [23]. For instance, an image could be related to road accidents, crime scenes, public gatherings and other significant events [4]. This diverse range of *contexts* underscores the profound impact of visual content on modern communication and societal trends, reflecting how images on social media have become integral to shaping our collective understanding of the world. Additionally, the *image service* abstraction proposed in [32] aids in effectively handling the context of an image, enhancing our ability to interpret and utilize visual information.

Given the flood of social media images on our screens, a key concern is their *trustworthiness* [1,10]. The accessibility of digital manipulation tools has led to an alarming increase in *manipulated* images, undermining users' trust in the online visuals [22]. Whether for minor enhancements or *deceptive* alterations, distinguishing real from manipulated content has become increasingly difficult [21]. In some cases, a manipulative image might not contain changes in the image but could be misleadingly reused out of context, such as using an old image to falsely represent a recent incident [39]. This decline in trust affects both users and the credibility of information shared online, highlighting the urgent need for more rigorous scrutiny of digital images. Addressing the trust issue in social media images is essential for cultivating a discerning online community, given the highly contextual nature of image changes and manipulations.

Several approaches are employed to detect *fake* images, focusing primarily on image processing and digital forensics techniques [16]. Image processing is usually *computationally* expensive. Forensic analysis of metadata, such as date, time, and location information embedded in image files, has been a common method for assessing image authenticity [11]. However, the limitations of traditional forensic analysis have become increasingly evident in the face of advanced manipulation techniques. Recent studies use deep learning algorithms for image forensics, leveraging the power of convolutional neural networks to identify subtle alterations indicative of image tampering [5]. While these approaches perform well, they often lack the contextual awareness necessary for distinguishing manipulated images within the intricate landscape of social media. To overcome these issues, some metadata-based service frameworks have recently been proposed to determine the trust of social media images. For instance, a word2vec model is trained on image metadata to determine contextual inconsistencies [34]. However, these models are trained on a general corpus and are not completely capable of detect subtle *contextual* image changes.

The existing solutions face significant challenges when applied to social media contexts, where images are frequently shared and re-shared, introducing additional layers of *contextual* complexity [18]. Additionally, the models must be highly *scalable* to handle the massive volume of social media content [26]. Current image processing solutions lack the *semantic* awareness needed to understand the context of an image completely. Moreover, the lack of service-based solutions further complicates the detection of fake images. Recognizing these limitations, this research aims to develop a lightweight model by integrating context-aware datasets and a context-based algorithm. This approach ensures both scalability and a deeper understanding of the image's contextual nuances. We aim to improve the precision and adaptability of image forensics in social media, offering a more nuanced and effective approach to identifying *fake* images in the dynamic digital landscape.

Our solution relies *exclusively* on the *non-functional attributes* of an image service. The non-functional attributes reflect the content in the picture [20]. For instance, *inks* reflect the colors used in the picture. The non-functional attributes are highly qualitative in nature. For instance, GPS location is correlated with the name of the city. If an image is changed with good intentions, there is no need to change it's metadata to make it align with the changes in the image. However, an attempt to change the metadata with *ill-intentions* may introduce *inconsistencies* among these non-functional attributes. For instance, changing the country name may make it inconsistent with *GMT* offset. Our designed framework identify and investigate these inconsistencies to ascertain the *trust* of an image service.

We introduce a novel context-aware service framework designed to assess the trustworthiness of social media images. Our approach incorporates context through a specialized algorithm and training methodology tailored to the specific context under study. To achieve this, we utilize a state-of-the-art transformer model, BERT trained on an image metadata corpus, focusing specifically on subsets that align with the relevant contextual parameters. In this context-based approach, the model is trained on specific categories, such as crime scenes, road accidents, medical images, etc. to ensure accuracy within those contexts. This targeted training enhances the model's ability to accurately analyze and evaluate social media images within their specific contexts. For instance, to detect fake images related to road accidents, the model is only trained on images related to road accidents rather than training on the entire corpus. The training process consists of two phases. In the first phase, the model is trained on metadata attributes to learn their interrelationships, utilizing the Multimodal C4 dataset. In the second phase, the pre-trained model is fine-tuned on a fact-checked fake image dataset to understand how inconsistencies in the metadata correlate with image trustworthiness, employing the image verification corpus. Results validate that the effectiveness of the model increases when trained on a specific context.

Below, we summarize our main contributions:

– We propose a novel service framework to ascertain the trust of social media images by identifying the inconsistencies among image metadata attributes.
– The uniqueness of this solution lies in its exclusive reliance on image metadata, setting it apart from traditional vision-based approaches.
– The proposed model is context aware, which can detect the manipulations in an image given a specific context.

We propose this model from the perspective of social media owners, assuming full access to image metadata attributes. It is important to note that our goal is not to compete with vision-based approaches, but to complement existing image processing solutions. Additionally, we acknowledge that some changes may not be captured in the non-functional attributes of an image service. Hence, the proposed framework works is more efficient and accurate in detecting those changes that are reflected in the non-functional attributes.

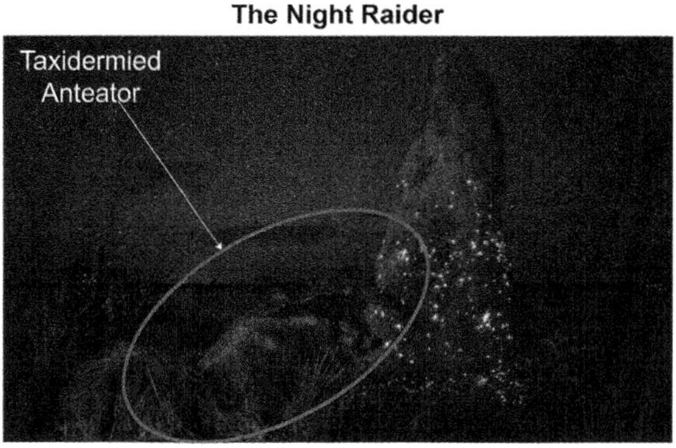

Fig. 1. A motivating example

2 Motivating Scenario

We use a *manipulative* award winning picture as our motivating example. Figure 1 shows the photograph titled "The Night Raider". In 2017, this photograph won a prestigious award in the Wildlife Photographer of the Year competition. Subsequently, it was revealed that the photograph depicted a taxidermy anteater (a preserved specimen) rather than a live animal, leading to its disqualification from the competition. This incident not only prompts scrutiny of ethical standards in wildlife photography but also underscores a notable gap in the field of digital forensics, particularly in detecting and analyzing manipulated images. While current algorithms excel at identifying digital alterations in images, significant advancements in these technologies have not fully addressed certain types of photographic manipulations found in competition submissions. This gap is notably evident in cases where the context or authenticity of the subject matter itself is in question, rather than the digital integrity of the image file. The Stuffed Anteater case underscores the necessity for a context-aware approach in verifying image authenticity, an approach that transcends the limitations of context-free ML techniques. Unlike context-free methods, which analyze images and metadata in isolation, a context-aware strategy integrates and analyzes metadata in conjunction with external contextual information, offering a more nuanced and comprehensive understanding of the image's authenticity.

To bridge this gap, we propose a novel *context-aware* service framework that leverages the metadata of images as a pivot for authenticity verification. This framework differs fundamentally from existing ML techniques by incorporating a broader range of contextual cues derived from metadata, such as geographical location, date and time, and even camera settings. By analyzing the GPS data and timestamps in an image's metadata and comparing them with environmental data, wildlife databases, and historical weather conditions, it's possible to ascertain the plausibility of the photograph's setting and timing. For instance, the presence of certain wildlife in a region where they are not known to exist, or the depiction of an animal in conditions that are inconsistent with the timestamped weather conditions, would signal a red flag. Evaluating the camera settings (e.g., exposure, focal length) recorded in the metadata against the visual content of the photograph can provide insights into the authenticity of the image. Discrepancies between the documented settings and the expected visual outcomes (e.g., depth of field, motion blur) can indicate potential manipulation.

3 Related Work

Detecting fake images on social media has been an essential research topic and many techniques have been employed [7]. Below are some of the most popular techniques that are used to detect changes in images.

3.1 Types of Image Forgeries and Vision-Based Detection Methods

Image forensic solutions compare the image with the metadata. To understand it better, we need to first know the different types of image manipulations.

Copy-Move Detection. In copy-move forgery, a section of an image is duplicated, altered, and then reinserted into a different location within the same image. To detect such cloning, there are primarily two methods: one based on identifying unique features and another reliant on hashing techniques. The majority of detection algorithms focus on analyzing distinct features, while hashing is reserved for detecting straightforward cloning where the copied segment hasn't been modified. Initially, Fridrich and colleagues developed a detection method for copy-move forgery that utilized quantized coefficients from the Discrete Cosine Transform (DCT) applied to overlapping blocks of the image [12]. This process involves scanning the image with blocks of size BxB, computing feature vectors through DCT, and then comparing blocks after the feature vectors are sorted in a lexicographical order, with matching blocks indicating potential tampering.

Resampling. Resampling is a process used to generate a modified version of an image with altered dimensions, either in terms of height or width. When the image size is enlarged, it is referred to as upsampling, whereas downsampling denotes the process of reducing the image size. Additionally, image rotation involves resampling, where rotating an image by any given angle results in a transformed appearance. To identify resampling in images, Popescu and Farid employed an expectation-maximization (EM) algorithm to generate probability maps that reveal specific patterns of correlation within the image [28]. This approach has been proven effective only for basic resampling techniques and is not suitable for analyzing compressed images.

Generative Adversarial Networks (GANs). Detecting images created by Generative Adversarial Networks (GANs) through forensic techniques presents significant challenges. Although traditional forensic methods have achieved some success, deep learning approaches consistently produce superior results. McCloskey and colleagues analyzed GAN generators and noted that such images often have a limited frequency of saturated pixels and employ weightings for RGB channels that diverge from those typical in digital camera sensors [27].

The challenges faced by forensic methods in analyzing images from social media platforms are multifaceted. Firstly, these images often lack specialization due to undergoing numerous manipulations, making them non-ideal examples for forensic analysis. The quality of social media images is frequently compromised due to the platforms' size limitations, resulting in images with less than optimal resolution. Additionally, these images are subject to high levels of compression, and in some cases, may undergo multiple compressions, further degrading their quality. The application of noise through blurring and edge removal techniques leads to the loss of visual features, essential for forensic examination. Cropping is commonly used to obscure specific details and emphasize emotional content, thereby altering the image's context. The extent of manipulation can vary significantly, with some images featuring large, altered regions while others contain small, discreetly tampered areas.

3.2 Machine Learning Based Solutions

Fake news on social media often involves a mix of elements such as text, images, videos, audio, and links. Sometimes, these elements are combined, for example, text overlaying images or irrelevant images paired with *misleading text* in comments, leading to challenges in detecting fake news based solely on images. The effectiveness of image-based fake news detection is not consistently high, as images might be authentic while the accompanying text or audio could be misleading or false [13]. To address these limitations, researchers are adopting a multi-modal approach that evaluates not just images but other content forms as well [14,37]. This approach necessitates a fusion classifier capable of integrating information from diverse sources to make an accurate classification. Several multi-modal strategies have been explored with promising results. For instance, frameworks that analyze both text and images have shown to outperform those utilizing other multi-modal features [41]. Despite considerable progress in machine learning (ML) and artificial intelligence (AI), a notable limitation persists in these technologies' capacity to identify specific kinds of manipulations in photographic content. This limitation becomes particularly apparent in situations where the question concerns the genuineness of the subject matter depicted, rather than any digital tampering with the image file itself.

3.3 Service-Based Solutions

Some service-based solutions have recently been proposed to ascertain the trust of social media images. For instance, *intention of changes* is introduced in [33].

The intention is derived by identifying the systematic changes in image metadata. A framework to determine the provenance of social media images for trust purposed is presented in [32]. Theory of algebraic matrix transformation is employed to model the transformation of an image into its versions. Another framework to detect inconsistencies in image metadata is proposed in [34]. These solutions are trained on a general corpus and are incapable of detecting highly contextual changes.

4 Image Service Abstraction

We abstract an *image as a service* having *functional* and *non-functional* attributes. Functional attributes represent the actions involved in capturing an image. Whereas, *non-functional* part of an image service can be represented as a function of spatio-temporal and contextual attributes:

$$\text{nf} = \{\zeta, \tau, c\} \tag{1}$$

where ζ represents the set of spatial attributes, τ is the set of temporal attributes, and c contains contextual attributes.

Definition of Image Service An **image service** is a digital service that enables the capture, processing, storage, retrieval, and delivery of images. It provides functionalities to manage the lifecycle of images, ensuring they are accessible, and relevant for various applications. The service is characterized by its ability to handle both functional operations related to image management and non-functional requirements that define the quality and context of the images.

1. Functional Attributes. Functional attributes of an image service refer to the actions and operations directly involved in capturing, processing, and delivering an image. These actions can include:

2. Non-Functional Attributes. Non-functional attributes of an image service are related to the quality, context, and constraints under which the image service operates. These attributes can be categorized as spatio-temporal and contextual attributes:

- **Spatial Attributes (ζ)**
  - *Location*: Geographical coordinates where the image was captured.
  - *Orientation*: Camera angle, direction, etc.
  - *Coverage*: Area covered by the image (e.g., wide-angle, close-up).
  - *Resolution*: Spatial resolution, pixel density, etc.
- **Temporal Attributes (τ)**
  - *Timestamp*: Date and time of image capture.
  - *Duration*: If it's a sequence of images or a video, the duration of capture.
  - *Frequency*: Capture intervals for time-lapse photography.
  - *Lifespan*: How long the image is retained in the system.

– **Contextual Attributes** (*c*)
  • *Environmental Conditions*: Lighting, weather, etc. during capture.
  • *Event Context*: The event or situation being captured (e.g., wedding, sports).
  • *User Context*: Preferences or requirements of the user requesting the image.

5 Proposed Framework

We present a context-aware variant of BERT, a transformer model specifically trained on context-based image metadata attributes. This section details the proposed framework for context-aware BERT and describes the associated image metadata corpus used for its training. We start by detailing the construction of the image metadata corpus, followed by an in-depth discussion of the model training methodology. Our approach involves a two-stage training process as shown in Fig. 2, inspired by the methodology used in BERT. Initially, we conduct pre-training on a large-scale dataset. This is followed by fine-tuning the model using a more targeted and compact dataset specifically designed for fake image detection. We use the term 'context-aware Exif-BERT' to refer to our fine-tuned model.

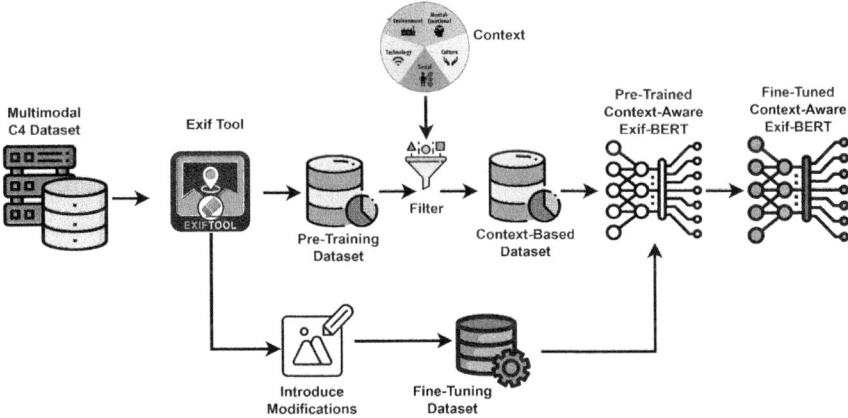

Fig. 2. The Proposed Framework

5.1 Dataset Construction

We construct our image metadata corpus using the Multimodal C4 (MMC4) dataset [42], derived from the C4 dataset, known for training models like T5 [29]. MMC4 includes both images and natural language, facilitating relationships between text and images. With over 100 million documents and 571 million images, it offers a diverse collection of diagrams, figures, and in-camera photographs. Despite many images lacking metadata, the large scale provides sufficient high-quality images. To reduce training costs, we use a subset of 36 million images from MMC4.

Building a Context-Based Dataset. We leverage BERTopic to group the images into contextually similar clusters based on their metadata and content. BERTopic uses advanced topic modeling techniques to analyze and categorize images according to their contextual themes and attributes [15]. This method enables us to organize the images into clusters where each cluster represents a specific context or topic, such as road accidents, crime scenes, or natural landscapes. By grouping images in this manner, we ensure that Exif-BERT is trained on data that is contextually relevant and coherent. Each cluster provides a focused set of images with shared characteristics and metadata attributes, allowing the model to learn more effectively about the relationships between metadata and the contextual significance of images. This context-based approach helps Exif-BERT better understand and interpret metadata in relation to specific image contexts, ultimately enhancing its performance in tasks such as fake image detection.

5.2 Metadata Extraction

We use ExifTool to extract metadata attributes from images in the MMC4 dataset [17]. After downloading and extracting Exif metadata for each image, we associate it with the most relevant sentence as defined by MMC4. Given the extensive range of unique metadata types, we focus on a pre-defined subset of attributes that are semantically significant and effective in representing the image, such as shutter speed, exposure time, and GPS data. Attributes with minimal semantic impact, like *filetype* and *filesize*, are excluded. The importance of metadata attributes varies by context; for example, *color* is significant in scenes involving blood, while timestamps are crucial in forensics. We determine the significance of attributes through domain expert opinions, contextual relevance, and their relationship with other attributes, using Latent Semantic Analysis to measure contextual relevance. This careful selection and analysis enhance the accuracy of our model, Exif-BERT, by enabling it to understand image semantics. The context-aware nature of BERT makes it suitable for this task, as it can interpret attributes differently based on context, such as "traffic-jam" versus "strawberry-jam". To further improve accuracy, we will train Exif-BERT on a context-specific corpus, ensuring the model is finely tuned to the nuances of various scenarios.

5.3 Pre-training

We begin the training of the Exif-BERT model on a very large image metadata corpus derived from the MMC4 dataset. During this phase, the model lacks a direct understanding of *trustworthiness* of images. Instead, we teach the model metadata attributes, words, and *relationships* based on real data found on the web. This pre-training equips the model with a foundational grasp of metadata relationships. To enhance its capabilities, we conduct pre-training on context-based datasets. For instance, the model is separately trained on datasets specific to road accidents, crime scenes, and other relevant contexts. This contextual pre-training allows Exif-BERT to develop a nuanced understanding of metadata within different scenarios. Following this, the pre-trained model can then be fine-tuned to learn specific tasks such as *fake image* detection, leveraging its foundational and contextual knowledge to improve accuracy and reliability in determining the trustworthiness of images.

Sequence Formation. MMC4 dataset contains sequences of text and images. When training BERT, constructing input sequence of text and metadata is crucial. Following BERT and RoBERTa's methodologies, we define an input sequence size of 512 tokens to balance efficiency and content inclusion [9]. This size accommodates at least one sentence and the full Exif metadata of an image per sequence, with few exceptions. For context-based pre-training, we use datasets specific to scenarios like road accidents and crime scenes, enhancing Exif-BERT's contextual understanding. Images generating sequences longer than 512 tokens are excluded, and rare instances exceeding this limit in fine-tuning are removed. Future efforts might consider truncating metadata attributes. Each input sequence includes only images and sentences from a single document, following RoBERTa's methodology [24], improving intra-document relationship understanding.

We use a Unigram tokenizer for its accuracy with qualitative and quantitative text [6], important for Exif-BERT due to mixed image metadata. Special tokens mark the start of each metadata attribute, with separators between sentences and images, and classifiers for fine-tuning. Padding tokens fill any remaining space, and a special masking token is reserved for pre-training.

Model Architecture. Our model architecture is based on BERT, with a focus on context-based training. We start with a learned embedding layer for token-specific and positional embeddings, tailored for contextual relevance. This is followed by 6 stacked multi-head attention layers, each with 4 heads, which process the embeddings. The output is passed through a single-layer feed-forward network, adapted for the specific task. The embedding layer includes 30,000 token-specific embeddings (512-dimensional) and learned positional embeddings for 512 positions, optimized for context-aware classification [40]. The attention layers capture metadata-word relationships crucial for context-based tasks.

Pre-Training. For the pre-training, we use the Masked Language Modeling task from BERT [9], masking 15% of tokens in an input sequence-80% with [MASK], 10% with random tokens, and 10% unchanged. Unlike BERT, we dynamically mask sequences each batch, as per RoBERTa's approach [24], and omit the Next Segment Prediction (NSP) task, which RoBERTa found to be detrimental [24]. We train with a batch size of 64 sequences for 3 epochs, using 80% of the dataset for training and reserving 20% for hyperparameter tuning and testing.

5.4 Fine-Tuning

After pre-training, we fine-tune BERT for the task of fake image detection. During this stage, the model leverages its learned metadata relationships to identify altered images. We replace the pre-training classification network with a new one tailored specifically for detecting fake images. Fine-tuning involves a smaller dataset with injected metadata changes, allowing the model to directly assess image trustworthiness.

Dataset Construction. For fine-tuning, we use a smaller, high-quality dataset of modified images. From the MMC4, we extract 1 million images and select 25,000 with the most metadata attributes (at least 25 tags each) to ensure diverse and rich examples. These selected images, distinct from those used in pre-training, are then modified using the ChatGPT API, which is trained on diverse real-world data. This ensures that modifications reflect genuine language patterns and semantics. The dataset is divided into three parts: one-third with no modifications, one-third with beneficial modifications (e.g., image brightening), and one-third with misleading modifications. The latter includes systematic changes to multiple metadata attributes to deceive viewers, reflecting the actions of unscrupulous actors.

Fine-Tuning. During fine-tuning, we adapt the pre-trained model by replacing its token classification network with one tailored to classify image modifications into three categories: *no modification, good modification,* and *bad modification.* Leveraging the model's pre-existing knowledge of metadata relationships, this phase is faster and requires less data. We use a batch size of 64 input sequences, each corresponding to a modification type, and train for 10 epochs with each epoch containing 32 sequences. Similar to the pre-training phase, 10% of the data is allocated for hyperparameter tuning and another 10% for testing, leaving 80% for training.

6 Experimentation and Results

6.1 Dataset Characteristics

Figure 3 shows that common metadata attributes like *XResolution* and *YResolution* are present in all images, including computer-generated ones. However, specialized attributes are exclusive to camera-captured photographs. The encouraging aspect is that a significant percentage of images contain a substantial number of important metadata attributes.

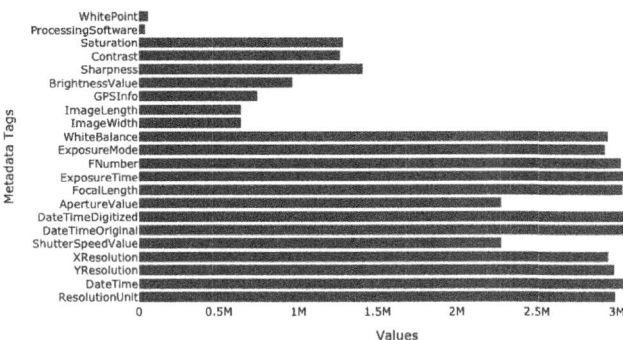

Fig. 3. Breakdown of important metadata attributes in the dataset

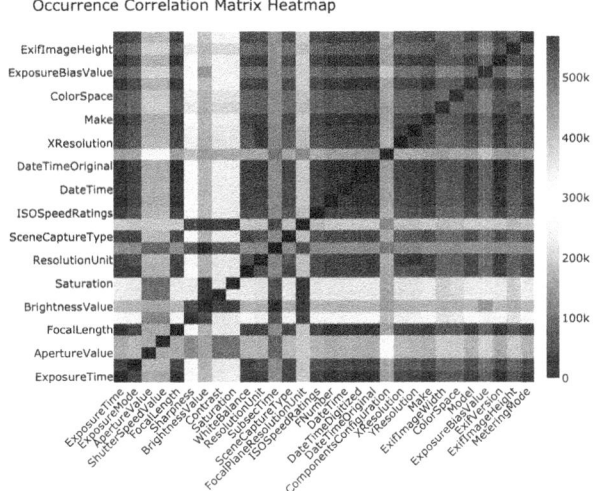

Fig. 4. Occurrence correlation of important metadata attributes

Certain metadata attributes frequently occur together, revealing how the model learns *relationships* between them. Figure 4 provides occurrence correlations among *lighting attributes*, such as *shutter speed* with *focal length* and *white balance*. It is essential to note that a weak correlation in this figure suggests a lower likelihood of these two attributes co-occurring in images from our dataset. However, our model demonstrates a robust performance, maintaining over 90% accuracy in detecting modifications. Some state-of-the-art approaches related to correlation studies could be explored to further investigate the relationships among metadata attributes [19,30].

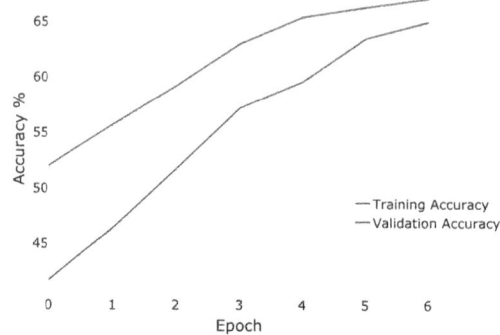

Fig. 5. Evaluation of pre-training accuracy

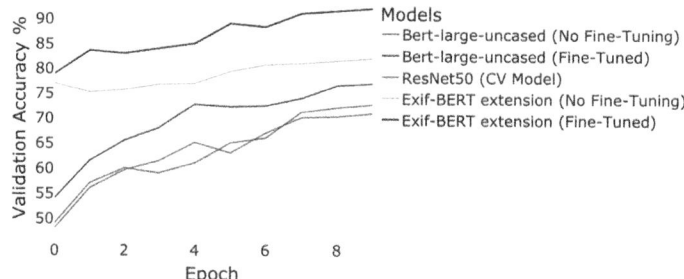

Fig. 6. Fine-tuning experiments: Analyzing different modalities

6.2 Pre-Training Effectiveness

Figure 5 shows the training and validation accuracy during the pre-training phase, achieving approximately 65%. This accuracy highlights the limitations of our computational resources (i.e., GPUs), which restricted the training to only three epochs. In the future, training can be accelerated by leveraging advanced distributed training techniques and more suitable training environments [2,3,36].

6.3 Fine-Tuning Effectiveness

Figure 6 shows validation accuracies of different variants of BERT for different number of epochs. We also provide a comparison of validation accuracy with that of ResNet which is a computer-vision-based model. It is evident from the figure that the validation accuracy of Exif-BERT is substantially better than the general BERT model. It is also clear from the figure that the fine-tuned models perform better than the pre-trained variants. Future research could explore whether more extensive pre-training is needed to strengthen the connections between text and image metadata.

7 Conclusion

We present a *context-aware* variant of Exif-BERT, an innovative pre-trained transformer designed for detecting fake images using only metadata. The model undergoes a two-step training: first, learning metadata relationships, and second, distinguishing real from fake metadata. Initial accuracy is 60–65%, improving to 95% in verifying image trustworthiness. Future fine-tuning on context-aware modifications enhance accuracy further, and the framework may aid in image provenance detection. Additionally, exploring dynamic weighted quadratic approaches in the attention layer could lead to further improvements in accuracy [31,35,38].

Acknowledgments. This research was partly made possible by LE220100078 and DP220101823 grants from the Australian Research Council. The statements made herein are solely the responsibility of the authors.

References

1. Abukari, A.M., Madavarapu, J.B., Bankas, E.K.: A lightweight algorithm for detecting fake multimedia contents on social media. Earthline J. Math. Sci. **14**(1), 119–132 (2024)
2. Afzal, B., Umair, M., Shah, G.A., Ahmed, E.: Enabling IoT platforms for social IoT applications: vision, feature mapping, and challenges. Futur. Gener. Comput. Syst. **92**, 718–731 (2019)
3. Akram, J., Umair, M., Jhaveri, R.H., Riaz, M.N., Chi, H., Malebary, S.: Chained-drones: blockchain-based privacy-preserving framework for secure and intelligent service provisioning in internet of drone things. Comput. Electr. Eng. **110**, 108772 (2023)
4. Amiruzzaman, M., Curtis, A., Zhao, Y., Jamonnak, S., Ye, X.: Classifying crime places by neighborhood visual appearance and police geonarratives: a machine learning approach. J. Comput. Soc. Sci., 1–25 (2021)
5. Bayar, B., Stamm, M.C.: A deep learning approach to universal image manipulation detection using a new convolutional layer. In: Proceedings of the 4th ACM Workshop on Information Hiding and Multimedia Security, pp. 5–10 (2016)
6. Bostrom, K., Durrett, G.: Byte pair encoding is suboptimal for language model pretraining. In: Findings of the Association for Computational Linguistics: EMNLP 2020, pp. 4617–4624. Association for Computational Linguistics, Online (2020). https://doi.org/10.18653/v1/2020.findings-emnlp.414, https://aclanthology.org/2020.findings-emnlp.414
7. Cao, J., Qi, P., Sheng, Q., Yang, T., Guo, J., Li, J.: Exploring the role of visual content in fake news detection. In: Shu, K., Wang, S., Lee, D., Liu, H. (eds.) Disinformation, Misinformation, and Fake News in Social Media: Emerging Research Challenges and Opportunities, pp. 141–161. Springer International Publishing, Cham (2020). https://doi.org/10.1007/978-3-030-42699-6_8
8. Choi, T.R., Sung, Y.: Instagram versus snapchat: self-expression and privacy concern on social media. Telematics Inform. **35**(8), 2289–2298 (2018)
9. Devlin, J., Chang, M.W., Lee, K., Toutanova, K.: BERT: pre-training of deep bidirectional transformers for language understanding. arXiv preprint arXiv:1810.04805 (2018)

10. Dootson, P., Thomson, T., Angus, D., Miller, S., Hurcombe, E., Smith, A.: Managing problematic visual media in natural hazard emergencies. Int. J. Disaster Risk Reduction **59**, 102249 (2021)
11. Ferreira, S., Antunes, M., Correia, M.E.: Exposing manipulated photos and videos in digital forensics analysis. J. Imaging **7**(7), 102 (2021)
12. Fridrich, J., Soukal, D., Lukas, J., et al.: Detection of copy-move forgery in digital images. In: Proceedings of Digital Forensic Research Workshop, vol. 3, pp. 652–663. Cleveland, OH (2003)
13. Ghai, A., Kumar, P., Gupta, S.: A deep-learning-based image forgery detection framework for controlling the spread of misinformation. Inf. Technol. People **37**(2), 966–997 (2024)
14. Giachanou, A., Zhang, G., Rosso, P.: Multimodal multi-image fake news detection. In: 2020 IEEE 7th International Conference on Data Science and Advanced Analytics (DSAA), pp. 647–654. IEEE (2020)
15. Grootendorst, M.: BERTopic: neural topic modeling with a class-based TF-IDF procedure. arXiv preprint arXiv:2203.05794 (2022)
16. Gupta, S., Mohan, N., Kaushal, P.: Passive image forensics using universal techniques: a review. Artif. Intell. Rev. **55**(3), 1629–1679 (2022)
17. Harvey, P.: ExifTool Documentation. ExifTool Development Team (2021). https://exiftool.org/
18. Hasan, R.: A Socio-Technical Approach to Protecting People's Privacy in the Context of Sharing Images on Social Media. Indiana University (2020)
19. Iqbal, H., Umair, M., Rizvi, S.A., Cheema, M.A.: A correlation study of COVID-19 in Europe considering different vaccines, age groups and variants including delta and omicron. BioMed **2**(2), 133–169 (2022)
20. Johnson, J., Ballan, L., Fei-Fei, L.: Love thy neighbors: image annotation by exploiting image metadata. In: Proceedings of the IEEE International Conference on Computer Vision, pp. 4624–4632 (2015)
21. Khan, S.A., et al.: Visual user-generated content verification in journalism: an overview. IEEE Access **11**, 6748–6769 (2023)
22. Kozyreva, A., Lewandowsky, S., Hertwig, R.: Citizens versus the internet: confronting digital challenges with cognitive tools. Psychol. Sci. Public Interest **21**(3), 103–156 (2020)
23. Li, Y., Xie, Y.: Is a picture worth a thousand words? An empirical study of image content and social media engagement. J. Mark. Res. **57**(1), 1–19 (2020)
24. Liu, Y., et al.: RoBERTa: a robustly optimized BERT pretraining approach. arXiv preprint arXiv:1907.11692 (2019)
25. Mahoney, L.M., Tang, T.: Strategic social media: from marketing to social change. John Wiley & Sons (2024)
26. Maqsood, T., Khalid, O., Irfan, R., Madani, S.A., Khan, S.U.: Scalability issues in online social networks. ACM Comput. Surv. (CSUR) **49**(2), 1–42 (2016)
27. McCloskey, S., Albright, M.: Detecting GAN-generated imagery using color cues. arXiv preprint arXiv:1812.08247 (2018)
28. Popescu, A.C., Farid, H.: Exposing digital forgeries by detecting traces of resampling. IEEE Trans. Signal Process. **53**(2), 758–767 (2005)
29. Raffel, C., et al.: Exploring the limits of transfer learning with a unified text-to-text transformer. J. Mach. Learn. Res. **21**(1), 5485–5551 (2020)
30. Rizvi, S.A., Umair, M., Cheema, M.A.: Clustering of countries for COVID-19 cases based on disease prevalence, health systems and environmental indicators. Chaos, Solitons Fract. **151**, 111240 (2021)

31. Umair, M., Afzal, B., Khan, A., Rehman, A.U., Sekercioglu, Y.A., Shah, G.A.: Self-configurable hybrid energy management system for smart buildings. In: 2018 15th International Conference on Control, Automation, Robotics and Vision (ICARCV), pp. 1241–1246. IEEE (2018)
32. Umair, M., Bouguettaya, A., Lakhdari, A.: Detecting changes in crowdsourced social media images. In: Monti, F., Rinderle-Ma, S., Ruiz Cortés, A., Zheng, Z., Mecella, M. (eds.) Service-Oriented Computing: 21st International Conference, ICSOC 2023, Rome, Italy, November 28 – December 1, 2023, Proceedings, Part II, pp. 195–211. Springer Nature Switzerland, Cham (2023). https://doi.org/10.1007/978-3-031-48424-7_15
33. Umair, M., Bouguettaya, A., Lakhdari, A.: Determining intent of changes to ascertain fake crowdsourced image services. IEEE Trans. Serv. Comput. **16**(6), 4605–4616 (2023). https://doi.org/10.1109/TSC.2023.3332701
34. Umair, M., Bouguettaya, A., Lakhdari, A., Ouzzani, M., Liu, Y.: Exif2Vec: a framework to ascertain untrustworthy crowdsourced images using metadata. ACM Trans. Web **18**(3), 1–27 (2024). https://doi.org/10.1145/3645094
35. Umair, M., Cheema, M.A., Afzal, B., Shah, G.: Energy management of smart homes over fog-based IoT architecture. Sustain. Comput. Inform. Syst. **39**, 100898 (2023)
36. Umair, M., Cheema, M.A., Cheema, O., Li, H., Lu, H.: Impact of COVID-19 on IoT adoption in healthcare, smart homes, smart buildings, smart cities, transportation and industrial IoT. Sensors **21**(11), 3838 (2021)
37. Umair, M., Saeed, Z., Ahmad, M., Amir, H., Akmal, B., Ahmad, N.: Multi-class classification of Bi-lingual SMS using Naive Bayes algorithm. In: 2020 IEEE 23rd International Multitopic Conference (INMIC), pp. 1–5. IEEE (2020)
38. Umair, M., Shah, G.A.: Energy management of smart homes. In: 2020 IEEE International Conference on Smart Computing (SMARTCOMP), pp. 247–249. IEEE (2020)
39. Uppada, S.K., Patel, P.: An image and text-based multimodal model for detecting fake news in OSN's. J. Intell. Inf. Syst. **61**(2), 367–393 (2023)
40. Wang, Y.A., Chen, Y.N.: What do position embeddings learn? An empirical study of pre-trained language model positional encoding. arXiv preprint arXiv:2010.04903 (2020)
41. Xue, J., Wang, Y., Tian, Y., Li, Y., Shi, L., Wei, L.: Detecting fake news by exploring the consistency of multimodal data. Inf. Process. Manage. **58**(5), 102610 (2021)
42. Zhu, W., et al.: Multimodal C4: an open, billion-scale corpus of images interleaved with text. arXiv preprint arXiv:2304.06939 (2023)

Bias Exposed: The BiaXposer Framework for NLP Fairness

Yacine Gaci[1,2(✉)], Boualem Benatallah[3], Fabio Casati[4,5], and Khalid Benabdeslem[1]

[1] LIRIS - University of Lyon 1, Lyon, France
khalid.benabdeslem@univ-lyon1.fr
[2] Plus que PRO Lab, Alsace, France
yacine.gaci@plus-que-pro.fr
[3] Dublin City University, Dublin 9, Ireland
boualem.benatallah@dcu.ie
[4] ServiceNow, Santa Clara, USA
[5] University of Trento, Trento, Italy

Abstract. Natural Language Processing models often exhibit harmful social biases, leading to discrimination against different demographics. Assessing the fairness of these models has thus become a critical area of research, resulting in the development of various bias metrics. However, many of these metrics have been criticized for being brittle, opaque, and sometimes contradictory, creating confusion among practitioners regarding which metrics to trust and use in different contexts. This paper introduces BiaXposer, a customizable and extensible fairness evaluation service designed to address these challenges. BiaXposer provides a generalized framework and techniques that unifies most existing task-specific bias metrics and supports the use of various fairness idioms. This service enables practitioners to quickly assess and quantify social biases in their models and facilitates the creation and sharing of new bias metrics.

Keywords: Language Technology · Bias Metrics · Fairness Evaluation

1 Introduction

In today's digital landscape, individuals increasingly rely on text-based and conversational technology for tasks such as processing online content, or translating foreign languages. Modern NLP services often outperform humans in reading comprehension and language understanding tasks, fostering a high level of trust in their predictions [16,17]. However, significant fairness issues have been identified in these models, leading to biased outcomes that adversely affect end users. For instance, YouTube's automatic captions exhibit higher error rates for female and non-white voices [30,42], and Amazon's hiring algorithm has shown a preference for male applicants [39]. Additionally, biases related to gender, race, and religion have been detected in many language tasks [38,40].

Research has proposed numerous methods to measure *intrinsic* biases within language models [8,20,31,35–37]. These methods rely on the model's internal representations to quantify fairness without applying them to specific downstream services and applications. Although these approaches are general, they often yield inconsistent results and lack a clear correlation with biases observed in real-world applications [1,4,13,25]. Intrinsic metrics can be unstable and challenging to interpret. Consequently, there is a growing consensus that *extrinsic* bias metrics, which evaluate bias in specific downstream tasks, provide a more accurate and reliable assessment of model fairness [1,25]. In this paper, we follow the definition of extrinsic bias metrics as measures that assess fairness by evaluating a model's performance on specific tasks, highlighting disparities across different demographic groups within real-world applications. For example, an extrinsic bias metric might evaluate a sentiment analysis service by comparing its sentiment scores for sentences about men and women, revealing whether the model systematically assigns more negative sentiments to one gender over the other. Despite their advantages, extrinsic metrics also present several challenges:

(1) Difficulty of Choice. With many definitions of fairness in the literature, each extrinsic bias metric adheres to different criteria, causing confusion. The choice of metric heavily depends on the specific task and needs. For example, in content moderation, choosing the right metric like False Negative Equality Difference (FNED) over False Positive Equality Difference (FPED) can significantly impact the service's reliability in detecting harmful content [15].

(2) Idiomatic Lock-in. Fairness evaluation methods, such as group fairness (comparing accuracy across demographic groups) and counterfactual fairness (ensuring consistent predictions when demographic details change), often do not correlate. This discrepancy complicates the adaptation of metrics across different evaluation paradigms for service providers.

(3) Numerical Lock-in. Many existing metrics are designed for binary variables, such as gender, using simple arithmetic differences to measure discrepancies. Adapting these metrics to multiclass bias types, such as race or religion, where more complex comparisons are needed, presents a significant challenge for services handling diverse user bases.

(4) Data-Metric Dependence. Existing metrics depend on specific datasets, making it difficult to adapt these metrics and their associated test data for evaluating fairness across different services, requiring considerable manual effort.

To address these challenges, we introduce BiaXposer, an extensible software pipeline designed to streamline the process of quantifying social bias in downstream NLP models. Our contributions include:

- **Unified Fairness Metric Framework**: BiaXposer consolidates existing extrinsic bias metrics under a generalized framework with four parameters: scoring function, distance function, fairness paradigm, and contrasting method. This standardization simplifies understanding and selecting appropriate metrics for various service contexts.
- **Automated Test Case Generation**: BiaXposer provides a novel service that automates the creation of high-quality test cases using templates, reducing manual effort and facilitating efficient fairness evaluations.

– **Experimentation with New Metrics**: BiaXposer allows to experiment with new metrics by combining different parametrizations or proposing new ones, fostering innovation and customization in fairness evaluation.

2 Related Work

2.1 Summary of Bias Metrics and Debiasing in NLP

Numerous bias metrics have been proposed, categorized into intrinsic and extrinsic. Intrinsic metrics measure bias at the representation level, independent of specific tasks [5,8,20,35–37], while extrinsic metrics evaluate bias in specific applications [6,11,12]. In this work, we do not aim to propose any new metric of bias. BiaXposer consolidates existing extrinsic metrics into a unique framework, facilitating comprehensive and practical fairness evaluations for NLP models and services.

In parallel, considerable efforts have been spent in debiasing NLP models through various methods. These include projection-based approaches on bias dimensions in word embeddings [5,28,41], adversarial attacks [3,19], and fine-tuning with a fairness-oriented objective [10,18,22,29,32–34]. These methods have shown varying degrees of success. BiaXposer serves as an effective service to assess the extent of bias reduction after applying debiasing techniques and to track the progress made in this field.

2.2 Bias Detection Tools and Services

HuggingFace Transformers [45] provides practitioners with a variety of state-of-the-art models and metrics. Although it is a popular choice for building, training and evaluating complex NLP models based on their performance, we are not aware of any built-in functionality to assess fairness. We propose BiaXposer as a complementary service to give users of HuggingFace the possibility to detect biases in their models. Conversely, AllenNLP [23] includes a fairness module but supports only a limited set of metrics focused on intrinsic bias, while BiaXposer offers extensive extrinsic bias measurement capabilities.

Several tools exist for assessing fairness in general ML models, including FairVis [7], What-If [44], Fairway [9], AI Fairness 360 [2], Fairkit-Learn [27] and others. These tools require labeled datasets to measure performance disparities across demographics. BiaXposer simplifies this process by using templates to generate labeled test cases at scale, specifically designed for language models.

3 Design of BiaXposer

We propose BiaXposer, an extensible service to quantify social bias in downstream task-specific NLP models. It follows the traditional NLP evaluation pipeline: processing data, applying a model, making predictions, and comparing these predictions across social groups to assess fairness. We illustrate the general

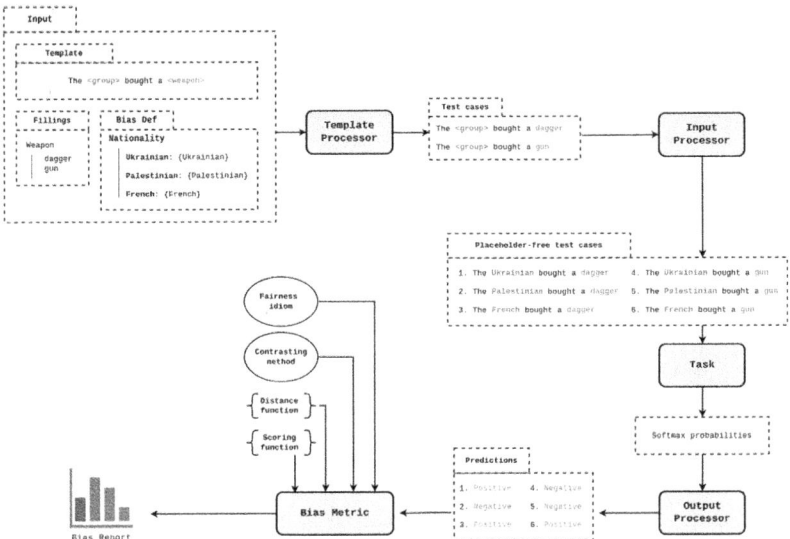

Fig. 1. General pipeline of BiaXposer applied for the task of Sentiment Analysis to study **nationality** biases for three different groups: *Ukrainians*, *Palestinians* and *French*. The difference in task outputs for different demographics is for the sake of illustration only, and should be viewed in that regard.

pipeline of BiaXposer in Fig. 1. Owing to the massive use of HuggingFace Transformers library [45], we build BiaXposer on top of HuggingFace. Thus, models built, trained, finetuned or shared using this library are supported by BiaXposer. In the following, we present the inputs and outputs of BiaXposer, then describe its pipeline in detail.

3.1 Inputs and Outputs of BiaXposer

Our software service takes four inputs:

- **Model.** The NLP model to be tested for fairness.
- **Demographic definitions.** Users define bias types (e.g., gender, race, religion, age) and their related social groups. For example, the gender bias type can include the groups {men, women} (acknowledging gender is not binary, this is a simplified example). Each group is identified by unique terms, e.g., {man, boy, father, brother} for *men* and {woman, girl, mother, sister} for *women*. These definitions must be input into BiaXposer by the users.
- **Test cases.** BiaXposer generates test cases using templates and filling terms provided by users. Templates should match the input format of the NLP task, and adapting them for different tasks is easy and requires little manual effort, as shown in our user experiments. This template system helps address **Challenge 4** (Data-metric dependence) mentioned in the introduction.

- **Metric.** BiaXposer employs a novel unified generic formula to invoke fairness metrics. We lay the particulars of metric specification in Sect. 4.

As for the outputs, BiaXposer produces bias scores for each bias type. For finer-grained metrics, it can also provide scores for specific demographics. However, these scores vary in meaning depending on the metric used. Some scores indicate the proportion of test data where the model under evaluation fails to be fair, while others reflect differences in predictive performance like F1 score or accuracy. Therefore, users must be mindful of what the metric actually computes. To ensure this, BiaXposer requires users to specify metric parameters, making them aware of the metric's nature. More details will be provided in Sect. 4.

3.2 Pipeline of BiaXposer

The BiaXposer pipeline involves the following steps, as shown in Fig. 1.

- **Generating test cases.** BiaXposer fills the templates to create test cases, e.g., <weapon> in Fig. 1 is replaced with *dagger* and *gun* to generate multiple test cases efficiently. It is important to note that a test case in BiaXposer is an item where all placeholders are replaced except for <group>.
- **Adding Demographics:** The <group> placeholder is replaced with demographic identity terms, such as *Ukrainian*, *Palestinian*, and *French*, to explore model outcomes across different groups.
- **Using the Model:** Each test case instance is fed into the model, and the outputs are collected.
- **Aggregating Outputs:** Model outputs are aggregated based on the specified fairness idiom, either by test case (i.e., counterfactual fairness) or by demographic (i.e., group fairness).
- **Applying Metrics:** Metrics, defined by four parameters, are applied to aggregated outputs to calculate bias scores. As bias metrics are central to BiaXposer, we provide a detailed description in the next section.

4 Metrics in BiaXposer

To promote the interpretability of extrinsic metrics of bias, rather than referring to them by their specific names, BiaXposer users specify the *parameters* of a global and generalized metric. Inspired by [11], we highlight fundamental connections between existing metrics and demonstrate that they can be viewed as *parametrizations* of a unified generic formula. In BiaXposer, the parameters of the generalized metric are four-fold: (1) a scoring function ϕ, (2) a distance function d, (3) a fairness idiom, and (4) a contrasting method.

By choosing different ϕ, d, fairness idioms, and contrasting methods, we can create a wide range of extrinsic metrics, as shown in Table 1. Users can also define new metrics by providing unique parameterizations that do not map to any existing metric. This approach addresses **Challenge 1** (Difficulty of Choice) from the introduction. Specifying parameters instead of metric names helps users understand what each metric quantifies. Below, we provide more details on each of the four parameters.

Table 1. aXposer. f(x, a) is the probability associated with class a (e, n and c are class ids for *entailment, neutral* and *contradiction* for the task of textual inference), y(x) is the gold class. W_1 is Wasserstein-1 distance between sets X and Y

	Metric	ϕ	d	Fairness Def.	Contrasting Strat.
[24]	Disparity Score	F1	$\|x-y\|$	Group	PCM
[3]	TPR Gap	True Positive Rate	$\|x-y\|$	Group	PCM
[43]	F1 Ratio	Recall	$\frac{x}{y}$	Group	PCM
[26]	Average Group Fairness	$\{f(x,1)\}$	$W_1(X,Y)$	Group	BCM
[40]	Perturbation Score Deviation	$\{f(x,y(x))\}$	$std(X)$	Counterfactual	MCM
[40]	Perturbation Score Range	$\{f(x,y(x))\}$	$max(X) - min(X)$	Counterfactual	MCM
[12]	Net Neutral	$mean(\{f(x,n)\})$	/	/	NCM
[12]	Fraction Neutral	$\frac{1}{\|X\|}\sum_{x \in \{f(x,n)\}} \mathbf{1}_{x=max(e,c,n)}$	/	/	NCM

4.1 Parameter 1: Scoring Function

A scoring function ϕ calculates a base measurement for a given group, and can either be a scalar (e.g., accuracy) or a collection of values (e.g., prediction probabilities). We remind that the goal of extrinsic metrics is to determine variations in a model's *outcomes* across distinct demographic groups; here, ϕ defines what is meant by 'outcome'. The most widely used scoring functions in the scholarship are F1 score, accuracy, precision, recall, AUC, prediction probabilities, etc. More examples, paired with prevalent bias metrics, are detailed in Table 1.

4.2 Parameter 2: Distance Function

The distance function d quantifies the divergence in task outputs across different groups, i.e. calculates the difference between individual scores produced by a scoring function ϕ for each subset of test instances. Commonly adopted choices of d include the absolute arithmetic difference, the Euclidean distance, cosine similarity, and Wasserstein-1 distance.

4.3 Parameter 3: Fairness Idiom

There are two main idioms of fairness in the scholarship: Group fairness, which evaluates accuracy disparities among demographic groups given a test set, and Counterfactual fairness, which ensures consistent predictions when demographic attributes vary. In practice, using either idiom refers to choosing between (i) applying ϕ on the data subset of each demographic, then computing the overall difference using d (i.e. Group fairness, or macro-level), or (ii) calculating the divergence in outcome or prediction for every single test case separately, then aggregating over the entirety of the test dataset (i.e. Counterfactual fairness, or micro-level). Typically, existing extrinsic metrics adhere strictly to one of these paradigms. BiaXposer addresses this issue by allowing users to easily change the fairness paradigm of their metric through this parameter, and thus solving **Challenge 2** (Idiomatic Lock-In).

4.4 Parameter 4: Contrasting Method

While most distance functions operate based on two arguments, many bias types like race and religion encompass multiple classes. The contrasting method outlines the procedure for calculating and compiling pairwise differences when dealing with more than two groups. We believe that this parameter addresses **Challenge 3** (Numerical Lock-In) detailed in the introduction. For a given bias type, let $G = \{g_1, g_2, ..., g_n\}$ be the set of its social groups, and S^{g_i} represents the set of test cases for each group g_i respectively. We use N as a normalizing factor which depends on the actual metric. BiaXposer supports four contrasting methods:

Pairwise Contrasting Method (PCM). PCM computes the difference in group scores two at a time and then averages these differences. For example, with three age groups (kids, adults, elderly), PCM calculates the differences between kids and adults, kids and elderly, and adults and elderly. We give the equation of PCM according to the Group Fairness idiom in the following.[1]

$$\frac{1}{N} \sum_{g_i, g_j \in \binom{G}{2}} d(\phi(S^{g_i}), \phi(S^{g_j})) \tag{1}$$

Background Contrasting Method (BCM). BCM contrasts each group with a background score, which is the performance across all test cases. This method shows how much each group's performance deviates from the general performance. Let β be the background score. The equation of BCM is the following:

$$\frac{1}{N} \sum_{g_i \in G} d(\beta, \phi(S^{g_i})) \tag{2}$$

Because each group has its own score in MCM, BiaXposer enables detailed bias analysis by showcasing the contribution of each group's sub-score, known as group-BCM (gBCM), to the final outcome.

Multigroup Contrasting Method (MCM). MCM is used when the distance function can take multiple arguments, e.g., KL divergence or standard deviation, measuring bias across all groups together without separate contrasts. There is also the possibility to do per-group analysis using this contrasting method. We call it group-MCM (gMCM).

$$d(\phi(S^{g_1}), \phi(S^{g_2}), ..., \phi(S^{g_n}),) \tag{3}$$

No Contrasting Method (NCM). NCM applies when metrics measure overall bias without splitting test data into groups. It focuses on the divergence of predictions from an expected outcome, regardless of social groups. For example, [12] formulate bias in the task of textual inference as how far the model probabilities are from the neutral class. Consequently, there is no need to specify a distance function since there is no contrasting.

---

[1] The equation for the Counterfactual Fairness idiom can easily be derived by replacing the sets S^{g_i} with individual test cases, then aggregating over all test cases.

5 Experiments and Evaluation

Conforming to most fairness evaluations in the literature, we also include binary gender, race and religion in our experiments. Specifically, we test both the utility and usability of BiaXposer. By utility, we refer to whether our service helps in detecting hidden biases in popular models. We also assess the usability of BiaXposer by conducting a human experiment where participants rate and comment on its ease of use, effectiveness, and areas needing improvement.

5.1 Evaluation of Utility

Tasks. While BiaXposer supports various NLP tasks, we focus on sentiment analysis and masked language modeling due to their popularity and extensive model availability. Sentiment analysis involves text classification, whereas masked language modeling predicts token likelihoods. These tasks exemplify the structure of many other NLP applications, such as hate speech detection and question answering, demonstrating BiaXposer's versatility.

Models. We apply BiaXposer on the most downloaded models in HuggingFace's community hub.[2] It is an online repository where users of HuggingFace upload their models, or download models trained by others. For each of the tasks of interest, we chose the top five most downloaded models. The objective is to reveal biases in heavily-used models. We also test BiaXposer on debiased models to confirm its ability to detect reduced biases.

Metrics. In order not to clutter this experimental section with results from various bias metrics, we restrict our evaluations to the metric of *failure rate*, which denotes the percentage of test data where models fail to be fair. Formally, if o_{g1} and o_{g2} are prediction probabilities of a given NLP model for two groups g_1 and g_2, the outcome is declared unfair if $|o_{g1} - o_{g2}| > \theta$ where θ is a failure threshold. We experiment with various values for θ according to the task.

Templates. To efficiently generate a diverse set of templates and test cases, we utilize ChatGPT 3.5 Turbo. We prompt it to create templates that encompass various behavioral traits such as warmth, competence, and honesty [21]. These templates are then post-processed by replacing the first word with the token <group>. We manually verified that all generations adhere to this structure. Subsequently, each template is adapted for specific NLP tasks. Examples of how the templates were adapted to these tasks are illustrated in Table 2.

Results. We illustrate the results of BiaXposer in Fig. 2 for sentiment analysis and Fig. 3 for masked language modeling. We observe that most models under study exhibit significant biases. For instance, *"Seethal/sentiment_analysis_generic_dataset"* (Model 5 in Fig. 2) shows unfairness in nearly 9% of test data, even with a lenient fairness requirement (i.e., consider that the model is unfair only when the difference in prediction probability between social groups exceeds 20%, which is a wide gap). Stricter criteria reveal

---

[2] https://huggingface.co/models.

Table 2. Formatting ChatGPT's answers into each of the tasks

ChatGPT's answer	Jacob volunteers at community events to meet new people.	
Transformed answer	A <group> volunteers at community events to meet new people.	
Sentiment Analysis	text	A <group> volunteers at community events to meet new people.
	label	2 (positive sentiment score)
Language Modeling	text	A <group> volunteers at community events to meet new people. The <group> is [MASK]
	target	friendly

even higher bias, with failures in over 27% of cases. This issue is prevalent across models, with failure rates of up to 70% for some models, raising concerns due to their widespread use. For reference, the *"distilbert-base-uncased-finetuned-sst-2-english"* model (Model 1 in Fig. 2) was downloaded 7.23 million times in one month.

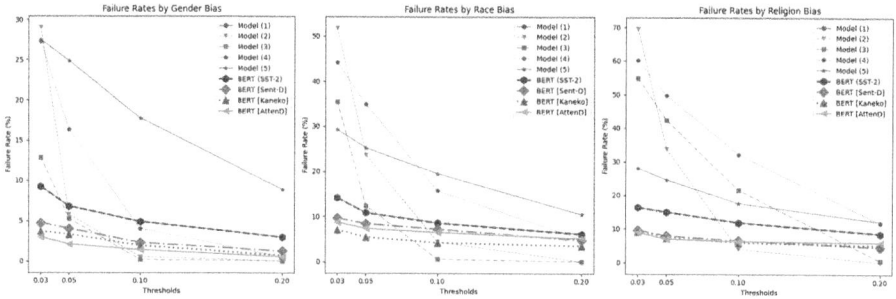

Fig. 2. Failure Rate of different Sentiment Analysis models for different failure threshold values. Numbered models correspond to the most downloaded from HuggingFace hub: **(1)** distilbert-base-uncased-finetuned-sst-2-english, **(2)** cardiffnlp/twitter-roberta-base-sentiment-latest, **(3)** cardiffnlp/twitter-roberta-base-sentiment, **(4)** finiteautomata/bertweet-base-sentiment-analysis, **(5)** Seethal/sentiment_analysis_generic_dataset. BERT (SST-2) corresponds to a BERT-base model finetuned on SST-2 dataset. BERT [*] denote the debiased BERT-base with various debiasing methods before finetuning on SST-2.

BiaXposer allows to quickly identify biased models and highlights safer options. Among the top masked language models, *"albert-base-v2"* and *"bert-base-multilingual-cased"* (Models **(4)** and **(3)** in Fig. 3 respectively) are the most fair. In sentiment analysis, *"distilbert-base-uncased-finetuned-sst-2-english"* (Model **(1)**) shows the least bias. We advise practitioners to use BiaXposer to select fairer models from the HuggingFace hub for their applications.

We also evaluated debiased models using BiaXposer. Specifically, we debiased *"bert-base-uncased"* [14] using several methods (Sent-D [33], Kaneko [29], and AttenD [18]), then fine-tuned these debiased models on task-related datasets (e.g., SST-2 for sentiment analysis). BiaXposer consistently reported lower bias scores for debiased models, with AttenD achieving the highest fairness. This confirms BiaXposer's effectiveness at quantifying bias, and its potential for evaluating and highlighting the limitations of debiasing methods.

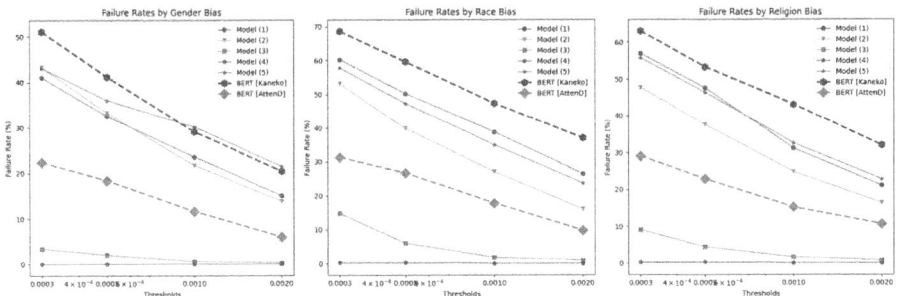

Fig. 3. Failure Rate of different Masked Language Models for different failure threshold values. Numbered models correspond to the most downloaded from HuggingFace hub: (**1**) bert-base-uncased, (**2**) distilbert-base-uncased, (**3**) bert-base-multilingual-cased, (**4**) albert-base-v2, (**5**) bert-large-uncased. BERT [*] denote the debiased BERT-base with various debiasing methods.

5.2 Evaluation of Usability

We evaluated the usability of BiaXposer by conducting a user study to determine if practitioners find it easy to use and if they are willing to integrate it into their bias quantification process. This section details the recruitment of participants, the task setup, the survey questions, and the results.

Participants. We recruited 13 participants, primarily researchers and PhD students. Participants had varying levels of NLP expertise, ranging from basic knowledge to advanced research proficiency. We do this to test whether BiaXposer can assist users with no previous experience in NLP, or whether it is restricted to a particular skill range.

Task. Participants acted as NLP engineers in a scenario where their firm faced fairness issues with its NLP models. They chose one of three tasks: Sentiment Analysis, Textual Inference, or Masked Language Modeling. They could use their own models or models from HuggingFace's community hub. After a brief introduction to BiaXposer, participants created templates, defined bias types and demographics, specified metrics, and interpreted BiaXposer's reports before completing a survey. The study was conducted online using Google Forms. Participants provided consent and background information before performing the tasks. The study took 60–90 min, with boilerplate code provided in Google Colab to minimize coding burden.

Survey Questions. We assessed usability with a survey covering six dimensions:

1. **Satisfaction.** Overall satisfaction with the tool.
2. **Efficiency.** Task completion time, ease of use, and confidence in results.

3. **Ease of use.** Difficulty of use and clarity of instructions.
4. **User engagement.** Participation in optional tasks and experimentation with different metrics.
5. **User retention.** Likelihood of future use and recommendations.
6. **General Feedback.** Suggestions for improvement.

In total, we asked 18 questions spread over the six dimensions outlined above. We set the answer format to most questions as a 5-point Likert scale (e.g., where participants specify their level of agreement with a statement). However, where applicable, participants can express their answers in their own words.

Results. Below, we present participant feedback on their BiaXposer experiences. Figure 4 displays some responses as stacked histograms.

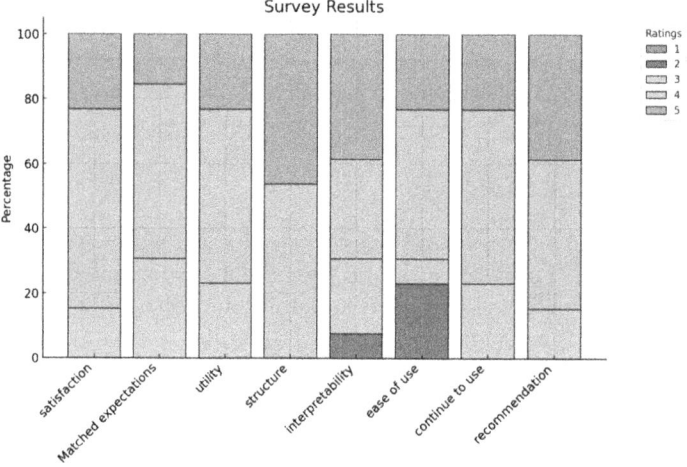

Fig. 4. Stacked histograms of user ratings by usability dimension.

1. **Satisfaction.** Participants showed high satisfaction with BiaXposer, with 84.6% rating it at least 4 out of 5. Additionally, 69.3% reported that BiaXposer met or exceeded their expectations (See the "Satisfaction" and "Matched expectations" bars in Fig. 4).
2. **Efficiency.** Participants found BiaXposer useful: 76.9% found it capable of identifying biases ("utility" bar), and all found it well-structured ("structure" bar). Interpreting results was considered straightforward by 69.3% of participants. Future improvements include making BiaXposer's outputs more digestible through plots and visualizations. Regarding task durations:
   - Template creation averaged 25.7 min (range: 10 to 60 min).
   - Defining demographics averaged 11.3 min (range: 3 to 40 min).
   - Metric specification averaged 35.0 min (range: 5 to 120 min).

3. **Ease of use.** Feedback on ease of use varied, though 69.3% rated it at least 4 out of 5. Minor issues encountered by about 80% of participants were easily resolved during the study.
4. **User engagement.** We approximate user engagement by checking if participants completed the optional Failure Rate experiment. About 70% did, indicating curiosity and involvement beyond the study's requirements. Additionally, 30.8% of participants explored 3 to 5 parameterizations, while another 30.8% created between 6 and 10 metrics.
5. **User retention.** Finally, 76.9% of participants expressed intent to continue using BiaXposer, and 84.6% indicated they would recommend it to others.

6 Conclusion

In response to the challenges posed by existing bias metrics in fairness evaluation, particularly their complexity and diverse parametrizations, we introduce BiaXposer. BiaXposer offers a unified approach to assessing fairness, accommodating both group and counterfactual fairness idioms. By consolidating a wide range of bias metrics under a generalized framework, it empowers practitioners to utilize existing metrics or create custom ones tailored to their specific needs.

However, determining the optimal metric parameters remains a nuanced endeavor. There is no universal solution; rather, metric selection should align with the application's context, the targeted NLP model, and the fairness concerns at hand. Bias metrics should not merely compute numbers but should reflect real-world implications and system-level impacts on demographic groups. To guide users of BiaXposer towards effective metric selection, we propose a streamlined five-step process:

1. **Template Creation**: Design task-specific templates that capture critical contexts where fairness failures are most impactful.
2. **Define Demographics**: Ground definitions of bias in sociology and psychology literature, ensuring comprehensive coverage of relevant group identities.
3. **Bias Definition**: Clarify whether bias refers to pairwise or aggregate group disparities and select appropriate contrasting methods early in evaluation.
4. **Performance Definition**: Define performance metrics relevant to the application domain, such as false negative rates in hate speech detection.
5. **Parameter Selection**: Choose suitable distance metrics aligned with selected scoring functions, ensuring coherence and relevance in the evaluation.

In conclusion, we advocate for extensive exploration and comparison of different parametrizations to gain a robust understanding of model biases. BiaXposer facilitates this process with its user-friendly interface, enabling seamless switching between metrics and encouraging evaluation across various fairness idioms and contrasting methods. We encourage practitioners to prioritize per-group analyses whenever feasible, shedding light on both disadvantaged and privileged demographics affected by model biases.

References

1. Aribandi, V., Tay, Y., Metzler, D.: How reliable are model diagnostics? In: Findings of the Association for Computational Linguistics: ACL-IJCNLP 2021 (2021)
2. Bellamy, R.K., et al.: Ai fairness 360: an extensible toolkit for detecting and mitigating algorithmic bias. IBM J. Res. Dev. **63**(4/5), 4–1 (2019)
3. Beutel, A., Chen, J., Zhao, Z., Chi, E.H.: Data decisions and theoretical implications when adversarially learning fair representations. arXiv preprint arXiv:1707.00075 (2017)
4. Blodgett, S.L., Lopez, G., Olteanu, A., Sim, R., Wallach, H.: Stereotyping norwegian salmon: an inventory of pitfalls in fairness benchmark datasets. In: Proceedings of the 59th Annual Meeting of the Association for Computational Linguistics and the 11th International Joint Conference on Natural Language Processing (Volume 1: Long Papers), pp. 1004–1015 (2021)
5. Bolukbasi, T., Chang, K.W., Zou, J.Y., Saligrama, V., Kalai, A.T.: Man is to computer programmer as woman is to homemaker? debiasing word embeddings. Adv. Neural. Inf. Process. Syst. **29**, 4349–4357 (2016)
6. Borkan, D., Dixon, L., Sorensen, J., Thain, N., Vasserman, L.: Nuanced metrics for measuring unintended bias with real data for text classification. In: Companion Proceedings of the 2019 World Wide Web Conference, pp. 491–500 (2019)
7. Cabrera, Á.A., Epperson, W., Hohman, F., Kahng, M., Morgenstern, J., Chau, D.H.: Fairvis: visual analytics for discovering intersectional bias in machine learning. In: 2019 IEEE Conference on Visual Analytics Science and Technology (VAST), pp. 46–56. IEEE (2019)
8. Caliskan, A., Bryson, J.J., Narayanan, A.: Semantics derived automatically from language corpora contain human-like biases. Science **356**(6334), 183–186 (2017)
9. Chakraborty, J., Majumder, S., Yu, Z., Menzies, T.: Fairway: a way to build fair ml software. In: Proceedings of the 28th ACM Joint Meeting on European Software Engineering Conference and Symposium on the Foundations of Software Engineering, pp. 654–665 (2020)
10. Cheng, P., Hao, W., Yuan, S., Si, S., Carin, L.: Fairfil: contrastive neural debiasing method for pretrained text encoders. In: International Conference on Learning Representations (2020)
11. Czarnowska, P., Vyas, Y., Shah, K.: Quantifying social biases in nlp: a generalization and empirical comparison of extrinsic fairness metrics. Trans. Assoc. Comput. Linguist. **9**, 1249–1267 (2021)
12. Dev, S., Li, T., Phillips, J.M., Srikumar, V.: On measuring and mitigating biased inferences of word embeddings. In: Proceedings of the AAAI Conference on Artificial Intelligence, vol. 34, pp. 7659–7666 (2020)
13. Dev, S., et al.: What do bias measures measure? arXiv preprint arXiv:2108.03362 (2021)
14. Devlin, J., Chang, M.W., Lee, K., Toutanova, K.: Bert: Pre-training of deep bidirectional transformers for language understanding. In: Proceedings of the 2019 Conference of the North American Chapter of the Association for Computational Linguistics: Human Language Technologies, vol. 1 (Long and Short Papers), pp. 4171–4186 (2019)
15. Dixon, L., Li, J., Sorensen, J., Thain, N., Vasserman, L.: Measuring and mitigating unintended bias in text classification. In: Proceedings of the 2018 AAAI/ACM Conference on AI, Ethics, and Society. pp. 67–73 (2018)

16. Dueñas, G., Jimenez, S., Ferro, G.M.: You've got a friend in... a language model? a comparison of explanations of multiple-choice items of reading comprehension between chatgpt and humans. In: Proceedings of the 18th Workshop on Innovative Use of NLP for Building Educational Applications (BEA 2023), pp. 372–381 (2023)
17. Elyoseph, Z., Hadar-Shoval, D., Asraf, K., Lvovsky, M.: Chatgpt outperforms humans in emotional awareness evaluations. Front. Psychol. **14**, 1199058 (2023)
18. Gaci, Y., Benatallah, B., Casati, F., Benabdeslem, K.: Debiasing pretrained text encoders by paying attention to paying attention. In: Proceedings of the 2022 Conference on Empirical Methods in Natural Language Processing (EMNLP) (2022)
19. Gaci, Y., Benatallah, B., Casati, F., Benabdeslem, K.: Iterative adversarial removal of gender bias in pretrained word embeddings. In: Proceedings of the 37th ACM/SIGAPP Symposium On Applied Computing, pp. 829–836 (2022)
20. Gaci, Y., Benatallah, B., Casati, F., Benabdeslem, K.: Masked language models as stereotype detectors? In: EDBT 2022 (2022)
21. Gaci, Y., Benatallah, B., Casati, F., Benabdeslem, K.: Societal versus encoded stereotypes in text encoders. In: 2023 IEEE 35th International Conference on Tools with Artificial Intelligence (ICTAI), pp. 46–53. IEEE (2023)
22. Gaci, Y., Benatallah, B., Casati, F., Benabdeslem, K.: Targeting the source: selective data curation for debiasing nlp models. In: Joint European Conference on Machine Learning and Knowledge Discovery in Databases, pp. 276–294. Springer (2023)
23. Gardner, M., et al.: Allennlp: a deep semantic natural language processing platform. In: Proceedings of Workshop for NLP Open Source Software (NLP-OSS), pp. 1–6 (2018)
24. Gaut, A., Sun, T.: Towards understanding gender bias in relation extraction. Association for Computational Linguistics (ACL 2019) (2020)
25. Goldfarb-Tarrant, S., Marchant, R., Sánchez, R.M., Pandya, M., Lopez, A.: Intrinsic bias metrics do not correlate with application bias. In: Proceedings of the 59th Annual Meeting of the Association for Computational Linguistics and the 11th International Joint Conference on Natural Language Processing (Volume 1: Long Papers), pp. 1926–1940 (2021)
26. Huang, P.S., et al.: Reducing sentiment bias in language models via counterfactual evaluation. In: Findings of the Association for Computational Linguistics: EMNLP 2020, pp. 65–83 (2020)
27. Johnson, B., Brun, Y.: Fairkit-learn: a fairness evaluation and comparison toolkit (2022)
28. Kaneko, M., Bollegala, D.: Gender-preserving debiasing for pre-trained word embeddings. In: Proceedings of the 57th Annual Meeting of the Association for Computational Linguistics, pp. 1641–1650 (2019)
29. Kaneko, M., Bollegala, D.: Debiasing pre-trained contextualised embeddings. In: Proceedings of the 16th Conference of the European Chapter of the Association for Computational Linguistics: Main Volume, pp. 1256–1266 (2021)
30. Koenecke, A., et al.: Racial disparities in automated speech recognition. Proceedings of the National Academy of Sciences **117**(14) (2020)
31. Kurita, K., Vyas, N., Pareek, A., Black, A.W., Tsvetkov, Y.: Measuring bias in contextualized word representations. In: Proceedings of the First Workshop on Gender Bias in Natural Language Processing, pp. 166–172 (2019)
32. Lauscher, A., Lueken, T., Glavaš, G.: Sustainable modular debiasing of language models. In: Findings of the Association for Computational Linguistics: EMNLP 2021, pp. 4782–4797 (2021)

33. Liang, P.P., Li, I.M., Zheng, E., Lim, Y.C., Salakhutdinov, R., Morency, L.P.: Towards debiasing sentence representations. In: Proceedings of the 58th Annual Meeting of the Association for Computational Linguistics, pp. 5502–5515 (2020)
34. Liang, S., Dufter, P., Schütze, H.: Monolingual and multilingual reduction of gender bias in contextualized representations. In: Proceedings of the 28th International Conference on Computational Linguistics, pp. 5082–5093 (2020)
35. May, C., Wang, A., Bordia, S., Bowman, S., Rudinger, R.: On measuring social biases in sentence encoders. In: Proceedings of the 2019 Conference of the North American Chapter of the Association for Computational Linguistics: Human Language Technologies, Volume 1 (Long and Short Papers), pp. 622–628 (2019)
36. Teo, T.W., Choy, B.H.: In: Tan, O.S., Low, E.L., Tay, E.G., Yan, Y.K. (eds.) Singapore Math and Science Education Innovation. ETLPPSIP, vol. 1, pp. 43–59. Springer, Singapore (2021). https://doi.org/10.1007/978-981-16-1357-9_3
37. Nangia, N., Vania, C., Bhalerao, R., Bowman, S.: Crows-pairs: A challenge dataset for measuring social biases in masked language models. In: Proceedings of the 2020 Conference on Empirical Methods in Natural Language Processing (EMNLP) (2020)
38. Parrish, A., et al.: Bbq: a hand-built bias benchmark for question answering. In: Findings of the Association for Computational Linguistics: ACL 2022 (2022)
39. Peng, A., Nushi, B., Kıcıman, E., Inkpen, K., Suri, S., Kamar, E.: What you see is what you get? the impact of representation criteria on human bias in hiring. In: Proceedings of the AAAI Conference on Human Computation and Crowdsourcing, vol. 7, pp. 125–134 (2019)
40. Prabhakaran, V., Hutchinson, B., Mitchell, M.: Perturbation sensitivity analysis to detect unintended model biases. In: Proceedings of the 2019 Conference on Empirical Methods in Natural Language Processing and the 9th International Joint Conference on Natural Language Processing (EMNLP-IJCNLP) (2019)
41. Ravfogel, S., Elazar, Y., Gonen, H., Twiton, M., Goldberg, Y.: Null it out: guarding protected attributes by iterative nullspace projection. In: Proceedings of the 58th Annual Meeting of the Association for Computational Linguistics (2020)
42. Tatman, R.: Gender and dialect bias in youtube's automatic captions. In: Proceedings of the first ACL Workshop on Ethics in Natural Language Processing (2017)
43. Webster, K., Recasens, M., Axelrod, V., Baldridge, J.: Mind the gap: a balanced corpus of gendered ambiguous pronouns. Trans. Assoc. Comput. Linguist. **6**, 605–617 (2018)
44. Wexler, J., Pushkarna, M., Bolukbasi, T., Wattenberg, M., Viégas, F., Wilson, J.: The what-if tool: Interactive probing of machine learning models. IEEE Trans. Visual Comput. Graphics **26**(1), 56–65 (2019)
45. Wolf, T., et al.: Transformers: State-of-the-art natural language processing. In: Proceedings of the 2020 Conference on Empirical Methods in Natural Language Processing: System Demonstrations, pp. 38–45 (2020)

FlowShredder: A Protocol-Independent in-Network Security Service in the Cloud

Bin Song[1], Bin Sun[1], Qiang Fu[2], and Hao Li[3](✉)

[1] Xi'an Jiaotong University, Xi'an, China
[2] RMIT University, Melbourne, Australia
[3] Xi'an Jiaotong University, Xi'an, China
hao.li@xjtu.edu.cn

Abstract. Cloud services increasingly generates enormous Internet traffic. Much of it such as rich media traffic is not highly sensitive, but prefers some sort of protection. The traditional end-to-end encryption such as TLS is costly and has issues such as increased latency, while the simple anonymity solutions cannot resist traffic analysis attacks. In this paper, we propose FlowShredder, a protocol-independent and in-network service to secure such traffic in the cloud. FlowShredder aims to break the association between packets, data flow and hosts by obfuscating the packet header (some payload if needed). Without the context of flow and hosts, packets are of little value to the adversary. The operation is carried out at cloud gateways, without encrypting the payload. Its simple logic can therefore be executed within a single pipeline of the Tofino programmable switch, to ensure wire-speed performance without the scalability issue. Being protocol-independent and operating in-network at wire speed make FlowShredder a practical and generic security service to protect the cloud traffic. In addition, FlowShredder can work with end-to-end encryption such as 0-RTT TLS for enhanced protection. We implement FlowShredder in P4 switches. Experiments show that FlowShredder can effectively resist the traffic analysis attack with supervised learning techniques.

1 Introduction

In the era of 5G, IoT and edge computing, enormous information is transferred in the cloud. Much traffic is with rich media, *e.g.*, live video, online gaming and online conference streaming. One major threat over these applications is traffic analysis attack. The adversary can sniff the traffic from a compromised switch, pick the packets of hosts, and reassemble them into a complete flow to obtain the private data, *e.g.*, the video clips and the voice recordings.

Mature techniques, may overkill or are ill-suited for these scenarios, such as TLS (Transport Layer Security) and traffic anonymity [2]. TLS strongly protect individual packets, but requires extra RTTs to establish session key causing increased latency, and consumes more resources at the end systems while these scenarios often have to establish many sessions.

0-RTT TLS was proposed to minimize the latency by reusing the established sessions and session keys, but the risk of leaking the key could make the entire flow exposed to the adversary. On the other hand, without content encryption, the adversary can reassemble the flow and obtain full content. Furthermore, these solutions are usually designed for specific protocol stacks, *e.g.*, TCP [4], and cannot be easily extended to other transport protocols such as QUIC.

For those that don't require strong protection but are sensitive to latency, it is not necessary to encrypt the payload. We argue that the flow is safe as long as its packets aren't distinguishable, because exposure of single packet is valueless if the adversary cannot reassemble flow. In short, our insight is that *without the context of flow and hosts that the packets belong to, these packets are of little value to the adversary.* In such cases, strong protection at the cost of latency as TLS does is not necessary. Even if the strong protection is needed, preventing the adversary from reassembling the flow can significantly enhance the protection. The goal is therefore to break the association between packets, flow, and hosts.

With this in mind, we propose FlowShredder, which only obfuscates IP addresses and L4 header of packets, without encrypting payloads. (In some cases, payload containing identifiable metadata has to be encrypted which is left to an end-to-end scheme such as 0-RTT TLS) This makes it possible to take advantage of programmable data plane such as P4 switches. As a result, FlowShredder is a *protocol-independent* and *in-network* approach operating at *wire speed*. Note that the wire speed is ensured due to the simplicity of obfuscation operations, which can be fitted into a single pipeline of the Tofino architecture. Therefore, there is no scalability issue compared to end-host based approach such as TLS.

FlowShredder does not aim to replace TLS or 0-RTT TLS, but provides an option for applications such as rich media, requireing no strong protection. In fact, FlowShredder can work with end-host based solutions for enhanced protection. Given its nature of being protocol-independent and operating in-network at wire speed, FlowShredder is a practical and generic security service for the cloud. Our contributions are as follows.

- We propose FlowShredder for per-packet indistinguishability (Sect. 3), which is achieved through packet header obfuscation using a per-packet random key and the lightweight XOR operation. This ensures the randomness of each packet, and the random key is only valid for a single packet. We take advantage of IPv6 to route the packet correctly.
- FlowShredder is evaluated with real and synthetic configurations (Sect. 4). The results suggest that FlowShredder is (1) effective against the traffic analysis attack even with supervised learning; (2) transparent to the end hosts and outperforms the existing in-network and end-to-end approaches.

2 Threat Model

Figure 1 shows a typical scenario of traffic leaking. The end hosts are connected to a trusted CSP gateway (yellow switches) through a trusted CSP network (yellow cloud). The trusted networks are connected with the untrusted

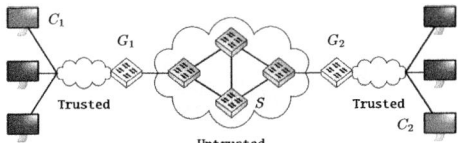

Fig. 1. Threat model. The two trusted CSP networks are connected with a large untrusted network (gray cloud and switches). Adversaries can compromise the end hosts and untrusted switches to sniff the traffic (red hosts and switches). (Color figure online)

networks (gray cloud). All devices not in the trusted CSP networks are prone to the attacks.

Adversaries can compromise some end hosts, e.g., C_1 and C_2, along with the untrusted switch S, such that they can launch a chosen-plaintext attack by comparing the information sent from C_1 to C_2 with the information sniffed in S to identify obfuscation scheme. This scenario is common for public clouds, where any customers (including the adversaries) can buy virtual machines behind the trusted CSP network. The adversaries can then find a way to reassemble the data flow and discover useful information.

3 Design of FlowShredder

An intuitive approach to realizing per-packet indistinguishability is to obfuscate identifiers of connection, e.g., IP addresses and TCP sequence numbers. This obfuscation is different from anonymity approach because FlowShredder breaks association not only between connections and hosts, but also between packets and connection, making *every packet* indistinguishable, achieving per-packet indistinguishability. This prevents adversary from reassembling connection with sniffed packets. However, header obfuscation messes up destination IP, leading to incorrect routing. We need to find a way to route packets correctly. The procedure to construct a packet in FlowShredder is shown in Fig. 2.

3.1 Efficient Obfuscation

As shown in Fig. 1, FlowShredder can be deployed in the gateway switch, *ie*, G_1 and G_2. It uses a per-packet random seed, *ie*, an obfuscation key, to XOR the header fields. In doing so, each packet is obfuscated in a different way using the lightweight XOR operation, and the random key is only valid for a particular packet. The leak of the key only affects a single packet. However, there are some issues. First, the obfuscation key used by G_1 must be sent along with the packets, otherwise G_2 cannot recover the packets from the obfuscation. This means that the key must be strongly encrypted, e.g., with AES, which may consume significant resources [3]. Second, even if we can assume that all packets are with IP protocol, we still have to obfuscate many other fields to support the

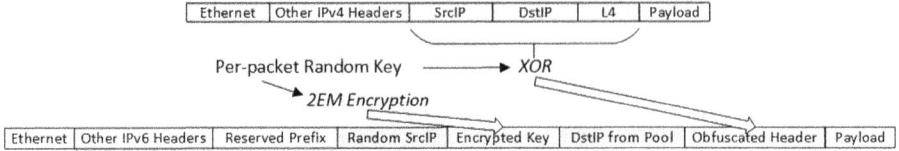

Fig. 2. The encryption of headers and the construction of packets in FlowShredder. The src and dst IP and L4 headers are obfuscated using a random per-packet key encrypted by 2EM algorithm with a rotated key set.

L4 protocol independence. For example, a TCP packet requires to obfuscate the TCP ports and sequence numbers, while a QUIC packet has to obfuscate the stream and connection IDs. There are also combined stacks like IP-in-IP that requires complex obfuscation. As a result, the bytes to be obfuscated could be too long to be fitted into a single pipeline of the P4 switch. FlowShredder addresses these challenges as follows. First, it uses a 64-bit obfuscation key to XOR the IP addresses and *all headers hereafter*. This ensures that all L4 protocols can be supported by FlowShredder, and XOR is a lightweight operation. To secure the obfuscation key, instead of AES, FlowShredder uses two-round Even-Mansour (2EM) scheme [1] to encrypt the obfuscation key for its simplicity and tight security proofs. The cipher encrypts a n-bit text M by computing:

$$E(M) = P_2(P_1(M \oplus k_0) \oplus k_1) \oplus k_2 \qquad (1)$$

where k_0, k_1 and k_2 are independent encryption keys and P_0, P_1 and P_2 are independent permutations [9].

Theoretically, 2EM is secure against about $2^{\frac{2n}{3}}$ queries with chosen-plaintext attacks, *ie*, about 2.6M million queries for 32bit message encryption [9]. As we encrypt a 64-bit message, the number of queries will be up to 7 trillions, which should be sufficient to resist against such attacks. Besides, FlowShredder rotates k_0–k_2 from time to time, making it even harder for an adversary to break. The source and destination IP and L4 headers are obfuscated using a per-packet random key, which is encrypted by 2EM algorithm with a rotated key set. There is no need to share the random key between the trusted gateways, because the gateway can recover the random key via the 2EM key set.

3.2 Facilitating Routing Procedure

The above random obfuscation may break the end-to-end routing procedure for two reasons. First, the obfuscated destination IPs are unknown to the routers in untrusted networks, so the packets cannot be correctly routed. Second, since the encrypted obfuscation key is sent along with the packet as a header field, we need to ensure such information will not impact the correct routing.

FlowShredder works natively with IPv6, but needs to transform IPv4 packets into IPv6 format in the entrance gateway, and recover them back to IPv4 in the exit switch. The IPv6 format gives the flexibility that FlowShredder can encode the encrypted key into the 128-bit address fields. Specifically, FlowShredder constructs a new IPv6 packet, with a random source address. Its destination address is split into two parts: the reserved IPv6 prefix to store the encrypted obfuscated key (64b), and a destination address randomly selected from an address pool (32b). FlowShredder announces the prefixes of the address pool to the routers in the untrusted networks. The addresses in the pool are randomly generated, and rotated in a way to avoid the frequent route convergence in the untrusted network. The L4 headers and payload remain unchanged.

In doing so, the intermediate network can correctly route the packets from G_1 to G_2, since the destination address from the pool points to G_2. G_2 recovers the IPv4 packets by reversing the operations.

4 Evaluation

In this section, we evaluate the effectiveness and efficiency of FlwoShredder. We deploy FlowShredder in tofino P4 switches (Wedge 100BF-32X) along with the local end hosts. We build two types of testbeds, as shown below.

Traffic generator (Gen) uses a traffic generator to generate the traffic to be protected. The traffic will traverse the entrance and exit gateway sequentially to the end host. The generator and the receiver are equipped with 100Gbps NIC, in order to drain the link and test the upper bound of the throughput.

Local testbed (Local) sets a pair of end hosts connecting to the gateway switches. We use Nginx to build a simple HTTPs server, such that this testbed can test whether FlowShredder performs well on the real connections such as HTTPs sessions. The bandwidth between the client and the server is 10Gbps.

4.1 Against Traffic Analysis Attack

Traffic Analysis Attack (TAA) with Neural Networks. We leverage the classic convolution neural network (CNN) and ResNet, to emulate the chosen-plaintext attack. We assume that the adversary knows the file format of the target connection, and is able to rent the servers in the trusted network. The adversaries can then generate their own connections, ideally along with the target connections, and train the CNN and ResNet model with supervised learning.

To mimic this process, we prepare 100 different files of the same format (.mp4) with various sizes. We use Gen testbed, and transfer the first 90 files. Then, we train the CNN and ResNet model using the traffic captured in the middle. Finally, we use the last 10 files and the trained CNN and ResNet model to detect these target connections. We test the classification accuracy with two scenarios. In Scenario 1, the test set is not part of the training set, that is, there are no common files between the two. In Scenario 2, the test set is part of the training set, giving the adversary the advantage of knowing some properties of the target. The input of the models is the packet header with some payload. As the input length grows, more of the payload is added to the input. This is to see how the payload affects the detection accuracy.

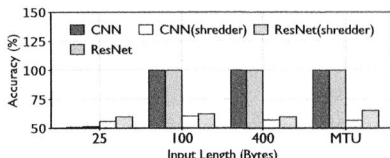
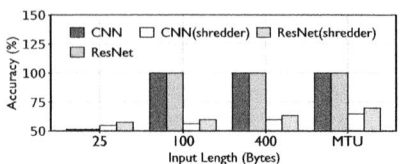

Fig. 3. CNN and ResNet can achieve a high accuracy on original packets, but fail on the traffic protected by FlowShredder, as the features to distinguish the connections are obfuscated.

Fig. 4. If trained over the target traffic, ResNet can improve its accuracy on FlowShredder. However, it is still challenging to reassemble the connection even in this simplistic setting.

Per-Packet Indistinguishability Against TAA. Figure 3 shows the testing accuracy of the raw traffic and FlowShredder in Scenario 1, when the test set is not part of the training set. The share of the background and target traffic is 1:1. Thus, the accuracy of a random guess is 50%. Both CNN and ResNet have a high accuracy (nearly ∼100%), when dealing with the raw traffic, indicating that the traffic analysis with supervised learning is quite effective. The only exception is when the training input length is 25B, as it only covers the first two header fields in Fig. 2, which have no valid information for detection. The accuracy is essentially a random guess, ∼50%. However, for FlowShredder, the accuracy is slightly better than a random guess. This indicates that the knowledge learned from the 25B sample traffic is not quite meaningful for the testing traffic, as the headers of all packets are completely random.

Figure 4 shows the testing accuracy in Scenario 2, when the test set is part of the training set. ResNet, performs much better in this scenario with the highest accuracy of ∼70%. We reckon that this is related to the size of the training set and the diversity of the traffic. As the training set is relatively small and the test set is already a significant part of it, this makes it relatively comfortable to learn and recognise the target traffic. Nevertheless, even with this accuracy in such a simplistic setting, it is difficult to reassemble the whole connection.

4.2 In-Network Capabality

Comparison with P4-AES. P4-AES [3] is an in-network encryption approach that leverages Tofino chips to encrypt the packet payload, and can be used to offload the end hosts for encryption. We compare FlowShredder with P4-AES using Gen testbed, where the generator sends fix-sized UDP packets to the receiver. The P4 switches encrypt or decrypt every packet. For FlowShredder, S_1 obfuscates the headers. For P4-AES, S_1 encrypts the fixed-sized payload. S_2 performs the reverse operations accordingly. Figure 5 measures the throughput of FlowShredder and P4-AES by transferring UDP packets with 16- and 32-byte payload. It can be seen that P4-AES suffers from a significant penalty as the packet size or the input rate increases. For example, it can only achieve 3.3Mpps for 16-byte payload and 1.45Mpps for 32-byte payload, at the input

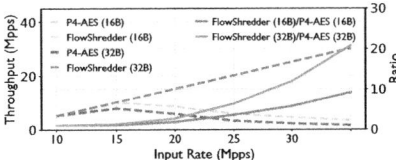
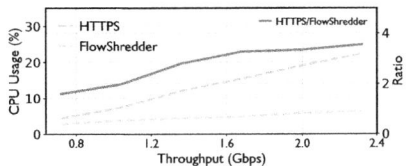

Fig. 5. Comparison with P4-AES on different packet sizes. FlowShredder's performance is irrelevant to packet size.

Fig. 6. Comparsion with HTTPS on CPU usage at server side. HTTPS consumes a lot more CPU cycles.

rate of 30Mpps. The root cause is that P4-AES has to recirculate the packets for many rounds to encrypt the payload, ie, 10 rounds for 16-byte encryption and 20 rounds for 32-byte. Larger packets lead to more recirculation rounds, and higher input rate increases the possibility to drop the packet in the recirculation. In the worst case, the packet is eventually dropped before finishing the recirculation, and the throughput may drop to zero. In contrast, the performance of FlowShredder is irrelevant to the packet size, which always catches up with the input rate. The reason is that FlowShredder only obfuscates the packet header.

Comparison with TLS. HTTPS/TLS may consume a large number of CPU cycles at the end hosts. To reveal the benefit of the in-network approach, we compare FlowShredder with HTTPS/TLS using Local testbed, where the client uses 8 processes to retrieve the 1MB file from the server at various rates. We measure the average CPU usage of the server during the transmission. Figure 6 shows that, compared to FlowShredder when the throughput is 1.6Gbps, HTTPS/TLS consumes more than 3× of CPU cycles, and the factor is still growing as the throughput increases. This is largely because the server is busy encrypting and decrypting the payload with its CPU.

5 Related Work

Anonymity. Anonymity systems, such as LAP [6], Dovetail, HORNET and TARANET, obfuscate the IP addresses to break the association between the connection and the hosts. However, the association between the packets and the connection can still be discovered. In addition, these systems usually require host intervention. Some systems are based on the programmable data plane, e.g., ONTAS, PANEL, and MIMIQ [5]. These efforts suffer the same problem of traditional anonymity approaches.

Encryption with Programmable Data Plane. P4-AES [3] is a P4 version of TLS, which inherits its limit of requiring powerful computation capability. Moreover, the AES encryption in P4 cannot complete within a single pipeline, even for a 16B message. As a result, P4-AES cannot achieve wire-speed encryption. PINOT [9] is a DNS-privacy approach that obfuscates the IP addresses of the DNS requests. However, it does not aim to protect the content. SPINE [4] aims to protect IP addresses but avoid the high overhead of IPSec. It obfuscates the IP address and TCP sequence number for each packet. SPINE does break the association between the flow and the hosts, but relies on TLS for payload encryption. Some studies leverage the programmable data plane to obfuscate the topology [8], or adjust end-to-end encryption schemes [7]. These studies are orthogonal and complementary to FlowShredder.

6 Conclusion

We introduced FlowShredder, a protocol-independent, in-network security service to protect cloud traffic by separating packets from connection context. This achieves per-packet indistinguishability through header obfuscation. FlowShredder uses IPv6 with randomized IP addresses for accurate routing, ideal for latency-sensitive applications like rich media and real-time apps. For stronger protection, it can integrate with end-to-end encryption schemes like 0-RTT TLS to enhance security and reduce latency.

Acknowledgement. This paper is supported by the National Key Research and Development Program of China (2022YFB2901403) and NSFC (62172323).

References

1. Bogdanov, A., Knudsen, L.R., Leander, G., Standaert, F.X., Steinberger, J., Tischhauser, E.: Key-alternating ciphers in a provable setting: encryption using a small number of public permutations. In: International Conference on the Theory and Applications of Cryptographic Techniques (2012)
2. Bromberg, Y.D., Dufour, Q., Frey, D., Rivière, É.: Donar: Anonymous VoIP over tor. In: USENIX NSDI (2022)
3. Chen, X.: Implementing AES encryption on programmable switches via scrambled lookup tables. In: ACM SIGCOMM Workshop on Secure Programmable Network Infrastructure (2020)
4. Datta, T., Feamster, N., Rexford, J., Wang, L.: SPINE: surveillance protection in the network elements. In: USENIX Workshop on Free and Open Communications on the Internet (2019)
5. Govil, Y., Wang, L., Rexford, J.: {MIMIQ}: Masking {IPs} with migration in {QUIC}. In: USENIX Workshop on Free and Open Communications on the Internet (2020)
6. Hsiao, H.C., et al.: LAP: lightweight anonymity and privacy. In: IEEE Symposium on Security and Privacy (2012)
7. Liu, G., Quan, W., Cheng, N., Lu, N., Zhang, H., Shen, X.: P4NIS: improving network immunity against eavesdropping with programmable data planes. In: IEEE INFOCOM Workshops (2020)
8. Meier, R., Tsankov, P., Lenders, V., Vanbever, L., Vechev, M.: {NetHide}: secure and practical network topology obfuscation. In: 27th USENIX Security Symposium (USENIX Security 18), pp. 693–709 (2018)
9. Wang, L., Kim, H., Mittal, P., Rexford, J.: Programmable in-network obfuscation of DNS traffic. In: NDSS Workshop on DNS Privacy (2021)

Processes and Workflows

HiGPP: A History-Informed Graph-Based Process Predictor for Next Activity

Jiaxing Wang[1,2], Chengliang Lu[1], Yifeng Yu[1], Bin Cao[1], Kai Fang[3], and Jing Fan[1(✉)]

[1] College of Computer Science and Technology, Zhejiang University of Technology, Hangzhou, China
[2] School of Information Science and Technology, University of Science and Technology of China, Hefei, China
[3] College of Mathematics and Computer Science, Zhejiang A&F University, Hangzhou, China
{wjx,clianglu,yuyifeng,bincao,fanjing}@zjut.edu.cn,kaifang@ieee.org

Abstract. Next activity prediction in business process monitoring is crucial for optimizing resource allocation and decision-making in service-oriented environments. Existing approaches often fail to integrate control flow with event attributes, resulting in incomplete modeling of process dynamics and inability to capture temporal dependencies between events. We propose **HiGPP** (**H**istory-**i**nformed **G**raph-based **P**rocess **P**redictor), a novel method that constructs unified history-informed graphs from event logs, incorporating both control flow and multi-view event attributes. **HiGPP** innovatively encodes the temporal sequence and contextual data of event attributes using attribute-specific embedding layers and gated recurrent units (GRUs), effectively capturing historical dynamics within node embeddings. By leveraging GraphSAGE to aggregate neighborhood information, **HiGPP** refines embeddings to capture both local and global graph structures. **HiGPP** achieves superior performance in next activity prediction, with an average improvement of more than 2% in all evaluation metrics compared to the best baseline method. Our code is available at https://github.com/HiGPP/HiGPP.

Keywords: Process mining · Predictive business monitoring · Graph convolutional network · Deep learning · Next activity prediction

1 Introduction

Predictive business process monitoring, an advanced analytical approach rooted in process mining [1], has become crucial in today's dynamic service-oriented environments. This field aims to forecast future behaviors in ongoing process instances [2,3], with next activity prediction emerging as a key focus due to its direct impact on resource allocation, task prioritization, and proactive process management [4,5]. The complexity of modern service ecosystems, characterized by distributed processes and intricate service compositions, amplifies the importance and challenges of next activity prediction. For example, in a microservices-based order fulfillment process, predicting the next activity (e.g., fraud check, inventory allocation, or shipping service selection) enables proactive service orchestration and optimized process execution, enhancing overall service efficiency.

Despite significant advancements in deep learning techniques for next activity prediction [5–11], current approaches often overlook critical structural information inherent in process models. This oversight presents a significant challenge in accurately predicting process behaviors, particularly in the context of service composition and orchestration. Recent research has explored the use of process graphs derived from event logs, such as directly-follows graphs (DFGs) [12], Petri nets [13], and instance graphs [14], to enhance predictive capabilities. However, these approaches often separate control flow from event attributes, necessitating additional integration efforts and complicating the management of graph-based models. The separation of control flow and event attributes leads to two issues: (1) It hinders the effective modeling of complex process dynamics, particularly in service-oriented systems where the interplay between different service components is crucial. (2) It fails to adequately capture historical dependencies between events, essential for accurate next activity prediction, especially in long-running or intricate business processes. These limitations reduce prediction accuracy in complex service environments. In cloud-based services, failing to integrate execution sequences with performance data leads to inaccurate predictions and suboptimal service allocation.

To address these limitations, we propose **HiGPP** (**H**istory-**i**nformed **G**raph-based **P**rocess **P**redictor), a novel approach aimed at improving next activity prediction in business processes. The core of **HiGPP** lies in its construction of history-informed graphs that integrate control flow and multi-view event attributes into a unified model, ensuring a comprehensive view of process dynamics. **HiGPP** employs a novel history-informed graph embedding model to capture both the temporal evolution and contextual data of events. This model utilizes independent embedding layers and gated recurrent units (GRUs) for each attribute type to transform historical sequences of event attributes into node embeddings. By doing so, **HiGPP** effectively encodes the temporal dependencies, capturing the dynamic nature of business processes. Furthermore, **HiGPP** utilizes an iterative refinement process with the GraphSAGE network. This process incorporates local neighborhood information and global graph architecture, enabling robust next activity predictions by leveraging comprehensive historical insights and the structural relationships in business processes.

In summary, the main contributions of our work are as follows:

- We design history-informed graphs constructed from the event log, integrating control flow with multi-view attributes and ensuring comprehensive modeling of historical dependencies and intricate relationships between events.
- We propose a novel history-informed graph embedding model that enhances node representations using attribute-specific embedding layers and GRUs, effectively capturing temporal dependencies within business processes.

– Extensive experimental evaluations across diverse real-life datasets demonstrate that **HiGPP** outperforms state-of-the-art methods in next activity prediction tasks.

2 Related Work

Recent advancements in predicting the next activity in business processes have primarily followed two categories: sequence-based and graph-based methods.

Sequence-Based Methods. These approaches focus on the temporal order of activities in business processes, leveraging the inherent sequential nature of event logs. Pasquadibisceglie et al. [5,15] pioneered the use of convolutional neural network (CNN) and multi-view learning with long short-term memory (LSTM) for process prediction. Bukhsh et al. [6] introduced Transformer models to overcome the limitations of recurrent neural networks (RNNs) in learning from long sequences, which Wang et al. [7] further enhanced by integrating multi-view information fusion. Aversano et al. [16] proposed a data-aware explainable method leveraging LSTM and Layer-Wise Relevance Propagation, while Gunnarsson et al. [8] utilized all available attributes from past events for more accurate predictions. Rama-Maneiro et al. [11] introduced a deep reinforcement learning-based system optimizing sampling strategies for suffix prediction. Seidel et al. [10] combined process model analysis with predictive monitoring to recommend the next best action, and Kosciuszek et al. [9] developed an online prediction framework addressing dynamic concept drift with a PrefixTree method and Weibull distribution for retraining parameters.

Graph-Based Methods. Recognizing the importance of structural information, researchers have begun exploring graph-based methods. Peeperkorn et al. [17] investigated the ability of LSTMs to learn process model structures from event logs. They concluded that LSTMs encounter difficulties generalizing to unseen behaviors, particularly when learning complex process structures. Venugopal et al. [12] leveraged deep learning techniques for predicting the next activity and timestamp by transforming event logs into directly-follows graphs (DFGs). Rama-Maneiro et al. [13] integrated process structures using process discovery techniques to create place graphs from Petri nets. Chiorrini et al. [14,18] employed instance graphs combined with deep graph convolutional neural networks for next activity prediction.

Unlike previous methods treating temporal and structural aspects separately, **HiGPP** integrates multi-dimensional process data in a unified framework. Introducing a history-informed graph structure and embedding model, **HiGPP** captures temporal dynamics and structural relationships in business processes. This approach bridges sequence-based and graph-based methods, opening possibilities for modeling complex process dynamics.

3 Preliminaries

This section introduces the basic concepts essential for understanding **HiGPP**.

Event. An event e is defined as a tuple $(c, a, t, \boldsymbol{v})$, where $c \in \mathcal{C}$ is the case identifier from the set of all case IDs $\mathcal{C}$, $a \in \mathcal{A}$ is the activity from the set of all activities $\mathcal{A}$, $t \in \mathbb{T}$ is the timestamp from a totally ordered set of timestamps $\mathbb{T}$, $\boldsymbol{v} = (v_1, ..., v_m) \in \mathbb{R}^m$ is an m-dimensional attribute vector representing various event characteristics.

Trace. A trace $\sigma = \langle e_1, ..., e_i, ..., e_n \rangle$ ($1 \leq i \leq n$) is an ordered sequence of events, where $\forall e_i, e_j \in \sigma : e_i.c = e_j.c$ (all events in a trace have the same case ID), and $\forall i < j : e_i.t \leq e_j.t$ (events are ordered by timestamp).

Prefix Trace. Given a trace $\sigma = \langle e_1, ..., e_n \rangle$, a prefix trace $\sigma^{(k)} = \langle e_1, ..., e_k \rangle$ is the subsequence of the first k events of σ, where $1 \leq k \leq n$.

Event Log. An event log $\mathcal{L}$ is defined as a set of traces $\mathcal{L} = \{\sigma_i | \sigma_i \in \mathcal{S}, 1 \leq i \leq N\}$, where $\mathcal{S}$ is the trace set, and N is the total number of traces.

Next Activity Prediction. Given an event log $\mathcal{L}$, the next activity prediction task is to find a function $\Omega_A : \mathcal{S} \times \mathbb{N} \to \mathcal{A}$ such that: $\Omega_A(\sigma^{(k)}) = a_{k+1}$, where $\sigma^{(k)}$ is a prefix trace of length k, and a_{k+1} is the activity of the $(k+1)$-th event in the trace σ.

Table 1. Event log example from the BPI2012W dataset

Case ID	Activity	Timestamp	$attr_1$	$attr_2$
1	Completeren aanvraag-SCHEDULE:0	2012/01/16 18:31:38	112	1
1	Completeren aanvraag-START:1	2012/01/16 19:49:51	11201	1
1	Nabellen offertes-SCHEDULE:3	2012/01/16 20:01:26	11201	1
1	Completeren aanvraag-COMPLETE:2	2012/01/16 20:01:27	11201	1
1	Nabellen offertes-START:5	2012/01/16 20:01:39	11201	1
1	Nabellen offertes-SCHEDULE:3	2012/01/16 20:02:52	11201	1
1	Nabellen offertes-COMPLETE:4	2012/01/16 20:02:54	11201	1
1	Nabellen offertes-START:5	2012/01/24 19:30:02	11203	2
1	Nabellen offertes-COMPLETE:4	2012/01/24 19:32:10	11203	2
1	Nabellen offertes-START:5	2012/01/25 19:54:13	10909	3

Consider Table 1 as an illustration of a trace of the event log derived from the BPI2012W dataset[1]. In this example, each row represents an event e_i, where the

---
[1] https://www.win.tue.nl/bpi/2012/challenge.html.

"Case ID" column corresponds to c, the "Activity" column to a, the "Timestamp" column to t, and the "attr$_1$" and "attr$_2$" columns collectively form the attribute vector v. All events sharing the case ID "1" constitute a single trace σ.

4 Methodology

This section presents **HiGPP**, which uniquely integrates control flow and multi-view attributes to capture both structural and historical dependencies within event sequences of business processes. As illustrated in Fig. 1, **HiGPP** encompasses four key phases: attribute granular division, history-informed graph construction, history-informed graph embedding, and next activity prediction using GraphSAGE. By seamlessly combining history-informed graph with advanced deep learning techniques, **HiGPP** offers a comprehensive framework for predictive process monitoring in complex service-oriented environments.

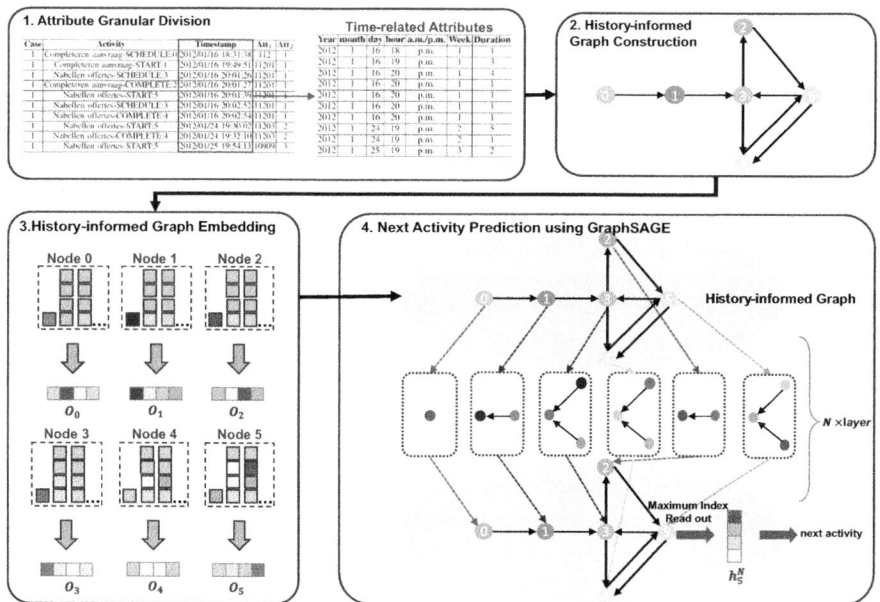

Fig. 1. The architecture of HiGPP

4.1 Phase 1: Attribute Granular Division

This phase divides the multi-view attributes of each event into three fine-grained groups, providing a comprehensive framework for capturing the nuanced characteristics of events across multiple dimensions: (1) *Basic attributes*: This group encompasses the core event information, including case ID, activity, and timestamp. Such fundamental attributes form the essential structure of the event log and are crucial for tracing the process flow. (2) *Domain-specific attributes*: These attributes are unique to the context of a particular log, such as the loan amount in a banking loan log or the order value in a retail process. They provide deep insights into the specific business domain and allow for more nuanced analysis of process variations. (3) *Time-related attributes*: Derived from the timestamp, these include year, month, day, hour, a.m./p.m., day of the week, and duration. These attributes are crucial for capturing temporal patterns, seasonality, and time-based dependencies within the process.

4.2 Phase 2: History-Informed Graph Construction

This phase presents an algorithm for constructing a graph from event log prefixes that captures historical dependencies by integrating control flow and event attributes. It extracts prefix traces of identical activities to construct the history information of nodes, with edges indicating transitions. Events are grouped by activity name based on predefined attribute sets, storing relevant attributes as historical data for each node. The algorithm primarily consists of four steps:

Step 1: Defining and Encoding Nodes. Given a trace $\sigma = \langle e_1, \ldots, e_n \rangle$, we first extract the activity-only trace $\sigma_a = \langle a_1, \ldots, a_n \rangle$ from σ, representing the chronological sequence of activities. To construct the history-informed graph, we define each unique activity as a node and employ a deduplication process that retains only the last occurrence of each activity, resulting in a unique node type sequence $\sigma'_a = [a_{i_1}, a_{i_2}, \ldots, a_{i_m}]$, where $i_1, i_2, \ldots, i_m$ are the indices of these last occurrences. We then encode σ'_a sequentially, starting from 1, while preserving the original activity order. This encoding scheme ensures that higher indices correspond to more recently active nodes, facilitating efficient retrieval of the most recent nodes for subsequent analysis in the history-informed graph.

Step 2: Generating Edges from Activity-only Trace. For each transition from activity a_i to activity a_{i+1} in the activity-only trace $\sigma_a = \langle a_1, \ldots, a_n \rangle$, we create the ordered pair (a_i, a_{i+1}). In a trace of length n, this results in $n - 1$ ordered pairs, collectively forming the edges of the history-informed graph. These edges precisely capture the sequential flow of activities, reflecting how activities progress in sequence within the business process.

Step 3: Establishing Historical Attribute Storage. To capture the temporal evolution of attributes for each activity, we create a historical attribute storage for each node, which records the chronological sequence of attribute values associated with events related to a specific activity. For each node a_{i_k} in the unique node type sequence $\sigma'_a = [a_{i_1}, \ldots, a_{i_k}, \ldots, a_{i_m}]$, we identify its corresponding event sequence E_{i_k}. This sequence includes all events from the original trace σ that are associated with activity a_{i_k}, maintaining their original order. Within E_{i_k}, we process each event e_j to extract its attributes p. The value $e_j.p$ is appended to the historical attribute storage H_p^k, preserving the temporal order:

$$H_p^k = H_p^k \cup \{e_j.p \mid e_j \in E_{i_k}, j = 1, 2, \ldots, |E_{i_k}|\} \qquad (1)$$

where $p = 1, 2, \ldots, N_A$ and N_A denotes the total number of attributes. Each H_p^k is padded to a maximum length $Repetition_{max}$, which reflects the highest occurrence count of any activity in the event log:

$$H_p^k = H_p^k \cup \{0\}^{Repetition_{max} - T}, \quad T = |H_p^k| \qquad (2)$$

where T represents the effective length of the sequence, excluding padding. Ultimately, the historical attribute storage for each node a_{i_k} is represented as a matrix $H_k = \{H_1^k, \ldots, H_p^k, \ldots, H_{N_A}^k\}$, where each $H_p^k \in \mathbb{R}^{Repetition_{max}}$ captures the sequence information of the p-th attribute associated with node a_{i_k}.

Step 4: Integrating Historical Attribute Storage into Graph Nodes. In this final step, we associate each node a_{i_k} in the history-informed graph with its corresponding historical attribute storage matrix H_k, as constructed in Step 3. Consider the event log provided in Table 1. The constructed history-informed graph $\mathcal{G} = (\mathcal{A}, \mathcal{E}, \mathcal{F})$ is illustrated in Fig. 2, where: The set of nodes $\mathcal{A} = 0, 1, 2, 3, 4, 5$ represents different activities, the set of edges $\mathcal{E}$ = {(0,1), (1,3), (3,2), (2,5), (5,3), (3,4), (4,5), (5,4), (4,5)} represents the potential transitions between these activities, the set of feature matrices $\mathcal{F}$

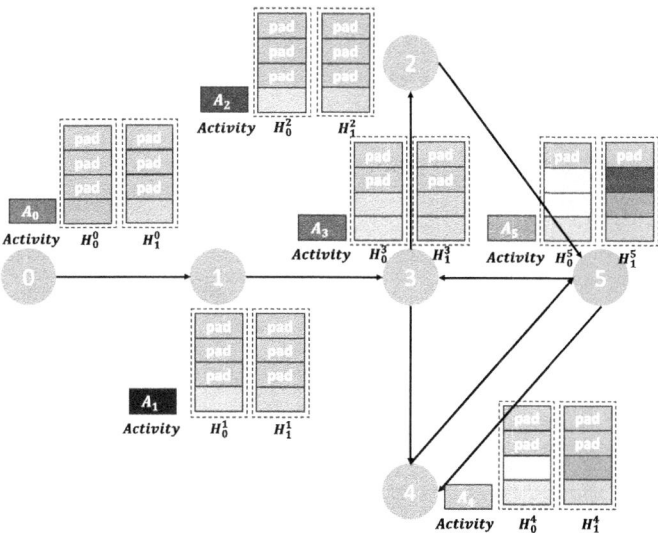

Fig. 2. History-informed graph transformed form the event log in Table 1

= {H_0:[[112,0,0,0], [1,0,0,0]], H_1: [[11201,0,0,0], [1,0,0,0]], H_2:[[11201,0,0,0], [1,0,0,0]], H_3: [[11201,11201,0,0], [1,1,0,0]], H_4: [[11201,11203,0,0], [1,2,0,0]], H_5: [[11201, 11203, 11209, 0], [1,2,3,0]]}. In this example, each H_k is the historical attribute matrix of node a_{i_k}, where each sequence is padded to $Repetition_{max}$ to ensure consistency. Each sequence is padded to length 4 (which is $Repetition_{max}$ in this case) to ensure consistency, with 0 used as the padding value.

4.3 Phase 3: History-Informed Graph Embedding

In our specially designed history-informed graph, each node's historical attribute storage sequentially records the attribute information of multiple historical events associated with it. This information is crucial for capturing the subtle temporal variations in node behavior. Therefore, we propose a historical information graph embedding method that integrates nodes' historical attribute data into the embedding process to enhance their representational capability. As illustrated in Fig. 3, our model consists of three key components: attribute-specific embedding layers, time dynamics captured by GRU, and feature interaction and integration.

Attribute Embedding Layer: For a node S associated with an activity A_S, we perform two types of embeddings: (1) *Attribute Historical Storage Embedding*: The node S has an attribute historical storage matrix $H_S = \{H_1^S, \ldots, H_{N_A}^S\}$, where N_A is the total number of attributes. Each historical sequence H_i^S is mapped to a vector representation by an embedding layer E_i, resulting in $E_i(H_i^S) = \{E_i(H_{i,1}^S), \ldots, E_i(H_{i,M}^S)\}$, with M being the length of the sequence. (2) *Activity Embedding*: Simultaneously, the activity itself A_S is embedded using a separate layer E_{act}, yielding the representation $E_{\text{act}}(A_S)$.

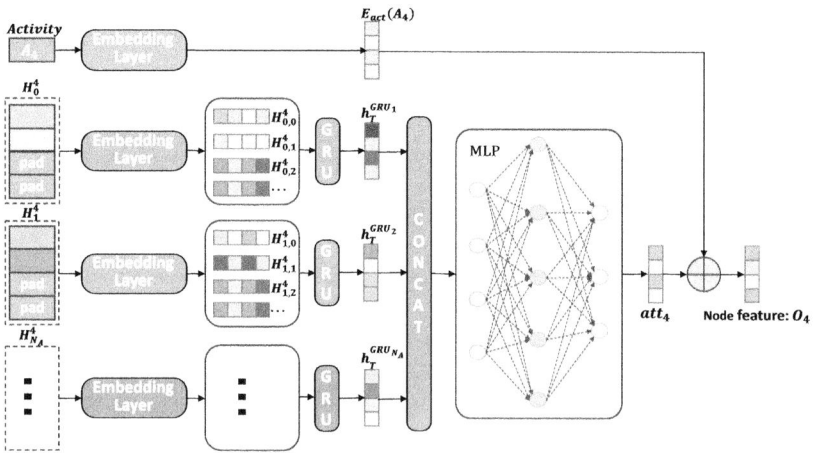

Fig. 3. The history-informed graph embedding component

Time Dynamics Captured by GRU: To capture the temporal dynamics of attribute values, we process each attribute's historical attribute storage independently using a GRU. For the i-th attribute, the hidden state $\boldsymbol{h}_t^{\mathrm{GRU}_i}$ of its corresponding GRU at time step t is computed as:

$$\boldsymbol{h}_t^{\mathrm{GRU}_i} = \mathrm{GRU}_i(E_i(H_{i,t}^S), \boldsymbol{h}_{t-1}^{\mathrm{GRU}_i}) \tag{3}$$

where $E_i(H_{i,t}^S)$ is the embedding at time t, and $\boldsymbol{h}_{t-1}^{\mathrm{GRU}_i}$ is the previous hidden state. To mitigate the impact of padding on sequence processing, we introduce T as the actual number of non-padded elements in the sequence. This T, which we call the effective length, is used as the maximum temporal step size for GRU processing. By doing so, we ensure that the GRU only processes meaningful data and not the padding values. After processing, we extract the final hidden state of each GRU and concatenate these states to form a multi-attribute vector $\boldsymbol{h}_S = [\boldsymbol{h}_T^{\mathrm{GRU}_1}; \boldsymbol{h}_T^{\mathrm{GRU}_2}; \ldots; \boldsymbol{h}_T^{\mathrm{GRU}_{N_A}}]$.

Feature Interaction and Integration. The concatenated multi-attribute vector $\boldsymbol{h}_S$ undergoes feature interaction through a multilayer perceptron (MLP), yielding an interacted information feature $\boldsymbol{attr}_S$. To synthesize complementary representations, we integrate the embedding feature $E_{act}(A_S)$ of the activity A_S corresponding to node S with the information feature $\boldsymbol{attr}_S$:

$$\boldsymbol{O}_S = \boldsymbol{W}\left(sum\left(E_{act}(A_S) + \boldsymbol{attr}_S\right)\right) + b, \quad \boldsymbol{attr}_S = MLP(\boldsymbol{h}_S) \tag{4}$$

where $\boldsymbol{W}$ and b are parameters of a linear layer, and sum denotes the element-wise sum operation. This embedding process captures both state (through activity embedding) and temporal (through attribute history) aspects of the process, resulting in rich node representations $\boldsymbol{O}_S$ that encapsulate historical information and time dynamics.

4.4 Phase 4: Next Activity Prediction Using GraphSAGE

We employ the GraphSAGE architecture [19] to predict the next activity based on node embeddings integrated with neighborhood information. This process involves the following steps:

Step 1: Neighborhood Sampling. For each node v, we uniformly sample a fixed-size subset S_v from its neighborhood $N(v)$. This ensures the incorporation of relevant contextual information from surrounding nodes.

Step 2: Feature Aggregation. We use an aggregation function $AGGREGATE_k$ at each layer k to consolidate features from the sampled neighbors S_v^k. The depth k represents the extent of graph traversal.

Step 3: Node Representation Update. We update each node's representation by combining its current features with the aggregated neighbor features:

$$\boldsymbol{h}_v^{(k+1)} = \sigma(\boldsymbol{W} \cdot sum(AGGREGATE_k(\{\boldsymbol{h}_u^{(k)}, \forall u \in S_v^k\}), \boldsymbol{h}_v^{(k)})) \tag{5}$$

where $\boldsymbol{h}_v^{(k)}$ is the representation of node v at the k-th layer, σ is a non-linear activation function, $\boldsymbol{W}$ is a trainable weight matrix, and sum denotes the vector summation operation.

Step 4: Aggregation Methods. We explore four $AGGREGATE$ functions: GCN, Mean, LSTM, and Pooling. These methods, although differing in implementation details, yield comparable results in final predictions.

Step 5: Graph Representation and Prediction. Our node encoding scheme ensures that the node with the maximum index corresponds to the most recently active node. To prevent information dilution and enhance predictive performance, we select the features of the node with the maximum index as the graph features to predict the next activity. Finally, we employ a linear layer for prediction and optimize the model using cross-entropy loss.

5 Experimental Result

This section presents the evaluation of **HiGPP**'s effectiveness through a series of rigorous experiments. We begin by introducing the benchmark event logs employed in this study, followed by a detailed description of the experimental setup and evaluation metrics. The experimental analysis is structured around four key investigations: performance comparison analysis, attribute impact analysis, sequential modeling technique analysis, and graph feature readout analysis.

5.1 Benchmark Event Logs

For our experimental evaluation, we leverage three representative benchmark event log datasets from the prestigious 4TU Centre for Research Data[2]. These datasets encompass a diverse spectrum of business process service scenarios, providing a comprehensive foundation for our analysis: (1)*BPI Challenge 2012*[3], from the financial domain focuses on loan application processes. We utilize three variants: i) *BPI2012Complete*, a subset containing all loan event instances that are in the "complete" status. ii) *BPI2012W*, a subset containing all loan event instances associated with the work item. iii) *BPI2012WComplete*, a subset that

---

[2] https://data.4tu.nl/.
[3] https://data.4tu.nl/articles/_/12689204/1.

includes all loan event instances associated with work items that are in the "complete" status. (2) *BPI Challenge 2013*[4], comprising IT service management processes from a large company. We utilize two subsets: i) *BPI2013Incidents*, focusing on incident management processes. ii) *BPI2013Problem*, concentrating on problem management processes. (3) *BPI Challenge 2020 Request for Payment*[5], representing payment request processes in a large multinational company.

5.2 Experimental Setup and Evaluation Metrics

We used 3-fold cross-validation to evaluate **HiGPP** and baseline methods. Traces were divided into three subsets: two for training and one for testing, repeated three times for comprehensive testing. Hyperparameters were a batch size of 64, embedding dimension and GRU hidden state size of 128, and two graph convolutional layers. The learning rate started at 0.001 and was adjusted based on validation accuracy. Training stopped early if no improvement was seen within ten epochs, capped at 100 epochs. These settings were effective across different data scales, as shown by experiments. We evaluated predictive efficacy using accuracy, Macro-precision, Macro-recall, Macro-Fscore, Macro-AUCROC, and Macro-AUCPR [5]. Macro metrics provided an equitable assessment across all classes. Metrics are reported as the average of three-fold cross-validation for a comprehensive view of performance and stability.

5.3 Results

Performance Comparison Analysis. We conducted a comprehensive performance evaluation of **HiGPP** against seven state-of-the-art baseline methods, encompassing both sequence-based and graph-based approaches. The sequence-based methods include MiDA [5], ProcessTransformer [6], MiTFM [7], and PREMIERE [15], while the graph-based methods comprise GCN-ProcessPrediction [12], BIGDGCNN [18], and Multi-BIGDGCNN [14]. These methods were selected based on their relevance to next activity prediction in business processes and the availability of their source code, ensuring reproducibility and fair comparison. All algorithms were tested under identical conditions across six diverse datasets, with baseline parameters set to their reported optimal values from respective code repositories.

Table 2 demonstrates that **HiGPP** outperforms all baseline methods across all metrics and datasets. **HiGPP** achieves improvements of approximately 2–3% across various performance metrics (accuracy, precision, recall, Fscore, AUC, and AUCPR) for all datasets. The performance advantage of **HiGPP** becomes more pronounced in complex datasets. For instance, in the BPI2013Problem dataset, **HiGPP** demonstrates an improvement of around 4% in accuracy and

---

[4] https://data.4tu.nl/articles/_/12693914/1
https://data.4tu.nl/articles/_/12688556/1
https://data.4tu.nl/articles/_/12714476/1.
[5] https://data.4tu.nl/articles/_/12706886/1.

Table 2. Performance comparison analysis: HiGPP vs. Baseline Methods

Eventlog		Approach	Accuracy	Precision	Recall	Fscore	AUC	AUCPR
BPI2012Complete	Sequence-based	MiDA	0.795	0.780	0.629	0.646	0.810	0.526
		MiTFM	0.799	0.776	0.635	0.658	0.812	0.531
		ProcessTransformer	0.767	0.724	0.591	0.604	0.790	0.481
		PREMIERE	0.789	0.761	0.625	0.640	0.807	0.516
	Graph-based	GCN-ProcessPrediction	0.655	0.287	0.260	0.234	0.621	0.187
		BIGDGCNN	0.659	0.478	0.474	0.448	0.729	0.353
		Multi-BIGDGCNN	0.714	0.545	0.502	0.497	0.744	0.376
		HiGPP	**0.801**	**0.798**	**0.642**	**0.666**	**0.816**	**0.535**
BPI2012W	Sequence-based	MiDA	0.909	0.755	0.693	0.693	0.844	0.623
		MiTFM	0.910	0.725	0.694	0.684	0.844	0.625
		ProcessTransformer	0.888	0.591	0.643	0.607	0.818	0.573
		PREMIERE	0.904	0.746	0.684	0.680	0.838	0.611
	Graph-based	GCN-ProcessPrediction	0.641	0.423	0.413	0.395	0.697	0.293
		BIGDGCNN	0.713	0.462	0.427	0.411	0.706	0.317
		Multi-BIGDGCNN	0.750	0.561	0.470	0.483	0.728	0.372
		HiGPP	**0.914**	**0.804**	**0.708**	**0.709**	**0.851**	**0.642**
BPI2012WComplete	Sequence-based	MiDA	0.842	0.790	0.684	0.699	0.824	0.586
		MiTFM	0.843	0.792	0.664	0.694	0.814	0.577
		ProcessTransformer	0.785	0.652	0.619	0.608	0.784	0.508
		PREMIERE	0.822	0.782	0.653	0.679	0.812	0.570
	Graph-based	GCN-ProcessPrediction	0.671	0.499	0.504	0.468	0.721	0.375
		BIGDGCNN	0.649	0.455	0.396	0.382	0.664	0.305
		Multi-BIGDGCNN	0.714	0.550	0.473	0.469	0.710	0.367
		HiGPP	**0.854**	**0.805**	**0.719**	**0.732**	**0.843**	**0.620**
BPI2013Incidents	Sequence-based	MiDA	0.724	0.455	0.423	0.435	0.698	0.297
		MiTFM	0.741	0.475	0.422	0.428	0.698	0.309
		ProcessTransformer	0.647	0.267	0.261	0.248	0.613	0.209
		PREMIERE	0.661	0.421	0.332	0.334	0.648	0.238
	Graph-based	GCN-ProcessPrediction	0.578	0.234	0.233	0.209	0.594	0.196
		BIGDGCNN	0.677	0.314	0.305	0.289	0.637	0.255
		Multi-BIGDGCNN	0.692	0.297	0.326	0.309	0.648	0.264
		HiGPP	**0.760**	**0.479**	**0.440**	**0.441**	**0.708**	**0.328**
BPI2013Problem	Sequence-based	MiDA	0.621	0.411	0.402	0.405	0.665	0.296
		MiTFM	0.627	0.424	0.403	0.409	0.667	0.300
		ProcessTransformer	0.519	0.266	0.263	0.221	0.584	0.212
		PREMIERE	0.595	0.404	0.374	0.381	0.648	0.278
	Graph-based	GCN-ProcessPrediction	0.527	0.237	0.281	0.237	0.602	0.221
		BIGDGCNN	0.596	0.322	0.340	0.317	0.638	0.271
		Multi-BIGDGCNN	0.607	0.351	0.351	0.333	0.644	0.275
		HiGPP	**0.667**	**0.452**	**0.440**	**0.442**	**0.689**	**0.331**
BPI2020Request	Sequence-based	MiDA	0.882	0.586	0.472	0.491	0.738	0.434
		MiTFM	0.885	0.559	0.481	0.489	0.736	0.441
		ProcessTransformer	0.855	0.390	0.417	0.402	0.703	0.390
		PREMIERE	0.856	0.500	0.420	0.411	0.704	0.393
	Graph-based	GCN-ProcessPrediction	0.852	0.377	0.385	0.375	0.688	0.339
		BIGDGCNN	0.839	0.324	0.319	0.330	0.654	0.284
		Multi-BIGDGCNN	0.850	0.331	0.361	0.367	0.678	0.314
		HiGPP	**0.908**	**0.611**	**0.539**	**0.553**	**0.766**	**0.489**

about 3.3% in Fscore over MiTFM. These improvements, while modest, are consistent and potentially significant in practical applications. The performance gap widens when comparing **HiGPP** with the best graph-based method, Multi-BIGDGCNN. **HiGPP** demonstrates more substantial gains: roughly 10% in accuracy, 22% in precision, 17% in recall, 18% in Fscore, 9% in AUC, and 16% in AUCPR. However, it is crucial to note that such notable percentage improvements might partly reflect the lower baseline performance of Multi-BIGDGCNN, rather than solely indicating the superiority of **HiGPP**.

The observed performance can be attributed to **HiGPP**'s innovative approach in integrating historical data and creating comprehensive node representations within the history-informed graph. By aggregating events with the same activity, the event log transforms into historical sequence information embedded in node features. This method enhances understanding of process dynamics, enabling robust analysis of interaction patterns and improving predictive accuracy.

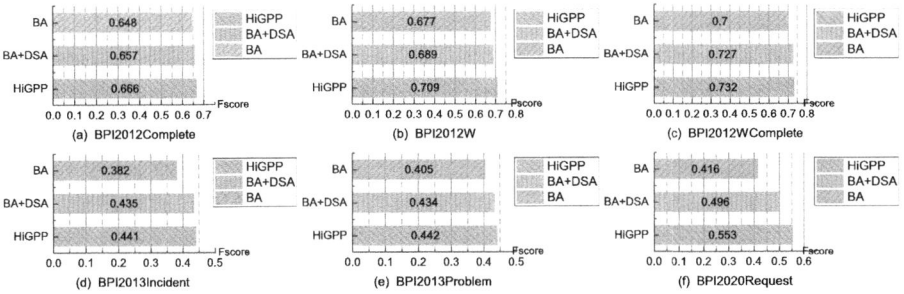

Fig. 4. Attribute-based prediction analysis

Attribute Impact Analysis. This study evaluates **HiGPP**'s predictive accuracy using three attribute combinations: basic attributes (BA), BA with domain-specific attributes (BA+DSA), and the full set including time-related attributes (BA+DSA+TA, i.e., **HiGPP**). Figure 4 illustrates the performance across six datasets, revealing a consistent improvement pattern as more attributes are incorporated. On average, BA+DSA improves Fscores by approximately 3.5% over BA alone, while **HiGPP** further enhances performance by approximately 1.8% over BA+DSA (approximately 5.3% over BA). This incremental improvement underscores the significance of domain-specific context and temporal information in refining predictive accuracy. Notably, the integration of DSA enriches the model's understanding of unique business characteristics, evident in complex datasets like BPI2013Problem (Fscore: 0.405 to 0.434). The addition of TA enables **HiGPP** to discern intricate temporal patterns, particularly beneficial in datasets such as BPI2020Request (Fscore: 0.496 to 0.553). These results demonstrate **HiGPP**'s ability to construct context-rich representations of business processes, leading to enhanced predictive accuracy across diverse scenarios.

Table 3. Sequential modeling technique analysis

Dataset	Metrics	Approach			
		HiGPP	LSTM	Average Pooling	Max Pooling
BPI2012Complete	Accuracy	0.801±0.001	0.801±0.003	0.793±0.004	0.796±0.002
	Fscore	0.666±0.005	0.661±0.004	0.653±0.009	0.655±0.003
BPI2012W	Accuracy	0.914±0.001	0.914±0.001	0.911±0.001	0.911±0.001
	Fscore	0.709±0.021	0.701±0.012	0.703±0.026	0.700±0.006
BPI2012WComplete	Accuracy	0.854±0.005	0.853±0.005	0.832±0.009	0.836±0.004
	Fscore	0.732±0.014	0.724±0.011	0.700±0.016	0.728±0.005
BPI2013Incident	Accuracy	0.760±0.002	0.758±0.005	0.732±0.004	0.737±0.002
	Fscore	0.441±0.014	0.418±0.012	0.396±0.018	0.407±0.028
BPI2013Problem	Accuracy	0.667±0.010	0.655±0.013	0.653±0.008	0.663±0.011
	Fscore	0.442±0.010	0.433±0.012	0.429±0.008	0.439±0.007
BPI2020Request	Accuracy	0.908±0.004	0.910±0.002	0.911±0.001	0.909±0.001
	Fscore	0.553±0.010	0.553±0.009	0.552±0.017	0.550±0.016

Sequential Modeling Technique Analysis. This experiment compares four sequential modeling techniques for learning historical attribute sequences within **HiGPP**: GRU, LSTM, average pooling, and max pooling. Table 3 shows that **HiGPP** with GRU outperforms other three sequential modeling techniques in accuracy and Fscore across most datasets. GRU's streamlined architecture, efficiently integrating hidden states and memory cells, proves particularly effective in capturing complex sequence dependencies, especially in datasets with strong temporal correlations. However, the performance gap narrows in datasets like BPI2020Request, where all sequential modeling techniques show similar results. This suggests that for processes with shorter execution cycles or trace lengths, the advantages of sophisticated recurrent architectures may be less pronounced, and simpler pooling techniques can adequately capture essential sequence patterns. These findings underscore the importance of selecting appropriate sequential modeling techniques based on the specific characteristics of the business process being analyzed, balancing model complexity with dataset requirements.

Graph Feature Readout Analysis. We evaluated three GraphSAGE readout strategies for next activity prediction: maximum index, max pooling, and average pooling. Figure 5 demonstrates that maximum index consistently outperforms the other strategies across all datasets. This strategy directly selects the features of the most recently active node as the graph readout features for predicting the next activity, obtaining relevant information without dilution. Max pooling shows a slight advantage over average pooling, as it preserves strong predictive signals. Average pooling, while least effective, smooths features and potentially reduces the impact of critical data points. These findings suggest that in process execution contexts, strongly activated features in graph representations are highly informative for next activity prediction, offering valuable insights for improving process monitoring in service-oriented architectures.

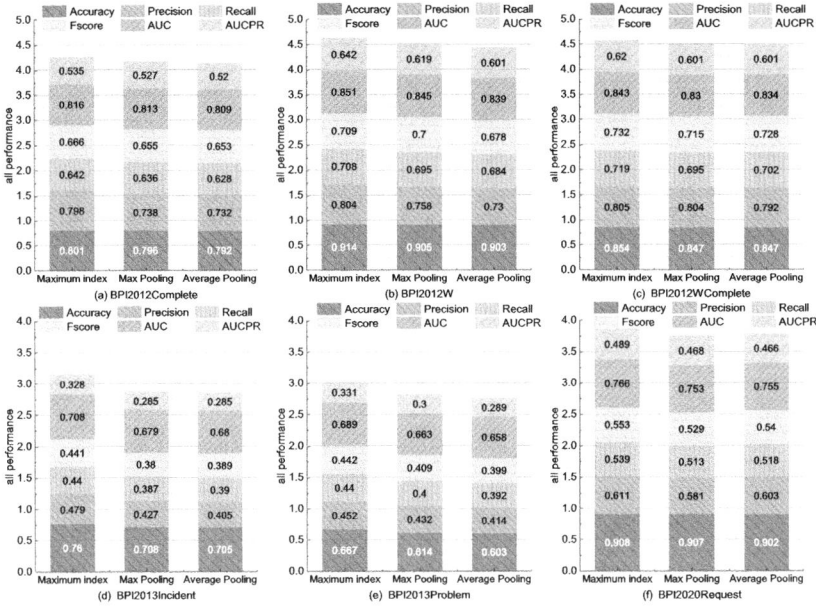

Fig. 5. Graph feature readout analysis

6 Conclusion

This paper introduces **HiGPP**, a novel approach for next activity prediction in business processes. **HiGPP**'s key innovations lie in constructing history-informed graphs that integrate structural process information with historical dependencies, and employing a specialized graph embedding model using attribute-specific layers and GRUs. This comprehensive approach captures both temporal and structural relationships in processes. Leveraging GraphSAGE for embedding refinement, **HiGPP** demonstrates superior predictive performance on real-life datasets, showcasing its potential for process monitoring and optimization in service-oriented architectures. Future work will focus on extending **HiGPP** to handle real-time streaming data and exploring model interpretability, further enhancing its applicability in dynamic service environments.

Acknowledgment. This work was partially supported by the National Natural Science Foundation of China (Grants Nos. 62102366, 62276233), the Natural Science Foundation of Zhejiang Province (Grant No. LQ22F020010), and Key Research Project of Zhejiang Province (Grant No. 2022C01145).

References

1. Van Der Aalst, W.: Process mining: overview and opportunities. ACM Trans. Manag. Inform. Syst. (TMIS) **3**(2), 1–17 (2012)
2. Cao, J., Wang, C., Guan, W., Qian, S., Zhao, H.: Remaining time prediction for collaborative business processes with privacy preservation. In: International Conference on Service-Oriented Computing, pp. 38–53 (2023)
3. Gherissi, W., El Haddad, J., Grigori, D.: Object-centric predictive process monitoring. In: International Conference on Service-Oriented Computing, pp. 27–39 (2022)
4. Rama-Maneiro, E., Vidal, J.C., Lama, M.: Deep learning for predictive business process monitoring: Review and benchmark. IEEE Trans. Serv. Comput. **16**(1), 739–756 (2021)
5. Pasquadibisceglie, V., Appice, A., Castellano, G., Malerba, D.: A multi-view deep learning approach for predictive business process monitoring. IEEE Trans. Serv. Comput. **15**(4), 2382–2395 (2022)
6. Bukhsh, Z.A., Saeed, A., Dijkman, R.M.: Process transformer: Predictive business process monitoring with transformer network. arXiv preprint arXiv:2104.00721 (2021)
7. Wang, J., Lu, C., Cao, B., Fan, J.: MiTFM: a multi-view information fusion method based on transformer for next activity prediction of business processes. In: Proceedings of the 14th Asia-Pacific Symposium on Internetware, pp. 281–291 (2023)
8. Gunnarsson, B.R., vanden Broucke, S., De Weerdt, J.: A direct data aware LSTM neural network architecture for complete remaining trace and runtime prediction. IEEE Trans. Serv. Comput. **16**(4), 2330–2342 (2023)
9. Kosciuszek, T., Hassani, M.: Online next activity prediction under concept drifts. In: International Conference on Advanced Information Systems Engineering, pp. 335–346 (2024)
10. Seidel, A., Haarmann, S., Weske, M.: Model-based recommendations for next-best actions in knowledge-intensive processes. In: International Conference on Advanced Information Systems Engineering, pp. 195–211 (2024)
11. Rama-Maneiro, E., Patrizi, F., Vidal, J., Lama, M.: Towards learning the optimal sampling strategy for suffix prediction in predictive monitoring. In: International Conference on Advanced Information Systems Engineering, pp. 215–230 (2024)
12. Venugopal, I., Töllich, J., Fairbank, M., Scherp, A.: A comparison of deep-learning methods for analysing and predicting business processes. In: International Joint Conference on Neural Networks (IJCNN), pp. 1–8 (2021)
13. Rama-Maneiro, E., Vidal, J.C., Lama, M.: Embedding graph convolutional networks in recurrent neural networks for predictive monitoring. IEEE Trans. Knowl. Data Eng. **36**(1), 137–151 (2023)
14. Chiorrini, A., Diamantini, C., Genga, L., Potena, D.: Multi-perspective enriched instance graphs for next activity prediction through graph neural network. J. Intell. Inf. Syst. **61**(1), 5–25 (2023)
15. Pasquadibisceglie, V., Appice, A., Castellano, G., Malerba, D.: Predictive process mining meets computer vision. In: Business Process Management Forum: BPM Forum 2020, Seville, Spain, September 13–18, 2020, Proceedings 18, pp. 176–192 (2020)
16. Aversano, L., Bernardi, M.L., Cimitile, M., Iammarino, M., Verdone, C.: A data-aware explainable deep learning approach for next activity prediction. Eng. Appl. Artif. Intell. **126**, 106758 (2023)

17. Peeperkorn, J., vanden Broucke, S., De Weerdt, J.: Can recurrent neural networks learn process model structure? J. Intell. Inf. Syst. **61**(1), 27–51 (2023)
18. Chiorrini, A., Diamantini, C., Mircoli, A., Potena, D.: Exploiting instance graphs and graph neural networks for next activity prediction. In: International Conference on Process Mining, pp. 115–126 (2021)
19. Hamilton, W., Ying, Z., Leskovec, J.: Inductive representation learning on large graphs. In: Advances in Neural Information Processing Systems, vol. 30 (2017)

From Visual Choreographies to Flexible Information Protocols

Tom Lichtenstein[1](✉), Amit K. Chopra[2], Munindar P. Singh[3], and Mathias Weske[1]

[1] Hasso Plattner Institute, University of Potsdam, Potsdam, Germany
{tom.lichtenstein,mathias.weske}@hpi.de
[2] Lancaster University, Lancaster, UK
amit.chopra@lancaster.ac.uk
[3] North Carolina State University, Raleigh, NC, USA
mpsingh@ncsu.edu

Abstract. Choreographies enable the coordination of interactions between business partners. Established modeling languages such as BPMN focus on a visual notation that may facilitate design but lacks formal semantics. Moreover, such notations encourage the explicit ordering of interactions, which often results in over-constrained models. In contrast, information protocols provide a precise and flexible operational model for interaction. This paper contributes a tool-supported, semi-automated mapping from object-aware BPMN choreography diagrams to information protocols. Our approach enables business experts to tailor the flexibility of the resulting protocols to their requirements.

Keywords: Business processes · Interaction protocols · Multiagent systems · Messaging · Information flow

1 Introduction

This paper focuses on modeling interactions between the business processes of collaborating organizations. Current business process modeling languages such as BPMN choreography diagrams [19] capture coordination requirements in terms of ordering constraints on message exchanges. The visual nature and wide adoption are significant strengths of these languages [8]. However, these languages often rely on explicit interaction sequencing, which can lead to complex models or overly constrained behavior [17]. The latter may interfere with the underlying business requirements, especially in light of changes in internal needs or the external environment [21]. Nonetheless, distinguishing between intended and arbitrary constraints is nontrivial, complicating the creation of flexible yet precisely constrained models. In addition, despite progress on object-aware choreographies [14], current models remain non-operational due to a lack of essential details about the information transferred in each interaction. Thus, providing operational semantics could facilitate the implementation of interaction behaviors by providing a clear interface to the processes involved.

Contributions. Consequently, this paper addresses the following research question: *How can we derive flexible and operational models from object-aware choreographies?* To this end, we adopt the idea of *information protocols* specified in the *Blindingly Simple Protocol Language* (BSPL) [22,23]. Information protocols are declarative, have a formal semantics, can be enacted by decentralized agents representing the parties, and can support highly flexible interactions—setting them apart from other protocol languages [4]. Unlike traditional business process models, which explicitly specify the ordering of tasks and messages, typically via control-flow abstractions, information protocols specify causal dependencies and integrity constraints declaratively based on information, thus avoiding unnecessary control-flow constraints while preserving necessary data constraints.

Our main contribution is an approach for generating information protocols from object-aware choreographies that preserves business meaning. Figure 1 provides our key intuitions: given a choreography (a), we generate a protocol (b) while ignoring control-flow constraints, allowing for a more flexible ordering of the choreography's interactions. Since not all the resulting flexibility may be desired by the business partners, our method supports business experts in fine-tuning the protocol by applying a modified or reduced set of relevant control-flow constraints discovered from the choreography. Thus, the refined protocol (c) can be tailored to the needs of the collaborating organizations.

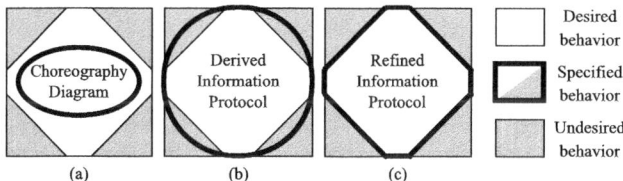

Fig. 1. The interaction behavior allowed by (a) a choreography, (b) a derived information protocol, and (c) a refined protocol, adapted from [17].

The paper is organized as follows: Sect. 2 introduces object-aware process choreographies and interaction protocols. Section 3 maps choreographies to BSPL. Section 4 identifies and integrates control-flow constraints. Section 5 evaluates our approach using two scenarios, and Sect. 6 reviews related work in the area. Finally, Sect. 7 concludes the paper and outlines directions for future research.

2 Preliminaries

We now introduce the core background for this paper.

2.1 Object-Aware Process Choreographies

Process choreographies define the ordering of message exchanges between collaborating *participants*. We focus on BPMN choreography diagrams, in the following referred to as *choreography*, as an interaction-oriented abstraction of BPMN collaboration diagrams [19]. A choreography comprises *choreography tasks*, each specifying a message sent by one participant to another (optionally with a response), as Fig. 2 shows. This choreography begins with the buyer placing an order. Next, the shop sends an invoice. The buyer either cancels the order (ending the choreography) or pays. When the invoice is paid, the shop forwards the order to the warehouse. Once packed and approved, the warehouse ships the parcel, and the buyer's confirmation of receipt completes the choreography. Sequence flow defines order constraints between tasks, while gateways indicate exclusive and parallel behavior.

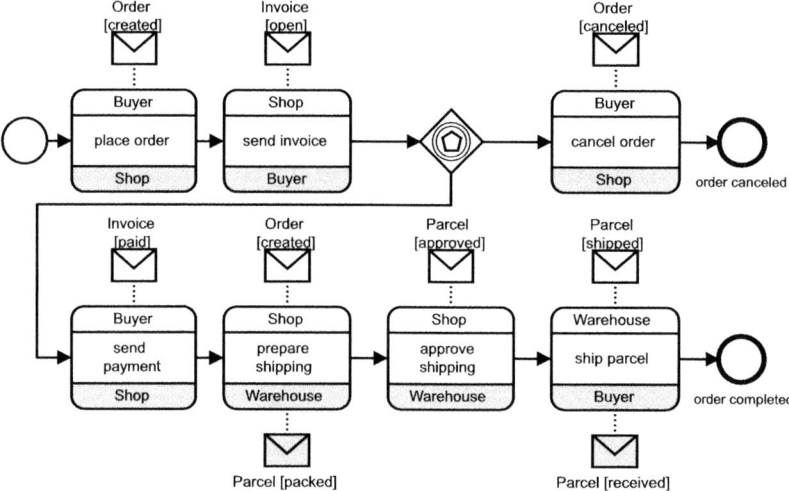

Fig. 2. A BPMN choreography diagram for an order management choreography between a buyer, a shop, and a warehouse. Participants in white bands initiate the respective task. Gray envelopes indicate response messages. (Color figure online)

Lichtenstein et al. [14] extend choreographies by incorporating a *shared data model* and *shared object lifecycles*. Each class in the shared data model specifies a type of message that is used to annotate the message elements in a choreography. Figure 3 shows a shared data model for the choreography in Fig. 2. The inclusion of attributes is discussed in Sect. 3.1. Relations between classes may impose ordering constraints on the creation of objects [14]. For example, according to Fig. 3, creating an *Invoice* or *Parcel* requires an existing *Order*.

Objects' states are modified during execution. A shared object lifecycle defines the allowed states and state transitions for each class, as exemplified in

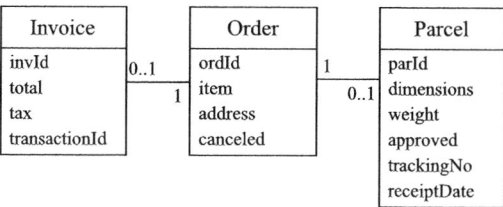

Fig. 3. A shared data model, as a UML class diagram, illustrating the structure of the data being exchanged for the order management choreography, including attributes.

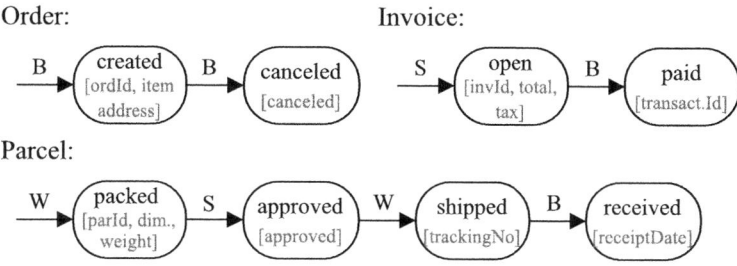

Fig. 4. Shared lifecycles for data objects of the classes *Order*, *Parcel*, and *Invoice* extended with attribute references. Participant names are abbreviated to initials.

Fig. 4. State transitions without a source state indicate the creation of objects. In addition, arc inscriptions specify the participant that can perform the transition. For example, only a *Buyer* (B) can create an order and only a *Warehouse* (W) can change a parcel's state to *shipped*. States are changed locally and synchronized with participants via messages. In a choreography, message annotations in square brackets indicate the state in which an object must be sent [14]. Section 3.1 discusses the associations between states and attributes shown in Fig. 4.

2.2 Information Protocols

Information protocols capture the ordering and occurrence of messages between autonomous parties while neglecting their internal reasoning [7]. The Blindingly Simple Protocol Language (BSPL) is an operational, declarative language to capture possible interactions based on the information available to the agents [22]. Listing 1 shows an example BSPL *protocol*. Each protocol consists of a name (Line 1), a set of roles (Line 2), a public (Line 3) and private (Line 4) set of parameters representing the units of information exchanged, and message schemas (Lines 6–9) or references to other protocols (Line 10) allowing composition. At runtime, each business partner would adopt a role. Message schemas define a sender, a receiver, and the parameters exchanged. In a protocol enactment, a parameter is either bound to a value (available for reading but not for writing) or unbound. An enactment is identified by a binding of the public *key* parameters.

For each interaction, *in*, *out*, and *nil* adornments specify requirements on the availability of the parameters. Parameters adorned with *in* must be bound to enable the interaction, e.g., in Listing 1, *ship* can be sent only if the *orderId* is bound. An *out* adornment binds an initially unbound parameter once the message is sent, e.g., sending an *order* message binds the parameters *orderId*, *item*, and *address* to their respective values. Finally, *nil* requires the parameter to be unbound for execution. Hence, *outcome* must not be bound to send *req_cancel*.

```
 1  OrderManagement {
 2    roles B, S
 3    parameters out orderId key, out item, out outcome
 4    private address, price, receipt, rescind
 5
 6    B→S: order       [out orderId, out item, out address]
 7    S→B: ship        [in orderId, in item, in address, in receipt, nil rescind,
          out outcome]
 8    B→S: req_cancel  [in orderId, nil outcome, out rescind]
 9    S→B: ack_cancel  [in orderId, in rescind, out outcome]
10    Payment(S, B, in orderId, in item, nil outcome, out price, out receipt)
11  }
```

Listing 1. Order management protocol adapted from [22].

Notably, *OrderManagement* supports concurrent sending of *cancel* and *ship* messages by different agents, with the shipping preventing *ack_cancel* by binding *outcome*. Traditional protocol languages based on communicating state machines do not allow for such concurrency [4]. Nonetheless, a protocol should never allow a parameter to be bound by multiple agents concurrently to ensure *safety*, which is crucial for operability and can be statically verified [25]. Therefore, prioritizing shipping in Listing 1 is essential to support concurrency without violating safety.

3 From Choreographies to Protocols

We now describe a semi-automatic approach to mapping object-aware choreographies to BSPL, using the example from Sect. 2.1. The supplementary models are first enriched with attributes and then mapped to a BSPL protocol.

3.1 Extending Object-Aware Choreographies with Attributes

Object-aware choreographies provide a high-level view of data using objects and states, whereas protocols rely on low-level parameters to specify the information to be exchanged. To bridge the gap between these levels of abstraction, we enrich shared data models and lifecycles with attributes. Each attribute represents a unit of information associated with an object that is exchanged via messages. Therefore, for the mapping, we interpret attributes as parameters. As depicted in Fig. 3, each class is associated with a set of attributes. Inspired by the work of Pérez-Álvarez et al. [20], we interpret the state of an object as a binding of attributes. The mapping of binding to state is defined in the corresponding object lifecycle (cf. Figure 4). Binding the respective attributes to a value changes the object's state accordingly. For example, an invoice in state *open* has only *invId*, *total*, and *tax* bound. Transitioning to *paid* requires binding *transactionId* as well. To avoid ambiguity, each state must be associated with a unique binding.

3.2 Mapping Object-Aware Choreographies to Protocols

A protocol defines the legal interactions in a choreography. Hence, our mapping uses the choreography tasks and the enriched shared data model and shared object lifecycles as input. Since BSPL supports composition [22], we create a *class protocol* for each class of the data model and compose them into the resulting protocol. A class protocol defines roles, parameters, and message schemas related to one class. Listing 2 illustrates the class protocol generated for the class *Order*. The mapping rules for class protocols and their composition are detailed below.

```
1 Order {
2   roles B, S, W
3   parameters out ordId key, out item, out address, out canceled
4   private fw_created
5
6   B→S: create     [out ordId, out item, out address]
7   S→W: fw_create  [in ordId, in item, in address, nil canceled, out fw_created]
8   B→S: cancel     [in ordId, in item, in address, out canceled]
9 }
```
Listing 2. Order class protocol.

Roles and Public Parameters. The roles are inferred from the participants involved in choreography tasks associated with the class. The class attributes of the shared data model serve as public parameters. These parameters are adorned *out*, as they are only bound by the respective class protocol. At least one class attribute must be selected as a key parameter for a protocol. Each key parameter must reflect an attribute associated with all possible initial states in the lifecycle. For our running example, we select *ordId*, *invId*, and *parId* as the key parameters for the respective class protocols.

```
1 Invoice {
2   roles S, B
3   parameters in ordId key, out invId key, out total, out tax, out transactionId
4
5   S→B: open  [in ordId, out invId, out total, out tax]
6   B→S: pay   [in invId, in total, in tax, out transactionId]
7 }
```
Listing 3. Invoice class protocol.

A class protocol may require key parameters of other class protocols as *in* parameters to express dependencies according to the shared data model [14]. Referencing other key parameters is required if there is a relation to another class with a multiplicity having a lower-bound greater than zero, as for *Invoice* and *Parcel* in Fig. 3. Consequently, as Listings 3 and 4 show, both class protocols take the key parameter *ordId* of the *Order* protocol as in. For one-to-one relations, the creation of both objects is merged into one message schema that is added to both class protocols, including the respective adaptation of the public parameters. For brevity, we do not discuss verifying upper bounds greater than one, as this requires more advanced language features [3].

```
Parcel {
  roles W, S, B
  parameters in ordId key, out parId key, out dimensions, out weight,
    out approved, out trackingNo, out receiptDate

  W→S: pack    [in ordId, out parId, out dimensions, out weight]
  S→W: approve [in parId, in dimensions, in weight, out approved]
  W→B: ship    [in parId, in approved, out trackingNo]
  B→W: receive [in parId, in trackingNo, out receiptDate]
}
```

Listing 4. *Parcel* class protocol.

Message Schemas. A class protocol defines message schemas based on the tasks associated with the class in the choreography, relations to other classes, and the state transitions in the shared object lifecycle. Figure 5 shows the message schemas for the *Invoice* protocol based on the tasks *send invoice* and *send payment*. For the mapping, we interpret two-way tasks as two sequential one-way tasks with alternating initiators [6]. Given a task with a class and a state, a message schema is created for each transition towards the state that can be performed by the task's initiator. For example, for *send payment*, the buyer can perform one state transition towards *paid* according to the lifecycle in Fig. 5. Hence, one message schema is added to the class protocol for this task.

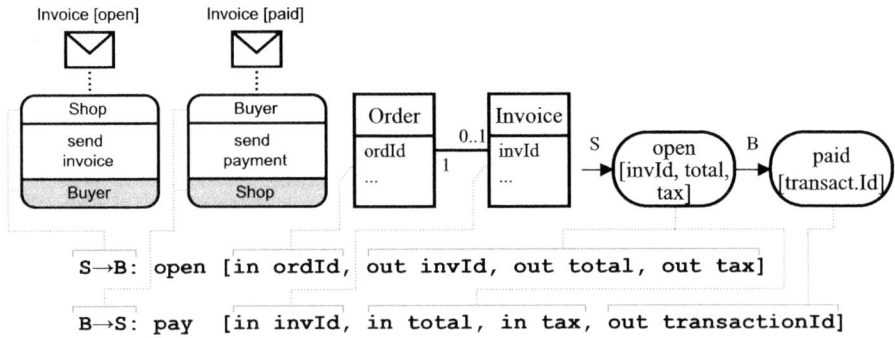

Fig. 5. Mapping rules for the message schemas of the *Invoice* class protocol.

Each message schema is named according to the state in which the task sends the object in active form. For example, the message sending an invoice in state *paid* is named *pay*. Sender and receiver are adopted from the task. The parameters of each message result from the state transition associated with the message schema. Each message schema specifies the parameters associated with the target state as *out*, e.g., *transactionId* for *pay*. Since *out* parameters can be bound at most once per enactment, only acyclic lifecycles are supported.

If a source state exists, the parameters associated with the source state and the key parameters of the class protocol are added as *in* parameters, e.g., *invId*, *total*, and *tax* (cf. Figure 5). If there are alternative transitions originating from the source of the transition associated with the message, all parameters of the alternative target states must be added as *nil* parameters to enforce exclusivity. If no source state exists, the key parameters of the class protocol are adorned *out* and the key parameters of the classes on which the considered class depends are added as *in* parameter. Considering the message *open* for the task *send invoice* in Fig. 5, *ordId* is adorned *in* to enforce a relation to an existing order.

Whereas most messages add information to the choreography, some only forward already exchanged information, e.g., as *prepare shipping* forwards an order to the warehouse (cf. Figure 2). A forwarding message schema takes all parameters associated with the required state as *in* and all parameters associated with directly succeeding states as *nil*, ensuring the object is in the correct state when forwarded. A private *out* parameter is added to capture that a forwarding took place. A forwarding message schema is added when (1) the initiator of a task cannot transition to the required state, or (2) multiple tasks can send the object in the same state, all of which have an initiator that can transition to that state. In the latter case, it is not clear which message performs the transition, so that forwarding messages are inserted in addition to the transitioning messages. Since a task can now be associated with both a transitioning and a forwarding message, both message schemas must contain the same private *out* parameter so that only one can be sent. Listing 2 shows an example of a forwarding message schema. For clarity, forwarding schemas are prefixed with *fw*.

Composition. Listing 5 shows the result of composing the class protocols into one. Some parameters are omitted due to space constraints.

```
RelaxedOrderManagement {
    roles B, S, W
    parameters out ordId key, out invId key, out parId key, out item, ...

    Order(B, S, W, out ordId, out item, out address, out canceled)
    Invoice(S, B, in ordId, out invId, out total, out tax, out transactionId)
    Parcel(W, S, B, in ordId, out parId, out dimensions, out weight, ...)
}
```

Listing 5. Relaxed order management protocol combining all class protocols.

4 Fine-Tuning Flexibility

The derived protocol may be more flexible than the original choreography, since it incorporates only the data-related constraints. However, as illustrated in

Fig. 1(b), the protocol may allow undesirable behavior that the choreography avoids via control-flow constraints. For example, Listing 5 allows the following sequence of interactions: ⟨create, fw_create, pack, approve, ship, receive, open, pay, cancel⟩, which permits shipping before payment and cancellation after shipping. This behavior may not be acceptable in a business context. We therefore propose an approach to identify relevant control-flow constraints from the initial choreography that can be used to constrain the derived protocol's behavior. By modifying or removing the identified constraints, the protocol can be refined according to business needs, as Fig. 1(c) shows.

4.1 Identifying Control-Flow Constraints

Given a protocol and a choreography, we derive constraints by detecting interaction sequences of a protocol that deviate from a given choreography. For each deviation, we extract the violated control-flow constraints from the choreography as output, as described in Algorithm 1. Lines 3–4 determine all possible sequences of interactions assuming synchronous communication, i.e., sent messages are received before the next message is sent. Lines 5–6 filter all interaction sequences produced by the protocol that are not supported by the choreography. For each filtered sequence, the first message that deviates from the behavior of the choreography is identified (Line 7) and the deviating message is associated with its corresponding task to derive the applicable control-flow constraints (Line 8). Lines 10–11 add constraints that are violated by the sequence to the output.

Algorithm 1: Identifying protocol constraints given a choreography.

Input: p (protocol), c (choreography)
Output: $\mathcal{C}$ (set of constraints)

1 **Function** identify_control_flow_constraints(p, c):
2     $\mathcal{C} \leftarrow \emptyset$; // Set of discovered constraints
3     $S_p \leftarrow$ determine_interaction_sequences(p);
4     $S_c \leftarrow$ determine_interaction_sequences(c);
5   **for** $\sigma_p \in S_p$ **do**
6   **if** $\sigma_p \notin S_c$ **then**
7            $m \leftarrow$ get_deviating_message(σ_p, S_c);
8            $\mathcal{C}_t \leftarrow$ infer_constraints(get_task(m, c), c);
9   **for** $k \in \mathcal{C}_t$ **do**
10   **if** sequence_violates_constraint(k, m, σ_p) **then**
11                    $\mathcal{C} \leftarrow \mathcal{C} \cup \{k\}$;

12 **return** $\mathcal{C}$;

We distinguish two types of control-flow constraints. A *precedence* constraint requires that the preceding task always occurs before the succeeding task. An *exclusion* constraint between the two tasks implies that no interaction sequence contains both. If the sequence flow arc connects two tasks, a precedence from the source to the target is identified, e.g., in Fig. 2, *send payment* precedes *prepare shipping*. In case the arc connects the observed task to a gateway, precedence is derived from the observed task to all tasks following the gateway. Similarly, if an arc connects a gateway to the observed task, precedence is imposed from the preceding tasks to the observed task; e.g., *send invoice* precedes *send payment*. To ensure that precedence constraints can be enforced, we only consider realizable choreographies [9]. In addition, if an exclusive or event-based gateway is connected to the observed task, exclusion is derived for all tasks connected to the gateway on exclusive paths, e.g., *cancel order* excludes *send payment* and vice versa.

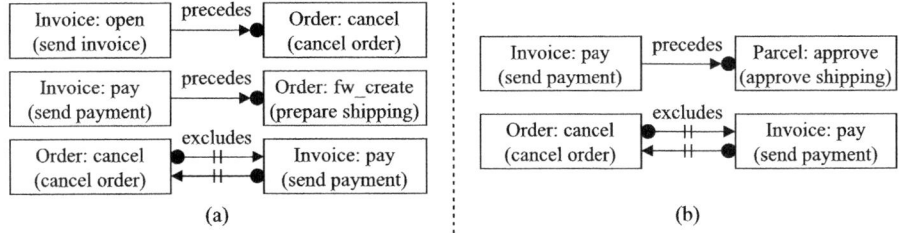

Fig. 6. Control-flow constraints for the protocol in Listing 5, in the notation of [17]: (a) derived from the control flow of Fig. 2 and (b) a possible relaxation of the constraints. Messages are associated with the respective class protocol name and task label.

Finally, all discovered constraints that are violated by the interaction sequence up to the deviating message are added to the output, essentially removing the interaction sequence from the protocol to achieve trace-based conformity with the choreography [6]. In case multiple precedences share the same target with the sources being exclusive, only one of the precedences must hold. Figure 6(a) illustrates the constraints discovered from Listing 5 and Fig. 2. Though the discovered control-flow constraints serve as a baseline for the refinement of the protocol, constraints might be modified or omitted by experts in accordance with business needs. Figure 6(b) shows a possible relaxation that allows for preparing the parcel before receiving payment: ⟨create, open, fw_create, pack, pay, approve, ship, receive⟩. Hence, the relaxed constraints allow for behavior beyond the choreography, while ensuring that the invoice is paid before a parcel is shipped and that a shipped order cannot be canceled (nor a canceled order shipped). In general, the realizability of the new constraints is crucial, but its verification is out of our present scope.

4.2 Refining Protocols

We can refine a protocol to satisfy additional control-flow constraints. In essence, the protocol is extended by parameters that are used to implement precedence and exclusion constraints to control message ordering. Specifically, precedence translates to an *out* parameter from the preceding message included as *in* in the succeeding message. Similarly, exclusion is achieved by adding the same *out* parameter to the exclusive messages. If multiple precede constraints share the same target, with the sources being exclusive, the target message is copied for all possible preceding messages. Each copy takes a parameter bound by a different preceding message as *in* parameter.

```
 1  RefinedOrder {
 2    roles B, S, W
 3    parameters ..., in cf_p1, in cf_p2, out cf_e
 4
 5    B→S: create     [...]
 6    S→W: fw_create  [..., in cf_p1]
 7    B→S: cancel     [..., in cf_p2, out cf_e]
 8  }
 9
10  RefinedInvoice {
11    roles S, B
12    parameters ..., out cf_p1, out cf_p2, out cf_e
13
14    S→B: open  [..., out cf_p2]
15    B→S: pay   [..., out cf_p1, out cf_e]
16  }
```

Listing 6. Refinement of the protocols in Listings 2 and 3 based on the constraints illustrated in Figure 6. Unchanged parameters are omitted.

Listing 6 refines Listings 2 and 3 based on the constraints in Fig. 6(a). Here, cf_p1 ensures that ⟨pay⟩ precedes ⟨fw_create⟩, cf_p2 guarantees that ⟨open⟩ precedes ⟨cancel⟩, and cf_e enforces exclusivity between ⟨pay⟩ and ⟨cancel⟩, thus implementing the constraints.

5 Evaluation

We evaluate the conformance, flexibility, and operability of protocols derived from object-aware choreographies to answer the research question presented in Sect. 1 based on two scenarios: S_1, an *Order Management* choreography described in Sect. 2.1, and S_2, a *Transport of Goods* choreography illustrated in Fig. 7.

We adopt the number of distinct interaction sequences that can be generated by a given model as the primary metric for evaluating flexibility [5]. Furthermore, we compare the behavior of models and protocols using trace-based conformance [6]. In this context, we consider polymorphic message schemas to represent the same interaction. Only interaction sequences of a single protocol enactment are considered, assuming synchronous communication. Therefore, we evaluate conformance and flexibility according to three criteria:

C_1 **Fitness**: Derived protocols cover the entire behavior of the choreography.
C_2 **Precision**: Protocols, when refined with control-flow constraints discovered from the choreography, match the behavior of the choreography.
C_3 **Relaxation**: Refined protocols with fewer control-flow constraints allow for more distinct interaction sequences.

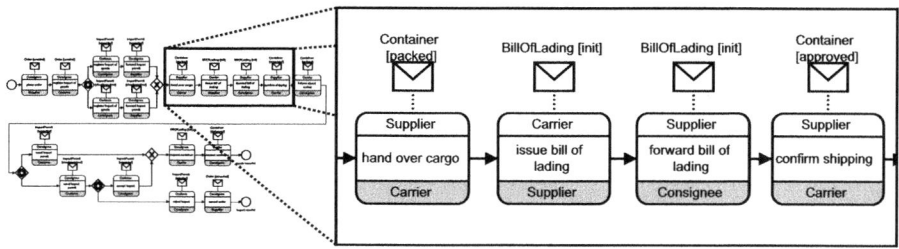

Fig. 7. Choreography adapted from [14], describing the interplay between a consignee, a supplier, a carrier, and customs to organize the transportation of goods. The model consists of 18 tasks and 5 gateways and 4 shared data model classes.

The first two criteria are adapted from the quality dimensions for process model discovery [2], while the third criterion assesses the degree of flexibility achieved by applying only a subset of discovered constraints [5]. To evaluate these criteria for the given scenarios, we developed a prototype to automate the mapping from choreographies to protocols, identify control-flow constraints, and create refined protocols. For S_1, we identified three constraints (two precedence and one exclusion), as shown in Fig. 6(a). For S_2, we identified 15 constraints (13 precedence and two exclusion). Based on the results, we derive three types of refined protocols for each scenario: (1) protocols containing only exclusion constraints, (2) protocols containing only precedence constraints, and (3) protocols containing both types of constraints. For each resulting protocol, we compute the number of distinct interaction sequences. The results are presented in Table 1.

Table 1. Distinct interaction sequences computed for both scenarios using choreographies, derived protocols, and refined protocols including (1) exclusion constraints only, (2) precedence constraints only, and (3) both types of discovered constraints.

Scenario	Choreography	Protocol	Refined Protocol		
			Exclusion	Precedence	Both
S_1	2	143	58	7	2
S_2	3	11,699,340	4,948,100	49	3

Our results show that for both scenarios, the derived protocols support significantly more interaction sequences than the original choreographies. We reason that the large number of tasks relative to the number of classes is responsible for the significant increase in interaction sequences for S_2. Since tasks operating on objects of different classes can act independently after object creation, S_2 allows for high concurrency, leading to the comparatively large number of different interaction sequences without control-flow constraints.

Furthermore, the interaction sequences derived from refined protocols represent a subset of the parent protocol's sequences. When all identified constraints are applied, the protocols exactly match the interaction sequences of the choreographies, thus confirming C_1 and C_2. In addition, removing exclusion, precedence or both types of constraints increases the behavioral flexibility of the protocols, confirming C_3.

By using tooling from [25], we verified that all derived protocols comply with BSPL syntax and are safe. In conclusion, our approach effectively derives flexible, operational models from object-aware choreographies, as demonstrated by the results for both evaluation scenarios.

Limitations. Despite promising results, this approach relies on consistency between the choreography, the shared data model, and the shared object lifecycle to form valid protocols. Conflicting models can lead to deadlocks. States currently require a unique set of attributes for clear separation, which may lead to artificial attributes that provide no value besides identifying the state. In addition, we associate one choreography instance with one protocol enactment, which prevents support for loops and many-to-one relationships between data objects. While BSPL allows expressing iterative behavior using multiple key bindings, relaxing this assumption requires further investigation.

When refining protocols, mapping each constraint to a parameter increases protocol complexity. Optimizing parameter introduction, such as reusing parameters for multiple constraints, could reduce protocol size. Furthermore, the relaxation of constraints is up to the end user. The approach could benefit from a methodology to guide the relaxation. Visual representations of protocol behavior could aid business experts in assessing the resulting protocols.

In addition, our discovery of control-flow constraints and evaluation assumes synchronous communication for computing possible interaction sequences. Given that protocols support asynchronous communication, the flexibility gains and limitations that asynchrony implies need further investigation. Finally, the evaluation is limited to two scenarios. Further validation with more complex scenarios, including consideration of applicability by business experts, would substantiate the results.

6 Related Work

Data-aware and declarative choreographies have garnered much attention. Knuplesch et al. [13] model interorganizational data exchange by extending choreographies with virtual data objects that act as variables for routing conditions. Similarly, Meyer et al. [16] enhance BPMN collaboration diagrams with a global data model to automate data exchange and transformation between global and local data. Adding to this, Nikaj et al. [18] incorporate RESTful specifications to coordinate data exchange in choreographies. Whereas these works model data exchange, they rely on explicit interaction ordering, limiting flexibility.

Montali et al. [17] propose DecSerFlow, a declarative language that uses linear temporal logic to constrain message ordering and logical expressions for data constraints. Building on this, Sun et al. [26] introduce artifact-centric choreographies, which treat interacting processes as artifacts that are accessed and manipulated via messages. Geatti et al. [10] extend DECLARE for collaborative processes, partitioning constraints into assumptions for external participants and guarantees for the local process using LTL on finite traces. Expanding further, Hildebrandt et al. [12] present a formal model for declarative choreographies based on dynamic condition response graphs, later extended with temporal and data constraints in [11]. While the approaches achieve flexibility through declarative constraints, they still rely on explicit message ordering. Since our approach aims to relax control-flow constraints while preserving data constraints, we chose BSPL as our target language. BSPL's inherent focus on specifying information dependencies allows us to naturally encode data dependencies without the need to infer explicit message ordering.

Bergman et al. [1] discover declarative control-flow constraints from BPMN process models to be used for conformance checking. Contrary to their work, we aim to discover control-flow constraints that affect flexibility in a distributed scenario, allowing for fine-granular relaxation of constraints. Meroni et al. [15] map BPMN process diagrams to more flexible E-GSM models for artifact-based monitoring of multi-party processes. Nonetheless, their approach abstracts from interaction behavior among collaborators. Finally, Singh [24] introduces Bliss, an extension of BSPL, providing a systematic methodology for specifying information protocols. The methodology iteratively identifies the required information to produce protocol artifacts, ensuring flexibility and avoiding over-constrained specifications. In contrast, our approach infers protocols from visual object-aware choreographies.

7 Conclusion

We propose a novel approach that maps object-aware BPMN choreography diagrams to BSPL information protocols to address the need for flexibility and operability in modeling collaborations between autonomous organizations. By initially neglecting control-flow constraints, the resulting protocol allows for more flexible behavior. To prevent undesirable behavior, constraints are identified that limit the protocol to the choreography specification. By selectively relaxing these constraints, business experts can refine the protocol's behavior to increase flexibility while avoiding undesired behavior. Evaluation shows that protocols refined with the identified constraints match the behavior of the original choreography, while removing constraints increases flexibility. Furthermore, all generated protocols are safe and adhere to BSPL syntax, validating operability.

Future research includes adding support for loops and investigating the impact of asynchronous communication on flexibility and conformance with the original choreography. Further enhancements include the development of constraint relaxation guidelines and visual representations of the resulting protocols to assist business experts in protocol design. Finally, user studies could validate the applicability of the approach.

Resources and Reproducibility. The source code of the prototype, all resources used for the evaluation, and a screencast demonstrating the prototype are available on GitHub[1].

Acknowledgements. This work was supported by DFG grant 450612067 (TL), EPSRC grant EP/N027965/1 (AKC), and NSF grant IIS-1908374 and a gift from SAS Institute (MPS).

References

1. Bergmann, A., Rebmann, A., Kampik, T.: BPMN2Constraints: breaking down BPMN diagrams into declarative process query constraints. In: BPM Demonstration & Resources Forum. CEUR-WS.org (2023)
2. Buijs, J.C.A.M., van Dongen, B.F., van der Aalst, W.M.P.: On the role of fitness, precision, generalization and simplicity in process discovery. In: Meersman, R. (ed.) On the Move to Meaningful Internet Systems: OTM 2012, pp. 305–322. Springer, Berlin, Heidelberg (2012). https://doi.org/10.1007/978-3-642-33606-5_19
3. Chopra, A.K., Christie, V., S.H., Singh, M.P.: Splee: a declarative information-based language for multiagent interaction protocols. In: AAMAS. ACM (2017)
4. Chopra, A.K., Christie V., S.H., Singh, M.P.: An evaluation of communication protocol languages for engineering multiagent systems. JAIR (2020)
5. Corea, C., Felli, P., Montali, M., Patrizi, F.: On the flexibility of declarative process specifications. In: Guizzardi, G., Santoro, F., Mouratidis, H., Soffer, P. (eds.) Advanced Information Systems Engineering: 36th International Conference, CAiSE 2024, Limassol, Cyprus, June 3–7, 2024, Proceedings, pp. 161–177. Springer Nature Switzerland, Cham (2024). https://doi.org/10.1007/978-3-031-61057-8_10
6. Corradini, F., et al.: Collaboration vs. choreography conformance in BPMN. Log. Methods Comput. Sci. (2020)
7. Desai, N., Mallya, A.U., Chopra, A.K., Singh, M.P.: Interaction protocols as design abstractions for business processes. IEEE Trans., Softw. Eng. (2005)
8. Dumas, M., Pfahl, D.: Modeling software processes using BPMN: when and when not? In: Kuhrmann, M., Münch, J., Richardson, I., Rausch, A., Zhang, H. (eds.) Managing Software Process Evolution, pp. 165–183. Springer International Publishing, Cham (2016). https://doi.org/10.1007/978-3-319-31545-4_9
9. Fu, X., Bultan, T., Su, J.: Conversation protocols: a formalism for specification and verification of reactive electronic services. Theor. Comput. Sci. (2004)
10. Geatti, L., Montali, M., Rivkin, A.: Foundations of collaborative DECLARE. In: BPM Forum. LNBIP, Springer (2023). https://doi.org/10.1007/978-3-031-41623-1_4
11. Hildebrandt, T.T., López, H.A., Slaats, T.: Declarative choreographies with time and data. In: Di Francescomarino, C., Burattin, A., Janiesch, C., Sadiq, S. (eds.) Business Process Management Forum: BPM 2023 Forum, Utrecht, The Netherlands, September 11–15, 2023, Proceedings, pp. 73–89. Springer Nature Switzerland, Cham (2023). https://doi.org/10.1007/978-3-031-41623-1_5

---

[1] https://github.com/bptlab/chor2bspl.

12. Hildebrandt, T.T., Slaats, T., López, H.A., Debois, S., Carbone, M.: Declarative choreographies and liveness. In: Pérez, J.A., Yoshida, N. (eds.) Formal Techniques for Distributed Objects, Components, and Systems: 39th IFIP WG 6.1 International Conference, FORTE 2019, Held as Part of the 14th International Federated Conference on Distributed Computing Techniques, DisCoTec 2019, Kongens Lyngby, Denmark, June 17–21, 2019, Proceedings, pp. 129–147. Springer International Publishing, Cham (2019). https://doi.org/10.1007/978-3-030-21759-4_8
13. Knuplesch, D., Pryss, R., Reichert, M.: Data-aware interaction in distributed and collaborative workflows: modeling, semantics, correctness. In: CollaborateCom. IEEE (2012)
14. Lichtenstein, T., Weske, M.: Execution semantics for process choreographies with data. In: Di Francescomarino, C., Burattin, A., Janiesch, C., Sadiq, S. (eds.) Business Process Management Forum: BPM 2023 Forum, Utrecht, The Netherlands, September 11–15, 2023, Proceedings, pp. 90–106. Springer Nature Switzerland, Cham (2023). https://doi.org/10.1007/978-3-031-41623-1_6
15. Meroni, G., Baresi, L., Montali, M., Plebani, P.: Multi-party business process compliance monitoring through IoT-enabled artifacts. Inf. Syst. **73**, 61–78 (2018). https://doi.org/10.1016/j.is.2017.12.009
16. Meyer, A., Pufahl, L., Batoulis, K., Fahland, D., Weske, M.: Automating data exchange in process choreographies. Inf. Syst. (2015)
17. Montali, M., Pesic, M., van der Aalst, W.M.P., Chesani, F., Mello, P., Storari, S.: Declarative specification and verification of service choreographiess. ACM Trans. Web (2010)
18. Nikaj, A., Weske, M.: Formal specification of RESTful choreography properties. In: Bozzon, A., Cudre-Maroux, P., Pautasso, C. (eds.) Web Engineering: 16th International Conference, ICWE 2016, Lugano, Switzerland, June 6-9, 2016. Proceedings, pp. 365–372. Springer International Publishing, Cham (2016). https://doi.org/10.1007/978-3-319-38791-8_21
19. OMG: Business Process Model and Notation (BPMN), V 2.0.2: Standard (2014)
20. Pérez-Álvarez, J.M., et al.: Verifying the manipulation of data objects according to business process and data models. Knowl. Inf. Syst. (2020)
21. Reichert, M., Weber, B.: Enabling Flexibility in Process-Aware Information Systems. Springer, Berlin, Heidelberg (2012). https://doi.org/10.1007/978-3-642-30409-5
22. Singh, M.P.: Information-driven interaction-oriented programming: BSPL, the blindingly simple protocol language. In: AAMAS. IFAAMAS (2011)
23. Singh, M.P.: Semantics and verification of information-based protocols. In: AAMAS, IFAAMAS (2012)
24. Singh, M.P.: Bliss: Specifying declarative service protocols. In: Proceedings of SCC (2014)
25. Singh, M.P., Christie V., S.H.: Tango: declarative semantics for multiagent communication protocols. In: IJCAI, ijcai.org (2021)
26. Sun, Y., Xu, W., Su, J.: Declarative choreographies for artifacts. In: Maglio, P.P., Weske, M., Yang, J., Fantinato, M. (eds.) Service-Oriented Computing: 8th International Conference, ICSOC 2010, San Francisco, CA, USA, December 7-10, 2010. Proceedings, pp. 420–434. Springer, Berlin, Heidelberg (2010). https://doi.org/10.1007/978-3-642-34321-6_28

Architectural Elements of Decentralized Process Management Systems

Kai Grunert[✉][ID], Janis Joderi Shoferi, Lucas Gold, Wolf Rieder[ID], and Axel Küpper[ID]

Service-centric Networking Technische Universität Berlin, Berlin, Germany
{kai.grunert,w.rieder,axel.kuepper}@tu-berlin.de
https://www.tu.berlin/snet

Abstract. In a decentralized Process Management System, several process engines cooperate to execute a single process instance by using direct Machine-to-Machine communication and local coordination of the process flow. In this paper, we analyze the software architecture elements of a decentralized Process Management System. We explain the involved components, connectors, data, and the relationships between them. We also describe the state transitions of decentralized processes during execution.

Keywords: decentralized Process Management System · Distributed Process Engines · Distributed and Heterogeneous Workflow Enactment Service · Business Process Management System · Process Automation · Process Execution System · Process Engine

1 Introduction

Process automation is an important topic in the digital world. This paper focuses on self-defined *processes* that consist of several steps to achieve a process goal and that use distributed computing systems for their automation. These processes are usually automated with the help of a centralized Process Management System (cPMS). For example, business processes are often automated using a Business Process Management System (BPMS) to coordinate internal company processes like a purchasing process in which different employees obtain, evaluate, approve offers, and buy a product. However, processes can also be routines in the smart home controlled by automation software such as IFTTT.

They all have in common that a logically centralized software, the process engine, interprets and runs the processes on the basis of a proprietary or standardized process description. The engine usually does not execute the respective steps by itself but instead passes instructions to external systems or human process participants who carry out the process step. Hence, the automation system typically only *coordinates* the process flow (and sometimes the data exchange).

A problem can arise if the cPMS runs in a different location than the distributed systems required for process automation. For example, a local switch in a smart home can no longer activate the music box if a centralized Process Management System in the cloud is supposed to coordinate this process, but the remote connection to the cloud fails. A *decentralized Process Management Systems* (dPMS), as defined in [8], can improve this situation (Fig. 1). Here, the specified process description is transferred to the involved distributed systems. They interpret the description, execute parts of it, coordinate, and communicate directly with each other without the need for a connection to a remote, centralized system.

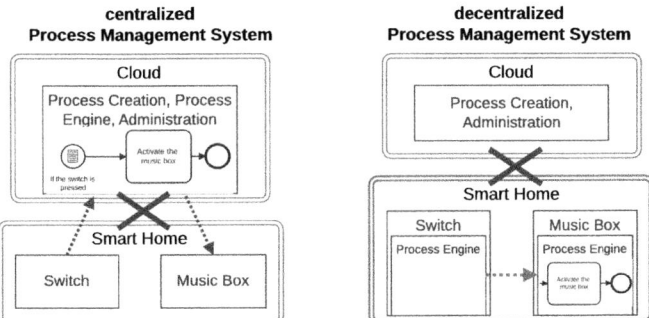

Fig. 1. The diagram shows one difference between a centralized and decentralized Process Management System during the execution of a process on the example of a simple self-defined smart home routine. In a cPMS, the process engine in the cloud environment coordinating the interaction between the switch and the music box can no longer reach the devices if the physical connection to the smart home fails (red arrows). In a dPMS, the process is first split up and deployed to the process engines on the local devices, which then coordinate the execution of the routine directly (green arrow), even if the connection between the cloud and the smart home is physically interrupted. (Color figure online)

To implement a decentralized Process Management System, most distributed Machines[1] must install process engines, so-called *Distributed Process Engines* (DPE). The DPEs are comparable to the process engine in a centralized automation architecture, with some additional functionalities for coordinating with other DPEs and for accessing Capabilities of the Machine they are running on [8].

There are several options for deploying the process description and additional items, the so-called Deployment Artifacts, to the Distributed Process Engines. For example, it is possible to specify the execution location, i.e. the selected DPE, of each process step statically at design time or to determine the execution

---

[1] We capitalize some terms in the text because they represent important components of a decentralized Process Management System, as explained in Sect. 3.

location for the next step dynamically at runtime. Due to the distribution of all process steps to different DPEs, there is generally not one engine that centrally coordinates the entire execution of one process execution (also called process instance); instead, different Distributed Process Engines can coordinate different parts of one process instance in a decentralized manner.

[8] defines the concept of decentralized Process Management Systems and explains the Distributed Process Engine with its software modules, the interfaces, and the various aspects of the process deployment. However, there is no description of the required Deployment Artifacts that enable the execution phase. This is important as it forms the basis for the decentralized execution behavior. Therefore, this paper analyzes the software architecture of a dPMS, i.e. it describes the required architectural elements for the decentralized process execution and coordination on multiple DPEs. We explain the components, connectors, and data as well as the possible state transitions of the process instance during the execution phase.

In the context of this paper, we use some terms interchangeably:

∗ Process Management System (PMS) and coordination/automation system
∗ Distributed Process Engine (DPE), process engine, and engine
∗ Process, and process definition/specification/description/model

2 Related Work

The basic idea of decentralized coordination of processes has already been covered in various works under different terms: distributed/heterogeneous/decentralized workflow enactment services, web service composition, and agent systems [1–4,7,9–13]. Most of these works focus very narrowly on a specific technology or problem. Furthermore, solutions are often proposed that only allow process descriptions with a limited set of workflow patterns and others that predefine various aspects for process deployment or splitting.

In [8], the authors explain the generalized concept of a decentralized Process Management System. The focus is on the description of the overall system, the structure of the Distributed Process Engines, and the various aspects of process deployment using a Decider that selects the optimal DPEs. However, the description of the runtime phase with the architectural elements and the instance state transitions was neglected.

This paper closes these gaps in the understanding of the necessary architectural elements for a decentralized Process Management System.

3 Architectural Elements of a Decentralized Process Management System

In this section, we describe the software architecture of decentralized Process Management Systems according to the definition of Fielding [6, sec. 1.2]:

"A software architecture is defined by a configuration of architectural elements – components, connectors, and data – constrained in their relationships in order to achieve a desired set of architectural properties."

The UML class diagram in Fig. 3 summarizes the components, data, and connectors of a dPMS. For a better understanding, Fig. 2 shows an example of how a process can be executed in a dPMS with some of these architectural elements (which are defined and explained in the following subsections). First, a Process Model and the additional Deployment Artefacts, such as the execution instructions for each Process Step, are created. Then, the preferred deployment location can be determined for each Process Step, i.e., the DPE that best fulfills the Constraints of the respective Step is selected. This assignment leads to splitting the Process Model into several Process Fragments that contain one or more Process Steps. Depending on the assessment and splitting algorithm, the same Process Model can be split in different ways and divided into completely different Process Fragments. Each Fragment is subsequently transferred to the selected Distributed Process Engine.

During execution, each DPE coordinates and runs its assigned Process Fragments. Several DPEs communicate to enact the full process. The Machines on which the DPEs are running are located in an Environment. However, some of these machines can be mobile. This means that mobile Machines may change the Environment and execute the process in a different Environment.

It is also possible that the process has not been split, but all Process Artefacts including the Process Model have been deployed to one DPE. This allows the DPE to pass the Process Artifacts on to another DPE if it is better to execute the following Process Steps at a different deployment location. This deployment decision can be made locally on a DPE with the help of the internal Decider component, resulting in processes that can migrate independently across multiple DPEs (so-called Portable Processes).[2]

3.1 Components of a dPMS

dPMS are executing decentralized processes that run in *Environments*. These are administrative domains and usually technical computer networks. However, they are also influenced by non-technical rules, resources, and interactions. Examples include company networks, cloud environments, the public vehicle-to-everything infrastructure, or private networks, e.g., a smartwatch connected to a smartphone.

An Environment is managed by an *Owner*. Owners can be private persons, governments, or companies. One Owner can have zero or more Environments. The Owner can also be the *Process Owner* and Creator to whom the executed process belongs. Sometimes, in the case of an individual, the Owner can also be the *Process Participant* who works on the Process Steps.

---

[2] The possible process splitting methods and deployment procedures are not discussed in this paper as they are already explained in [8].

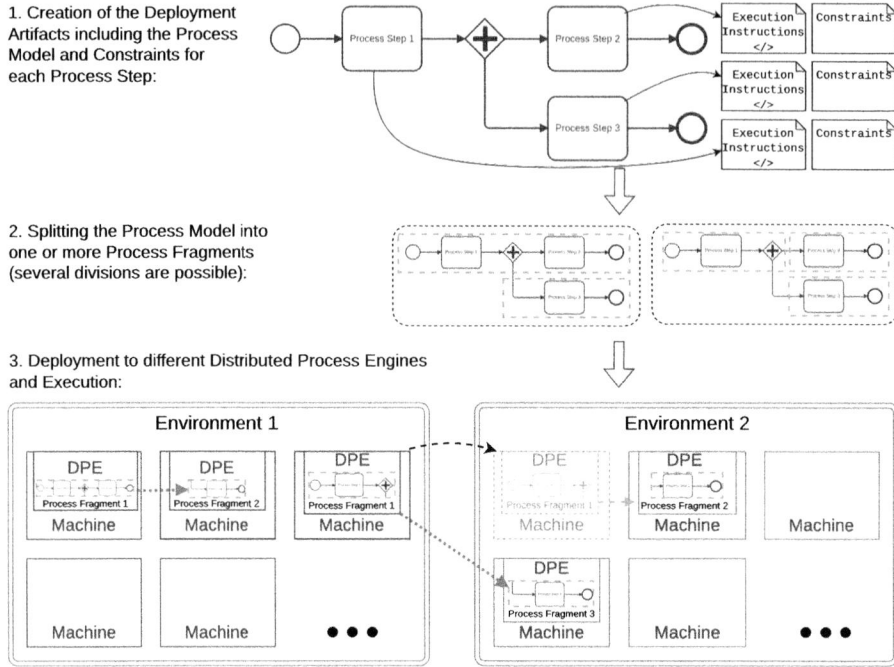

Fig. 2. To execute processes in a dPMS, a Process Model can be split into several Process Fragments and deployed to different Distributed Process Engines. Two splitting variants of the same Process Model are visualized in the diagram. Both fulfill the defined Constraints of the process steps (blue and orange). The DPEs coordinate the execution of the entire process among themselves (green arrow). The Machines running a DPE can be mobile and thus change location to a different Environment (black arrow). (Color figure online)

Machines are every kind of computing system with a processing unit and a network adapter, e.g., cloud or edge servers, laptops, smartphones, production machines, drones, microcontroller, or sensors. Even if the term Machine is often associated with physical, tangible objects, it can also refer to virtual entities. A Machine belongs to one Environment. Within Environments, Machines can communicate with other Machines. Some Machines are mobile and are able to move to another geographical location. Therefore, due to the location-independent nature of some Machines, they can run within multiple Environments during its lifetime. A Machine can also connect to multiple Environments simultaneously if it has multiple network adapters, like a smartphone connected to a local network via WiFi and to a headset via Bluetooth.

A Machine may have multiple *Capabilities*, i.e., functional abilities related to that Machine. These are physical properties like sensors, direct connections to other Machines, or installed applications. A running process instance can use such Capabilities during its execution.

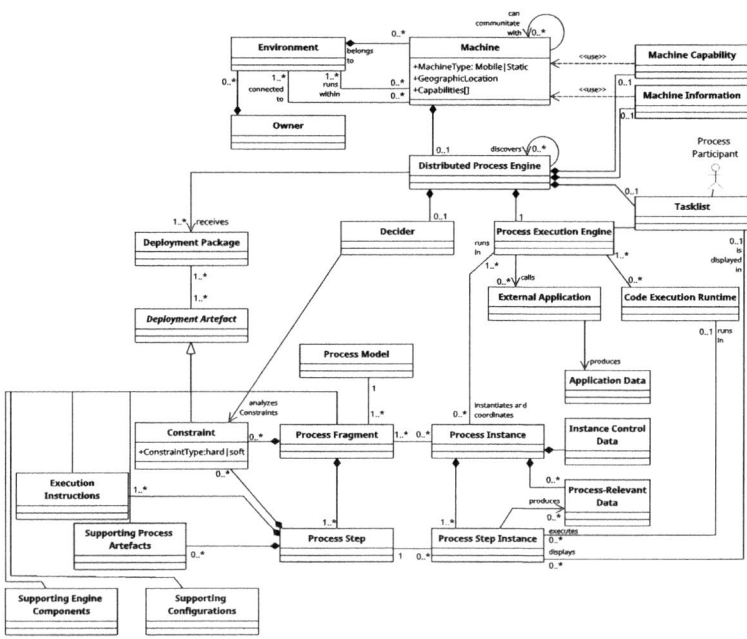

Fig. 3. The diagram shows the components, data, and connectors of a decentralized Process Management System with their relationships.

Machines in an Environment can have zero or one *Distributed Process Engine* installed; one DPE is always installed on one Machine. (In the following, we use "D/M" to indicate the one-to-one relationship of one DPE on one Machine.) In a decentralized Process Management System, this software component partially enacts *Process Instances* with its modules *Process Execution Engine, Decider, Machine Capability, Machine Information, Tasklist*, as well as its interfaces, which are described in detail in [8].

3.2 Data Elements Within a dPMS

To execute part of a Process Instance, a DPE must receive a *Deployment Package*, either at design time or runtime. The Package includes *Deployment Artefacts*, most notably the *Process Model*. However, the Deployment Package only needs to contain a part of the process description, known as the *Process Fragment*, which consists of one or more Process Steps. The splitting process during the deployment phase determines the number of Fragments that assemble the complete Process Model [8]. Note that a DPE can receive more Fragments/Steps than it will execute. For monitoring and transparency reasons, sending the entire Model to each D/M involved in a process flow often makes sense. So, a Process Model can consist of several Process Fragments, but it is also possible that the Model is not split up and is only represented by one Fragment.

A *Process Step* is an atomic unit that usually cannot be divided any further, meaning its execution is done exactly on one engine. (Nonetheless, a modeling language can have more high-level, non-atomic constructs, e.g., subprocesses in BPMN.) A Process Step is always linked to *Execution Instructions* such as interpretable source code, binary code, Capability calls, or user interface markup. The Instructions are executed within a (sandboxed) Code Execution Runtime or displayed via the Tasklist to the Process Participant. Sometimes, the Deployment Package contains additional Supporting Process Artefacts like pictures or documents that assist in executing a process step.

For the deployment, each Process Step and Process Fragment can have *Constraints* that restrict where and by whom it is processed. Constraints are either hard or soft. [8] explains the difference: Hard Constraints "are conditions that must be satisfied before a D/M is allowed to execute a step. ... hard constraints can refer to all possible properties of a Machine. Examples include the required Capabilities, a specific Machine address, a physical location, or - humanwise - a person/role that must work on a task. Soft constraints are optimization functions to select the best D/M for a criterion, e.g., the one with the highest battery status or the lowest workload."

A Deployment Package can also contain *Supporting Configurations*, such as settings, preferences, or security information that can adapt and protect the Instance execution. Furthermore, *Supporting Engine Components* are a potential extension mechanism for Distributed Process Engines, for example, to add additional networking protocols.

To enact a decentralized process, a DPE creates a *Process Instance* with the help of the Process Execution Engine, which is able to interpret the received Process Fragment. After executing the first *Process Step Instance*, the Decider needs to analyze the next Steps' Constraints and must find a suitable engine that can fulfill the requirements. If it is a different DPE, it must exchange the Deployment Package (optional, could have already been transmitted at design time) and the *Execution Data*. On the one hand, this is the *Instance Control Data*, and on the other, the *Process-Relevant Data*. The latter is the same as in the case of a centralized Process Management system, where it is used if the Process Steps' data is transferred via the process engine, e.g., to make decisions. The former is similar to the same data category in conventional cPMS. Most importantly, it includes information about the current process state, which a DPE needs to start the correct Process Step in the Process Model (assuming that the Process Model was not split). Following this procedure, one Process Instance is executed on one or more Distributed Process Engines, and one Process Step Instance is always executed on one DPE. As previously explained, this does not mean that all Process Instances of one Process Model are always executed by the same DPEs. The Constraints influence the execution path, and if they are defined openly, multiple DPEs may satisfy the requirements.

3.3 Connectors of a dPMS

DPEs need network functionality to discover and communicate with other process engines in the Environment. The specific network technology is determined by the Machine's network adapter and the software stack. A DPE is not tied to a specific technology, but can interact with other DPEs via different technologies.

The *Decider* module is responsible for initializing communication with other DPEs and must find the best process engine for the given Deployment Artefacts. From a high-level perspective, communication in a dPMS corresponds to an unstructured peer-to-peer system, where each DPE knows an ad hoc list of neighbors that can change over time [14, sec. 2.4.2]. The resulting network corresponds to a random graph which requires the Decider to use special methods such as flooding, random walk, or policy-based methods to search for suitable DPEs for the next process step.

For the actual execution and coordination of the process description, the Process Execution Engine can call external applications. The Tasklist controls the interaction with Process Participants and the Machine Capability module allows accessing the Machine's Capabilities.

3.4 State Transitions of Decentralized Process Instances

State diagrams are helpful for understanding the inner workings of the decentralized process execution. The status diagram of a Process Step does not change compared to an execution in a central automation system and is described, for example, in [9, sec. 3.3.3], [5, sec. 13.3.2], or [15, sec. 3.4].

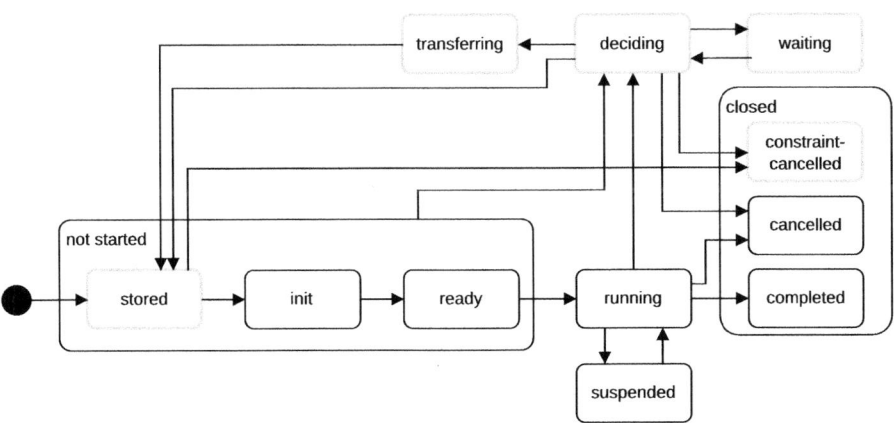

Fig. 4. The figure shows the possible status transitions that a single token of a process instance undergoes on a DPE. If there are several tokens in an instance, each token goes through this cycle. The green boxes indicate new states added by the decentralized execution. (Color figure online)

It is more interesting to examine the Process Instance state that results from the execution of each Instance part. Logically, the state is computed transparently across all distributed D/M on which the Instance runs. Since one Instance can be split into multiple parallel execution paths, it is difficult to calculate a single state. Instead, it is more beneficial to take the well-established concept of tokens and look at each execution path separately. Figure 4 depicts the token state diagram. The green boxes indicate new states added by the decentralized execution. *init, ready, running,* and *suspended* represent the usual states if a token controls the execution of a process step.

The *deciding* state is the most crucial extension, indicating the phase during constraint analysis, discovery, and evaluation after each process step. As a result of these tasks, the Decider can find and select one suitable DPE for the next step, which changes the state to the *transferring* mode or, in case the own D/M is the most fitting one, directly into the preparation phase for the next Process Step. When tokens arrive at a DPE, they enter a *stored* state, which is needed to wait for other tokens in case of an upcoming joining operation. If the Decider finds no suitable DPE, the token enters a *deciding-waiting* cycle, which is aborted by constraints defining the timescale for this cycle.

4 Discussion

In contrast to a centralized PMS, the steps of a Process Instance in a decentralized PMS are normally executed on several process engines. Whether this is decentralized or distributed is a matter of defining the terminology. As the opposite of "centralized", the term "decentralized" fits when an instance is no longer coordinated by one central engine but when different parts of an instance are coordinated on several engines. This use of the term also matches the definition of Steen and Tanenbaum [14, sec. 1.1.1], who differentiate between the "necessity" and "sufficiency" of distribution. A process instance is only executed on the necessary number of process engines, hence it is a "decentralized" process execution, but there are maybe more process engines in the Environment than those necessary for the execution of one instance, so the term "distributed" is suitable for the several process engines.

The big challenge for realizing and installing a complete decentralized Process Management System in reality is the necessary standardization of the data elements. Although a few collaborating companies could create a proprietary dPMS, it would only deliver some advantages. The dynamic integration of the surrounding context would not be possible, at least not until every other Machine is able to communicate a completely self-describing, machine-understandable interface.

Standardizing a dPMS would mean standardizing the engine's interfaces, the DPE's components, and the Deployment Artefacts. This work is quite challenging. Even today, after more than thirty years of research and application of process systems, it is often impossible to exchange every information within a process diagram between modeling tools. When using a standard like BPMN, software vendors like to incorporate vendor-specific extensions instead of working to extend the standard. This behavior makes sense for special use cases, but often it is more about the business model and the enforcement of customer loyalty.

In addition to the standardization, there must be an software implementation of a DPE for every Machine. Although reusable implementations for many general systems could be developed collaboratively, as with web browsers, the adaptation for special Machines would still involve much effort on the side of a vendor.

5 Conclusion

This paper described the software architectural components, connectors, and data used for process automation in a decentralized Process Management System. Unlike a centralized PMS, this system allows direct, peer-to-peer communication between Machines and the transmission of mobile code to other process engines. As a result, the system coordinates and executes Process Instances fragment by fragment on several Distributed Process Engines.

In our future work, we will compare the two PMS architectures with architectural properties commonly used to evaluate network-based software. The comparison will reveal several advantages and disadvantages of decentralized Process Management Systems that could be useful for certain application areas.

Acknowledgment. The research described here was conducted as part of the EvoFrame project funded by the German Federal Ministry of Education and Research (BMBF) (funding reference 02J21C101).

References

1. Baresi, L., Maurino, A., Modafferi, S.: Towards distributed BPEL Orchestrations. Electron. Commun. EASST **3** (2007). https://doi.org/10.14279/tuj.eceasst.3.7
2. Bauer, T., Dadam, P.: A distributed execution environment for large-scale workflow management systems with subnets and server migration. In: Proceedings of CoopIS 97: 2nd IFCIS Conference on Cooperative Information Systems, pp. 99–108 (1997). https://doi.org/10.1109/COOPIS.1997.613807
3. Bauer, T., Dadam, P.: Efficient distributed workflow management based on variable server assignments. In: Wangler, B., Bergman, L. (eds.) Advanced Information Systems Engineering, CAiSE 2000, pp. 94–109 (2000). https://doi.org/10.1007/3-540-45140-4_8
4. Binder, W., Constantinescu, I., Faltings, B.: Decentralized orchestration of composite web services. In: International Conference on Web Services, pp. 869–876 (2006). https://doi.org/10.1109/ICWS.2006.48
5. Business process model and notation (BPMN). Standard 2.0.2, Object Management Group (OMG) (2014)
6. Fielding, R.T.: Architectural Styles and the Design of Network-based Software Architectures. University of California, Irvine (2000)
7. Gokkoca, E., Altinel, M., Cingil, R., Tatbul, E., Koksal, P., Dogac, A.: Design and implementation of a distributed workflow enactment service. In: In: Proceedings of CoopIS 97: 2nd IFCIS Conference on Cooperative Information Systems, pp. 89–98 (1997). https://doi.org/10.1109/COOPIS.1997.613806

8. Grunert, K., Joderi Shoferi, J., Rohwer, K., Pankovska, E., Gold, L.: Architecture of decentralized process management systems. In: Di Ciccio, C., Dijkman, R., del Río Ortega, A., Rinderle-Ma, S. (eds.) BPM, pp. 436–452. Springer International Publishing, Cham (2022). https://doi.org/10.1007/978-3-031-16103-2_28
9. Hollingsworth, D.: Workflow management coalition: the workflow reference model. document number TC00-1003, **19**(16), 224 (1995)
10. Jennings, N.R., Norman, T.J., Faratin, P., O'Brien, P., Odgers, B.: Autonomous agents for business process management. Appl. Artif. Intell. 145–189 (2000). https://doi.org/10.1080/088395100117106
11. Joeris, G.: Decentralized and flexible workflow enactment based on task coordination agents. In: 2nd Int'l. Bi-Conference Workshop on Agent-Oriented Information Systems (AOIS 2000@ CAiSE∗ 00), pp. 41–62 (2000)
12. Khalaf, R., Leymann, F.: E role-based decomposition of business processes using BPEL. In: International Conference on Web Services (ICWS'06), pp. 770–780 (2006). https://doi.org/10.1109/ICWS.2006.56
13. Martin, D., Wutke, D., Leymann, F.: A novel approach to decentralized workflow enactment. In: Enterprise Distributed Object Computing Conference pp. 127–136 (2008). https://doi.org/10.1109/EDOC.2008.22
14. van Steen, M., Tanenbaum, A.S.: Distributed Systems. 4th edn., Distributed-systems.net (2023)
15. Weske, M.: Business Process Management: Concepts, Languages, Architectures. 2nd edn., Springer Berlin Heidelberg (2012). https://doi.org/10.1007/978-3-642-28616-2

LLM-Based Business Process Documentation Generation

Rui Zhu[1,2], Quanzhou Hu[1,2], Lijie Wen[3], Leilei Lin[4(✉)], Honghao Xiao[1,2], and Chaogang Wang[1,2]

[1] School of Software, Yunnan University Kunming, Yunnan, China
{hqz,wangchaogang0220}@mail.ynu.edu.cn, xiaohonghao@stu.ynu.edu.cn
[2] The Key Laboratory in Software Engineering, Yunnan, Kunming 650091, China
rzhu@ynu.edu.cn
[3] School of Software, Tsinghua University Beijing, Beijing, China
wenlj@tsinghua.edu.cn4
[4] School of Management, Capital Normal University Beijing, Beijing, China
leilei_lin@cnu.edu.cn

Abstract. Business processes underpin enterprise execution, coordination, and management. However, differing levels of familiarity with modeling languages among users can create an understanding gap, potentially disrupting the process flow. Business process documentation bridges this gap. Current methods, such as manual writing and rule-based generation, face inefficiency, errors, and limitations. We innovate by harnessing large language models for documentation generation. Our approach involves defining a Refined Process Structure Tree (RPST) meta-model and mapping rules, then constructing fine-grained RPSTs and crafting sentences using a hierarchical construction method. Finally, global optimization enhances the documentation. Tested on 100 diverse process models, our method outperforms benchmarks in robustness, and it achieves 6% and 1% higher semantic similarity scores by n-gram and semantics metrics.

Keywords: Business Process Documentation · Large Language Model · Hierarchical Construction · Prompt Learning

1 Introduction

High-quality business process documentation helps users understand the business process and is of great significance to the evolution of the business process [1]. As far as we know, there are two ways to obtain the documentation: (1) manual writing; and (2) rule-based generation. Figure 1 demonstrates the business process documentation generation task. Manually writing the documentation is inefficient, and current rule-based methods produce well-structured documentation but lack robustness and naturalness.

The current research spans three phases: business process model (e.g., BPMN [2] and Petri Net [3]) transformation into a Refined Process Structure Tree (RPST) [4], then RPST traversal using natural language processing tools and rules for Deep-Syntactic Tree (DSynT) [5] conversion. DSynT fuels RealPro's [6] sentence generation. Leopold et al. [1] pioneered a structure-based approach. They focus on BPMN's trivial, bond, and polygon structural components. The sequel [7] targeted BPMN's rigid aspects, adopting Petri Net conversion and the longest-first strategy. Qian et al. [8] introduced the Extended Process Structure Tree to augment RPST's expressiveness, emphasizing BPMN's unfolding model. While focusing on varied aspects, their sentence generation echoes [1]. When confronted with unmanageable circumstances, including typos (e.g., *receive order*), these methodologies are prone to yielding imprecise outcomes (e.g., *conducts receive order*). Analogously, upon encountering gateway descriptions that defy processing, like *Are beers ordered?*, they merely yield *In case*, thereby forfeiting crucial gateway details. Qian et al. [9] delved into the transformation of Petri Net, scrutinizing complex structures' behavior during linearization. Their documentation feature underscored task descriptions, e.g., *'receive_ order'*, enhancing robustness yet compromising on documentation's natural flow. The domain lacks ample data collection. Large language models (LLMs) [10,11] synthesize knowledge across disciplines, empowering them to encompass diverse topics. Their robust transference prowess ensures superior performance even in data-scarce domains [12]. However, owing to the limitation inherent in LLMs' capacity to adeptly process intricately recursive nested structures [13], GPT-4o [10], a multimodal model of unparalleled prowess, falls short of optimal performance when employed in conjunction with BPMN images and files. This limitation is highlighted in Fig. 2.

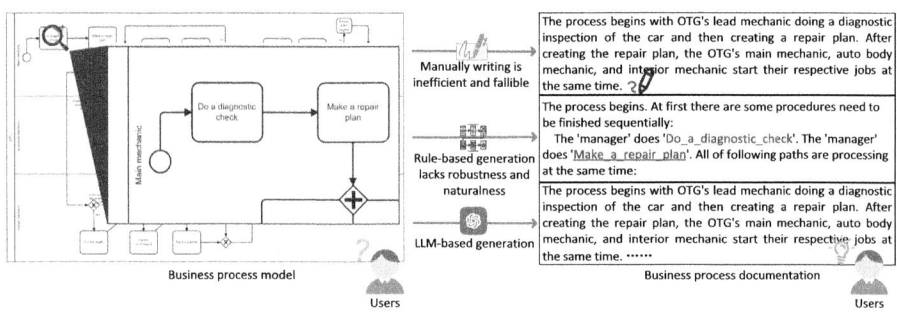

Fig. 1. Business process documentation generation task.

To our knowledge, we are the first to propose using LLMs to generate documentation. Our approach strengthens the robustness of documentation generation and makes it more natural. The meta-model and mapping rules of RPST are proposed. The meta-model will serve as the input for hierarchical construction methods. Within the method, RPST undergoes a process of decomposition, yielding finer-grained versions of itself. This initial phase results in the production of more detailed documentation. The complete documentation is further generated at the sentence level. While overlooking global information,

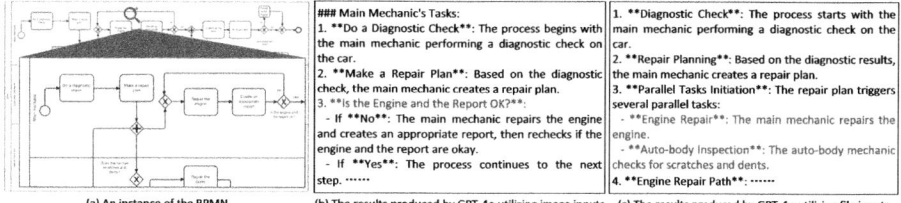

Fig. 2. GPT-4o-produced results using image or file input.

the method can be complemented by global optimization to enhance the documentation. Our approach aims to address the limitations of LLM in managing recursive nested structures, ensuring a more accurate documentation process. To summarize, the main contributions of this paper are listed as follows:

- We pioneered the approach of utilizing deep learning for the generation of business process documentation. This methodology surpasses traditional rule-based methods in terms of robustness, generalizability, and naturalness.
- The hierarchical construction method addresses the deficiency of LLM in handling recursive nested structures, enabling the accuracy of the generation.
- We gathered a real-world dataset and demonstrated proficiency in our proposed methodology in its application.

2 Preliminaries

2.1 In-Context Learning

In-Context Learning (ICL) [14] has emerged as minimizing data needs and eliminating the burden of intricate fine-tuning. This milestone facilitates profound investigations into the reasoning prowess of LLMs. Subsequently, advancements like chain-of-thought (CoT) [15] and self-consistency (SC) [16] streamline the landscape. The paramount challenge, however, lies in the inability of LLMs to reconstruct structural information from sequences [13]. ICL aims to improve LLMs performance by adding demonstrations $D = \{d_1, d_2, ..., d_n\}$ to the input, which can be expressed as $p_\theta(a|D,q)$, where answer a from a question q.

2.2 RPST

RPST [4] is a tree structure that indicates a process model's SESE (single entry, single exit) parts, which are called process components. A process component is canonical *iff* (i.e., if and only if) it does not overlap with any other process component, meaning that any two canonical process components are either disjoint or nested. Therefore, canonical process components naturally form a hierarchy.

3 Methodology

Figure 3 illustrates our proposed method. When confronted with problems that exceed the capabilities of LLMs, we seek to simplify them into smaller, solvable components. Since LLMs struggle with recursive nested structures [13], such as RPST, this can result in inconsistencies when documenting business processes. Our approach circumvents this limitation by avoiding LLM processing of such structures, thereby enhancing the accuracy of the resulting business process documentation. The code[1] and implementation[2] are publicly accessible.

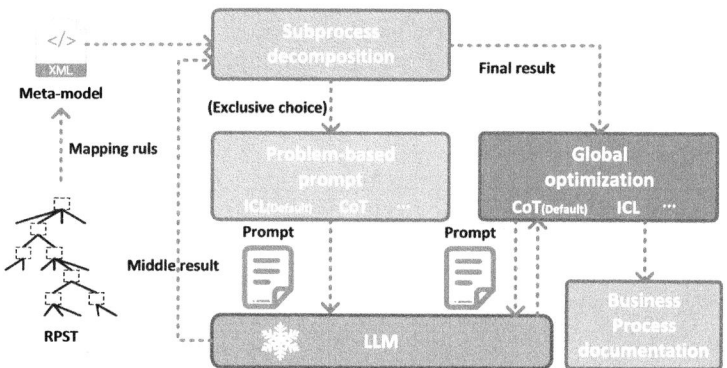

Fig. 3. The procedure of our method. (Converting RPST to its meta-model, we decompose it granularly through subprocesses. Leveraging ICL (default) and CoT, the prompt module employs LLMs to create detailed process documentation as an interim step. This intermediate output then frames the basis for sentence-level process documentation. Lastly, the global optimization module, also utilizing ICL and CoT (default), refines the end product, guaranteeing a holistic and optimized output.)

The composition of the business process documentation shall progress from the deep towards the superficial layers rather than adhering to a linear commencement at the model's inception. Figure 4 delineates this approach with tangible exemplification.

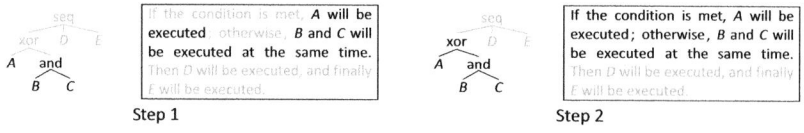

Fig. 4. A specific example of using our method.

---

[1] https://github.com/anonymous-1-a/BPDG.
[2] http://121.43.97.132:8080/ProcessModel/.

3.1 Meta-Model

We have delineated the meta-model of RPST and added the corresponding mapping rules based on [1]. This model comprises seven primary node types: <seq>, <xor>, <or>, <and>, <loop>, <rigid>, and <task>. Each node signifies a distinct function: for *Sequence, Exclusive choice, Inclusive choice, Parallel, Loop, Rigid*, and *Task*.

Unified Modeling Language schema of the main interface components of the RPST is demonstrated in Fig. 5. The seven node classes, descendants of *Process*, are formed by aggregating *Process* entities. This structure allows for intricate interconnections, creating a nested hierarchy. *RPST*, a *Process*, possesses a unique configuration, while *Xor, Loop, Task, Edge, Gateway*, and *Event* have extensible attributes. *Rigid* emerges from the union of *Vertex* and *Edge*, where *Vertex* encompasses *Gateway, Event*, and *Task*.

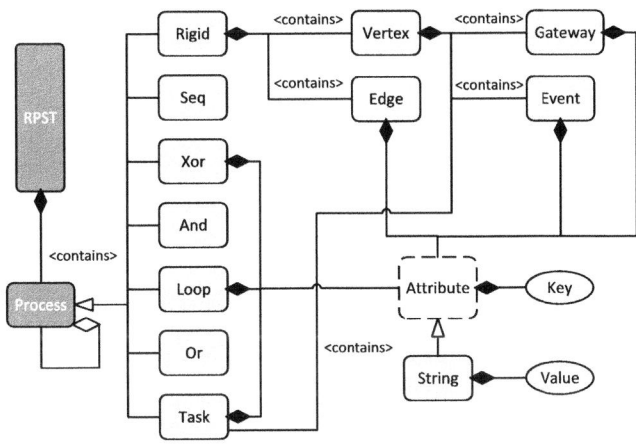

Fig. 5. Meta-model of RPST.

3.2 Hierarchical Construction Method

RPST boasts an optimal substructure, inspiring us to propose a hierarchical construction method based on the divide-and-conquer principle. Essentially, we decompose RPST into more refined components, producing granular documentation, which then enables the creation of complete documentation at the sentence level. The hierarchical construction method comprises three integral parts: subprocess decomposition, problem-based prompts, and global optimization.

1. **Subprocess decomposition** Based on [4], RPST exhibits an optimal substructure. *Task* and *rigid* nodes are non-decomposable, generating documentation directly. Other nodes, however, undergo decomposition into fine-grained RPST. Initially craft fine-grained documentation, then refine it further at the sentence level.

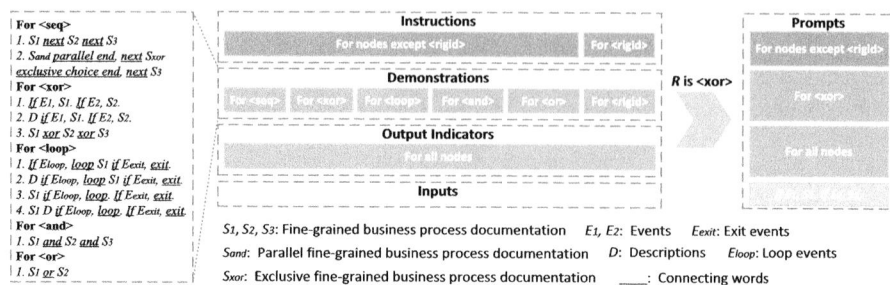

Fig. 6. The idea of the problem-based prompt. (Prompts are constructed based on R. *Instruction* is the task that an LLM is expected to complete. *Demonstration* are some examples. *Output Indicator* controls the output format. *Input* is the query.)

2. **Problem-based prompt** This part clarifies the process of generating business process documentation at the sentence level, utilizing finely detailed documentation as the foundation. Here, the core aim is to minimize distractions and noise, ultimately yielding more precise and reliable outcomes. Figure 6 illustrates the idea of the problem-based prompt module. In other words, we segmented the task of crafting documentation at the sentence level into six distinct categories. In this context, ICL (default), CoT, SC, and other techniques can be effectively employed.

3. **Global optimization** The hierarchical construction method lacks the perception of global information. This outcome inevitably leads to the proliferation of redundant material within the documentation, particularly about subjects, thereby detracting from its overall naturalness. The inherent redundancy in the document, while marginally enhancing its readability, fails to resonate with the natural reading patterns of humans. Consequently, the primary objective of this module is to meticulously eliminate such redundancy. In this context, ICL, CoT (default), SC, and other techniques can be effectively employed.

4 Experiments

4.1 Experimental Setup

Datasets. We gathered real-world business process models from SAP-SAM [17], focusing on two strategies: mirroring SAP-SAM's task distribution and sourcing models from diverse fields like industry and finance. We then manually annotated the corresponding business process documentation. Table 1 summarizes the dataset's key characteristics, including 100 model-text pairs. The abundance of <seq> nodes arises due to their encapsulation of every individual node.

Baseline Methods. We compare our proposed method with existing state-of-the-art methods. The most representative works are the following four papers: Leo [1], Hen [7], Goun [8], and BePT [9]. Our analysis also encompassed ICL [11], wherein the distinction lies in the treatment of RPST. ICL takes in the

Table 1. Dataset Statistics. (prop = proportion of the dataset; depth=max depth of an RPST; seq, xor, and, or, loop, rigid, and task=the number of <seq>, <xor>, <and>, <or>, <loop>, <rigid>, and <task> node.

	proportion	depth			seq			xor			and			or			loop			rigid			task		
		max	avg	min	max	avg	min	max	avg	min	max	avg	min	max	avg	min	max	avg	min	max	avg	min	max	avg	min
Industry	36%	10	5.56	2	13	5.0	1	7	1.5	0	3	0.53	0	1	0.11	0	3	0.36	0	1	0.11	0	30	12.36	3
Finance	13%	10	5.85	2	13	5.62	1	4	1.85	0	2	0.46	0	1	0.08	0	1	0.08	0	1	0.08	0	22	11.54	5
Logistics	12%	8	5.0	2	7	4.25	1	2	1.0	0	1	0.42	0	1	0.17	0	3	0.33	0	0	0.0	0	24	11.17	7
Pharmacy	7%	10	5.14	4	12	4.57	1	4	1.43	0	2	0.43	0	0	0.0	0	0	0.0	0	1	0.29	0	21	12.43	4
Insurance	6%	6	4.33	2	7	4.17	1	2	0.83	0	1	0.5	0	0	0.0	0	2	0.5	0	0	0.0	0	12	9.33	6
Education	5%	8	5.2	2	13	4.6	1	1	0.2	0	2	0.4	0	1	0.2	0	6	1.4	0	1	0.4	0	18	12.8	5
Others	21%	10	5.43	4	12	5.48	1	6	1.24	0	3	0.9	0	0	0.0	0	2	0.38	0	1	0.1	0	22	10.48	4

entire RPST, whereas our approach disassembles it, crafting fine-grained documentation, and then seamlessly fusing it into a coherent sentence-level structure.

Parameter Settings. *GPT-3.5 turbo* uses temperature sampling. The *temperature* is set to *0* to avoid randomness.

4.2 Results

Robustness. This section examines the robustness of methods, with a focus on converting business process models across domains. √ signifies a perfect conversion rate at 100%, while the underlined figure represents the second-highest value. Table 2 shows the conversion rates for all methods. The highest conversions belong to ICL and ours, trailed by BePT. Rule-based methods, faced with unconventional scenarios, often stumble upon unforeseen issues, disrupting the generation flow. This accounts for their inferior conversion rates.

Grammatical Correctness and Language Style. LanguageTool [18] identifies linguistic issues, encompassing grammar and style. Issue rate *i%* is

Table 2. Conversion rate.

	Leo	Hen	Goun	BePT	ICL	Ours
Industry	74%	80%	57%	<u>89%</u>	√	√
Finance	<u>92%</u>	<u>92%</u>	85%	<u>92%</u>	√	√
Logistics	73%	73%	73%	<u>91%</u>	√	√
Pharmacy	43%	43%	71%	<u>86%</u>	√	√
Insurance	<u>50%</u>	<u>50%</u>	17%		√	√
Education	60%	<u>80%</u>	40%		√	√
Others	74%	<u>79%</u>	63%		√	√
AVG	67%	71%	58%	<u>94%</u>	√	√

Table 3. Grammatical correctness & language style.

	Leo	Hen	Goun	BePT	ICL	Ours
Industry	0.68	0.67	0.61	<u>0.88</u>	**0.89**	<u>0.88</u>
Finance	0.51	0.51	0.39	<u>0.89</u>	**0.93**	<u>0.89</u>
Logistics	**0.84**	**0.84**	0.45	0.72	0.77	<u>0.81</u>
Pharmacy	0.87	0.87	0.64	**0.94**	<u>0.92</u>	0.89
Insurance	0.71	0.71	0.29	<u>0.76</u>	**0.83**	0.67
Education	0.5	0.6	0.64	**0.97**	<u>0.91</u>	0.79
Others	0.8	0.81	0.63	<u>0.88</u>	**0.94**	0.81
AVG	0.70	0.72	0.52	<u>0.86</u>	**0.88**	0.82

($issues \div sentences$) × 100%. We quantify correctness with $1-i\%$. This value may be negative, yet its maximum attainable value is 1, with the bolded numeral denoting the maximum and the underlined numeral, the second highest. Table 3 shows the results. The findings indicate LLM enhances documentation's naturalness and grammar. Our approach lags ICL and BePT, attributed to dataset noise, particularly in insurance. LanguageTool flags issues in process models' elements (e.g., pools and lanes). ICL mitigates by decreasing instances. Conversely, BePT evades detection with single quotes. In our endeavors to globally optimize the document, redundancy inevitably arises, yet interestingly, ICL paradoxically transforms errors into inconsequential pronouns, disrupting coherence.

Similarity. We opted for a multifaceted evaluation framework, integrating n-gram-based metrics like Meteor [19] and Rouge [19] alongside semantic methods. We introduced BERT-Score [20], SBERT [20], and BLEURT [20] for a semantic evaluation, transcending n-gram limitations. These incorporate softer evaluations than their n-gram counterparts. Our Rouge score encapsulates Rouge-1, -2, and -L, ensuring thoroughness. BERT-Score's F1 metric stresses precision and recall, bolstering the assessment rigor. The range of all values extends from 0 to 1, with bolded numerals signifying the utmost peak and underscored numerals indicating the second-highest tier. Tables 4 and 5 show the results. The BePT attains the lowest score in the n-gram metric owing to mechanisms like 'Send_rejection'. LLMs falter with recursive structures [13]. Erroneous parsing of RPST's layered architecture undermines documentation fidelity, underscoring ICL's inferiority against our methodology.

Table 4. Similarity n-gram-based.

	Rouge						Meteor					
	Leo	Hen	Goun	BePT	ICL	Ours	Leo	Hen	Goun	BePT	ICL	Ours
Industry	0.26	0.27	0.19	0.09	0.43	**0.53**	0.27	0.28	0.2	0.1	0.41	**0.5**
Finance	0.39	0.39	0.35	0.1	**0.47**	0.46	0.36	0.36	0.34	0.12	**0.4**	0.38
Logistics	0.27	0.27	0.26	0.08	0.49	**0.63**	0.31	0.31	0.32	0.09	0.53	**0.64**
Pharmacy	0.13	0.13	0.19	0.09	0.38	**0.45**	0.13	0.13	0.23	0.12	0.35	**0.4**
Insurance	0.16	0.16	0.08	0.12	0.38	**0.48**	0.17	0.17	0.07	0.11	0.42	**0.45**
Education	0.23	0.28	0.12	0.12	**0.45**	0.42	0.21	0.25	0.15	0.11	**0.38**	0.33
Others	0.23	0.24	0.18	0.1	0.41	**0.51**	0.24	0.25	0.19	0.11	0.38	**0.46**
AVG	0.24	0.25	0.2	0.1	0.43	**0.50**	0.24	0.25	0.21	0.11	0.41	**0.45**

Ablation Study. After ablating the global optimization module, we delved into its potential impact on enhancing the documentation. The incorporation of a global optimization module is projected to elevate grammatical correctness

Table 5. Similarity semantics-based.

	BERT-Score						SBERT						BLEURT					
	Leo	Hen	Goun	BePT	ICL	Ours	Leo	Hen	Goun	BePT	ICL	Ours	Leo	Hen	Goun	BePT	ICL	Ours
Industry	0.57	0.61	0.43	0.54	0.83	**0.86**	0.63	0.67	0.41	0.54	0.91	**0.92**	0.39	0.42	0.26	0.46	0.63	**0.66**
Finance	0.71	0.71	0.66	0.56	**0.84**	0.83	0.81	0.81	0.63	0.62	**0.92**	**0.92**	0.5	0.5	0.42	0.51	**0.63**	**0.63**
Logistics	0.56	0.56	0.56	0.56	0.86	**0.89**	0.58	0.58	0.52	0.58	0.93	**0.94**	0.39	0.39	0.35	0.48	0.67	**0.71**
Pharmacy	0.32	0.32	0.52	0.52	0.82	**0.85**	0.37	0.37	0.48	0.47	**0.92**	**0.92**	0.24	0.24	0.33	0.42	0.6	**0.65**
Insurance	0.37	0.37	0.14	0.62	0.81	**0.83**	0.4	0.4	0.12	0.69	**0.93**	0.92	0.26	0.26	0.08	0.52	**0.63**	**0.63**
Education	0.48	0.62	0.31	0.62	**0.82**	**0.82**	0.52	0.66	0.29	0.58	**0.9**	0.89	0.33	0.41	0.18	0.5	**0.6**	0.58
Others	0.56	0.6	0.47	0.61	0.84	**0.85**	0.62	0.66	0.42	0.59	**0.92**	**0.92**	0.4	0.43	0.29	0.5	0.63	**0.64**
AVG	0.51	0.54	0.44	0.58	0.83	**0.85**	0.56	0.59	0.41	0.58	**0.92**	**0.92**	0.36	0.38	0.27	0.48	0.63	**0.64**

and language style by a marginal 2%, yet it is anticipated to elicit a decline of 1% and 2% respectively in the Meteor and Rouge metrics while maintaining parity in the realm of semantic similarity indices.

5 Conclusion and Future Work

Business process documentation generation enhances user communications and drives business evolution. Our LLM-based method boosts robustness and naturalness. Though GPT-4o excels in multimodal, documentation from images and files falters due to noise. Our tactic mitigates noise and refines documentation accuracy. In the future, we will explore LLM's perception of graph structure and improve the correctness of converting *Rigid* components into documentation.

Acknowledgments. This work was supported in part by the National Natural Science Foundation of China under Grant 62362067, in part by the Science Foundation of Yunnan Jinzhi Expert Workstation under Grant 202205AF150006, in part by the Yunnan Provincial Key Laboratory of Software Engineering Open Fund Project under Grant 2023SE205, in part by Yunnan Xing Dian Talents Support Plan.

References

1. Leopold, H., Mendling, J., Polyvyanyy, A.: Generating natural language texts from business process models. In: Ralyté, J., Franch, X., Brinkkemper, S., Wrycza, S. (eds.) CAiSE 2012. LNCS, vol. 7328, pp. 64–79. Springer, Heidelberg (2012). https://doi.org/10.1007/978-3-642-31095-9_5
2. Schuster, D., van Zelst, S.J., van der Aalst, W.M.: Utilizing domain knowledge in data-driven process discovery: a literature review. Comput. Ind. **137**, 103612 (2022)
3. Zhu, R., et al.: Business process retrieval from large model repositories for industry 4.0. IEEE Trans. Serv. Comput. **17**(1), 306–321 (2024)
4. Corradini, F., Fornari, F., Polini, A., Re, B., Tiezzi, F., Vandin, A.: A formal approach for the analysis of BPMN collaboration models. J. Syst. Softw. **180**, 111007 (2021)

5. Velardi, P.: Acquiring a semantic lexicon for natural language processing. In: Lexical Acquisition, pp. 341–367. Psychology Press (2021)
6. Al-Thanyyan, S.S., Azmi, A.M.: Automated text simplification: a survey. ACM Comput. Surv. (CSUR) **54**(2), 1–36 (2021)
7. Leopold, H., Mendling, J., Polyvyanyy, A.: Supporting process model validation through natural language generation. IEEE Trans. Software Eng. **40**(8), 818–840 (2014)
8. Qian, C., Wen, L., Wang, J., Kumar, A., Li, H.: Structural descriptions of process models based on goal-oriented unfolding. In: Dubois, E., Pohl, K. (eds.) CAiSE 2017. LNCS, vol. 10253, pp. 397–412. Springer, Cham (2017). https://doi.org/10.1007/978-3-319-59536-8_25
9. Qian, C., Wen, L., Kumar, A.: BEPT: a behavior-based process translator for interpreting and understanding process models. In: Proceedings of the 28th ACM International Conference on Information and Knowledge Management, pp. 1873–1882 (2019)
10. Sonoda, Y., et al.: Diagnostic performances of GPT-4o, Claude 3 Opus, and Gemini 1.5 pro in "diagnosis please" cases. Jpn. J. Radiol. **42**, 1–5 (2024). https://doi.org/10.1007/s11604-024-01619-y
11. Brown, T., et al.: Language models are few-shot learners. Adv. Neural. Inf. Process. Syst. **33**, 1877–1901 (2020)
12. Zhu, R., Xiao, H., Hu, Q., Li, W., Wang, J., Bait, T.: SWDG: service workflow deep generation using large language model and graph neural network. In: 2024 IEEE International Conference on Software Services Engineering (SSE), pp. 153–159 (2024)
13. Lakretz, Y., Desbordes, T., Hupkes, D., Dehaene, S.: Can transformers process recursive nested constructions, like humans? In: Proceedings of the 29th International Conference on Computational Linguistics, pp. 3226–3232 (2022)
14. Dong, C., et al.: A survey of natural language generation. ACM Comput. Surv. **55**(8), 1–38 (2022)
15. Liu, Z., Liu, H., Zhou, D., Ma, T.: Chain of thought empowers transformers to solve inherently serial problems. In: The Twelfth International Conference on Learning Representations, Vienna, Austria, 7-11 May 2024. OpenReview.net (2024)
16. Wang, X., et al.: Self-consistency improves chain of thought reasoning in language models. In: The Eleventh International Conference on Learning Representations, ICLR 2023, Kigali, Rwanda, 1-5 May 2023. OpenReview.net (2023)
17. Sola, D., Warmuth, C., Schäfer, B., Badakhshan, P., Rehse, J.R., Kampik, T.: Sap signavio academic models: a large process model dataset. In: Montali, M., Senderovich, A., Weidlich, M. (eds.) International Conference on Process Mining, vol. 468, pp. 453–465. Springer, Cham (2022). https://doi.org/10.1007/978-3-031-27815-0_33
18. Madina, M., Gonzalez-Dios, I., Siegel, M.: LanguageTool as a CAT tool for easy-to-read in Spanish. In: Wilkens, R., Cardon, R., Todirascu, A., Gala, N. (eds.) Proceedings of the 3rd Workshop on Tools and Resources for People with REAding DIfficulties (READI), pp. 93–101. ELRA and ICCL, Torino, Italia (2024)
19. Briman, M.K.H., Yildiz, B.: Beyond rouge: a comprehensive evaluation metric for abstractive summarization leveraging similarity, entailment, and acceptability. Int. J. Artif. Intell. Tools **33**(05), 2450017 (2024)
20. Fikri, F.B., Oflazer, K., Yanıkoğlu, B.: Abstractive summarization with deep reinforcement learning using semantic similarity rewards. Nat. Lang. Eng. **30**(3), 554–576 (2024)

Author Index

A

Abdellatif, Takoua II-210
Abusafia, Amani I-125
Aiello, Marco II-276
Akram, Junaid II-323
Alqahtani, Daghash K. I-142
Alvarado-Valiente, Jaime II-195
An, Qi II-314
Anaissi, Ali II-323
Awanyo, Christson I-133

B

Baresi, Luciano I-3
Becker, Steffen II-276
Begoug, Mahi II-373
Ben Mrad, Ali I-253
Benabdeslem, Khalid I-312
Benatallah, Boualem I-312
Benblidia, Nadjia II-146
Benghazi, Kawtar I-168
Besbes, Olfa II-210
Bouguettaya, Athman I-125, I-296
Bradai, Salma II-331
Brandic, Ivona I-38

C

Caglayan, Bora II-357
Callejas, Zoraida I-168
Camilli, Matteo II-55
Cao, Bin I-337
Casati, Fabio I-312
Casco-Seco, Jorge II-195
Cavero, Francisco Javier II-260
Cheema, Muhammad Aamir I-142
Chen, Feifei I-263
Chen, Gang II-3
Chen, Guihai I-69
Chen, Shuaijun I-85
Cheng, Long II-87
Chopra, Amit K. I-354
Chung, Lawrence I-236

D

Ding, Hao I-202
Ding, Jiandong II-357
Dustdar, Schahram II-72

E

El Eze, Mohamed Salem II-331

F

Fan, Jing I-337
Fang, Kai I-337
Fei, Shen II-357
Fei, Yang II-72
Fekih, Rim Ben II-331
Felderer, Michael II-35
Firmani, Donatella II-287
Fu, Qiang I-327

G

Gacha, Yassine II-210
Gaci, Yacine I-312
Gao, Qiaomei II-314
Gao, Wentao I-85
Gao, Xiaofeng I-69, II-341
Gara Hellal, Yassmine I-116
Garcia-Alonso, Jose II-195
García-Fernández, Alejandro II-260
Georgievski, Ilche II-276
Giallorenzo, Saverio II-161, II-243
Gold, Lucas I-370
Graiet, Mohamed I-116
Gritsch, Philipp II-35
Grunert, Kai I-370
Guéhéneuc, Yann-Gaël II-123
Guermouche, Nawal I-133
Guo, Jiecheng II-341

H

Hamel, Lazhar I-116
Han, Boyang II-138

Hautz, Mika II-35
He, Qiang I-263
He, Xiang I-54
He, Xiangdong II-225
He, Yiyuan I-218
Herzwurm, Georg II-276
Hill, Tom I-236
Hnich, Brahim I-253
Hu, Quanzhou I-381

I

Ilager, Shashikant I-38

J

Jain, Prakhar I-21
Jiang, Tianyu II-176
Jmaiel, Mohamed II-331

K

Kanatbekova, Meerzhan I-38
Kelleher, John D. II-357
Kim, Donggyun I-100, II-19
Kim, Hyungjun I-100, II-19
Klein, Kevin II-276
Küpper, Axel I-370

L

Lahami, Mariam II-331
Lakhdari, Abdallah I-125
Lamari, Selena II-146
Lee, Eunyoung II-19
Leotta, Francesco II-287
Li, Hao I-327
Li, Hongfeng I-281
Li, Yanhui I-263
Li, Ying II-107
Li, Zhengquan II-87
Lichtenstein, Tom I-354
Lim, Gyujeong I-100
Lin, Leilei I-381
Liu, Mengjin II-341
Liu, Mingyi I-153, II-176
Liu, Sihao II-176
Lu, Chengliang I-337
Luccioletti, Fabio II-55
Luo, Yang II-341

M

Ma, Hui II-3
Ma, Yue I-69
Mahmoudi, Brahim II-123
Mandreoli, Federica II-287
Marchese, Angelo II-96
Mathew, Jerin George II-287
Mauro, Jacopo II-243
Mecella, Massimo II-287
Melis, Andrea II-243
Mirandola, Raffaela II-55
Mkaouer, Mohamed Wiem I-253
Moguel, Enrique II-195
Moha, Naouel II-123
Mombrey, Carolin II-276
Montesi, Fabrizio II-161, II-243
Monti, Flavia II-287
Morichetta, Andrea II-72
Murillo, Juan M. II-195

N

Nastic, Stefan II-35
Nivon, Quentin I-185

O

O. Thiombiano, Abdoul Majid I-253
Ouni, Ali II-373

P

Pandey, Divyansh I-21
Parejo, José Antonio II-260
Park, Hokun I-100
Peng, Wei I-281
Peressotti, Marco II-161, II-243
Pesl, Robin D. II-276
Pham, To Kim Bao I-236
Prandini, Marco II-243
Prodan, Radu II-35

Q

Qu, Xiaobo II-72
Quatrocchi, Giovanni I-21
Quattrocchi, Giovanni I-3

R

Rademacher, Florian II-161
Rattanavipanon, Norrathep II-299
Rauer, Julie I-236
Rieder, Wolf I-370

Author Index

Ristov, Sashko II-35
Rodríguez-Sánchez, María Jesús I-168
Romero-Álvarez, Javier II-195
Rong, Dunlei I-153, II-225
Ruiz-Cortés, Antonio II-260
Ruiz-Zafra, Angel I-168

S

Sa, Rula II-314
Sachweh, Sabine II-161
Salaün, Gwen I-185
Scandurra, Patrizia II-55
Sedlak, Boris II-72
Shen, Ya II-3
Shi, Weijia II-45
Shoferi, Janis Joderi I-370
Singh, Munindar P. I-354
Singh, Paramvir I-296
Singhal, Prakhar I-21
Sohrabi, Nasrin II-299
Song, Bin I-327
Song, Linxuan I-281
Song, Zheng II-87
Sui, Dianbo I-202
Sun, Bin I-327
Sun, Hongliang I-202
Supakkul, Sam I-236

T

Tamzalit, Dalila II-123
Tari, Zahir II-299
Tavallaie, Omid I-85
Tian, Cong I-263
Tibermacine, Chouki II-146
Ticongolo, Inacio Gaspar I-3
Tomarchio, Orazio II-96
Tong, Gui II-357
Toosi, Adel N. I-142
Trabelsi, Imen II-123
Tu, Zhiying I-202

U

Umair, Muhammad I-296
Urtado, Christelle II-146

V

Vaidhyanathan, Karthik I-21
Vauttier, Sylvain II-146

W

Wang, Can I-202
Wang, Chaogang I-381
Wang, Guiling II-138
Wang, Jiaxing I-337
Wang, Liang II-72
Wang, Mingxue II-357
Wang, Teng I-54
Wang, Xiao II-225
Wang, Yuhao II-72
Wang, Zhongjie I-54, I-153, II-176, II-225
Wen, Lijie I-381
Weske, Mathias I-354
Wizenty, Philip II-161
Wu, Daiqiang II-341
Wu, Jingfeng I-218
Wu, Suxiang II-107

X

Xi, Meng II-107
Xia, Geming I-281
Xiao, Honghao I-381
Xu, Chengzhong I-218
Xu, Hanchuan II-176, II-225
Xu, Minxian I-218
Xu, Xiaofei I-153

Y

Yang, Jiyu I-263
Yang, Yun I-263
Yang, Zhiqing I-54
Yao, Lina I-153
Ye, Kejiang I-218
Yin, Jianwei II-107
Yu, Chaodong I-281
Yu, Heonchang I-100, II-19
Yu, Jian II-138
Yu, Meiju II-314
Yu, Shuang I-153, II-176
Yu, Yifeng I-337

Z

Zhang, Bolin I-202
Zhang, Jin II-314
Zhang, Mengjie II-3
Zhang, Puchao II-357
Zhang, Yuqi II-138
Zhang, Yuze I-281

Zhao, Baokang II-45
Zhao, Yi II-314
Zhen, Peng II-341
Zheng, Wanyi I-218
Zheng, Xin II-138
Zheng, Yinting I-153

Zhou, Huan II-45
Zhu, Rui I-381
Zhu, Xinzhou II-107
Zomaya, Albert I-85
Zuo, Yuxin II-341
Zyberaj, Denesa II-276

Printed by Printforce, the Netherlands